challenges & future

challenges & future

RETHA WIESNER

BRUCE MILLETT

WILEY

John Wiley & Sons Australia, Ltd

First published 2003 by
John Wiley & Sons Australia, Ltd
42 McDougall Street, Milton, Qld 4064

Offices also in Sydney and Melbourne

Typeset in 10.5 pt Adobe Garamond

© Retha Wiesner, Bruce Millett 2003

National Library of Australia
Cataloguing-in-Publication data

Human resource management:
   challenges and future directions

   ISBN-13   978 0 470 80095 9
   ISBN-10   0 470 80095 X

   1. Personal management   2. Human capital.
   I. Millett, Bruce.   II. Wiesner, Retha.

658.3

Cover and internal images © 2002 Digital Vision

Printed in Singapore by
Seng Lee Press Pte Ltd

10 9 8 7 6 5 4 3

Contents

About the editors

Retha Wiesner

Retha Wiesner is Associate Professor in the Faculty of Business and Head of the Department of Management and Organisational Behaviour at the University of Southern Queensland. Before entering academia in 1989 she gained extensive experience in human resource management and organisational behaviour as an HR manager and industrial psychologist. Her current research interests include a major national and international study on employee management practices, and organisational change in small and medium-size enterprises. Dr Wiesner has published extensively in Australia and overseas. She was co-author, with Bruce Millett, of the successful *Management and Organisational Behaviour* readings, also published by John Wiley & Sons. She has taught human resource management and organisational behaviour courses in Australia and overseas. She continues to work as a consultant to many Australian organisations. (wiesner@usq.edu.au)

Bruce Robert Millett

Bruce Millett is currently Associate Dean (Teaching and Scholarship) in the Faculty of Business at the University of Southern Queensland. He earned his PhD in the management of organisational change at Griffith University. Dr Millett has published articles and book chapters on organisational change, performance management and the learning organisation. He has taught management courses in Australia and overseas. His current research interests include the learning organisation, organisational change and the work of consultants. (millett@usq.edu.au)

About the contributors

James Hunt

James Hunt (BA (Hons), MA (Mngt), Kent, UK) is a lecturer in management and organisational behaviour at the University of Newcastle's School of Business on the Central Coast campus. His research interests include the psychological determinants of leadership style, management competencies, international management issues, and organisational forms in the twenty-first century. He has published refereed articles in US, British and Australian management journals, and has written chapters for a number of management texts. James has lived and worked in Bahrain, Spain, England, Malaysia, the Philippines, Indonesia, Hong Kong, South Korea, South Africa and Australia. (mgjbh@cc.newcastle.edu.au)

Robin Kramar

Robin Kramar is Associate Professor in Management at the Macquarie Graduate School of Management. She has a special interest in strategic human resource management and has led Australian research in the longitudinal, comparative study on international strategic human resource management organised by the Cranet Network of Researchers since 1995. Other research interests include diversity management, work–life balance and the future of human resource management. Robin has published widely, including three textbooks (one with Peter McGraw and Randall Schuler, and another with Helen De Cieri) and two books of readings, both with Graham O'Neill. She has been involved with the *Asia Pacific Journal of Human Resources* for more than ten years, first as book review editor, then as an associate editor and now as editor. (Robin.Kramar@mq.edu.au)

Kerr Inkson

Kerr Inkson is Professor of Management at the Albany (Auckland) campus of Massey University. Kerr has held positions at the University of Aston (UK), the University of San Diego (US), and the universities of Otago and Auckland (New Zealand). His publications include eight books and more than 40 refereed journal articles. He was first author of *Theory K* (1986), the biggest selling management book in New Zealand history, and of *Management: New Zealand Perspectives* (1998), currently the country's leading management textbook. His most recent research has focused on careers in the contemporary work environment. His latest books are *The New Careers* (with Michael B. Arthur and Judith K. Pringle) and *Management: Perspectives for New Zealand* (with Darl Kolb). (K.Inkson@massey.ac.nz)

Margaret Patrickson

Margaret Patrickson is Associate Professor in Human Resource Management at the International Graduate School of Management at the University of South Australia. She is the author of four books and many articles in the field of human resource management. Her research interests are older workers, international diversity management issues and teleworking. (margaret.patrickson@unisa.edu.au)

Jarrod Haar

Jarrod Haar is currently employed at one of New Zealand's largest tertiary institutions, Te Wananga o Aotearoa, in the new Aotearoa Business School, in Hamilton. He has also taught in the Waikato Management School, University of Waikato (New Zealand). Jarrod's roles within the Business School include research leader, lecturer and academic manager (including program development). Jarrod has a Bachelor of Business, two postgraduate diplomas (Strategic Management and Organisational Behaviour), and a Master of Management Studies in Human Resource Management. His PhD research has examined the relationship between work–family practice and employee attitudes within a local government organisation. He is currently analysing post-doctoral data on work–family policies in New Zealand government departments. Other research interests include organisational adoption of work–family policies, employee stress and health, and employee drug testing in New Zealand. A paper from his PhD research findings has been published in the *New Zealand Journal of Human Resource Management*. (mhaar@wave.co.nz)

Chester Spell

Chester Spell is Assistant Professor of Management at Rutgers University. He has also taught at the University of Waikato (New Zealand) and Washington State University.

He received his PhD in Management from the Georgia Institute of Technology. His main research interest is the process by which managers come to adopt and accept management practices and how some of these practices eventually become popular. Other research interests include the interface between employee work and family roles, how organisations become involved in managing non-work-related roles, and problems and the diffusion of human resource management practices, especially employee substance abuse prevention programs. His work has appeared in publications such as the *Journal of Management*, the *Journal of Organizational Behavior*, *Human Relations* and the *Sloan Management Review*. (cspell@tricity.wsu.edu)

Ronel Erwee

Ronel Erwee was Professor in Organisational Behaviour in the Graduate School of Management at the University of Pretoria, South Africa, from 1989. In 1997 she joined the Department of HRM and Employment Relations, in the Faculty of Business, USQ. She served on the boards of the Small Business Development Corporation, Denel Informatics and the Women's Bureau. Professor Erwee's current research interests include entrepreneurship; career development of adults; diversity management; and organisational behaviour and leadership. She is currently the Director of the Australian Graduate School of Business, at the University of Southern Queensland. (Erwee@usq.edu.au)

Lesley Willcoxson

Lesley Willcoxson has worked in the private sector, the public service and universities. After completing her PhD she provided cross-cultural training for senior executives of some of Australia's largest companies in preparation for their leadership roles overseas. She then took up a staff development role at Sydney University before moving to Murdoch University to establish its academic staff development program. She currently works at the University of Southern Queensland, where she has developed the Leadership and Management evaluation instrument, which forms part of the university's performance management system. Her research and consultancy interests are in the areas of knowledge management, organisational learning, organisational change, organisational culture, leadership and teaching development. She has published widely in these areas. (lesley.willcoxson@usq.edu.au)

Heather Maguire

Heather Maguire is currently Head of Department, Economics and Resources Management, and lecturer in Administrative Management at the University of Southern Queensland. Her main research interests are psychological contracting, organisational restructuring and the impact of information management on corporate risk. Her recently completed PhD studies examined the impact of restructuring on the psychological contract of managers in the banking industry. Her current research investigates the role played by the psychological contract in creating or obstructing the type of organisational culture needed to bring about agility in manufacturing. (maguireh@usq.edu.au)

Ray Fells

Ray Fells currently holds the position of Associate Director of the Graduate School of Management, at the University of Western Australia. His primary responsibility is the quality of the School's MBA program. Associate Professor Fells has taught a wide range of workplace relations and negotiation courses both at the university and for public and private sector organisations. He has recently returned from teaching at the Judge Institute, University of Cambridge (UK). His current research interests are in the practice of negotiation and mediation, particularly in the workplace. He has published extensively both in Australia and overseas. He has worked in the UK as an adviser and conciliator in workplace relations, and he continues this aspect of his work by providing advice and training and by serving as a mediator. (rfells@ecel.uwa.edu.au)

Mark Bray

Mark Bray lectures in industrial relations, human resource management and research methodology in the Employment Relations Group of the Newcastle Business School at the University of Newcastle. Professor Bray's empirical research has explored the role of unions and the regulation of employment across a range of industries, including road and air transport, manufacturing and health care. He has also published 'macro' and interpretative analyses of unions, industrial relations policy and bargaining structures in Australia and overseas. (mgmdb@cc.newcastle.edu.au)

Peter Waring

Peter Waring is a lecturer in the Employment Relations Group of the Newcastle Business School at the University of Newcastle. He lectures in industrial relations, human resource management and other general management areas. Peter has diverse research interests across areas such as industrial relations policy, bargaining structures, coal industry employment relations and the employment relations implications of mergers and acquisitions. He is currently particularly interested in researching the dynamics of financial markets and their consequences for human resource management. (pwaring@mail.newcastle.edu.au)

Linley Hartmann

Linley Hartmann is a senior lecturer in the School of International Business at the University of South Australia. Her research concerns human resource management issues including workforce diversity, empowerment, work values and decision making. (Linley.Hartmann@unisa.edu.au)

Simon Peel

Simon Peel is a lecturer in the Department of Education and Professional Development at University College London. He has previously held positions at the University of Auckland and Massey University, New Zealand. Dr Peel has taught in the areas of management and organisation, organisational behaviour and human resource management. His research interests have included the management of contractors and employment structure choice, as well as cross-cultural and cross-national differences in psychological contracts. Additional research interests include organisational justice and performance management issues. (s.peel@ucl.ac.uk)

Suzanne Jamieson

Suzanne Jamieson is a senior lecturer in work and organisational studies at the University of Sydney. After graduating from law school she worked in trade unions covering the telecommunications and maritime industries. She became a senior bureaucrat in the New South Wales workers compensation administration, where she held a number of legal and management jobs, and in the federal Department of Industrial Relations. In 1996 she was appointed to the Pay Equity Task Force and the Occupational Health, Safety and Rehabilitation Council of New South Wales. In 1998 she was appointed by the state attorney-general to the Operations Review Committee of the Independent Commission Against Corruption. More recently she has been a Deputy Chair of the Nurses Tribunal and the Psychologists Tribunal. Her main current research interests are in occupational health and safety law and the position of women in the paid workforce. (s.jamieson@econ.usyd.edu.au)

Diana du Plessis

Diana du Plessis is a consultant, human resource practitioner and researcher with more than 15 years' experience in strategic HR management and HR project management, organisational change, training and development, executive search and selection, and recruitment. She has degrees in politics and psychology and is completing a Master of Business degree specialising in HR management. She has extensive international experience in the private, public and government sectors, and has consulted in numerous industries including financial services, consulting engineering, medical, maritime, universities and education, and local and state government bodies. Diana has published more than a dozen papers and made numerous conference presentations. She is currently employed in a senior HR management role in a New South Wales government corporation. (dupless@optusnet.com.au)

Susan Hinton

Susan Hinton is a lecturer in the Department of Management at Monash University's Peninsula Campus. Dr Hinton teaches in the areas of general management, human resource management and organisational behaviour. Her current research focuses on the use of electronic recruitment (e-cruitment) in the Australian and New Zealand recruitment industry. (susan.hinton@buseco.monash.edu.au)

Graham O'Neill

Graham O'Neill leads the Reward and Recognition Practice for Hay Pacific. He has some 25 years' consulting experience in areas related to employee, management and executive reward planning, and is Hay Group's client manager for firms such as Amcor, BankWest, BHP Billiton, National Foods and RACV. In addition to his client consulting roles, Graham has appeared as an expert witness in legal cases relating to employee remuneration, and before the AIRC on issues related to enterprise bargaining. Graham has a first-class BA (Hons) degree in psychology and a postgraduate diploma in applied psychology. He was elected a Fellow of the Australian Human Resource Institute in 1988, and in 1999 was appointed Adjunct Professor in RMIT University's School of Management. He has published three books — *Corporate Remuneration in the 90s: Strategies for Decision Makers* and (with Robin Kramar of Macquarie University) the two-volume *Australian Human Resource Management: Trends in Management Practice*. He is the author of some 40 papers, which have appeared in magazines, professional journals and books in Australia and overseas. He is a past editor of *Asia Pacific Journal of Human Resource Management* and remains on the editorial board of the journal.

Brian Delahaye

Brian Delahaye is Associate Professor, Adult and Workplace Education, in the School of Professional Studies at the Queensland University of Technology. Before taking up this position in 1990, he was senior training officer, staff development officer and administration manager with Telecom Australia. He also taught human resource management in the School of Management at QUT for eight years. Brian's research, including his doctoral thesis, has concentrated on self-directed learning, developing human resource developers, and the management of knowledge capital. He has published more than 30 articles in national and international refereed journals, is author of the text *Human Resource Development: Principles and Practice*, and is co-author of the texts *How to Be an Effective Trainer* and *Applied Business Research*. He consults widely with commercial, non-profit and government organisations on the management of change, managing knowledge, management development and human resource development. (b.delahaye@qut.edu.au)

Brian Hansford

Brian Hansford (BCom, BEd (Melb), MEd (Calg), PhD (NE)) was Professor and Head of the School of Professional Studies, Faculty of Education, at Queensland University of Technology from 1992 to 2000. He has had considerable experience in the supervision of staff and mentoring of new appointments. His Master of Educational Administration focused on decision making in organisational settings, and his PhD examined change in affective attributes during a structured training program. (bc.hansford@qut.edu.au)

Lisa Catherine Ehrich

Lisa Catherine Ehrich (DipT, BEd (Brisbane CAE), MEd Admin (QLD), PhD (QUT)) is a senior lecturer in the School of Professional Studies at Queensland University of Technology. She teaches in the areas of leadership and management, teacher education, and adult and workplace education. Her research interests include human resource management in education, women in management, mentoring and adult learning theories and practices. (l.ehrich@qut.edu.au)

Lee Tennent

Lee Tennent (BA (CQU), GradDip Ed (QUT), MEd (Research) (QUT)) is a doctoral student and senior research assistant in the Faculty of Education at Queensland University of Technology. Her research interests are in educational and business mentoring and the use of technology in teacher education, and early childhood care and education. (l.tennent@qut.edu.au)

Susan Long

Susan Long is Professor of Management (Organisation Dynamics) in the Australian Graduate School of Entrepreneurship at Swinburne University in Melbourne, where she teaches in postgraduate programs and supervises research candidates. Originally trained as a clinical psychologist, she has worked for more than 20 years as a group and organisation consultant and researcher. As a consultant, she works on organisational change, role analysis, team development and management training. Professor Long has extensive experience in the field of group relations and has directed several conferences through the Australian Institute of Socio-Analysis. She has been a staff member of group relations conferences in the United States (Bridger Workshop), the UK (Leicester), the Netherlands and Israel. She is President of the International Society for the Psycho-analytic Study of Organisations, is on the editorial board of two international journals and is editor of *Socio-Analysis*, the journal of AISA. She has published three books and many articles in collections and scholarly journals. (slong@groupwise.swin.edu.au)

Dianne Lewis

Dianne Lewis is a senior lecturer in management at the Queensland University of Technology. She researches and publishes widely in the areas of organisational culture, change and leadership and has extensive experience in the analysis of documentation providing insights into corporate culture. Dr Lewis specialises in the study of public-sector and not-for-profit organisations. In both her research and her consultancy she has had experience in analysing these types of organisations structurally, culturally and strategically with the aim of helping them plan for the future. She is currently executive committee editor (Asia–Pacific region) of the international journal *Strategic Change*. (d.lewis@qut.edu.au)

Dianne Waddell

Dianne Waddell is an Associate Professor and Director of Graduate Management Programs at Edith Cowan University, Perth. She is responsible for the development, implementation and evaluation of postgraduate courses, including the MBA, and teaches in the areas of quality management, change management and strategic management both on and off campus. She holds a PhD (Monash), Master of Education Administration (Melbourne), Bachelor of Education (Melbourne) and BA (LaTrobe). She has published and presented papers on resistance to change, leadership, e-business, quality management and forecasting for managers. Her publications include two textbooks, Organisation Development and Change and E-Business in Australia: Concepts and Cases. She has taught for many years in both public and private education systems, as well as presenting specifically designed industry-based courses. (Dianne.Waddell@buseco.monash.edu.au)

Michelle Greenwood

Michelle Greenwood is a lecturer in the Department of Management, Faculty of Business and Economics, at Monash University. Her research areas include management ethics, stakeholder theory, corporate social responsibility, social and ethical auditing, and ethical issues in HRM. Among her most recent publications are a review and conceptual analysis of ethics and HRM, and examinations of the community as a stakeholder in focusing on social and environmental reporting and citizenship, and the importance of stakeholders according to business leaders. She teaches management ethics and managing people and organisations. (Michelle.Greenwood@buseco.monash.edu.au)

Denice Ellen Welch

Denice Ellen Welch has a Bachelor of Business from the University of Southern Queensland, a Master of Management from Brunel University, and a PhD from Monash University. She is Professor of International Management at the Mt Eliza Business School in Melbourne, a conjoint appointment with the University of Queensland. Denice is co-author (with Peter Dowling and Randall Schuler) of the leading textbook *International Human Resource Management*. She has taught IHRM courses at the Norwegian School of Management in Oslo, Norway; the Copenhagen Business School in Denmark; and the Helsinki School of Economics in Finland. Her current research interests centre on the impact of the psychological contract on expatriate performance, the role of language standardisation in MNEs, and the link between IHRM strategies and international business operations. (Dwelch@mteliza.com.au)

Marilyn Fenwick

Marilyn Fenwick has a conjoint Bachelor of Business (Mngt) / BA degree from the Chisholm Institute of Technology and a PhD from the University of Melbourne. She is a senior lecturer with the Department of Management at Monash University, Melbourne. Marilyn designs and delivers undergraduate, master's and MBA courses in international management and IHRM. She has published international journal articles and book chapters in the areas of performance management, IHRM and international management. Her current Monash research projects concern expatriate performance management, forms of international assignment, and strategic IHRM in networking multinational organisations. Marilyn convenes the AHRI Special Interest Group in International Human Resource Management in Victoria. (Marilyn.Fenwick@buseco.monash.edu.au)

Beverley McNally

Beverley McNally is a lecturer in management at the Open Polytechnic of New Zealand and a doctoral researcher with the Centre for the Study of Leadership at Victoria University, Wellington. She is completing her doctorate in business in association with the University of Southern Queensland. Her research focuses on the development of global leadership competencies in New Zealand multinational companies and the role of HR in developing appropriate leadership development programs. Other research interests include the role of IHRM in New Zealand, CEO derailment and board–CEO relationships. (beverley.mcnally@paradise.net.nz)

Patrick Dawson

Patrick Dawson holds the Salvesen Chair of Management in the Department of Management Studies at the University of Aberdeen and is Guest Professor on the Danish research program 'Working Environment and Technological Development'. Professor Dawson has held positions at the universities of Adelaide, Wollongong, Surrey, Southampton, Edinburgh and Roskilde, and at the Danish Technical University. His main research interest centres on various aspects of organisational change. He has published numerous articles in scholarly books and refereed journals. (pdawson@abdn.ac.uk)

Preface

There is a great deal at stake in human resource management. The quality of the HR practices in organisations has a direct impact on people's physical and emotional health, their careers, and the effectiveness and viability of their organisations. Increasingly, the study of HRM deals with fundamental organisational processes that are developed and managed not only by HRM professionals but by all managers. The management of these organisational processes is geared to the search for competitive advantage. The challenge for managers is to develop the skills to unleash the potential of the people around them and throughout the organisation.

HR practices are under increasing scrutiny. HRM as we know it is changing, and these changes require new capabilities from all managers. The success of managers, and HR professionals in particular, depends on their ability to transform themselves and their organisations. HR professionals in organisations are continually challenged to prove that the HR practices they develop and implement deliver value. This book has been prepared to assist managers and HR professionals to do just this. The book does not simply replicate those formulas for success provided in HRM texts. It goes one step further, bringing together a highly qualified group of academics and practitioners to outline emerging issues and trends in their respective areas of expertise. The contributors discuss the challenging issues and controversies related to the HRM topics found in most HRM textbooks, and they identify future directions and implications for the management of human resources. This book provides students, HR professionals and managers with an authoritative reference source for their work in managing people and HR practices in organisations.

Retha Wiesner
Bruce Millett
June 2003

Acknowledgements

I wish to thank my husband, Johan, and daughter, Anchen, for their enthusiastic support, which made the completion of this project possible. I also wish to thank Janine Spencer-Burford and Jem Bates from John Wiley & Sons for their professional support and patience.

Retha Wiesner

I wish to thank my family, Jennifer, Rachael, Scott and Jessica, for their patience during this project.

Bruce Millett

The authors and publisher also wish to thank the following copyright holders, organisations and individuals for their permission to reproduce copyright material in this book.

Images
Page 60/ Bruce Millett, B (1999) *Strategic Human Resource Planning*, Study Book GSN216, University of Southern Queensland, Toowoomba. Reproduced with permission of Bruce Millett. Page 66/ Adapted from A Nankervis, RL Compton and TM McCarthy (1999), *Strategic Human Resource Management*, 3rd edition (Melbourne: Nelson), p.158. © Thomson Learning. Further copying, reproduction, downloading or transferring requires permission from Thomson Learning. Page 87/ Adapted from DM Rousseau and KA Wade-Benzoni (1994), Linking strategy and human resources practices: how employees and customer contracts are created, *Human Resources Management*, 33 (3), p. 464. Reproduced with permission of Denise Rousseau & Kimberly Wade-Benzoni. Pages 89, 96 (top), 96 (bottom)/ From L Shore and L Tetrick (1994), in CL Cooper and DM Rousseau (Eds), *Trends in Organisational Behaviour*, 1. Reproduced with permission of John Wiley & Sons Ltd (UK). Page 99/ W Turnley and D Feldman (1998), Psychological contract violations during corporate restructuring, *Human Resource Management*, 37 (1), p. 82. Used by permission of John Wiley & Sons, Inc. Page 294/ From B Kedia and A Mukherji (1999), *Journal of World Business* 34 (3), p. 235. Reproduced with permission from Elsevier.

Page 298/ Adapted from JA Quelch and H Bloom (1999), *Strategy & Business*, 14 (1). Reproduced with permission of John Quelch. Page 301/ Adapted from DT Hall (1986), *An Overview of Current Career Development Theory, Research and Practice* (San Francisco: Jossey-Bass), p. 4. Reproduced by permission of Douglas T Hall.

Text
Pages 61, 68/ Ronel Erwee (2000), *Education Victoria: Managing and valuing diversity policy and guidelines*. Report no. 2. Toowoomba: University of Southern Queensland, pp. 1–9. © R Erwee. Reproduced with permission. Page 78/ From D Binney (2001), The knowledge management spectrum — understanding the KM landscape, *Journal of Knowledge Management*, 5 (1), pp. 33–42. Reproduced with permission of Derek Binney. Page 112, figures 9.5 and 9.6/ Adapted from R Fells (1999), The process of negotiation, in R Thorpe (Ed.), *Managing Diversity*. Proceedings of the British Academy of Management Conference, Manchester. Adapted and reproduced with permission of Ray Fells. Page 180/ From RL Compton, WJ Morrissey and A Nankervis (2002), *Effective Recruitment and Selection Practices*, 3rd edition (Sydney: CCH), pp. 134–5. Reproduced with permission of CCH Australia Limited. Page 262, figures 21.2 and 21.3/ From JV Saraph and RJ Sebastian (1993), Developing a quality culture, *Quality Progress*, 26 (9), p. 74. Adapted and reprinted with permission from *Quality Progress* magazine, © 1993 American Society for Quality. Page 300, table 24.1, figures 24.3 and 24.4/ From K Inkson, J Pringle, M Arthur and S Barry (1997), *Journal of World Business*, 32 (4), pp. 352, 358, 364. Reproduced with permission from Elsevier.

Every effort has been made to trace the ownership of copyright material. Information that will enable the publisher to rectify any error or omission in subsequent editions will be welcome. In such cases, please contact the Permissions Section of John Wiley & Sons Australia, Ltd, who will arrange for the payment of the usual fee.

Introduction

Human Resource Management: Challenges and Future Directions is a book of invited chapters about aspects of HRM, a book that raises challenges and offers advice to managers, and in particular HR managers, of contemporary organisations. First, it provides valuable insights into managing people. Second, it addresses current challenges that HR and other managers face every day. Third, it outlines the practical implications of these challenges for organisations. Fourth, it identifies future directions for managers, and particularly HR managers, to consider in their quest to develop high-performance workplaces.

We believe the book fulfils a real need for both HR managers and students of HRM. It complements current HRM texts by offering a range of alternative views and perspectives. Uniquely, it provides an authoritative, up-to-date commentary from a selection of noted authors on significant issues relating to HRM.

The chapters have been grouped into four parts.

Part 1 • The changing context of HRM

What are the main features of the changing context of HRM? What does it take for organisations, HR managers and employees to succeed in these changing environments? Part 1 provides answers to these questions. In chapter 1, James Hunt emphasises the importance for modern managers of understanding the origins and forces driving organisational change. He identifies three broad groups of forces propelling organisational change: global economic forces, individual forces and technological forces. He examines the phenomenon of rapid organisational change in the context of the rise of the modern management consultancy industry and the blossoming of the global organisational solutions market by exploring five related organisational responses. He argues that it is individuals who can think fast and harness their intellectual capacity to generate solutions and identify opportunities who will excel in the future world of work. They will need to be alert, informed and capable of assuming a leadership role when the opportunity presents itself. James sets the scene for the new world of work in which if you don't seize control of your own destiny, somebody else will.

In chapter 2, Robin Kramar focuses on changing organisational practices by examining the extent to which formal HR policies and practices in large Australian organisations changed during the 1990s, particularly between 1993 and 1999, and by comparing these changes with those in 21 other countries. She explores the characteristics of the 'ideal' model or vision of people management practice developed by employers in the 1980s. She then examines the findings of an international study to determine the extent to which large Australian organisations have moved towards this 'ideal' model. She identifies the implications of these developments for employees, the challenges they pose for management and possible future directions for people management in Australia. She concludes that although there is considerable variation among the countries in the international study, it appears that more organisations in Australia have developed policies consistent with the American model than with those associated with other countries in the study.

Kerr Inkson's chapter focuses on taking responsibility for one's own career within a changing workplace environment. In chapter 3, he asks the question: is the main responsibility for your career yours, or your company's, or is it a shared obligation? He argues that, contrary to the traditional view, the responsibility lies with the individual. In answering the question, 'What, if anything, is the role of HRM in an individual's career?', he argues that there is a role in assisting individual career development through opportunities for motivation, education, skills development, access to networks, evaluation and reputation. He asserts that good HR can 'partner' employees' career development by ensuring the individuals are aware of and able to utilise these opportunities appropriately. Conversely, employees can do much to assist their organisations through their own personal career development and decision making. Kerr concludes that career development will in future become less the responsibility of the organisation and more that of the individual; less a local matter and more an external matter; less about the management of human and organisational resources and more about the development of human and organisational partnerships across boundaries.

In chapter 4, Margaret Patrickson explores the challenges facing Australian HR practice in the twenty-first century as a result of workforce ageing. She argues that those aged over 50 could soon form the largest cohort in the workforce, and that this demographic change will have important ramifications for HRM as older workers approach a majority in the workforce. Unlike in the previous generation, older workers' contributions will add value to business, and they will be needed. In view of this, providing them with a healthy work environment, working within the terms of their financial situation, and stimulating their motivation and commitment will be important challenges for HRM. She offers suggestions on how to manage this group effectively and integrate its contribution with that of others to gain maximum value from all staff. The chapter also outlines the desirable changes in HRM policy and practice as the over-40 cohort comes to form at least half the workforce and as those aged over 50 become a political force in the workplace. Margaret concludes that organisations will need to adapt their staff management activities to retain this group for as long as possible. She provides a snapshot of the future in which organisations' efforts are supported by governments who have a vested interest in reducing the numbers of those receiving social security payments. Community attitudes will need to be supportive and work patterns flexible during this period of change.

Another important issue facing organisations today is how to assist employees to balance their work and family commitments. This question is addressed by Jarrod Haar and Chester Spell in chapter 5. He argues that as employees' lives become increasingly complicated both in the workplace and at home, their capacity to provide unrestricted and energised labour is affected. He stresses the need for business leaders, HR managers and employers to be aware of their employees' work and family issues. Forward-thinking leaders and their HR counterparts recognise that work–family policies may provide the key to correcting the imbalance that many employees now face. Jarrod identifies the major influences on organisations that have facilitated the development and proliferation of work–family policies, and he discusses the major practices themselves. He also explores the reported effects of work–family policies and the future direction of this progressive HRM practice. He concludes that managers who ignore the concerns of their workers, especially in industries with a tight labour market, will experience negative repercussions, while organisations that embrace work–family policies may achieve a competitive advantage over other firms that their resources might not suggest.

In chapter 6, Ronel Erwee examines the debate on how diversity management initiatives can be integrated with strategic human resource management (SHRM), and how SHRM is linked to organisational strategy. To what extent

are processes associated with managing diversity an integral part of the strategic vision of management? Ronel argues that there is no consensus on how a corporate strategic plan influences or is influenced by SHRM, and how the latter integrates diversity management as a key component. Organisations tend to be understood either as linear, steady-state entities or as dynamic, complex and fluid entities. Approaches to SHRM are influenced by these contrasting paradigms. She explores SHRM's links to both corporate strategy and diversity management. She also considers how managing diversity should address sensitive topics such as gender, race and ethnicity. Finally, she considers whether an integrative approach to SHRM can be achieved and how to overcome the obstacles to making this a reality. She concludes that managers need to establish whether their organisations have formulated strategic priorities that will sustain them over the next decade. Managers should assist organisations to design and implement a range of SHRM policies and programs to ensure they provide high-quality services to their staff, customers and the community.

In chapter 7, Lesley Willcoxson examines the concepts of organisational learning and the learning organisation and how these relate to the concept of knowledge management. She establishes the similarities and differences between the three concepts and reviews the reported reasons for failure to achieve organisational learning or create a learning organisation. She then outlines the HRM strategies conducive to the achievement of a learning organisation or organisational learning and, against this background, examines the HRM strategies associated with effective knowledge management within organisations. Drawing on the reasons given for failures to achieve learning in organisations, she derives additional conclusions about the HRM strategies needed to promote knowledge management. She argues that knowledge management, like organisational learning, holds out to organisations the potential for fully capitalising on the intangible assets implicit in the knowledge and experience of their employees. For employees, knowledge management, like organisational learning, holds out the prospect of invigorating the organisational environment in which communication would be rich and productive, personal growth would be assured and rewards would come to those who contribute most effectively. She concludes, however, that, like the learning organisation, knowledge management initiatives currently deliver to employees much less than promised.

Part 2 • *Contemporary issues in employment relations*

Part 2 explores the challenging issues and future directions associated with employment relations. Heather Maguire, writing on the changing psychological contract in organisations, sets the scene for the rest of the section. In chapter 8, she outlines the function, development and content of the psychological contract; the 'old' versus the 'new' psychological contract; change and the psychological contract; challenging issues associated with the changing psychological contract and implications for the management of human resources. She argues that the co-dependency between employee and organisation that once underpinned the psychological contract has weakened considerably, and if employees move towards the new protean career, organisations may be unwilling to invest in training and development programs for employees because of a perceived lack of continuing commitment among them. She further argues that, taken to the extreme, this trend could produce a highly transient workforce in which employees are simply attracted to the organisation offering the highest rewards; in this situation, the psychological contract may take on far less importance than it did traditionally. Heather recognises, however, that an increasingly transient workforce has considerable dollar costs for organisations. She identifies the need for organisations to research the types of rewards that will attract employee loyalty.

Ray Fells focuses on the collective aspects of employment in chapter 9. He explores a number of issues relating to the management of a collectively organised workplace, developing his arguments around three themes: the organisational need to negotiate; the need for a strategic, or at least well-considered, approach; and the importance of integrating management–union relations and manager–employee relations. He provides clear frameworks for the strategic options explored in this chapter. He concludes by arguing that, given the importance of negotiation in all aspects of managing an organisation, the HR manager has an obligation to establish a preferred way of negotiating.

In contrast to the preceding chapter, Peter Waring and Mark Bray focus on the individualisation of the employment relationship. In chapter 10, they make a thoughtful assessment of individualism in employment relations, and of the strategic choices available when managing human resources, by exploring the recent growth in individualism

of the employment relationship. After defining and identifying three main types of individualism, they examine the various arguments used to support and oppose individualisation. They explore the question: are the critics right when they claim that individualism is about excluding trade unions from representing members and permitting employers to exploit their superior bargaining power, or are its supporters closer to the truth when they argue that individual contracts encourage a closer, more trusting relationship between employers and their employees? They examine in depth the Australian experience of individualism in its various forms. They conclude that a growing number of Australian employers have individualised the employment relationship in response to economic imperatives, although there is little evidence to support claims that substantial benefits accrue as a result of individualisation.

The transformation of the Australian labour market from a highly unionised, centrally regulated, male-dominated, mainly full-time workforce has resulted in a diverse range of direct employment and contractual arrangements that, it has been argued, better meet the needs of employers and employees. HRM in contemporary organisations therefore frequently involves managing a workforce that incorporates a variety of employment relationships including, for example, part-time, casual and fixed-term staff. In chapter 11, Linley Hartmann explores the challenges of mixed employment relations. She begins by outlining alternative forms of employment and organisational employment structures. She examines Atkinson's organisational framework depicting the alternative employment relationships available to organisations before discussing the differences these alternatives bring to the employment relationship. The focus of the chapter then moves to the incidence of alternative forms of employment in Australia and the issues and challenges of multiple employment relationships for organisations, for managers and for individual workers. She discusses organisational challenges including determining the right employee mix, contracts and commitment, equity and fairness, broader social impacts, and legal implications as illustrated by occupational health and safety issues. She explores these challenges in terms of their implications for managers and employees. Linley argues that Australian organisations have rapidly adopted alternative forms of employment, and that this development has created a great deal of uncertainty within the labour force. The extent to which different sections of the workforce, and individuals within them, will find these changes to their advantage or disadvantage may shift as their experience and understanding of these new labour market dynamics develop. She makes it clear that managing these changing mixed employment relationships requires new levels of adaptability.

Simon Peel takes the theme of mixed employment relations one step further by examining a contemporary issue — the widespread use of contractors — and exploring some of the related concerns and implications for managers and organisations. He argues that the use of contractors in organisations presents challenges of a theoretical and practical nature. Contracting has costs as well as benefits. Although the costs may not outweigh the real and tangible benefits of using contractors, Simon asserts that they should nonetheless be acknowledged, because the costs are often hidden and will be revealed only by close examination. Nowhere is this more apparent than when considering the paradoxical nature of employment flexibility, with managers challenged to balance the multiple ways in which flexibility can be gained or lost. The chapter suggests that contemporary employment practices such as the use of contractors challenge some traditional views of what HRM is about and force a re-examination of fundamental concepts such as what we mean by the business 'core' and what we mean by referring to people as 'resources'. Simon outlines how those responsible for managing the firm's most important resources might accept the challenge of considering alternative employment structures. He concludes that they should do so by employing a more rigorous style of analysis that accounts for the many ways in which people add value to organisations.

Part 2 concludes with Suzanne Jamieson's analysis of the legal context of HRM. She begins by discussing the powers with which the Constitution provides the various parliaments to address labour and HRM issues, and raises the important question of just who is a worker. She then maps out the way in which the law regulates the employment relationship in Australia — from the creation of the contract through to its conclusion. Having provided a 'broad brush' picture of the current law regulating the workplace, she argues that the reality is necessarily complex because of the federal–state dichotomy. The picture is also constantly changing, with regulation now increasingly reflecting the individualist approach. Change, in any case, is endemic to labour law, which is always subject to changing political attitudes.

Part 3 • Contemporary issues in managing performance and development

Part 3 focuses on contemporary challenges in managing performance and development in organisations, such as recruitment and selection, e-cruitment, implementing a total reward framework, company change, understanding the dynamics of the internal team, and HRM and the legal environment.

The first challenge facing any organisation undertaking recruitment and selection is how to attract and select the right people. Diana du Plessis focuses on this very important HR issue in chapter 14. Organisations today face greater challenges from both their external and their internal environments. She argues that it is easier for organisations to duplicate competitors' technology or manufacturing processes than to replicate their unique combination of human resources. She demonstrates why it is crucial for organisations to hire the right mix of employees in terms of their knowledge, skills and abilities. She also outlines the relevant recruitment and selection processes needed to obtain a competitive advantage.

In chapter 15, Susan Hinton takes the theme of recruitment one step further by delving into the issue of e-cruitment. She provides answers to the following questions: What are the costs and benefits of e-cruitment? To what extent do recruiters rely on the Internet as a recruitment tool, and for what purpose? What kind of recruitment outcomes does e-cruitment provide? She addresses these questions by first providing an overview of 'e-cruitment' and then examining claims that it is an effective, low-cost alternative to traditional (face-to-face and paper-based) recruitment methods. She argues that despite the hype surrounding the popularity and effectiveness of e-cruitment methods, the take-up of Internet technology in the recruitment industry is relatively slow. She makes the point that e-cruitment is best understood as a new method of recruitment (one of many available to employers) that brings new challenges to an already complex and increasingly strategic process. She concludes by examining a number of issues of importance to job seekers, employers and HR professionals such as privacy, access and diversity.

Graham O'Neill addresses the complex issue of reward strategies in chapter 16. He argues that if there is one major global trend in the broad arena of employee rewards it is the notion of Total Rewards, and that one of the surest ways to maximise return on investment in employees is to develop a deliberate framework that includes all reward mechanisms available to the organisation. Graham asserts that experience in working with clients on issues of management style and work climate over the past decade or so suggests there are some specific characteristics that differentiate high-performing organisations. He proposes that there are two critical design factors related to performance-based pay at all levels within the organisation. With the growing trend towards team-based work structures, he identifies the management of team performance as a major issue. He concludes that the successful organisation today provides a genuinely rewarding work environment that encourages employees to become committed to the objectives of the enterprise. Such an organisation offers a significant contrast to those firms that maintain a simplistic reliance on individual financial reward as the basis for managing people and their work experience.

In chapter 17, Brian Delahaye addresses management of the knowledge capital (sometimes referred to as the 'knowledge asset' or 'knowledge resource') of an organisation and demonstrates why this has become one of the key activities for organisations in the twenty-first century. He argues that the human resource development (HRD) function has a central role in managing the critical asset of knowledge. Brian first examines the change in organisational emphasis from the early-twentieth-century concept of 'training and development' to 'human resource development' to 'managing knowledge'. He then discusses the unique nature of knowledge as an asset and presents a basic model as a means of examining the processes involved in managing an organisation's knowledge capital. He uses this model of two interacting systems — the legitimate and the shadow — to examine the critical role each has to play in managing the organisation's knowledge capital. Brian concludes that HRD is pivotal to the successful management of the organisation, and to fulfil this central role effectively the HR developer must become the steward of the organisational knowledge capital.

Brian Hansford, Lisa Ehrich and Lee Tennent report on findings from empirical research conducted in the area of mentoring in chapter 18. They begin their chapter by defining mentoring and identifying the two types of mentoring arrangements that operate in organisations — formal and informal mentoring. They then provide a brief dis-

cussion on some of the theories and conceptual models that have been proposed to explain the mentoring phenomenon. An analysis of the research literature identifies the benefits and drawbacks of mentoring for key stakeholders such as mentors, 'mentees' (traditionally known as 'protégés') and the organisation. They draw upon findings from their structured analysis of 151 pieces of mentoring research. Finally, they discuss some important issues, implications, challenges and future directions associated with mentoring for HRM. They conclude that the successful implementation and management of any mentoring program requires a careful mix of many important ingredients.

A lot of work in contemporary organisations is performed by teams. In chapter 19, Susan Long asks: what is the specific nature of a team, and how are the team members related to one another? She argues that effective and satisfying team-work relies on a complex and specific psychological capacity among team members — that is, the ability to work creatively with other team members and the team-as-a-whole as internalised objects. When this capacity is not exercised or cannot be achieved, teamwork is impaired. She also examines the nature of work and in doing so asserts that, in essence, psychic work involves transformative and representative processes that engage the psyche (or mind) with reality. She then explores the nature of the team as a special form of group and illustrates through research examples the complex dynamic of work with internal objects. She draws the conclusion that the key to successful teamwork is to establish conditions under which each member can understand and internalise the roles of other team members vis-à-vis the common task. As well as communicating with others, team members should have an understanding of the other roles in the system. A helpful HR consultant can provide supportive conditions to aid this process. These conditions allow team members to develop and change their internal objects in the light of current realities. She concludes that team training and mentoring should advance such processes.

Part 4 • Managing for the millennium

The twenty-first century brings many new challenges for HR managers and students of HRM. More than ever we need to identify and discuss these HRM issues if we are to take advantage of the opportunities that abound. Part 4 explores some of these critical issues.

In the opening chapter of this part, Dianne Lewis addresses the issue of power and politics in organisations. She argues that understanding power is an important survival tactic. While a knowledge of power has traditionally been considered essential for general managers, it is also important for HR managers and indeed all individuals in organisations to understand its workings. Many individuals may never aspire to managerial positions, but this does not mean they will never want to use power. And even if they have no desire to use it, they need to know how it affects outcomes in organisations. Within this context, Dianne discusses the nature of power and politics, the different forms of power and where power comes from. She also examines such challenging issues as how to recognise and assess power, the relationship between power and conflict, and how to understand when to use power. Controversial areas such as the unsettling nature of power and politics and the place of politics in organisational life are also discussed. She assesses the directions the study of power seems to be taking in the literature for general managers, HR managers and practitioners, women and individuals who work in the public sector. She concludes with a discussion of the implications of power and politics for organisations, managers (both general and HR) and individuals. The message in this chapter is that power exists in organisations for good and for ill, and managers and other individuals need to understand the threats and the opportunities that power presents. Rather than trying to eliminate it altogether, we need to see it as a source of both positive and negative outcomes. Future HR professionals will need to recognise power's influence and learn to use it to implement organisational policies and handle conflicts. At the same time, all organisational members will need to understand its workings and how they may use it either in pursuit of their own ambitions or simply to survive in a power environment. Power is indeed a 'two-edged sword'.

Dianne Waddell addresses one of the hottest topics in the media today — quality. In chapter 21, she argues that if the culture of the organisation does not support and reinforce a quality philosophy, the entire quality effort will be significantly undermined. She further maintains that it is important to identify which quality culture factors (top management leadership, teamwork, employee empowerment and commitment to customers) have the greatest impact on quality performance outcomes (financial performance, service performance, employee satisfaction and customer satisfaction). Dianne concludes by arguing that quality is predominantly about people, not processes. It is about behaviour, attitude, involvement, empowerment, commitment and, above all, change. To this end, the HR manager must be a proactive champion of quality and a catalyst for continuous improvement in the organisation.

In chapter 22, Michelle Greenwood explores another hot media topic, namely the issue of ethics in contemporary organisations. Accepting that many corporate mission statements contain claims that the organisation values and cares for its employees, she asks the question: what do these claims imply about the ethical responsibility of the organisation to its employees? The answers to this and other questions, she argues, are the subject of the developing ethical perspective of HRM. This perspective has been differentiated in the HRM literature only recently, and in this chapter Michelle analyses and further develops the conceptualisation of the main issues. She gives particular emphasis to the use of stakeholder theory, which has so far been neglected in the literature. She explores the pervasive positivist perspective of HRM, the response of an alternative critical paradigm and the development of the ethical perspective of HRM. She also examines the gaps and challenges in the existing ethical discourse of HRM and discusses the implications for organisations, managers and employees. Finally, she identifies future directions for the ethical perspective of HRM.

The next two chapters explore HRM within an international and global context. Denice Welch and Marilyn Fenwick examine the issue of virtual assignments in chapter 23. They draw on the results of a recent survey suggesting that the use of what is being termed 'non-standard' international assignments is growing, partly as a substitute for the more traditional form of longer term expatriate assignments. These non-standard forms include short-term, contractual, rotational, commuter and virtual assignments. They draw out the HR management implications of what is emerging as a new form of international assignment — the 'virtual assignment'. Within this context they investigate a central question: is the virtual assignment a new form of international assignment initiated to complement existing forms as the organisational context of multinational enterprise changes, or does it merely repackage elements of existing practice to capitalise on advances in communication media to overcome barriers to staff mobility and contain the rising cost of expatriate management? If the former, what are the implications for IHRM? They explore the emergence of the virtual assignment as part of the trend towards non-standard assignments by questioning whether the virtual assignment is a new form — a logical extension of improved communication systems and new forms of multinational enterprise that are conducive to the achievement of strategic objectives without the need for a longer term physical presence in the host country. They conclude that from the limited data available it seems that the virtual assignment is a variation of the traditional, standard assignment — the spatial dimension being its main distinction, in that a geographical distance separates the assignee from the organisation's day-to-day operations located in a foreign country. They close by posing an even more relevant question: what makes a virtual assignment different from situations in which international activities are supervised from a central location?

In chapter 24, Beverley McNally addresses the challenges of globalisation and its implications for HRM. This chapter outlines several HRM challenges relating to globalisation, including the development of an international human resource management (IHRM) discipline and an HR system with global strategies, a strategic partnership, the global HR specialist and the global employee. Beverley argues that the development of global capabilities will greatly depend on the organisation's approach to IHRM. She identifies numerous challenges, including rapid growth, issues of culture and diversity, new technology, globalisation and competitive pressures. She asserts that given these challenges managers may have to struggle to keep up with the new skills required of them, and the challenge for business will be to fundamentally change the way in which people understand doing business in this environment. Business in the new global environment, she concludes, is no longer about taking frequent short business trips, attending conferences or meeting people from other cultures at company headquarters. It is about developing a geocentric mindset,

which requires a global perspective; it is about being comfortable doing business in a country with a different culture, and on that country's terms.

Flexibility is a key business concept in the twenty-first century. In chapter 25, Patrick Dawson questions both traditional change models and modern change initiatives advocating a human-centred approach that, while supporting strategies that supposedly promote flexibility and empowerment, actually result in an intensification of work and an increase in employee pressure to conform to new, imposed behaviours. He examines key HR dimensions to change management, and in particular the growing pressure for employees to adapt to flexible work practices and job arrangements. He argues that although it is not uncommon for change models to recognise the importance of gaining the support of employees, from the perspective of those on the shop floor or in the branch office there is a growing weariness and cynicism over what appears to be an endless barrage of change initiatives to extract ever more from a dwindling pool of employees. In critically evaluating some of these issues, he begins by examining the main reasons why companies embark on change initiatives. He addresses a number of definitional concerns and change strategies that seek labour flexibility yet stress the importance of the human dimension, such as employee participation, communication and building collaborative relationships at work. He then critically appraises the push towards flexible working arrangements, the benefits to employees of such changes, employee resistance to change, change theories that emphasise the importance of communication and employee involvement, and the planned organisational development approach to change. He concludes by charting the benefits of a processual approach that draws attention to the lived experience of change and unmasks the rhetoric behind many of the change initiatives associated with the 'culture-excellence' school.

The changing context of HRM

part 1

CHAPTER I

The anatomy of organisational change in the twenty-first century

by James B. Hunt
University of Newcastle

Introduction

Over the past 20 years, the world of work has been immersed in a process of dynamic and sometimes turbulent change, reflecting the shift from the industrial era to the information age. Despite their profound effects, many of the changes that have emerged in organisations over this period have been largely unrecognised in some quarters, so that change itself is now accepted as an indispensable feature of today's professional arena. *Downsizing, delayering* and *outsourcing* are all part of today's business lexicon, and yet these are terms that would have been unfamiliar even to senior executives in the early 1980s.

Organisations today are far less hierarchical than they were in the past. Large international organisations in the 1970s typically consisted of approximately 15 layers of management; today these firms have just five or six managerial levels. The result is that *delegation* is far more important now than it ever was, since managerial spans of control have been extended considerably, making it impossible for managers to rely exclusively on their own specialist expertise to achieve organisational goals. This structural shift has made *reciprocal interdependence* an important feature of modern organisational effectiveness, and has significantly weakened the once unchallenged potency of autocratic management approaches, thus placing a premium on interpersonal skills at all levels.

It is important for modern managers to understand the origins and forces driving these changes, primarily because such an understanding enables executives and professionals to better equip themselves to remain effective today and into the future. Three broad groups of forces propelling organisational change are identified in this chapter. These are *global economic forces*, *individual forces* and *technological forces*. The phenomenon of rapid organisational change is examined in the context of the rise of the modern management consultancy industry and the blossoming of the global organisational solutions market. Five related organisational responses are noted, providing evidence of the dominance of the North American model of management in organisations throughout the world today. These forces for and consequences of change combine to define in organisational and managerial terms what is commonly referred to as the knowledge economy, the information age or the digital era.

The Japanese ascendancy

Before the 1980s the United States dominated the world in terms of its multinational business empires and, beyond a handful of successful European companies, large US corporations had very few serious commercial rivals. All this changed in the early 1980s when several large Japanese manufacturing firms emerged on the world stage. For the first time, US car manufacturers lost significant market share to their Japanese counterparts. The emergence of successful firms such as Toyota, Nissan and Mitsubishi sparked a serious re-examination of management and manufacturing processes at Chrysler and Ford. At the same time, Sony emerged as a world leader in consumer electronics, provoking US-based business schools and management consultants to explore the reasons behind the Japanese ascendancy.

Over the decade of the 1980s Western organisations, and in particular US-based firms, learned from the meticulous Japanese approaches to organisational management. Western firms began to successfully incorporate into their own organisations those aspects of Japanese management practice that suited their culture. William Ouchi (1981) referred to this process of adaptation as 'theory Z management'. This phase of international business development marked the start of a significant acceleration in competitiveness among multinational firms around the world. The Japanese had thrown down the gauntlet in the early 1980s, effectively challenging US corporate hegemony on the world stage. This unleashed a frenzy of hyper-competitiveness that passed largely unnoticed before the worldwide recession of the early 1990s consigned many white-collar workers to the ranks of the unemployed. Downsizing and outsourcing initiatives were not just 1990s management fads; they were products of the accelerated competitiveness set in train in the early 1980s. What was once predominantly a North American approach to management (slimming down organisational hierarchies, speeding up innovation and outsourcing non-core functions) has now begun to take hold in countries such as France, Germany and Japan.

Global economic forces for change

One of the most important sparks to ignite the flame of managerial best practice, and therefore fuel the pace of change in organisations, was the shift by Western nations towards low-inflation economies at the beginning of the 1990s. Another factor contributing to ongoing organisational change has been the continuing reduction in tariff barriers and the move towards free trade agreements.

In the early 1970s Australia and the United States were known as high-inflation economies, a characteristic they shared with a number of other Western nations. In 1991 inflation collapsed in these countries, reflecting the deep resolve on the part of national governments to hold inflation down. The reasons behind this move are complex, but they include the realisation that *management* in a high-inflation environment can become careless and wasteful. In such an environment there is little incentive to contain costs. This meant that management could avoid making tough decisions to enhance organisational competitiveness, as was the general approach in Australia in the 1970s. High-inflation environments tended to encourage borrowing, because inflation simply eroded the value of debt

over time. Good growth in business revenue tended to occur predominantly as a result of inflation, rather than as a result of tangible productivity increases.

In 1991 central banking authorities in a number of prominent Western nations committed themselves to maintaining limits on inflation. Managers quickly learned that borrowing in a low-inflation environment is much tougher than borrowing in a high-inflation environment. In the low-inflation environments that have emerged in modern economies since 1991, managers have been required to become very good at containing costs within organisations. As a result, wage increases, for example, are now normally linked to demonstrated improvements in productivity. Productivity, which refers to the efficiency with which people and organisations operate, is an important driver of change in modern organisations. Productivity increases are now sought in most organisations on a continuous basis, thus perpetuating the change process.

The second global economic force for change influencing today's organisations is the continued movement towards reducing tariff barriers between nations. This has the effect of exposing domestic manufacturers and service providers to international competition, which in turn tends to reveal the lack of efficiency in domestic operations. When tariff barriers remain high, they tend to sustain enterprise performance below the level of international best practice and act as a disincentive to lifting productivity levels. Thus, the reduced tariff barriers emerging in today's world of commerce are further fuelling the process of change in terms of internal structural adjustments at the organisational level.

Individual forces for change

At the individual level, it is often overlooked that shareholders and consumers alike continue to exert considerable pressure, both directly and indirectly, on organisations to transform their internal processes in order to raise productivity levels and increase the competitiveness of their goods and services. The closure of bank branches throughout Australia, for example, is sometimes portrayed by the media as evidence of unbridled corporate greed, but such an analysis ignores the forces that have ignited this heightened pursuit of profit.

Shareholders today are not just more demanding in relation to their expected return on investments; they are also often more impatient and more unforgiving, as well as better equipped to gain real-time information about corporate performance. They also have greater freedom to move their investment dollars to capitalise on alternative opportunities if existing investments fail to perform according to expectations. In addition, there are many more shareholders around the world now than ever before, boosting the potential flow of capital around the globe. Even individuals who don't own shares directly can exert an influence on corporations through their pension funds, which are expected to be managed for growth and typically include a portfolio of share-based investments. Friedman (2000) refers to this movement of capital in search of the highest return as *the electronic herd,* effectively capturing the devastating pace at which money-market psychology can operate on organisations as a catalyst for change.

Today's consumers constitute the second major individual set of forces for change in modern organisations. The demand for newer, better, faster products and services is evident everywhere — from the fashion industry to children's toys, from fast foods to the computer software market. Tighter and tighter product life cycles, and increasing consumer demand for service innovations, ensure that organisations remain constantly engaged in the process of change (Bridges 1995). Internal organisational response systems are now required to manage the pursuit of creativity and simultaneously adhere to high levels of productivity in the form of annual efficiency gains.

Technological forces for change

The rapid transformation of the world's central nervous system has touched individuals from Washington to Tuvalu, one of the world's least developed countries. The digital revolution has resulted in developments that have helped to transform the way in which work is carried out in and between organisations. Satellite linkages, cellular phone networks and high-speed fibre-optic cables have enabled business transactions to gain the kind of momentum never before witnessed in the modern commercial world. These technological changes, exemplified by the rapid developments in computer processing capabilities, have sustained and enabled the global economic forces for change previously identified, and have also contributed to the individual forces for change. More importantly, however, they contributed to ongoing rapid organisational change throughout the 1990s by creating a heightened awareness of the importance of advanced technology to the world's commercial environment. Investment in new forms of enabling infrastructure (computer networks, software, telecommunications) allowed Western organisations in the second half of the 1990s to defy cyclical economic downturns and continue to realise productivity increases, further fuelling organisational transformation and change.

Before the advent of the information era, with its high-speed modems and the emergence of e-commerce, organisations had already begun to require their employees at every level to think for themselves, to exercise initiative, to innovate, and to solve problems at their source as quickly and as effectively as possible. Modern information and communications technology (ICT) has simply enabled more employees to respond to these demands with greater efficiency than was previously possible.

The more obvious signs of the growing reliance on ICT around the world today are apparent everywhere. The mobile telephone, a luxury item just 15 years ago, has now become the quintessential instant communications tool for the modern world of work and is enjoying explosive growth around the world. Even more revealing is the phenomenal growth of the Internet. China, which is still in transition from a centrally planned economy to a market economy, had an estimated 18 million Internet users in 2000 and is expected to have 200 million users by 2005 (Elliott & Hiscock 2000). There are currently 147 million Internet users worldwide; by 2005 this figure is expected to reach 1 billion (Gottliebsen 2000). Business-to-business e-commerce is now a US$131 billion industry, and according to the Forrester Research Group will reach $1.5 trillion by 2003 (Krantz 2000). In 1998 just 17 per cent of Fortune 500 firms used the Internet for recruitment purposes; by 2000, 70 per cent of these corporations were recruiting on-line. The magnitude of organisational change that these figures suggest is difficult to determine with accuracy, but far-reaching structural and procedural organisational transformation processes are already evident at the dawn of what may well become known as the *new* information age.

The rise of the modern management consultancy industry

Managers in organisations today have come to rely increasingly on expert advice, often provided by external experts, partly because downsizing has meant that organisations no longer have internal access to the variety and depth of expertise required to meet the challenges created by continuous innovation and change. In particular, senior executives in US and Australian organisations have depended to a remarkable extent on management consultants to assist in the generation of organisation-wide strategies and solutions. The management consultancy industry has thrived as a result of this dependence.

Modern management consultants command premium rates for assisting organisations with the process of managing change today, mainly because they are usually able to demonstrate the effectiveness of their role in the change process. They do this initially through the intelligent diagnosis of pockets of inefficiency and through the detection of systems that may be expected to fail. Above all, modern management consultants are astute diagnostic specialists. They are able to isolate key problem areas, break these down in order to identify their respective root causes and quantify the relative magnitude of each required change initiative.

The management consultancy industry today consists of a wide range of smaller players (companies employing between 2 and 20 individuals) and a narrower range of dominant global players. The biggest of these are Accenture (formerly Andersen Consulting), the Boston Consulting Group (BCG), McKinsey & Co., Ernst & Young and Bain & Co. These global players are prominent in many of the world's largest organisations, assisting with strategic repositioning and restructuring initiatives, frequently on an ongoing basis. The role they play in driving organisational change, therefore, cannot be understated.

Figure 1.1 depicts the projected steady revenue growth for the management consultancy industry to the year 2002, based on data from the Kennedy Research Group (1997) and the United Nations Conference on Trade and Development (UNCTD 1993). It is evident that consultancy services will continue to grow over the next ten years, in line with the trend for organisations to under-utilise their existing intellectual capital to generate internal solutions to problems and opportunities, and therefore to rely on external assistance to manage the process of accelerated change.

The various large-scale consultancy firms have different strategies for managing knowledge generated from the collective experience of their employees. McKinsey & Co., for example, is less likely to store the individual wisdom and expertise generated from fieldwork electronically than is Accenture. Instead, McKinsey uses face-to-face meetings and other forms of direct dialogue to spread expertise throughout their organisation (Hansen, Nohria & Tierney 1999).

One of the reasons that McKinsey has acquired such a formidable reputation for managing change is that its consultants are constantly exposed to the dynamics of organisational transformation, and when they sell their expertise in the form of a solution to an organisational problem, they don't lose that solution; they take it with them and are able to adapt it and use it again, so their expertise literally snowballs. This deep experience helps them to understand and diagnose organisational change issues with greater and greater speed and accuracy.

Irrespective of the strategy they utilise to manage their own knowledge reservoirs, management consultancy firms remain at the forefront of organisational change initiatives and leaders in the management advice industry around the world, particularly when it comes to acquisitions, mergers and strategic alliances, as well as downsizing and general restructuring projects (Tisdall 1982; Wooldridge 1997; Head 1998). Total quality management, re-engineering, matrix management and management competency profiling are examples of the applied organisational solutions promoted by consultants over the past 20 years to enable firms to lift their levels of competitiveness and respond to environmental imperatives for change.

The organisational responses to consultancy-based change initiatives have not always been entirely successful in commercial terms (O'Shea & Madigan 1997). Nonetheless, management consultants around the world continue to enjoy strong reputations for effective cost-cutting initiatives. Their efforts have generally produced organisational responses in keeping with the increasing competitiveness of the modern commercial world. In particular, the downsizing initiatives of the early and mid 1990s, and the outsourcing drives of the late 1990s and beyond, reflect a hyper-competitive modern commercial world wired for immediate communication with suppliers, customers, clients, partners and competitors (Rifkin 1996; Littler et al. 1997). In the new information age, often appropriately referred to as the knowledge economy, information is readily digitised and traded at market prices. Whether you're buying the latest hit single or a university degree, the

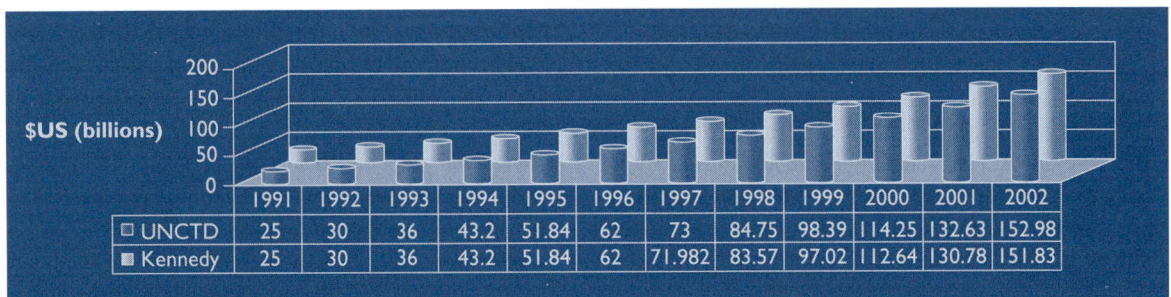

$US (billions)	1991	1992	1993	1994	1995	1996	1997	1998	1999	2000	2001	2002
UNCTD	25	30	36	43.2	51.84	62	73	84.75	98.39	114.25	132.63	152.98
Kennedy	25	30	36	43.2	51.84	62	71.982	83.57	97.02	112.64	130.78	151.83

Figure 1.1: Global revenue growth in the management consultancy industry

product or service is now available online. As organisations scramble to maintain pace with accelerated market demands, management consultants have positioned themselves as dominant players in the organisational solutions market, and are increasingly viewed as necessary agents of change. Figure 1.2 illustrates the rise of the modern management consultancy industry.

Conclusion

In the world we live in today, business priorities, productivity and the drive for efficiency are much more important than they were 10 or 15 years ago. This increasingly accepted perspective, which is the ultimate catalyst for change, has come to dominate managerial and organisational thinking, permeating both private and public sectors around the globe. As a consequence, the less developed economies of the world appear to be falling further and further behind, while the advanced nations continue to widen their competitive advantage.

The global convergence of industries bears testimony to the dominance of the *North American model of management* — a model that advocates uncompromising efficiency, continuous improvement and the outsourcing of human resources to drive down fixed costs. Kanter (1990), in the United States, was one of the first to call on organisations to shed their bureaucratic structures in order to become 'lean and mean'. Her book *When Giants Learn to Dance* sparked unprecedented downsizing initiatives around the world. These initiatives went into overdrive between 1990 and 1995, and continued throughout the 1990s in virtually every advanced nation other than Japan. Charles Handy's model of the shamrock organisation, with its core and outsourced workers, offered an accurate template for the evolution of organisations towards this super-competitive structure. It is a paradigm that even the Japanese began to embrace in 1999 when it became clear that they could no longer compete globally by adhering to culturally entrenched tenets of lifelong employment.

By 2000 corporate giants such as Sony, Mitsubishi and Oji Paper announced that they would be eliminating thousands of jobs from their respective organisations. These

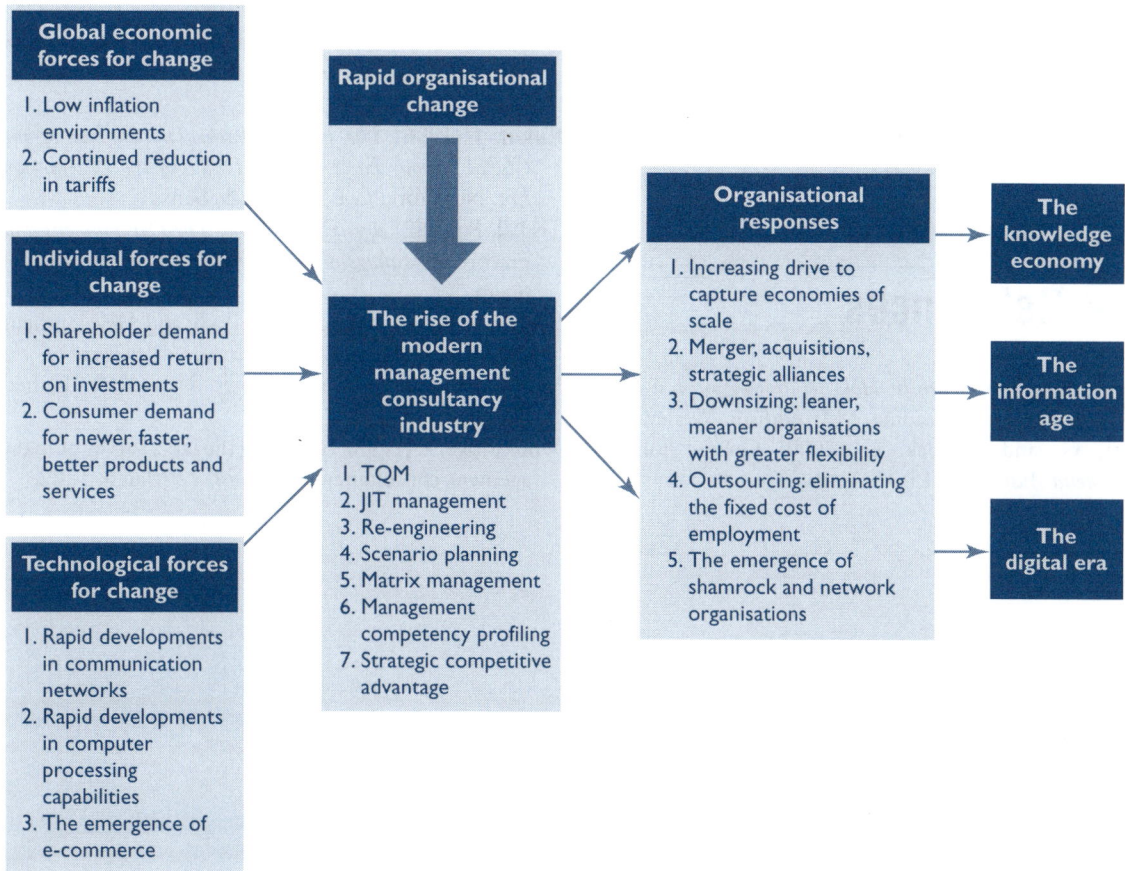

Figure 1.2: Forces for and consequences of organisational change, 1980–2002

initiatives marked the beginning of Japan's recognition that it, too, would need to adopt the 'lean and mean' corporate model in order to remain competitive at the global level.

Management consultants have played a very influential role in this process of organisational change and, as premium providers of expert advice, will no doubt continue to do so in the foreseeable future. Basing their intervention techniques on accelerated versions of organisational development, the large consultancy firms around the world collaborate with often desperate executive corporate teams to re-engineer organisations, providing advice that is often strategic in nature in an uncompromising effort to extract further efficiency gains from the organisation.

This rapid structural change at the organisational level has unequivocally transformed the world of work; along with advances in information technology, these changes have produced more obvious winners and losers within and between nations. While the philosophical implications of these massive changes are worth considering, it is the pragmatic lessons that are likely to be of most interest to those in the corporate front line. Individuals who can think fast and harness their intellectual capacity to generate solutions and identify opportunities are the ones who will excel in the future world of work. They will need to be alert, informed and capable of assuming a leadership role when the opportunity presents itself. In the new world of work, if you don't seize control of your own destiny, somebody else will. At least in this respect, little has changed since the world's earliest civilisations.

References

Bridges, W (1995) *Jobshift: How to Prosper in a Workplace without Jobs*. Reading, MA: Addison-Wesley.

Elliott, G, and Hiscock, G (2000) Guanxi jump. *Weekend Australian*, 15–16 April, 33.

Friedman, T (2000) *The Lexus and the Olive Tree*. New York: HarperCollins.

Gottliebsen, R (2000) Clinton's boom crash. *Australian,* 18 April, 32.

Hansen, T, Nohria, N, and Tierney, T (1999) What's your strategy for managing knowledge? *Harvard Business Review*, March–April, 106–116.

Head, B (1998) How the consultant's role just grows and grows. *Australian Financial Review,* 15 June, Supplement, 14.

Kanter, RM (1989) *When Giants Learn to Dance.* New York: Simon & Schuster.

Kennedy Research Group (1997) *The Global Management Consulting Marketplace: Key Data, Forecasts and Trends*. Peterborough, NH: Kennedy Information.

Krantz, M (1999) The next e-volution. *Time*, 12 July, 154 (2) 47.

Littler, C, Dunford, R, Bramble, T, and Hede, A (1997) The dynamics of downsizing in Australia and New Zealand. *Asia Pacific Journal of Human Resource Management,* 35 (1) 65–79.

O'Shea, J, and Madigan, C (1997) *Dangerous Company: The Consulting Powerhouses and the Businesses They Save and Ruin*. London: Nicholas Brealey Publishing.

Ouchi, W (1981) *Theory Z: How American Business Can Meet the Japanese Challenge*. Reading, MA: Addison-Wesley.

Rifkin, J (1996) *The End of Work: The Decline of the Global Labour Force and the Dawn of the Post-market Era*. New York: G.P. Putnam & Sons.

Tisdall, P (1982) *Agents of Change: The Development and Practice of Management Consultancy*. London: Heinemann.

United Nations Conference on Trade and Development (1993) *Management Consulting: A Survey of the Industry and Its Largest Firms*. New York: United Nations.

Wooldridge, A (1997) Trimming the fat: a survey of management consultancy. *Economist*, 22 March, 1–22.

CHAPTER 2

Changes in human resource policies and practices: management's dream come true?

by Robin Kramar
Macquarie University

Introduction

During the 1980s and early 1990s employers advocated changes in people management practices in Australia. They argued that the centralised industrial relations system produced inefficiencies. Remuneration arrangements through awards, grievance management procedures, working hours, narrow job design and trade union roles, employers claimed, did not meet the requirements of business (Hilmer 1989; Business Council of Australia 1989; Drago, Wooden & Sloan 1992). In addition, there was considerable pessimism about the low level of training in Australia (Dawkins 1988) and the failure to align performance appraisals to the business needs of an organisation (Scotts 1999). Reviews of recruitment and selection techniques used in Australia (Haydon & Patrickson 1988; Vaughan & McLean 1989; Di Milia & Smith 1997; Wooden & Harding 1998) have found that employers rely on suspect methods 'conducted without much objectivity, technical sophistication or scientific rigour' (Vaughan & McLean 1989, p. 31).

This chapter examines the extent to which formal human resource (HR) policies and practices in large Australian organisations changed during the 1990s, particularly between 1993 and 1999. These changes are compared with changes in 21 other countries. The first part briefly discusses the characteristics of an 'ideal' model or vision of people management practice developed by employers in the 1980s. The dimensions examined include the focus and rationale for people management policies, job design, employment tenure, performance feedback, compensation and communication. The second part examines the findings of the study to determine the extent to which large Australian organisations have moved towards this 'ideal' model of people management. The third part examines the implications of these developments for employees and the challenges they pose for management. The final part explores possible future directions for people management in Australia.

A vision of people management

Central to the vision of people management espoused by many employers in Australia during the late 1980s was the notion that employers should be free to develop policies that best suited the needs of the business. Consequently, people management policies were expected to support the achievement of the corporate strategy and objectives rather than some broader national standard (Hilmer 1989). The implications of this vision for people management practices were as follows:

- People management needed a strategic orientation based on corporate strategy.
- Policies should provide flexibility in the hours and design of jobs so that the needs of customers could be most effectively met.
- A process enabling evaluation of employee performance was needed.

- Employees should be paid for their contribution to the performance of the organisation rather than solely for 'the value of the job'.
- Organisations required mechanisms for direct communication and the settlement of differences between management and employees that did not involve outside parties such as trade unions.

The ideal role of the HR manager was not explicitly elaborated. However, one of the consequences of this vision was that those responsible for managing people issues, such as the HR or industrial relations manager, would need to fulfil a proactive, strategic role rather the traditional reactive, administrative role (Dabscheck & Niland 1981, pp. 168, 171). Since some of the work previously undertaken by the HR manager would need to be done by others, this expanded HR role could be expected to have implications for other managers and staff. In addition, the role of trade unions could be expected to change and their influence decline. Human resource management (HRM) policies and practices would be critical for the organisation's financial success. Certain policies could enhance customer and other stakeholder satisfaction The HR manager would work in partnership with other managers and employees to foster the achievement of organisational objectives.

This vision of people management was based on three propositions: First, it espoused a unitarist philosophy, proposing that employers and employees shared common interests in the workplace (BCA 1989, p. 6). Second, it adopted a narrow view of success, defined in terms of satisfying customers and shareholders and competing successfully in the marketplace (BCA 1989, p. 5). Third, it contended that there was one best way of managing people (BCA 1989, pp. 8–10). These propositions reflected a 'universalist' approach to people management (Mayrhofer, Brewster & Morley 2000), an approach proposed by many American writers at the time (Tichy, Frombrun & Devanna 1982; Schuler & Jackson 1987; Ulrich 1987).

It also reflected an approach to people management evident in many organisations in the United States. Employers in the US had always accepted unions grudgingly, out of necessity, but since the mid 1970s they had increasingly resorted to anti-union activities (Wheeler & McClenon 1998, pp. 72–3). Also, HR issues were now viewed as part of the strategic planning process (Kochan & Dyer 1994, p. 227). Work was redesigned to boost productivity; cost-cutting efforts, including outsourcing, downsizing and contingent employment, were increasingly adopted; management power was growing and union power declining (Wheeler & McClenon 1998; Kochan & Dyer 1994).

The vision proposed by many employers fundamentally challenged the pluralist view that underpinned the management of people in Australia, and especially the traditional view that the success of employment policies needed to take into account their impact on employees, the community and the economy. By challenging the pluralist view, the employers emphasised the role of management in formulating employment policies, and at the same time implied that the role of trade unions and industrial tribunals should be minimised. This vision challenged the approach adopted under the Accords determined by the federal Labour government and the ACTU. It also challenged the view of the ACTU, who, following a mission to European countries, argued for continued support for centralised wage determination and the linking of wages policy to training and skill development (Davis & Lansbury 1998, p. 136).

This chapter draws on the results of two surveys conducted in Australia as part of the Cranfield Network's International Strategic Human Resource Management Survey. The surveys were conducted in 1996 and 1999 by the Centre for Australasian Human Resource Management at Macquarie University in conjunction with PricewaterhouseCoopers. They included questions on changes in HRM practices in the previous three years. Senior HR directors or managers were sent a standardised questionnaire that was slightly modified to suit local conditions. In 1999 PricewaterhouseCoopers provided a database of more than 5000 public and private sector organisations with 100 or more employees, and 1120 questionnaires were distributed. Telephone reminders were made two weeks and four weeks after the questionnaires were sent out. Two hundred and forty questionnaires were returned. All industries except agriculture were represented in the sample.

Mining, electricity, gas and water, construction, communication services, finance and insurance and government administration were slightly overrepresented in the sample, while agriculture, transport and storage, wholesale and retail trade, property and business services, accommodation, cafes and restaurants, health and community services, education, cultural and recreational services and personal services were under-represented. The manufacturing industries were represented to the same extent as they were in the Australian market.

In 1999, 29 countries in the Cranfield Network distributed questionnaires as part of the survey. As of the end of February 2000 the data for 22 countries had been analysed, and the results for these countries are used for comparison with the Australian results. These countries were Austria, Australia, Belgium, Bulgaria, the Czech Republic, Denmark, Finland, France, East Germany, Greece, Italy, Japan, the Netherlands, Norway, Northern Ireland, Portugal, the Republic of Ireland, Spain, Sweden, Switzerland, Turkey and the United Kingdom. In addition to the results of the survey, this chapter draws on the findings of six focus groups involving 28 HR managers. These focus groups explored some of the issues raised by the results of the questionnaire.

Trends in Australian human resource management: vision achieved?

The vision of people management developed in the late 1980s challenged many of the traditional values and practices in Australia. It explicitly emphasised the importance of policies enhancing organisational performance by changing work and management practices. By doing this, it focused on assessing, improving and rewarding individual contributions to the organisation. The focus on improving organisational and individual performance required that people management policies support and enhance the organisation's strategy and objectives. Such a vision required a change in the role of the HR manager.

The results of the 1999 Cranfield–Pricewaterhouse-Coopers survey indicate that this vision has been in many respects achieved in Australia. Table 2.1 describes the characteristics of the vision and the extent to which it was achieved in 1999 and, where possible, in 1996.

Table 2.1: Characteristics of Australian people management — 1996, 1999

	1996	1999
	Percentage of organisations	
Strategic orientation		
Written and unwritten mission statement	92 (w) 2 (u)	89 (w) 1 (u)
Written and unwritten corporate strategies	89 (w) 5 (u)	87 (w) 9 (u)
Written and unwritten human resource strategies	70 (w) 14 (u)	70 (w) 17 (u)

	1996	1999
Flexible job design and tenure		
Job design		
Open-ended jobs — increase		
managers	56	56
professionals	49	50
clerical	56	52
manual	42	35

Contract and working hours — increase		
subcontracting and outsourcing	51	62
temporary / casual	53	58
part time	59	57
fixed-term contracts	52	57
Performance assessment		
Performance appraisals		
managers	91	96
professionals	86	94
clerical	77	86
manual	47	66
Use of performance appraisals		
individual training needs	94	95
career development	79	79
promotion potential	62	65
organisational needs	64	62
Compensation		
Variable pay and non-monetary benefits		
variable pay — increase	32	52
non-monetary benefits — increase	30	24
Incentive schemes		
Merit/performance based		
managers	63	70
professionals	53	63
clerical	40	53
manual	21	24
Profit sharing		
managers	12	18
professionals	7	13
clerical	6	12
manual	4	10
Employee share ownership		
managers	22	35
professionals	14	24
clerical	14	17
manual	11	13
Group bonus		
managers	21	33
professionals	15	27
clerical	12	21
manual	10	17
Communication		
Increasing use of		
team briefing	63	64
computer/electronic mail	64	83
direct verbal methods	67	66
written direct methods	62	61
Decreasing use of		
representative staff bodies	15	23
influence of trade unions	28	42

Source: CRANET data sets, 1999 (unpublished).

Trends in strategic orientation

A strategic orientation to people management policies would require at least a mission statement, a corporate strategy and an HR strategy that would provide the formal basis for the development of HRM policies (Storey 1992; Walker 1992). Written and unwritten mission statements, corporate strategies and HR strategies were widely used, with about 90 per cent of organisations reporting on these in 1999. This result was very similar to the findings in 1996. However, mission, corporate and HR strategies were much more widespread in Australia than in any other country in the survey other than Sweden.

Trends in flexible job design and employment tenure

Another indicator of this vision is the presence of a flexible labour supply facilitated by employment arrangements that provide employers with labour when required. This elasticity could be achieved through task flexibility, created by open-ended jobs, and through working time and contract flexibility.

Between 1996 and 1999 growing numbers of organisations developed working arrangements that provided employers with a flexible labour supply. This continued the trend identified between 1993 and 1996. Between 1996 and 1999, 62 per cent of Australian organisations increased their use of subcontracting/outsourcing, 58 per cent increased their use of temporary/casual work, 57 per cent increased their use of part-time work and 57 per cent increased their use of fixed-term contracts.

Australian organisations were more likely to introduce a range of flexible employment practices, particularly those resulting in insecure employment, than organisations in other countries. Australia had the highest increase in the use of subcontracting, temporary/casual employment and weekend work, and showed one of the highest increases in the use of shift work, job sharing and fixed-term employment. These practices were viewed by many HR managers not only as an effective way of securing labour when required by the customer and the business, but also as an efficient way of securing very specialised skills that become obsolete quickly.

Although 21 per cent of organisations in Australia had increased their use of telecommuting and 28 per cent had increased their use of home-based work, these arrangements were not widely adopted. More than 90 per cent of organisations either did not adopt these arrangements or used them for less than 1 per cent of their workforce. In comparison, temporary/casual and part-time employment were used more commonly for a higher proportion of the workforce. Ten per cent of organisations either did not use temporary/casual work or used it for less than 1 per cent of the workforce; for part-time work the figure was 22 per cent.

In 1996 there was a marked trend towards wider, more open-ended jobs for managerial, professional/technical, clerical and manual employees. This trend continued between 1996 and 1999, with jobs becoming broader or more flexible for managers in 56 per cent of organisations, for professionals/technical in 50 per cent of organisations, for clerical workers in 52 per cent of organisations and for manual employees in 35 per cent of organisations.

As to the open-endedness or specificity of jobs for the four occupational groups, there was considerable variation between the countries in the survey, making it difficult to draw comparisons.

Trends in performance assessment

Scotts claims that during the 1990s Australian organisations began to recognise the need to manage employee performance as a way of building an organisational culture 'that aligns employee behaviours with organisational objectives' (1999, p. 60). An indicator of the vision articulated in the 1980s is the presence of performance appraisals as part of this performance management process. The appraisals are then used in a variety of employment decisions. It has been recognised that obtaining feedback about the performance of individuals or teams from a range of sources provides a fuller picture of performance (Kramar, McGraw & Schuler 1997, p. 399).

The percentage of organisations conducting performance appraisals for all occupational groups between 1996 and 1999 is summarised in table 2.1, which charts their increasing use between these years. Performance appraisals for managers were used more widely in Australia than in other countries in the survey. The second most widespread use was for professionals; the third for clerical staff. Five other countries used performance appraisals more frequently for manual employees than did Australian organisations. Sweden and Switzerland used performance appraisals extensively for all four occupational groups.

The sources of information for the performance appraisal process were similar in 1999 to those in 1996. However, it appeared that groups associated with 360-degree feedback were more widely represented in 1999. Feedback from the immediate supervisor and from the employee were the most common sources of information for performance appraisals.

A higher percentage of Australian organisations sought information from employees, subordinates and peers than in organisations in any other country. The focus groups revealed conflicting opinions about the value of collecting information from a variety of sources. Some HR managers found the process difficult, while others found it was an invaluable tool for providing information for career development. The information generated from the appraisal process was used for a variety of HRM decisions. The percentage of organisations making use of appraisal results changed little between 1999 and 1996, with almost all organisations using the information for decisions on individual training needs and almost 80 per cent using the information for career development.

The use of formal performance appraisals was widespread in Australia in 1999. Focus groups indicated that the feedback process was a useful way of establishing guidelines on individual performance standards and outcomes.

Trends in compensation

A compensation system that rewards people on the basis of behaviours and capabilities supporting organisational objectives was an indicator of the vision articulated by some employers in the 1980s. The trend during the past decade to introduce more variable pay based on performance signified an attempt to align the interests and financial wellbeing of employees with those of owners and shareholders (Lawler 1990; Schuster & Zingheim 1992; Kanter 1989).

The survey found that a greater percentage of organisations offered variable pay and non-monetary benefits in 1999 than in 1996. Change in total reward packages in Australia grew, too, with more than 50 per cent of organisations increasing their use of variable pay between 1996 and 1999.

Although a higher proportion of organisations in Italy, Switzerland and Spain increased their use of variable pay, organisations in Australia were more likely to introduce variable pay than any of the remaining 18 countries in the survey. Similarly, a higher percentage of organisations in Greece and Bulgaria introduced non-monetary benefits to a greater extent.

In Australia, the alignment of employee behaviour with organisational objectives has been sought not only through performance appraisals, but also through the growing use of incentive schemes (O'Neill 1995, p. 20). These schemes take a variety of forms, including merit/performance-related pay, employee share options, and group bonus and profit sharing. Table 2.1 indicates that managers and professional/technical employees were most likely to receive incentive rewards, but that more than half the organisations provided

merit/performance-related pay to clerical/administrative employees, and almost a quarter of the organisations provided these payments to manual employees.

Countries in the survey varied in their use of incentive schemes. In Japan, incentive rewards were used widely in all four occupational groups, and although they were not adopted as widely in Australia as in Japan, compared with the other countries their use was high, particularly for managers and professionals. Similarly, the use of group bonuses and merit pay in Australia for managers and professionals compared favourably with other countries.

Research (Cohen Mason 1993; Friedman 1991) indicates that individual performance is improved through the introduction of policies that seek to satisfy employees' personal needs and at the same time satisfy organisational needs. Policies making it easier for individuals to manage their work and non-work needs include leave for family reasons, time for study or education, and flexibility in benefit package design. In 1999, 43 per cent of organisations provided education/training breaks, 12 per cent provided career break schemes, 30 per cent provided maternity leave in excess of statutory requirements, 67 per cent provided paternity leave in excess of statutory requirements, 67 per cent provided superannuation in excess of statutory requirements and 55 per cent provided flexible benefit packages.

Trends in communication

As already noted, the vision of people management articulated in the 1980s encompassed direct communication between employees and managers and a reduced role for trade unions. The trend towards greater communication between employers and employees evident between 1993 and 1996 continued between 1996 and 1999. Table 2.1 indicates that organisations were making increasing use of team briefings, computer/electronic mail systems, and direct verbal and written methods. On the other hand, between 1996 and 1999 almost one in four organisations decreased their use of staff representative bodies such as trade unions, and about one in three organisations did not use these bodies at all.

The role of trade unions in representing employees and the influence of trade unions in Australian organisations continued to decline between 1996 and 1999. In 1999 only 17 per cent of organisations had more than 50 per cent of their workforce represented by trade unions, compared with 40 per cent of organisations in 1996. At the other extreme, 52 per cent of organisations in 1999 had fewer than 25 per cent of their employees in trade unions, while in 1996 the proportion of organisations with this level of trade union representation, at 27 per cent, was a little more than half the 1999 percentage.

Trade union influence decreased in 42 per cent and increased in only 8 per cent of organisations between 1996 and 1999. This trend towards reduced trade union influence was stronger in the period 1996–99 than in 1993–96, when 28 per cent of organisations reported that trade union influence had decreased and 17 per cent claimed it had increased. In 1999, 15 per cent of organisations stated that trade unions had no influence in their organisations.

The decrease in trade union influence in Australia (42 per cent) was by far the highest among the 22 countries in the survey. For instance, after Australia the greatest decrease in influence was experienced in Bulgaria (29 per cent), the Czech Republic (27 per cent) and Italy (27 per cent). The increasing use of direct communication with employees — using verbal or written methods or team briefings — was higher in Australia than in any other country in the survey.

Factors contributing to the changes in HRM practices

In many respects the employers' vision for people management articulated in the late 1980s has been realised in large Australian organisations. In many organisations policies have been developed within the framework of a mission, a corporate strategy and a broader HR strategy. Policies that provide flexibility in working hours and job design, assessment of employee performance, linking of employee compensation to individual and organisational performance, and direct communication between employees and managers have increasingly been adopted. On the other hand, trade union influence has declined. These developments reflect the characteristics of writers in the universalist paradigm and are similar to US trends.

Arguments for the reform of people management practices in the mid to late 1980s and the 1990s were couched in terms of the need for Australia to become internationally competitive as a consequence of 'globalisation'. Workplace reform was seen as necessary for improving workplace productivity and increasing efficiencies in the labour market. However, 'there is no inevitability about workplace change and the direction it has taken' (ACIRRT 1999, p. 8).

The vision pursued in the late 1980s and practically realised in 1999 is based on the view that the free market is the most efficient way of managing the economy, and that managers should be able to develop employment policies that best suit the business. Profit and short-term economic results became two of the most important criteria for evaluating organisational success. According to this view, the role of national policymakers is to create an environment in which managers may achieve this (Hilmer 1989; BCA 1989). A number of political, legislative, economic and social developments interacted during the 1980s and 1990s to encourage the implementation of this view.

Throughout the 1980s and early 1990s a Labour government fostered reforms in employment policies at the workplace level by supporting enterprise bargaining and limiting the role of industrial tribunals. The conservative Coalition government enhanced this trend with the introduction of the Workplace Relations Act and subsequent amendments. This legislation further emphasised that employment policies should be based on the needs of the enterprise and that the security of trade unions should be reduced.

At the same time the federal industrial tribunal had facilitated workplace reform in the late 1980s by reflecting a policy of 'centrally managed decentralisation of award adjustments' (Isaac 1998, p. 713). The Australian Industrial Relations Commission repeatedly observed, however, that these decentralised adjustments, conditional on workplace reform, were not a sufficient condition for increased productivity generally. The average rate of productivity growth increased during the 1990s, but this was most likely a result of the changed economic environment of the labour market. High unemployment, greater exposure to international competition and tight monetary policies encouraged management and employees to implement more efficient work practices (Isaac 1998, pp. 713–14).

The transformation of the labour market from one equated with full employment to one associated with long-term unemployment in the 1970s adversely affected many Australians. It was the major cause of poverty, it lowered living standards by exerting downward pressure on living standards, and it signalled the death knell of 'Keynesian demand as an economic tool' (ACIRRT 1999, pp. 17–18). It has been argued that the loss of full employment undermined government intervention in general and provided the basis for microeconomic reform (Quiggin 1996, p. 26). In this environment, governments were concerned with the process of wealth creation rather than wealth distribution in the labour market. The reform of employment practices, seen as a means of creating wealth, became an area for negotiation between trade unions and employers.

In addition to the re-emergence of neo-liberal ideas about economic management during the mid 1980s and the

1990s, ideas about how to better manage organisations were emerging. These included support for flattening the organisational structure, taking action directed towards achieving a vision, adopting 'best practice' policies, creating a culture based on shared values and preventing managers from influencing the Board of Directors (Hilmer & Donaldson 1996, pp. 3–5; Peters 1988). Many Australian organisations adopted these ideas and implemented them through their employment practices (Wright 1995, pp. 134–43).

A recurring management idea was the need for flexibility and organisational restructuring. During the 1990s the proportion of Australian organisations restructuring their workplaces increased, with more than a quarter of employers reducing their workforces (Morehead et al. 1997). As demonstrated in this chapter and supported by other research, increasingly non-standard forms of employment were being introduced through the greater use of part-time and casual employment (ABS 1998) and external providers of labour (Kramar 1997; Kramar 2000; Vanden-Heuval & Wooden 1995; ACIRRT 1999).

Social changes were also taking place: significant changes in the demographics of the workforce occurred during the 1990s. One of the reasons given for introducing flexible working arrangements was the need to accommodate employees' domestic, family and work commitments. During the 1990s an increasing percentage of women with children aged 0–4 years were working, and participation rates for couple families in the workforce increased (ABS 1998; ABS 1988–98).

Accompanying these demographic changes were changes in attitudes and expectations in the workforce. Each generation within the workforce has been found to have different expectations and attitudes towards work, living standards and quality of life. The baby boomers, those born between 1946 and 1964, tend to value material comfort, personal happiness and combining work and family. On the other hand, those born between 1965 and 1983 value personal freedom, flexibility and individuality; they like to keep their options open, postponing long-term commitments in favour of short-term goals and temporary solutions (Mackay 1997, pp. 59–140).

Changes in perspective are particularly marked in attitudes to parenting. For example, there has been a significant change in expectations about male involvement in domestic responsibilities. Men spend more time with their children and are closer to them now than in the mid 1980s. Most fathers want to be more involved with their children, although the requirements of their employment may limit this ability (Russell & Bowman 2000).

A range of social, economic, ideological, legislative and organisational developments facilitated and encouraged the changes in people management practices. Many of these developments were mutually supportive. For instance, while many employers introduced more flexible working hours and job structures in order to satisfy customer demands, many employees, particularly women, sought more flexible working arrangements in order to fulfil their domestic and family responsibilities. However, as indicated in the next section, the consequences of the changes in HRM policies for managers and employees differed.

Implications of the changes in approach to people management for managers and employees

Implications for managers

Changes in HR policies during the past decade have had significant implications for managers, particularly line managers and HR managers. In many organisations line managers are undertaking more HRM work and the role of the HR professional is changing. At the same time, the changes have decidedly affected employees, particularly their well-being and their experience in the workplace.

One of the implications of people management policies being used to enhance business outcomes is that the HR manager can become involved in translating organisational priorities into HR priorities or in assisting with the development of organisational strategies based on the capabilities of the people in the organisation. Ulrich (1997) argues that HR managers need to become strategic partners in order to improve organisational performance. Two indicators of HR managers behaving as strategic partners are their involvement in the 'Executive Team' and in the development of strategy.

In 1999, 49 per cent of the surveyed HR managers were represented on the Board or the Executive Team, compared with 40 per cent in 1996. In those organisations in which the HR manager was not represented on the Executive Team, the Chief Executive or Managing Director took responsibility for people management issues in 59 per cent of organisations. The Board representation of HR managers in Australia was similar to that in the United Kingdom, Denmark, Switzerland, Austria and Turkey. However, it was much lower than in France, Sweden, Spain, Finland, Belgium and Japan, where the HR manager was represented on the Board in about four out of five organisations.

Another indicator of HR managers serving as strategic partners is their strategic involvement. Table 2.2 indicates that the HR manager was involved in the development of corporate strategy:

- from the outset in 54 per cent of organisations in 1999 compared with 47 per cent in 1996
- in a consultative way in 30 per cent of organisations in 1999 compared with 31 per cent in 1996
- at the implementation stage in 7 per cent of organisations in 1999 compared with 8 per cent in 1996.

Table 2.2: Role of human resource managers

HR managers as strategic partners	Percentage of organisations	
	1996	1999
Member of executive team	40	49
Involvement in development of strategy		
from the outset	47	54
in consultative way	31	30
at implementation stage	8	7
Shared responsibility		
HR dept/manager present	98	99
Use of external providers in the increasing role of line managers	n/a	44
Recruitment and selection	44	50
Training and development	50	44

Source: CRANET data sets, 1999 (unpublished).

In 9 per cent of organisations in 1999 the HR manager was not consulted but in 1996 only 14 per cent of organisations did not consult.

This level of involvement was comparable to that experienced in the United Kingdom, Denmark, Ireland, Belgium, Japan and Portugal. The involvement from the outset of HR managers in the development of corporate strategy was much more widespread in France, Sweden, Italy, Norway, Finland and East Germany, where this occurred in about two out of three organisations.

Ulrich (1997, p. 234) claims: 'Human resources is no longer the sole responsibility of the HR department'. This certainly appears to be the case in Australia, where line managers are taking an increasing role in managing people, and where external providers are increasingly used to undertake people management activities. However, almost all organisations in the survey still have an HR department or HR manager.

The 1996 survey. This proportion rose to 99 per cent in 1999. This situation is very similar to that in the United Kingdom, France, Switzerland, the Netherlands, the Czech Republic and Portugal, but unlike the experience of Finland,

Bulgaria, the Republic of Ireland and Northern Ireland, where less than one in four organisations had an HR department and/or HR manager.

In 1999, 51 per cent of HR managers had been recruited from outside the organisation and 22 per cent from within the organisation's HR department. In 1996 almost 47 per cent of HR managers were recruited from an HR department outside the organisation and almost 23 per cent from the organisation's own HR department.

The results indicate that the HR manager is part of an emerging HR community involving a series of partnerships with outsourcing partners, line managers and senior executives. Between 1996 and 1999 more than 44 per cent of organisations increased their use of external providers of HR services and 10 per cent reduced their use. Only 6 per cent of organisations used no external HR providers. Training and development, recruitment and selection, and outplacement were the activities most commonly outsourced, with:

- 83 per cent of organisations increasing their use of external providers in training and development
- 78 per cent of organisations increasing their use in recruitment and selection
- 58 per cent of organisations increasing their use in outplacement or workforce reduction
- 31 per cent of organisations increasing their use with regard to pay and benefits.

This growing use of external providers was greater than the levels reported in the United Kingdom, France, the Scandinavian countries of Denmark, Norway, Sweden and Finland, Greece, the Czech Republic, Portugal, East Germany, Bulgaria and Japan, where less than one in three organisations had increased their use of external providers for HR services. However, the level of increase was lower than in the Netherlands, Turkey and Belgium, where more than half the organisations increased their use of external providers.

In 1999 in Australia the primary responsibility for most HR policy decisions remained with HR managers rather than with line managers. The sharing of responsibilities between line and HR managers in Australia was similar to the experience in the United Kingdom but unlike that of the other countries, where line managers took greater responsibility for pay.

Although HR managers consistently took primary responsibility, line managers increased their involvement in HR decisions between 1996 and 1999. As in 1996, there was a difference in emphasis, with HR managers more likely to oversee the industrial relations and pay and benefits areas, while line managers were more likely to take responsibility for decisions for workforce expansion or reduction. These results support Ulrich's (1997, pp. 236–7) claim that there is an emerging partnership between line managers and HR managers.

Between 1996 and 1999 in Australia the responsibility for HR issues continued to increase for line managers. This was reflected in at least 3 out of 10 organisations, with responsibility for recruitment and selection increasing in half of the organisations and responsibility for training and development increasing in 44 per cent of organisations. Figures 2.1(a) and 2.1(b) illustrate the extent of the changes in line managers' responsibilities in 1993–96 and 1996–99.

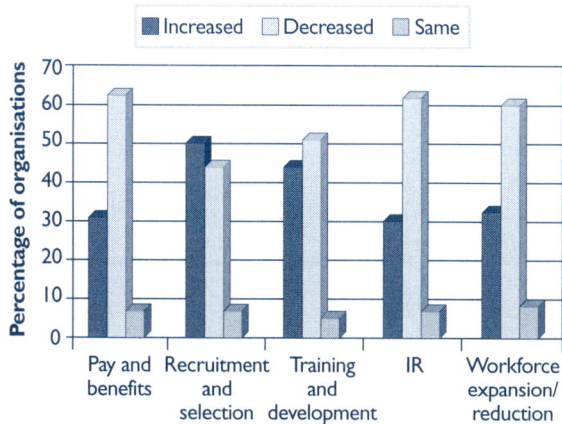

Figure 2.1(a): Changes in responsibilities of line managers, 1996–1999

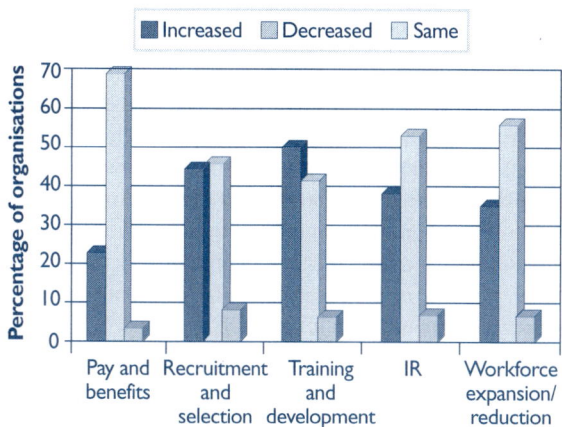

Figure 2.1(b): Changes in responsibilities of line managers, 1993–96

All 22 countries in the Cranfield–Pricewaterhouse-Coopers survey reported an increase in the responsibility of line managers for HR decisions. However, the increase in East Germany was lower than any other country. The increase in line managers' responsibility for industrial relations in Australia was similar to increases reported in the Netherlands, Sweden, Ireland and Bulgaria and higher than that in the other 17 countries.

The changing roles of HR managers and line managers require the development of additional skills, knowledge and methods of communication. HR managers need to understand the strategic issues confronting the organisation in order to operate as strategic partners. They therefore need to understand business issues, to think strategically and in the long term, to understand the impact of employment practices on the organisation and on its finances, and to be able to communicate in a variety of ways so that the different stakeholders understand the benefits of particular policies. HR managers are required to manage the paradox of, on the one hand, representing the needs of the business and, on the other, being employee advocates. This paradox can be managed by devolving responsibility for employee advocacy to the line manager, so that HR managers may focus on improving the quality of the management and workplace culture through sponsorship of employee surveys, work–life balance programs and initiatives supporting manager and employee development.

Similarly, line managers require many more skills. They are often expected to make decisions about selection, training, rewards and performance feedback. This requires technical skills as well as the ability to manage conflict, negotiate, communicate information to their employees and communicate with the HR manager on employee-related issues. Line managers are also at the frontline of managing change through the implementation of new policies. Many line managers are uncomfortable with these responsibilities and report that they are 'struggling to adjust to a wide range of responsibilities and challenges' (Sheldrake & Saul 1995).

Managers must also work longer hours. In 1997 about half of all managers worked more than 49 hours a week, and an additional 25 per cent worked between 41 and 48 hours a week. Unlike blue-collar employees, who are likely to receive overtime payments, managers generally do not receive overtime (ACIRRT 1999, pp. 103–5).

The changes in people management policies during the 1990s changed the nature of the work of managers, including line and HR managers. Managers require a greater range of skills and knowledge and an ability to cope with change and long work hours. HR managers are increasingly required to develop partnerships with line managers and external providers to fulfil their role.

Implications for employees

The changes in HR practices have implications for the skills required of employees, too. Many employees are required to deal directly with their managers through their open-ended jobs, through general communication about organisational affairs, and through processes such as the performance appraisal. Consequently, employees require negotiation and communication skills that enable them to work effectively with their managers. In addition, the decline in the role and influence of trade unions has meant diminished collective negotiation and employee protection. Therefore, if employees are to adequately represent themselves in performance appraisal, performance pay and training needs discussions, they will require additional negotiation and advocacy skills.

Many employees have experienced workplace reforms, introduced on the understanding that everyone would benefit, in terms of incurred costs rather than received benefits. Consequently, they feel less satisfied with management and the nature of communication and consultation, and believe they have less job security than in the past (ACIRRT 1999, Department of Industrial Relations 1995; Morehead et al. 1997; Sheldrake & Saul 1995). Many employees feel overworked and more stressed, experiencing lower morale, loyalty and trust in the workplace. Many also feel that the balance between work and family life is uneven (ACIRRT 1999; Department of Industrial Relations 1995; James 1990; Sheldrake & Saul 1995; Morehead et al. 1997).

The introduction of greater flexibility in working hours and job structures has been found to have adverse affects on the health and safety of employees. In situations where work intensification is associated primarily with cost cutting and improved productivity, functional flexibility has had detrimental effects on employees. Flexible working hours can benefit employees; however, in many circumstances they have resulted in unregulated extended hours and shiftwork-like arrangements (Heiler 1995).

Despite the promotion of direct communication methods with employees, this communication is often experienced as one-way rather than two-way. Many employees feel that there is little consultation about workplace change (Morehead, Steele, Alexander, Stephen & Duffin 1997; ACIRRT 1999). The decline in representative bodies in the workplace could contribute to this experience of lack of participation.

At the broader level of the labour market, these changes could also be seen to be affecting the structure of the labour market and the availability of jobs. There is evidence that the 'economy is creating two nations, those with jobs and those without jobs and with little hope of getting one in the future' (Editorial 1999, p. 14). In addition, the growth in non-traditional forms of work, such as part-time, casual, contract and fixed-term employment, is further segmenting the labour market. People in these sorts of employment arrangements could be regarded as a third nation. They experience even greater employment insecurity than other people in the labour market.

Future directions

One of the advantages of a comparative global study is that it is possible to assess the developments in Australia in the light of alternative approaches to people management. Australian organisations appear to have followed the United States path to people management — a path based on freedom and autonomy (Guest 1990) and the enhancement of management's 'right to manage' and to maximise the benefits to the organisation. Although there is considerable variation among the countries in the Cranfield survey, it appears that more organisations in Australia have developed policies that are consistent with the American model than with those associated with other countries in the survey.

People management in many European countries has retained higher levels of participation of trade unions and other bodies representing employees and a lower propensity to introduce employment arrangements that increase job insecurity. Also, there does not appear to be a strong reliance on articulating the purpose of the organisation through mission statements, corporate strategies or formal evaluations of employee performance. For many years there have been calls to examine people management from a European rather than an American perspective (Brewster 1995; Hickson 1993). Although there is considerable diversity in people management practices across Europe, the Cranfield–PricewaterhouseCoopers results provide a welcome reminder that there are ways of managing people that reflect values other than those promoted in Australia during the past decade.

The European comparison raises the question of whether the vision articulated in the late 1980s is the vision Australians wish to drive change in the next decade. An alternative vision is based on the need to build social cohesion through long-term partnerships within economic and social communities, rather than relying on glib mission statements about corporate responsibility (Trinca 1999, p. 5s). There is a common view among many policy makers, politicians, executives and analysts that such partnerships will be needed to cope with the future impact of 'globalisation', particularly the growing inequities within society and between countries (Shanahan 1998, pp. 1–6). Such a view has implications for people management policies, including criteria for assessment, the nature of employment contracts and methods of pay determination. Some organisations have begun to introduce measures, such as the balanced scorecard approach, that enable the assessment of performance in terms of a range of short- and long-term criteria not limited to economic indices. However, it is a time-consuming process and in turbulent times can take second place to the quarterly financial results.

References

ABS (Australian Bureau of Statistics) (1998) *Social Trends*. Cat. no. 4102.0. Canberra: ABS.

ABS (1988–98) *Labour Force Australia*. Cat. no. 6203.0. Canberra: ABS.

ABS (1999) *Labour Force Status and Other Characteristics of Families: June 1998 and 1999*. Cat. no. 6244.0. Canberra: ABS.

ACTU/TDC (1987) *Australia Reconstructed*. Canberra: Australian Government Publishing Service.

ACIRRT (1999) *Australia at Work: Just Managing*. Sydney: Prentice Hall.

Adams, R. (1999) Employment relations: is individualization inevitable? In R Tripples and H Shrewsbury (Eds), *Global Trends and Local Issues*. Proceedings of the Seventh Annual Conference of the International Employment Relations Association, 13–16 July, Canterbury, New Zealand.

Brewster, C (1995) Developing a 'European' model of human resource management. *Journal of International Business Studies*, 21, (6) 1–21.

Brewster, C, Larsen, HH, and Mayrhofer, W (1997) Integration and assignment: a paradox in human resource management. *Journal of International Management*, 3 (1) 1–23.

Business Council of Australia (1989) *Enterprise Bargaining Units: A Better Way of Working*. Melbourne: BCA.

Campion, M, Palmer, D, and Campion, J (1997) A review of structure in the selection interview. *Personnel Psychology*, vol. 50.

Cohen, Mason J (1993) Working the family way. *Management Review*, July.

Davis, E, and Lansbury, R (1998) Employment relations in Australia. In GL Bamber and RD Lansbury (Eds), *International and Comparative Employment Relations*, Sydney: Allen & Unwin.

Dawkins, JS (1988) *Industry Training in Australia*. Canberra: AGPS.

Department of Industrial Relations (1995) *Enterprise Bargaining Annual Report 1994*. Canberra: AGPS.

Di Milia, L, and Smith, P (1997) Australian management selection practices: why does the interview remain popular? *Asia Pacific Journal of Human Resources*, 35 (3).

Drago, R, Wooden, M, and Sloan, J (1992) *Productive Relations?* Sydney: Allen & Unwin.

Editorial (1999) Work-poor. *Sydney Morning Herald*, 16 July, 14.

Friedman, D (1991) *Linking Work–Family Issues to the Bottom Line*. Report no. 962. The Conference Board, New York.

Guest, D (1990) Human resource management and the American dream. *Journal of Management Studies*, 27 (4) 377–97.

Heiler, K (1995) *Is Enterprise Bargaining Good for Your Health?* Sydney: ACIRRT.

Hickson, DJ (Ed.) (1993) *Management in Western Europe: Society, Culture and Organisation in Twelve Nations*. Berlin: de Gruyer.

Hilmer, F (1989) *New Games, New Rules*. Sydney: Angus & Robertson.

Hilmer, F, and Donaldson, L (1996) *Management Redeemed*. Sydney: The Free Press.

Isaac, J (1998) Australian labour market issues: an historical perspective. *Journal of Industrial Relations*, 40 (4) 690–715.

James, D (1990) Study shows success is in the balance. *Business Review Weekly*, 13 April.

Kanter, RM (1989) *When Giants Learn to Dance*. London: Unwin.

Katz, H, and Darbishire, O (2000) *Converging Divergences: Worldwide Changes in Employment Systems*. Ithaca, NY: Cornell University Press.

Kochan, T, and Dyer, L (1994) Managing transformational change: the role of human resource professionals. In JR Niland, RD Lansbury and C Verevis (1994), *The Future Role of Industrial Relations*. Thousand Oaks, CA: Sage Publications.

Kramar, R (2000) *Cranfield–PricewaterhouseCoopers Survey on International Strategic Human Resource Management*. North Ryde, Sydney: Centre for Australasian Human Resource Management.

Kramar, R, and Lake, N (1997) *The Pricewaterhouse-Coopers–Cranfield Project on International Strategic Human Resource Management*. Sydney: Macquarie University.

Kramar, R, McGraw, P, and Schuler, R (1997) *Human Resource Management in Australia*. Melbourne: Addison-Wesley Longman.

Lawler, EE (1990) *Strategic Pay: Aligning Organisational Strategies and Pay Systems*. San Francisco, CA: Jossey-Bass.

Mackay, H (1997) *Generations: Baby Boomers, Their Parents and Their Children*. Sydney: Macmillan.

Mayrhofer, W, Brewster, C, and Morley, M (2000) The concept of strategic European human resource management. In C Brewster, W Mayrhofer and M Morley (Eds), *New Challenges for European Human Resource Management*. Hampshire, UK: Macmillan.

Morehead, A, Steele, M, Alexander, M, Stephen, K, and Duffin, L (1997) *Changes at Work: The 1995 Australian Workplace Industrial Relations Survey*. Canberra: Department of Industrial Relations and Small Business.

O'Neill, G (1995). Linking pay to performance: conflicting views and conflicting evidence. *Asia Pacific Journal of Human Resources*, 33 (2) 20–35.

Peters, T (1988) *Words*. Palo Alto, CA: The Tom Peters Group.

Quiggin, J (1996) *Great Expectations: Microeconomic Reform and Australia*. Sydney: Allen & Unwin.

Russell, G, and Bowman, L (2000) *Work and Family: Current Thinking, Research and Practice*. Canberra: Department of Family and Community Services.

Schuler, R, and Jackson, S (1987). Linking competitive strategies with human resource management practices. *Academy of Management Executive*, 1, 207–19.

Schuster, J, and Zingheim, P (1992) *The New Pay: Linking Employee and Organisational Performance*. Lexington, NY: Lexington.

Scotts, H (1999) Planning and managing employee performance. In G O'Neill and R Kramar (Eds), *Australian Human Resources Management*, vol. 2. Sydney: Business and Professional P/L.

Shanahan, D (1998) Australia unlimited: a fair and decent place. *Weekend Australian*, 8–9 May, 1–6.

Sheldrake, P, and Saul, P (1995) First line managers: a study of the changing role and skills of first line managers. In *The Report on the Industry Task Force on Leadership and Management Skills*. Canberra: AGPS.

Smith, A (1999) Development training and learning. In G O'Neill and R Kramar (Eds), *Australian Human Resources Management*, vol. 2. Sydney: Business and Professional P/L.

Storey, J (1992) *Developments in the Management of Human Resources*, Oxford: Blackwell.

Sunoo, BP (1996) Panel interviews: are four heads better than one? *Personnel Journal*, vol. 75.

Taylor, P (1999). Providing structure to interviews and reference checks. *Workforce*.

Tichy, N, Frombrun, CJ, and Devanna, MA (1982) Strategic human resource management. *Sloan Management Review*, 23 (2) 47–60.

Trinca, H (1999) A kinder capitalism. *Sydney Morning Herald*, 17 July, 5s.

Ulrich, D (1997) *Human Resource Champions*. Boston: Harvard Business School Press.

Ulrich, D (1987) Organizational capability as competitive advantage: human resource professionals as strategic partners. *Human Resource Planning*, 10, 169–84.

VandenHeuval, A, and Wooden, M (1995) *Self-Employed Contractors in Australia: What Are the Facts*, NILS working paper no. 136. Adelaide: National Institute of Labour Studies.

Vaughan, E, and McLean, J (1989) A survey and critique of management selection practices in Australian business firms. *Asia Pacific Human Resource Management*, vol. 27, November, 20–33.

Walker, J (1992) *Human Resource Strategy*. New York: McGraw-Hill.

Wooden, M, and Harding, D (1998) Recruitment practices in the private sector: results from a national survey of employers. *Asia Pacific Journal of Human Resources*, 36 (2).

Wheeler, HN, and McClendon, JA (1998) Employment relations in the United States. In GJ Bamber and RD Lansbury (Eds), *International and Comparative Employment Relations*. Sydney: Allen & Unwin.

Wright, C (1995) *The Management of Labour*. Melbourne: Oxford University Press.

CHAPTER 3

Human resource management and the new careers

by Kerr Inkson
Massey University

Introduction

The new approach to career development is based on an underlying assumption that would have been considered heresy 10 or 20 years ago — that each employee is responsible for his or her own career development. (Cascio 1995, p. 307)

A key feature of the new concept is that the company and the employee are partners *in career development.* (Cascio 1995, p. 308; original emphasis)

A career is not something that should be left to each employee: instead it should be managed *by the organisation to ensure the efficient allocation of human and capital resources.* (Cascio 1995, p. 310; original emphasis)

Confused? You ought to be. Are those HR people schizophrenic, or *what*? Is the main responsibility for your career yours, or your company's, or is it a shared obligation? Here is the conventional HRM answer to that question.

It is part of the conventional wisdom of human resource management that HRM should always be aligned with the organisation's strategy and that, in support of that strategy, human resources can be recruited, developed and deployed within an HR system. Because of the long-term nature of strategy and the desire of organisations to survive and grow over the long term, HRM needs to consider human resources not just in terms of their immediate performance, training and welfare, but also in terms of their career development over many years. Companies can plan and develop their supply of key competencies and committed employees far into the future. Sophisticated companies therefore have career development systems from which their employees can benefit — to mutual advantage. Thus, the *organisation* should manage its employees' careers.

Here is a different answer to the question.

The view expressed above may represent a benefit for the company but is not necessarily good for the individual or for society as a whole. In a companion article to this one (Inkson 2000), I argue that the primary responsibility for a career is the individual's. There is an ethical basis for this statement: it concerns concepts of individual liberty and personal choice. After all, how many of us really want our careers to be 'managed by the organisation to ensure the efficient allocation of human and capital resources' (Cascio 1995, p. 310)? That turns ordinary employees, apparently, into pawns without the power of self-determination. Unfortunately, it is typical of the kind of mindset we adopt if we pay too much attention to the strategy-spouting, systems-generating, Big Brother concept of HRM advanced in some texts.

In addition, developments over recent years have strongly discouraged organisations from managing their employees' careers. Globalisation, restructuring, delayering, downsizing and outsourcing have cut a swathe through companies around the developed world, displacing many employees from careers they imagined they might have for life. Employees' loyalty to their companies has consequently decreased. The organisation's 'core' of permanent full-time employees has shrunk, while their 'periphery' of casual workers, part-timers and contractors — whose careers tend to be unstable and hard to manage — have grown.

In this changed context, careers have become increasingly 'boundaryless' (Arthur & Rousseau 1996). The 'new careers' are demonstrably more improvisational than planned, and personally rather than organisationally controlled (Arthur, Inkson & Pringle 1999). In a recent article, Michael Arthur and I advocate that people develop their own careers by means of 'career capitalism' (Inkson & Arthur 2001). This philosophy turns on its head the conventional HRM wisdom that companies should invest in their people with a view to developing a high-value workforce. It proposes instead that people should invest in their companies with a view to building a high-value career.

Of course, the career capitalism model will not serve for those with little capital to invest (e.g. low-skilled people). But it works well for the high-calibre staff in whom companies tend to be most interested. Unfortunately for the companies, though, it puts the individual in charge. There are many reasons why such people should be mobile in pursuit of good investments for their career capital. They may be able to increase their career capital to a greater extent by investing in a wide portfolio of career opportunities than by 'putting all their eggs in the one basket' of a single organisation or occupation. This may have advantages for both the individual and society as a whole, as individuals cross-pollinate business and industry with their knowledge and expertise while developing their careers across boundaries. But for the company it may seem all bad, because it produces employees who want to follow their own paths rather than the company's, and causes unacceptable labour turnover as they move around, searching for new investment opportunities.

Career development and HRM

So what, if anything, is the role of HRM in careers? There *is* a role in assisting individual career development. The organisation is often able to provide individuals with access to resources — opportunities for their motivation, education, skills development, access to networks, evaluation and reputation — that they could not find elsewhere. Good HR can therefore 'partner' employees' development of their careers by ensuring the individuals are aware of these opportunities and assisting them to utilise them appropriately. Conversely, employees can do much to assist their organisations through their own personal career development and decision making. The trick is to integrate the individual's

often informal and idiosyncratic processes for self-development and career decision making with the organisation's plans and activities.

A model of this type of collaboration was developed more than twenty years ago by MIT professor Edgar Schein (1978). So effectively did Schein represent the integration of individual career planning activities with organisational HRM activities that, according to the authors of a recent major text on career management, his model remains 'the most comprehensive approach to the integration of the two components' (Greenhaus, Callanan & Godschalk 2000, p. 402). Schein's model is reproduced as figure 3.1.

Figure 3.1 shows, on the left, a set of 'organisational activities' — a conventional system of strategy-based planning, followed by HR planning. Gaps between current and desired resources are assessed, and recruitment and development activities are adopted to fill them. The outcomes are then evaluated. The right-hand side of the figure outlines a set of individual processes, as the individual employee makes his or her career plans in the light of previous experiences, development and personal self-assessment. In the middle is a set of 'matching processes' linking the two sets of activities together.

For example, performance appraisal assists the company to match the person's performance and potential to its own map of future needs, while at the same time giving the employee much-needed feedback for his or her career-related self-assessment. Later in the process there is a 'dialogue' about issues such as job rotation and employee development, to which the organisation brings its HR plans, and the individual brings his or her career plans. The result, ideally, is the implementation of plans that will benefit both sides. As Greenhaus, Callanan and Godschalk (2000) put it, the model is useful 'because it demonstrates the fundamental interdependence between individuals' career plans and organisations' human resource plans' (p. 404).

At the same time, in relation to the new world of inter-organisational careers, Schein's system is idealistic. Seeing models like this, I imagine that good HR managers, when they die, must go to a kind of human resources heaven where textbook 'systems' — these wonderful assemblages of boxes and arrows beloved of business academics — actually *work*. In HR heaven systematic, well-intentioned HR programs — renamed 'AR' for 'angelic resources' — are accepted by St Peter and the other senior managers and utilised daily to give heaven a resource-based competitive advantage over the other place. The rank-and-file angels, of course, are enthusiastic about planning their heavenly careers. They are conscious of their strengths and weaknesses (though they don't have many of these!) and are keen to develop further. And, of course, having been recruited and selected for heaven, they don't want to leave and work for the competition! In HR heaven the HR managers preside over individual performance evaluation and career planning sessions guided by clear and compatible plans from both sides. Occasionally, a bit of give-and-take may be needed, but the outcome is always a synergistic win–win — thanks, of course, to the transcendent skills of the HR manager. Heavenly!

In fact, in my Earth-bound experience I have found few companies that come close to creating the HR nirvana that theorists assume. The small and medium-sized enterprises in which most people work don't even have an HR function to provide this kind of discipline. In larger companies, senior management often pays no more than

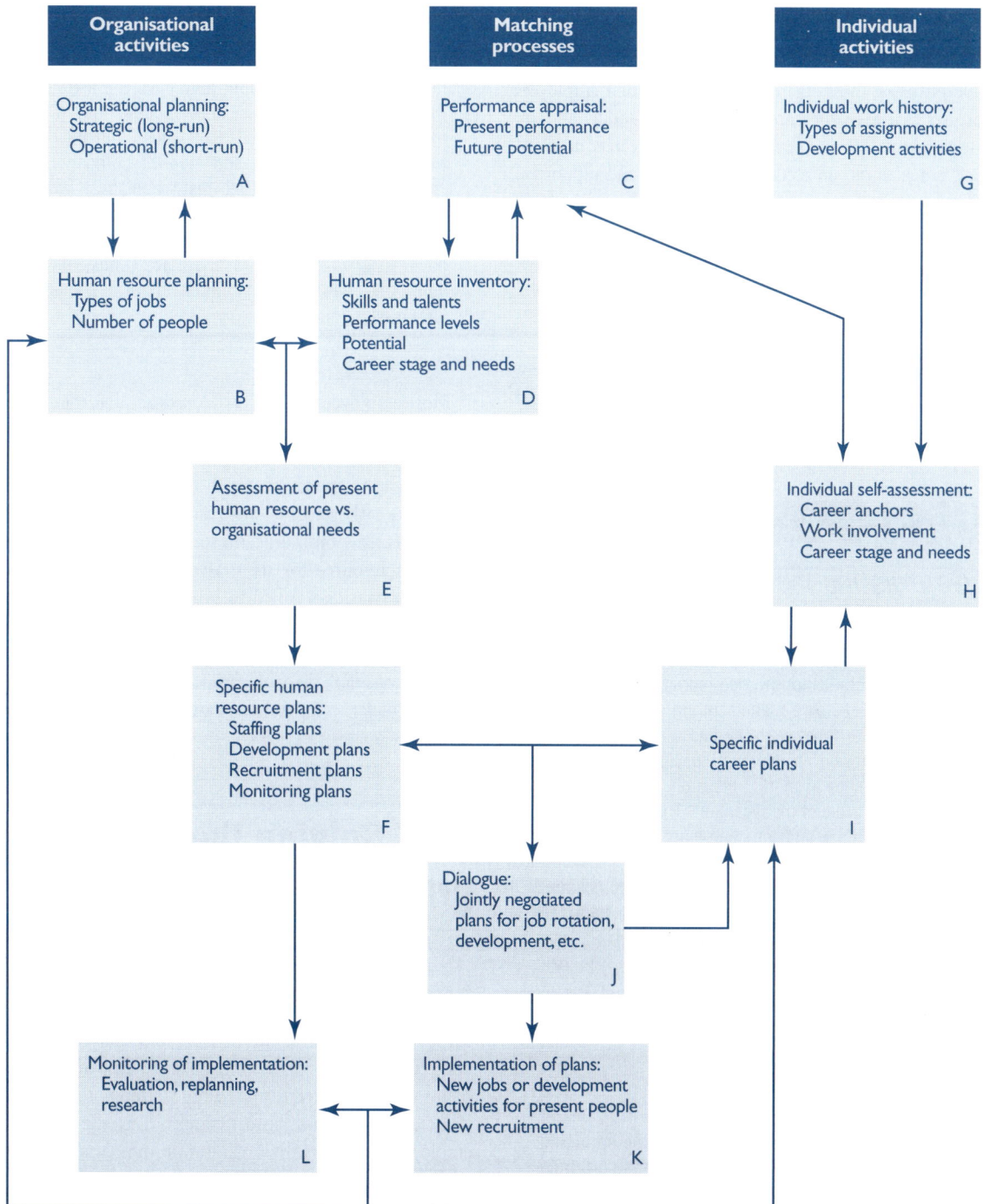

Organisational activities	Matching processes	Individual activities
Organisational planning: Strategic (long-run) Operational (short-run) **A**	Performance appraisal: Present performance Future potential **C**	Individual work history: Types of assignments Development activities **G**
Human resource planning: Types of jobs Number of people **B**	Human resource inventory: Skills and talents Performance levels Potential Career stage and needs **D**	
Assessment of present human resource vs. organisational needs **E**		Individual self-assessment: Career anchors Work involvement Career stage and needs **H**
Specific human resource plans: Staffing plans Development plans Recruitment plans Monitoring plans **F**		Specific individual career plans **I**
	Dialogue: Jointly negotiated plans for job rotation, development, etc. **J**	
Monitoring of implementation: Evaluation, replanning, research **L**	Implementation of plans: New jobs or development activities for present people New recruitment **K**	

Figure 3.1: Model of a human resource planning and development system

lip-service to HR in its strategic policy, and planning is rudimentary. The 'individual activities' are generally little better. Employees don't often understand or respect the HR systems the way the systems hypothesise they should. As for individual career planning, since time immemorial this has been known to be based on good techniques of self-assessment and opportunity assessment, followed by a matching process (Parsons 1909; Arnold 1997). But most people lack the disciplined approach and training to make it work.

Nevertheless, most organisations *do* offer their employees processes that are represented in the Schein model and are clearly potentially valuable to the employees' career development. For example, an accurate, informative and supportive performance evaluation can greatly assist the individual's self-assessment. A company-initiated opportunity for transfer to a new job or involvement in a task force can help the employee to develop 'career capital'. Potentially, many companies are good organisational resources for their employees' careers.

The problem, in a career-mobile society, is that the new, mobile employee may take all the assistance on offer, and then move on and use it for his or her own benefit and that of some other employer. Here is a case in point:

CASE

Contrasting views of commitment

Don is a graduate in marketing from an Australian university. After graduation he was recruited directly as a marketing trainee by a manufacturing company in the same city. Over three years he had a number of jobs and was involved in various special projects. He gained experience in market research, database management and product management. Then, abruptly, he left to work for a smaller competitor. Here are two views of his departure.

HR Manager, Allied Electro-Communication: 'When Don joined us, we thought he had the makings of a good marketing professional. He was smart, well-presented and eager to learn. He had interests in high tech that fitted in with our long-term strategy. So, as well as giving him the advantages of the normal HR systems, we tried to create a fast track for him — rapid promotions, special development experiences, that kind of thing. But in the end he lasted only three years, then he was off to one of those smaller competitors that seem to be springing up everywhere. It seems he just wasn't the corporate type. In the end we put far more into him than we ever got out.'

Don, former employee, Allied Electro-Communication: 'Yeah, Allied was a good company to work for. They certainly had the knowledge I needed for my career. And they really knew how to look after their people. I had a performance and development review session with my bosses every six months. We'd work out where I was going, and what development I needed. I volunteered for courses all over, learned a wide range of new skills. If I felt I wasn't going fast enough or wanted to learn a new facet of the business, I'd pester them until they gave me a transfer. But in the end it was like they thought they owned me, with their vision and their values and their culture and their politics, and love-the-company, we-can-get-you-to-the-top, all that rubbish. I worked hard while I was there, doubled my market value, but I was glad to leave. Anyway, it doesn't do, these days, to stay too long in one place. Looks bad on your c.v. People might think there's something wrong with you.'

Most employees believe, as Don does, that their careers belong to them rather than to the organisation for which they currently work. Many consider, as Don does, that it is a mistake to spend too much of that career — particularly in its early stages — with a single employer. Much as Allied Electro-Communication may like to consider Don a human resource for its strategic initiatives, it is clear that Don considers Allied to be no more than an organisational resource for his career. Don apparently has skills in demand and is able to choose his employers for himself. He considers that the competitor has more to offer at this particular stage in his career development. So he leaves.

Solving the turnover problem

For the company, the corollary to the mobile careers of Don and others like him is of course high levels of employee turnover. By and large, organisations dislike turnover. It causes them to lose important knowledge and skills that those leaving have developed. It incurs major costs in recruiting and training replacements (Cascio 1991). And unfortunately, it is the most able employees, the ones the organisation most wants to keep, who are the most likely to be 'headhunted' by other organisations or choose to leave in pursuit of personal goals. So, it is apparently in the interests of organisations to encourage staff to develop their long-term careers within the organisation.

As the HR manager at Allied Electro-Communication discovered in relation to Don, the usual contemporary HR practices of appraisal and development are by themselves often insufficient to prevent high levels of labour turnover as ambitious employees seek to advance their mobile, non-traditional careers. What else can HR do? Here are a few suggestions:

1. Stop thinking of Don and others as 'human resources'

'Resource' means 'a stock or supply that can be drawn on' (*Concise Oxford Dictionary*). Resources don't stick two fingers up at management, as Don did, and walk out of the door. Don is an autonomous person, who makes his own decisions about his own life. The use of the term 'resources' and the way of thinking it encourages imply the organisation's 'ownership' of the person as part of its stock, to be drawn on and developed for organisational ends. If there is a future for organisations' involvement in their employees' career development, it is not in the *management* of their careers as resources but in *partnership* with them as equals. You can't partner a resource, and Don's rejection of Allied was clearly determined in part by his rejection of its attempts to own him.

2. Listen to employees' career anxieties and aspirations

Discussion with individuals about their careers is 'off limits' in many organisations. Even when companies like Allied try to hold meaningful dialogue with employees about their careers, the discussion is likely to be confined to prospective careers *within the company*. Employees often do not want it to be known that they are considering leaving the organisation; and some managers regard such talk as evidence of 'disloyalty'. HR managers should seek to educate managers to understand that open discussion is vital in their career dialogues with employees. They should seek to cultivate an atmosphere of trust in which employees know that if they discuss their career aspirations openly they will not be 'jumped on'. If Don had felt able to express and discuss his desire to escape what he saw as the nonsense of Allied's culture and vision, perhaps a solution might have been found before he left.

3. Learn about the dynamics of careers

If we understand how careers work, then we are in a better position to help people to solve their career problems.

Career studies is the counterpart to HR studies, in that it examines issues from the perspective of the individual rather than the organisation. This mirror-image provides managers with a new, complementary understanding of people at work, and enables them to develop greater empathy with the concerns, particularly the longer-term concerns, of organisation members (Arnold 1997; Greenhaus, Callanan & Godschalk 2000).

Career theory is fascinating (Arthur, Hall & Lawrence 1989). For example, we can differentiate between the 'objective' career of defined positions, advances in status, salary and so on, and the 'subjective' career of emotions, satisfactions and aspirations (Bailyn 1989). There are predictable age-related stages in many careers as workers change their circumstances and priorities over a lifetime (Levinson et al. 1978). There are other predictable sequences as people go through the job-to-job transition points in their careers (Nicholson 1984). We can 'profile' people in terms of their suitability for specific careers (Holland 1985). New theories show how mobile careers are articulated in people's lives (Arthur & Rousseau 1996; Arthur, Inkson & Pringle 1999). There are common problems, such as those of the 'career plateau' (Feldman & Weitz 1988) and the 'dual career couple' (Sekaran & Hall 1989), that cause major difficulties for organisations and individuals alike. Surely, therefore, education about career principles ought to be undertaken by every HR manager. Unfortunately, career studies for some reason does not feature strongly in business curricula or HR education. HR managers, in particular, must make their own efforts to understand careers.

4. Devise programs to fit known problems

HR managers who have good information about the real career issues of current staff and understand how careers advance are well placed to develop programs that are oriented to the real issues. For example, why do companies that lose their mobile younger workers like Don persist in trying to solve the problem by hiring *more* mobile younger workers? Contrary to some of our 'ageist' prejudices about the 'problems' of older workers, research indicates that, by and large, older workers not only are less mobile but exhibit less absenteeism, have fewer accidents, and demonstrate better interpersonal relationships and equal job performance and trainability (Cascio 1995, pp. 322–4). A number of organisations have solved critical turnover problems by recruiting older staff. Also, there are programmable solutions to such common career problems as 'career plateau' workers and dual careers.

5. Proactively facilitate career development

Part of the problem is that many employees do not know how to go about developing their own career (see the right-hand part of Schein's 'system' in figure 3.1). Organisations can assist them here. Techniques include the use of assessment centres and workshops that involve the person in competing and getting feedback on tests of such attributes as abilities, aptitudes, personality and vocational interests. Alternatively, employees may complete workbooks asking them provocative questions about their careers, and discuss the results in groups or with a trained facilitator. Arnold (1997, chapter 4) provides a summary of the opportunities. The World Wide Web has many sites that feature opportunities for self-assessment, but guidance may be needed to assist employees to make effective use of these resources.

6. Encourage stability by promoting mobility

Today's employees recognise that in the fast-changing business scene they need development that is broad, varied and challenging. They seek employability rather than employment, and career knowledge capital that is portable beyond the boundaries of their present employer. Yet the conventional HR wisdom is that:

> *training and development must be aligned with corporate objectives if the organisation is to gain any real benefit . . . HR managers must be obsessive about linking individual and organisational development to the bottom line.'* (Stone 1998, pp. 318–19)

Unfortunately, it is in organisations that focus employee training and development most obsessively on the *organisation's* needs and goals that employees are most likely to find that their *own* career development needs are neglected.

An alternative view is that employee development should be aimed at cultivating 'career resilience' (Waterman, Waterman & Collard 1994). Development opportunities that take a more lateral view, reducing internal boundaries to the acquisition of new skills, and assisting employees to find opportunities to develop skills that are transferable outside the organisation, are paradoxically more likely to encourage loyalty among employees who can see that their longer term needs are being looked after (Parker & Inkson 1999). A more genuine and consistent management approach to employee development can encourage stability and a work environment based on trust, loyalty and mutual commitment.

New forms of organisational career

In the second half of this paper, I will develop the argument that the fundamental nature of careers is undergoing massive change and that the implications for HRM are profound. The 'new careers' are inter-organisational and frequently inter-occupational. They are mediated by broad networks rather than narrow, company-based HR systems. They are individually controlled. They are increasingly the causes rather than the effects of organisational change. They provide major opportunities for organisations to develop new, more flexible forms, and to let organisational activity follow and benefit from, rather than control, the enterprise of talented individuals pursuing career goals.

Nowadays people very seldom have career histories confined to a single occupation or organisation. Getting people — especially experienced people — to tell you their career histories is fascinating. There are so many unexpected twists and turns, idiosyncrasies and chance events. Frequently, there are periods of major uncertainty, insecurity and turbulence. But usually, with the benefit of hindsight, one can see some kind of logic behind the pattern of career development. The underlying patterns observed in a recent study of the new careers based on 75 cases were related not so much to organisations or occupations as to the sometimes purposive and sometimes accidental acquisition of the career competencies of motivation, skills and networks (Arthur, Inkson & Pringle 1999; Inkson 2000).

One feature of 'the new careers' identified in the latter study is that respondents seldom attributed their career decisions or outcomes to activities by their organisations. And they never attributed them to their organisation's HR departments (except in the event of redundancy or dismissal); rather, they nearly always ascribed them to their own initiatives and actions. This finding may depress some readers. It is partly caused by the well-known 'attribution error' through which individuals credit favourable events to their own agency and unfavourable events to outside circumstances (Miller & Lawson 1989). The absence of HR influence on people's perceptions of their own careers is nevertheless salutary for those who see careers as outcomes of beneficent HRM activities.

Individual career narratives also allow us to explore the interactions of individuals with their organisations in new ways. They enable us to learn new patterns of organisational operation that affect individual careers and new ways of pursuing a career that affect organisational functioning. Consider the following case.

Navigating the organisation

Heather, aged 28, is on the lower rungs of a major television organisation, which we will call BroadCaster. BroadCaster is very big and has operations in a number of countries. Heather is a BA graduate with an interest, and some 'amateur' experience, in video production — hence her attraction to BroadCaster. However, Heather's initial work qualification was as a chef (in which she qualified when taking a year out from her BA studies), and it was in that capacity that she commenced work in the staff restaurant of a major BroadCaster facility. She joined Broad-Caster because she hoped in due course to be able to make a lateral move into television production work. To her consternation, she discovered after she had joined that her employer was not BroadCaster but the contract catering company that ran the BroadCaster restaurants. Opportunities for transfer were nonexistent. Still, it was an interesting place to be. Heather spent two years as a chef, and was able to see the potential of the organisation.

'BroadCaster is in the field of work that most interests me. It employs thousands of people, in many different locations. Once you are in the company, all sorts of transfers to new types of work and new opportunities become possible. It's a company that is worth sticking with . . .'

So, while working as a chef, Heather retrained herself (at home in her spare time) in office and secretarial skills that she felt would provide her with greater mobility and, eventually, higher earnings. Through a contact in Broad-Caster, she was soon able to find work within the company, as a mobile, project-to-project secretary/PA. Again, she was not employed by BroadCaster but by a 'temp' agency that supplies temporary secretarial and administrative staff, with BroadCaster as its main client. The agency recognises that many of its temps are attracted to it by the prospect of assignments in the high-profile production side of the client organisation. The agency therefore assigns routine administrative projects and jobs to new temps and then, once they have proved their worth, offers them the assignments they really want, on the production side. Heather has made good progress and is now temporary PA to a senior project manager. She has also learned office and support skills usable across a range of industries, as well as commonly used IT applications such as SAP. Thus, her administrative career has advanced considerably. But she still awaits her first production-related assignment.

What can we learn from this case?

1. BroadCaster is evidently pursuing a strategy of focusing on its own core competency (television broadcasting), and outsourcing activities such as catering and administration in which it has no particular background or expertise. This kind of thinking changes career pathways, which increasingly run through networks of linked organisations rather than within organisations. The company-to-company job-hopping that provides much of the intellectual energy of the Silicon Valley regional semi-conductor industry is a spectacular example of this phenomenon (Saxenian 1996).

2. Although she has never been employed by the organisation in question, Heather is beginning to see herself as having a form of organisational career. But unlike those pursuing traditional organisational careers, she defines her organisational career not in terms of upward mobility through different levels in a stable hierarchy, but as a series of self-redeployments through a range of different opportunities towards a vaguely defined ultimate goal. She perceives the company, like the broader world of employment opportunities, not as a defined structure of pathways, but as a reservoir of ever-changing opportunities that can be better accessed from the inside rather than the outside.

3. Heather has, in her use of personal time and resources to re-skill from chef to secretary/PA, explicitly recognised that in the end it is she and not any of her employers who is responsible for her personal and career development. On the other hand, she has used BroadCaster and her employment opportunities within it effectively to improve her wider career prospects and skills.

4. Heather's current work is based not on a single job in a single location but on a series of 'projects'. She is not employed by BroadCaster, yet is mobile within it. Each project presents a new challenge, new learning opportunities. Each takes place in a fresh location and puts her in touch with new contacts. She is probably getting to know BroadCaster a lot better than many of its permanent employees, and is certainly learning a wider and more varied range of skills.

5. It may be that Heather will be able to engineer pathways that will take her towards her current career goals. Alternatively, she may find new, unanticipated opportunities for career fulfilment within the organisation. And if neither of these courses works out, she appears likely to acquire inside the organisation a range of skills relevant

to an inter-organisational career. If her outlook and the possibilities she sees for herself are characteristic — as I believe they are — of organisational careers nowadays, then it is clear that these careers are similar in many respects to the inter-organisational or 'boundaryless' careers with which they are often contrasted.

6. What does Heather need from HRM? So far it has apparently impinged on her career very little. Perhaps HR managers were involved in her initial recruitment as chef and secretary, and in the provision of the limited training and evaluation opportunities she has had. Basically, however, she has taken charge of her own career, found her own opportunities and ensured her own development. Now she most needs guidance about opportunities to secure the kind of work she aspires to in BroadCaster and the kind of self-development she might undertake in order to get there. She acquires that assistance in her own way from informal sources. Yet Heather, unusually for a 'new careers' person, does at least identify a single organisation within which she seeks to develop her career. If HRM is irrelevant to Heather's career, whose is it relevant to?

The core and the periphery

Heather is typical of those pursuing new careers. A recent book by Hall (1996) is entitled *The Career Is Dead — Long Live the Career*. Paraphrasing Hall, we might suggest that the organisational career is dead, but that the *inter*-organisational, or boundaryless, career is very much alive. One way of conceptualising these major changes to business forms in recent years has been to distinguish between the organisational 'core' and the 'periphery'. These terms identify different types of employment relationships.

The core of an organisation structure largely comprises its 'permanent' workers — those whose employment contracts are of indefinite duration. The longer people have been in the organisation, the more central their work and the more senior their position, the more they can be considered to be core staff members. These employees typically have 'relational' contracts with the company — that is, contracts based on an ongoing relationship of mutual respect and trust, and not just a simple exchange of money for work (Rousseau 1995). It is in these employees that the organisation's memory resides. They typically act as guardians of its culture and values. They can justifiably be considered the 'heart and soul' of the company.

The periphery consists of workers who contribute effort to the company but are more marginal. Part-time workers, temporary workers, casual workers dealing with special orders or seasonal fluctuations in demand, contractors employed to do a specific project only — all these are part of the periphery. These employees are sometimes known as 'contingent' workers, because their employment is contingent on changing organisational needs. They typically have 'transactional' contracts with the company; that is, contracts defined by clear expectations of immediate exchange — in essence, 'this amount of dollars for that output' — with no anticipation of an ongoing relationship (Rousseau 1995). These employees may seek to do their jobs well, but they are likely not to have the same long-term concern for the organisation that the core workers have.

Core workers typically understand what the organisation is about, have much useful 'local' knowledge, and are likely to be loyal and committed members. Peripheral workers, however, are more flexible. They can be called in at short notice; they can provide 'special skills' that may be needed only for one-off jobs; and they require no long-term financial or psychological commitment by the employer — when the company no longer needs them or cannot afford them, they can be got rid of quite easily, because their employment relationship guarantees them nothing.

It is clear that each type of worker can make different contributions to the business. But in recent years, the overriding priority of reducing overheads and maximising flexibility for competitive advantage has led to a considerable growth in the peripheries of organisations relative to their cores. The problem with this, from an HRM perspective, is that the desirable integrated HR model provided by Schein implicitly assumes that everyone in the company is a 'core' organisation member, whose long-term development and career needs it is in the company's interests — as well as his or her own — to consider.

Furthermore, peripheral workers are no longer — as used once to be the case — only unskilled seasonal and casual workers and junior office 'temps'. The periphery now contains many well-educated people with high skills that are in strong demand. For example, in the computer programming/systems analysis areas, job advertisement pages nowadays contain nearly as many advertisements for short-term contracts as for full-time positions.

Traditional HRM is largely focused on the management of core workers. How relevant is it to contingent workers? To illustrate the special problems involved in HR and career management, consider the following case, based on research reported by Inkson, Heising and Rousseau (2001) and also summarised by Inkson (2001).

CASE

Leased executives in Auckland

A leased executive (LE) is a management professional, usually with a specific area of expertise, who contracts to provide a client company with short-term cover, trouble-shooting in an area of expertise, or completion of a pre-defined project. Typically, the LE is leased to the client company by an agency, which receives a fee for supplying the resource. The executive can be hired for specific skills related to a short-term project. Clearly, a leased executive is part of an organisation's 'periphery'.

The following description of LE work is based on interviews with a sample of 50 LEs, all working or available for work through a major agency in Auckland. (See Inkson, Heising & Rousseau (2001) for further details.)

Typically, the LE receives, as compensation for the insecurity involved, a salary somewhat higher than that for the equivalent 'permanent' job. On the other hand, the client will not have to contribute superannuation payments or staff development costs or any other overheads of permanent employment, or have to worry about any expenditure at all once the current project is over. There is no commitment to the future — if the person's skills are no longer required after the project is over, he or she can be easily disposed of. An executive who doesn't perform or fails to develop on the job does not become part of the company's 'dead wood'. The company will not end up in court facing charges of wrongful dismissal or become liable for redundancy payments.

Another advantage of LEs to organisations is that because of their mobility between companies, they often have a wider range of expertise than the typical core worker. Because they don't have a lot of time to make a difference, they have an ability to 'hit the ground running' and focus on the key project tasks. Because they are temporary they also tend to keep out of company politics and are willing to speak their minds.

There are also advantages for the LE. Being basically self-employed gives them a welcome autonomy. Their hours tend to be flexible, enabling them to do more than one contract simultaneously or to cultivate personal consultancies or small businesses. They are able to keep out of company politics, which many consider a real blessing. Exposure to a range of industries and organisations broadens their skill base and widens their networks. They learn to get things done quickly. They become more versatile, more employable and less dependent on a single company. And, of course, the pay is significantly higher.

To balance these benefits there are also disadvantages. There is no guarantee that a suitable new contract will coincide with the completion of the previous one. In the eyes of the world, and particularly of the agency, LEs are only as good as their last job. They often find it difficult to become 'part of the scene' in a company, and may find that colleagues are not just indifferent but hostile. They worry about how much real impact they make in their client companies. After they have completed their contracts, there is no guarantee that the client company will follow up their projects properly.

Like an increasing number of twenty-first-century workers, LEs construct their careers not on a job-to-job basis but on a project-to-project basis. They are 'hired guns' — proud of their skills, and anxious to develop these and their reputations through further gunfights. The career thus becomes an exercise in project learning. Every project provides opportunities — for example, mastery of new computer packages or familiarity with a new industry. Even more important, in a world where most career transitions are assisted by personal networking, is the development of new contacts with each fresh project.

Responsibility for the career development of the LE devolves squarely on the individual. If an LE wants to go to a management seminar, he or she will normally have to find the time and money to do so; neither the client company nor the agency is likely to support the development of such a short-term appointee. LEs accept this responsibility in theory but do little about it in practice, maintaining that the extent and variety of their on-the-job experience compensates for any deficiencies in formal qualifications.

In the LE context, the agency is a 'matchmaker'. Based on a project description supplied by the client organisation, the agency selects the LE from a database to which it has access. The client pays a fee to the agency and the agency pays a fee to the LE. The agency's interest in the relationship does not end when the match is made. It has a responsibility to the client organisation to ensure that the LE does a good job, a responsibility to the LE to assist him or her to find further projects, and a responsibility to itself to cultivate ongoing contracts between the organisation and the LE. Where the traditional employment relationship involves two parties, this one — typical, I believe, of future structures — has three, as shown in figure 3.2.

Note that the relationship of the employer with the LE is explicitly 'transactional' rather than 'relational' (Rousseau 1995). Interestingly, the agent may well be interested in developing a longer term relationship with both LE and company than they do with each other. This is typical of the way in which restructuring and mobile careers change HRM.

(continued)

The agency has sophisticated systems of data storage and retrieval relating to both temporary positions and potential leased executives. A systematic profile of project tasks and associated skill requirements can be matched against a similar profile of every LE on the agency's books. The agency seeks to remain attractive to the LE, and to keep the LE on the agency's lists. In the long term, therefore, the agency may have more to gain from the career development and effective HRM of the LE than does the client company. Support activities by the agency may include ongoing support on projects, information about further project opportunities and even some support for inexpensive elements of personal development.

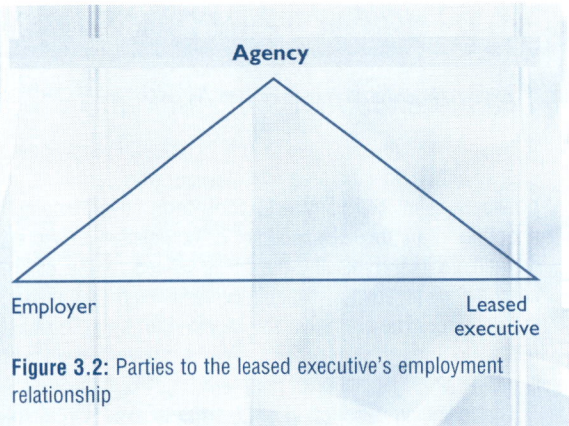

Figure 3.2: Parties to the leased executive's employment relationship

Looking at the leased executive, you may be looking at your own future, and that of much of the workforce: project-based organisations creating and being created by project-based careers; a premium on flexibility, versatility and inter-organisational learning as people seek to match their own competitive advantage to the requirements of the new economy; and more and more of everything — careers, collaboration, knowledge development and HRM — taking place *between* rather than within organisations.

The outsourcing of HRM

In the core-and-periphery world, companies have to decide whether to 'buy, make or lease' their own professional employees — that is, whether to recruit them on permanent employment, develop them from within the firm or hire them on a short-term contingency basis. Such decisions are best made on the basis of HR policies that rationally evaluate the strengths and weaknesses of the alternatives in relation to the company's wider strategy. HR systems that have been explicitly devised to foster loyalty and assume permanence may be inappropriate to the handling of temporary staff.

In the above case, much of the traditional HR function is now the responsibility of the leased executive him- or herself. But the new career mobility also means that organisations must staff themselves increasingly through *external* labour markets. In the past, vacancies could be filled from within the company, and career development was identical to staff development. Nowadays more and more posts are filled through tapping into the external, even international, labour market, and agencies with good external networks and knowledge are vital. Agencies such as the one referred to in the case take on more and more of the HR support function that has traditionally been discharged by the employing organisation. The above case therefore illustrates an inexorable trend for HRM to be located outside rather than inside company boundaries.

As the trend to larger peripheries and smaller cores continues, more and more HRM-type activities will be conducted by these types of intermediary agencies (often with offices in many countries), which are better equipped to deal with internationalised and mobile workforces and staff who are operating in 'boundaryless career' mode. These agencies operate in broad, often international, labour markets, have access to large databases of potential applicants and understand the wider industry contexts in which the new mobile professionals work. They can take account of the strategic HR plans and needs of client organisations, but their competitive advantage vis-à-vis 'internal' company HRM is in their greater knowledge of wider contexts and individual professional needs.

Students of HRM frequently see their own future careers as taking place within work organisations where they expect to operate as professional managers and advisers of the organisation's internal HR function. But there is no reason, in principle, why any part of HR should not be outsourced to another organisation with greater competency in the area. Indeed, good HR departments already hire external specialist consultants to do much of their work. As one HR manager in a large company with 16 specialist HR staff put it:

You can outsource everything. You can contract in training and development. You can get employment relations specialists when you need them. In our organization you could get rid of most of the HR people. You'd need someone like me in a go-between role. But even I could be on contract. The same model applies to finance, IT, property... HR specialists aren't needed in-house. (Parker & Inkson 1999, p. 36)

An organisation that goes to this extreme may, of course, pay the price in poor coordination, lack of appreciation of the organisation's history and culture, close personal relationships between HR people and other staff and so on. Yet such scenarios are not just possible, but increasingly standard. A growing proportion of HR-type jobs exist outside traditional organisational boundaries, as agents, contractors and consultants. These people require a much wider focus than a specific company's current objectives. They need to interact both with client companies and with the current and potential employees of these companies as partners rather than managers. In a few years' time, there may not be much left of the cosy world of internally focused company HR departments.

Conclusion

Prophets of future organisational forms foresee a time when organisations will no longer be composed — as they tend to be now — of employees doing their jobs within an ongoing company structure of plans, authority relationships, procedures and job descriptions, supported by a benign HR department. Rather, they will consist of autonomous professionals completing short-tem contracts with the company on an evolving basis. Rather than long-term company strategies creating pathways for good careers, enterprising and knowledgeable individuals will create opportunities for the incremental development of company strategy through their short-term entrepreneurial or 'intrapreneurial' career moves (Miles & Snow 1996).

If this is the case, career development will become less the responsibility of the organisation and even more that of the individual; less a local matter and more an external matter; less about the management of human and organisational resources and more about the development of human and organisational partnerships across boundaries. The aspiring HR professional setting a course for his or her own career development would do well to consider these trends and their implications for the future.

References

Arnold, J (1997) *Managing Careers into the 21st Century.* London: Paul Chapman.

Arthur, MB, Hall, DT, and Lawrence, BS (1989) *Handbook of Careers.* Cambridge: Cambridge University Press.

Arthur MB, Inkson, K, and Pringle, JK (1999) *The New Careers: Individual Action and Economic Change.* London: Sage.

Arthur, MB, and Rousseau, DM (Eds) (1996) *The Boundaryless Career: A New Employment Principle for a New Organizational Era.* New York: Oxford University Press.

Bailyn, L (1989) Understanding individual experience at work: comments on the theory and practice of careers. In MB Arthur, DT Hall and BS Lawrence, *Handbook of Careers.* Cambridge: Cambridge University Press.

Cascio, WF (1991) *Costing Human Resources: The Financial Impact of Behavior in Organizations* (3rd ed.). Boston, MA: PWS-Kent.

Cascio, WF (1995) *Managing Human Resources: Productivity, Quality of Work Life, Profits* (4th ed.). New York: McGraw-Hill.

Feldman, DC, and Weitz, BA (1988) Career plateaux reconsidered. *Journal of Management,* 14, 69–80.

Greenhaus, JH, Callanan, GA, and Godschalk, VM (2000) *Career Management* (3rd ed.). Fort Worth, TX: Dryden Press.

Hall, DT (1996) *The Career is Dead — Long Live the Career.* San Francisco: Jossey-Bass.

Holland, JL (1985) *Making Vocational Choices: A Theory of Personality and Work Environments.* Englewood Cliffs, NJ: Prentice Hall.

Inkson, K (2000) Rewriting career development principles for the new millennium. In R Wiesner and B Millett (Eds), *Contemporary Challenges and Future Directions in Management and Organizational Behaviour.* Brisbane: John Wiley & Sons.

Inkson, K (2001) The rent-a-managers. In G Elkin (Ed.), *Human Resource Management in Action, Volume 2.* Palmerston North, NZ: Dunmore Press.

Inkson, K, and Arthur, MB (2001) How to be a successful career capitalist. *Organizational Dynamics,* 31 (3) 48–61.

Inkson, K, Heising, A, and Rousseau, DM (2001) The interim manager: prototype of the twenty-first century worker? *Human Relations,* 54 (3) 259–84.

Levinson, DJ, Klein, CN, Levinson, MH, and McKee, B (1978) *The Seasons of a Man's Life.* New York: Knopf.

Miles, RE, and Snow, CC (1996) Twenty-first century careers. In MB Arthur and DM Rousseau (Eds), *The Boundaryless Career: A New Employment Principle for a New Organizational Era.* New York: Oxford University Press.

Miller, AG, and Lawson, T (1989) The effect of an informational option on the fundamental attribution error. *Personality and Social Psychology Bulletin,* June, 194–204.

Nicholson, N (1984) A theory of work role transitions. *Administrative Science Quarterly,* 29, 172–91.

Parker, P, and Inkson K (1999) New forms of career: the challenge to human resource management. *Asia-Pacific Journal of Human Resources,* 37 (1) 67–76.

Parsons, F (1909) *Choosing a Vocation.* Boston, MA: Houghton-Mifflin.

Rousseau, DM (1995) *Psychological Contracts in Organizations.* Thousand Oaks, CA: Sage.

Saxenian, AL (1996) Beyond boundaries: open learning and labor markets in Silicon Valley. In MB Arthur and DM Rousseau (Eds), *The Boundaryless Career: A New Employment Principle for a New Organizational Era.* New York: Oxford University Press.

Schein, EH (1978) *Career Dynamics: Matching Individual and Organizational Needs.* Reading, MA: Addison-Wesley.

Sekaran, U, and Hall, DT (1989) Asynchronism in dual-career and family linkages. In MB Arthur, DT Hall and BS Lawrence, *Handbook of Careers.* Cambridge: Cambridge University Press.

Stone, RJ (1998) *Human Resource Management* (3rd ed.). Brisbane: John Wiley & Sons.

Waterman, RH, Waterman, JA, and Collard, BA (1994) Toward a career-resilient workforce. *Harvard Business Review,* July–August, 87–95.

CHAPTER 4

Human resource management and the ageing workforce

by Margaret Patrickson
University of South Australia

Introduction

This chapter explores the challenges facing Australian human resource practice in the twenty-first century as a result of workforce ageing. During the past two decades work and personal circumstances have propelled many older individuals to leave the workforce by opting for early retirement, but the next two decades seem poised to reverse this process.

Indications are that both the global economic outlook (United Nations 1990) and the Australian economy (Larkin 1995) are improving, which should increase the demand for labour. United States projections (Friedman 1992) suggest that the high-skill market will provide expanding opportunities for those who are flexible, but that fewer opportunities will be generated in the contingent labour area; and Australia seems to be similarly positioned (Patrickson & Hartmann 2001). At the same time the age profile of the workforce continues to increase steadily. By 2030 the median age of the Australian population is expected to rise to 40.1 years, up from 33.6 years in 1995 (United Nations 1995). Life expectancy is also set to rise from 81.5 in 1995 to 84.0 in 2025 (United Nations 1994). Clearly these figures have implications for workforce management as the numbers of younger individuals entering the workforce fall (ABS 1999) and the immediate post–World War 2 baby-boomer generation heads into the 'older worker' category. Those aged over 50 could soon form the largest cohort in the workforce.

An ageing workforce will have important ramifications for human resource management (HRM) as older workers move from a minority situation to a potential majority in the workforce. Nor should the current generation of older workers be as vulnerable to job loss as its predecessor. During the past 20 years the work experience of those now aged over 50 has led to a higher rate of computer literacy. They are more accustomed to reskilling and multiskilling, and they have had to come to terms with flexible usage of labour with its potential consequences for their employment. They have matured in a climate of multiculturalism, they are more aware of the principles of workforce diversity increasingly adopted by Australian business (Australian Business 1999), and many are going back to the classroom. Unlike the previous generation, their contribution will add value to business and they will be needed. In view of these issues, providing them with a healthy work environment, working within the terms of their financial situation, and stimulating their motivation and commitment will be a challenge for HRM. This chapter addresses the challenge by suggesting how to manage this group effectively and integrate its contribution with that of others to gain maximum value from all staff.

Contemporary challenges for HRM and the ageing workforce

Deploying this cohort competitively, efficiently and effectively presents HRM with a challenge. Policies and practices directed towards finding and developing them, measuring their contribution, rewarding their performance and retaining them will need to be formulated, adopted and monitored. Formally, this means revisiting the functions of recruitment, selection, training, career development and management, performance appraisal, occupational health and safety management, salary and benefits administration, and disengagement.

This chapter considers how each of these activities might be so designed that worker contribution is valued, satisfaction is high, and both employer and employee benefit. Good HRM practice will involve providing a supportive environment, adopting a careful and flexible approach, using open channels of communication and, where possible, involving older staff in designing and implementing changes (Walker 1999). The chapter concludes by addressing the potential impact of changes in HR practice on the health, financial needs and motivation of older workers, concerns that previous research has established as major influences on any decision to remain in the workforce (Taylor & Walker 1996; Patrickson 1998; Yeats, Folts & Knapp 2000).

Recruitment and older workers

Older workers seeking to rejoin the workforce have experienced discrimination and have found it very difficult to find work following a period of unemployment (Moore, Tilson & Whitting 1994; Worsley 1996; Kinsella-Taylor 1998). Bishop (1999) cites ABS figures that show the average spell of unemployment for people over 55 as 121.9 weeks compared with 55.0 weeks for other job seekers. Discrimination against older employees is rife. Australian organisations have been reluctant to hire older staff (Pickersgill et al. 1996) in spite of evidence that assumptions about their reduced capacity are false. This reluctance disregards the experience of a number of overseas companies such as B&Q, Glaxo Wellcome, WH Smith, Ford and Tesco in the United Kingdom (Jobs East 1998); Days Inn in the United States (Barth, McNaught & Rizzi 1993); and IBM Italy and Stahlwerke Bremen in Germany (European Foundation 1997). Those companies that have set out to deliberately attract older staff have been surprised by the benefits that have accrued. These include reduced turnover, consistent and reliable performance, a depth of experience and team benefits.

Pickersgill's data demonstrate that Australian employers have shown themselves especially reluctant to seek older individuals for long-term positions or leadership roles in middle management. Older workers are viewed as lacking

'drive'; they are not associated with the future. Such stereotypes are difficult to challenge or to change, yet they need to be if older workers are to improve their success in job seeking. Efforts by the federal government to promote the cause of the older worker have generated publications, conferences and seminars, but employers have a poor attendance record. At two recent seminars in Melbourne organised by Jobs East, in 1998 and 2000, the audience consisted largely of those seeking work rather than those seeking workers.

Job seeking by older workers is more likely to be successful when vacancies remain unfilled. Change will accelerate if labour shortages become acute and only older people are available. Foot and Venne's (1991) research predicted that labour shortages would begin in the 1990s, but more recent ABS data suggest this forecast may have been premature and that shortages are more likely to be experienced early in the current decade (ABS 1999). Inglis (2000) suggests there is already evidence that labour shedding has stabilised, and this may be a precursor to a shortage.

Positive experiences, by employers or their colleagues, or desperation, may act eventually to convince employers that they need to eliminate prejudice in their pre-judgements of the performance of older applicants. Any evaluation of anticipated performance should be made on the same basis as for other applicants — in other words, judgements should be reached on past achievements and present capacity and not on the basis of age. Outstanding older workers can point to their record and need not rely on potential. They stand to benefit from the trend towards contract employment, now that recruitment has broadened from purely entry-level positions to seeking talent at all levels of experience (Patrickson & Hartmann 2001). If current trends towards contract-style jobs continue, little long-term commitment by either party can be expected. Consequently any risk is reduced. Another group likely to yield suitable applicants for contract positions is the organisation's former full-time permanent staff. The performance levels of experienced staff are known, and often they can provide scarce skills or fill temporary positions. This may help some older people to rejoin the workforce.

However, indications are that any such change in existing recruitment practice is likely to happen slowly. Anti-discrimination legislation in the 1990s, which called upon employers to be less discriminating in their recruiting activities, has until recently had little impact on their prejudice against hiring older workers (Bennington 1998). Discrimination charges are difficult to prove, since any complaint can be refuted by the employer on the grounds that the hiring decision was made on the basis not of age but of unsuitability or simply that another applicant was preferred (Matthews 2000).

It may be premature to suggest that managers seek to deliberately target older workers for recruitment, as has been the case in the United States (Gilbert & Ivancevich 2000). Sullivan and Duplaga (1997) recommend that organisations use recruitment pictures featuring older individuals, or alternatively ask for 'mature, experienced and reliable employees'. They also note efforts to target the hidden retired by placing advertisements in magazines typically read by older individuals. Such messages would be heeded only by those already ideologically supportive. Change in Australia is more likely to follow a recommendation that applications from older individuals to join an organisation be treated on their merit and not automatically downgraded because the applicant is no longer young. Slow change *is* happening. Tabakoff and Skeffington (2000) note the examples of Qantas, BP and Macquarie Bank, who have all recruited older managers because of their experience.

But there is less movement at the lower end of the job market. Ingles (2000) reports on the ABS Survey of Employment and Unemployment Patterns 1995–97, which showed that 19 per cent of job seekers were aged 45 to 59. Of these, approximately one quarter were successful in finding work, if not always a stable or well-paid job, yet those aged 55 to 59 were generally unsuccessful. These applicants were predominantly unskilled or semi-skilled and lacked experience in service-type jobs involving people contact, where most of the vacancies occurred.

RECOMMENDATIONS

HR managers should:

- ensure that ageing is included in the diversity policy on recruitment as a key variable to promote workforce balance
- ensure that job applicants are evaluated on the basis of ability, not age
- insist that recruitment policies address only the competencies required for the job, not irrelevant personal characteristics
- insist that any decision against a qualified and experienced older individual is justified on criteria other than age
- where possible, consider recruiting former full-time staff in temporary, part-time or contract roles
- consider recruiting unknown older individuals for interim contract positions to enable their performance to be evaluated
- if recruiting from an agency, insist that the agency send a mix of applicants, not simply younger individuals.

Implementing the recommendations outlined will not be easy since they challenge deep-seated prejudices, but recent advances in two areas should help. The development and regular use of performance measurement systems should facilitate the collection of reliable information concerning individual performance levels (Nankervis & Leece 1997). Job applicants can use data on recent performance to substantiate any claim about their competence. Grueller (1999) claims many studies show that older workers regularly equal or outperform their younger colleagues when attention is given to quality rather than quantity. Pressures to raise awareness of the benefits of a balanced workforce may also help counteract the worst excesses of discrimination (Taylor & Walker 1993; Heilman, McCullough & Gilbert 1996).

Records of past performance should help dispel myths of incompetence that persist when supervisor ratings contain in-built prejudice. Such performance indicators have proved especially relevant in computing, where applicants can supply prospective employers with samples of proficiency and speed in various software packages (Pierce 2000). The more objective performance measures are developed and used routinely, the greater the likelihood that applicants will seek to provide potential employers with this type of evidence rather than rely on unsubstantiated claims. Within information processing this evidence is relatively easy to obtain, although it is not so accessible in more indeterminate skill areas. Shortages of skilled staff in computing have led contract agencies that supply staff with performance guarantees to develop reliable measures of competency. This strategy could also benefit other skill areas and stimulate the search for similarly effective measures in other industries.

Selection and older workers

Older workers need more than encouragement to apply for work; they need to be hired. Hiring is the ultimate recognition of potential suitability to remain part of the workforce. For many older workers, despite innumerable applications, getting hired when the economic climate is poor and discrimination is rife has proven an insurmountable task. Some simply either cease to search in despair or are galvanised to investigate an alternative such as self-employment (ABS 1996–2000).

Those seeking work do not conform to a uniform pattern. For every job seeker hoping to find something similar to an earlier job experience, there are others who are changing their skill portfolio, or who seek only a part-time or contract position (Tabakoff & Skeffington 2000). Inglis (2000) found that older women have generally been more successful in their quest for employment than older men. His research shows that the proportion of older women employed has risen by 20 per cent in the 45–54 age group and by 10 per cent among those aged 55–64. The proportion of full-time jobs held by 45- to 54-year-olds has grown by 10 per cent; those held by 55- to 64-year-olds has increased by 15 per cent. Arthur, Inkson and Pringle (1999) found that women tend to approach their work roles with more flexibility and versatility, and this allows them greater freedom of choice when seeking employment. Women have dominated the part-time sector and shown themselves more adaptable to opportunities on offer. Many have spent a period out of the workforce while raising a family, so that when they return they are conscious of obsolescent skills and often retrain. This flexibility can make them more attractive to employers.

In the 1980s and 1990s employers became accustomed to discarding applications from older individuals and hiring younger people. As mentioned above, this bias looks set to change. Once it does, older job applicants may find themselves courted, rather than being downgraded or ignored. Selection approaches will shift from reflexively eliminating older applicants to developing a strategy to identify *all* those offering potential value.

Selection strategies that measure performance and capacity may need to be adapted for use with older applicants. Sullivan and Duplaga (1997) suggest the simple expedient of not using young interviewers. Where possible, objective performance measures need to be developed. The opinions of former managers or colleagues who know an applicant well should be canvassed. High-value applicants may need to be enticed to join. They may even ask for special conditions; if so, negotiating to incorporate their needs will add to the HRM task.

The role of human resource managers in selecting job applicants should therefore change in three ways. First, they must educate managerial staff concerning the potential contribution of older subordinates and help them to reduce any existing bias. This should involve providing information to debunk some of the common myths noted above. If possible, the HR manager should ensure that older candidates are always included in those shortlisted for appointment, and should promote their hiring if skill portfolios are appropriate. Second, HR managers should develop selection measures that are free of age bias. Third, they should assist in the negotiation of employment contracts that reflect these values.

RECOMMENDATIONS

HR managers should:

- ensure their policy on diversity precludes age bias
- insist that selection be based on merit
- promote a balanced workforce
- alert organisational managers to the benefits of hiring older workers if older staff numbers are low
- supply feedback to any unsuccessful applicants to enable them to present more effectively in the future
- re-examine selection criteria to ensure freedom from age bias
- keep statistics on the subsequent performance of older hires, using these data for mutual benefit.

None of the above recommendations is likely to involve a radical departure from existing practice, since they mainly revolve around ensuring that selection practices are professional and up to date. But proactive HR managers might also declare their position on diversity issues and take steps to promote a more egalitarian, performance-based culture that reinforces performance, rather than immutable characteristics such as age, as the preferred basis for differentiating between job applicants.

Keeping statistics, and publishing them widely and regularly, will contribute to this effort. Such factual evidence ensures that assessments of competency are based on evidence rather than unsubstantiated and possibly mistaken beliefs that older individuals are 'past it'.

Training, development and career management for older workers

Organisations have been urged to provide more opportunities for training and development (Curtain 2000). Methodologies more suited to the learning styles of older participants have been recommended (WHO 1993; Warr 1994), and organisations that make it difficult for older employees to attend training sessions have been berated (Itzin & Phillipson 1993; Hutchens 1993). Complaints about the lack of opportunity for training and development, or its unsuitability, underlie the majority of discrimination issues raised by existing employees (New Zealand Employers Federation 1998; EEO Report 1999–2000).

Access to training and the mode of its delivery have been sources of dissatisfaction and unrest for many older employees. Human resource practitioners will need to address this issue if they are to retain valued staff and fulfil their obligations regarding diversity issues.

A key question is how to apportion the responsibility for training. In the past, almost all responsibility for the acquisition of general or transferable skills has been borne by the employee, and all firm-specific skills by the employer (Grueller 1999). Throughout the twentieth century most Australian organisations provided limited staff training, below the level of comparable nations overseas and restricted largely either to specific skill acquisition or to management development (Smith 1992). Recent Australian data (Patrickson & Hartmann 2001) indicate that more individuals have begun to assume responsibility for their own development, and this trend has accelerated as more jobs have changed from full-time to contract positions. Numbers involved in post-secondary education continue to soar. Labour hire agencies now offer training for registered job seekers (Pierce 2000).

These developments have occurred while greater attention is being paid to notions of lifelong learning (Senge 1990). Recognition that many job skills have a limited life has grown steadily, spurred by rapid technological change. Training is gradually coming to be viewed as less a current expense than an investment in future staff performance (Smith 1996). In consequence, employers are starting to cut back on programs where the links between cost and subsequent performance improvement are difficult to demonstrate. The employer needs to see that the value of the firm's human capital has risen. Organisations will support only those programs likely to provide staff with additional skills that will more than repay the cost of delivery.

Employees, too, need to see a return for the time, effort and perhaps even loss of income associated with their involvement in a training program. They need to see that it will lead to positively valued outcomes such as job retention, a pay increase or career development; if not, then it may be difficult to stimulate their interest. Both employer and employee may assess the period remaining in the employee's work life in late career to be insufficient to justify further training costs. Furthermore, the longer time required to achieve full proficiency in the newly acquired skills, the lower will be the enthusiasm of both employer and employee. The more firm specific the training, the more the employer will evaluate the outlay in terms of forecast improvement in employee value. Neither manager nor worker will be attracted unless positive outcomes, either economic or psychological, are anticipated.

A second consideration is employee commitment to further learning. Not all older staff will want further training. Some will have reached a plateau in their careers (Savery & Luks, 1998), while an even greater number will be *perceived* as having done so. Such judgements often justify the decisions of managers not to underwrite training costs for older staff. But unless these assessments are founded on performance-based criteria, they are inappropriate. Just as some older staff may not perceive any benefit in undertaking further training, others would learn, enjoy and subsequently apply new skills effectively. Performance and a keenness to learn, rather than age, should distinguish these two groups. Organisational learning is about the acquisition, maintenance and nurturing of valued skill sets, while at the same time helping position participants so they can take advantage of present and future opportunities (Tovey 1997). Some older individuals will want to participate as active learners; others, especially those with long tenure, may be better placed to contribute to formal or informal mentoring schemes in which their knowledge and skills are passed on to younger staff.

Since they prepare individuals to tackle more demanding tasks, learning and development are linked to career management. In recent decades organisations have broadened their career management activities (Patrickson 1994). In addition to formal training sessions, larger organisations in both private and public sectors offer sessions on successfully managing the transition from full-time employment to partial or full retirement. Counselling for older staff, addressing financial and psychological issues, is becoming a popular HRM service, whether provided in-house or subcontracted to an external provider. To be effective, this service needs to be offered confidentially and without penalty. (Some workers have indicated to the writer that they were reluctant to show interest in these programs in case this was used to target them for redundancy offers.)

Training, development and career management practices can be structured to offer older workers a number of benefits. These include further skill acquisition and extension, opportunities to share their knowledge through mentoring others, and assistance with retirement planning or scaling back to part-time, sessional or short-term contract employment. Such services will be in increasing demand as this segment of the workforce grows. Compared with the United States, where services for older workers are rapidly expanding (Barth, McNaught & Rizzi 1993; Elliott 1995), in Australia the area is still relatively underdeveloped, but this will change.

Career planning options for older staff should be geared to their needs (Patrickson 1994). HRM practices should recognise that the needs of all older staff are not identical. Different groups desire different programs depending on their skill portfolio and its transferability; the terms of their employment contract; how long they intend to keep working; and their health, financial position and commitment to ongoing development. Best practice will require the provision of a range of counselling services to help employees resolve issues associated with disengagement.

Performance appraisal

Performance appraisal is that aspect of HR practice that audits the quality and quantity of the employee's work output. Its aim is to measure the degree to which the workforce, as both units and individuals, has fulfilled managerial goals and to suggest remedies for any deficiencies. A subsidiary aim is to distinguish better performers for encouragement, reward and development. It is an area fraught with operational problems, chief among them the difficulties in establishing objective measures of work performance.

Computer operators can be evaluated in terms of speed and accuracy. Sales staff can be assessed in terms of the dollar value of sales and the number of satisfied customers. Production staff can be evaluated by the number of perfect products they produce in a given time. Such measures are reasonably objective, although problems of comparison arise when the conditions under which each individual works are not identical. By contrast, it is very difficult to evaluate the work of managers, clerical staff or team leaders, and even more so to use them for comparative purposes.

Ratings substitute for more objective measures, but ratings are subject to bias.

Older staff can be disadvantaged in subjective ratings by the myth of declining competence; if supervisors believe the myth, they may underrate them. Clearly objective measures help both parties, giving workers the evidence to underpin any claim concerning their value, and the manager the evidence to justify any decision on the employee's future. Without objective measures, these decisions are susceptible to bias and subjective interpretation. When numeric measures are not possible, multi-source measures should be used.

Multi-source assessments are used to overcome bias from any one source (Hoffman 1995); they help reduce prejudice but still do not eliminate it. Common prejudices that older workers are less physically capable and have high rates of accidents and absenteeism are simply not supported by objective measurements (Peterson & Coberly 1988), but this does not stop them being believed. The relationship between age and performance depends on the type of measure used and on occupation. Waldman and Avolio (1986) found only supervisor ratings correlated negatively. Ratings from co-workers, customers or the self may provide a more balanced evaluation.

Appraisal is also important as a means of ranking workers for the purposes of reward and promotion. The use of objective measures encourages the acceptance of such decisions, since the connection between performance and reward is less ambiguous. Targeting poor performers for redundancy is more equitable and acceptable than targeting older workers.

Occupational health and safety

The belief that older workers have more accidents than younger ones is strong, yet it is not supported by the evidence. WHO (1993) found that overall accident rates are lower for older workers than younger workers (under 24) and equal to the accident rate of prime-aged workers (25–44). The results vary according to occupation, but when they are adjusted for the fact that older workers are often given higher-risk tasks because of their experience, the differences are negligible. There is evidence, however, to suggest that the recovery rate for older workers who do have an accident is slower (WHO 1993; Ringenbach & Jacobs 1995).

Since the creation of the National Health and Safety Commission in 1985, Australian industry has improved its safety record and intensified its efforts towards the prevention of work-based illness (DeCieri 1998). Cigarette smoking has been banned in many workplaces, and efforts to improve job design have increased. Still to be addressed, and especially relevant for an ageing workforce, are the implementation of practices that compensate for failing acuity in the senses with age, and the introduction of wellness promotion into the occupational health portfolio. Deteriorating vision and hearing, difficulties with lifting and stress-related illness may lead to the need to further review existing practices in work design. Wellness promotion programs may include screenings for diabetes and other insidious diseases, support for fitness programs, seminars to assist in coping with stress, and the provision of healthy food in the staff canteen (Sherman 1990).

WHO (1993) recommends a combination of health promotion and job redesign. They suggest regular health examinations to detect any muscle deficit and vision or hearing problems, or other conditions that may affect staff well-being either in or outside the workplace. Too much demand and too little control also present potentially high-risk situations for health (Griffiths 1999). Flexible work practices should be investigated and adopted where possible. Older staff should also avoid night shifts, since these may negatively affect their health (WHO 1993).

In recent years many Australian workers, especially those seeking career advancement, have experienced pressure to work longer hours. It is a demand that many older individuals have resisted, but media reporting suggests this resistance is now also shared by younger staff opting for greater balance in their lives (Steggall 2000; *Weekend Australian*, 27 January 2001, pp. 17, 21). If so, then this trend will need to be addressed given its potentially divisive effect on the workforce, since only those without family commitments are able to work regularly outside normal hours.

Employers will clearly be expected to play a more responsible role in staff health in the future. Those who wish to promote themselves as employers of choice will introduce more health promotion programs, offer more health benefits and tailor work practices to employee capacity, where possible compensating for any deterioration in competency as a result of ageing. High-technology jobs are often more demanding than those they have replaced (Yeats, Folts & Knapp 2000), and adapting to new forms of job design may prove stressful for some. Employers should ensure the work climate is supportive of these changes, and that learning programs are appropriate and do not add to staff stress levels.

RECOMMENDATIONS

HR managers should:

- regularly review occupational health and safety activities to ensure they provide maximum staff benefit
- examine work practices to ensure these can be undertaken without unnecessary strain
- promote a healthy lifestyle by supporting activities that have proven health benefits
- eliminate smoking in the workplace
- adjust individual work practices to compensate for any health problems
- keep up-to-date records and use them to introduce new health practices
- work towards a more health-conscious culture
- consider providing special services for older staff, such as eye or hearing tests, or disease testing programs
- ensure their workplace is ergonomically sound
- consider moving older staff out of physically demanding jobs or not assigning them to night shifts (WHO 1993)
- ensure training programs are sympathetic to the needs of older workers and are not stressful.

Salary and benefits administration

Older workers tend to have long tenure, and long tenure is more likely to be coupled with higher earnings. Until recently older staff have often earned marginally more than younger people doing the same or comparable work. O'Neill (1998) reports that this is changing, since wages no longer rise consistently with age and experience. He adds that wages are not the only form of employee payment; older workers have consistently expressed interest in tax-effective indirect salary benefits.

Most older workers face different financial pressures from younger staff. Their children may have grown and left home, their mortgage is paid or almost paid, their retirement is looming and their need to save has increased (Ekerdt & Koslowski 2000). Employees whose salary is not consumed in daily living will be interested in any indirect financial benefits their employer may provide. Salary packaging will be particularly attractive. Non-remunerative benefits such as salary sacrifice, assistance with private health insurance, share options, vehicle subsidy and subsidised learning activities can encourage saving and add to the quality of working life.

Given that superannuation coverage became universal only in 1989, many workers who were previously excluded are especially interested in the level of their entitlement and in ensuring that this is maximised before their retirement. Recent contributors who can afford it are attracted by the tax-effective impact on savings of salary sacrifice (O'Neill 1998). Many others, especially high-income earners who can manage on less, are discovering that they prefer to work fewer hours and trade off additional income for increased leisure (Burbury 2000).

Yet even among older employees financial needs vary widely. Larger employers are beginning to offer staff opportunities to vary income packaging, and the indications are that this policy will become increasingly popular (Tabakoff & Skeffington 2000).

RECOMMENDATIONS

HR managers should:

- examine the range of non-salary benefits and offer as many variations as possible. (Information processing systems now make these variations less costly to administer.)
- encourage older staff to consider alternatives to direct income payments, such as salary sacrifice or reduced hours, which have both proved to be effective motivators.

Disengagement

Cordial disengagement of staff who are no longer needed is the hope of every HR manager confronted with the task of managing staff reduction. Being able to choose who to let go and who to retain is another. In recent decades whole

departments have been outsourced, but this practice appears to be waning as organisations have become sufficiently 'lean' (Cascio 1996; Littler 1996). Future restructuring programs are likely to feature fewer wholesale staff departures and more selective determination of who to retain and who to let go (Patrickson 1998). The traditional industrial relations practice of 'last on, first off' is gradually being replaced by new, performance-based practices that rely on accurate, objective measures to determine who to let go. This shift has been aided by the development of measures that can accurately track any deterioration in performance. If performance is deteriorating, then the evidence is there to support discussions of possible solutions. The worker may be asked to undertake additional training or be transferred to another, less demanding role; hours may be reduced; or he or she may be targeted for redundancy. The choice will depend on the wishes of the individual, the availability of alternatives and the capacity of the organisation to absorb flexible work practices.

Recent trends indicate that Australian organisations are increasingly exploring flexible work practices and phased disengagement of older staff (Morehead et al. 1997). Workers, too, are initiating these arrangements (Tabakoff & Skeffington 2000), and certainly this is the trend overseas (Delsen 1996; Moore, Tilson & Whitting 1994). It seems likely that this development will continue and expand; if so, it will need to be incorporated into HRM policy as part of its diversity management policy.

RECOMMENDATIONS

HR managers should:

- ensure redundancy decisions are based on objective measures of performance
- examine the feasibility of offering phased retirement for older workers
- where possible, adopt flexible work practices.

This chapter has considered a number of likely trends in HRM to accommodate and respond to the ageing of the workforce. Ageing will become an integral component of the management of workforce diversity. Suggested changes are directed towards greater recognition of issues of equity and access, and include greater flexibility in staff deployment and a stronger emphasis on performance measures to distinguish between individuals. The next section considers the potential impact of these changes on the health, financial circumstances and motivation of older workers.

Impact on health, financial position and motivation of older workers

As already discussed, forecasts indicate that the input of older workers will be greatly needed, and for many of them the decision of whether or not to remain in the organisation will be voluntary. HR practitioners will need to ensure that employment conditions are sufficiently attractive to persuade them to stay rather than to choose early retirement.

Impact on health

Older workers are more likely to suffer from nuisance conditions than severe health problems (Swirling, Sprince, Davis & Whitten 1998). Physiological health problems may involve declining vision, hearing or mobility (Stalnaker 1998). Potential psychological problems include stressors associated with long hours, pressures to achieve high levels of quality output and interpersonal difficulties with other staff (Chouros & Gold 1992).

The recommended changes in occupational health and safety practices will do much to improve the physiological environment and ensure work design is ergonomically sound. Providing regular health checks and improving lighting and sound will help in the detection and reduction of workplace hazards. The provision of phased retirement, a reduction in shift work, and a willingness to explore flexible working arrangements will reduce pressures and compensate for any declining capacity. This will enable those who can contribute less than a full week's work to do so.

The key factor is that the employer communicates a willingness to accommodate health needs. So long as this is part of the prevailing culture of the organisation, the task for older workers in declining health is one of finding a solution rather than coping with inevitable separation. A willingness by the employer to embrace flexible work practices will confirm and enhance this orientation.

Financial impact

The recommendations above emphasise the important role of indirect financial payments in providing individuals with benefits, such as learning opportunities and salary sacrifice, that would be unavailable if they were unemployed. These benefits can act as powerful incentives.

The recommendations also advocate encouraging those wishing to work less than a full week. However, such an option may be realistically available only to those not receiving social security transfer payments (Patrickson 1998). Government policy is to penalise those who earn small amounts, so unless the number of hours worked is very small, or the individual is a self-funded retiree, it is unlikely that such an option will be financially attractive.

It is difficult to generalise about the finances of older workers, given the variety of combinations of asset and income portfolios available, other than to observe that those excluded from superannuation before 1989 can now improve their position in retirement by continuing to work and contribute to superannuation schemes for as long as possible. The key determinant of financial position is residual income after tax, and this can vary between individuals undertaking similar jobs if they have private investments.

Impact on motivation

Making work sufficiently attractive that an older individual will choose to follow this path rather than to retire is the factor most likely to be adjustable by the employer. The recommendations in this chapter suggest adopting a strong diversity management philosophy that emphasises inclusiveness and encourages age balance. They also suggest offering continuous learning and further skill development, possible mentoring roles, flexible work arrangements, regular measures of performance based on objective criteria, and efforts to reduce environmental stressors.

Individuals are thus offered greater choice. With acceptable flexible work arrangements, provided they are employed in a core area and can maintain performance levels, older workers can choose their degree of involvement and whether or not to participate in further learning, and can help contribute to any decision on how best to utilise their skills. So long as former work attitudes were positive, such options should continue to be attractive. They should have most impact on those for whom working is a central part of their identity (Meaning of Working Research Team 1987).

Conclusion

This chapter has explored desirable changes in HRM policy and practice as the over-40 cohort comes to form at least half the workforce and those aged over 50 become a political force in the workplace. Unlike former generations, the skills of older workers today are current and their future contribution will be needed. Organisations will need to adapt their staff management activities to retain this group for as long as possible. Their efforts will be supported by governments who have a vested interest in reducing the numbers of those receiving social security payments. Community attitudes should also be supportive. Flexible work patterns will play an important role in this change.

References

ABS (1996, 1997, 1998, 1999, 2000) *Labour Force Australia*. Cat. no. 6203. Canberra: AGPS.

ABS (1999) *Labour Force Projections, Australia 1999–2016*. Cat. no. 662600.0. Canberra: AGPS.

Australian Business (1999) *Productive Diversity: Benefits to Your Business*. Australian Business and NSW Department of Education and Training.

Bishop, B (1999) *The national strategy for an ageing Australia: independence and self-provision*. Discussion paper. Canberra: Commonwealth of Australia.

Burbury, R (2000) Grey power buys it all, except time. *Australian Financial Review*, 11 March, 4.

Cascio, W (1996) *Seminar on Organisational Restructuring*. Sydney: Australian Human Resources Institute.

Chouros, G, and Gold, P (1992) The concepts of stress and stress symptoms disorders: overview of physical and behavioral homeostasis. *Journal of the American Medical Association*, 267, 1244–52.

Delsen, L (1996) Gradual retirement: lessons from the Nordic countries and The Netherlands. *European Journal of Industrial Relations*, 2 (1) 55–67.

Ekerdt, D, and Koslowski, K (2000) The normative expectation of retirement by older workers. *Research on Aging*, 22 (1) 3–23.

Elliott, R (1995) Human resource management's role in the future aging of the workforce. *Review of Public Personnel Administration*, Spring.

Equal Employment Opportunity (EEO) Commission (2000) Report of the Equal Opportunity Commission of South Australia, 1999–2000.

European Foundation for the Improvement of Living and Working Conditions (1997) *Combating Age Barriers in Employment, Research Summary*. Office for the Official Publication of the European Communities, Luxembourg.

Friedman, B (1992) Job prospects for mature workers. *Journal of Aging and Social Policy*, 4 (3/4) 53–73.

Gilbert, J, and Ivancevich, J (2000) Valuing diversity: a tale of two organizations. *Academy of Management Executive*, 14 (1) 93–105.

Griffiths, A (1999) Work design and management: the older worker. *Experimental Aging Research*, 25 (4) 11–21.

Grueller, M (1999) In search of late career: a review of contemporary research applicable to the understanding of late career. *Human Resource Management Review*, 9 (3) 309–348.

Heilman, M, McCullough, M, and Gilbert, D (1996) The other side of affirmative action: reactions of non-beneficiaries to a sex-based preferential selection. *Journal of Applied Psychology*, 81 (4) 346–57.

Hoffman, R (1995) Ten reasons you should be using 360 degree feedback. *HR Magazine*, 40 (4) 82–85.

Hutchens, R (1993) Restricted job opportunities and the older worker. In O Mitchell (Ed.), *As the Workforce Ages*. New York: ILR Press, 81–102.

Itzin, C, and Phillipson, C (1993) *Age barriers at work*. Metropolitan Authorities Recruitment Agency. Exeter, UK: Short Run Press.

Jobs East (1998) *Achieving an Age Balance in the Workforce*. Melbourne: Jobs East.

Kinsella-Taylor, L (1998) *Profiting from maturity: the social and economic costs of mature age unemployment*. Melbourne: Jobs East.

Larkin, J (1995) Major issues concerning the global economy. In P Ruthven, J Larkin, T Dwyer, C Rameau and A Soutter (1995), *Workplace 2010: Forces That Will Shape the Future of Work in Australia*. Melbourne: Business Council of Australia, 23–38.

Littler, C (1996) Downsizing: a disease or a cure? *HR Monthly*, August, 8–10.

Matthews, L (2000) Interview on ABC Radio, September.

Meaning of Working Research Team (1987) *The Meaning of Working*. London: Harcourt, Brace and Jovanovich.

Moore, J, Tilson B, and Whitting, G (1994) *An international review of employment policies and practices toward older workers*. London: Department of Employment.

Morehead, A, Steele, M, Alexander, M, Stephen, K, and Duffin, L (1997) *Changes at Work: The 1995 Australian Workplace Industrial Relations Survey*. Melbourne: Longman.

Nankervis, A, and Leece, P (1997) Performance appraisal: two steps forward, one step back. *Asia Pacific Journal of Human Resources* 35 (2).

New Zealand Employers Federation (1998) *Employment of older workers and retirement: a guide for employers*.

Patrickson, M (1994) Workplace management strategies for a new millennium. *International Journal of Career Management*, 6 (2) 25–32.

Patrickson, M (1998) Reversing the trend to early retirement. In M Patrickson and L Hartmann (Eds), *Managing the Ageing Workforce*. Melbourne: Woodslane, 106–120.

Patrickson, M, and Hartmann, L (forthcoming) HRM in Australia: future directions. *International Journal of Manpower*.

Peterson, D, and Coberly, S (1988) The older worker: myths and realities. In R Morris and S Bass (Eds), *Retirement Reconsidered: Economic and Social Roles for Older People*. New York: Springer.

Pierce, J (2000) *Contract employees and perceived responsibility for reskilling and training*. Unpublished Master of Business thesis, University of South Australia.

Ringenbach, K, and Jacobs, R (1995) Injuries and aging workers, *Journal of Safety Research*, 26 (3) 1699.

Savery, L, and Luks, A (1998) Plateauing: a potential risk for the older worker. In M Patrickson and L Hartmann (1998), *Managing an Ageing Workforce*. Melbourne: Woodslane, 193–204.

Senge, P (1990) *The Fifth Discipline: The Art and Practice of the Learning Organization*. New York: Doubleday.

Sherman, M (1990) *Wellness in the Workplace*. Los Altos, CA: Crisp Publications.

Smith, A (1992) Australian training and development in 1992. *Asia-Pacific Journal of Human Resources*, 31 (2) 71–2.

Smith, A (1996) *Training and Development in Australia*. Sydney: Butterworths.

Stalnaker, C (1998) Safety of older workers in the twenty-first century. *Professional Safety*, 43 (6) 28–31.

Steggall, V (2000) Curing the body corporate. *HR Monthly*, July, 16–21.

Sullivan, S, and Duplaga, E (1997) Recruiting and retaining older workers for the new millennium. *Business Horizons*, 40 (6) 65–70.

Swirling, C, Sprince, N, Davis, C, and Whitten, P (1998) Occupational injuries among older workers with disabilities: a prospective cohort study of the Health and Retirement Survey, 1992–1994. *American Journal of Public Health*, 88 (11) 1691–5.

Tabakoff, N, and Skeffington, R (2000) The wise old heads are back. *Business Review Weekly*, 11 March, 60–6.

Taylor, P, and Walker, A (1993) The employment of older workers in five European countries. In *Age and Employment*. Institute of Personnel Management. Exeter, UK: Short Run Press.

Taylor, P, and Walker, A (1996) Policies and practices toward older workers: a framework for comparative research. *Human Resource Management Journal*, 8 (3) 61–76.

Tovey, M (1997) *Training in Australia*. Sydney: Prentice Hall.

United Nations (1990) *Global Outlook 2000: An Economic, Social and Environmental Perspective*. New York: United Nations Publications.

United Nations (1994) *The Sex and Age Distributions of the World's Populations*. New York: United Nations Publications.

United Nations (1995) *World Population Prospects*. New York: United Nations Publications.

Waldman, D, and Avolio, B (1986) Meta-analysis of age differences in job performance. *Journal of Applied Psychology*, 71 (1) 33–8.

Walker, A (1999) Combating age discrimination in the workplace. *Experimental Aging Research*, 25 (4) 367–78.

Weekend Australian, 27 January 2001, pp. 17, 21.

Worsley, R (1996) Only prejudices are old and tired. *People Management*, 2 (1) 18–23.

Yeats, D, Folts, W, and Knapp, J (2000) Older workers' adaptation to a changing workplace: employment issues for the twenty-first century. *Educational Gerontology*, 26 (6) 565–83.

CHAPTER 5

Contemporary issues regarding work–family policies

by Jarrod Haar and Chester Spell

University of Waikato, New Zealand | Rutgers University, New Jersey

Introduction

One of the main issues facing organisations today is how to assist employees to balance their work and family commitments. As employees' lives both in the workplace and at home become increasingly complicated, their capacity to provide unrestricted and energised labour is affected. Business leaders, human resource (HR) managers and employers need to be aware of the work and family issues related to organisations and employees. Forward-thinking leaders and their HR counterparts are realising that work–family policies may provide the key to rectifying the imbalance that employees now face. This chapter seeks to identify the major influences on organisations that have facilitated the development and proliferation of work–family policies, and to identify the major practices themselves. It will also discuss the reported effects of work–family policies and the future direction of this progressive human resource management (HRM) practice.

The rationale behind work-family policies

While the United States has led the proliferation of work–family or family-friendly practices, countries like Australia and New Zealand are also adopting these pro-gressive HR policies. Work–family policy adoption has grown markedly in the past two decades, with the 1990s being an era of unparalleled growth. A number of demographic changes, including increases in participation rates of women, dual-career couples, single-parent families and the elderly, as well as changing employee attitudes towards work and family, have provided the impetus for developing work–family policies. Each of these issues is discussed in the following sections.

Participation rates of women

An increase in participation rates of working women and working mothers has been a major influence in developing work–family policies (Milliken, Martins & Morgan 1998; Ingram & Simons 1995; Osterman 1995). In the US, employed women aged 16 years and above increased from 38 per cent in 1960 to 54 per cent in 1991 (Ingram & Simons 1995) and rose to 61 per cent by 1996 (Greenhaus, Callanan & Godshalk 2000). Of this group, working mothers with children aged under six years increased dramatically from 19 per cent in 1960 to 60 per cent in 1991 (Ingram & Simons 1995), and up to 63 per cent by 1996 (Greenhaus, Callanan & Godshalk 2000) and married women with children between the ages of 6 and 17 years rose from 39 per cent to 77 per cent between 1960 and 1996 (Greenhaus, Callanan & Godshalk 2000).

These trends are reflected in other Pacific Rim countries. In New Zealand, work participation rates of women increased from 54 per cent in 1988 to 57 per cent in 1998 (Statistics New Zealand 1998). In Malaysia women made up 49 per cent of the workforce in 1993 (Michaels 1995). It is predicted that in the future, women with children will be the primary source of growth in the number of workers (Magid & Codkind 1995). This group accounted for two-thirds of new employees in 2000 (Greenhaus, Callanan & Godshalk 2000). Four reasons have been offered for the increase in participation rates of women in paid employ-ment (White, Cox & Cooper 1992). First, technological changes enable employers to replace highly skilled male workers with cheaper, semi-skilled female workers. Second, because they are marrying and having fewer children later, women are freeing themselves from lifelong domestic work. Third, women are seeking work-related self-identities as opposed to marriage-related identities. Finally, economic factors are becoming increasingly important; for example, 40 per cent of married women in the US have husbands earning less than $15 000 per annum, with the result that most of these women will return to work within a year after maternity leave owing to financial pressures (Magid & Codkind 1995).

It is estimated that 75 per cent (Greenhaus, Callanan & Godshalk 2000) of women workers will become pregnant during their working lives. Yet it is well documented that working women continue to perform the majority of household and child-rearing duties (Kossek, Huber-Yoder, Castellino & Lerner 1997). The combination of pregnancy, work and childcare responsibilities pose particular diffi-culties for working women, and this problem will require organisations to develop new ways of working (Magid & Codkind 1995). Work–family policies may help organ-isations deal with the complexities of this expanding work-force segment.

Dual-career couples

The increase in participation rates of working women has seen the traditional family roles of the husband in paid employment and the wife staying home being replaced by a developing neo-traditional family in which both parents work (Goodstein, 1994; Morgan & Milliken 1992; Magid & Codkind 1995). The US has experienced the most notable increases; figures show that the total number of dual-career couples with children under 18 years was almost 60 per cent in 1993, up from 32 per cent in 1973 (Larkin 1996). In 1992 the figure for dual-career couples with children under three years was 67 per cent (O'Sul-livan 1996). Similar trends are also evident elsewhere in the Pacific Rim, with Singapore reporting an increase in dual-career couples to 44 per cent in 1993 (Michaels

1995). In Australia, dual-career couples rose from 53 per cent in 1990 (Moore 1997) to 59 per cent in 1993 (Michaels 1995). Similarly, in 1997 New Zealand dual-career couples accounted for more than 50 per cent of households (Henderson 1997).

Single-parent families

The large increase in the number of single-parent families has also influenced work–family policies (Goodstein 1994; Morgan & Milliken 1992). It has been suggested that working mothers head almost 25 per cent of all US families (Michaels & McCarthy 1993). New Zealand is very similar, with 27 per cent of New Zealand families headed by just one parent (Henderson 1997). In 1996 nearly 70 per cent of women who were divorced, sepa-rated or widowed, with children under six years old, worked; this figure increases to more than 80 per cent for women with children aged between 6 years and 17 (Greenhaus, Callanan & Godshalk 2000). Importantly, at some time in their childhood, more than half of US chil-dren will live in a single-parent family (Kossek, Noe & DeMarr 1999). In the United Kingdom, the proportion of people living in one-parent families has increased 400 per cent between 1961 and 1991 (Cooper 1998). As single-parent families continue to proliferate, employers must accept that a more flexible way of managing employees will produce better results.

Increase in the elderly

An emerging demographic trend that is likely to influence work–family policies is the projected increase in the elderly population. This is a worldwide phenomenon. With people living longer, the number of elderly in the US requiring care is projected to increase from 35 million to 70 million by 2030, with the cost of nursing-home services set to sky-rocket by more than 400 per cent (Hendrickson 2000). As a result of the combination of increased elderly population and higher cost of care, it is likely that the burden of elder-care will fall on families. Traditionally, it has been women who have fulfilled these caregiver roles but, as already noted, more women are in paid employment now than ever before. As more of these caregivers join the workforce, there will be additional pressures on employers to facilitate solu-tions (Magid & Codkind 1995). Work–family expert Ellen Galinsky, co-president of the New York–based Families and Work Institute, warns that in the United States, elder-care is going to eclipse child-care as a work–family practice (Smith 1996).

Changing employee attitudes

Aside from the demographic changes that have influenced work–family policy adoption, employee attitudes towards work and their family and personal time have also influenced change. Family and personal leisure time may be more prized now than at any time in US history (Magid & Codkind 1995). As more men share in work–family responsibilities because more women are part of the workforce, it has been suggested that there has been a shift in priorities by men towards work. Because more fathers have spouses in the workforce and supposedly share directly in family care responsibilities, work schedules are affected, since these employees are less available for extended travel on short notice, overtime work and relocation (Magid & Codkind 1995). Employees are reported to be more concerned with 'quality of life', both at work and in their personal lives, suggesting that work may no longer be the sole focus for employees today (Magid & Codkind 1995).

These five factors have together significantly reshaped the landscape of organisations. It is almost impossible for organisations to be unaware of the changes that are occurring among their employees in terms of both demographics and changing attitudes towards work. These changes have led employees to experience increased levels of work–family conflict, when work and family priorities prove to be mutually incompatible (Greenhaus & Beutell 1985). Organisations must seek to rectify or improve the balance as best they can; those that ignore or evade these factors may be destined to falling productivity and even business failure.

Work–family policies

At the heart of work–family policies is the necessity for these programs to help employees balance their changing work and family roles (Goodstein 1994; Judge, Boudreau & Bretz 1994; Moore 1997; Osterman 1995).

Work–family policies are defined as arrangements that make it easier for employees to manage the conflicting worlds of work and family (Moore 1997). By embracing work and family issues, organisations can mediate this conflict. Also known as 'family-friendly' policies, these programs deal with issues of conflict centred on the family, such as child-care concerns. Work–family policies aim to improve the balance between employees' work and personal lives, from child- and elder-care, to pregnancy leave and flexitime. Family-friendly workplaces have been

defined as those that make a deliberate attempt to assist employees to balance their work and family responsibilities (Ryan & Torrie 1999). The following section discusses major work–family practices in seven distinct categories.

Pregnancy policies

Pregnancy-related work–family policies can involve both pre- or post-pregnancy employee needs. Paid parental leave gains the most attention among pregnancy-related policies (Berns & Berns 1992; Chiu & Ng 1999; Goodstein 1994; Hall & Parker 1993; Hand & Zawacki 1994; Ingram & Simons 1995; Mason 1993; Milliken, Martins & Morgan 1998; Overman 1999) and takes two distinct forms: paid maternity leave (specifically for the mother) and paid paternity leave (specifically for the father). Only five United Nations countries, including the US, New Zealand and Australia, do not legislate for maternity leave payments (International Labour Organization 1997). Despite the policy's popularity in the work–family literature, it is quite uncommon in both the US, where it is estimated to be available in only 23 per cent of firms (Wood 1999), and New Zealand, where it is offered by an estimated 18 per cent of firms (Sheeran 1996). In Australia, paid paternity leave is very rare, with fewer than 10 per cent of firms offering it (Crichton 1998). Naturally, given that it presents no direct cost to the organisation, unpaid parental leave is more common, with up to 95 per cent of firms offering it (Morgan & Milliken 1992). Other pregnancy-related policies include breastfeeding rooms, staggered return to work after parental leave, car parks for new/expectant parents, adoption assistance and special pregnancy programs, which can include 24-hour nurse hotlines and pagers for fathers.

Child-care policies

Child-care needs affect a large proportion of employees. Between 1988 and 1992 in the US (Kossek, Dass & DeMarr 1994) there was an almost 300 per cent increase in child-care programs, but although this growth appears significant, actual practice varies considerably, with the majority of this increase in the lower cost range (Hall & Parker 1993). The most expensive child-care policies, and typically the most sought after by employees, involve childcare centres. Organisational adoption of on-site child-care centres .is driven by the twin problems of quality and availability of child-care in the United States, which have reached near-critical stage (Mason 1993). The availability of convenient, moderately priced day care for preschoolers is considered the most pressing problem faced by most US employees (Elsberry 1999) and appears universal in most Western societies. Child-care centres are a popular work–family focus (Goodstein 1994; Ingram & Simons 1995; Cole 1999). These may be on-site, off-site or near-site child-care centres (Milliken, Martins & Morgan 1998) and usually involve a major organisational financial commitment. Because of this expense, child-care centres are uncommon even in the US and are usually limited to large corporations (1000 employees and above). Adoption estimates vary considerably between 1 and almost 11 per cent of employers offering on-site child-care centres (Kossek, Dass & DeMarr 1994). Some corporations, such as Toyota, operate 24-hour child-care centres to meet the demands of shiftworkers (Elsberry 1999). Some firms have collaborated to fund a child-care centre for their combined workforces. A more popular policy is for an organisation to contribute financially towards the cost of employee child-care. Almost 75 per cent of large companies, 33 per cent of medium and 14 per cent of small firms in the US offer child-care subsidies (Crispell 1996). Less expensive policies include reserving places in child-care facilities, after-school child-care, holiday care, emergency care for dependants and child-care by a parent on-site (for example an office worker bringing her baby to work). Even cheaper policies focus on supplying child-care information. Exceptionally rare programs offer nanny services and satellite schools — for example, Hewlett-Packard operates a satellite school on-site for employees' children from kindergarten age through to school year three (Elsberry 1999).

Flexible work policies

Flexible work practices allow workers to vary their work hours and location from the traditional on-site, 9 to 5, Monday to Friday model to enable them to manage their work and family commitments. Telecommuting, also known as work from home or telework, is the most recognised practice.

Telecommuters are commonly company employees who regularly work from a location other than the workplace (Tapsell 1999) such as home or a car or hotel. Advances in technology such as laptop computers, modems, fax machines, the Internet and e-mail make telecommuting a realistic option for many organisations, and it has become very popular among large US corporations (Durst 1999). Flexitime allows for variable starting and finishing times, is low cost, and is popular among government departments and employees because it provides a degree of freedom in

their timetables. It is most popular in the US, where adoption rates have been as high as almost 80 per cent (Hall & Parker 1993). Job sharing, through which two or more people share a single job, is one of the most complex flexible options available to firms (Sheley 1996) but despite this it is popular in the US, Australia and New Zealand, although normally within larger organisations. Part-time work, which allows employees to work fewer hours, is offered by a high proportion of organisations (Bencivenga 1995) again because of its minimal costs. However, this practice does not constitute a work–family practice unless employees use it on a voluntary basis rather than its being imposed by management (Goodstein 1994). Flexible work scheduling policies include four-day weeks (four ten-hour days), variable week scheduling (40 hours in *any* combination are worked a week) and maxiflex scheduling (employees may vary the number of hours worked each day and the number of days worked each week). Other practices include part-time work for senior staff (phased retirement) and downshifting, in which employees can decide to reduce their work commitments either temporarily or permanently.

Financial policies

Financial policies in relation to work–family practice provide a monetary gain to employees or payments on their behalf. Typically, the US leads the adoption of financial work–family policies owing to legislated tax advantages. For example, US firms can offer pre-tax payroll deduction for dependent care that can shelter from income tax up to US$5000 of an employee's earnings used for child-care expenses. Some organisations offer an elder-care subsidy, which, like child-care subsidies, involves a financial contribution towards the care of the elderly, for example a nursing home subsidy. While financial support for elder-care is quite rare (Hall & Parker 1993), given the projected demographic increase in the elderly over the next twenty years, employees will undoubtedly place greater pressure on organisations to contribute financially towards elder-care costs. This pressure will intensify as these costs increase dramatically in conjunction with reduced government funding. Other related policies include the reimbursement of family costs due to work, payment of extraordinary family costs and dependent health care.

Leave policies

Leave policies provide specialised leave for employees but do not include pregnancy-related leave. A common policy is family leave, or domestic leave, which refers to leave provisions for domestic reasons such as a sick child or spouse, a family emergency or other personal commitments. Elder-care leave is similar but caters specifically for the care of the elderly. Unpaid leave for the care of family, including the elderly, is quite common (Morgan & Milliken 1992). While sabbaticals were once considered the exclusive domain of the teaching world, this flexible leave practice is used by organisations to provide executives and top employees with a way of temporarily escaping the pressures of corporate life. Sabbaticals can be either paid or unpaid, and vary in length from months to years, with longer periods typically unpaid but sometimes still retaining benefits. A quarter of large US firms with 1000 or more employees have a sabbatical leave program, which they use to address issues including employee stress, burnout and morale problems (Vincola 2000). Smaller firms can also utilise this practice. For example, New Zealand firm Wheeler Campbell Consulting Ltd offer a one month's paid sabbatical to staff at the end of five years' service to allow them to reflect on their career and aspirations (EEO Trust 1998). Other types of programs include social leave policies, which encourage workers to take a break from their jobs and work full-time for a non-profit organisation, school or university. For example, Xerox pays employees their full salaries while they spend time contributing to the community (Vincola 2000). Because firms offering this leave tend to see it as a philanthropic gesture for the benefit of society, it typically carries full pay and benefits. Other policies include special days off (for employee birthdays or other personal obligations), career break schemes, company-funded vacations and leave bank programs, where employees' total leave (including sick and holiday dues) can be used as they see fit.

Information and support policies

Policies within this category tend to be those requiring fewer resources, and have been referred to as 'cheap practices' (Ingram & Simons 1995) or at the cheaper end of the spectrum (Osterman 1995). Because of this, they are also more accessible to smaller organisations. Informational policies include work–family seminars or orientations at which approaches and organisational programs that allow for a better balance of work and family roles are discussed. Support programs include elder-care referrals, which provide both information and support on elder-care concerns. Employee Assistance Programs (EAPs) are a formal intervention system that identifies and assists organisational members with a wide range of personal problems affecting their job-related behaviours (Milne, Blum & Roman 1994). New Zealand firms categorise this form of employee support as a work–family policy, but because they were originally designed to treat alcoholism among employees, these policies are not always so classified internationally. Other forms of support include time for family social events, a dedicated family area within a work site, and mentoring and networking for female employees. Finally, a simple support policy is to allow employees access to family calls, a practice that has been found to improve productivity and efficiency (Henderson 1997).

Other work–family policies

This section outlines all those work–family policies that do not fit neatly into the previous six categories, including work–family workplace policy statements, support staff, management training and domestic service provisions. A work–family workplace policy is a formalised document indicating an organisation's commitment to work–family policies. These policies constitute the first step in organisations' recognising the changing forces on workers, and their determination to address them. Such policies formalise an organisation's commitment to balancing work–family issues. Work–family support staff are typically found in government organisations, and are often incorporated with Equal Employment Opportunity positions. These staff provide a more formal HR department commitment to work–family policies, and communicate and liaise with employees and management. Work–family management training seeks to provide to managers and supervisors training on existing policies on work–family fundamentals as a means to encourage acceptance and utilisation. For example, Johnson & Johnson offer managers training in responding to employee family issues (Mason 1993). One of the more unusual work–family policies involves organisations providing their employees with domestic services, ranging from housekeeping and laundry to home repairs, legal services and even pet care (Hammonds 1996). Others programs include travel support for employees with families (such as short business trips), family-oriented meeting schedules (for example no meetings before 9 am and after 3 pm), and relocation assistance for the entire family, such as spousal job assistance. Fitness and medical services, teenage children initiatives and employer-sponsored family meals are examples of other work–family policies that can allow employees to better balance their work and life commitments.

Advantages of work–family policies

Increasingly, business leaders understand that success today relies on efficient employees, and that employees who are distracted by work–family conflict may be less competent and effective than required. A leading work–family expert warns:

> The workforce of the future will include more people of colour, more women, more new immigrants, more special needs employees — in short, more diversity than the current norm. It follows, then, that the companies that can attract, retain, motivate, and engage the most talented within these groups will be most likely to succeed, while those that do not may not even survive. (Hall & Parker 1993, pp. 4–18)

This section seeks to provide an indication of the types of advantages that have been associated with work–family policies. This, is turn, may provide a better understanding of why organisations adopt such policies. An organisation that improves employee job satisfaction while reducing turnover and increasing productivity may make considerable efficiency gains through work–family policies. It should be noted that few organisations would register more than a few of these benefits, and some may register none at all. The impact of these policies will be specific to each organisation; this section should be seen as highlighting *potential* rather than *guaranteed* benefits. The advantages of work–family programs are grouped into three distinct areas: internal organisational benefits, external organisational benefits and employee benefits. These areas, in turn, are assessed in terms of overall organisational performance impact (see figure 5.1).

Internal organisational benefits

This category focuses on those benefits that occur internally within an organisation and in which the major beneficiary is the organisation. For example, organisations may promote a more loyal and committed workforce, and while this requires the participation and support of employees, typically it is the organisation that benefits. Efficiency gains and improved attitudes have been attributed to work–family policies, but they can also improve the working lives of employees while providing the organisation with additional benefits.

Reduced employee tardiness

This advantage refers to reducing the frequency and number of employees who are repeatedly late for work. When work or family problems overwhelm employees, they may try to avoid job stress through physical actions such as tardiness (Bhagat, McQuaid, Lindholm & Segovis 1985). Work–family programs have been repeatedly successful in reducing employee tardiness (Michaels & McCarthy 1993), since they help employees to better balance their personal and work commitments.

Reduced employee absenteeism

Many studies have examined the causes of absenteeism (Bhagat, McQuaid, Lindholm & Segovis 1985), with a number of authors specifically identifying work–family practices as a means of reducing the phenomenon (Cutcher-Gershenfeld, Kossek & Sandling 1997). This may be because studies of absenteeism have often found that less-satisfied employees are more likely to abstain from work (Waters & Roach 1971). A Canadian study found that employee difficulty in managing their work and personal responsibilities resulted in reduced performance through absenteeism (Paris 1990). Business units from Xerox have reduced absenteeism rates by 30 per cent through planning based on employees' work–family needs (Shellenbarger 1999).

Improved employee morale

Many organisations have achieved improved employee morale through the introduction of work–family policies, particularly flexible work policies.[1] Employees feel that flexible policies allow them greater freedom and responsibility, which in turn improves morale.

Improved employee loyalty

Work–family policies have also been found to increase employee loyalty (Gordon & Whelan 1998; Tenbrunsel, Brett, Maoz, Stroh & Reilly 1995). Employee loyalty can be enhanced through the adoption of work–family programs, particularly those that employees value, such as flexible scheduling (McNerney 1994). This highlights an important aspect of these advantages: if employees are not enthusiastic about the policy, then benefits gained may be weaker than if strongly desired policies are adopted.

---

1. See Shellenbarger, S (1999), op. cit.; Hall, DT, and Parker, VA (1993), op. cit.; McNerney, DJ (1994) A strategic partnership: Clean Air Act and work–family. *HR Focus,* 71 (11) 22–3; Leonard, B (1998) Royal Bank's workers laud flexibility. *HR Magazine,* 43 (13) 30–31; Collins, RC, and Magid, RY (1989), op. cit.

Improved employee motivation

Work and family issues are among the root causes of critical workplace problems such as lack of motivation (Cutcher-Gershenfeld, Kossek & Sandling 1997). Employees may be more motivated when they have control over their working schedule, which can be achieved through practices like flexitime (Overman 1999). In addition, it has been suggested that lifestyle issues are of increasing importance in defining what keeps employees motivated (Vincola & Farren 1999). Therefore organisations that adopt work–family policies in an effort to improve employees' balance of work and family priorities may enhance their employees' motivation.

Increased employee commitment

Another common benefit associated with work–family policies is an increase in employee commitment. Recent studies have linked work–family practices with improved employee commitment (Scandura & Lankau 1997), since employees become more committed to their organisation if it makes an effort to address their work and family needs.

Improved employee retention

There is strong support for a link between work–family policies and employee retention (Berns & Berns 1992; Gordon & Whelan 1998). SAS Institute estimates that work–family policies create US$50 million savings annually as a result of reduced employee attrition (Cole 1999). Corning Inc. believes it lost millions of dollars each year through high turnover among women professionals, and the associated costs of recruiting and training replacements, before they adopted work–family policies (Hall & Parker 1993). Specific policies such as job sharing have also reduced employee turnover rates (Flynn 1997).

Competitive advantage

The Canadian Royal Bank believes it has turned flexible work arrangements into a real competitive advantage (Leonard 1998). Work–family policies that improve employee performance and work enjoyment may offer firms significant advantages over their competitors and provide a necessary edge in business.

Other internal benefits include employees with a broader range of skills, trained replacements for job cover, reduced office space, improved customer service and reduced health costs. This is the largest category of benefits associated with work–family policies.

External organisational benefits

This category focuses on those benefits that occur outside an organisation and in which the major beneficiary is the organisation. Typically, work–family policies have been seen to have positive impacts on the image of organisations that provide and promote them. The benefits include the following:

Enhanced corporate image

It has been argued that work–family policies have the ability to enhance an organisation's corporate image (Faught 1995). Organisations that strive to improve the balance of work and family concerns for employees through these policies are perceived as progressive on employee issues and as being concerned about their employees. The outcome is that the public will see these organisations in a more positive light.

Improved employee recruitment

Supporters of work–family policies maintain that these policies improve an organisation's ability to attract the best applicants (Hall & Parker 1993). Organisations that offer these policies are also perceived by stakeholders both inside and outside the organisation as caring about their employees. Through work–family policies an organisation can gain a reputation as an employer of choice. For example, *Fortune Magazine* publishes an annual list of the 'top 10 companies to work for'. Organisations that appear on this list typically champion work–family policies and supposedly attract a higher quality of applicant to their organisation.

Other external benefits include improved CEO image, usually linked to corporate image, and environmental advantages, such as less travel and pollution through telecommuting.

Employee benefits

This category focuses on those benefits that provide a major benefit to organisational members in addition to balancing their work and family commitments.

Increased job satisfaction

Many studies find links between work–family policies and increased job satisfaction (Mason 1993; Overman 1999; Thomas & Ganster 1995; Kossek & Ozeki 1998) with some experts suggesting work–family policies can significantly influence job satisfaction (Judge, Boudreau & Bretz Jr.

1994). Employee job satisfaction increases, it is claimed, as organisations take steps to alleviate work–family conflict, leading to a general flow-on effect from improved loyalty, morale and commitment. Employees see organisations that offer work–family policies as caring about their personal and family commitments, and this approach generates greater feelings of job focus and satisfaction.

Decreased stress

Job stress can elicit negative behaviours such as tardiness, absenteeism or leaving the job altogether (Bhagat, McQuaid, Lindholm & Segovis 1985). Because work and family conflict can lead to increased stress both in the workplace and at home, work–family policies have been found to reduce employee stress (Hand & Zawacki 1994). Since organisations are increasingly aware of the link between employee stress and increased health-care costs, many employers see work–family policies as a means of combating stress and increased costs (Phillips 1993).

Improved physical health

A major study examined the connection between work–family policies and the physical health of employees. Findings suggest that these policies allow employees greater control over work and family issues, which, in turn, was found to be associated with enhanced physical health through reduced somatic complaints, depression and blood cholesterol levels (Thomas & Ganster 1995). Work–family policies, then, may improve both the physical and mental health of employees.

Improved organisational performance

The combination of benefits discussed above can lead to improved organisational performance throughout all phases of the HRM process. Through decreasing costs and increasing benefits to organisations, work–family programs can have positive bottom-line consequences (Gordon & Whelan 1998). Linkages between work and family have been shown to affect organisational performance (Edwards & Rothbard 2000). There is much support for the contention that work–family programs contribute to greater productivity or improved organisational performance (Daley 1998; Lapin 1996). They improve recruitment, affording organisations more efficient employees. Employees have greater motivation, satisfaction and commitment, which

also influence performance (Durst 1999). IBM believes work–family programs have enhanced employee productivity (Mason 1991). Productivity gains are also made through reducing lost work hours and improving employee focus on job rather than on family issues (Daley 1998). Further cost savings are made from reduced employee turnover (Cole 1999). Overall, the advantages and benefits noted above may provide a significant collective impact on firm performance. From these benefits, firm operations improve through greater efficiency, effectiveness and cost reductions. This impact is well supported by major US corporations, with 75 per cent perceiving a positive or very positive impact on bottom-line profits from work–family programs.[2] This interpretation of the benefits of these policies has been summarised in the figure below.

Figure 5.1: Work–family policy framework

This policy framework encapsulates the various advantages that firms report they receive through adopting work–family policies. The implication that these policies lead to improved organisational performance is often overlooked. This may limit the adoption of work–family policies within otherwise progressive organisations that seek a competitive edge. For example, recruitment and retention are often cited as benefits of work–family policies. Some organisations operating in competitive industries that are desperate for high-quality staff, such as the computer industry, are failing to attract and retain scarce employees. The adoption of work–family policies may be an effective HR strategy to attract and retain employees. A major success story is the largest privately owned US computer software company, SAS Institute, with 3800 employees. Regarded as a leader in work–family practices, SAS bucks the industry norm of 20 per cent per annum staff turnover by maintaining a 4 per cent average (Cole 1999). As already noted, this company has gained such an enhanced reputation through its work–family policies that it is listed among *Fortune Magazine*'s top 10 companies to work for in the US (Cole 1999), saving US$50 million per annum through reduced turnover.

---

2. Hall, DT, and Parker, VA (1993), op. cit.

Issues concerning work–family policies

When examining work–family policies, some issues need to be addressed. One particularly negative aspect of work–family policies is the perception that such policies produce a 'family-friendly backlash' among employees who do not use the policies. As companies set up flexible schedules, child-care or paid parental leave, childless workers and older employees have asked what benefits are available for them (Kirkpatrick 1997). Yet researchers have found no support for a family-friendly backlash and have attributed the claim to media sensationalism (Rothausen, Gonzalez, Clarke & O'Dell 1998). Despite this conclusion, organisations need to be aware that work–family policies that are targeted solely at certain employees, such as those with dependent children, may create some negative feelings. Offering a range of benefits that can be utilised by the greatest number of employees may be a way for organisations to reduce resentment and enhance employee acceptance of work–family programs.

The costs associated with work–family policies must also be considered. Although SAS Institute provides a 3000-square-metre fitness centre, on-site medical clinic, unlimited sick days (which may be used to care for sick family members) and on-site day care, these benefits would be beyond the financial resources of most organisations. So companies looking to adopt work–family policies may initially seek to target less expensive policies. For example, instead of building and operating an on-site creche, an alternative might be for the organisation to research (possibly through its own employees) the best creches in the vicinity, and provide a child-care subsidy instead. Once the benefits of these policies have been observed, it may also be easier for the HR department or employee advocates to press for expanded programs. Importantly, work–family policies have a greater likelihood of organisational success if driven by employees rather than the employer. For example, if employees prefer child-care subsidies to an on-site child-care centre, the organisation would be wise to concede. Work–family policies that respond to employee requests have been found to be more popular, well used and successful than the best employer-driven ideas. When seeking to adopt these policies, an organisation should survey employees to see what issues are important to them. While we naturally assume flexible work practices and child-care to be important, as the population ages, elder-care issues may become more critical for organisations to consider. For organisations with limited resources, a few cheap policies may be a good starting point, and if successful they may encourage management acceptance and lead to program expansion.

Some organisations pay their employees increased wages in lieu of offering on-site work–family programs. These firms suggest that they allow their employees to *buy* their way out of work–family conflict through paying for housekeeping, good child-care or even the services of a nanny. This approach allows employees to target those areas that affect them most, whether elder-care, child-care or housekeeping support. Since most work–family programs provide services that would be prohibitively expensive to lower paid employees if they themselves had to provide them, this course has some merit. Nonetheless, our study found that lower paid employees are more likely to use a greater number of work–family policies, and realistically, most organisations could not pay all their employees enough money to meet all employee requests. Larger organisations enjoy economies of scale over smaller companies; we therefore suggest that this option is unlikely to help any but the highest paid employees. This conclusion emphasises the impact of organisational size on adoption. Larger organisations have greater resources to spend on work–family policies and have been found to adopt more such policies than smaller organisations (Goodstein 1994). To counter this imbalance, smaller organisations may need to focus on lower cost policies until such time as additional policies are warranted, or to collaborate with other small firms to gain economy-of-scale advantages.

It should be noted that although work–family policies have been linked to the many advantages and benefits already discussed, such outcomes are by no means a guaranteed consequence of policy adoption. Firms that adopt a few practices and attempt to utilise them simply to enhance their public image may experience both positive and negative effects, since an enhanced public image may be coupled with employee disillusionment and high turnover. Alternatively, firms that adopt policies that are desired by employees and widely available may well enjoy a variety of benefits from work–family policies so long as they constantly strive to address the work and family concerns of employees.

Finally, some critics have noted that work–family policies may have a short-term focus without improving employee conditions over the long term. For example, an employee who takes domestic leave to care for a sick family member may return to work to find that all his or her work is still waiting to be done, requiring increased output to catch up. So while this particular policy allowed the employee to meet family responsibilities at one point, it failed to provide the employee with needed support at work. Again, careful consideration by management and supervisors can alleviate these concerns and improve the overall performance of work–family policies.

The authors researched work–family policies and their effects on employees of a New Zealand local government organisation in 2000–2001. The organisation is a major employer in a rural region, with 450 employees, 65 per cent of these full time. The organisation offers several family-friendly practices including unpaid parental leave (up to 52 weeks unpaid), paid parental leave (six weeks paid), domestic leave (up to five days of personal sick leave per year for the care of spouse, child or parent), bereavement leave (leave for funeral but includes special cultural requirements), flexible work hours (variability of hours, location and negotiated leave without pay to fulfil family commitments), and a before- and after-school room (for children over 10 years, usable before and after school for a maximum of two hours per session). Data were collected in two stages; from a total sample of 206 employees, 100 responses were collected for both surveys, representing a response rate of 48.5 per cent. The average age of these respondents was 42 years, with 69 per cent of respondents female, and 77 per cent married.

The utilisation rates of the work–family practices are listed below ($n = 100$):

Practice	Percentage of employees
Bereavement leave	74
Flexible work arrangements	60
Domestic leave	36
Paid parental leave	19
Unpaid parental leave	19
Before- and after-school room	14

Work–family practice findings by demographics:
- More men (81 per cent) than women (71 per cent) use bereavement leave.
- Flexible work arrangements are used more often by men (68 per cent) than by women (57 per cent).
- A similar proportion of men (39 per cent) and women (35 per cent) use domestic leave.
- A greater proportion of women (23 per cent) use unpaid parental leave than do men (10 per cent), but more men (29 per cent) than women (14 per cent) use paid parental leave.
- More women (16 per cent) than men (10 per cent) use the before- and after-school room.
- Married employees are more likely to use a greater number of work–family policies.
- Employees who are parents are more likely to use greater numbers of work–family policies.
- There was no difference between male and female employees regarding the use of greater numbers of work–family policies.

- Employees earning $25 000 to $45 000 per annum accounted for 67 per cent of all users of work–family policies.
- Those employees with the lowest levels of education utilise the greatest number of practices, with 57 per cent of all work–family practices used by those with a college education or a diploma/certificate.

Work–family conflict findings:
- Work to family conflict was higher than family to work conflict, which indicates that workplace–related stress causes greater conflict on the family than family stress causes in the workplace.
- Factors such as long working hours, communication stress, job burnout and emotional demands in the workplace all had a statistically significant relationship to work–family conflict.
- Work–family conflict was related to job satisfaction.
- Stress originating with family roles was found to be associated with use of work–family policies, but workplace stress was not.

Work–family benefits findings:
- The perceived recruitment and retention benefits of work–family policies were significantly related to use of these policies. Employees who use these policies believe they offer recruitment and retention benefits to their organisation.
- Employees who use work–family policies report greater satisfaction with support of work–family issues by their organisation, as well as greater satisfaction with benefits.
- There was no significant link found between employee use of work–family policies and increased organisational commitment and job satisfaction, or decreased employee turnover.
- Overall, the findings suggest the benefits are linked more to specific attitudes than global attitudes, at least in this local government organisation.

Work–family/family-friendly backlash findings:
- Overall, there was little evidence of family-friendly backlash.
- Employees who do not use work–family policies did not register significant differences towards the organisation with regard to commitment, satisfaction and turnover from users of work–family policies.
- Employees who do not use work–family policies did register statistically significant differences towards organisational benefits, work–family support and work–family benefits.

Figure 5.2: Current research findings: work–family policies inside a New Zealand local government organisation

The future of work–family policies

Work–family policies have undoubtedly become a fundamental aspect of the HRM field and an issue of concern for all businesses today. There are indications that adoption of these policies will increase over the next few decades. A driving force behind this growth will be the ageing population. It has been suggested that as the population grows, shortfalls will become evident in the workforce population. These deficits will escalate as the workforce confronts both child-care and, increasingly, elder-care challenges. Despite this daunting prospect, the outlook is not entirely problematic. Both Australia and New Zealand have the advantage of being able to draw on the extensive work–family research conducted internationally, especially in the United States. Although differences in organisational size between these countries can be significant, the US still provides evidence of successful programs, identifying positive and negative aspects of work–family policies whose relevance transcends national boundaries.

This chapter has sought to highlight the policies and advantages that have been observed both internationally and within Australia and New Zealand. Organisations that adopt work–family policies sooner rather than later, and work continuously with their employees to create the best policies their resources will allow, may enjoy a competitive advantage over competitors who choose to ignore these concerns. The future for business leaders, managers and HR specialists is to encourage firm adoption of programs that will enhance their employees' working and personal lives. Such programs may provide organisations with tangible benefits that deliver an edge in an increasingly competitive global market.

It is our belief that work–family policies will continue to expand both in the number of organisations adopting them and in the range of programs offered. The use of such policies by employees will also increase. These programs may become more integrated into HRM strategies, being linked to employee recruitment, selection and remuneration. Managers who ignore the concerns of their workers, especially in industries with a tight labour market, will experience negative repercussions, while organisations that embrace work–family policies may achieve a competitive advantage over other firms that their resources might not suggest. Whether choosing to start and finish work early, taking time off to enjoy the birth of a child, or helping to meet the needs of elderly parents, we will all require work–family programs in the future. Poll after poll indicates that employees increasingly feel a loss of control over their lives, and work–family policies with full organisational support may provide the answer (Hammonds 1996).

References

Bencivenga, D (1995) Summer hours, compressed weeks: boutique work schedules fill an HR niche. *HR Magazine,* June 1995.

Berns, P, and Berns, J (1992) Good for business: corporations adopt the family. *Management Review,* 81 (9) 34–8.

Bhagat, RS, McQuaid, SJ, Lindholm, H, and Segovis, J (1985) Total life stress: a multimethod validation of the construct and its effects on organisationally valued outcomes and withdrawal behaviours. *Journal of Applied Psychology,* 70 (1) 202–214.

Chiu, WCK, and Ng, CW (1999) Women-friendly HRM and organisational commitment: a study among women and men of organisations in Hong Kong. *Journal of Occupational and Organisational Psychology,* 72, 485–502.

Cole, J (1999) Case study: SAS Institute Inc. uses sanity as strategy. *HR Focus,* 76 (5) 6.

Cooper, CL (1998) The 1998 Crystal Lecture: the future of work — a strategy for managing the pressures. *Journal of Applied Management Studies,* 7 (2) 275–81.

Crichton, S (1998) Pioneer firms see benefits in paid parental leave. *Evening Post,* 16 September, p. 5.

Crispell, D (1996) How to manage a chaotic workplace. *American Demographics,* 18 (6) 50–52.

Cutcher-Gershenfeld, J, Kossek, EE, and Sandling, H (1997) Managing concurrent change initiatives: integrating quality and work/family strategies. *Organizational Dynamics,* 25 (3) 21–37.

Daley, D (1998) An overview of benefits for the public sector: not on the fringe anymore. *Review of Public Personnel Administration,* 19 (3) 5–22.

Durst, SL (1999) Assessing the effects of family friendly programmes on public organisations. *Review of Public Personnel Administration,* Summer, 19–33.

Edwards, JR, and Rothbard, NP (2000) Mechanisms linking work and family: clarifying the relationship between work and family constructs. *Academy of Management Review,* 25 (1) 178–89.

EEO Trust (1998) *New Zealand's Best Employers in Work and Family (1998).* Auckland: EEO Trust.

Elsberry, R (1999) The family-friendly office. *Office Systems,* 16 (3) 42–5.

Faught, L (1995) Elder care benefits excelling in the '90s. *Human Resource Professional,* 8 (6) 3–6.

Flynn, G (1997) A bank profits from its work/life programme. *Workforce,* 76, 49.

Greenhaus, JH, and Beutell, NJ (1985) Sources of conflict between work and family roles. *Academy of Management Review,* 10 (1) 76–88.

Greenhaus, JH, Callanan, GA, and Godshalk, VM (2000) *Career Management* (3rd ed.). Orlando, FL: The Dryden Press.

Goodstein, JD (1994) Institutional pressures and strategic responsiveness: employer involvement in work–family issues. *Academy of Management Journal,* 37 (2) 350–82.

Gordon, JR, and Whelan, KS (1998) Successful professional women in midlife: how organisations can more effectively understand and respond to the challenges. *Academy of Management Executive,* 12 (1) 8–27.

Hall, DT, and Parker, VA (1993) The role of workplace flexibility in managing diversity. *Organisational Dynamics*, 22 (1) 4–18.

Hammonds, K (1996) Balancing work and family: big returns for companies willing to give family strategies a chance. *Business Week*, 16 September.

Hand, S, and Zawacki, RA (1994) Family-friendly benefits: more than a frill. *HR Magazine,* 39 (10) 79–84.

Henderson, M (1997) Employer help with juggling act is vital. *Sunday Star Times,* 13 July, p. 16.

Hendrickson, R (2000) What does the future hold for health care, elder care, and long-term care coverage for workers and their families? *Perspectives on Work,* 4 (2) 16–17.

Ingram, P, and Simons, T (1995) Institutional and resource dependence determinants of responsiveness to work–family issues. *Academy of Management Journal,* 38 (5) 1466–82.

International Labour Organization (1997) *Maternity Protection at Work: Report of the Maternity Protection Convention (Revised), 1952 (No. 103) and Recommendation, 1952 (No. 95).* Geneva: International Labour Office.

Judge, TA, Boudreau, JW, and Bretz Jr., RD (1994) Job and life attitudes of male executives. *Journal of Applied Psychology,* 79 (5) 767–82.

Kirkpatrick, D (1997) Child-free employees see another side of equation. *The Wall Street Journal Interactive Edition,* 2 April.

Kossek, EE, Dass, P, and DeMarr, B (1994) The dominant logic of employer-sponsored work and family initiatives: human resource managers' institutional role. *Human Relations,* 47 (9) 1121–49.

Kossek, E, Huber-Yoder, M, Castellino, D, and Lerner, J (1997) The working poor: locked out of careers and the organisational mainstream? *Academy of Management Executive,* 11 (1) 76–92.

Kossek, EE, Noe, RA, and DeMarr, BJ (1999) Work–family role synthesis: individual and organisational determinants. *International Journal of Conflict Management,* 10 (2) 102–129.

Kossek, EE, and Ozeki, C (1998) Work–family conflict, policies, and the job-life satisfaction relationship: a review and directions for organisational behaviour–human resources research. *Journal of Applied Psychology,* 83 (2) 139–49.

Lapin, H (1996) Fringe benefits offer low cost morale booster for employers. *The CPA Journal,* 66 (5) 66–7.

Larkin, J (1996) Human Resources. *Pennsylvania CPA Journal,* 67 (3).

Leonard, B (1998) Royal Bank's workers laud flexibility. *HR Magazine,* 43 (13) 30–31.

Magid, RY, and Codkind, MM (1995) *Work and Personal Life: Managing the Issues.* Menlo Park, CA: Crisp Publications.

Mason, JC (1993) Working in the family way. *Management Review,* 82 (7) 25–8.

McNerney, DJ (1994) A strategic partnership: clean air act and work–family. *HR Focus,* 71 (11) 22–3.

Michaels, B (1995) A global glance at work and family. *Personnel Journal,* 74 (4).

Michaels, B, and McCarthy, E (1993) Family ties and bottom lines. *Training and Development,* March, 70–72.

Milliken, FJ, Martins, LL, and Morgan, H (1998) Explaining organisational responsiveness to work-family issues: the role of human resource executives as issue interpreters. *Academy of Management Journal,* 41 (5) 580–92.

Milne, S, Blum, T, and Roman, P (1994) Factors influencing employees' propensity to use an employee assistance programme. *Personnel Psychology,* 47, 123–45.

Moore, T (1997) Work and family — a balancing act. *Asia Pacific Journal of Human Resources,* 34 (2) 119–25.

Morgan, H, and Milliken, FJ (1992) Keys to action: understanding differences in organisations' responsiveness to work-and-family issues. *Human Resource Management,* 31 (3) 227–48.

O'Sullivan, K (1996) Life based on a false economy. *Evening Post,* 14 August, p. 24.

Osterman, P (1995) Work/family programmes and the employment relationship. *Administrative Science Quarterly,* 40 (4) 681–700.

Overman, S (1999) Make family-friendly initiatives fly. *HR Focus,* 76 (7).

Paris, H (1990) Balancing work and family responsibilities: Canadian employer and employee viewpoints. *Human Resource Planning,* 13 (2) 147–57.

Phillips, T (1993) Cut costs, not programmes. *Human Resources Professional,* 6 (2) 21–3.

Rothausen, TJ, Gonzalez, JA, Clarke, NE, and O'Dell, LL (1998) Family-friendly backlash — fact or fiction? The case of organisations' on-site child-care centres. *Personnel Psychology,* 51, 685–706.

Ryan, R, and Torrie, R (1999) *How Can We Help?* Auckland: EEO Trust.

Scandura, TA, and Lankau, MJ (1997) Relationships of gender, family responsibility and flexible work hours to organisational commitment and job satisfaction. *Journal of Organisational Behaviour,* 18, 377–91.

Sheeran, G (1996) Oh baby, it's hard for Kiwis to get paid parental leave. *Sunday Star Times,* 19 May, p. 50.

Sheley, E (1996) Job sharing offers unique challenges. *HR Magazine,* January.

Shellenbarger, S (1999) *Work and Family: Essays from the 'Work and Family' column of The Wall Street Journal.* New York: The Ballantine Publishing Group.

Smith, A (1996) Family-friendly staff policies come of age. *Dominion,* 24 June, p. 25.

Statistics New Zealand (1998) *Household Labour Force Survey.*

Tapsell, S (1999) How do I know they're working? *Management,* July 1999, 38–41.

Tenbrunsel, AE, Brett, JM, Maoz, E, Stroh, LK, and Reilly, AH (1995) Dynamic and static work–family relationships. *Organisational Behaviour and Human Decision Processes,* 63 (3) 233–46.

Thomas, LT, and Ganster, DC (1995) Impact of family-supportive work variables on work–family conflict and strain: a control perspective. *Journal of Applied Psychology,* 80 (1) 6–15.

Vincola, A (2000) *Sabbatical, anyone? Increasingly, companies use sabbatical programs to fight burnout, raise productivity,* womenConnect.com (viewed 20 January 2000).

Vincola, A, and Farren, C (1999) Good career/life balance makes for better workers. *HR Focus,* 76 (4) 13.

Waters, LR, and Roach, D (1971) Relationship between job attitudes and two forms of withdrawal from the work situation. *Journal of Applied Psychology,* 55, 92–4.

White, B, Cox, C, and Cooper, G (1992) *Women's Career Development: A Study of High Flyers.* Cambridge, MA: Blackwell.

Wood, S (1999) Family-friendly management: testing the various perspectives. *National Institute Economic Review,* April 1999, 99–116.

Integrating diversity management initiatives with strategic human resource management

by Ronel Erwee
University of Southern Queensland

0101
01010
0101001
010101
1010011
0111010

Introduction

Managing diversity is usually viewed in broad conceptual terms as recognising and valuing differences among people; it is directed towards achieving organisational outcomes and reflects management practices adopted to improve the effectiveness of people management in organisations (Kramar 2001; Erwee, Palamara & Maguire 2000). The purpose of the chapter is to examine the debate on how diversity management initiatives can be integrated with strategic human resource management (SHRM), and how SHRM is linked to organisational strategy. Part of this debate considers to what extent processes associated with managing diversity are an integral part of the strategic vision of management. However, there is no consensus on how a corporate strategic plan influences or is influenced by SHRM, and how the latter integrates diversity management as a key component. The first section of the chapter addresses the controversy about organisations as linear, steady state entities or as dynamic, complex and fluid entities. This controversy fuels debate in the subsequent sections about the impact that such paradigms have on approaches to SHRM. The discussion on SHRM in this chapter will explore its links to corporate strategy as well as to diversity management. Subsequent sections propose that managing diversity should address sensitive topics such as gender, race and ethnicity. Finally, attention is given to whether an integrative approach to SHRM can be achieved and how to overcome the obstacles to making this a reality.

Strategic management in a turbulent world

The first challenge is to clarify the different approaches to organisational strategy as they affect both SHRM and the management of diversity. Strategic management is usually understood as the formulation, implementation and evaluation of cross-functional decisions that enable an organisation to achieve its objectives (David 2001; Hubbard 2000). Strategy formulation includes developing a mission and vision, identifying external opportunities and threats, determining internal strengths and weaknesses, establishing long-term objectives, generating alternative strategies, and choosing particular corporate- or business-level strategies on which to focus.

During strategy implementation, employees and managers are mobilised to set annual objectives, devise policies and allocate resources to achieve objectives. Managers are required to develop 'a strategy-supportive culture, create an effective organisational structure, prepare budgets, develop and utilise information systems and link employee compensation to organisational performance' (David 2001, p. 6). Strategy evaluation reviews external and internal factors on which current strategies are based, measures performance and takes corrective action.

It is usually during the strategy implementation phase that issues such as leadership, people, culture and change management are incorporated, and these issues form the link between strategy implementation and the concept of SHRM. As Hubbard (2000) observes, 'Leadership is one of the elements in determining whether or not an organisation can carry out its chosen strategy', and 'the introduction of a new CEO will often lead to a change in the required information systems, a restructure of positions, some changes in the key personnel reporting to the CEO, a change in one or more of the key values of the organisation and different use of the communication vehicles available' (pp. 213–14).

If the first challenge is to clarify different approaches to organisational strategy, a related issue is the traditional view of strategy formulation and implementation as a linear but dynamic process that evolves over time (Kramar, McGraw & Schuler 1997). It is influenced both by external environmental issues, such as competitive behaviour, and by internal changes within the company. 'We are becoming a borderless world with global citizens, global competitors, global customers, global suppliers and global distributors' (David 2001, p. 8). Organisational strategy attempts to anticipate issues and events in an uncertain future, so strategy must be flexible (Anthony, Perrew & Kacmar 1999; David 2001). Intended strategies are those that are planned; 'realised strategies' are those that actually take place in the real world. Strategists must take into account the fact that the business environment is highly dynamic and often changes before a strategy can be fully implemented. Therefore, all strategies are subject to future modification.

Organisations are experiencing a turbulent period of accelerated change, and these disruptive conditions tax their ability to survive crisis, renew themselves and function under changing conditions (Dunphy & Griffiths 1998). The linear but dynamic paradigms traditionally used to understand organisations cannot do justice to the complexity of organisations or suggest ways to become more adaptable to meet the demands of disjunctive environments. Chaos and complexity theories that focus on emergent and fluid living systems assist in understanding the changes in organisations and in guiding managers towards increasing their sustainability (Briggs & Peat 1999; Gleick 1998). Referring to chaos theory, Merry states that a 'new paradigm of organizational theory and practice is gradually beginning to take shape', and organisations have to deal with 'multi-layered, non-linear, interconnected, dynamic, complex problems, that Modern Science has difficulty dealing with' (Merry 1999, cited in Heaton 2001, p. 34).

The literature on chaos and complexity does not contain many explicit references to corporate or human resource management strategy. Briggs and Peat (1999) comment that, 'in a chaotic system, everything is connected, through negative and positive feedback to everything else' (p. 34), and 'chaos shows that when diverse individuals self-organise, they are able to create highly adaptable and resilient forms' (p. 39). Further:

> the structures we work in and that govern our society are derived from a markedly different set of assumptions about reality... It's a reality where we form ourselves into groups and social organs that resist diversity and where our social structures operate as closed entities, many deriving their identity from their opposition to other groups. (p. 68)

The implication is that turbulent environments necessitate a questioning of previous linear but dynamic approaches in order to evolve approaches to strategy formulation that are more flexible, dynamic, complex, non-linear and multilayered. Not only the paradigms of SHRM but also its implications for the interrelationships between corporate, business and human resource strategies need to be examined.

Linking SHRM to corporate strategy

A further challenge is to explore the links between corporate strategy and SHRM. Among the external variables in organisational strategy formulation are the labour market, educational structures, technological and political change, and societal issues that affect human resources. One of the aims of strategic management is to coordinate and align all the firm's resources, including its human resources, to work towards fulfilling the organisational goals (Hubbard 2000; Kramar 2001).

Stone (1995) initially argued that SHRM objectives are determined by the organisational objectives and need to be linked to the organisation's strategic planning in an ongoing cycle. Other proponents of SHRM confirm that it is concerned with ensuring a strategic alignment between business and HR strategies and policy, and acknowledge people as a strategic resource (Nankervis, Compton & McCarthy 1999; Walker, in Albrecht 2001). They believe that HR plans and policies should be formulated within the context of organisational strategies and objectives, and should be responsive to the organisation's changing external environment. This approach argues that corporate strategy drives HRM strategy. Therefore, an organisational strategy of innovation would require employees to show a degree of creative behaviour, and HRM policies would then need to ensure there is close interaction and coordination among groups of people. This perspective is usually signified by an 'accommodative' linkage between SHRM and organisational strategy (Nankervis et al. 1999, p. 43).

According to another view, SHRM should have an input in determining corporate strategy. Initially, the perspective was that HRM specialists and practitioners should work together, contributing to the formulation of strategy and ensuring the 'best' outcomes for all stakeholders. Stone (1995) later emphasised a reciprocal relationship, arguing that the HRM unit had achieved greater say in influencing organisational objectives. This development highlights the fact that in the mid 1990s, SHRM was not clearly differentiated. A more recent perspective is that HRM gathers invaluable information on the external environment, such as labour market data, and internal information such as HR allocation. The capabilities and predictive knowledge and skills of the HRM department can be invaluable to strategy formulation. Proponents of this perspective argue that HR specialists should become strategic partners with all levels of management. Such partnerships may include devolving practical functions such as recruitment to line managers, or outsourcing specialist activities such as payroll administration, but also forming close relationships with senior management to contribute to the formulation of strategic plans. The perspective is generally described as an 'interactive' linkage and is depicted in a Nankervis et al. (1999, p. 48) model of SHRM. Although the model recognises the need for flexibility to cope with dynamic external environments, it is essentially a linear model.

A third set of views, developed in the Strategic International Human Resource Management (SIHRM) literature, argues that in the competitive process of globalisation and complexity, it is becoming critical to manage sustainable multinational organisations more effectively by using SHRM, and to link this with strategic needs in the larger organisational context (Adler 1997; Albrecht 2001; Briscoe 1995; Schuler, Dowling & De Cieri 1993). If a multinational organisation fails to gain strategic control of its dispersed operations and to manage them in a coordinated manner, it cannot succeed. The arguments in this literature for developing SIHRM are that human resource management at any level in a multinational corporation is important to strategic implementation. However, a wide variety of factors complicate the relationship between the multinational organisation and SIHRM.

Many multinationals opt for an integrative framework of SIHRM that takes into account the linkages between their offices in different states and, in some cases, their complex internal operations. If workplaces in specific countries or states have different legal frameworks, union demands or demographics, the multinational organisation may have to differentiate its SIHRM policies. In addition to working together, each international workplace must operate within the confines of its local environment as well as the range of laws, politics, culture, economy and practices between societies.

The issue then becomes how the multinational's increasingly diverse HRM policies and practices are to be integrated, controlled and coordinated across countries (Walker, in Albrecht 2001). Questions of differentiation and integration are especially important because they acknowledge the complexity of multinational environments but also point up the need to formulate guiding principles that may be used to manage the complexity of divergent policies and practices. In this international context, the key to strategic management is coping with change (requiring flexibility) and continual adaptation to achieve a fit between the multinational's changing internal and external environments.

The integrative framework has three major components of SIHRM: issues, functions, and policies and practices (Schuler et al. 1993). All three components must be included because they are all influenced by the multinational's strategic activities, and because they in turn influence the concerns and goals of this type of organisation. Walker (in Albrecht 2001, p. 75) notes that 'sustained performance requires superb implementation on a global basis. This requires effective human resource management in several areas … cross-cultural leadership … a workforce with global business savvy … individuals with sensitivity to work in diverse environments … global networks … [and] a capacity to change rapidly …'. This view assumes that there is a movement towards a 'fully integrated' linkage between corporate strategy and SHRM (Nankervis et al. 1999, p. 43), especially in multinational corporations.

It is especially in the SIHRM literature that references occur to cultural diversity, cross-cultural management, transnational teams, managing diversity and multicultural organisations (Adler 1997; Briscoe 1995; Cox 1993; Cox, in Albrecht 2001; Hernandez 1993; Hofstede 1991; Hofstede, in Albrecht 2001). The contradictions in the current paradigms, such as universalism in management and organisation theories with local realities, are noted:

In reality, the problem is complex because a diverse world co-exists simultaneously with an organisation logic that presumes and assumes a universal character, one, however, that can only really find its specific forms in the institutional and cultural context of every local reality … the contrast between the fashionable recipes and the results of their translations to these diverse locales, establishes the terms of this ambivalence. (Clegg, Ibarra-Colado & Rodriquez 1999, p. 7)

The implications are that universalism should not be assumed but that organisations should adapt their SHRM policies and practices to take account of diversity in each location.

Corporate strategy, SHRM and performance management

To what extent is an effective performance management system part of strategic HRM in an organisation, and to what extent is diversity management incorporated into such a performance management system? Millett (1999) argues that performance management is a vital part of not only SHRM but also the corporate strategic management process. Performance management incorporates activities such as setting organisational, organisational unit and individual performance standards that link to the overall organisational strategic plan. Organisational, team and individual performance measurement is included, as are strategies for managing underperformance and rewarding excellent performance. One perspective suggests it is the responsibility of a line manager or leader who influences staff to ensure that outcomes match strategic aims and expectations (see figure 6.1).

The primary focus of performance management is not to monitor or control people, but to work with them either individually or as a group in a cooperative way to better align work outcomes with the organisational strategy. This implies continuous improvement and a participative, strategic approach to the changes that are recognised as necessary to achieve a more effective management of human resources and diversity in the workplace (Millett 1999; Schuler et al. 1993).

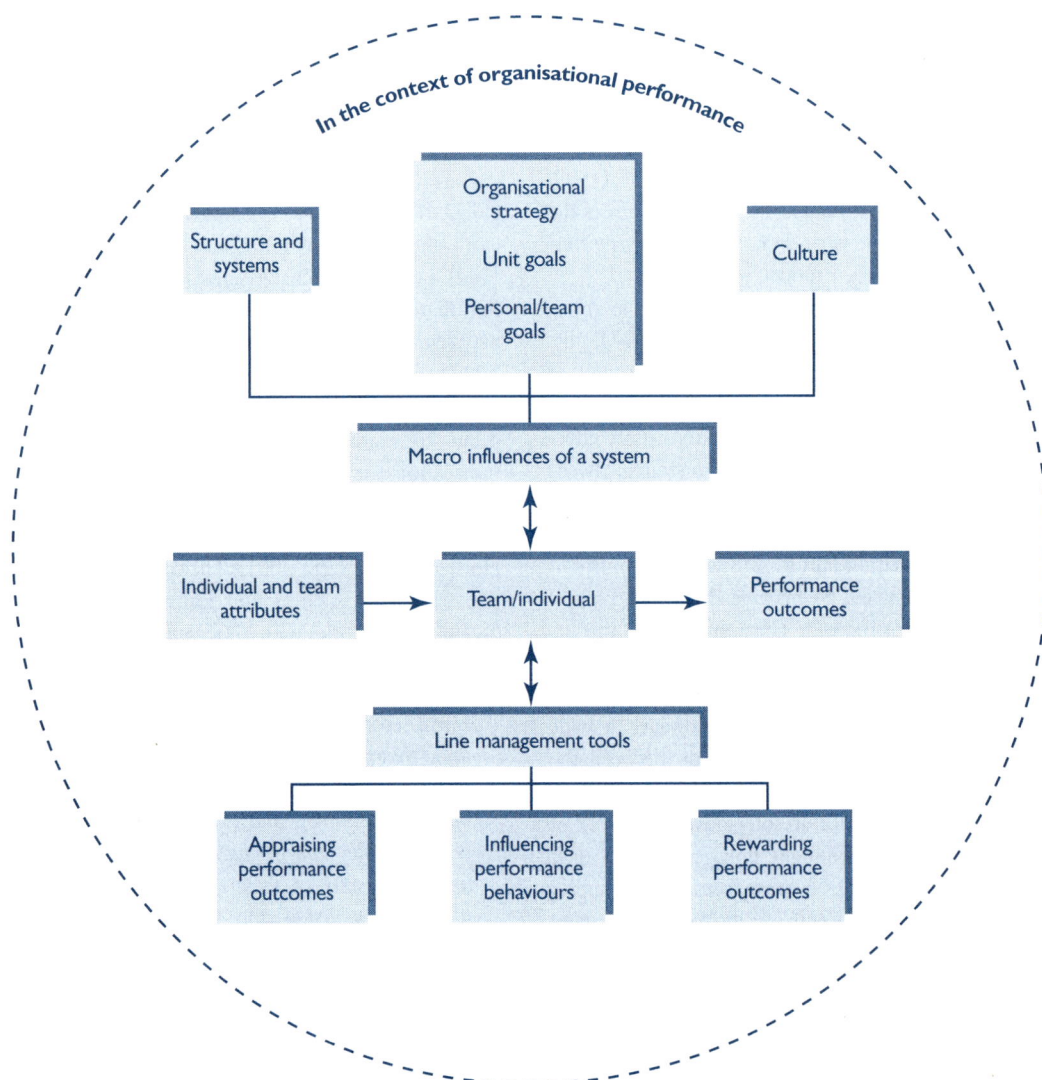

Figure 6.1: Performance management tools for line managers *Source:* B Millett (1999).

Diversity management must fit into the performance management system of an organisation. This implies that an organisation has an effective and supportive performance management system in relation to managing overall system performance, and that concepts of diversity management are integrated into these systems. It also implies that there is an active involvement by line managers in managing the performance of those people and systems for which they have responsibility in order to achieve diversity and other organisational goals (Erwee 2000). Depending on the specific purposes for which the organisation chooses to use the performance management system, outcomes may or may not be linked to administrative systems such as remuneration and promotion (Millett 1999).

CASE

The Human Resources Division, Department of Education, Employment and Training, Victoria, formulated a People Management Framework to enhance the capacity of the Department to achieve its strategic priorities in 1999. The framework embraced four key components of people management, namely workforce planning, performance excellence, professional development and work environment. Objectives and actions for improved practice are formulated for each component. *Managing and valuing diversity* was one of the action categories in the Performance Excellence component. The intended outcomes for each component were specified. Accountability mechanisms aimed to test the alignment between values, strategies and practices as well as provide guidelines for improvement. This framework was adapted when the Department restructured in 2000. (Erwee 2000)

The model in figure 6.1 does not refer to the challenges created by cultural diversity, cross-cultural management or multicultural organisations, but the author acknowledges that linear models of organisations are being challenged by paradigms of non-linear, interconnected, dynamic, complex systems. Such models of the linkages between corporate strategy, strategic HRM and performance management will be adjusted to incorporate diversity maangement in addition to the new focus on non-linear and complex elements of systems.

Operationalising SHRM

The next challenge is to put into practice, or 'operationalise', SHRM at the managerial level in an organisation. If the perspective is that SHRM is a major contributor to the setting of organisational objectives, then it needs to be clarified how its policies can contribute to the emergence of business strategy. Managers could explore how HR strategy contributes to organisational goals, how organisational goals drive or influence the aims of SHRM, and how well the elements of the HR system fit together to support the accomplishment of organisational goals (Baron & Kreps 1999).

If senior managers believe that they are responsible for making decisions based on the SHRM agenda, but this belief is not supported by the organisational structure, culture or perceptions, then it is unlikely that SHRM will be effectively implemented. The lack of clarity on managerial responsibility for SHRM may explain why some research indicates that little implementation of SHRM is carried out in certain organisations (Heaton 2001).

The notion that turbulent environments necessitate a flexible and dynamic approach should also be applied to operationalising strategy and SHRM. This confirms that the links between organisational and HR strategies are complex and fluid. A further complexity that emerges during an operational stage is that the concept of diversity management may have been ignored as part of corporate strategy formulation or during SHRM formulation.

In the previous sections it has been established that organisations are evolving as more complex, multi-layered systems, which has led to changes in corporate strategy. The adaptation of corporate strategy again influences and is influenced by concomitant changes in SHRM. The role of diversity management within these complex systems needs to be highlighted.

Diversity management: concepts and controversies

Kramar (in Wiesner & Millett 2001, p. 62) defines managing diversity and highlights a linkage with strategic HRM:

Managing diversity can be regarded as a process of management based on certain values that recognise differences between people and identities as a strength but at the same time is directed towards the achievement of organisational outcomes. The processes associated with managing diversity become an integral part of management. When managing diversity is understood from this perspective it is framed as a broad term that refers to management practices used to improve the effectiveness of people management in organisations.

Following this broad approach to conceptualising 'managing diversity', Griggs and Louw (1995, p. 19) argue that HR and management interventions should maximise the potential of the workforce in all its diversity and that any intervention should take into account 'the critical area of human diversity and the concomitant reality of changing relationship patterns'. Their model assumes that the philosophy of valuing diversity and the reality of managing diversity are key components in dealing with SHRM development challenges. Their view is that although specific strategies may be used in certain areas of an organisation, 'an integrated response embedded in the context of the organisation's broader strategic challenges and objectives can achieve long term results' (p. 20). Although they then tend to focus on 'diversity initiatives', they place these initiatives in a strategic context. For example, strategic questions linking diversity management with organisational strategy are posed:

What are the broader challenges facing the organisation? Is the diversity initiative managed as an integral part of the organisation's total system change and ... other key human resource strategies? How is the diversity intervention perceived by leaders and employees: as an organisational development intervention, a human resource intervention, a skills development-educational intervention, a public relations effort, a bottom-line business opportunity or a way to avoid discrimination suits? How consistent are these reasons with the strategic direction of the organisation? (Griggs & Louw 1995, pp. 22–3)

Diversity management as specific programs or strategies

One of the controversies in diversity management is that a number of researchers focus on *diversity management* or *managing diversity* as a series of steps or specific programs in organisations. Examples of specific programs classified as diversity management are:

Providing training and development

The provision of training and education in managing and valuing diversity is an often-noted aspect of organisational diversity strategy (D'Netto, Smith & Da Gama Pinto 2000; Kramar 2001; Griggs & Louw 1995). Awareness training focuses on creating an understanding of the importance and meaning of diversity, and increases participants' self-awareness of diversity-related issues such as stereotyping and cross-cultural insensitivity. Skill-building training educates employees on specific cultural differences and how to respond to differences in the workplace. These two types of training are often combined. In addition, legal awareness training informs employees of the law and the consequences of breaking the law, and encourages employees to engage in appropriate behaviours. Such training would not necessarily be enough to change employees' attitudes about diversity. Practitioners caution that these workshops do not achieve their objective of improved cohesion between individuals, but instead heighten tensions, sharpen differences and increase competition and hostility when members of these groups view themselves as competing for jobs.

CASE

The Californian based grocery chain, Lucky Stores instituted diversity training sessions designed to teach their employees to acknowledge and cope with their racist and sexist assumptions about women and minority groups. Unfortunately, some employees sued the company for discrimination and used the notes taken during the training as evidence. Lucky Stores was found guilty of discrimination and ordered to pay $90 million. (see Kramar 2001, p. 66)

In an Australian study, the majority of managers noted that their organisations focus on diversity-related training opportunities, with emphasis on cross-cultural training and anti-racism training (D'Netto et al. 2000). While managers in some organisations believed that their company had provided the appropriate training and support resources to ensure that diversity is managed and integrated at all levels of the business, respondents from other organisations suggested that additional training was needed to help employees attain diversity management skills and awareness. Education techniques varied, and included focus groups and round-table discussions, facilitated workshops, meetings, more standard training, and meetings of single identity groups followed by mixed groups to discuss an issue (for example, a women's group and a men's group would meet separately, then as a mixed group, to discuss gender dynamics in an organisation). Only two private sector organisations noted a comprehensive diversity education program that included in-depth education sessions, a leadership diversity component that included coaching, and special focus groups for newcomers.

Cox (1993, in Albrecht 2001) and Griggs and Louw (1995) suggested that diversity training and development programs needed to be integrated with the organisation's diversity management strategy and should not be seen as solutions in themselves.

Leadership and organisational policy

The general view is that management's support and genuine commitment to cultural diversity is crucial, and that they should take strong personal stands on the need for managing diversity and change and should role model the behaviours required for change (Cox & Blake 1991; Cox 1993; Sinclair 1998). It follows that human, financial and technical resources should be provided, and that diversity should form part of corporate strategy and should consistently be made a part of senior-level meetings. HR practices such as recruitment, training, performance management and compensation are expected to change to respond to diversity-related issues. Managers are encouraged to demonstrate a willingness to sustain management diversity efforts over a long period, not just in the short term (Cox & Blake 1991).

The absence of leadership and organisational policy was illustrated by the D'Netto et al. (2000) study. They found that the third most widely reported response to questions on diversity issues was that no formal strategy existed. Australian managers shared a concern that the organisation responded to the issues in a piecemeal way and had no formalised strategies, while acknowledging that a more systemic and strategic approach needed to be implemented. Some respondents noted that their organisation had no strategies to deal with the effect of the changing composition of the workforce on its business, whereas others did not seem overly concerned by the lack of strategy. This finding reinforces Smith's (1998) suggestion of a high level of denial or inclination to dismiss diversity issues among Anglo-Australian management. This phenomenon was described as:

> 'The privilege of oblivion'; that is — if an issue, such as subtle discrimination, is not happening to me (as is the case with most white men), I don't see it (I am oblivious), I don't believe it really exists, and as such I don't need to do anything about it. Hence the lack of investment of time or resources in the development and implementation of strategies to make the most effective use of a diverse workforce. (D'Netto et al. 2000, p. 23)

Organisational research or cultural audits

This program or strategy assumes that the collection and analysis of data on diversity issues within the organisation is essential. Data collection would, for example, include equal opportunity profile data, analysis of attitudes and perceptions of employees and the career expectations of different cultural groups. The analysis could identify departments where certain groups are clustered, monitor the effectiveness of and

progress with diversity programs, and assist in designing organisation specific training and development programs. Furthermore, a comprehensive analysis of the organisation's culture and HR systems such as recruitment, performance appraisal, career planning and promotion, and compensation are envisioned. The primary objectives of a cultural audit are to uncover sources of potential bias against members of certain cultural groups and to identify ways that corporate culture may inadvertently put some members at a disadvantage (Thomas 1991; Cox 1993; Griggs & Louw 1995).

Cultural audits are seen as an integral part of managing diversity; however, they are not sufficient in themselves to build a culture that allows all members of the organisation to contribute to their fullest potential. For a cultural audit to be effective, formal procedures such as HR policies need to be assessed. This assessment provides the means to examine the extent to which an organisation's policies support or hinder the desired culture to value diversity. There is a danger that a cultural audit will leave the impression that the 'white male culture is the problem and that the white men in the organisation must bear the burden of most of the change' (see Kramar 2001, p. 66). However, if managing diversity is a mutual process, then the process must be inclusive, allowing all members to contribute to their fullest potential. Cultural audits therefore need to focus on both differences and similarities between groups, and encourage HR policies and practices to incorporate both aspects.

Diversity enlargement or target group employment strategies

Diversity enlargement programs refer to increasing the representation of groups with particular personal characteristics such as ethnic or gender backgrounds. Usually the organisation's demographic composition is changed, but other HR practices may remain unchanged. Such a strategy will not be effective if there is an assumption that increasing diversity and exposure to certain groups will automatically result in increased performance, particularly if this assumption is combined with a perception that it is a forced change effort in order to be politically correct. Although the Australian equal employment opportunity (EEO) and discrimination legislation in the federal and state jurisdictions does not require forced adherence to quotas, it is possible that some employers would feel coerced by expectations in the labour market and among customers to increase the representation of particular groups (Kramar 2001).

Several managers in the D'Netto et al. (2000) research reported efforts to increase the representation of specific target groups, including women in management, Indigenous employees, people with disabilities, or people from non-English-speaking backgrounds (NESB). While many of these initiatives occurred in government organisations subject to EEO legislation, others were voluntary initiatives in the private sector. Another approach involved assisting in the development of supplier organisations owned and run by target groups, such as Indigenous organisations or organisations run by ethnic minorities, and then using these organisations as preferred suppliers. D'Netto et al. (2000) argue that while the idea of quotas is anathema to most Australians, such an approach is a practical step towards overcoming potential systemic bias in corporate supply chains.

In these perspectives of diversity management as special programs there are references to cultural diversity and cross-cultural management, yet they do not occur within the same paradigms of organisational complexity as those in SIHRM or within chaos theory. Within these perspectives there are few direct linkages to SHRM or organisational strategy. Most of the implicit assumptions are of organisations as relatively linear and static, with little fluidity or complexity.

Diversity management as a series of steps or stages

In contrast to the perception of diversity management as a specific program is the debate about stages or states in managing diversity.

Some researchers argue that certain organisational forms are relevant in an organisation's transformation process towards greater diversity. Adler (1997) refers to a parochial form, an ethnocentric organisation or a synergistic organisation, whereas Cox (1993, in Albrecht 2001) describes the characteristics of monolithic, plural and multicultural organisations. All argue that organisations experience three stages in the evolution towards a diversity sensitive environment. In the monolithic or monocultural stage the organisation acts as though all employees are the same. There is an expectation that all staff will conform to a standard (for example a white male model), and success will be achieved by following the expectations and norms of this model. *Others* are expected to assimilate and adopt the dominant style of the organisation.

In the plural or non-discriminatory stage, it is assumed that organisations begin to adhere to affirmative action or EEO regulations usually as a result of government regulations or the threat of employee grievances. They meet quotas in hiring and promotions and remove obstacles to equal advancement opportunities. Employees of non-mainstream groups experience the need to assimilate as well as a desire for the organisation to accommodate their needs. Conflict is usually alleviated through compromise. In the multicultural stage, differences are recognised while culture,

background, preferences and values are respected. Assimilation is viewed not as the way to deal with conflict, but rather as the creation of new norms that allow employees freedom of choice. Policies and procedures are flexible, applied equitably, and no one is exploited (Gardenswartz & Rowe 1993; Cox, in Albrecht 2001).

The researchers cited above suggest that an organisation can be classified using a specific typology of organisational forms. The organisation is therefore monocultural, plural or multicultural. One measuring instrument in Gardenswartz and Rowe (1993) assumes that a company can be classified according to its score on the status quo of diversity management in that organisation.

In contrast to the classification approach, other researchers suggest that a company can move from being a monocultural to being a multicultural organisation by following certain steps, namely from monocultural to 'lip service given to inclusion' to 'tokenism' to 'a critical mass' to 'tolerating/accepting diversity', and eventually to a multicultural approach that values diversity (Esty, Griffin & Hirsch 1995, p. 189). The objective of managing diversity is seen as the creation of a multicultural organisation in which members of all social backgrounds can contribute and achieve their full potential (Jackson & Ruderman 1997; Prasad, Mills, Elmes & Prasad 1997). These statements seem to suggest a gradual evolutionary process with no definitive demarcations. The continuum is seen as bipolar, starting from an exclusive organisation and evolving into an inclusive organisation. The focus shifts from merely complying with legislation to valuing diversity.

Smith (1998) also uses 'stages' in his description of a process to manage diversity. However, the term is used not to classify companies; rather, it identifies seven steps in a process (or phases in a program) to manage diversity. For example, the first step is ensuring that organisation leaders are committed and personally involved in the process of managing diversity. The next step is ensuring that a 'Diversity Council' representative of diverse groups is involved in setting business reasons for managing diversity. A third step involves conducting employee surveys, focus groups or targeted interviews to assess the climate for diversity management. In the fourth step a range of measures are suggested, such as performance evaluations and bonuses tied to achievement of diversity goals and growth measures such as retention and turnover figures. Certain programmatic measures associated with the outcomes of diversity management, such as flexible work practices and mentor programs, are also included in this phase. The next step is described as an intervention stage, with the range of targeted actions including awareness training, changing the workforce profile and creating developmental opportunities. Major organisation-wide programs, such as changing the organisational culture or performance management systems, may be involved. The final steps focus on progress checks on different levels and the ongoing maintenance of programs. Cox (in Albrecht 2001) describes similar key components of multicultural organisations, whereas Griggs and Louw (1995, pp. 50–53) construct a 'Diversity Journey Learning Map' with 10 major steps, or modules.

Erwee, Perry and Tidwell's (1999) results on the formation and maintenance of Asian–Australian networks support the idea that cross-cultural business relationships evolve through unprogrammed, dynamic *states* rather than a sequential, linear progression of clearly defined and predetermined *stages*. The contention is that it is difficult to classify an organisation categorically as 'monocultural', 'non-discriminatory' or 'multicultural' in its management of diversity. The first adaptation is to assume that an organisation displays a continuum of progress rather than discrete categories or demarcated stages. A more realistic approach is to assume that an organisation is gradually evolving over time through unprogrammed, dynamic *states.*

A further complicating factor is the multidimensionality of diversity as a concept and the interrelationships among diversity dimensions. Jackson & Ruderman (1995, p. 237) pose the question, 'Which types of diversity have effects on which organisational outcomes?' to illustrate the multidimensionality of the concept.

The organisational context for diversity management

One of the aims of an Australian study was to explore the perspectives of managers on the management of diversity in a sample of Australian companies by using a Diversity Survey (Erwee & Innes 1998). The Australian managers depicted the majority of the 277 companies as 'Open but not embracing change' or indicated that the companies needed to be quicker to implement change initiatives such as diversity management. The sample was split almost evenly between respondents from private sector and public sector organisations. The highest proportion of respondents believed that their companies are primarily in the monocultural phase of evolution towards a diversity sensitive workplace.

According to the Diversity Survey research, two factors were important in determining perceptions of the stage of diversity, namely the sector and the extent of organisational change (Erwee & Innes 1998). The extent of organisational change was also differentially associated with the phase or stage of diversity. For example, companies in the multicultural and non-discriminatory stages of evolution were more open to change. These results were confirmed by results relating to valuing diversity. Equal proportions of managers in public sector organisations described such institutions as monocultural, non-discriminatory or multicultural. In contrast, managers in private sector companies were more likely to describe their company as monocultural. Middle, senior and first-line supervisors noted that their companies are monocultural, whereas chief executive officers believed that their companies are multicultural.

This Diversity Survey research still used the concept of classifying organisations according to stages. Yet the fact that the subscale that had one of the highest reliabilities was 'Openness to change' suggests that diversity management is part of a larger organisational context. What is important in this macro organisational context is the flexibility of the organisation to adapt to a changing environment.

From the above statements, the proposition formulated was that an organisation's attitude towards internal and external change creates the context in which diversity is managed in the company.

In the Diversity Survey research managers stated that companies' procedures and policies comply mainly with legal imperatives, and the respondents believed that individual managers are more enlightened than the trends reflected in their organisations' policies and practices (Erwee & Innes 1998). This suggests that organisational values and norms and management practices were slower to change within companies despite legislation inducing compliance. Organisations differ on the extent to which they are complying with legislation and on whether they have acted out of a conviction that diversity should be valued. This could be seen from the different reactions by companies on the 'Openness to change' subscale, since companies that are open to change had contrasting responses to those that resist change. Each organisation has its own benchmarks to measure its progress on the continuum, and research needs to identify these 'indicators' or benchmarks of progress.

Future directions

In relation to future directions, two themes are identified.

Creating linkages in SHRM policy and practices with diversity management

The discussion so far has noted many divergent opinions of the linkages between corporate strategy, SHRM and 'managing diversity', or 'diversity management'.

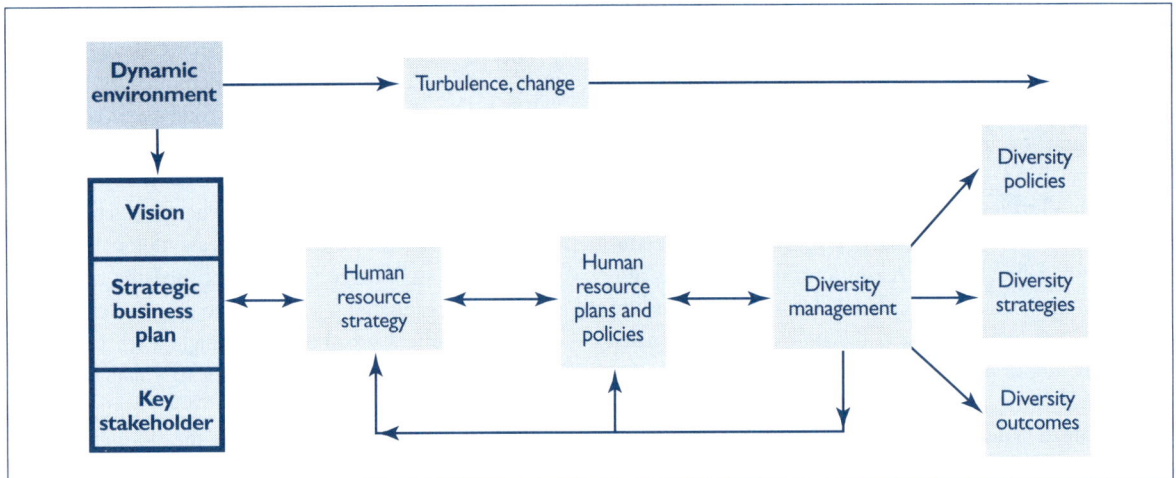

Figure 6.2: A strategic model of diversity management ***Source:*** Adapted from Nankervis, Compton and McCarthy (1999), 158.

Nankervis et al.'s model (1999, p. 115) assumes reciprocal linkages between HR strategy and a strategic business plan, giving rise to HR plans and policies that have a reciprocal influence on strategy. Such HR plans and policies set the stage for diversity management but are influenced by the latter. Diversity management policies, strategies and outcomes flow from the previous processes, but a feedback loop influencing HR plans, HR strategy or the strategic business plan was not included. The model is based on the assumption that working arrangements and management styles have to be flexible to accommodate the range of employee work attitudes and religious and cultural requirements, and is designed to optimise and liberate human potential in order to maximise productivity while at the same time satisfying individual employee desires. The model has been adapted for this chapter (see figure 6.2) to emphasise organisational turbulence and change and to incorporate more linkages between components to suggest a fully integrated approach.

Griggs and Louw (1995) include a module on 'Initiating systemic change' that identifies systemic barriers in organisations to the organisation's ability to value and manage diversity. It focuses on implementing a diversity strategy and managing this specific change process. They question whether the diversity initiative is managed as an integral part of the organisation's total system change, but they explore this issue no further. Jackson and Ruderman (1995, p. 239) suggest that a key determinant of how increasing diversity will affect work team and organisational performance is the extent to which the organisation consciously manages diversity by creating a supportive climate.

Very few of the sources make specific reference to links between SHRM and diversity management. However, Kramar, McGraw and Schuler (1997) note that affirmative action programs that are integrated with organisational objectives and strategic plans require an analysis of the organisation's employment profile and employment policies. They still focus on either AA or EEO, but they acknowledge that the development of EEO in the future will involve management's dealing with EEO as an integral part of business activity and success.

Fernandez (1995) argues that the key strategy for forming high performance teams is for corporations to understand the link between diversity, team building and total quality management. He emphasises that managing diversity should be a corporate strategy tied directly into the business strategy for managing organisational change and improving productivity. From the statements in this section, it seems likely that diversity management programs or initiatives will be more successful if they are integrated into the strategic human resource programs that support organisational strategic plans.

The notion that turbulent environments necessitate a flexible and dynamic approach was not consistently noted in the above sources and should therefore be applied to the linkages between strategy, SHRM and managing diversity. Again, the assumption is that links between organisational, HR and diversity management strategies are complex and fluid. This suggests, again, that diversity management policies, practices and strategies become an integral part of corporate strategy and SHRM formulation and implementation.

Acknowledging the controversies about colonialism, race and gender

Hofstede's early research (1991, in Albrecht 2001) proposed that national identity is part of the mental programming (collective pattern of thinking, feeling and acting) shared by people in a group, and that this influences management culture in organisations in a society. Hall and Hall argue that the cultures of the world can range from high context to low context, with 'context as the information that surrounds an event' (in Albrecht 2001, p. 26). Using the argument that management philosophies and practices are culturally conditioned, Fernandez (1995) states that the United States has a history and philosophy of embracing diversity — in contrast to Europe and Japan, who have a limited history of laws and programs that respect and utilise diversity.

Docker and Fisher (2000) found many contradictions in their study of race, colour and identity in Australia and New Zealand, noting:

> colonial versus post-colonial, old settlers versus new settlers, indigenous people versus invaders, majority versus innumerable minorities, white against black or coloured, the search for a collective, inclusive or national identity (in an era of post national globalisation) vis-à-vis the search for individual and personal or group identity based on ethnicity, language, country of origin or religion. (p. 6)

However, many of the researchers and arguments cited in the preceding sections of this paper are criticised for a lack of attention to gender, racism and colonialism. For example, Adler and Izraeli (1994) argue that women's under-representation, under-utilisation and skewed distribution in management are often explained by four perspectives, namely individual differences between the sexes, organisational context problems, institutionalised discrimination and as a consequence of power dynamics.

> Yet, while outstanding human resource systems provide competitive advantages, companies worldwide draw from a restricted pool of potential managers. Although women represent over 50 percent of the world population, in no country do women represent half, or even close to half, of the corporate managers ... beyond the international commonalities underlying women's exclusion from the centres of managerial power and authority lies the uniqueness of local conditions in each country that produces the variety of women's experiences worldwide. (Adler & Izraeli 1994, pp. 3–4)

Although the Australian workforce is among the most culturally and linguistically diverse in the world, Sinclair (1998) contends that the traditional notions of leadership have not developed to keep pace with an internationalised and multicultural workplace:

> ... there is a close but obscured connection between the constructs of leadership, traditional assumptions of masculinity and a particular expression of male heterosexual identity ... our conceptions of leadership are locked in a time-warp, constrained by lingering archetypes of heroic warriors and wise but distant fathers ... homogeneity in the characteristics of leadership in an environment of dramatic change and a workforce of increased diversity, is a major liability ... (pp. 1–2)

In a discussion of the construction of race in Australia, Docker and Fisher (2000, p. 266) state that 'whiteness is represented as mainstream Australia and under threat, the extreme has moved to the centre and the privilege of whiteness is hidden', and 'a common theme within this narrative is fear and politics of division'.

Some critics deride the 'managerial focus', 'strategic perspectives', the focus on 'bottom line success' and the 'neo-unitarist approach to the management of employees' in SHRM (Nankervis et al. 1999, p. 45). Mills and Hatfield (in Clegg et al. 1999, p. 36) state that current textbooks on management are built around a 'white, male, liberal American view of reality', that a 'generalised Cold War mentality' strengthened tendencies to avoid concerns with broader socio-political issues (p. 49), and that even in the better texts, 'gender — along with race, age, sexual preference and ethnicity — is becoming subsumed under "diversity" and problematised anew' (p. 56). What discussions there are on race, ethnicity or national origin are framed according to a 'eurocentric, assimilationist perspective', and discussion about diversity is a 'newer, more subtle form of cultural imperialism' (Mills & Hatfield, in Clegg et al. 1999, pp. 57–8).

In an Australian study, managers identified a total of 23 separate discussed or 'visible' diversity issues in their organisations (D'Netto et al. 2000, p. 32). Most issues dealt with culture or gender, while others included general themes such as differences, organisational culture and flexible response to change. The managers also singled out 23 'undiscussable' or taboo diversity issues in their organisations. Nearly all undiscussables were specific issues such as race, cultural bias, sexual orientation or age.

Certain authors are concerned that case studies of companies that celebrate their achievements in managing diversity cloak problems of diversity, gender, or racial tension and cultural friction in organisations. Although many organisations profess to be multicultural and to manage diversity, they are monocultural entities whose organisational policies, norms and values do not adequately reflect the realities of a multicultural workforce. Prasad,

Mills, Elmes and Prasad (1997) discuss the negative effects of a monocultural organisation:

> More than anything, organisational monoculturalism leads to institutional resistance against workplace diversity. Institutional resistance can be distinguished from individual resistance by the structural potency of the problem. Organisational monoculturalism therefore results in innumerable routine workplace processes (such as reward systems) that are systematically hostile to the cultural values and lifestyles of different groups. The ultimate result is a structural failure to accommodate difference in the workplace. (pp. 15–16)

This pessimistic perspective regarding the discourse on race, gender, ethnicity and colonialism in a society will negatively affect beliefs about organisational strategy and its links to SHRM, as well as to the reality of managing diversity.

Implications for managers

In Australia a variety of federal or state Acts influence the SHRM policies, performance and diversity management systems that a human resource or line manager designs. In the Australian public sector there may also be existing minimum standards formulated in a Commissioner for Public Employment's directions. A manager should ensure that there are direct linkages between the organisation's vision, mission and values statements and the relevant Acts, institutional or organisational documents (public sector), or industry or professional society benchmarks or quality standards (private sector).

Another way of establishing linkages is to develop a values statement that incorporates respect for the individual, teamwork and a positive work environment. A values statement should comprise a good progression of commitments — from the broad general value of, for example, performance excellence to a focus on the individual (respect and customer service), before moving to values pertaining to groups and management systems (teamwork, work environment, quality management, valuing diversity). This statement could form the basis for linkages between corporate strategy, SHRM and policies on managing diversity. In contrast to the sometimes adversarial nature of workplace relations, the tone of policy documents could emphasise cooperation between staff and management and between internal and external stakeholders.

A manager could further exemplify efficient management communication by focusing attention on the organisation's vision, mission and values. Is the vision inspirational, customer focused and cooperative in intent, and does it specify realistic current and future outcomes?

CASE

In the Department of Education, Employment and Training, Victoria, the mission of the department influences the missions of Offices and Divisions within Offices. For example, in 1999 the mission of the Office of Departmental Services was to ensure that the 'core support services of the Department are delivered smoothly and effectively by providing support to those delivering educational services in a way that adds value to the operations of schools and services'. The Human Resources Division's mission was a concise statement on 'improving the quality of teaching and learning in schools and institutes by providing high quality services in human resource management for all Department staff'. (Erwee 2000, p. 2)

Many organisations include diagrams to clarify the complex relationship between government policy, the organisation's corporate and business or operational plans, and SHRM practices. Specific strategic priorities in particular time frames, for example managing diversity in 2000 to 2002, are often highlighted. References to other documents can serve to focus on the interrelatedness of strategies within the organisation.

CASE

The Human Resources Division, Department of Education, Employment and Training, Victoria's 1999 document had some notable strategies. There were attempts to draw every member of staff into the Performance Management Framework by clarifying their personal responsibility at the onset. The importance of cooperation to succeed and joint ownership of the PMF were often illustrated by the use of terminology such as 'our success' or 'our mission'. This subtle personal appeal is incorporated before emphasis was placed on the role of leadership. (Erwee 2000, p. 4)

Few documents of this nature state so directly that quality of leadership can have an impact on both the culture of the organisation and the performance of staff. However, specific references to characteristics of effective leaders seemed to place the burden of the outcomes on the leader, rather than on a cooperative effort by leaders and their teams.

Managers could include a diagram to demonstrate that the full spectrum of HR policies and practices, such as workforce planning, job design, staff selection and placement, developing and managing staff, performance management, review and recognition processes, are incorporated. Note how the components and actions have a direct effect and link to other actions. The manager needs to indicate in either the diagram or its detailed discussion how diversity management is incorporated in each policy and set of practices. Some organisations include the use of performance measures to test progress, and a few also specify the relevant performance measures within each component.

A manager could present the information in terms of best practice or of objectives, immediate tasks and indicators to measure progress. This will enhance staff members' comprehension and acceptance of such a document.

Managers could investigate whether key elements of effective HR strategy can be identified in their policies and systems. They could:

- acknowledge the impact of the outside environment, for example the needs of customers or clients
- note the dynamics of internal and external labour markets, for example references to workforce planning and professional development
- have a long-range rather than a short-range focus to continuous improvement
- emphasise the significance of choice and decision making in strategic activity by noting, for example, consumer choice or staff responsibility for personal development
- consider involving all levels of staff, leaders and managers
- integrate a human resource framework and strategies within the overall corporate or organisational and functional strategies and policies
- note that planning is contingent on changing strategic priorities; that implementing plans may be more difficult than initially anticipated; that paradoxes in planning may occur and need to be acknowledged; and that various stakeholders may have to be consulted during the planning process.

Implications for employees

Employees in multicultural or monocultural organisations need to monitor the degree to which organisational policy on strategy, SHRM and diversity management emphasises the interdependence between management and staff. For example, staff might be consulted during policy develop-ment or review. Documents usually include statements about the responsibility of management for providing acceptable work environments and sufficient support to staff. Staff could be afforded the opportunity to plan their own performance and development within the organisation. However, care must be taken not to create the impression that the burden of responsibility for their development is only on staff, but rather that it is the outcome of a process of consultation.

Implications for organisations, managers and employees

Managers need to establish whether their organisations have formulated strategic priorities that will sustain them in the next decade. They can assist organisations to design and implement a range of SHRM policies and programs to ensure that they provide high-quality services to their staff, customers and the community. One of their aims will be to create a commitment to developing a competent team of leaders, managers and staff members. Their organisational strategy, human resource and performance management framework and strategic policies must align with the relevant Acts, public sector directions or private sector benchmarks and a government's employment and management framework. Managers could ensure they gain the support of important stakeholders and assist colleagues and staff to play a critical role in designing and implementing SHRM and diversity policies and practices that align with the strategic priorities of their organisation.

This author's view is that an organisation's attitude towards change and SHRM creates the context in which diversity is managed in the company. A company's policies and beliefs about the management of diversity gradually evolve over time, developing unique benchmarks to track the process. Finally, researchers should acknowledge Prasad et al.'s (1997) concern that:

Only by examining the social, political, cultural and historical context in which workplace diversity has evolved can academics and practitioners move beyond a managerialist discourse which all too frequently seeks to obscure, conceal, and deny the real human differences that inhabit today's organisations, and which seem to equate diversity management with 'learning to get along' in organisations that have theoretically been sanitised. (p. 373)

References

Adler, NJ (1997) *International Dimensions of Organisational Behaviour.* Cincinatti, OH: South Western Publishing.

Adler, NJ, and Izraeli, DN (1994) Competitive frontiers: women managers in a global economy. Cambridge, MA: Blackwell Business.

Albrecht, MH (2001) *International HRM: Managing Diversity in the Workplace.* Oxford: Blackwell Business.

Anthony, W, Perrew, P, and Kacmar, K (1999) *Human Resource Management: A Strategic Approach.* Fort Worth, TX: The Dryden Press.

Baron, JM, and Kreps, DM (1999) Consistent human resource practices. *California Management Review*, 41 (3) 25–53.

Briggs, J, and Peat, FD (1999) *Seven Lessons of Chaos: Timeless Wisdom from the Science of Change.* St Leonards, NSW: Allen & Unwin.

Briscoe, DR (1995) *International Human Resource Management.* Englewood Cliffs, NJ: Prentice Hall.

Clegg, S, Ibarra-Colado, E, and Rodriquez, L (Eds) (1999) *Global Management: Universal Theories and Local Realities.* London: Sage, pp. 1–16.

Cox, T, and Blake, S (1991) Managing cultural diversity: implications for organizational competitiveness. *Academy of Management Executive*, 5 (3) 45–56.

Cox, T (1993) *Cultural Diversity in Organizations.* San Francisco: Berret-Koehler Publishers.

Cox, T (2001) The multicultural organisation. In MH Albrecht, *International HRM: Managing Diversity in the Workplace.* Oxford: Blackwell Business.

David, FR (2001) *Strategic Management Concepts* (8th ed.). Englewood Cliffs, NJ: Prentice Hall.

D'Netto, B, Smith, D, and Da Gama Pinto, C (2000) Diversity management: benefits, challenges and strategies. *Proceedings of the 21st Century Business: Delivering the Diversity Dividend Conference.* Department of Immigration and Multicultural Affairs, Commonwealth of Australia, CD-ROM 1–80. Melbourne, 11–12 November.

Docker, J, and Fischer, G (2000) *Race, Colour and Identity in Australia and New Zealand.* Sydney: University of New South Wales Press, 1–20.

Dunphy, D, and Griffiths, A (1998) *The Sustainable Corporation: Organisational Renewal in Australia.* St Leonards, NSW: Allen & Unwin.

Erwee, R (2000) Education Victoria: Managing and valuing diversity policy and guidelines. Report no. 2. Toowoomba: University of Southern Queensland, 1–9.

Erwee, R, and Innes, P (1998) Diversity management in Australian organisations. *Proceedings of the 12th ANZAM International conference*, CD-ROM 1–8. Adelaide, 6–9 December.

Erwee, R, Palamara, A, and Maguire, B (2000) The process of designing a self-assessment strategy for diversity management. In R Dunford (Ed.), The leap ahead: managing for the new millennium. *Proceedings of the Australian and New Zealand Academy of Management*, Macquarie Graduate School of Management, CD-ROM 1–10. Sydney, 4–6 December.

Erwee, R, Perry, C, and Tidwell, P (1999) Forming and maintaining interorganisational business networks. *Proceedings of the Pan Pacific Conference XVI*, Fiji, 31 May–3 June.

Esty, K, Griffin, R, and Hirsch, MS (1995) *Workplace Diversity.* Holbrook: Adams Media Corporation.

Fernandez, C (1997) 'Avoid EEO flak over promotions'. *Government Executive*, March, 29 (3) 47.

Gardenswartz, L, and Rowe, A (1993) *Managing Diversity.* New York: Business One, Irwin Pfeiffer & Company.

Gleick, J (1998) *Chaos: The Amazing Science of the Unpredictable.* London: Vintage.

Griggs, LB, and Louw, L (1995) *Valuing Diversity: New Tools for a New Reality.* New York: McGraw-Hill.

Heaton, R (2000) The operationalisation of strategic human resource management in a large public service organisation. Unpublished honours dissertation, University of Southern Queensland.

Hernandez, JP (1993) *The Diversity Advantage.* New York: Lexington Books.

Hofstede, G (1991) *Cultures and Organisations: Software of the Mind.* London: McGraw-Hill.

Hofstede, G (1993) Cultural constraints in management theories. *Academy of Management Executive*, 7 (1) 81–94.

Hofstede, G (2001) Difference and danger: cultural profiles of nations and limits to tolerance. In MH Albrecht, *International HRM: Managing Diversity in the Workplace.* Oxford: Blackwell Business.

Hubbard, G (2000) *Strategic Management: Thinking, Analysis and Action.* Frenchs Forest, NSW: Pearson Education.

Jackson, SE, and Ruderman, MN (Eds) (1997) *Diversity in Work Teams: Research Paradigms for a Changing Workplace.* Washington: American Psychological Association.

Kramar, R (2001) Managing diversity: contemporary challenges and issues. In R Wiesner and B Millett (Eds), *Contemporary Challenges in Organisational Behaviour.* Brisbane: John Wiley & Sons.

Kramar, R, McGraw, P, and Schuler, RS (1997) *Human Resource Management in Australia* (3rd ed.). Melbourne: Addison-Wesley Longman.

Merry, U (1999) The Information Age, New Science and Organizations, Part Two, cited in Heaton (2001, p. 32).

Millett, B (1999) *Strategic Human Resource Planning*, Study Book GSN216, University of Southern Queensland, Toowoomba.

Mills, AJ, and Hatfield, J (1999) From imperialism to globalisation: internationalisation and the management text. In S Clegg, E Ibarra-Colado and L Rodriquez (Eds), *Global Management: Universal Theories and Local Realities*. London: Sage.

Nankervis, A, Compton, RL, and McCarthy, TM (1999) *Strategic Human Resource Management* (3rd ed.). Mebourne: Nelson ITP.

Prasad, P, Mills, AJ, Elmes, M, and Prasad, A (1997) *Managing the Organisational Melting Pot: Dilemmas of Diversity*. Thousand Oaks, CA: Sage.

Schuler, R, Dowling, PJ, and De Cieri, H (1993) An integrative framework of strategic international human resource management. *Journal of Management*, 19 (2) 419–59.

Sinclair, A (1996) *Journey without Maps: Transforming Management Education*. Published inaugural professorial lecture delivered at the Melbourne Business School, University of Melbourne, 23 April.

Sinclair, A (1998) *Doing Leadership Differently: Gender, Power and Sexuality in a Changing Business Culture*. Carlton South: Melbourne University Press.

Smith, D (1998) The business case for diversity. *Monash Mt Eliza Business Review*. 1 (3) 72–81.

Stone, RJ (1995) *Human Resource Management* (2nd ed.). Brisbane: John Wiley & Sons.

Thomas, RR Jr. (1991) *Beyond Race and Gender*. New York: Amacom.

Walker, JW (2001) Are we global yet? In MH Albrecht (Ed.), *International HRM: Managing Diversity in the Workplace*. Oxford: Blackwell.

CHAPTER 7

Creating the HRM context for knowledge management

by Lesley Willcoxson
University of Southern Queensland

Introduction

It is now a cliché to point to knowledge as the new organisational wealth and the fulcrum of success in the global economy. OECD figures indicate that the service sector is playing an increasingly significant role in the economy, and competitive advantage is increasingly tied to innovation even in previously labour-intensive sectors such as agriculture, mining and manufacturing (Burton-Jones 1999). In 'a shift in the locus of economic power as profound as that which occurred at the time of the Industrial Revolution', knowledge has displaced labour, materials and money as the key input into organisations' income-generation processes (Burton-Jones 1999, p. 3). Intangible intellectual resources, it is argued, will underpin the future wealth and power of both organisations and individuals (Sveiby 1997; Burton-Jones 1999; Horibe 1999).

The recognition of knowledge as a discrete resource, and the consequent shift in focus from manpower to brainpower, has generated many prescriptions designed to assist learning and development of the capacity for learning. After the 1980s' team focus of *total quality management* (Deming 1982), in the 1990s came the wider focus implied in the notion of the *learning organisation* (Senge 1990) and the revitalised interest in *organisational learning* (Argyris & Schön 1996). From the late 1990s, following Leonard-Barton's (1995) and Nonaka and Takeuchi's (1995) lead, effective knowledge management became the goal of many organisations, and a clear focus for human resource management (HRM) efforts. Just as managers of human resources were urged to review recruitment and selection and career management processes, compensation and performance management systems, and training and development strategies when seeking to build learning organisations or achieve organisational learning, so now they are again being urged to engage these aspects of HRM for the achievement of effective knowledge management.

If organisations have already engaged in HRM activities designed to produce learning organisations and promote organisational learning, however, why is there now a need for knowledge management? One possible answer is a claim that learning organisations, organisational learning and knowledge management are merely sequential 'management fads' to which HRM is responding. However, this claim ignores the evidence that during the past decade learning and knowledge have been a (if not *the*) key source of competitive advantage (Binney 2001), and consequently there have been many serious attempts within organisations to increase organisational capacity to recognise, develop and use knowledge (Starkey & McKinlay 1996; Tushman & Nadler 1996). Many HRM practitioners have already devoted considerable effort and expertise to creating the conditions for learning within organisations (Mumford 1996); yet, despite this prior investment in the development of learning capacity, knowledge management has still found a place on the HRM agenda. Perhaps it is hoped that if organisations have not yet learnt how to learn, knowledge management may provide a viable alternative. But can it? What lessons for the implementation of knowledge management can be learned from the apparent failures to achieve organisational learning or develop learning organisations?

In this chapter we look first at the concepts of organisational learning and the learning organisation, and relate these to the concept of knowledge management. Having established similarities and differences between the three concepts, we review the reported reasons for failure to achieve organisational learning or create a learning organisation. Next we briefly examine the HRM strategies identified as conducive to the achievement of a learning organisation or organisational learning and, against this background, we examine the HRM strategies associated with effective knowledge management within organisations. Drawing on the reasons given for failures to achieve learning in organisations, we derive additional conclusions about the HRM strategies needed to promote knowledge management. In conclusion, we briefly discuss the implications for employees of organisational moves to manage knowledge more effectively.

Charting the territory: learning organisations, organisational learning and knowledge management

Despite significant variations in use of the concepts by different writers (Garavan 1997), and a tendency to use the terms interchangeably, broadly speaking *organisational learning* refers to processes or activities through which an organisation learns, while a *learning organisation* is an organisational form (Ortenblad 2001) defined by the capacity to learn and outcomes of learning. As initially conceived by Senge, the learning organisation has a strongly humanist orientation, being a place where

> people continually expand their capacity to create the results they truly desire, where new and expansive patterns of thinking are nurtured, where collective aspiration is set free, and where people are continually learning how to learn together. (Senge 1990, p. 2)

In Senge's (1990, pp. 6–11) model, the learning organisation is achieved through personal mastery ('clarifying and deepening personal vision, focusing energy, developing patience and seeing reality objectively'), awareness of mental models (assumptions and generalisations that affect ways of seeing and interacting with 'the world'), building a shared vision (leadership that develops commitment through shared 'pictures of the future'), team learning (dialogue leading to creative thought and recognition of patterns that undermine learning), and systems thinking (an awareness of

the intrinsic interconnectedness of people, processes and events). The learning organisation makes 'intentional use of learning processes at individual, group and system level to continuously transform the organisation in a direction that is increasingly satisfying to its stakeholders' (Dixon 1994, p. 5). The learning organisation as Senge conceives of it, however, is an idealised organisational form, for as Kofman and Senge point out:

> when we speak of a 'learning organization' we are not describing an external phenomenon or labelling an independent reality...we are taking a stand for a vision, for creating a type of organization we would truly like to work within and which can thrive in a world of increasing interdependency and change. (1995, p. 32)

Despite Kofman and Senge's disclaimer about its potential for realisation, several subsequent writers have built on Senge's original concept to produce alternative pictures of learning organisations and suggestions about how a learning organisation might be developed. Watkins and Marsick (1993, p. 11), for example, provide a practice-oriented, people-focused sketch of the learning organisation. In their view, the learning organisation is defined by and dependent on structures and processes that:

- create continuous learning opportunities
- promote inquiry and dialogue
- encourage collaboration and team learning
- establish systems to capture and share learning
- empower people toward a collective vision
- connect the organisation to its environment.

Dixon (1994, 1998), who eschews use of the term 'learning organisation' and refers instead to 'an organisation that is learning', takes a similarly people-focused approach to the learning organisation, emphasising the need for dialogue, continuous and collaborative learning, and involvement in organisational governance processes. Garvin (1993), however, defines the learning organisation in far more instrumental terms than those employed by Senge (1990) or Watkins and Marsick (1993). In a portent of things to come (under the banner of knowledge management), he describes a learning organisation as 'an organization skilled at creating, acquiring, and transferring knowledge, and at modifying its behaviour to reflect new knowledge and insights' (Garvin 1993, p. 80). Again foreshadowing the concerns of knowledge management practitioners and theorists, the activities that Garvin (1993) identifies as essential for the creation of his learning organisation are systematic problem solving, experimentation, learning from the organisation's experience and history, learning from other organisations and best practice, and transferring knowledge efficiently and effectively.

Despite the tendency of many writers to relate organisational learning to processes claimed as necessary to achieve a 'learning organisation' (e.g. Garvin 1993; Fulmer et al. 1998; Reynolds & Ablett 1998), Argyris and Schön's (1978) original conception of organisational learning focused on examining the quality and long-term sustainability of learning in an organisation. Unlike discussions of organisational learning focused on utilising specified strategies to promote learning (Dixon 1994), their description of organisational learning provided a lens through which to examine the nature and long-term productiveness of learning in an organisation. They argued for the existence of three levels of learning: *single loop learning*, characterised by correction of errors but no fundamental change to the underlying system; *double loop learning*, characterised by questioning of the assumptions that gave rise to the error and subsequent change to the system; and *deutero double loop learning*, which relates to meta-cognition or learning how to learn (Argyris & Schön 1978).

Argyris and Schön's assumption was that individual learning underpins organisational learning, but organisational learning is the collective learning and action of groups of individuals on behalf of the organisation. The combination of collective and individual learning leads to change in collective (organisational) theories about how things should be done (Argyris 1999), and to the embedding of this learning into changed organisational routines (March 1999). Both Argyris (1999) and March (1999), however, point to the potential for organisational learning impairments to result in flawed learning. March (1999) describes the tendency for individuals and organisations to use lessons from their own history to develop increased competency in established procedures even when these procedures are fundamentally flawed. He also points to the tendency to interpret or rewrite history so that it conforms to existing values or can be construed as evidence of the success of those who hold power. Argyris (1999) describes 'organisational defensive routines' that serve to prevent embarrassment or threat to individuals with power and status to the extent that anticipated results may be reported even when factual evidence is available to contradict these reports. In other words, irrespective of the strategies put in place by organisations to foster learning, it may be assumed that in most organisations there are forces actively (if unconsciously) working to prevent learning for the purpose of conserving power and maintaining the status quo.

As will be discussed later in this chapter, the issue of defensive routines has profound implications for the success or otherwise of knowledge management initiatives, just as it has had profound implications for the success or otherwise of organisational learning and learning organisation

initiatives. However, discussion of knowledge management is currently linked to organisational learning and learning organisation literature primarily by its focus on the themes of collective learning, learning processes and learning infrastructure.

'Knowledge management' was conceived to signify (usually computer-based) management strategies for capturing, codifying and distributing organisational data and information. However, since the mid 1990s knowledge management has come to imply a focus not just on the technical capacity for distribution of data and information, but also on the education and innovation processes that lead to the creation of knowledge (McElroy 2000). This additional focus on knowledge — data and information interpreted and given meaning by people through reference to their experience, values, expertise and understanding of context (Davenport & Prusak 2000) — has led 'knowledge management' down a path that weaves across those already taken by organisational learning and the learning organisation. Indeed, several writers observe links between the concepts of knowledge management, organisational learning and the learning organisation (Godbout 1998; Harrison 1998; McAdam & McCreedy 1999), and one commentator describes knowledge management as 'a kind of implementation strategy for OL — a tool kit for how to get there from here if what you want is to be a learning organization' (McElroy 2000, p. 200). Such links are easily made because much writing about organisational learning, learning organisations and knowledge management is characterised by either limited or no definition of terms. Nevertheless, various aspects of knowledge management have clear parallels in concepts of the learning organisation or organisational learning.

As with organisational learning and the learning organisation, the keys to unlocking the gateway to effective knowledge management are described in one of three different ways — using knowledge category models, socially constructed models or intellectual capital models (McAdam & McCreedy 1999). Early writers on knowledge management and on learning in organisations have tended to describe it primarily in terms of:

- an understanding of learning processes (compare Nonaka & Takeuchi's (1995) focus on tacit versus explicit knowledge with Dixon's (1994) organisational learning cycle)
- an understanding of learning as a social phenomenon (compare Wenger's (1998) communities of practice with Senge's (1990) utopian focus on learning communities)
- in terms of the organisational elements that need to be mobilised to achieve desired outcomes (e.g. compare intellectual capital models of knowledge management (Klein 1998) with Garvin's (1993) prescription for the learning organisation).

However, as Pan and Scarbrough's (1999) analysis of the knowledge management initiatives at Buckman Laboratories shows, successful knowledge management requires understanding and action in all three areas, which these authors neatly summarise (moving progressively from the technical, objective to the socially determined, subjective) as infrastructure, infostructure and infoculture. Increasingly, writers on knowledge management are drawing together the various threads of the knowledge management discussion. Davenport and Prusak (2000), for example, point to the need for a knowledge-oriented culture, a technical and organisational infrastructure, and a process orientation based on an understanding of the steps involved in achieving knowledge management.

It is perhaps because the most recent discussion on knowledge management offers diverse points of entry, diverse foci for activity and diverse desirable outcomes that knowledge management has been able to take centre stage and push its more esoteric yet often more prescriptive relatives into the wings. While knowledge management may be conceptualised as an entire organisation development strategy involving infrastructure, infostructure and infoculture, it may equally be conceptualised as the establishment of communities of practice in a limited area of 'knowledge work', or as the building of technical infrastructure related to specific identified organisational needs such as analysis, asset management, development or innovation (Binney 2001). For example, while Buckman Laboratories took a holistic approach to knowledge management (Pan & Scarbrough 1999), organisations such as Anglian Water (Mayo 1998) and British Telecom have focused on developing communities of practice among specifically targeted research groups, and many more organisations have invested in the building of technological infrastructure. Compared with the organisational learning and learning organisation concepts, knowledge management thus offers its proponents within organisations a more manageable implementation task and more clearly identifiable and measurable targets, yet it also holds out the possibility of human development within organisations (albeit in a less idealised context than that offered by the learning organisation).

In summary, there are clear parallels between the concepts and practices associated with the learning organisation, organisational learning and knowledge management, although knowledge management appears to offer practitioners more flexibility in determining the focus of activity and therefore more capacity to establish limited, achievable targets. Although the establishment of limited targets related to the implementation of knowledge-capturing infrastructure or learning processes (infostructure) undoubtedly go some way towards achieving good knowledge management, it is

the development of an appropriate infoculture — a culture of knowledge sharing — that unlocks the final door to fully effective knowledge management. Given the parallels already established, discussion of the behavioural impediments to the development of learning organisations or the achievement of organisational learning may thus provide helpful insights into barriers likely to block the implementation of knowledge management strategies. The following section therefore explores impediments to learning by and within organisations as a precursor to examining HRM strategies that may be used to overcome these impediments and assist in the development of effective knowledge management.

Challenges and impediments to learning by and within organisations

Fragmentation, reactiveness and competition

Reflecting on the impediments to learning by organisations and within organisations, Kofman and Senge (1995) identify factors that they argue also form the basis of learning disabilities in society as a whole, namely:
- fragmentation, resulting from linear thinking, specialisation and independent, warring fiefdoms within the organisation
- reactiveness, reflecting a fixation on problem solving, rather than creation and innovation
- competition, creating an environment in which looking good is more important than being good; measurable, short-term gains count more than long-term achievement; and problems are solved by individuals in isolation.

Such learning disabilities are probably immediately recognisable to employees within organisations divided along functional lines. Functional areas gain their status and power from the division of knowledge into distinct, specialist areas, which often fight each other for recognition and funds. Modes of inquiry in most organisations are dominated by rational/analytical problem solving, possibly because problem solving provides more easily measurable outcomes, but this orientation towards rational analysis often leads to the neglect of intuition and creativity, which may provide far more effective tools for radical change or development.

In many areas of public sector enterprise, exemplified by higher education, competition between institutions is encouraged by external political pressures and funding processes, leading to institutional separation and an emphasis on quantity rather than quality of production. Often, in the public sector, government-imposed quality measurements focus on processes, but the lack of triangulation of processes with inputs and outputs may result in institutional process 'window-dressing' in time for inspection. In both the public and private sectors, the absence of triangulation or effective measures of quality in many areas of professional endeavour (such as leadership or management) results in individual claims for selection or promotion being based on looking good rather than being good, and on demonstration of short-term achievements rather than long-term development and change. Despite the increasing emphasis on teamwork in recent years, within most organisations career progress and financial rewards still accrue to individuals in competition with others; thus, there is little incentive for these individuals to engage in collaborative learning or the sharing of knowledge. In other words, fragmentation, reactiveness and competition are hardwired into the mental and functional architecture of most organisations, and clearly these dominant structures will not be readily demolished. To these impediments to learning deriving from social norms are added challenges arising from issues of power, politics and time.

Power, politics and time

In addition to the impact of societal characteristics such as fragmentation, reactiveness and competition that militate against learning within organisations, issues of power, politics and time also fundamentally determine the amount and nature of learning that can take place. In organisations under stress, challenged to find new directions and respond to frequently changing environmental pressures as well as increased scrutiny — such as many public sector organisations — it is likely that much time will be spent on 'firefighting' and 'window dressing'. For both individuals pursuing their own career goals and groups of individuals attempting to advance organisational goals under such conditions, it is even more likely that looking good will become more important than being good, for the former can be evaluated in the short term whereas the latter requires a longer term assessment process. If rewards are perceived to accrue or do accrue on the basis of appearance rather than performance, or short-term rather than long-term achievement, there may be few incentives to engage in the behaviour necessary for learning within and by organisations.

Dunphy and Griffiths (1998) argue that the current emphasis on short-term exchanges and competing interests limits the capacity of organisations to respond effectively to a changing environment, and therefore limits their sustainability. Quoting Block (1990), they point out that 'production generally depends on some degree of stability in the relations among a group of people and it is this stability that is undermined by rapid recalculations of self interest' (Dunphy & Griffiths 1998, p. 165). Although their argument is focused on the sustainability of organisations as a whole, it has clear implications for the conduct of relationships within organisations.

Hodgkinson (2000) points to the difficulties of achieving a shared vision in the face of personal agendas, and achieving team learning when information can be used as power. Conscious and subconscious 'defensive routines', which serve to prevent embarrassment or threat to individuals with power and status, do much to preserve the status quo even when this is demonstrably antithetical to the interests of the organisation as a whole (Argyris & Schön 1996). Thus, individuals with power and status often seek to surround themselves with those who will reinforce their own perceptions and not challenge their actions; those who choose not to challenge are often pursuing an agenda of self-interest at the expense of organisational interest, but rationalise this in terms of the futility of speaking out in the face of immovable conviction (Argyris 1999).

Compounding learning impediments arising from the pursuit of self-interest or the removal of threat are structural distortions that facilitate or deny access to decision-making power and strategic influence, independent of expertise (Ryan 1995). Thus, as Ryan points out, those in the research and development sections of organisations are often kept at a distance from strategic management decisions, even when their specialist expertise could contribute vital information to the decision-making process. Similarly, those in designated senior management positions within a university may develop teaching-related policy with little input from those whose discipline expertise lies in the field of education or from those who daily confront the effects of growing student numbers and relatively decreasing resources. This failure to seek wider input into the decision-making process and the maintenance of structures that undermine learning potential can probably be explained partly by defensive routines, but also by perceptions that management and employee visions for the future are invariably different and employee input is therefore of limited value (Steiner 1998). The latter view is a reasonable argument in most organisations, since few employees at a non-management level are exposed to the type of information necessary for the creation of an organisation-wide vision that challenges their own assumptions of what 'management' is doing, could do or should be doing.

It is not easy to overcome these impediments to learning, as they have historically conditioned the interactions within organisations. Organisations seeking to capitalise on knowledge must nevertheless find strategies for overcoming these aspects of organisational behaviour that impede learning and sustainability. Given that the impediments to learning are located primarily within the sphere of personal interactions, HRM thus provides the key to unlocking organisational learning and, together with the development of appropriate technological infrastructure, the key to truly effective knowledge management.

Using HRM to develop learning in organisations and effective knowledge management

The literature on the learning organisation and organisational learning consistently identifies appropriate structures and culture as keys to unlocking the possibility of ongoing learning (Senge 1990; Watkins & Marsick 1993; Garavan 1997; Applebaum & Reichart 1998; Reynolds & Ablett 1998; Grieves 2000). Within the scope of structure, recurring themes are the need for teamwork (Senge 1990; Watkins & Marsick 1993), work across traditional functional and other boundaries, a systems approach, and organisational structures that encourage openness and bottom-up as well as top-down flows of information (Senge 1990; Watkins & Marsick 1993; Rolls 1995; Applebaum & Reichart 1998; Goh 1998; Teare & Dealtry 1998). Within the scope of culture, recurring themes are the need for involved leadership and openness, a risk-taking and action-learning approach, awareness of existing mindsets, empowerment and continuing education (Redding & Catalanello 1994; Senge 1990; Watkins & Marsick 1993; De Geus 1996; Applebaum & Reichart 1998; Teare & Dealtry 1998).

In what may serve as a summary of most of the recurring themes, Watkins and Marsick (1993, p. 8) outlined eight imperatives for the achievement of a learning organisation:
- leaders who model calculated risk taking and experimentation
- decentralised decision making and employee empowerment
- skill inventories for sharing learning and using it
- rewards and structures for employee initiatives
- consideration of long-term consequences and impact on the work of others

- frequent use of cross-functional work teams
- opportunities to learn from experience on a daily basis
- a culture of feedback and disclosure.

These themes are repeated in the knowledge management literature that extends beyond discussion of infrastructure (computer software and hardware) to consideration of a facilitating infostructure and infoculture. Although it is acknowledged that different organisational cultures will require and produce different knowledge-sharing strategies (McDermott & O'Dell 2001; Lang 2001), there is broad agreement in the knowledge management literature about the issues that underpin development of a knowledge-sharing culture. Paralleling the concerns of the learning organisation and organisational learning literature, researchers and practitioners highlight the critical roles played by senior management support and role modelling (Pan & Scarbrough 1999; Davenport & Prusak 2000; McDermott & O'Dell 2001), communities or networks of practice and learning (Brown & Duguid 2000; Davenport & Prusak 2000; Wenger 2000; Lang 2001), recognition and reward (McDermott & O'Dell 2001; Scarborough 1999), risk taking (Pan & Scarbrough 1999; Lang 2001), empowerment and trust (Pan & Scarbrough 1999; Lang 2001; Lesser & Prusak 2001), and the need for ongoing education and personal development (Davenport & Prusak 2000).

Practitioners and researchers focusing on the development of knowledge-facilitating structures point to the need for less hierarchical organisational structures (Davenport & Prusak 2000), more cross-functional teams (Master 1999), development of top-down and bottom-up information flow (Rogers & Wolff 1996), and systemic thinking (Davenport & Prusak 2000). Indicating the ways in which systemic thinking might be demonstrated, Davenport and Prusak (2000) suggest that although an organisation may choose to initiate knowledge management through any one of a number of strategies — for example the development of information-sharing technology, the sharing of best practice, the tracking of decision points, the use of accounting that takes into account intellectual capital, or organisational learning strategies — concurrent multiple approaches to knowledge management are ultimately needed:

To begin knowledge management with a focus on organizational learning would be a good idea … but it is rare for organizational learning initiatives to lead to knowledge management because many learning-oriented organizations ignore the possibilities for structuring and leveraging knowledge. Only a few firms, such as Coca-Cola and Monsanto, are working simultaneously on organizational learning issues and the more tangible knowledge management issues. (Davenport & Prusak 2000, p. 169)

The challenge thrown out by Davenport and Prusak to HRM specialists is to develop an understanding of knowledge management infrastructure and then look beyond standard HR learning organisation change strategies to become active partners in developing the infostructure and infoculture necessary for effective knowledge management. The parallel concerns of the learning organisation/organisational learning and the knowledge management literatures suggest that HR practitioners are already aware of the infostructure and infoculture issues involved in developing knowledge within organisations. Despite this, results of several European surveys indicate that HR departments are the least likely of all organisational functions to be involved in knowledge development initiatives (Geraint 1998). Such missed opportunities have clear implications not just for the credibility of HR practitioners, but also for the perceived viability of the HR function within organisations. The following sections examine the role that HR practitioners might play in developing the structures and culture necessary for effective knowledge management.

HRM and infrastructure

As a starting point for the involvement of HR practitioners in the development of knowledge management initiatives, the development of some understanding of knowledge management infrastructure is essential. Only with this understanding does it become possible for HR practitioners to communicate effectively with potential partners in knowledge development, such as IT specialists, and make a case for partnership in the development of knowledge strategies. Only with this understanding does it become possible for HR practitioners to envisage the particular HR strategies necessary to leverage and capture knowledge within an organisation, for neither HR strategies nor technological strategies alone are sufficient to achieve this end. Binney's (2001) diagrammatic representation of the relationship between knowledge management technology and applications provides guidance for HR practitioners on how

	Transactional	Analytical	Asset management	Process	Developmental	Innovation and creation
Knowledge management applications	• Case-based reasoning (CBR) • Help desk applications • Customer service applications • Order entry applications • Service agent support applications	• Data warehousing • Data mining • Business intelligence • Management information systems • Decision support systems • Customer relationship management (CRM) • Competitive intelligence	• Intellectual property • Document management • Knowledge valuation • Knowledge repositories • Content management	• TQM • Benchmarking • Best practices • Quality management • Business process (re)engineering • Process improvement • Process automation • Lessons learned • Methodology • SENCMM ISO9XXX, Six Sigma	• Skills development • Staff competencies • Learning • Teaching • Training	• Communities • Collaboration • Discussion forums • Networking • Virtual teams • Research and development • Multidisciplined teams
Enabling technologies	• Expert systems • Cognitive technologies • Semantic networks • Rule-based expert systems • Probability networks • Rule induction, Decision trees • Geospatial information systems	• Intelligent agents • Web crawlers • Relational and object DBMS • Neural computing • Push technologies • Data analysis and reporting tools	• Document management tools • Search engines • Knowledge maps • Library systems	• Workflow management • Process modelling tools	• Computer-based training • Online training	• Groupware • E-mail • Chat rooms • Video conferencing • Search engines • Voice mail • Bulletin boards • Push technologies • Simulation technologies
	• Portals, Internet, Intranets, Extranets					

Figure 7.1: The KM Spectrum: Knowledge management technologies and applications *Source:* D Binney (2001).

technological infrastructure might be used to support the human infrastructure necessary to achieve effective knowledge management.

It is to discussion of the human infrastructure — the infostructure and infoculture — that this chapter now turns.

HRM, infostructure and infoculture

It has been suggested that, as a result of the implementation of learning organisation and organisational learning concepts, HR practitioners have a well-developed repertoire of strategies able to be used to assist in the development of the infostructure (learning processes) and infoculture necessary for effective knowledge management. Indeed, many suggestions for HR approaches to knowledge management look suspiciously like recycled learning organisation approaches. There is, however, a significant difference between learning organisation approaches and knowledge management approaches to HR. Whereas the former have the ubiquitous goal of increasing learning within an organisation and usually offer a systematic, all-or-nothing approach to implementation, knowledge management approaches to HR inevitably draw upon similar strategies but the goals are more circumscribed, making them more implementable in sections of an organisation and, at least superficially, more achievable. Thus, even though Davenport and Prusak (2000) talk about the need for systemic thinking, they are able to provide a limited set of HR strategies for enhancing knowledge management, with each strategy related to a specific desired infostructure or infoculture outcome. These strategies are:

- *building relationships and trust* through face-to-face meetings
- *creating common ground* through education, discussion, publications, teamwork and job rotation
- *establishing times and places for knowledge transfer*, such as knowledge fairs, talk rooms or conference reports
- *building knowledge and increasing knowledge sharing* by evaluating performance and providing incentives based on sharing
- *developing knowledge absorption capacity* by educating employees for flexibility, providing time for learning, hiring for openness to ideas
- *creating widespread knowledge-building and innovation capacity* by dissociating the prerogative to know from specified groups and ensuring that the quality of ideas is recognised as more important than the status of the source
- *building risk-taking and collaborative capacity* by accepting and rewarding creative errors and collaboration.

The other major but often neglected distinguishing feature of HR approaches to knowledge management is the requirement that knowledge development and retention be linked to technological strategies for knowledge management. Thus, while the learning organisation literature may provide a useful base for the development of HR approaches to knowledge management, the facilitating role of technology needs to be recognised. The challenge for HR practitioners is to identify what alliances can be formed between human and technological infrastructures in order to enhance the effectiveness of each and, ultimately, to deliver added value to the organisation. Binney's (2001) schema, reproduced opposite, gives an indication of the relationships that may be drawn between technology and human resource management. The following discussion will therefore focus primarily on aspects of HRM that can be used to promote knowledge management, but it will also make reference to facilitating technology as appropriate.

Leadership for knowledge sharing

Critical to the development of effective knowledge management is the development of a knowledge-sharing culture and the support and role modelling for knowledge sharing provided by those in designated leadership positions. A tale circulating in British Telecom sums up the issues involved in knowledge sharing. Touring the research facility, a senior manager observed a research scientist sitting under his desk holding a document he was working on close to his chest. When she asked what he was doing the researcher replied, 'Last time I came up with a good idea my superior looked over my shoulder, stole the idea, used it as his own and I didn't get any credit, so this time I'm making sure no one can see what I'm doing and steal my ideas' (Fitzgerald 2002).

Leadership for knowledge management involves not only a demonstrated willingness to facilitate the sharing of knowledge by others, but also a commitment to ethical behaviour and to personally sharing valuable knowledge rather than hoarding it and using it for personal power.

The effective knowledge leader is therefore, like the leader of the learning organisation, not necessarily a charismatic visionary able to enthuse others for learning, but rather a collaborating designer (of organisational values, policies, strategies and learning), a steward (who leads by explicitly and visibly serving the interests of the organisational and wider community) and a teacher (who helps others discover their assumptions about the world and develop their full potential) (Senge 1996; Tichy & Cohen 1998). The effective knowledge-sharing leader is motivated primarily by what Sashkin (1992) describes as a 'prosocial power motive' — that is, the desire to foster the interests of the organisation and its staff over and above self-interest. The effective knowledge leader is also open to bottom-up flows of information and ideas, not just top-down flows of information, and puts in place strategies to achieve this.

Appropriate selection processes can go some way towards ensuring appropriate leadership and enhancing the knowledge-sharing capacity of an organisation, and training and development can go some way towards enhancing the knowledge-sharing capacities of leaders throughout an organisation. However, as has been discussed with reference to the learning organisation, impediments to learning and sharing — competition, fragmentation and reactiveness — are hardwired into the mental and functional architecture of most organisations. Unless these issues are addressed in a systemic fashion, starting at the top but also at the bottom, it is likely that the experience of the British Telecom research scientist will be duplicated in other organisations over and over again, rendering other knowledge management tools ineffectual. Fundamental to the facilitation of knowledge sharing, therefore, is a focus on long-term rather than short-term performance, the giving of rewards for sharing and for being good rather than looking good, the creation of meaningful links between diverse organisational functions, and the development of leadership characterised by open inquiry, testing of assumptions and minimisation of 'defensive routines'. In the absence of these characteristics, HRM or technological strategies may be used to facilitate limited knowledge management processes and outcomes, and to put 'runs on the board' for IT or HR practitioners. However, knowledge management, like the learning organisation, will fail to reach its potential organisational utility unless HR practitioners also use their HR tools to develop a fundamental organisational capacity for learning and knowledge sharing. This is, of course, not an easy undertaking, for it exposes HR practitioners to questioning of their own assumptions and implies the danger of assisting those in leadership positions to also question their own assumptions (Argyris 2000). Nevertheless, long-term and full effectiveness in knowledge management is necessarily underwritten by the removal of impediments to learning and sharing, so HR practitioners need to keep their eyes not just on the immediate scoring opportunities but also on whole game strategies.

HRM for knowledge sharing

While ongoing development of leadership for knowledge sharing plays a vital role in organisational knowledge management capacity, HR practitioners have to do more than develop strategies for encouraging knowledge sharing. They need also to proactively make a case for their involvement in knowledge management, and this case needs to be made on the basis of a clear business imperative for the sharing of knowledge (McDermott & O'Dell 2001). Subsequently, development of knowledge sharing capacity has to be embedded in all HR activities. Thus, selection processes need to be used to investigate the knowledge-sharing orientation of would-be employees, and compensation, performance management and promotion systems need to encourage and reward ongoing sharing as well as ongoing implementation of the outcomes of learning. Performance appraisal can be used to require and track the willingness of employees to share knowledge, use knowledge and engage in collaborative learning. This willingness may be demonstrated and tracked not only by recording contributions to communities of practice or cross-functional teams, but also by recording contributions made to organisational databases, electronic discussion forums or peer-assisted learning through virtual teamwork such as that used by British Petroleum (Davenport & Prusak 2000). Above all, rewards such as incentive payments and bonuses, recognition, and career progression must accrue for knowledge sharing rather than knowledge hoarding. The converse is also true: sanctions must be applied when knowledge is hoarded and used for personal gain rather than shared and used for organisational gain (Scarborough 1999). It must be recognised, however, that the measurement of knowledge sharing remains a difficult task. Sharing does not equate to clear organisational outcomes, especially in organisations where risk taking is rewarded even if it results in 'creative error'. Clearly, measurement and consequent reward or sanction cannot be the only factors impelling knowledge sharing and generation. HRM strategies must be designed to achieve an organisational culture in which sharing is an expectation.

Currently, although performance management systems have the capacity to identify and reward extraordinary performance, the individualistic focus of the systems existing in many organisations serves to reinforce barriers to sharing, teamwork and thus learning. It also serves to reinforce existing hierarchical structures and poor management through the use of one-way (up-down) review and feedback processes rather than 360° feedback processes. Hand in hand with the development of knowledge-sensitive performance management and reward systems, therefore, must also go the development of team-based organisational structures, training for effective teamwork and team-based performance management and reward. Even where a whole organisation approach to knowledge management is not feasible, HR practitioners can nevertheless play a role in the development of teamwork structures and capacity within limited contexts.

One possible approach to teamwork that has been the subject of considerable discussion in recent times is the *communities of practice* concept, which seeks to transfer to an organisation the benefits obtained by individuals through the voluntary sharing of knowledge with professional peers. The challenge for HR practitioners and others involved in setting up communities of practice, however, is that they necessitate considerable time commitment for uncertain organisational outcomes. As Brown and Duguid (2000) indicate, under conditions of perceived marginalisation, their 'stickiness' and 'leakiness' may lead to knowledge being secreted in corners inaccessible to the organisation or shared with professional peers employed by competitor organisations. More certain transfer of knowledge may occur through the use of mentoring or of cross-functional teams that come together to solve specific problems or develop creative new approaches. The work of cross-functional teams may occur face to face but may also be facilitated and documented electronically, offering the possibility of more effective retention of knowledge within the organisation. Empowerment of work teams may also be used to generate new approaches to problems as well as to increase the likelihood of a two-way rather than top-down flow of information and ideas. In each case, training for teamwork forms the linchpin of team success, but crucial to the creative and open discussion is the development of strategies to address 'defensive routines' and provide for open inquiry. While knowledge management may succeed to some extent through the use of HRM strategies designed to support teamwork and empowerment, it is likely that success will be limited and knowledge management programs will deliver less than promised unless impediments to inquiry and learning are also removed.

In summary, knowledge management, like organisational learning, holds out to organisations the potential for fully capitalising on the intangible assets implicit in the knowledge and experience of their employees. For employees, knowledge management, like organisational learning, holds out the prospect of an envigorating organisational environment in which communication would be rich and productive, personal growth would be assured and rewards would come to those who contribute most effectively. Like the learning organisation, however, knowledge management initiatives currently deliver to employees much less than promised.

In many Australian organisations, knowledge management is associated primarily with the development of technology for information sharing or with resource centre or library-based initiatives for information gathering and collation. To date only a few organisations have provided time for staff to share knowledge or supported the widespread use of knowledge databases through the provision of necessary training. Even fewer organisations have implemented HRM strategies designed to encourage knowledge development and sharing. Thus, for many employees, knowledge management initiatives offer, not a panacea for intellectual isolation or under-utilisation, but the threat of having to give away personal expertise that forms the basis of their professional standing and employability.

For employees, there will continue to be little incentive to share knowledge unless issues of teamwork, recognition, reward and defensive routines are dealt with, and thus organisations will continue to make less effective use of their intellectual and knowledge assets than they might. As Lesser and Prusak (2001) observe, too often valuable organisational knowledge walks out the door during periods of downsizing, not just because organisations have in place no strategies for pre-exit knowledge transfer, but also because the organisational climate during periods of downsizing makes knowledge hoarding emotionally desirable. At any time it is impossible to estimate how much knowledge is being hoarded to be used as a saleable commodity either internally for career advancement purposes or externally when in pursuit of alternative employment opportunities. The real challenge for HRM practitioners is not simply to implement HR strategies designed to support good knowledge management. It is to understand the human factors that work to subvert the effective implementation of these strategies and to produce new strategies designed to address these deeper issues of organisational culture.

References

Applebaum, S, and Reichart, W (1998) How to measure an organization's learning ability: a learning orientation: part 1. *Journal of Workplace Learning,* 10 (1) 15–28.

Argyris, C (1999) *On Organisational Learning.* Oxford: Blackwell Business.

Argyris, C, and Schön, D (1978) *Organisational Learning.* Reading, MA: Addison-Wesley.

Argyris, C, and Schön, D (1996) *Organisational Learning II.* Reading, MA: Addison-Wesley.

Binney, D (2001) The knowledge management spectrum — understanding the KM landscape. *Journal of Knowledge Management,* 5 (1) 33–42.

Brown, JS, and Duguid, P (2000) *The Social Life of Information.* Boston, MA: Harvard Business School Press.

Burton-Jones, A (1999) *Knowledge Capitalism.* Oxford: Oxford University Press.

Coopey, J (1996) Crucial gaps in 'the Learning Organization': power, politics and ideology. In K Starkey (Ed.), *How Organizations Learn*. London: International Thomson Business Press.

Davenport, T, and Prusak, L (2000) *Working Knowledge: How Organisations Manage What They Know*. Boston, MA: Harvard Business School Press.

De Geus, A (1996) Planning as learning. In K Starkey (Ed.), *How Organizations Learn*. London: International Thomson Business Press.

Deming, W (1982) *Quality, Productivity, and Competitive Advantage*. Cambridge, MA: MIT Center for Advanced Engineering Study.

Dixon, N (1994) *The Organizational Learning Cycle: How We Can Learn Collectively*. London: McGraw-Hill.

Dixon, N (1998) The responsibilities of members in an organization that is learning. *The Learning Organization: A Review and Evaluation*, 5 (4) 161–7.

Dunphy, D, and Griffiths, A (1998) *The Sustainable Corporation*. Sydney: Allen & Unwin.

Fitzgerald, E (2002) A critique of the role of communities of practice in knowledge sharing (forthcoming paper).

Fulmer, R, Gibbs, P, and Keys, J (1998) The second generation learning organizations: new tools for sustaining competitive advantage. *Organisational Dynamics*, 27 (2) 6–21.

Garavan, T (1997) The learning organization: a review and evaluation. *The Learning Organization*, 4 (1).

Garvin, D (1993) Building a learning organization. *Harvard Business Review*, 71 (4) 78–91.

Geraint, J (1998) Share strength. *People Management*, 4 (16) 44–7.

Godbout, A (1998) An integrative approach to effective knowledge management. *Optimum*, 28 (2) 11–19.

Goh, S (1998) Toward a learning organization: the strategic building blocks. *SAM Advanced Management Journal*, 63 (2) 15–20.

Grieves, J (2000) Navigating change into the new millennium: themes and issues for the learning organization. *The Learning Organization*, 7 (2).

Harrison, R (1998) Intellectual assets. *People Management*, 4 (5) 33.

Hodgkinson, M (2000) Managerial perceptions of barriers to becoming a 'learning organization'. *The Learning Organization*, 7 (3) 156–67.

Horibe, F (1999) *Managing Knowledge Workers: New Skills and Attitudes to Unlock the Intellectual Capital in Your Organization*. Toronto: John Wiley & Sons.

Klein, D (Ed.) (1998) The Strategic Management of Intellectual Capital. Boston, MA: Butterworth-Heinemann.

Kofman, F, and Senge, P (1995) Communities of commitment: the heart of learning organizations. In S Chawla and J Renesch (Eds), *Learning Organizations*. Oregon: Productivity Press.

Lang, JC (2001) Managerial concerns in knowledge management. *Journal of Knowledge Management*, 5 (1) 43–57.

Leonard-Barton, D (1995) *Wellsprings of Knowledge: Building and Sustaining the Sources of Innovation*. Boston, MA: Harvard Business School Press.

Lesser, E, and Prusak, L (2001) Preserving knowledge in an uncertain world. *MIT Sloan Management Review*, 43 (1).

March, J (1999) *The Pursuit of Organisational Intelligence*. Oxford: Blackwell Business.

Mayo, A (1998) Memory bankers. *People Management*, 4 (2) 34–8.

McAdam, R, and McCreedy, S (1999) A critical review of knowledge management models. *The Learning Organization*, 6 (3) 91–101.

McDermott, R, and O'Dell, C (2001) Overcoming cultural barriers to sharing knowledge. *Journal of Knowledge Management*, 5 (1) 76–86.

McElroy, M (2000) Integrating complexity theory, knowledge management and organisational learning. *Journal of Knowledge Management*, 4 (3) 195–203.

Mumford, A. (1996) Creating a learning environment. *Journal of Professional Human Resource Management*, 4, 26–30.

Nonaka, I, and Takeuchi, H (1995) *The Knowledge-Creating Company*. New York: Oxford University Press.

Ortenblad, A (2001) On differences between organizational learning and learning organizations. *The Learning Organization*, 8 (3) 125–33.

Pan, S, and Scarborough, H (1999) Knowledge management in practice: an exploratory case study. *Technology Analysis and Strategic Management*, 11 (3) 359–74.

Redding, J, and Catalanello, R (1994) *Strategic Readiness: The Making of the Learning Organization*, San Francisco: Jossey-Bass.

Reynolds, R, and Ablett, A (1998) Transforming the rhetoric of organisational learning to the reality of the learning organization. *The Learning Organization*, 5 (1) 24–35.

Rogers, D, and Wolff, M (1996) Knowledge management gains momentum in industry. *Research Technology Management*, 39 (3): 5–7.

Rolls, J (1995) The transformational leader: the wellspring of the learning organization. In S Chawla and J Renesch (Eds), *Learning Organizations*. Oregon: Productivity Press.

Ryan, M (1995) Human resource management and the politics of knowledge: linking the essential knowledge base of the organization to strategic decision making. *Leadership and Organization Development Journal,* 16 (5) 3–10.

Sashkin, M (1992) Strategic leadership competencies. In R Phillips and J Hunt (Eds), *Strategic Leadership. A Multiorganizational-Level Perspective.* Connecticut: Quorum Books.

Scarborough, H (1999) System error. *People Management,* 5 (7) 68–72.

Senge, P (1990) *The Fifth Discipline: The Art and Practice of the Learning Organization.* Sydney: Random House.

Senge, P (1996) The leader's new work. In K Starkey (Ed.), *How Organizations Learn.* London: International Thomson Business Press.

Starkey, K, and McKinlay, A (1996) Product development in Ford of Europe. In K Starkey (Ed.), *How Organizations Learn.* London: International Thomson Business Press.

Steiner, L (1998) Organisational dilemmas as barriers to learning. *The Learning Organization,* 5 (4) 193–201.

Sveiby, KE (1997) *The New Organizational Wealth: Managing and Measuring Knowledge-Based Assets.* San Francisco: Berret-Koehler Publishers.

Teare, R, and Dealtry, R (1998) Building and sustaining a learning organisation. *The Learning Organization,* 5 (1) 47–60.

Tichy, N, and Cohen, E (1998) The teaching organization. *Training & Development,* 52 (7).

Tushman, M, and Nadler, D (1996) Organizing for innovation. In K Starkey (Ed.), *How Organizations Learn.* London: International Thomson Business Press.

Watkins, K, and Marsick, V (1993) *Sculpting the Learning Organization.* San Francisco: Jossey-Bass.

Wenger, E (1998) *Communities of Practice: Learning, Meaning, and Identity.* Cambridge: Cambridge University Press.

Wenger, E (2000) Communities of practice: the organisational frontier. *Harvard Business Review,* 78 (1) 139–45.

Contemporary issues in employment relations

part 2

CHAPTER 8

The changing psychological contract: challenges and implications for HRM, organisations and employees

by Heather Maguire

University of Southern Queensland

Introduction

Organisations and their employees face ongoing challenges in the form of new strategic initiatives designed to keep pace in an increasingly complex business environment. In order for these challenges to be successfully met, new behaviours are required on the part of employees (Sims 1994). Defining these new behaviours is initiated through the organisation's human resource (HR) practices (Rousseau & Wade-Benzoni 1994). However, *actual* change in individual employees' behaviour is determined by *interpreting* their employers' HR practices. Such interpretation affects employee behaviour by altering perceptions of the terms of the individually held *psychological contract* (figure 8.1).

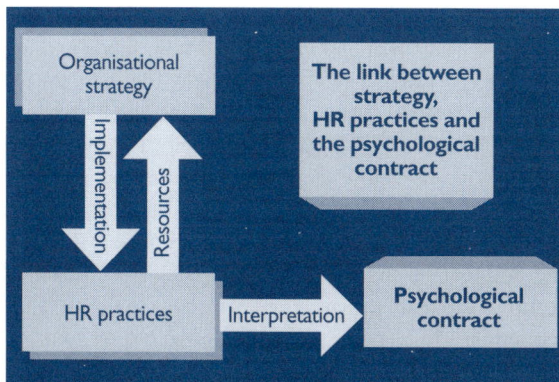

Figure 8.1: Relationship between strategy and employee's psychological contract *Source:* Adapted from Rousseau and Wade-Benzoni (1994), 464.

This chapter focuses on the following issues: defining the psychological contract; the function, development and content of the psychological contract; the 'old' versus the 'new' psychological contract; change and the psychological contract; challenging issues associated with the changing psychological contract; implications for the management of human resources; and future directions.

Defining the psychological contract

The exchange relationship between organisation and employee ranges the entire contract spectrum from strictly legal to purely psychological (Spindler 1994). Many aspects of this relationship are shaped by legislation, enterprise agreements and/or an employment contract signed by the employee detailing issues such as hours, salary and benefit plans. However, other aspects of the employment relationship are likely to be confined to the subconscious (Spindler 1994). The term *psychological contract* (Argyris 1960; Schein 1980; Rousseau 1989) refers to a commonly used exchange concept providing a framework for understanding the 'hidden' aspects of the relationship between organisations and their employees (Shore & Tetrick 1994).

The literature provides a number of definitions for psychological contract. For example:

- 'the set of expectations held by the individual employee that specify what the individual and the organisation expect to give to and receive from each other in the course of their working relationship' (Sims 1994, p. 375)

- 'an individual's system of belief, shaped by the organisation, regarding terms of an exchange agreement between him/herself and the organisation' (Rousseau 1989; Rousseau & Aquino 1993, p. 122)
- 'what employees are prepared to give by way of effort and contributions in exchange for something they value from their employer, such as job security, pay and benefits or continuing training' (Newell & Dopson 1996, p. 25)
- an emotional bond between employer and employee. It is implicit and thus unofficial and includes mutual responsibilities and expectations. Compliance motivation reflects the degree of shared belief and trust (DeMeuse & Tornow 1990).

The common theme underlying these definitions is that the psychological contract refers to an *employee's* unexpressed beliefs, expectations, promises and responsibilities with respect to what constitutes a fair exchange within the boundaries of the employment relationship.

Psychological contracts differ from other types of contracts not only because of the innumerable elements they may contain but also because the employee (the contract taker) and the employer (the contract maker) may have differing expectations with respect to the employment relationship. Few of these elements are likely to have been specifically discussed; most are inferred only, and are subject to change as both individual and organisational expectations change (Goddard 1984; Rousseau 1990; Sims 1990, 1991, 1992).

Psychological contracts differ from legal contracts with respect to procedures followed in the event of breach of contract. Breach of a legal contract allows the aggrieved party to seek enforcement in court. Breach of a psychological contract, however, offers no such recourse, and the aggrieved party may choose only to withhold contributions or to withdraw from the relationship (Spindler 1994).

The psychological contract is a complex phenomenon. Considerable debate has taken place during the past decade over the validity of the concept in the new 'lean and mean' organisation. Assessing its validity requires an understanding of the role played by the psychological contract in the organisational context.

The function of the psychological contract

The primary function of the psychological contract has been described in a number of ways. For example:
- Psychological contracts represent an essential feature of organisational life, serving to bind individuals and organisations together and to regulate their behaviour (Robinson, Kraatz & Rousseau 1994).

- The psychological contract acts to sustain the employment relationship over time (Rousseau & Wade-Benzoni 1994).
- The psychological contract enables the human side of organisations to function smoothly and is particularly important in times of uncertainty and risk such as during corporate restructuring (Morrison 1994).
- Psychological contracts act in a similar manner to hygiene factors. Good contracts may not always result in superior performance but poor contracts tend to act as demotivators and can be reflected in lower commitment and heightened absenteeism and turnover (Sparrow 1996).
- Psychological contracts help to accomplish two tasks — i.e. they help to predict the kinds of outputs employers will get from employees, and they help to predict what kind of reward the employee will get from investing time and effort in the organisation (Sparrow & Hiltrop 1997).

Predictability, as suggested by Sparrow and Hiltrop, contributes significantly to the employment relationship created by psychological contracts. Predictability is a critical underpinning to motivation. To be motivated, an employee should be able to predict that performance will result in desired outcomes (Vroom 1964). Predictability, understanding and a sense of control are also key factors in preventing stress (Sutton & Kahn 1986) and in developing trust (Morrison 1994). Morrison argues that predictability, reliability, credibility, loyalty and trust all reinforce one another. These factors are essential for a continued harmonious relationship between the employee and the organisation.

The need for predictability may in fact underlie the development of psychological contracts. It has been suggested (Shore & Tetrick 1994) that psychological contracts give employees the feeling that they are able to influence their destiny in the organisation, since they are party to the contract and can choose whether to carry out their obligations.

It is commonly proposed that the psychological contract affects employee satisfaction, attitudes and behaviour through constant review of the exchange relationship between employer and employee (Anderson & Schalk 1998). The idea of this exchange relationship is derived from models arising out of social psychology — for example, the inducement-contribution model (March 1958), Homans' Social Exchange Theory (Homans 1974) and Adams Equity Theory (Adams 1965). Without consideration being given to the 'employer perspective', the development of a psychological contract in the minds of employees — that is, a picture of what they owe the organisation and what the organisation owes them in return — can result in perceptions of inequity in the exchange relationship. To retain balance in the psychological contract, any perceived increase in employee obligations to the organisation needs to be matched by a perception of increased rewards. If increases in employee obligations are determined as exceeding increases in employee rewards, it is possible to assume that a negative shift has occurred in the psychological contract. This situation, in turn, is likely to result in a decrease in perceived obligations to the organisation, as witnessed in employee withdrawal of organisational citizenship behaviours (OCBs) or in employees' leaving the organisation. Organ (1988) proposes that the withdrawal of OCBs will negatively affect organisational performance.

The potential cost to organisations of withdrawal of OCBs may explain why much of the literature relating to psychological contracting emphasises the importance of employee commitment. Commitment, as an employee obligation, can be defined as the relative strength of an individual's identification with and involvement in a particular organisation characterised by:

- strong acceptance or a belief in an organisation's goals and values that is often operationalised in terms of attachment to or pride in the organisation — that is, affective commitment (Meyer & Allen 1984)
- willingness to exert effort on behalf of the organisation
- a strong desire to maintain membership of the organisation, or continuance commitment (Meyer & Allen 1984).

Continuance commitment, which may exist with or without associated affective commitment, may be maintained by a lack of alternatives to the employee's current job (Newell & Dopson 1996). In this case, negative attachment, characterised by an intention to remain accompanied by little intention of meeting organisational demands, may exist (Newell & Dopson 1996). These writers suggest that in times of recession and rationalisation, when a negative shift is perceived in the psychological contract, managers in particular are likely to move from affective to continuance commitment (and possibly negative attachment).

In the next section we will look at the way in which the complex phenomenon of the psychological contract develops before and during an employee's term of employment with an organisation.

The development of the psychological contract

Psychological contracts first emerge during pre-employment negotiation and are refined during the initial period of employment. The development of the psychological contract is illustrated in figure 8.2. Potential employees and organisational agents enter the employment relationship with a set of expectations about the potential relationship. These expectations may be transactional (monetary) and/or relational, and will influence the development of the psychological contract. The dynamic nature of the interaction between the parties to the contract, together with organisational goals and environmental conditions and the goal orientation of the individual, influence the development of the psychological contract (Shore & Tetrick 1994). During their employment with a particular organisation, employees will seek, process, integrate, interpret and derive meaning from information gained from a number of sources, such as co-workers, supervisors and recruiters, as well as the implied and formal employment contract. From this process employees will create their individual interpretations of their obligations and entitlements — that is, their psychological contract with the organisation.

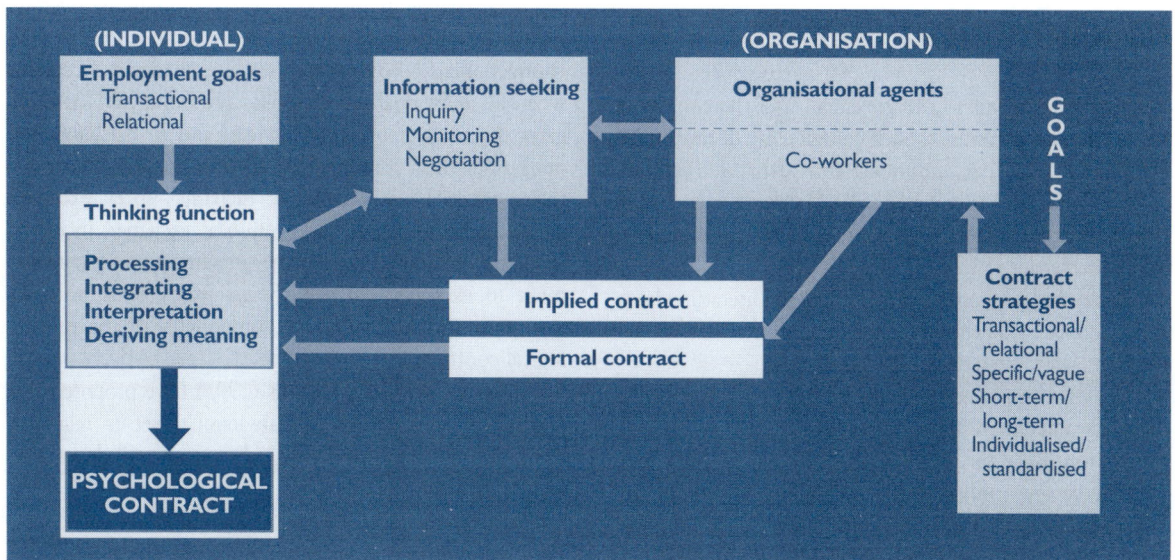

Figure 8.2: The development of the psychological contract *Source:* Shore and Tetrick (1994), 97.

Figure 8.2 illustrates the link between organisational goals and psychological contracts. In times of organisational change, particularly in large, previously stable organisations such as banks and insurance companies, a change in organisation goals can lead to the development of a mismatch in perceptions of obligations between employer and employee. This occurs in part because the development of a psychological contract is a 'deliberate, goal-oriented process' (Shore & Tetrick 1994) through which employees attempt to establish an agreement with their employing organisation to suit their own employment objectives. It might be suggested that this, in turn, influences the type of person who applies for work with an organisation. The concept of particular types of psychological contracts prevailing within a given organisation is supported in the literature (McLean Parks 1993; Mclean Parks, Tsui, Porter, Pearce & Tripoli 1993; Rousseau & Wade-Benzoni 1994).

Employees often hold on to the terms of the psychological contract that operated at time of hire, and subcultures can form around employees according to time served in the organisation, since those with similar tenure can be expected to share similar perceptions of the terms of the psychological contract (Rousseau & Greller 1994b). Tenure, and perhaps age, may therefore influence employee perception of the terms of the psychological contract.

Given the importance to the employee–employer relationship of the psychological contract, attention will now be turned to the content of the psychological contract.

The content of the psychological contract

The literature provides little agreement over the content of the psychological contract. Such contracts are deemed to be voluntary, subjective, informal and dynamic (Hiltrop 1996), with elements being added and deleted over time as employee and employer expectations change (Robinson et al. 1994; Herriot 1995).

Considerable agreement does exist in the literature, however, on the following components of the 'traditional' psychological contract:

- Individual employees are expected to provide hard work, loyalty and commitment, or sacrifice.
- The organisation is expected to provide high pay, advancement, training and development, and job security (Randle 1997; Rousseau 1989; Makin, Cooper & Cox 1996) in Marks, Findlay, Hine, McKinlay & Thompson 1997).

The current relevance of these components of the traditional psychological contract will be discussed in a later section of this chapter.

Contracts can be categorised as either transactional or relational (MacNeil 1985). *Transactional* contracts contain terms of exchange that can be given a monetary value, are specific and exist for a limited duration. The essence of the transactional components of the psychological contract can be expressed as 'a fair day's work for a fair day's pay' (Rousseau & Wade-Benzoni 1994) or as the 'effort exchange/effort bargain' — that is, the reciprocal process of exchanging effort for reward (Marks et al. 1997). By contrast, *relational* contracts contain terms that may not be easily monetisable, and broadly concern the relationship between the individual employee and the organisation (Guzzo & Noonan 1994). This type of contract can be characterised by a focus on open-ended relationships involving considerable investments by employees and employers (for example, loyalty, commitment and trust in management on behalf of the employee, and job security and training on behalf of the employer (Rousseau & Wade-Benzoni 1994).

The distinction between these two types of contracts can also be drawn with respect to the type of exchange. Transactional contracts are linked with *economic exchange*, while relational contracts are associated with *social exchange* (McLean Parks & Kidder 1994; Rousseau 1989; Rousseau & McLean Parks 1993). Economic exchange is based on the assumption that transactions between parties are not long-term or ongoing events (Emerson 1981). Emerson suggests that 'obligations, trust, interpersonal attachment or commitment to specific exchange partners are not incorporated into economic exchange frameworks' (p. 35). Economic exchange frameworks are commonly believed to typify the transactional components of the psychological contract. Blau (1964) defines social exchange as occurring when an individual who supplies rewarding services obligates the receiver of these services, and to discharge this obligation, the 'receiver' must, in turn, furnish benefits to the supplier. Unlike economic exchange, social exchange focuses on contingent and reciprocal exchange incorporating mutual obligation, trust, attachment and commitment to exchange partners. Social exchange is normally associated with the relational components of the psychological contract.

Rousseau and McLean Parks (1993) have proposed that the relative proportion of transactional versus relational elements within the psychological contract will depend on factors such as:

- employment status
- duration of the employer–employee relationship
- the HR benefits and practices of the organisation.

HR practices that are limited to basic work-related needs, and that may be described as fulfilling the explicit employment contract, concern the transactional component of the psychological contract. Those HR practices that exceed the employee's basic needs and are not contained in the employment agreement comprise the relational component of the contract.

The transactional and relational components of the psychological contract are not independent (Guzzo & Noonan 1994). The transactional terms of the contract can influence the kinds of relational rewards expected by the employee. For example, a manager who is asked to take on additional responsibilities may expect his or her chances of promotion to be increased. Guzzo and Noonan (p. 452) stress that the fulfilment of the psychological contract in both transactional and relational terms influences employee loyalty and commitment. In the context of the impact of restructuring on middle management positions, it could be hypothesised that when a negative shift occurs in the transactional component of an employee's psychological contract, there is little he or she can do to address the imbalance in transactional elements. For example, decreased effort or performance may worsen the situation. Hence, employees facing such a situation may withdraw some or all of their contribution to the relational component of the psychological contract with their employer.

Considerable debate has focused on the content of the transactional and relational components of the psychological contract. Table 8.1 provides an overview of elements that have been proposed by a selection of authors as transactional or relational components of the psychological contract.

Herriot and Pemberton (1995a) argue that employers are becoming less committed to a relational framework. Empirical evidence of this trend can be found in finance sector organisations where long-term, loyalty-based relationships for middle managers in particular are being abandoned in place of more monetisable and specific transactional agreements that emphasise explicit links between extrinsic rewards and employee performance (Hallier & James 1997; Turnley & Feldman 1998). This type of transition from the 'old' to the 'new' psychological contract will be discussed further in the following section.

Table 8.1: Summary of psychological contract content elements

Author	Transactional		Relational	
	Employee contribution	Employee reward	Employee contribution	Employee reward
Robinson 1996; Robinson, Kraatz and Rousseau 1997	Giving advance notice of intention to leave Willingness to accept a transfer Refusal to support organisation's competitors Protection of proprietary information	Promotion and advancement High pay Pay based on current level of performance	Spending a minimum of two years with the organisation Working extra hours Loyalty Volunteering to do non-required tasks	Training Long-term job security Career development Sufficient power and responsibility Support with personal problems
Randle 1997; Rousseau 1989 Makin 1996 Marks et al. 1997	Sufficient effort		Loyalty Commitment (affective) Commitment (continuance)	Opportunity for advancement Training and development Job security
Mumford 1995	Skills and knowledge	Good working conditions Satisfactory relationship with work (job satisfaction)	Loyalty Enthusiasm Motivation	Sense of achievement Responsibility Recognition
McFarlane Shore 1994		Competent management Opportunity to demonstrate competence		
Maguire 1998	Reasonable workload Reasonable number of hours worked Moderate level of stress	Appropriate level of autonomy Affiliation with colleagues	Trust in management	Sense of belonging

Note: Items are not repeated for each author (i.e. only those items not already included by previous authors are listed for each author).

The 'old' versus the 'new' psychological contract

Spindler (1994, p. 328) claims that the 'old' psychological contracts based on the exchange of security for compliance have been shattered, with the new contract only now being established. Considerable agreement can be found in the literature for such a proposition. For example:

- 'The old cradle-to-grave psychological contract ... is gone' (Waxler & Higginson 1993, p. 19).
- 'the bond between employer and employee has significantly changed, if not weakened' (DeMeuse & Tornow 1990, p. 203).
- 'the traditional bond between employers and employees rested upon a premise that has been revealed as unworkable' (Sorohan 1994, p. 28).
- 'Loyalty to the company has given way to looking out for oneself' (Kanter & Mirvis 1989, p. 5).
- The psychological contract between employer and employee in terms of reasonably permanent employment for work well done is truly being undermined (Cooper 1997).

Sims (1994) describes traditional psychological contracts as having existed in organisations characterised by stability, predictability and growth. The workforces of such organisations were seen as permanent, and employee loyalty was built on guarantees of long-term employment and investment in training. Employee commitment was the norm and employees expected advancement within the organisation. Sims adds that today's leaner organisations offer limited opportunities for advancement, and employees have learned that job security can no longer be guaranteed even for good performers.

Several authors refer to a dramatic revision in psychological contract provisions (DeMeuse & Tornow 1990; Burack 1993; Burack & Singh 1995). In the past the psychological contract was characterised by employees exchanging cooperation, conformity and performance for tenure and economic security. Such a dependent relationship virtually assured employee loyalty (Singh 1998). The terms of the new contract are not yet settled, but the new responsibility of employers is said to be evolving towards creating opportunities for employees to take care of themselves (Ehrlich 1994). The following summary of this evolving relationship between employer and employee (Kissler 1994) is based on the work of a number of authors (see table 8.2).

Sparrow (1996) also attempts to differentiate between old and new contracts (see table 8.3) based on the work of a range of authors (Rousseau 1989; Ehrlich 1994; Kissler 1994; Morrison 1994; Sims 1994; Rousseau & Greller 1994b; Sparrow 1996a).

In a further attempt to differentiate between old and new psychological contracts, Hiltrop (1996) questioned a group of middle managers attending a workshop at the International Institute for Management Development in Lausanne. She found that the keywords used to describe the old contract were stability, permanence, predictability, fairness, tradition and mutual respect, while the new contract was described as a short-term relationship with an emphasis on flexibility, self-reliance and achievement of immediate results (Hiltrop 1996)

Table 8.2: Kissler's (1994) distinction between old and new characteristics of psychological contracts

Old contract	New contract
Organisation is 'parent' to employee 'child'	Organisation and employee enter into 'adult' contracts focused on mutually beneficial work
Employee's identity and worth are defined by the organisation	Employee's identity and worth are defined by the employee
Those who stay are good and loyal; others are bad and disloyal	The regular flow of people in and out is healthy and should be celebrated
Employees who do what they are told will work until retirement	Long-term employment is unlikely; expect and prepare for multiple relationships
The primary route for growth is through promotion	The primary route for growth is a sense of personal accomplishment

Hiltrop describes the new 'self-reliance' orientation as far removed from the 'organisation man' (Whyte 1956) concept of the 1960s, according to which employees were expected to invest themselves completely in their company while the company did whatever was necessary to ensure that the employee succeeded in his or her job and career. This increased need for self-reliance among employees permeates most distinctions between the traditional and emerging psychological contracts.

Perry Pascarella (1988), editor-in-chief of *Industry Week*, sums up the terms of the new psychological contract from the perspective of employer obligations (see figure 8.3).

The way in which the psychological contract changes in response to organisational employment practices and other factors will be discussed in the next section.

Table 8.3: Sparrow's (1996) differentiation between old and new psychological contracts

Contract element	Old contract	New contract
Change environment	Stable, short-term focus	Continuous change
Culture	Paternalism, time served, exchange security for commitment	Those who perform get rewarded and have contract developed
Rewards	Paid on level, position and status	Paid on contribution
Motivational currency	Promotion	Job enrichment, competency development
Promotion basis	Expected, time served, technical competence	Less opportunity, new criteria, for those who deserve it
Mobility expectations	Infrequent and on employee's terms	Horizontal, used to rejuvenate organisation, managed process
Redundancy/ tenure guarantee	Job for life if perform	Lucky to have a job, no guarantees
Responsibility	Instrumental, employees exchange promotion for more responsibility	To be encouraged, balanced with more accountability, linked to innovation
Status	Very important	To be earned by competence and credibility
Personal development	The organisation's responsibility	Individual's responsibility to improve employability
Trust	High trust possible	Desirable, but expect employees to be more committed to project or profession

- We can't promise you how long we will be in business.
- We can't promise you we won't be bought by another company.
- We can't promise there will be room for promotion.
- We can't promise you your job will exist until you reach retirement age.
- We can't promise the money will be available for your pension when you retire.
- We can't expect your undying loyalty, and we're not even sure we want it.

Figure 8.3: The new psychological contract — employer obligations *Source:* P Pascarella (1998).

Change and the psychological contract

While the content of the psychological contract may be difficult, if not impossible, to define in periods of stability, the perceived terms often become painfully obvious when a breach of the contract is believed to have occurred. In such a case, the contract may be portrayed as a 'highly emotionally charged construct' (Sparrow 1996a).

In times of organisational change, psychological contracts assume an increasingly important role in employment relationships (Robinson 1996). The terms of the employment agreement are being repeatedly managed, renegotiated and altered to fit changing circumstances (Tichy 1983; Altman & Post 1996). Within such a dynamic environment, organisations may become less willing and/or less able to fulfil all of their promises to employees. Non-fulfilment of promises is referred to as 'breach of contract', and evidence has been found that the majority of employees currently believe that their employer has breached some aspect of their employment agreement (Robinson & Rousseau 1994).

Much of the concern that has been focused on the changing nature of the employment relationship over the past decade has concentrated on decreased job security and the associated lower levels of employee commitment that are claimed to be caused by organisational restructuring. There is widespread acknowledgement in the literature that changes in the *psychological contract* between workers and their organisations have not benefited employees (Turnley & Feldman 1998). Employees appear to be disadvantaged by a situation in which employers want employee involvement and loyalty but without offering in return a guarantee of job tenure and advancement (Hiltrop 1996). While employee entitlements appear to be decreasing, competitive pressures are leading organisations to demand greater commitment, initiative and flexibility from their employees (Schor 1992).

As described in the previous section, psychological contracts are not static (Guzzo; Noonan & Elron 1994). As the HR practices of an organisation respond to changing environmental conditions and as employees gain experience, employees will closely scan their existing psychological contracts in order to re-evaluate and renegotiate both their own and their employer's obligations (Rousseau & McLean Parks 1993). This process is supported in the literature by social information processing theory (Salancik & Pfeffer 1978), which suggests that information obtained by employees through observing their own behaviour and that of their employer will alter employees' perceptions of what they owe the employer and what they are owed in return (Robinson et al. 1994).

As HR practices and societal changes bring about alterations to employees' expectations of what they owe and are owed by the organisation, a sense of employee outrage commonly emerges (Rousseau & Greller 1994b). Rousseau and Greller explain that such a reaction results from the fact that employees are being asked to bear risks that were previously carried by the organisation. At the same time, reward systems do not appear to have compensated for this situation. Even if, in future, greater employee risk is offset by the opportunity for greater rewards, some employees may be 'so risk averse that no amount of reward sharing would offset the discomfort' (Rousseau & Greller 1994b).

The impact of HR or societal change on the psychological contract is complicated by the diversity of such contracts that may exist within the organisation. Since employment conditions change over time, different generations of employees may have varying expectations of obligations and entitlements (Rousseau & Greller 1994a). However, Rousseau and Greller suggest that even where varying expectations exist, organisations will normally support a number of core contract terms, such as job security, that create a status quo that becomes extremely difficult to change without contract violation.

The terms of the contract may also be affected by growing resentment among employees facing constant, often mismanaged change. Turnley and Feldman's study revealed that bank managers had developed high levels of resentment because they felt that the organisation was continually revising its performance criteria (Turnley & Feldman, 1998). Resentful employees are likely, subconsciously at least, to downgrade their perceived obligations and to increase perceptions of their entitlements.

Employee cynicism about organisational change has been defined as 'an attitude of pessimism and hopelessness towards future organisational change induced by repeated exposure to mismanaged change attempts' (Wanous, Reichers & Austin 1994). Cynicism has been described as both a generalised and specific attitude involving frustration, disillusionment and negative feelings towards, and distrust of, a person, group or objects (Andersson & Bateman 1997). Andersson and Bateman (1997) point out that job dissatisfaction and cynicism share an element of frustration. However, cynicism is anticipatory and directed outward while job dissatisfaction is retrospective and self-focused (Wanous et al. 1994). Results of a study by Reichers et al. (table 8.4) show that cynicism about organisational change has negative consequences for commitment, satisfaction and motivation among employees.

Table 8.4: Reichers, Wanous and Austin's 1997 study of cynicism in the workplace

	High cynicism N = 209	Low cynicism N = 226
High job satisfaction	42.8%	85.3%
Organisational commitment	38.9%	84.9%
Participation in decision-making	28.5%	53.2%

When one considers the two concepts of psychological contracting and cynicism, a somewhat negative prediction can be made about the success of organisational change. Previous sections have addressed the trend from relational to transactional contracts brought about by organisational change. This trend is reinforced by the likelihood that cynicism will also decrease commitment and credibility for organisational leaders. However, the literature would also suggest that more transactional contracts focusing on the exchange relationship might enjoy limited success given, for example, the decreased effectiveness of compensation systems as a motivator. The essential difference between the two concepts may lie in the fact that cynicism is created through a response to a 'history of change attempts', whereas a single change initiative may bring about changes in the psychological contract. Does it then follow that change to the psychological contract results from initial change but if employees see such change as mismanaged, then subsequent change efforts may result in both changed psychological contracts and organisational cynicism?

Sims (1994) summarises the effects of change on the psychological contract as follows:

The unilateral cancellation of the implied contract profoundly affects the surviving employees. Some of their most basic tenets — beliefs in fairness, equity and justice — have been violated. Their sense of security has been destroyed; their identity and self-esteem are threatened; and they mistrust their organisations' managements. For some, the contract has become null and void.

There is general agreement within the literature that psychological contracts are changing as a result of organisational change initiatives and societal factors. In the next section, the challenges posed by the changing psychological contract are discussed. The challenges relate to the role of middle managers and employee response to change and alterations to the psychological contract.

Challenging issues associated with the changing psychological contract

The role of middle management

Middle managers play a critical role in redefining and regulating change in the employee–employer relationship (Hallier & James 1997). Therefore, in times of organisational change the attitudes and behaviours of middle managers assume great importance.

For middle managers, the traditional psychological contract has been based on loyalty and commitment to the organisation in return for strong expectations of job security and career progression linked to increased status and increased rewards (Newell & Dopson 1996). Such strong expectations do not sit well with a workforce experiencing layoffs at record rates (McLean Parks & Schmedemann 1994). Recent economic conditions have resulted in the demise of jobs that once offered real, long-term security (Fetterman & Lawlor 1991). Consequently, the preferential treatment once afforded managers has diminished and become less easy to distinguish from the conditions of subordinate workers (Hallier & James 1997). The removal of middle management positions from organisations has been referred to as the 'massacre of the mid-ranks' (Toffler 1990) and as 'organisational liposuction' (Kissler 1991).

Middle managers appear not only to have become more vulnerable to job loss but also to have become the group whose psychological contract has been most severely violated. Research has shown that changes to the psychological contract between managers and their organisations have left managers feeling that they work harder and under tighter controls but without receiving compensation for the increased job pressure. A 1998 study by Turnley and Feldman found that managers in restructured organisations felt that their psychological contract had been violated in a number of areas, including:

- responsibility and power
- input into decision making
- job security
- opportunities for advancement.

The strong sense among middle managers of violation of the psychological contract may be the result of a number of factors. First, middle managers, as stated above, have been disproportionately affected by changes such as restruc-

turing, downsizing, redundancy and outsourcing. Second, middle managers are a group of employees who had previously been 'immune' from the effects of organisational restructuring. Third, middle managers, particularly in the finance sector, are likely to have had lengthy tenure within their organisations. These employees may therefore have become 'bound to specific jobs through such standard personnel policies as seniority policies' (McLean Parks & Schmedemann 1994). Human capital theory explains that the longer an employee stays with a specific employer, the fewer are his or her options in the job market. Long-serving employees are therefore likely to both expect and depend on job security (Gordon & Lee 1990; Glendon & Lev 1990; Shapiro & Tune 1974). Part of the difficulty experienced by managers in downsized and/or restructured organisations may also stem from the fact that these employees may hold dual allegiances — that is, allegiance to their employing organisation and loyalty to the employees they manage (Rousseau & Wade-Benzoni 1994). It could be argued that managers in service organisations may also hold a third allegiance — to their customers. With two or three layers of allegiance, adjustments to the psychological contract are likely to become more complex.

Managing employee response to change and alterations to the psychological contract

Two approaches can be taken to determining how employees will respond to changes in the psychological contract. The *situational* approach suggests that situational variables play a crucial role in determining employee responses by modifying the relationships between violations of the psychological contract and employee reactions. The *content* approach posits that the type of violation will determine how employees will respond (Turnley 1996).

The literature suggests that there are five potential employee responses (figure 8.4) to contract violation (Robinson & Morrison 1993) — voice, silence, retreat, destruction and exit. *Voice* is described as an action orientation in which an attempt is made to maintain and reinstate the psychological contract. *Silence, retreat, destruction* and *exit* are referred to as state orientations in which employees attempt to survive the violation by lowering their, or their employer's, perceived obligations or by withdrawing from the employment relationship (Shore & Tetrick 1994).

Shore and Tetrick's first proposition in the model illustrated in figure 8.4 is that employee response will in part be affected by the type of violation. Based on the organisational justice literature (Bies 1987; Greenberg 1990; Sweeney &

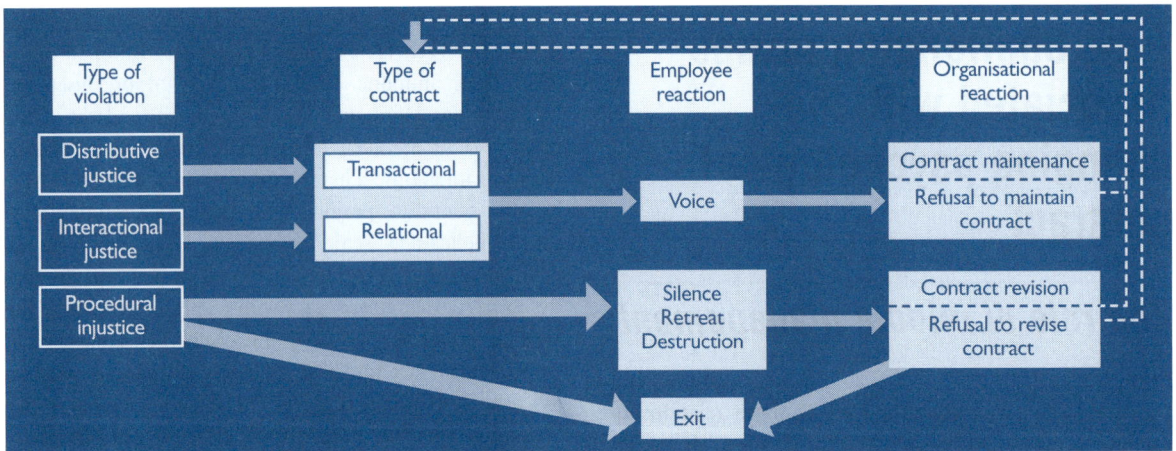

Figure 8.4: Shore and Tetrick's schematic representation of the response to violation of the psychological contract
Source: Shore and Tetrick (1994), 103.

McFarlin 1993), Shore and Tetrick (1994, pp. 103–4) argue that there are three types of violation. These are:

- distributive injustice, comprising unfulfilled transaction obligations that usually have specific monetisable outcomes
- interactional justice, which assesses the interpersonal treatment received during implementation (Bies 1987)
- procedural justice, comprising an assessment of the fairness of procedures through which outcomes have been allocated.

A fourth type of justice needs to be considered with respect to violation of the psychological contract. The effort by one party to the contract to inhibit contract violation by imposing significant and potentially painful consequences is referred to as retributive justice (Leatherwood & Spector 1991; Trevino 1992). The existence of retributive justice may explain why employees who believe their psychological contracts have been violated, and who as a consequence demonstrate a lack of loyalty and commitment to their organisations, continue to

contribute considerable effort. The consequences of reduced effort (which is far more observable than commitment or loyalty) could well be the loss of their jobs or demotion. McLean Parks and Kidder (1994) illustrate the relationship between the various types of justice/injustice in figure 8.5.

Parks and Kidder argue that in transactional contracts procedural justice and interactional justice may not be considered, irrespective of symmetric or asymmetric power, because of the short-term nature of the contract. They also suggest that, in the case of relational contracts with symmetric power, an assessment of procedural justice may not occur. Symmetric power produces a state comparable to bilateral deterrence (Lawler 1986). The fact that one's contracting partner holds equal power discourages contract violations, so that if a perceived breach does occur the violated party will attempt to restore balance in accordance with equity theory (Adams 1965) or to renegotiate the terms of the contract. However, situations of symmetric power are rare under current labour market conditions.

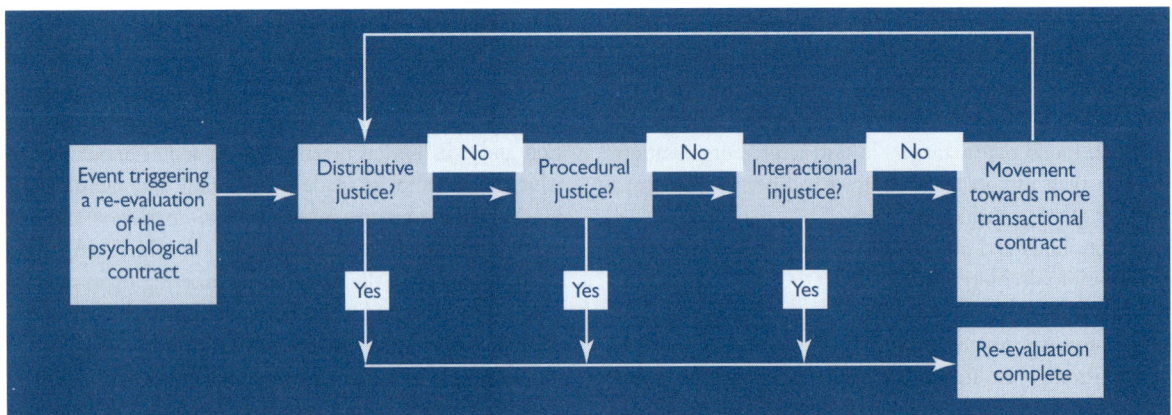

Figure 8.5: Re-evaluation of relational psychological contracts in asymmetric power situations
Source: Adapted from Shore and Tetrick (1994).

Following an event trigger, such as organisational restructuring or downsizing, it is hypothesised that employees assess the event outcomes. If principles of distributive justice appear to have been upheld, the re-evaluation may be completed at this point. If, however, an employee perceives distributive injustice (a discrepancy between employee and employer contributions), procedural justice will then be assessed. If the procedures used to allocate outcomes are understood as fair, the re-evaluation process may terminate. If, however, procedural justice is perceived as not being upheld, the employee will assess interactional justice. If this assessment reveals that the interpersonal treatment received during implementation was beyond reproach, the re-evaluation process will be complete. In the event of perceived interactional injustice, however, there is likely to be a marked shift towards a more transactional contract, with employees withdrawing from the relational aspects of their psychological contract. This will create a much more critical assessment of distributive justice.

The Shore and Tetrick model (figure 8.4) suggests that, after the type of violation, the next most significant influence on employee response to violation may be the type of contract — specifically, whether the contract is largely transactional or relational in nature. McFarlane, Shore and Tetrick draw here on the work of Robinson, Kraatz and Rousseau (1994), which suggested that reactions to violation of short-term transactional contracts may be less intense and more 'amenable to revision' than violation of long-standing relational contracts based on mutual trust. Shore and Tetrick's work also suggests that distributive injustice is of greater importance to employees whose psychological contracts are principally transactional, whereas interactional and procedural injustices will assume greater importance for those with relational contracts who may be prepared to discount small incidents of distributive injustice.

Shore and Tetrick's model (figure 8.4) suggests that employee voice response may be met by the organisation's agreeing to maintain or reinstate the contract, or by its refusal to maintain the contract, in which case the employee response may change to a state orientation — that is, silence, retreat or destruction. Organisational reaction to a state orientation could mean a revision of the terms of the psychological contract (which is likely to occur where employees have considerable power — perhaps in the form of rare skills or expertise). Alternatively, the organisation may refuse to revise the contract. Theoretically, this would lead to employee exit; however, such a reaction is largely determined by labour market conditions and how long the employee has worked in the organisation.

There is general agreement in the literature that violations of the psychological contract are negatively related to trust, organisational citizenship behaviour, employee relational obligations and employee withdrawal behaviour, as well as to intentions to quit and other disaffections (Robinson & Morrison 1993; Robinson & Rousseau 1994; Robinson et al. 1994; Guzzo et al. 1994).

There is also general agreement that employee response to perceived violation will be influenced by:
- the type of violation
- the size of discrepancy
- the degree of assessed organisational responsibility for the unmet obligations (Shore & Tetrick 1994)
- the likelihood of future violations (Floodgate 1994)
- positive working relationships with colleagues (Floodgate 1994).

Norm of reciprocity

Robinson et al.'s study found greater support for the fact that employees' perceptions of their obligations decreased over time while their employers' obligations increased (instrumental perspective), than for the norm or reciprocity perspective, which suggests that both employee and employer obligations would increase over time (p. 145). This finding confirms employees' perception of tenure, or time spent with the organisation, as itself an important contribution in that it should be reciprocated with increasing entitlements over time.

From an instrumental perspective, it could be argued that employees would be likely to increase their expectations of their employer in proportion to their time spent with a particular organisation. Robinson, Kraatz and Rousseau (1994) suggest that this occurs because of employees' desire to maintain equity between contributions and rewards. Continued employment (continuance commitment — a component of the psychological contract) is an increasingly valuable contribution that the employee perceives as enhancing their entitlement. A change in a relational component of the psychological contract (in this case, continuance commitment) therefore influences employees' perception of equity, which may in turn lead to a change in perception of entitlement under the transactional (increased pay) and relational (increased opportunity for advancement) components of the psychological contract.

Identifying the terms of the new contract

Uncertainty over the terms of the psychological contract is not new. However, it is increasingly unclear what employees and organisations owe one another 'because the traditional assumption of job security and steady rewards in return for hard work and loyalty no longer exist in most cases' (Sims 1994).

The common perception among employees that their psychological contracts have been breached may result from the fact that while the expectations that organisations have of their employees for hard work, loyalty and commitment are basically unchanged, the benefits exchanged for such contributions have changed. In the case of middle managers, for example, increased hours and stress levels have commonly been met with reduced opportunities for advancement, minimal job security, and reduced training and development.

It could be assumed that if the types of inducements offered by the organisation change, a change in employee contributions could be expected in order to maintain perceived equity in the relationship.

Employee commitment

In times of recession and rationalisation, managers may suffer 'unilateral variations of their psychological contracts' that result in a move away from affective commitment towards continuance commitment (Newell & Dopson 1996). Given their perception that hard work is no protection from layoff, employees are no longer prepared to attach themselves to the organisation (Waxler & Higginson 1993). Such negative impacts of restructuring could have serious consequences, since the very factors that are causing the change in role and psychological contract of middle managers mean that organisational survival is increasingly dependent on the innovation, creativity and commitment of this group of workers (Newell & Dopson 1996).

Organisations have been accused of treating employees as 'emotionally anorexic' (Kidd 1998). Such accusations result from the fact that HR departments have tended to ignore the implications of HR practices on the creation of psychological contracts (Fineman 1995). Failure to consider the implications for the psychological contract could prove costly for organisations in the current changing organisational environment, and this makes it difficult for organisations to specify all conditions of employment at time of hire. Lack of definition of conditions may lead employees to 'psychologically' fill in more of the blanks in the employment contract, creating a strong possibility of divergence between the organisation's and the employee's understanding of the contract (Rousseau & Greller 1994b). From the HR perspective, managing the psychological contract is about managing the relationship between mutual trust, commitment and rewards — that is, aligning employee and organisational needs.

Implications for HR management

Often in managing organisational change, HR practices focus clearly on changes to employees' jobs and career prospects. Situational factors such as commitment of employees to the change process and satisfaction with the change process make important contributions to withdrawal of employee commitment, loyalty, trust, pessimism and powerlessness. HR managers need to pay increased attention to the development of employee trust and the management of situational factors to avoid many of the negative consequences of organisational change.

Developing employee trust

Considerable research has been conducted into the impact on organisations of psychological contract breach (Robinson & Rousseau 1994; Robinson 1996; Sparrow 1996a). It has been argued that the intensity of the reaction to these violations results not only from unmet expectations of entitlements but also from 'more general beliefs about respect of persons, codes of conduct and other patterns of behaviour associated with relationships, involving trust' (Rousseau 1989).

Robinson (1996, p. 2) integrated various definitions of trust (e.g. Frost, Stimpson & Maughan 1978; Barber 1983; Gambetta 1988) to coin her own definition of trust:

One's expectations, assumptions or beliefs about the likelihood that another's future actions will be beneficial, favourable, or at least not detrimental to one's interests.

Robinson (1996) suggests that trust plays a significant role in the subjective experience of psychological contract breach by one's employer. Robinson claims that employees with low levels of trust are likely to be more vigilant in identifying breaches and more likely to perceive a breach even when there is none because such a finding would be consistent with low levels of trust. Lack of trust results in employees losing confidence that their contributions will be reciprocated as promised by the employer (Robinson 1996). Trust is based on the implicit assumption that others in one's social relationships have respect and concern for one's welfare (Barber 1983; Gambetta 1988). Such an assumption is taken for granted and usually unacknowledged until violated (Garfinkel 1963; Luhmann 1979; Zucher 1986).

Monitoring the situational factors

Turnley and Feldman (1998) draw on previous research in the area of layoffs (Leana & Feldman 1992; Brockner, Grover, O'Malley, Reed & Glynn 1993) to support the findings of their own study, which suggested that 'employees react less negatively to changes in psychological contracts when they attribute the violations to legitimate, external events outside the organisation's control' (p. 81). Turnley and Feldman's model is illustrated in figure 8.6.

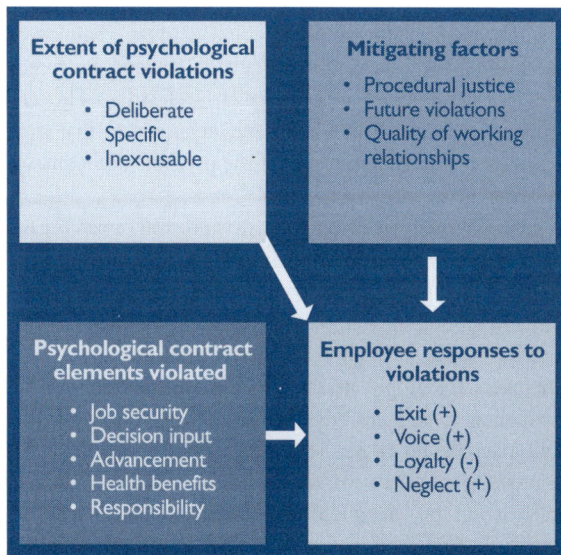

Figure 8.6: Turnley and Feldman's model summarising results of their 1998 study *Source:* Turnley and Feldman (1998), 82.

If the Turnley and Feldman model is placed within the context of the *type* of psychological contract (i.e. largely relational or transactional) and if interactional justice is added to the list of mitigating factors, a succinct summary of much of the literature on psychological contract violation is created. It should be noted, however, that the 'psychological contract elements violated' would depend not only on the type of contract involved but also on the organisational context in which the violation occurred. The model, which adopts the situational approach, also has much to offer management of those organisations involved in change events that are likely to trigger breach and/or violation of the psychological contract. If management can convince employees that:

- obligations cannot be met because of compelling external environmental factors, and the organisation was compelled to introduce such change in order to survive
- procedures allocating the outcomes of such change were fair and open

- people involved in the change process were managed in a manner consistent with the notions of trust
- future violations were unlikely,

then negative consequences of violation of the psychological contract could be minimised. This is important at a time when employees are being told there is no job security and no chance of promotion and that no job is safe from being reorganised, re-engineered, recombined, flattened or simply eliminated (Navran 1994). Reactions in such circumstances may include distrust resulting from the breach of implied promises, vulnerability or powerlessness, pessimism and loss of morale and motivation. Such reactions can result in dire consequences for restructured or downsized organisations that need the efforts and commitment of remaining employees in order to survive in a highly competitive environment. Turnley's work suggests that employee perceptions of the way in which the restructuring process is managed may be an important determinant of employee reaction.

Future directions

The human resource objectives of the organisation of the future are likely to emphasise guiding employees towards an attitude of 'self-employment' (Kets de Vries & Balazs 1997). Employees are encouraged to keep their work experience as up-to-date as possible so that they are better equipped to secure a new job if laid off. Kets de Vries suggests that shorter term employment contracts may be initiated, offering limited job security for a defined period of time. The ramifications of such contracts are yet to be fully understood, but concern has been expressed about the following aspects of the 'new' psychological contract:

- Increasing demands for a flexible workforce create a need for additional skills training. However, skills are expensive to develop and, in the absence of job security, newly trained employees may not remain long enough for the organisation to recoup the training costs (Cappelli 1997).
- The new contract may not prove suitable for those who have a strong need for connectedness and affiliation (Kets de Vries & Balazs 1997).

The new contract may prove unworkable. Employers, under increasing pressure in dynamic environments of increasing competition, will want an agreement under which they will pay salaries for only as long as necessary and will opt out of the burden of providing more than minimal employee benefits, while employees will have little incentive to do more than the minimum and will be unlikely to develop loyalty or to be highly productive (Tornow & DeMeuse 1994).

The role of the organisation in the new psychological contract is subject to debate. If the new 'protean' career contract is with the self rather than with the organisation (Hall & Moss 1998), what role will the organisation play? Hall and Moss define the protean career as being independent and directed by the needs and values of the individual, with success described as internal (psychological). Given this definition, the organisation may be seen as having an obligation to provide the opportunity for continuous learning to assist in employability. However, as argued earlier, organisations may question the financial incentive for developing their employees' careers; what little research has been done suggests that organisations do not see career development as an important part of their business strategy (Smith 1997).

In most discussions of the new psychological contract, the term 'employability' has replaced the concept of job tenure. William J. Morin, Chair and CEO of Drake Beam Morin, describes this new concept as 'non dependent trust', whereby employees take responsibility for their own careers and organisations give them the tools to do so.

Employee perceptions of obligations and entitlements may also be affected by changes that transcend the workplace (Cappelli 1997). Cappelli claims that the Protestant work ethic may have been replaced by a view of work as a source of personal satisfaction. Empirical data appear to support this claim; in a US survey of workers 49 per cent of respondents regarded having a job that they enjoyed as a measure of personal success, yet a decade earlier the percentage of respondents in this category barely registered (Yankelovich 1993). If work is becoming an increasingly important source of personal satisfaction, it is likely that intrinsic rewards such as recognition, sense of achievement, relationship with colleagues, autonomy and opportunities for personal growth will become important employee expectations along with job satisfaction. These rewards are rarely mentioned in the literature with respect to the content of the psychological contract, yet one could expect that they are of considerable importance to employees, and particularly to middle managers. In addition, as the ability of organisations to promise traditional employee rewards such as job security and extensive training diminishes, new rewards are likely to be sought, and these traditional intrinsic employee rewards are more likely to find their way into the psychological contract through information gained by employees through organisational agents at the recruitment and induction stages of their working life.

As a result of the negative shift in the terms of their employment relationship, many workers are now staying with their organisations only because alternative opportunities are so poor that they have nowhere else to go (Morrison 1994). The sense of dependency and fear experienced by these employees reflects a perceived employer breach of the employment contract that workers feel powerless to redress (Kissler 1994). In order to secure and retain a committed workforce, organisations need employees who are working for the organisation because they want to, not because they have no other option (Spindler 1994). Morrison (1994) poses the question of whether, when the economy improves, there is likely to be an exodus of leadership from downsized organisations in which the terms of the psychological contract have deteriorated.

Conclusion

The relationship between organisations and their employees has undoubtedly undergone dramatic change in recent decades, particularly in white-collar industries. The co-dependency between employee and organisation that provided the major underpinning of the psychological contract has weakened considerably.

If employees move towards the new protean career, organisations may be loath to invest in training and development programs because of a perceived lack of continuance commitment among their employees. Taken to the extreme, this could produce a highly transient workforce in which employees are simply attracted to the organisation offering the highest rewards. In this situation, the psychological contract may take on far less importance than traditionally. An increasingly transient workforce, however, has considerable dollar costs for organisations. Careful research may be needed by organisations into the types of rewards that will attract employee loyalty and both affective and continuance commitment, and into the content, operation and organisational advantages offered by the psychological contract.

References

Adams, J (1965a) Inequity in social exchange. In L Berkowitz (Ed.), *Advances in Experimental Social Psychology*. New York: Academic Press.

Altman, BW, and Post, JE (1996) Beyond the social contract: an analysis of executives; views at 25 large companies. In DT Hall (Ed.), *The Career is Dead — Long Live the Career: A Relational Approach to Careers* (pp. 46–71). San Francisco: Jossey-Bass.

Anderson, N, and. Schalk, R (1998) The psychological contract in retrospect and prospect. *Journal of Organisational Behaviour*, 19 (special issue), 637–47.

Andersson, LM, and Bateman, TS (1997) Cynicism in the workplace: some causes and effects. *Journal of Organisational Behaviour*, 18 (5) 449–69.

Argyris, CP (1960) *Understanding Organisational Behaviour*. Homewood, IL: Dorsey Press.

Barber, R (1983) *The Logic and Limits of Trust*. New Brunswick, NJ: Rutgers University Press.

Bies, RJ (1987) The predicament of injustice: the management of moral outrage. *Research in Organisational Behaviour*, 9, 289–319.

Blau, PM (1964) *Exchange and Power in Social Life*. New York: John Wiley & Sons.

Brockner, J, Grover, S, O'Malley, M, Reed, T, and Glynn, M (1993) Threat of future layoffs, self-esteem and survivors' reactions: evidence from the laboratory and the field. *Strategic Management Journal*, 14 (special issue), 153–66.

Burack, E (1993). *Corporate Resurgence and the New Employment Relationships*. New York: Quorum Press.

Burack, E, and Singh, R (1995) The new employment relations contract. *Human Resource Planning*, 18 (1), 12–19.

Cappelli, P (1997) Rethinking the nature of work: a look at the research evidence. *Compensation & Benefits Review*, July/August, 50–58.

DeMeuse, K, and Tornow, W (1990) The tie that binds has become very, very frayed. *Human Resource Planning*, 13, 203–213.

Ehrlich, CJ (1994) Creating an employer–employee relationship for the future. *Human Resource Management*, 33 (3), 491–501.

Emerson, R (1981) Social exchange theory. In M Rosenberg and R Turner (Eds), *Social Psychology: Sociological Perspectives* (pp. 30–65). New York: Basic Books.

Fetterman, M, and Lawlor, J (1991) Workforce redefined by rough times. *USA Today*, 12, 12–20, 1B–2B.

Fineman, S (1995) Stress, emotion and intervention. In T Newton, J Handy and S Fineman, *Managing Stress: Emotion and Power at Work* (pp. 120–35). London: Sage.

Floodgate, JNA (1994) Personal development plans: the challenge of implementation — a case study. *Journal of European Industrial Training*, 18 (11), 43–7.

Frost, T, Stimpson, DV, and Maughan, MRC (1978) Some correlates of trust. *Journal of Psychology*, 99, 102–8.

Gambetta, D (1988). *Trust: Making and Breaking Co-operative Relations*. New York: Basil Blackwell.

Garfinkel, H (1963) A conception of, and experiments with, trust as a condition of stable concerted actions. In OJ Harvey (Ed.), *Motivation and Social Interaction: Cognitive Determinants* (pp. 187–238). New York: Ronald.

Glendon, M, and Lev, E (1990) Changes in the bonding of the employment relationship: an essay on the new property. *Boston College Law Review*, 20, 457–84.

Goddard, RW (1984) The psychological contract. *Management World*, 13 (7), 12–14.

Gordon, M, and Lee, B (1990) Property rights in jobs: workforce, behavioral and legal perspective. In G Ferris and K Rowland (Eds), *Research in Personnel and Human Resources Management: A Research Annual* (vol. 3, pp. 141–83). Greenwich, CT: JAI Press.

Greenberg, J (1990) Organisational justice: yesterday, today and tomorrow. *Journal of Management*, 16, 399–432.

Guzzo, RA, and Noonan, KA (1994) Human resource practices as communications and the psychological contract. *Human Resource Management*, 33 (3), 447–62.

Guzzo, RA, Noonan, KA, and Elron, E (1994) Expatriate managers and the psychological contract. *Journal of Applied Psychology*, 79.

Hall, DT, and Moss, JE (1998) The new protean career contract: helping organisations and employees adapt. *Organisational Dynamics*, 26 (3), 22–37.

Hallier, J, and James, P (1997) Middle managers and the employee psychological contract: agency, protection and advancement. *Journal of Management Studies*, 34 (5), 703–729.

Herriot, P (1995) Psychological contracts. In N Nicholson (Ed.), *Encyclopaedic Dictionary of Organisational Behaviour*. Oxford: Basil Blackwell.

Herriot, P, and Pemberton, C (1995) A new deal for middle managers. *People Management*, 1 (12), 32–5.

Hiltrop, JM (1996) Managing the changing psychological contract. *Employee Relations*, 18 (1), 36–50.

Hirsch, P (1988) *Pack Your Own Parachute*. Boston: Addison-Wesley.

Homans, G (1961) *Social Behaviour: Its Elementary Forms*. New York: Harcourt, Brace & World.

Kanter, DL, and Mirvis, PH (1989) *The Cynical Americans*. San Francisco: Jossey-Bass.

Kets de Vries, MFR, and Balazs, K (1997) The downside of downsizing. *Human Relations*, 50 (1) 11–50.

Kidd, JM (1998) Emotion: an absent presence in career theory. *Journal of Vocational Behaviour*, 52, 275–88.

Kissler, GD (1991) *The Change Riders*. Reading, MA: Addison-Wesley.

Kissler, GD (1994) The new employment contract. *Human Resource Management*, 33 (3), 335–51.

Lawler, E (1986) Bilateral deterrence and conflict spiral: a theoretical analysis. In E Lawler (Ed.), *Advances in Group Process* (vol. 3, pp. 107–130). Greenwich, CT: JAI Press.

Leana, CR, and Feldman, DC (1992) *Coping with Job Loss: How Individuals, Organisations, and Communities Respond to Layoffs*. New York: Macmillan / The Free Press.

Leatherwood, M, and Spector, L (1991) Enforcements, inducements, expected utility and employee misconduct. *Journal of Management*, 17, 553–70.

Luhmann, N (1979) *Trust and Power.* New York: John Wiley & Sons.

MacNeil, IR (1985) Relational contract: what we do and do not know. *Wisconsin Law Review*, 483–525.

Makin, PM, Cooper, C, and Cox, C (1996) *Organisations and the Psychological Contract.* Leicester: BPS.

March, JG, and Simon, HA (1958) *Organisations.* New York: John Wiley & Sons.

Marks, A, Findlay, P, Hine, J, McKinlay, A, and Thompson, P (1997) *You Always Hurt the One You Love: Violating the Psychological Contract at United Distillers.* Paper presented at ERU Conference.

McLean Parks, J (1993) Organisational contracting: a 'Rational' exchange? In J Halpern and B Stern (Eds), *Non-rational Elements of Organisational Decision Making.* Ithaca, NY: ILR Press.

McLean Parks, J, and Kidder, D (1994) 'Till death us do part …' — Changing work relationships in the 1990s. In C Cooper and D Rousseau (Eds), *Trends in Organisational Behaviour*, vol. 1 (pp. 111–36). New York: John Wiley & Sons.

McLean Parks, JM, and Schmedemann, D (1994) When promises become contracts: implied contracts and handbook provisions on job security. *Human Resource Management*, 33 (3).

Meyer, J, and Allen, N (1984) Testing the side-bet theory of organisational commitment: some methodological considerations. *Journal of Applied Psychology*, 69, 372–8.

Morrison, DE (1994) Psychological contracts and change. *Human Resource Management*, 33 (3), 353–71.

Mowday, RT, Porter, LW, and Steers, RM (1982) *Employee–Organisation Linkages: The Psychology of Commitment, Absenteeism and Turnover.* New York: Academic Press.

Navran, F (1994) Surviving a downsizing. *Executive Excellence*, 11 (7), 12–13.

Newell, H, and Dopson, S (1996) Muddle in the middle: organisational restructuring and middle management careers. *Personnel Review*, 25 (4).

Organ, DW (1988) *Organisational Citizenship Behaviour: The Good Soldier Syndrome.* Lexington, MA: Lexington Books.

Pascarella, P (1988) Lesson from the fifties generation. *Industry Week*, 4 April.

Reichers, AE, Wanous, JP, and Austin, JT (1997) Understanding and managing cynicism about organisational change. *Academy of Management Executive.* 11 (1) 48–59.

Robinson, SL (1996) Trust and breach of the psychological contract. *Administrative Science Quarterly*, 41 (4), 574–600.

Robinson, SL, Kraatz, SM, and Rousseau, MD (1994) Changing obligations and the psychological contract: a longitudinal study. *Academy of Management Journal*, 37, 137–51.

Robinson, SL, and Morrison, EW (1993) The effect of contract violation on organisational citizenship behaviour. Unpublished manuscript, New York University.

Robinson, SL, and Rousseau, DM (1994) Violating the psychological contract: not the exception but the norm. *Journal of Organisational Behaviour*, 15, 245–59.

Rogers, RW (1995) The psychological contract of trust: Part 1. *Executive Development*, 8 (1), 15–19.

Rousseau, DM (1989) Psychological and implied contracts in organisations. *Employer Responsibilities and Rights Journal*, 2, 121–39.

Rousseau, DM (1990) New hire perceptions of their own and their employer's obligations: a study of psychological contracts. *Journal of Organisational Behaviour*, 11, 389–400.

Rousseau, DM, and Greller, MG (1994a) Guest editors' overview: psychological contracts and human resource practices. *Human Resource Management*, 33 (3) 383–4.

Rousseau, DM, and Greller, MG (1994b). Human resource practices: administrative contract makers. *Human Resource Management*, 33 (3) 385–401.

Rousseau, DM, and McLean Parks, JM (1993) The contracts of individuals and organisations. *Research in Organisational Behaviour*, 15, 1–43.

Rousseau, DM, and Wade-Benzoni, K (1994) Linking strategy and human resource practices: how employee and customer contracts are created. *Human Resource Management*, 33 (3) 463–89.

Salancik, GR, and Pfeffer, J (1978) A social information processing approach to job attitudes and task design. *Administrative Science Quarterly*, 23, 224–53.

Schein, EH (1980) *Organisational Psychology.* Englewood Cliffs, NJ: Prentice Hall.

Schor, J (1992) *The Overworked American.* New York: Basic Books.

Shapiro, J, and Tune, J (1974) Implied contracts rights to job security. *Stanford Law Review*, 26, 335–69.

Shore, LM, & Tetrick, LE (1994) The psychological contract as an explanatory framework in the employment relationship. In C Cooper and DM Rousseau (Eds), *Trends in Organisational Behaviour.* New York: John Wiley & Sons.

Sims, RR (1990) *An Experiential Learning Approach to Employee Training Systems.* Westport: Greenwood/ Quorum Press.

Sims, RR (1991) The institutionalisation of organisational ethics. *Journal of Business Ethics*, 10 (7), 493–506.

Sims, RR (1992) Developing the learning climate in public sector training. *Public Personnel Management*, 21 (3), 335–46.

Sims, RR (1994) Human resource management's role in clarifying the new psychological contract. *Human Resource Management*, 33 (3), 373–82.

Singh, R (1998) Redefining psychological contracts with the US work force: a critical task for strategic human resource management planners in the 1990s. *Human Resource Management*, 37 (1), 61–9.

Smith, A (1997) Auld Lang Syne. *Management — Auckland*, 44 (11) 130.

Sorohan, EG (1994) When the ties that bind break. *Training & Development*, February, 28–33.

Sparrow, PR (1996) Transitions in the psychological contract: some evidence from the banking sector. *Human Resource Management Journal*, 6 (4) 75–92.

Sparrow, PR, and Hiltrop, JM (1997) Redefining the field of European human resource management: a battle between national mindsets and forces of business transition. *Human Resource Management*, 36 (2), 201–219.

Spindler, GS (1994) Psychological contracts in the workplace — a lawyer's view. *Human Resource Management*, 33 (3), 326–34.

Sutton, R, and Kahn, RL (1986) Prediction, understanding, and control as antidotes to organisational stress. In J Lorsch (Ed.), *Handbook of Organisational Behaviour*. Englewood Cliffs, NJ: Prentice Hall.

Sweeney, PD, and McFarlin, DB (1993) Workers evaluation of the 'ends' and the 'means': an examination of four models of distributive and procedural justice. *Organisational Behaviour and Human Decision Processes*, 55, 23–40.

Tichy, NM (1983) *Managing Strategic Change*. New York: John Wiley & Sons.

Toffler, A (1990) *Power Shift*. New York: Bantam Books.

Tornow, WW, and DeMeuse, KP (1994) New paradigm approaches in strategic human resource management: a commentary. *Group and Organisation Management*, 19 (2), 165–71.

Trevino, L (1992) The social effects of punishment in organisations: a justice perspective. *Academy of Management Review*, 17, 647–76.

Turnley, WH (1996) Reconceptualizing the nature and consequences of psychological contract violations (loyalty). Unpublished doctoral dissertation, University of South Carolina.

Turnley, WH, and Feldman, DC (1998) Psychological contract violations during corporate restructuring. *Human Resource Management*, 37 (1), 71–83.

Vroom, VH (1964) *Work and Motivation*. New York: John Wiley & Sons.

Wanous, JP, Reichers, AE, and Austin, JT (1994) Organisational cynicism: an initial study. *Academy of Management Best Papers Proceedings*, 269–72.

Waxler, R, and Higginson, T (1993) Discovering methods to reduce workplace stress. *Industrial Engineering*, 25 (6), 19–22.

Whyte, W (1956) *The Organisation Man*. New York: Simon & Schuster.

Yankelovich, D (1993) How changes in the economy are reshaping American values. In HJ Aaron, TE Mann and T Taylor (Eds), *Values and Public Policy*. Washington, DC: The Brooking Institution.

Zucher, LG (1986) Production of trust: institutional sources of economic structure, 1980–1990. In BM Staw and LL Cummings (Eds), *Research in Organisational Behaviour* (8th ed., pp. 53–111). Greenwich, CT: JAI Press.

CHAPTER 9

Human resource management and the collective employment relationship — a negotiation perspective

by Ray Fells
University of Western Australia

Introduction

This chapter focuses on the collective aspects of employment. Despite the trend towards individualisation, statistics show that a significant majority of non-managerial employees in Australia still have their terms and conditions of employment determined through collective agreements or awards. To quote a recent report on the operation of the federal *Workplace Relations Act 1996*, 'Formalised bargaining has progressively expanded into new areas of the labour force' (DEWRSB 2000, p. 1). Although union membership has now fallen to about one employee in four, there are indications that the ACTU strategy of focusing on the workplace is beginning to have an effect. This strategy is outlined in Unions@work (ACTU 1999; Cooper 2000; Holland 1999) and recognises the need for unions to reallocate resources particularly into workplace organisation, recruiting in previously non-unionised areas and involvement in broader social campaigns. Although union density figures are still declining slowly, the actual number of union members has increased marginally (ABS 2000). In addition, evidence is emerging that the process of collective negotiation is associated with higher wage outcomes and that as a consequence, 'the attractiveness of union membership to workers will be enhanced' (Wooden 2001, p. 16). Taking a broader perspective, Kelly (1998) points to the underlying 'long wave' dynamics that lead to mobilisation and collectivism in the workplace, while Peetz's major study of Australian unions similarly concludes that the continued decline in union membership is not inevitable (Peetz 1998).

Many factors besides the wage differential contribute to an employee's decision to join a union. Peetz found that 'Around half of employees would rather be in a union than not in one and when free to choose in a workplace with a union presence, around half of the employees belong to a union.' (Peetz 1998, p. 54).

These factors, together with the continuing influence of the institutionalised industrial relations system in Australia, require human resource (HR) managers to be aware of the implications of the collective dimension to the employment relationship. This chapter will explore a number of issues that emerge in the management of a collectively organised workplace. It will be developed around three themes: the organisational need to negotiate; the need for a strategic, or at least well-considered, approach; and the importance of integrating management–union relations and manager–employee relations. The chapter provides frameworks that will enable the strategic options to be explored. First, we must address a rather more philosophical though nevertheless practical issue, namely the nature of organisational relationships.

The organisation as a negotiated order

Dunn (1990) presents an interesting contrast between industrial relations and the HR perspective. He asks us to imagine the steady migration and settlement across the United States. Industrial relations, he suggests, can be likened to the early days when the settlers were trapped between the east coast and the impenetrable Appalachian Mountains. With nowhere to go and a shortage of resources, conflict between the settlers was perhaps inevitable. In words used to describe industrial relations, it was a 'them and us', zero-sum situation. When the settlers broke through the mountain chain, resources became plentiful; it was simply a question of working together so that all would benefit — the human resource paradigm. Dunn went one step further in his metaphor to make the point that it was the journey rather than the destination that mattered, because the human resource management (HRM) journey is the continual search for improvement.

There has indeed been improvement for both employers and employees through the development of constructive HR practices, but questions such as 'Will we ever arrive?' or 'Why are we still trying to overcome the same old problems?' are not often asked. Perhaps these questions are best left unasked, because, to continue Dunn's metaphor, the settlers eventually reached California. The west coast was El Dorado for some, but it did not last, so where to next? The next stage of development was to populate all the places that had been bypassed en route to California; but this brings us back — conceptually if not geographically — to our point of departure. (Please hang in there; we will get to the workplace in a moment!) This 'filling in' again put pressure on resources, and the potential for tension and disharmony, which had been there all along, surfaced once more. No matter how much resources are increased through innovation, joint effort and sheer hard work, there remains the question of share — of how to distribute the newly created wealth.

The relevance to the workplace should now be clear. While employer and employee may have a common interest in wealth creation, they have divergent interests over its distribution. There is nothing particularly special about employees in this regard. The tax office wants a share of the organisation's wealth; the CEO acts[1] in the same way, as do the suppliers of raw materials — they want as high a price for their products as possible. The customer wants to pay as low a price as possible for the organisation's product or service. All parties want their share — this is the essence of the capitalist system. An organisation is pluralist, not unitarist, and the role of the manager is to balance and utilise these competing interests for the organisational benefit (Fox 1966, 1985; Mansfield 1980, p. 4; Purcell 1987; Saul 1996).

The conclusion is a practical one: The social or people dimension of an organisation is a complex web of negotiations rather than a team or family[2] or any of the other common 'working together' conceptions (Brown 1993; Morgan 1997; Mangham 1979; Strauss 1978). The CEO negotiates future strategy with the Board; the production manager negotiates with the marketing manager over production priorities; everybody negotiates with the finance manager over budgets; the supervisor negotiates with a staff member over the need to change shifts. Even teams become groups that negotiate within and among themselves (Barker 1993; Casey 1999). Most of these negotiations are resolved amicably to the mutual benefit of those concerned.[3] The significance for the HR manager, and for managers in general, is that their role in managing — particularly in managing employees — is to negotiate agreement, not to secure compliance. This is, of course, a challenge to management prerogative as well as to management competence.

The same point can be made in other ways. Work is often organised as a collective activity, or at least with interdependence and connectivity between work tasks and therefore between the people carrying out those tasks. In consequence, employees have common interests not only with the organisation but also with each other. Collectivisation starts in the workplace, not when the union official first knocks on the door. The employment relationship is an effort bargain (Behrend 1957) that remains inherently contradictory despite attempts to restructure the way work is done (Gallie et al. 1998). Workplace negotiations concern not only the terms and conditions of employment but also who decides those terms (Flanders 1968). From another perspective, the legal basis for an employment contract is, in essence, one of control (Macken, McCarry & Sappideen 1984; Merritt 1982; Sorrell 1979) that recognises and maintains profound differences of interest between employer and employee. Additionally, social attitudes from outside the workplace may give rise to different employee priorities. As an example, community opposition to long working hours or to permanent casual employment may grow steadily. As a result, employees may feel more confident in resisting these conditions at their place of work, particularly when the union movement builds campaigns around the issue — as expressed, for example, in the ACTU's Blueprint for Fairness (ACTU 2001). These issues may be dealt with on an individual basis — sometimes by the employee finding another job, but there is often sufficient commonality among employees for them to develop a collective response to management.

---

1. And often irrespective of the actual performance of the company they are overseeing.
2. It has been said that some workplaces are like families, while in other workplaces the people get on quite well together!
3. Though perhaps not for employees who, while part of the 'team', are casual employees and know that if they refuse to change shifts they may not appear on the next roster at all.

Alternative approaches to the management of union relations

Enough has been said, I hope, to establish that HR managers should recognise the collective dimension of the employment relationship and be in a position to manage it. How, then, might management–union relations best be organised?'[4]

In the Australian context many of the key decisions on management–union relations were made for the employer by virtue of the arbitration system. Questions such as whether to negotiate with a union and, if so, which union and over which issues were, by and large, determined by the tribunals. Employers could easily find themselves in a passive role. The situation has changed to some extent with the evolution of enterprise bargaining and the development of a legislative framework for individual employment arrangements, so it is instructive to examine the key strategic choices now available. In doing this we should again remember that the workplace is a negotiated order, and the outcome of any strategy is contingent upon the reactions of the employees and unions present.

There are three main alternatives for the management of unions in an organisation: to manage the organisation's union relations externally; to manage them internally through a specialist department; or to manage them internally through line management (see table 9.1). A fourth strategy is included for completeness, although it is a strategy for avoiding or dispensing with the union relationship rather than managing it.

The first option is to handle the organisation's union relations externally. This would normally be done though an employer association, which would act as the principal agent in any negotiation with unions. Should the union make a claim against the dismissal of one of its members, management would refer the matter to the employer association. The process would be handled by the association representative, whose professional advice would be relied upon; ideally, the matter would be dealt with through the legislative procedures for unfair dismissal, with an arbitrated decision preferred to a conciliated one. A further dimension to this externalisation of industrial relations might be a decision to follow industry-wide standards and agreements.

As a general approach the external model has a number of advantages. For smaller organisations it provides access to expertise in an area of operation that can cause significant costs if not handled properly. Bringing in an employer association (or, increasingly, an industrial lawyer) is no different from hiring a marketing consultant to advise on the promotion of a new product or a financial adviser to guide the company in raising funds. Further, it is at times convenient for employers to invoke industry standards and tribunal decisions as a defence against union claims: 'In unity is strength' applies as much to employers as to workers. An industry-wide floor to labour costs 'takes wages out of competition', which is particularly important in service industries in which companies compete for contracts. On the other hand, it might inhibit an organisation from developing work arrangements that suit its particular circumstances. Another disadvantage is that it tends to remove issues from the workplace, which turns small issues into big ones that are then harder to settle.

The thrust of recent reforms in workplace relations has been to move away from this external management model. The other two options involve managing workplace relations internally by having an organisation-specific focus and negotiating directly with the unions. In the first variant, internal

Table 9.1: The management of union relations — summary of options

	Decision making	Conduct of IR issues	Processes
External option	principally by third party or by industry body	by employer association	negotiation; preference for conciliation and arbitration
Internal option — specialist	by specialists	by specialists	negotiation
Internal option — line management	by line manager	by line manager	negotiation
Avoidance	by line manager		internal: consultation external (union): arbitration, courts

4. The reader will have noted that we have moved directly from collective relationships to union involvement. There are forms of purely non-union collective representation, and arrangements in which union and non-union representation are combined. The essential considerations are the same as for formal union representation.

specialists such as the HR manager handle the negotiations and the relationship with the unions generally. Here the expertise that was bought in as the need arose in the external model is provided 'in house', so that the strategies and practices are more clearly focused on the needs of the organisation. In this case, if a manager dismissed an employee and the union complained, the matter would be dealt with by the HR manager. Indeed, it might be the case that no dismissal could take place without the approval of the HR department. Among the significant advantages in having an internal specialist are that it improves the quality of management–union relations and ensures that negotiations are conducted properly, with outcomes resolved on the basis of accepted practice — hence, the number of 'unfair' dismissals is reduced. Additionally, having a specialist take control of issues reduces disputes by ensuring consistency and fairness in decisions across the organisation. This approach to managing union relations should allow management to think ahead and plan its workplace relations strategically rather than reactively. However, there are also disadvantages. It might so encourage the growth and importance of the union within the organisation that the HR department and union representatives have a high degree of control, vetting all management decisions; in such a case, industrial peace, rather than more significant organisational objectives, would become the overriding goal.

To overcome these disadvantages the second variant of the internal model places responsibility for industrial relations on line management. In other words, line managers have to handle the workplace issues themselves rather than calling in a specialist manager to do it for them. So, in our example, where a manager is considering dismissing a worker, the manager would have to take responsibility for the outcome. If the union complains, the manager handles the negotiations. A small specialist department may be available for advice but, crucially, if there is an unfair dismissal claim, the manager has to front up at the commission, and if compensation is awarded, then it comes from the manager's own departmental budget. The advantages of the line management approach is that it leads to issues being resolved early, builds up communication between management and workers, increases cooperation, and reduces disputes *if* — and it is a big 'if' — management is competent. One disadvantage is that the unions may feel that their access to senior levels of management is being constrained and that they are being marginalised. A more significant disadvantage is that if line managers are given the responsibility but do not then prove to be competent,

the result is likely to be increased conflict and dispute. This option, therefore, has the potential either to provide very good workplace relations or to result in the worst.

There is one further option that builds on the line management model (and is why unions are sometimes suspicious of this approach). This option tries to dispense with industrial relations and the union altogether and get managers to deal with employees individually and exclusively, so that employees question the need for a union at all. The implementation of this approach often involves a combination of internal and external strategies. Within the organisation the focus is on the individual, while typically a hard line is taken against unions in the industrial tribunals and the courts (see, for example, Bennett 1994, chapter 7).

Contemporary challenges in the management of collective employment relationships

Developing a strategic approach to the management of collective relations

One critical feature of the internal approach is that it provides an opportunity to bring the management of unions and of the workplace into closer alignment. It provides the HR manager with the opportunity to ensure that workplace relations contribute to, rather than detract from, the strategic direction of the organisation.[5] The opportunity to exercise influence over the nature of these relationships (rather than have them fundamentally structured by the formal industrial relations system) requires HR managers to take a strategic or at least a well-considered approach involving an analysis of the desired outcomes and of how they may be achieved.

Walton, Cutcher-Gershenfeld and McKersie (1994) developed a theory of strategic negotiation to analyse a number of longitudinal case studies involving change in management–union relations. They built on their earlier work on negotiation (Walton & McKersie 1965) and on the work of Kochan, Katz and McKersie (1986) to construct a

---

5. However, an important element in the avoidance approach is to create tension in management–union and manager–employee relations, casting the former as externally oriented and therefore detracting from the organisation's and employees' wellbeing.

framework with three main elements — the forces shaping the negotiator's choices, the interaction system and the outcomes. Their framework also incorporates both institutional (union) and individual (employee) levels, and identifies various 'social contract' or relational outcomes ranging from containment to cooperation at the union level and from compliance to commitment at the employee level (Walton et al. 1994, p. 58). This distinction between managing the union relationship and managing the employee relationship is important, given the need to manage both workplace and union relations in tandem as part of an integrated strategy.

The Walton et al. framework (with some modifications) can be usefully employed to analyse an organisation's workplace relations. A modified portrayal of their framework is presented in figure 9.1. Management first identifies its substantive and relational objectives, but the framework recognises that although particular objectives may be regarded as desirable, feasibility also has to be taken into account. Whether a particular objective is feasible depends, in large part, upon the expected response from employees and unions, and although these responses should not be regarded as immutable, they will have an impact. Walton et al. suggests three main negotiating strategies — *forcing change*, *fostering change* and *escape* (which, because it involves not negotiating at all, is not included here). The negotiations themselves can be either distributive (generally competitive) or integrative (cooperative), and will involve negotiations within each group as well as between management and union. These negotiations do not occur in a vacuum, so consideration

must be given to the frequency of negotiation and to the levels at which the negotiations take place. An addition to the Walton et al. framework is the management structure element to incorporate the specialist or line management options, either of which management can adopt as the preferred structure for implementing its workplace relations strategy.

Walton, Cutcher-Gershenfeld and McKersie draw upon their case studies to make a number of important points about the change process. Four of their conclusions are particularly relevant in that they support the point made earlier in the chapter about an organisation being a negotiated order. First, management change is a negotiated process, not a directed one; it is a process of mutual influence, with initiatives shifting back and forth between the stakeholders, and management can pay a price for failing to recognise that this is so. Second, they point to the indeterminacy of the change process, noting that 'outcomes are often unanticipated and unwelcome, not merely disappointing' (Walton et al. 1994, p. 343). Third, the contexts themselves are dynamic and so influence both the process and the outcome. Fourth, they note that resistance to change is often rational and so should be regarded as legitimate; this view challenges the unitarist management perspective that resistance to change is passive and is based on emotional or irrational factors. They conclude that 'successful change will depend upon how well management modifies its change proposals to accommodate labor's interests as well as its attempts to reduce labor's resistance to the proposals as they were originally formulated' (Walton et al. 1994, p. 344).

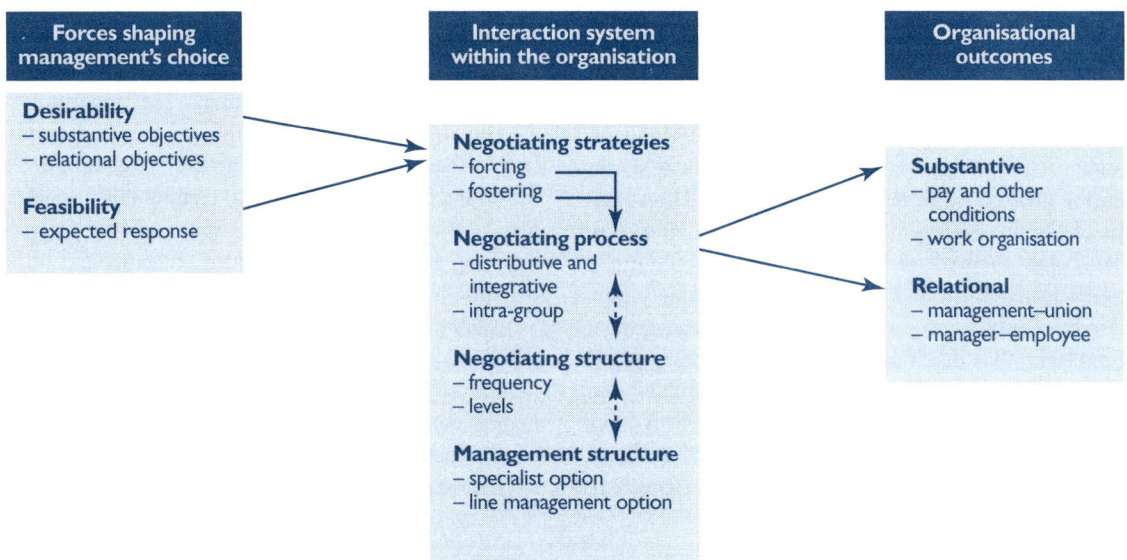

Figure 9.1: Framework for the analysis of workplace relations strategy *Source:* Developed from Walton, Cutcher-Gershenfeld and McKersie (1994), 58.

Different perspectives on the processes for managing change

The insights provided by Walton, Cutcher-Gershenfeld and McKersie can be developed still further. Their framework, essentially a model of *management*-initiated change, explores the strategic options open to a management seeking to bring about change in union and employee relationships. The framework gives less attention to union and employee perspectives, which suggests that it can be enhanced by making the place of employee and union participation in the process of change more explicit. In doing so we can also highlight the role of incentives and resistance to change, which Walton et al. themselves recognised and which feature in many models of the organisational change process. (Robins & Barnwell 1998, chapter 14; Mabry, Salaman & Storey 1998, chapters 13 and 14, provide examples and reviews of the change process.)

Where management drives change, the process might be as portrayed in figure 9.2. In simple terms, management sees the need for change in the organisation, perhaps arising out of new technology or a new competitor in the marketplace, and develops a plan to achieve the necessary changes in the workplace. A broad strategy — either forcing or fostering — is developed to secure employee acceptance of this plan and that the appropriate management structures are established. All these aspects of the change process may be regarded as the management dimension. The employee dimension of the process then focuses on the incentives to change through a process of consultation and persuasion (processes that recognise the ultimate control of management) to overcome employee resistance. The workplace outcomes are substantive changes to the way work is performed and rewarded together with changes to the relationships between employees and management. There is, of course, nothing deterministic in this process that guarantees that the desired substantive and relational outcomes will, in fact, be achieved.

If the change process is envisaged in this way, then when a union dimension is added we can see how easily the union can be regarded as a problem. The union may have an impact in a number of ways. It may stiffen employee resistance to change by making them aware of what has happened when similar changes were proposed elsewhere. It may introduce other concerns that the employees come to view as important. Third, the union may look more closely at the financial or longer term implications. As a result of union involvement, the incentives needed to accept change would be greater. Additionally, the union might be able to bring its negotiating expertise to bear, and so make the task of persuading the employees that much more difficult. In effect, achieving change will take longer, cost more and be likely to achieve less. Such is the typical employer's perspective of the impact of unions on workplace change, a portrayal often based on solid experience. The point being made here is that such a dynamic is inevitable if the management's starting point is to put the union outside the process — all that is left for the union to do is to resist.

In terms of the four approaches to managing union relations outlined earlier in this chapter (see table 9.1), we might expect the process of change to be management driven in the manner portrayed in figure 9.2 when management is pursing either external or avoidance options. Such a situation is not necessarily a stable one. If the union, through its level of membership or through its negotiating ability, forces management to give formal recognition to its role in representing the employees, then the union is no longer an external influence on the employees but is an integral part of the process of change. In this case, the place of the union in the overall process can be portrayed as shown in figure 9.3.

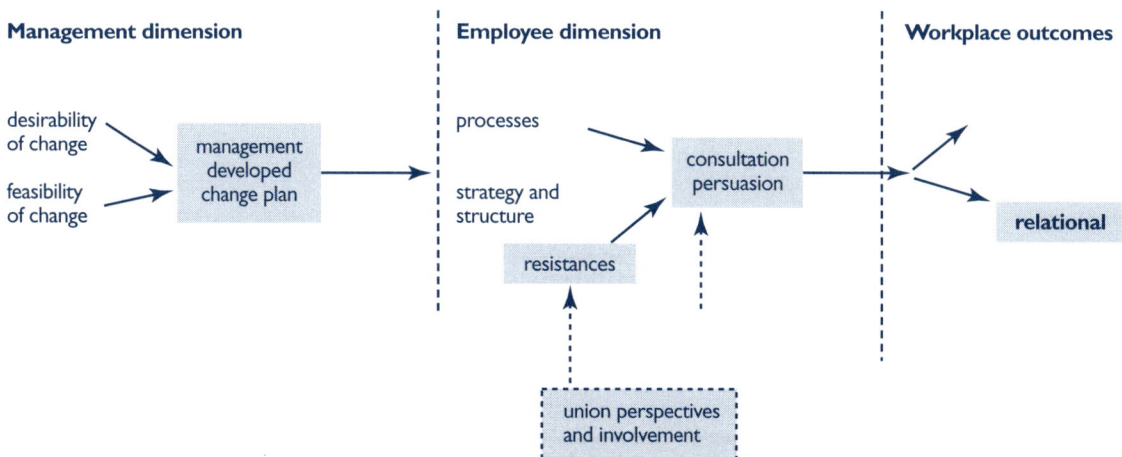

Figure 9.2: Elements of the process of workplace change — management-driven change

Figure 9.3: Elements of the process of workplace change — the union as gatekeeper

As a result of the union being cast in, and acting in, a role of stiffening employee resistance to management plans for change, the union is now clearly placed as the gatekeeper to change. The other difference that will be noted is that the employee consultation process no longer exists; the forum for persuasion is now the management–union negotiating committee; the coordination between the two levels of interaction (management–union and manager–employee) has been lost.[6]

An alternative evolution of the situation, as illustrated in figure 9.3, is a process in which there is a more explicit integration of the union into the change process. The expressions 'partnership' and 'mutual gains' are often used in this context, but these terms probably overstate the common interest and understate the power imbalance involved. The parties are independent but also interdependent, so the pragmatic image of an alliance or confederation is probably more appropriate.

There are two important points to note about this situation (which is portrayed in figure 9.4) and it is these points that make the difference, not the particular name used to describe the relationship. The first is union involvement early in the decision-making process. In practice, management will still — and ought to still — make most of the running on change issues, and the

desirability of change from a management perspective will remain the key driver. There will still be times when the union articulates resistance to some of management's plans but, through its earlier input into the shape of these plans or even the determination of their feasibility, the role of the union is recast. Rather than being viewed by management as a gatekeeper or hurdle to be overcome, the union is viewed as a means by which the employees can make a positive input. Second, employee consultation and persuasion reappear from the management-driven process (figure 9.2). We have noted that it is important for the change processes to occur at two levels — in the management–union committee and at the manager–employee/workgroup level. There is, of course, the union fear that management will 'get at' the employees and so subvert the negotiation process, which is no different from management's fear that the union does not properly represent the views of the employees but brings 'outside' agendas to the negotiations. However, the maintenance of an ongoing, mutually beneficial alliance between management and union and between manager and employee needs the checks and balances of the processes operating at both levels.

Three points should be made about these different approaches to change. First, change is not an end in itself but a means to an end, namely the achievement of desired

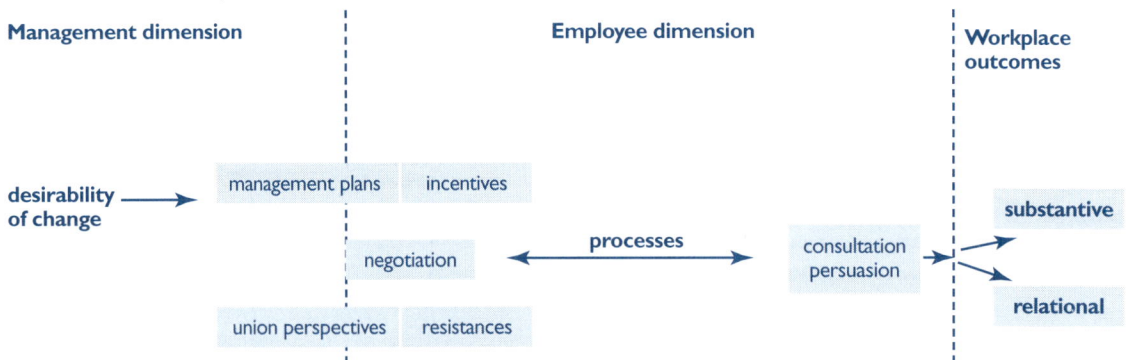

Figure 9.4: Elements of the process of workplace change — management–union alliance

---

6. The question of union recognition is a critical issue and needs careful management at the enterprise level to avoid the creation of adversarial relations at the outset (Fells 1999i).

substantive and relational objectives. Second, the development of workplace change processes is evolutionary and dynamic. Management-driven change can lead to the union's adopting a gatekeeper role. A management–union alliance that becomes too constricting for management will lead to pressure for a more aggressive period of management-driven change. Third, as in all areas of strategy, the actual outcome is determined as much by other participants, in this case the employees and their union, as it is by management.

The nature of cooperation in the alliance

Having outlined three different ways in which management may view the process of workplace change and the union's possible role in it, it is appropriate to take a cautionary look at the nature of possible cooperation in a management–union alliance. The use of the term *alliance* rather than 'partnership' or 'mutual gains' is intended to reflect the independence of the two parties, management and union, as well as their interdependence. It acknowledges that one party may have more power than the other and that one may gain more than the other, but it also recognises that each party has to get something out of the relationship over time. If not, then that party will seek to restructure the relationship. For example, if by 'cooperating' with management the union and employees come to believe that they are not being treated fairly, they may adopt a more forceful strategy to improve their position without necessarily moving to a stance of outright opposition to management on every issue.

Clearly, the nature of the relationship, and elements of it such as cooperation and trust, are fluid. The term *cooperation*, for example, has a wide range of meanings. Voos and Cheng (1989), in a study of the attitudes of management and union officials, found that managers viewed unions as cooperative when they made concessions and worked towards increasing productivity. However, as far as their own behaviour was concerned, making concessions was not seen as part of what management needed to do in order to be cooperative. Nor did they consider implementing plans to undermine the union's position in the workplace to be uncooperative. This research was conducted in the United States, and no similar work has been undertaken in Australia, but there is no reason to suppose that Australian managers' views are any less ambivalent. Indeed, despite all the rhetoric about the need for cooperation, consultation and involvement in the workplace, such ideals are not the dominant practice (Gollan &

Davis 1999, pp. 75–77). Data from the Australian Workplace Industrial Relations Survey indicate that employees were generally more likely only to be informed about those changes that affected them rather than to be consulted or to have any greater input (Morehead 1997, p. 244). Another survey revealed that employees are as likely to report that there had been less involvement and cooperation as that there had been more (DIR 1995, p. 225). It is therefore not surprising that Peetz (1996) found that union members wanted their unions both to cooperate with management (i.e. to work towards increasing productivity) and also to be strong enough to take industrial action, if necessary, to make sure that management cooperated with their employees.

This tension over the nature of cooperation means that management and union will continually 'define or redefine the terms of their interdependence' (Walton & McKersie 1965, p. 3). One aspect of the institutional nature of Australian industrial relations has been that many of these terms of interdependence have been determined by the legislation and the tribunal. As the focus shifts to the enterprise, both management and unions have to consider not only the outcome of their periodic enterprise negotiations but also the type of relationship they wish to maintain. In fact, the nature of their cooperation will itself be a matter for negotiation, and the parties may consider negotiating some form of constitutional agreement. Such an agreement might outline the parties' objectives in maintaining their relationship, their respective rights and responsibilities, the facilities that will be afforded to the union, the nature and extent of information that management gives to the union negotiators, the frequency of meetings and, particularly, the processes to be followed when significant differences occur. HR managers will have to give explicit consideration to the skills and abilities that will be needed in line management to implement the agreement, and they will also need to constantly examine the interface between what is agreed through negotiation with the union and other HR systems.

As pointed out earlier in this chapter, there is a danger that the organisation's relationship with the union, if not handled properly, can develop into one in which the HR department and union representatives exercise an undue influence on management decision making. An agreement giving formal and extensive recognition to the role of the union as representing the employees can, on occasion, contribute to this. On the other hand, a balanced agreement that is negotiated separately from substantive issues and recognises the rights and responsibilities of both parties can lay the foundation for a stable, constructive relationship.

The competitively cooperative process of collective negotiation

If the organisation is a negotiated order, and if the nature of the relationship with the union must itself be negotiated over, what sort of negotiations should be expected? Management–union negotiations are commonly portrayed as being distributive and competitive (following the analysis of collective bargaining by Walton & McKersie 1965). The adversarial nature of this type of bargaining stems in part from the zero-sum nature of the issues being negotiated (primarily pay and conditions) and in part from the fact that the non-negotiation options — the strike or lockout — are designed to cause economic hardship to the other party. The core elements of the distributive model are shown in figure 9.5.

An alternative portrayal of the negotiation process is as some form of integrative bargaining (again following Walton & McKersie 1965) in which the parties work together to explore ways through the problems they jointly face. The problem-solving model of Walton and McKersie has been enhanced by drawing upon Fisher, Ury and Patton's (1991) principled negotiation approach. One of the key elements of this approach is that the parties don't present their positions to be haggled over but instead explore the underlying interests or reasons motivating their respective demands. In the industrial relations context, this approach has been termed *mutual gains bargaining*. When carried through properly, this process involves management and union negotiators being trained to approach negotiations differently (Susskind & Landry 1991; Heckscher & Hall 1994). Heckscher (1993) suggests that key process skills are an ability and willingness to exchange information early and to engage in exploratory discussion before formal bargaining begins; an ability to undertake a discussion of each other's interests rather than engaging in a search for hidden positions; and an ability to make and receive proposals without commitment. This approach provides a better understanding of the context within which the negotiation is to take place; exploring interests allows new perspectives on issues to emerge; and regarding proposals as simply suggestions (rather than new positions) provides a basis for exploration of new solutions. The core elements of the integrative, mutual gains model are shown in figure 9.6.

This distinction between competitive and cooperative ways of negotiating has been utilised in attempts to reform workplace relations. Competitive negotiation is associated with the 'old' industrial relations, whereas the 'new' workplaces should achieve much more through cooperative bargaining approaches. However, the contrasts between competitive and cooperative approaches to negotiation are not so clear-cut in practice. Negotiation is a form of mixed-motive interaction that provides opportunities for both conflict and cooperation (Cutcher-Gershenfeld 1991; Fells 1998a). Competitive and cooperative actions sometimes seem to feed off each other as part of the process of achieving an agreement (Putnam 1990). This is consistent with the view that an organisation is a negotiated order, involving a mix of cooperative and more competitive interactions among those within the organisation.

Research into enterprise bargaining suggests that a typical negotiation involves a complex interaction of competitive and cooperative strategies (Barrett & Mutabazi 1998; Fells 1995; 1998a, 1998b, 2000). The parties *do* work together to find an outcome, but not in the sense of an around-the-table problem-solving group. The starting point for the negotiations is typically the existing agreement, and the negotiations consist of debating clauses in turn until issues are either agreed upon through compromise or dropped from the agenda. Where an interest-based approach is

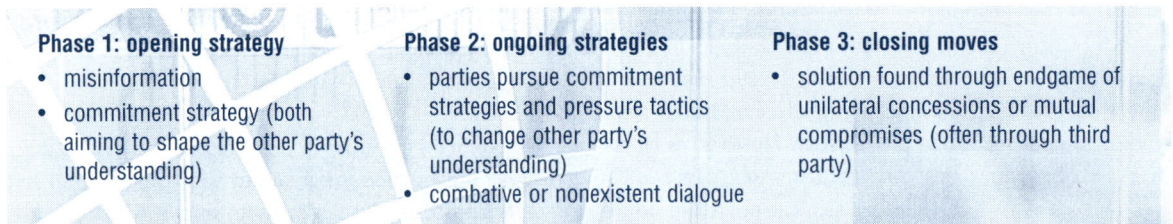

Phase 1: opening strategy	Phase 2: ongoing strategies	Phase 3: closing moves
• misinformation • commitment strategy (both aiming to shape the other party's understanding)	• parties pursue commitment strategies and pressure tactics (to change other party's understanding) • combative or nonexistent dialogue	• solution found through endgame of unilateral concessions or mutual compromises (often through third party)

Figure 9.5: The core elements of the model of distributive (competitive) bargaining *Source:* Adapted from RE Fells (1999b).

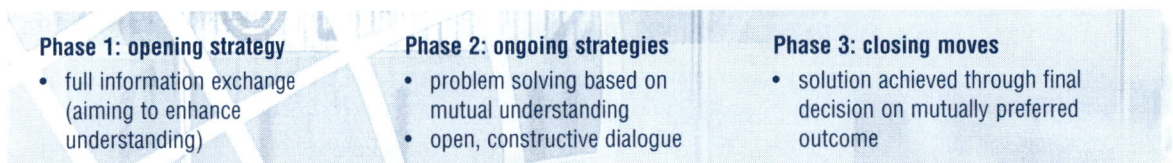

Phase 1: opening strategy	Phase 2: ongoing strategies	Phase 3: closing moves
• full information exchange (aiming to enhance understanding)	• problem solving based on mutual understanding • open, constructive dialogue	• solution achieved through final decision on mutually preferred outcome

Figure 9.6: The core elements of the model of integrative (mutual gains) bargaining *Source:* Adapted from RE Fells (1999b).

adopted and the issues are considered more broadly at the beginning of the negotiation, competitiveness will eventually emerge, usually when the broad issues are translated into specific proposals, because at this point the employees can calculate exactly what the offers mean to them and can make a judgement about the fairness of the proposal.

The approach that management takes to the negotiations will, of course, reflect their underlying perspective of the workplace. If this perspective is fundamentally unitarist, then disagreements that emerge during the course of the negotiation will be attributed to the employees not fully understanding or to the union's 'outside agendas'. The unitarist manager will regard negotiation as an unwelcome intrusion into management prerogative, and this will show in the strategies and behaviours exhibited across the bargaining table. The employee negotiators will react accordingly, and even though an agreement might be reached on the substantive terms, the relational outcome is likely to be one of low trust rather than cooperation. On the other hand, managers who accept the pluralist perspective and regard negotiation as a legitimate process within the organisation are more likely to view disagreements with the employees or union negotiators as a situation to work through, keeping focused on the longer term substantive and relational objectives.[7] The HR manager has an obligation to ensure that line managers have a proper understanding of this negotiation process, even though they might not be directly involved.

The collective or intra-organisational aspects of management–union negotiation

It has already been said that negotiation is a complex mix of cooperative and competitive strategy. Regrettably, this complexity is only part of the process of how managements and unions reach agreement. The key structural factor in these negotiations is that the negotiators are both acting on behalf of others, namely their respective constituencies of the management team on one side and the workforce (or at least the union membership) on the other (see figure 9.7).

When negotiators act on behalf of others (whether in management–union or any other negotiations), the level of competitiveness is likely to be higher than if the negotiators were acting on their own account (Klimoski & Ash 1994; Friedman 1994; Lewicki, Saunders & Minton 1999, pp. 289–314). The negotiating team may experience difficulties in developing the stance their party will take into the

negotiations; it is easier to secure broad support for a position than it is to get endorsement for a broad statement of interests. Management can 'get behind' a proposal to introduce a new shift pattern more easily than a general proposal to review working arrangements. Employees will more readily put their support behind negotiators seeking a $10 wage increase than if they are asking for something less specific such as a 'substantial' wage improvement. This also tends to lead to the development of high opening positions, since these will have broad support. Negotiators acting on behalf of others feel the need to convey an image of strength and the impression that they fully represent their constituents' views. The knowledge that they will have to report back to their constituents on the progress of the negotiations encourages firmness at the bargaining table, not only as a tactic but also in order to avoid loss of face with constituents. For their part, the constituents generally expect their negotiators to 'act tough'.

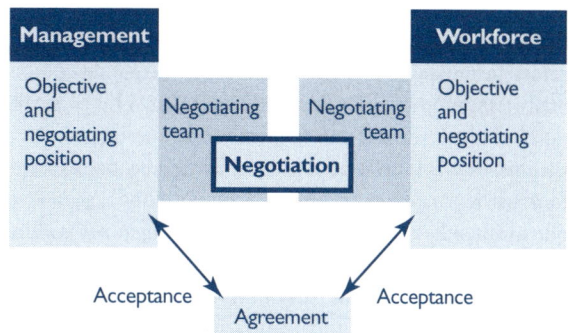

Figure 9.7: The agreement-making structure of a collective negotiation

Any collective negotiation will, in effect, involve three parallel negotiations — that between the two parties, and those within each party to ensure acceptance of the proposed agreement. These three negotiations have to be managed so as to get to a point of agreement at broadly the same time (see figure 9.8). Difficulties arise when the negotiators stray too far from the wishes and expectations of their constituents and then find that their proposed solution is rejected. This has been found to be a particular difficulty when negotiators embark upon the process of mutual gains bargaining, and it is one of the reasons why this form of bargaining is not more pervasive, despite its obvious attractions (Ancona, Friedman & Kolb 1991; Hescker 1993). In these negotiations, the negotiators (especially those on the union side) risk losing touch with their constituency for two reasons. First, the outcome of the negotiations may be quite innovative, including issues that were not on the original agenda, so the

---

7. In case this should be regarded as implying making concessions to the union, it should be noted that one of the prerequisites for generating creative outcomes is that both parties maintain a commitment to their underlying interests.

constituents feel their particular issues have not been addressed. Second, the negotiators are seen as not having negotiated 'properly', and in a low trust environment this may be interpreted as their having been seduced by the other side.

It is therefore important that the pace of the negotiations allows negotiators on both sides to ensure that their constituents are comfortable with the directions the negotiation is taking. Any planning for a negotiation must give consideration to how strong links can be built between the negotiating process and the workplace. In one case, for example, the following structure evolved (figure 9.8). At the first level, all managers and employees were involved in the information and discussion processes. The next level of processes involved determining who should be the negotiators for management and for the unions. Ideally, all managers and all employees would be involved in selecting representatives and conveying to them issues or concerns they believe should be on the agenda. Again ideally, all managers and all employees should continue to monitor the progress of the actual negotiations in anticipation of participating in the final ratification of the negotiated agreement. Only a small number of individuals will be involved in the negotiations themselves, the third level of process. These negotiators have to translate constituency demands into positions that can be put to the other side; they then negotiate outcomes within the parameters of what they understand their constituents will accept. An important part of this process is maintaining links with their constituents, so time and facilities for genuine feedback and constituency discussion must be allowed. In practice, it would be unusual for all the discussions to take place around the negotiating table, so there is a fourth level of process at which leading negotiators from each side may work together through informal discussion, particularly to break deadlocks on key issues.

Conclusion

This chapter has explored some aspects of managing the collective employment relationship. The fundamental premise has been that an organisation is a negotiated order, a pluralist coalition within which employees have collective interests that should be properly managed. Little has been said about the union perspective or about the role of the tribunals or industrial law; rather, the focus has been on the development of frameworks that provide a means for analysing the complex dynamics of management–union and manager–employee relationships.

The shift in emphasis in Australian industrial relations towards a workplace focus has provided the opportunity for both management and unions to develop new strategies. In general, the unions have not embraced the workplace focus as wholeheartedly as have employers. For their part, HR managers now have greater freedom to choose how they will approach the task of managing their relationship with the union — externally, internally or through avoidance. This chapter has concentrated on how the internal management of union and workplace relations might be developed, and in doing so has drawn attention to the need to integrate the management–union relationship with that between manager and employee.

The availability of a range of structures, processes and potential outcomes gives rise to the need for a strategic approach to be developed. In this respect, the Walton et al. (1994) framework provides a useful starting point that can be developed to give greater emphasis to the employee dimension in the change process. The three options — management-driven change, the union as gatekeeper and the management–union alliance — reflect different attitudes that

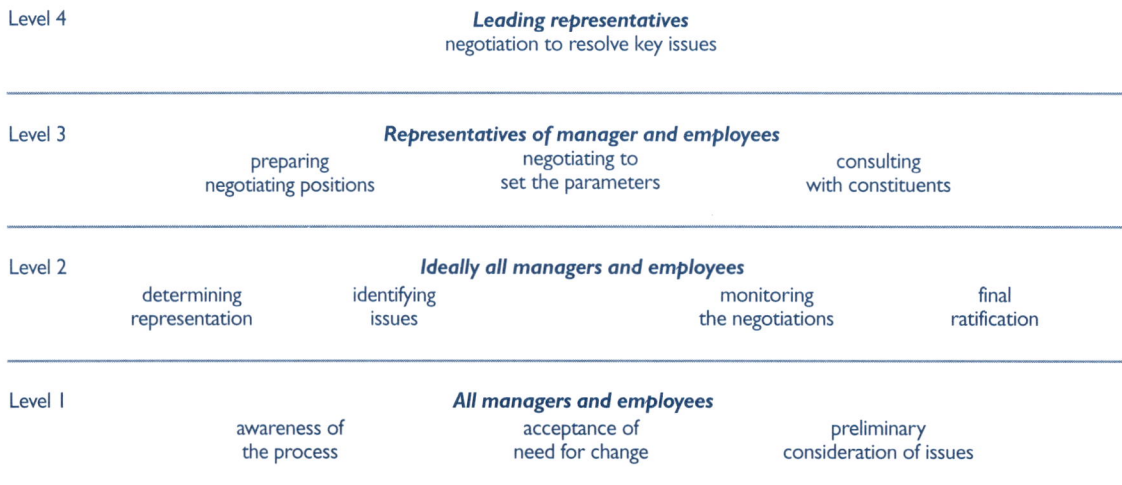

Level 4	*Leading representatives* negotiation to resolve key issues		
Level 3	*Representatives of manager and employees*		
	preparing negotiating positions	negotiating to set the parameters	consulting with constituents
Level 2	*Ideally all managers and employees*		
	determining representation	identifying issues	monitoring the negotiations	final ratification
Level 1	*All managers and employees*		
	awareness of the process	acceptance of need for change	preliminary consideration of issues

Figure 9.8: Levels of involvement in the collective negotiation process *Source:* Adapted from Fells and Robson (1995).

management might hold about its own role and that of the employees. The role of the HR manager in this respect is to ensure a consistency of approach across the organisation.

Given the importance of negotiation in all aspects of managing an organisation, the HR manager also has an obligation to establish a preferred way of negotiating. A simple preference for 'cooperative' over 'competitive' negotiation is not sufficient. Any negotiation is a complex mix of cooperation and competitiveness, a process made even more complex in workplace negotiations in which the negotiators are acting on behalf of others. As a result, the HR manager must ensure that line managers are competent in this aspect of their work and develop structures and processes to ensure that the links between the workplace and the negotiating table are maintained.

References

ABS (2000) *Employee Earnings, Benefits and Trade Union Membership*. Cat. no. 6310.0. Canberra: Australian Bureau of Statistics.

ACTU (1999) *Unions@work*. Melbourne: Australian Council of Trade Unions.

ACTU (2001) *Our Future at Work: A Union Blueprint for Fairness*. Melbourne: Australian Council of Trade Unions.

Ancona, DG, Friedman, RA, and Kolb, DM (1991) The group and what happens on the way to 'yes'. *Negotiation Journal*, 7 (2) 155–73.

Barker, JR (1993) Tightening the iron cage: concertive control in self-managing teams. *Administrative Science Quarterly*, 38, 408–473.

Barrett, R, and Mutabazi, C (1998) Enterprise bargaining in action. *Asia Pacific Journal of Human Resources*, 36 (1) 93–103.

Behrend, H (1957) The effort bargain. *Industrial and Labour Relations Review*, 10, 503–515.

Bennett, L (1994) *Making Labour Law*. Sydney: Australia Law Book Co.

Brown, RK (1993) The negotiated order of the industrial enterprise. In H Martins (Ed.), *Knowledge and Passion*. London: I.B. Touris.

Casey, C (1999) 'Come, join our family': discipline and integration in corporation organizational culture. *Human Relations*, 52 (2) 155–77.

Cooper, R (2000) Organise, Organise, Organise! ACTU Congress 2000. *Journal of Industrial Relations*, 42 (4) 582–94.

Cutcher-Gershenfeld, J (1991) The impact on economic performance of a transformation in workplace relations. *Industrial and Labor Relations Review* 44, 241–60.

DIR (1995) *Enterprise Bargaining in Australia*. Canberra: Department of Industrial Relations.

DEWRSB (2000) *Agreement making in Australia under the Workplace Relations Act*. Canberra: Department of Employment, Workplace Relations and Small Business.

Dunn, S (1990) Root metaphor in the old and new industrial relations. *British Journal of Industrial Relations*, 28 (1) 1–31.

Fells, RE (1995) Enterprise bargaining and the process of negotiation. *Journal of Industrial Relations*, 37 (2) 218–35.

Fells, RE (1998a) Overcoming the dilemmas in Walton and McKersie's mixed bargaining strategy. *Relations Industrielles — Industrial Relations*, 53 (2) 300–322.

Fells, RE (1998b) A critical examination of the process of workplace negotiation. *Labour and Industry*, 9 (1) 37–52.

Fells, RE (1999a) Competitive negotiation and the question of union negotiating rights. *Labour and Industry*, 9 (3) 99–122.

Fells, RE (1999b) The process of negotiation — an Australian and North American comparison. In R Thorpe (Ed.) (1999), *Managing Diversity*. Proceedings of the British Academy of Management Conference, 207–228.

Fells, RE (2000) Labour–management negotiation: some insights into strategy and language. *Relations Industrielles — Industrial Relations*, 55 (4) 583–603.

Fells, RE, and Robson, S (1995) Being realistic: the task of negotiating an enterprise agreement. Report prepared for the Department of Industrial Relations Workplace Bargaining Progam, Canberra.

Fisher, R, Ury, W, and Patton, B (1991) *Getting to Yes*. New York: Penguin.

Flanders, A (1968) Collective bargaining: a theoretical analysis. *British Journal of Industrial Relations*, 6, 1–26.

Fox, A (1966) *Industrial Sociology and Industrial Relations*. Research Paper No. 3. Royal Commission on Trade Unions and Employers' Associations. London: HMSO.

Fox, A (1985) *Man Mismanagement*. London: Hutchinson.

Friedman, RA (1994) *Front Stage Backstage* Cambridge, MA: MIT Press.

Gallie, D, White, M, Cheng, Y, and Tomlinson, M (1998) *Restructuring the Employment Relationship*. Oxford: Clarendon Press.

Gollan, PJ, and Davis, E (1999) High involvement management and organizational change: beyond rhetoric. *Asia Pacific Journal of Human Resources*, 37 (3) 69–91.

Heckscher, CC (1993) Searching for mutual gains in labor relations. In L Hall (Ed.), *Negotiation: Strategies for Mutual Gain*. Newbury Park: Sage, 86–104.

Heckscher, C, and Hall, L (1994) Mutual gains and beyond: two levels of intervention. *Negotiation Journal*, 10 (3) 235–48.

Holland, P (1999) 'Organising works': meeting the challenge of declining trade union membership. *International Employment Relations Review*, 5 (1) 63–74.

Kelly, J (1998) *Rethinking Industrial Relations*. London: Routledge.

Klimoski, RJ, and Ash, RA (1974) Accountability and negotiator behaviour. *Organizational Behavior and Human Performance*, 409–425.

Kochan, TA, Katz, HC, and McKersie, RB (1986) *The Transformation of American Industrial Relations*. New York: Basic Books.

Lewicki, RJ, Minton, JW, and Saunders, DM (1999) *Negotiation*. Burr Ridge, IL: Richard D. Irwin.

Mabey, C, Salaman, G, and Storey, J (1998) *Human Resource Management*. Oxford: Blackwell.

Macken, JJ, McCarry, GJ, and Sappideen, C (1984) *The Law of Employment*. Sydney: Law Book Co.

Mangham, I (1979) *The Politics of Organizational Change*. London: Associated Business Press.

Mansfield, R (1980) The management task. In M Poole and R Mansfield (Eds), *Managerial Roles in Industrial Relations*. Farnborough, UK: Gower.

Merritt, A (1982) 'Control' v. 'economic reality': defining the contract of employment. *Australian Business Law Review*, 10, 105–124.

Morehead, A, Steele, M, Alexander, M, Stephen, K, and Duffin, L (1997) *Changes at Work*. Melbourne: Longman.

Morgan, G (1997) *Images of Organisation*. Thousand Oaks, CA: Sage.

Peetz, D (1996) Unions, conflict and the dilemma of cooperation. *Journal of Industrial Relations*, 38 (4) 548–70.

Peetz, D (1998) *Unions in a Contrary World*. Melbourne: Cambridge University Press.

Purcell, J (1987) Mapping management style in employee relations. *Journal of Management Studies*, 23 (5) 533–48.

Putnam, LL (1990) Reframing integrative and distributive bargaining: a process perspective. In BL Sheppard, MH Bazerman and RJ Lewicki (Eds), *Research on Negotiations in Organizations*. Greenwich, CN: JAI Press, 3–30.

Robbins, SP, and Barnwell, N (1998) *Organisation Theory*. Sydney: Prentice Hall.

Saul, P (1996) Managing the Organisation as a Community of Contributors. *Asia Pacific Journal of Human Resources*, 34 (3) 19–36.

Sorrell, GH (1979) *Law in Labour Relations: An Australian Essay*. Sydney: Law Book Co.

Strauss A (1978) *Negotiations*. San Francisco: Jossey-Bass.

Susskind, LE, and Landry, EM (1991) Implementing a mutual gains approach to collective bargaining. *Negotiation Journal*, 7 (1) 5–10.

Voos, PB, and Cheng, T (1989) What do managers mean by cooperative labor relations?' *Labour Studies Journal*, 14 (1) 3–18.

Walton, RE, Cutcher-Gershenfeld, JE, and McKersie, RB (1994) *Strategic Negotiations*. Boston, MA: Harvard Business School Press.

Walton, RE, and McKersie, RB (1965) *A Behavioral Theory of Labor Negotiations*. New York: McGraw-Hill.

Wooden, M (2001) Union wage effects in the presence of enterprise bargaining. *The Economic Record*, 77 (236) 1–18.

CHAPTER 10

Human resource management and the individualisation of the employment relationship

by Peter Waring and Mark Bray
University of Newcastle

Introduction

Individual contracts, individual performance reviews and individualised reward schemes have all become part of contemporary human resource management (HRM) discourse, and in many instances they are viewed as the natural tools of the modern HRM professional. In Australia, the past decade has witnessed significant growth in the number of employers consciously choosing to individualise the employment relationship, as is indicated by new, increasingly popular legal options for individual employment contracts, as well as by survey and case study findings that reveal the adoption of many other individualistic HRM practices.

It is most often employers who are promoting the individualisation of the employment relationship, and their stance embodies a rejection of one hundred years of collective regulation and bargaining arrangements in Australia. Until very recently, the Australian system of industrial relations encouraged 'collectives' to represent both employees and employers, while collective bargaining, under the scrutiny of a network of industrial tribunals, was the *modus operandi* of industrial negotiation. Collectivism was, of course, far from complete — before the introduction of the state and federal conciliation and arbitration laws at the turn of the twentieth century, individual contracts mediated by the Masters and Servants Acts predominated, while collectives of employees (i.e. unions) were repressed by the common law. Even during the hundred-year history of compulsory conciliation and arbitration, individual common law contracts underpinned the employment of all employees and remained the sole form of regulation for some employees. In short, individualising the employment relationship is not totally new. Yet the most recent push for individualisation is novel, and acknowledgement of historical continuities does not explain this new phenomenon.

This chapter aims to develop an understanding of the recent growth in individualism of the employment relationship. The first step is to define individualism and identify three main types of individualism. The next step is to explore the various arguments used to support and oppose individualisation. Are the critics right when they claim that individualism is about excluding trade unions from representing members and permitting employers to exploit their superior bargaining power, or are its supporters closer to the truth when they argue that individual contracts help to induce a closer, more trusting relationship between employers and their employees? Next, the Australian experience of individualism in its various forms is examined in more depth. The conclusion that emerges is that a growing number of Australian employers have individualised the employment relationship in response to economic imperatives, although there is little evidence to support claims that substantial benefits accrue as a result of individualisation. Finally, the implications of the analysis for the practice of HRM within Australian organisations is explored.

What is individualism?

The term *individualism* is conceived in this chapter as a particular means of organising and structuring employment relations. This approach is necessarily broad. Too often in the past individualism, or the individualisation of employment relations, has been narrowly conceptualised in terms of the formation and regulation of individual employment contracts. In contrast, we argue that contemporary forms of individualism go beyond the use of individual employment contracts. Typically, individual contracts are merely one dimension of an HR strategy that incorporates other practices, which together have the effect of individualising the employment relationship. More particularly, individual contracts and individualistic HR practices, we contend, individualise different dimensions of the employment relationship (Waring 1999).

The key to understanding this approach to individualism is to recognise the dual nature of the employment relationship (see Bray 1986 & Edwards 1995b). On the one hand, there is the *exchange* dimension of the employment relationship, which encapsulates the sale of labour power (the potential of employees to work) in exchange for wages. The site of this exchange is the labour market. On the other hand, the *production* dimension of the employment relationship captures the way in which labour power converted into actual labour (i.e. work itself) in order to produce goods and services. The site of this second dimension is the production process in the factory or office or shop. Individualism can be the means by which either the exchange or the production dimension of the employment relationship is organised and structured, and this distinction allows us to identify three different types of individualism.

Procedural and substantive individualism

In the literature on individualism the dichotomy developed by Brown (1998) of 'procedural' and 'substantive' individualism has been highly influential. Put simply, *procedural individualism* refers to an individualised mechanism used to determine the content of employment contracts. In other words, when negotiating the terms and conditions of employment, the bargaining is conducted by employers and individual employees; this contrasts with collective bargaining, a process in which groups of workers combine to negotiate with their employer or employers. *Substantive individualisation* refers to the differentiation of terms and conditions of employment that results from the process of individual bargaining. In other words, each individual employee has wages or working conditions that are different from those of his or her fellow employees, even if these colleagues are performing similar work tasks.

This procedural/substantive distinction is useful in gauging the extent of individualisation in the labour market — in the 'exchange' dimension of the employment relationship. Brown (1998, p. 6), for instance, reports a British study of 15 firms that had used individual employment contracts. The study found, however, that standardisation of non-pay terms and conditions had actually increased rather than diminished. In other words, despite high *procedural* individualisation there was low *substantive* individualisation.

Process individualism

Although Brown's (1998) typology encapsulates the means by which the contract of employment is developed (procedural individualism) and considers the degree to which contractual terms and conditions are differentiated between contracts (substantive individualism), it does not accommodate the means by which the work performance of employees is secured within the production process. Consequently, individualistic management practices, that may or may not be referred to in the contract of employment, but that have the effect of individualising employment relations, are not captured. There is, then, a need for a third category — what might be called 'process' individualism (see Waring 1999, 2000) — that recognises the importance of individualistic approaches to managing the employment relationship in reshaping and possibly shifting employment relations away from collectivist foundations.

The saliency of process individualism can be seen in many of the more sophisticated versions of HRM that present a collection of practices designed to elicit individual mental, emotional and physical labour from the labour power of individual employees within the production process (Storey 1992; Townley 1994; Guest 1987; Legge 1995). Individual performance reviews and performance management systems generally, reward systems, communication and consultation mechanisms, and career development schemes are just some of the HR practices that arguably have the effect of individualising the employment relationship.

Why individualisation?

It is mainly employers who have sought to individualise the employment relationship. Why do they do this? Answering this question by identifying the underlying motives of employers is always a complex and problematic task. In this case, this complexity is compounded by the contentious nature of the subject and the notion that many of these explanations are interrelated. At the risk of some simplification, this section identifies three principal explanations for recent employer interest in individualisation.

The economic imperative

The declared motivation of many advocates of individualisation is to improve both firm and national economic performance. According to supporters, individualisation (and especially individual contracts) contribute to more flexible, and therefore more productive, working relationships. Central to this notion is the argument that the collectivism, and the capacity of third parties to intervene in and regulate employment relations, unduly restricts managerial prerogative and the ability of firms to respond to changing market circumstances.

One aspect of this argument is that collective bargaining, in itself, is an inefficient and cumbersome process that prevents employees from achieving their productive potential. Giudice (advocate for Comalco during the Weipa dispute and currently President of the Australian Industrial Relations Commission) advanced this argument when he stated:

> ... the employee ceases to be in a work environment in which improvements in work have a tradeable value in the collective context and are therefore to be hoarded up and sold in the collective negotiations ... In a staff relationship ... the inbuilt constraints on the free flow of work improvements are removed because each individual knows that he or she will be subjectively judged on his or her work performance ... We know that that form of employment is more productive for the company and therefore more cost effective, more enjoyable for employees, and enables the company to grow, to be more internationally competitive, and to make a greater contribution to the Australian economy. (J Giudice, cat. no. 20166 of 1994, cited in Hamberger 1995)

Thus, according to Giudice (1994), individual contracts encourage maximisation of individual effort because they do not permit the individual's contributions to be obscured by the work group. They also remove from the employment relationship the collective bargaining habit of trading stored inflexibilities for wage increases. In other words, collective bargaining — especially the 'productivity bargaining' approach that operated in Australia in the late 1980s and early 1990s — is repugnant as it encourages employees to 'slow release' work improvements over successive bargaining rounds. This argument is, of course, silent on whether such complete access to work improvements should be reciprocated through equal sharing of the fruits of productivity increases. It also presupposes that all productivity gains can be realised at a particular point in time. Nevertheless, individual employment contracts are said to encourage a more productive labour process, which is causally linked to international competitiveness and superior national economic performance.

The link between individualisation and national economic performance is explained in detail in the neo-liberalist literature of economist Fredrich Hayek. As Weeks (1995, p. 220) has noted, Hayek's ideas gained currency in Australia when he conducted a lecture tour in Australia in 1976. Three of these lectures were subsequently published by the Melbourne-based Centre for Independent Studies. According to Wailes (1997, p. 37), Hayek believed that trade unions distort prices in the labour market, which causes inefficiencies in other factor markets. In order to remove this distortion, the monopoly power that trade unions exert over labour market outcomes must be replaced with individual freedom of contract. If this were achieved, the superior bargaining power of employers would be counterbalanced by the weight of contract law and heightened labour mobility. Hayek was convinced that employers who took advantage of their superior economic power over individuals would lose quality labour as disgruntled workers would glide effortlessly into alternative employment. Similarly, Epstein (1983) has suggested that employees are free to strike a new bargain with an alternative employer should they be unhappy with their present employment arrangements. There are remarkable similarities between the doctrines of Hayek and Epstein and the arguments used by an Australian advocate for individualization, Des Moore. In challenging the existence of bargaining inequalities, for instance, Moore argues that 'unless an employer treats his employees fairly and provides employment conditions ... he risks losing workers ...' (Moore 1998, p. 34).

Economic theory may also suggest that individualisation is a means of internalising market forces to drive competition between employees and hence encourage productivity improvements. Under this approach, producing substantive individualism, remuneration should be highly differentiated and tied to individual performance. In this way, management are able to more easily reward employees according to their individual contributions. The veracity of this simplistic argument, however, is questionable. As Brown (1998, p. 5) has argued, more sophisticated economic theory presents good reasons why firms would want to limit 'individualisation'. For example, highly individualised contracts have transaction costs that may be expensive and problematic to administer. Moreover, high substantive individualism can create perceptions of inequity among employees that are highly de-motivating, producing poor performance outcomes (Adams 1965).

An additional economic reason for the current interest in individualism may lie in globalisation theory. The steady removal of tariffs, the privatisation of the public sector and the deregulation of certain industries have exposed Australian firms to heightened international competition over the past few decades. This increased competition has had the effect of exposing investors to greater risk. In order to protect shareholders, managers in some firms have attempted to redistribute this risk among the firm's suppliers and subcontractors and, most importantly, employees of the firm. This risk-averse behaviour often comes in the form of contingent pay arrangements by which a proportion of employees' wages becomes contingent on achieving certain sales, productivity or other relevant targets. In the past, contingent pay arrangements were usually linked to firm or work group performance, but increasingly, it seems, these are being devolved to the level of the individual. For instance, van Barneveld and Arsvoska's (2001) comparison of AWAs (federal individual contracts) with collective agreements discovered that AWAs were more likely to contain 'at-risk' pay arrangements than were collective agreements. Moreover, they found that AWAs (discussed more fully in a later section of this chapter) were more likely to link risk-based wage increases to the performance of individual employees as opposed to group performance. The strong correlation between individual contracts and at-risk pay arrangements indicates an attempt to shift or redistribute risk from shareholders to employees.

In summary, advocates of individualisation are firmly convinced of its potential to deliver productivity and work improvements that are superior to those that can be extracted from workers under collective bargaining. This key to improved productivity, they declare, also contributes to high national economic performance. The power of this argument would be greatly increased if there were empirical evidence to support it, but there is little such evidence. Furthermore, some critics have suggested that such an argument is merely a 'smokescreen' used to disguise the real underlying motivation of employers — to individualise power relations and avoid collectivism.

Individualising power relations and avoiding collectivism

In industrial relations scholarship, most discussion of individualisation rests on the assumption that a structured inequity exists in the employment relationship. This assumes that employees, as individuals, have far less power in the labour market than employers and therefore do not come to the bargaining table on equal terms. As early as 1897, Sidney and Beatrice Webb, described as the parents of industrial relations, observed this imbalance:

> … in the absence of any common rule, the conditions of employment are left to 'free competition'; this always means in practice, that they are arrived at by individual bargaining between contracting parties of very unequal strength. Such a settlement, it is asserted, invariably tends, for the mass of the workers, towards the worst possible conditions of labor. (p. 192)

Similarly, Fox (1974) is noted for his succinct characterisation of the employment relationship in which the 'weakness of the individual worker makes the individual agreement for sale of his labour power "asymmetric"… which cannot be gauged by reference to the so-called contract of employment' (p. 191). Moreover, Crouch has argued that although the employment contract 'pretends to be an even-handed relationship between two equal partners, this is purely a legal fiction' (p. 45).

Collectivism can be seen as a direct consequence of these inequalities — workers attempted to redress the power imbalance by combining to form trade unions and by agitating for state intervention and regulation of both the labour market and the labour process.

In this context, it can be argued that the pursuit by employers of procedural individualism is designed to dismantle collectivism in the labour market and to return the employment relationship to the free market in which employers inevitably dominate. The use of individual contracts in Australia can certainly be interpreted this way. Recent case studies by Waring (2000), for example, show that employers in the Australian coal industry attempted to individualise employment relations in order to weaken or even wholly displace union power at the workplace. Similar motives can be recognised when individual contracts were actively sought by some of Australia's largest employers, such as Patrick's Stevedoring during the bitter waterfront dispute in 1998 (see Ellem 1998), BHP Ltd in its iron ore facilities in Western Australia (see Riley 2000) and, most recently, the Commonwealth and ANZ banks.

Process individualism can also be associated with employer efforts to reduce collectivism. Human resource management, for example, has been described by some observers (Townley 1994; Purcell 1995) as offering a set of practices that privilege the individual in the production process and undermine collective organisation among workers. A particularly sophisticated version of this argument is Townley's (1994) Foucaldian analysis of HRM practices (such as performance appraisal, advanced selection techniques and employee counselling), which reveals them as attempts by employers to gain greater 'knowledge' about individual employees. This knowledge increases management's power over individual employees, in that managers are better placed to develop policies and practices that better motivate, more closely monitor and more effectively control the work performance of individual employees. These practices are considered to offer greater certainty to managers in their attempts to extract discretionary effort.

Clearly, to suggest that employers seek individualisation because it has the effect of undermining collectivism among employees — and thereby improves the market power and workplace authority of employers — is rarely accepted by employers. Strategies to de-unionise workplaces and achieve greater control over employees may not be judged favourably by the wider community and, indeed, may even tarnish the public image of organisations. Hence, more publicly palatable arguments focusing on the potential of individualisation to increase trust between employer and employee are often advanced in support of individualisation. This argument is evaluated in the next section.

Closer relations through individualisation?

A popular proposition used by advocates of individualisation is that it permits managers to introduce desirable 'cultural change' within organisations that in turn encourages the development of closer relationships with their employees. In a recent case involving the Commonwealth Bank's attempt to 'roll out' individual contracts to its staff, the Federal Court summarised this view in the following terms:

Individual employment contracts are justified on various bases. The most generous view holds that such arrangements promote a high level of trust and coincidence of purpose between employer and employee. It is said that those employment contracts encourage individual responsibility for quality and performance and develop employees who are organisationally committed and encouraged to pursue not only their own interests but also those of their employer.[1]

This 'generous' view of why employers use individual contracts was also articulated by the Employment Advocate, Johnathan Hamberger, in a presentation to the Australian Human Resources Institute on 8 May 2001. During this speech, Hamberger suggested that the individual contract:

encourages 'buy-in' to the needs of the enterprise and fosters a more co-operative approach to the employer–employee relationship. It could be argued that there is the potential to foster a cultural change through the introduction of AWAs.

The notion that individualisation is a precursor to the development of trust, and hence improved employee commitment, was also the primary argument relied upon by Comalco to defend the use of individual contracts during the 1995–96 Weipa dispute. In this watershed dispute the company, Comalco (a subsidiary of CRA, now Rio Tinto), had offered higher remuneration to 'staff employees' (those who had accepted common law employment contracts) than to comparable employees who worked under awards. As part of their defence for this seemingly inequitable situation, the company argued that a staff employee differed from an award employee because of the special commitment they had made to the organisation, demonstrated through the acceptance of individual contracts and adherence to core corporate values (Ludeke 1996).

An example of this 'special commitment' emerged during cross-examination conducted by the ACTU's advocate, and former prime minister, Bob Hawke, in an Australian Industrial Relations Commission hearing of the Weipa dispute. A Comalco employee who had committed to an individual contract declared that, in doing so, he had accepted the company's 'love' and made the 'paradigm shift' (Transcript, AIRC Print No. M8600, 1996).

Dr Ian Macdonald, an organisational psychologist consulting to Comalco/CRA, gave evidence to the commission outlining the importance and benefits of a 'staff relationship'. For Macdonald (1995), collectively negotiated agreements

---

1. *Finance Sector Union v Commonwealth Bank of Australia* [2000] FCA 1372 (28 September) para 3.

only maximise the problems associated with ignoring individual differences:

> *A collective agreement which minimises individual differences also stifles creativity and diversity and has the potential to wrap the company in red tape and bureaucratic systems. Thus, this form of work relationship cannot be expected to be as productive. The staff relationship is more efficient and productive provided the leadership accepts the accountabilities discussed above.* (Macdonald 1995, pt 35)

> *Thus the staff relationship must be founded four-square on trust. Trust in the leadership of the company and its ability to act fairly and with courage. The fear or anxiety aroused by such relationships is that this trust may be betrayed or is dependent on the good will or fairness of a particular manager/leader.* (Macdonald 1995, pt 19)

Not only does the staff relationship offer a pathway to increased trust, according to Macdonald, but the relationship removes the adversarial assumption that natural antagonisms exist between employers and labour:

> *In contrast to the relationship described above, a mediated relationship is essentially adversarial. It assumes that a group has to be represented by a third party if the members are to be treated fairly. It is, therefore, a relationship, which necessarily assumes an absence of trust. It assumes that neither side can be trusted not to exploit the other. It results from a fundamental assumption that capital and labour have contrary interests. The employee's view is that there is strength in numbers, as a necessary defence against the company. Individual differentiation is minimised in contrast to a staff relationship, which does not have this adversarial assumption.* (Macdonald 1995, pt 31)

The idea that trust is central to an individualised employment relationship conforms closely to the unitarist vision of organisations held by many managers. Clearly, Rio Tinto and its predecessors provide one example, but there are many others. A recent Federal Court case revealed that Telstra is another:

> *He [a senior Telstra manager] instructed managers by email that they should take into account the loyalty of Telstra employees who had signed contracts when implementing 10,000 redundancies. Non-union contract workers had shown 'trust' in the company by accepting Telstra's 'preferred model of individual employment'.* (Norington 2001)

However, this idealised picture of individualisation becomes more difficult to accept when the broader context of individual contracts in such organisations is considered. Waring and Lynch (1997), for example, argue that the offer of individual contracts at the Rio Tinto–owned Hunter Valley mine occurred against a background of stalled collective bargaining. Workers who accepted individual contracts stood to gain pay rises of more than $170 per week, while no wage increases were forthcoming through collective bargaining. Likewise, at Weipa, contract workers earned $10 000 to $15 000 more than workers whose conditions were governed by the award (Gorman 1996). More recently, at BHP's iron ore facilities in Western Australia, workers were offered considerable sums to sign up to individual contracts (Riley 2000, p. 94). Finally, Telstra employees on individual contracts could clearly expect greater employment security than their award counterparts. These examples suggest that strong instrumental factors — as opposed to high trust relations — often lie behind the offer (and acceptance) of individual contracts.

Finally, an associated argument that is sometimes used to support individualisation is the idea that an individualised employment relationship can better reflect the needs and circumstances of particular employees. For instance, individual contracts can be uniquely tailored to provide flexible, 'family-friendly' work arrangements for employees with family responsibilities. Additionally, reward systems can be designed to suit the individual wishes of employees. For example, some older employees may wish to have a higher proportion of their salary paid as superannuation, while other employees may wish to 'cash-out' certain conditions. This kind of flexibility is frequently highlighted to support claims that individual contracts are 'good' for employees. However, the second imputation here is that tailoring individual contracts to workers' needs is an expression of commitment from the employer that ought to be reciprocated, drawing both parties into a closer, more trusting relationship capable of producing mutual gains.

The notion that employers are willing to substantively individualise employment contracts, however, is not supported by research on individual contracts. As we shall see in the following sections on the Australian experience of individualism, the literature suggests that employers generally offer only highly standardised individual contracts, with very little scope for variation between comparable employees. This finding lends support to the contention that individual contracts have more to do with individualising power relations than assisting employees to cope with competing life demands.

The Australian experience

In Australia, calls for individualised employment relations are a fairly recent phenomenon. During the 1980s there was considerable criticism of compulsory arbitration and unions from a vociferous and relatively marginal group of commentators and employers associated with the 'New Right' (Dabscheck 1995). This clearly represented an attack on collectivism in the name of individualism, but at that stage there was little to suggest that the critics had seriously considered the legal and institutional reforms required to implement their dreams. Indeed, mainstream employer associations considered the demands of the New Right to be naïve. In 1986, for example, Bryan Noakes, the Director-General of the Confederation of Australian Industry, stated:

> The notion that industrial relations should be a matter for the individual employer and the individual employee is one which strikes many responsive chords, but it is so far removed from reality that it is a dangerous distraction. (cited in Houlihan 1986, p. 91)

It was only in the 1990s that the possibility of over-turning the dominant collectivist system of industrial relations in favour of individual employment contracts was more clearly articulated. A major catalyst for this transformation was the deregulatory experience of New Zealand after the introduction of the *Employment Contracts Act* in 1991. In May 1992, for example, the Business Council of Australia sponsored a study commission to New Zealand that praised the New Zealand system and argued for 'an efficient mechanism for removing award coverage in favour of enterprise and individual arrangements' (BCA 1993, p. 19). Hamberger (1995, p. 35) (now the Employment Advocate) also observed a significant change in the attitudes of employers towards individualism in the early 1990s. He noted that in 1988 individual contracts did not rate at all among the ten most preferred changes to Australian industrial relations identified by a survey of the chief executive officers (CEOs) of BCA members. By 1992, however, individual contracts were number eight on the list, and 25 per cent of CEO members agreed with the proposition that 'truly achieving world class productivity in my company requires individual employment contracts' (ibid.).

This marked the entrance of individualisation into the mainstream of Australian public policy debate. Major employer associations, which had previously been critical of such notions, moved in behind the Business Council and quickly became supporters of individualisation. The two most important examples were the Australian Chamber of Commerce and Industry, formed in 1991 by the merger of the Confederation of Australian Industry and the Australian Chamber of Commerce, and the Australian Industry Group, formerly the Metal Trades Industry Association (Thornthwaite & Sheldon 1996).

At the same time, conservative political parties were adopting individualism. Newly elected state governments in Victoria and Western Australia introduced legislation providing for individual contracts in 1992 and 1993 respectively. The then federal Coalition opposition adopted a policy supporting individual contracts in their controversial 'Jobsback!' policy of 1993 (Dabscheck 1995), while their apparently less radical policy stance in their victorious election campaign of 1996 also supported individual bargaining (Bray & Waring 1998). The *Workplace Relations Act 1996* subsequently introduced individual contracts for the first time at federal level in the form of Australian Workplace Agreements. Apparently, this initiative was not sufficient, because on re-election in 1998 the Coalition federal government commissioned Des Moore, one of the most strident of contemporary advocates for individualised arrangements, to prepare a report on the need for further labour market deregulation (Moore 1998). In the report, he parodied a well-known argument by Justice Higgins by claiming that Australia needs:

> a new start that would provide the opportunity for establishing a new province of law and order based on voluntarily agreed exchanges of individual rights and obligations by the parties directly involved. (Moore 1998, p. 160)

Similarly, the BCA sought further individualisation. In September 2000 it released a report entitled *Managerial Leadership in the Workplace* (BCA 2000), whose main theme was that the international competitiveness of Australian enterprises depended on the capacity of Australian managers to effectively lead their organisations. In quintessentially unitarist fashion, it argued that the most important test of leadership was to unite employees behind the vision and values of management. This task was conceived as a direct relationship between individual employees and managers, while anything impeding the development of this relationship — such as unions and external regulation — was considered damaging. The logical extension was the urgent need for further legal and institutional reform to better facilitate individualisation.

In summary, the unambiguous tide of employer and political opinion in Australia during the 1990s supported individualisation. The following section will examine in more detail the legal and institutional changes that emerged from this trend and the extent to which they have produced new employment practices.

Procedural individualism: the experience of individual contracts in Australia

The starting point for an account of procedural individualism must be the law. The common law, but especially statute law, determines the procedural options available to the parties, and also embodies preferences as to how the employment relationship should be organised. Central to such issues is the legal status of individual employment contracts. Once the legal situation is specified, the actual practices of the parties can be described and explained. In exploring the law and practice of individualism in Australia, this section will begin with the pre-1992 period, when both the legal options for individual contracts and their actual use was fairly limited. Developments in the years since 1992 will then be exposed first at the level of the state jurisdictions and then at the Commonwealth level.

The pre-1992 situation

During the pre-1992 period (and still today) persons hired to perform work on behalf of an employer were engaged under a contract of employment and consequently became 'employees'; to use a building metaphor, the individual common law employment contract provides the foundation upon which the house of employment law is built (see Creighton & Stewart 2000). However, statutory law substantially modifies the common law. In particular, the legal effect of the collectivist conciliation and arbitration system was to set minimum standards of wages and working conditions and, thereby, to vary individual employment contracts that did meet these standards. It was not legally possible for employees to 'contract out' of awards; if they were found to be covered by an award or collective agreement, their employers could not 'confer less beneficial treatment on a worker than that demanded by a statute award or registered agreement' (Stewart 1999, p. 19).

The reality of Australian industrial relations in this period was that most employees were covered by an award or a collective agreement. Australian Bureau of Statistics surveys suggested that up to 90 per cent of all employees fell into this category and were part of the collectivist system; as late as 1990 this figure was as high as 80 per cent, with the remaining 20 per cent of employees being covered solely by an individual contract of employment, and therefore being part of an individualised system (see Bray & Waring 1998, pp. 75–6). Although little is known about them, these 'non-award' workers appear to have been mostly managerial and professional employees along with some workers from a small number of award-free industries. Because of their location in the wages hierarchy and the legal regime just described, which at least legally did not allow wages and conditions below award minimums, common law employment contracts typically provided terms of employment superior to those under awards or collective agreements.

The post-1992 experience at the state level

The passing of the *Employee Relations Act 1992* in Victoria was the first major departure from the traditional, collectivist regime in Australia. This legislation closely resembled the New Zealand *Employment Contracts Act 1991* and sought to provide an individual agreement-making option while diminishing the status of awards and the role of trade unions (Fox & Teicher 1994). Victorian individual contracts, or Individual Employment Agreements (IEAs) as they were known, could be entered into by employees and employers whether or not either party was covered by a collective agreement. The agreements could be negotiated by either party or employees could authorise any representative to negotiate on their behalf. The Act provided that certain minimum terms and conditions of employment were to be met or exceeded in IEAs. Employers were obliged to inform the Administration Officer of the number of IEAs to which they were a party. Fox and Teicher (1994, p. 196) report that around 200 000 employees were covered by IEAs at October 1993, although many of these were the result of the operation of the Act, which deemed employees to be covered by IEAs when agreements and/or awards had expired.

Not much is known, however, about the real impact of this early legislative experiment with individual agreement making, partly because of the prohibitions on divulging the contents of agreements. More importantly, in what was described as 'the exodus to federal regulation' (Fox & Teicher, 1994, p. 205), hundreds of thousands of Victorian employees escaped the Victorian legislation — a move facilitated by the Keating Labor Government through amendments to the federal legislation in the form of the *Industrial Relations Legislation Amendment Act (No. 2) 1992* (Cth). This flight to the federal jurisdiction was a factor in convincing the Kennett Victorian government in 1996 to repeal the *Employee Relations Act of 1992 (Vic.)* and effectively hand over most of their industrial powers to the federal government. This means that the *Workplace Relations Act 1996* (Cth) now covers all Victorian workers regardless of whether an interstate dispute exists or whether Victorian employees are employed in constitutional corporations (Stewart 1999).

The next attempt to provide a jurisdiction for individual contract formation came with the election of the Court Coalition government in Western Australia in 1993. The Court government immediately passed three pieces of industrial relations legislation: the *Industrial Relations Amendment Act 1993*, the *Minimum Conditions of Employment Act 1993* and the *Workplace Agreements Act 1993* (Ford 1998, p. 2). Of these, the last, the *Workplace Agreements Act*, provides for individual contract making through Individual Workplace Agreements (IWAs). Employees and employers can enter into IWAs whether or not they are covered by an award or collective workplace agreement. IWAs have the effect of displacing inconsistent terms of a collective agreement and wholly displacing relevant awards. IWAs, however, must contain at least the statutory minimums provided for in the *Minimum Conditions of Employment Act 1993*. The task of comparing IWAs with the provisions of this Act is the responsibility of the Office of the Commissioner for Workplace Agreements.

By the end of 1998 the number of IWAs lodged with the Commissioner of Workplace Agreements had reached 166 843, covering 174 211 employees and 4597 employers (Department of Productivity and Labour Relations, December 1998.) In terms of the sheer numbers of individual contracts registered, the Western Australian system represents the longest and most developed Australian experience with individual contracts. However, as Ford (1998, p. 47) argues, it would be a mistake to judge the importance of IWAs merely by counting their number. Indeed, he argues that 'their very existence has changed fundamentally the dynamics of bargaining collectively' (p. 47). The election of the Gallop Labor government in 2000, however, is likely to stem the growth of Western Australian individual contracts. Under changes proposed by the Labor government, individual workplace agreements are to be abolished and replaced by a new form of individual contract known as employer–employee agreements (EEAs). In contrast to IWAs, EEAs must meet a 'no-disadvantage test' and cannot be used as a condition of employment. Moreover, unlike IWAs, they will be available for public inspection.

In Queensland, the conservative Coalition government moved to mirror the federal *Workplace Relations Act 1996* by passing its own *Workplace Relations Act* in 1997. However, unlike Western Australia, the adoption of Queensland Workplace Agreements (QWAs) has been quite limited, with only 1516 registered as at December 1998, covering just 245 employers, or 0.2 per cent of the Queensland workforce (ACCIRT 1998). An ACCIRT analysis of these agreements revealed that the majority (57.8 per cent) did not provide for any wage movement, and that most were narrow in scope. The election of the Beattie Labor government in Queensland in the middle of 1998 stimulated debate over the future of QWAs (Industrial Relations Taskforce 1998), but they were subsequently retained in the new Queensland *Industrial Relations Act 1999,* albeit with some modifications. The most important of these modifications was to allow the Queensland Industrial Relations Commission to take into account the relative bargaining power of the parties when approving QWAs (s. 203(6)).

The post-1992 experience at the Commonwealth level

According to Williams (1997), the industrial relations policy of the federal Coalition parties was radically altered at a policy development forum on 3 January 1996. The then shadow minister for industrial relations, the Honourable Peter Reith, urged his Coalition colleagues to partly abandon their failed 'Jobsback!' industrial relations policy, which was associated with the Coalition's defeat under the leadership of John Hewson in the 1993 federal election. In its place would be a commitment from the Coalition not to reduce the take-home pay of working Australians. The commitment was an important part of the Coalition's strategy to counter any 1993-like industrial relations scare campaign from the Australian Labor Party (see Bray & Waring 1998).

The new Coalition government sought to implement its policy platform through the *Workplace Relations Act 1996* (WRA). One of the most controversial provisions of that act, and the one most relevant to individualism, was the inclusion of individual agreement instruments known as Australian Workplace Agreements (AWAs). According to Ronfeldt (1997, p. 5), AWAs replicate the main elements of individual contracts available under Western Australia's *Workplace Agreements Act 1993* by providing a voluntary means for parties to contract out of awards and collective agreements. Indeed, under the WRA, AWAs override expired certified agreements, awards and state employment agreements to the extent of any inconsistency. The AWA provisions are therefore apparently directed at those parties already covered by traditional regulative mechanisms, such as awards and collective agreements, rather than extending regulation to those covered by common law employment contracts and unregistered agreements. For employers in the latter category, there will be little benefit in seeking AWAs. Although there are significant jurisdictional impediments for employers to conclude AWAs with employees, they will be, and have been, used as tools within highly unionised workplaces to remove mainly blue-collar workers from awards and/or collective bargaining processes (see Waring 2000).

The safeguard provisions in the WRA, however, mean that employers and employees do not have the unfettered right to write AWAs containing provisions solely of their own making. Rather, the WRA introduced a 'no-disadvantage test' that must be met if the AWA is to be registered, and thereby gain legal status. Unlike its more radical counterparts in Victoria and Western Australia, where individual agreements are compared with very simple legislative minimum standards, the WRA provides that AWAs must 'on balance' offer the same or better conditions than a relevant award. The no-disadvantage test is administered by the Office of the Employment Advocate (OEA), but where the OEA is uncertain, the AWAs are referred to the AIRC (s. 170VPC[3]).

Several other features of the WRA affect the attractiveness of AWAs to employees and especially employers. First, there are constitutional problems that limit the coverage of AWAs. Since the legislation is made under the 'corporations power' of the constitution, an employer must be incorporated under company law in order to legitimately be a party to the agreement. Estimates vary (see, for example, CCH 1996; Workforce 1997), but this provision excludes many firms. Second, in the interests of extending a degree of equity to employees entering individual contractual arrangements, the legislation allows employees (and employers) to appoint a 'bargaining agent' to negotiate on their behalf; this agent can be anyone from a solicitor to a union representative to someone's next-door neighbour. Under the Act, employers are prohibited from refusing to recognise an employee's nominated bargaining agent, although this prohibition does not compel employers to negotiate with bargaining agents. Third, there is also a capacity for employers and employees to undertake protected industrial action in support of claims when negotiating an AWA (s. 170WC). This is perhaps a prime example of the incompatibility of collectivist notions inserted into provisions facilitating individualisation. Very few employees faced with the prospect of negotiating an individual contract will attempt to take individual strike or other industrial action. Exceptions to this might include collectively negotiated AWAs or situations in which individual employees have expert power or hold a strategic position within an organisation. It is also easier for the employer to retaliate against a striking individual employee. While an employer must not dismiss or prejudice an employee for taking action (s. 170WE), they can stand down or lock out an employee in response. Moreover, the economic consequences of taking action against an individual employee are minor in comparison to locking out an entire workforce under collective bargaining conditions.

Finally, an additional reason why some employers may be attracted to AWAs concerns their ability to be used even when they fail the no-disadvantage test. Section 170LT of the WRA permits the commission to certify an otherwise unacceptable AWA where it is part of a strategy to meet a short-term business crisis. On 26 September 1997 the AIRC approved the first AWAs referred to it by the Employment Advocate because of his concerns over the agreement's compliance with the no-disadvantage test. The AIRC approved these AWAs, despite concluding that they failed the no-disadvantage test, because they were part of a strategy to deal with a crisis in the business. The Commission also took into account evidence of working patterns at the site, and the fact that the AWAs were claimed to be for a short term of one year (Workforce, 3 October 1997). Waring and Lewer (2001) have calculated that over 2000 of these 'suspect' AWAs have been certified by the AIRC since their introduction.

While the Workplace Relations Act 1996 and its associated rhetoric emphasises a 'hands-off' role for the state in employment relations, the federal government has adopted a highly interventionist role in encouraging (some might suggest forcing) the use of individual contracts. This has been most noticeable in the Howard government's instructions to federal departments to offer AWAs to public servants, particularly senior public servants (Macdonald 1998). Moreover, in the construction industry, government tender specifications have included a requirement that construction contractors strictly observe and implement workplace relations practices in accordance with the WRA.

Despite the best efforts of the federal government, AWAs underpin the employment of only about 1.8 per cent of Australia's workers, which demonstrates the resilience of collective bargaining and award regulation. The actual numbers of AWAs registered each quarter between their introduction in March 1997 and 2001 is detailed in table 10.1. The table shows that after a relatively slow start, the number of AWAs being registered by the OEA has grown significantly. However, it must be remembered that each AWA represents a single employee, so that the final cumulative total of 160 349 AWAs by March 2001 *potentially* only equates to the same number of employees. Yet even this figure is not a true indication of the number of AWAs in force. A significant proportion of the cumulative total may have expired or may have become nugatory owing to firms going out of business or employees becoming redundant.

Table 10.1: Number of federal AWAs, 1997–2001

As at the end of:	Total no. of AWAs approved	No. of employers covered by approved AWAs
September 1997	1 281	79
December 1997	4 393	225
March 1998	10 790	425
June 1998	22 471	700
September 1998	34 426	899
December 1998	45 089	1 163
January 1999	47 491	1 228
April 1999	55 548	1 436
June 1999	61 264	1 360
September 1999	73 042	1 567
December 1999	84 864	1 747
January 2000	90 562	2 017
February 2000	94 990	1 899
March 2000	98 708	1 961
January 2001	150 079	2 798
March 2001	160 349	3 012

Source: Derived from CCH/ACIRRT ADAM Report No. 20, March 1999; and Office of the Employment Advocate, 'Current Status of AWAs as at 01 April, 2001', www.oea.gov.au.

Table 10.2 presents data on the distribution of AWAs by industry sector. The clear picture that emerges is that the highest proportions of employees who are a party to AWAs come from the government sector, communication services and the retail trade. The large number of AWAs in the government sector is probably to be expected given the federal government's heavy promotion of AWAs in the public service. Similarly, the large number of AWAs in the

communication services industries is most likely due to significant growth in the award-free call centre industry.

Table 10.2: Distribution of employees with AWAs by industry sector, 2001

Industry sector	Percentage of all AWAs
Accommodation, cafes and restaurants	6.6
Agriculture, forestry and fishing	1.0
Communications services	11.4
Construction	2.0
Cultural and recreational services	4.4
Education	0.9
Electricity, gas and water supply	1.3
Finance and insurance	5.4
Government, administration and defence	16.0
Health and community services	4.7
Manufacturing	8.6
Mining	3.8
Personal and other services	5.2
Property and business services	9.6
Retail trade	11.6
Transport and storage	5.4
Wholesale trade	2.0

Source: Derived from Office of the Employment Advocate (2001), 'Current Status of AWAs as at 01 April, 2001', www.oea.gov.au.

Table 10.3 presents some early evidence on the number and type of bargaining agent being used in AWA negotiations. The overwhelming number of employees covered by an AWA (91.8 per cent) did not appoint a bargaining agent. This may imply that individual employees negotiate AWAs without the assistance of a bargaining agent. However, a more plausible explanation, which is supported by case study evidence and by the New Zealand experience (McAndrew & Ballard 1995), is that AWAs are rarely negotiated at all — they are simply offered to employees by employers and accepted without any substantive exchange. This was certainly the situation in Waring's case studies of mining companies utilising AWAs (Waring 2000), and it is also consistent with van Barneveld's (2000) discussion of Federal Court cases concerning duress and the offer of AWAs.

Table 10.3: Employees appointing bargaining agents in AWA negotiations

Bargaining agent	Percentage of all AWAs
None	91.8
Union	1.7
Family/friend	0.4
Lawyer/consultant	0.5
Other	5.4
Data missing	0.1

Source: Derived from ACIRRT (1998).

Further evidence on bargaining agents and the process of bargaining comes from Gollan (2000), who undertook a recent survey for the Office of the Employment Advocate of 500 managers representing Australian organisations with registered AWAs. He found that the majority of employers (65 per cent) held discussions with their employees before commencing the drafting of their AWAs. In 59 per cent of all cases, these discussions led employers to make changes to the AWAs, which Gollan interpreted as evidence demonstrating a degree of employee consultation and influence when drafting AWAs. An alternative interpretation of these data is that at least 40 per cent of employers offered AWAs on a 'take-it-or-leave-it' basis. As well, these data do not reveal the number of employees involved in these AWAs, and Gollan's survey says little about the quality of such consultation or the extent of influence exerted by individual employees. Moreover, the evidence does not support a causal relationship between reported employee consultation and subsequent changes made to AWAs, which might have indicated that actual bargaining had taken place. Finally, it is important to acknowledge that Gollan's findings are the result of a survey of management, who, understandably, may have an interest in overstating the extent of discussions held with employees over AWAs.

In summary, as a result of employer lobbying and increasingly neoliberal policies of governments, there have been significant changes in the law since 1992 that have fundamentally changed the legal status of individual bargaining in Australia and dramatically increased the opportunities for employees and employers to negotiate individual contracts. At the same time, the incidence of individual contracts has been remarkably limited. This could easily lead to the conclusion that procedural individualism in Australia is unimportant. This is not the case, however, because it ignores the significant role of individualism in reshaping the form, function and underlying dynamics of the employment relationship.

Substantive individualism

If new laws in Australia since 1992 have increased the procedural opportunities for individual bargaining, and growing (if not overwhelming) numbers of employees and employers are accepting these new opportunities, what of the outcomes of these new bargaining arrangements? In particular, has individual bargaining produced greater substantive individualism? Unfortunately, there has been little research in Australia designed to answer such questions. The limited evidence that is available, however, suggests that the growth of individual contracts has not produced significant differentiation in the wages and working conditions among the workers affected. In other words, the extent of substantive individualism appears to be quite limited.

The main sources on which such conclusions are based are case studies by Waring (2000; 2001) and van Barneveld (1999). Waring (2000; 2001) conducted case study research of two large organisations in the Australian black coal mining industry and discovered extremely low substantive individualisation in the AWAs used by these firms. The only source of contractual differentiation was in terms of provisions for rewards linked to individual employee performance. In all other cases, the AWAs were identical, leading Waring (2001, p. 290) to conclude that management were using AWAs to extend managerial prerogatives while reaping the administrative benefits that arise from contractual standardisation. Indeed, in the case of a firm in the construction industry reported by van Barneveld, not only were AWAs standardised, but their terms and conditions were exactly the same as a previously applicable certified agreement.

Clearly, there is a need for considerably more research on substantive individualism, but the available Australian evidence seems to support recent British research. For example, in a detailed study of so-called 'individualisers' — companies that had introduced individual contracts — Brown (1998) found limited differentiation in the wages paid to employees, but even less differentiation in non-pay issues:

These firms showed no tendency at all to differentiate between their employees in terms of non-pay terms and conditions. Indeed, the standardisation of substantive non-pay terms has increased rather than diminished at firms which claimed to have taken steps to individualise contracts. (Brown 1998, p. 6)

This pay/non-pay distinction was explained by Brown (1998) by reference to the widespread inclusion in individual contracts of performance-based pay arrangements. This is consistent with van Barneveld and Arsvoska's (2001) findings in Australia, which indicate that pay terms are more likely to be individualised (linked to individual performance) than collective agreements.

Explanations of substantive standardisation, to the extent that standardisation is confirmed by research, would hardly be surprising. In Australia, there is a specific legal reason why differentiation may be rare — that is, s. 170VPA(1)(e) of the WRA actually requires an employer to offer the same AWA conditions to comparable employees. However, there are many other more general possibilities. For example, even if employers introduce individualisation in a genuine effort to develop closer relations with employees, there are significant costs associated with negotiating and administrating individual agreements. Many potential morale problems can also be created among employees who discover that their colleagues enjoy better wages or conditions than they do. Finally, it is clear that employers who use individualisation to avoid unions or to reduce labour costs are unlikely to seek or deliver differentiated wages and conditions.

Process individualism

The previous sections have discussed the Australian experience of procedural and substantive individualism in the labour market, but the discussion of individualism as a management strategy is incomplete without consideration of what has been referred to as process individualism in the labour process. This term refers to the individualisation techniques of management, which are used to secure work performance on a day-to-day basis. Sophisticated HRM generally involves the use of a number of practices such as individual performance appraisals, performance-linked pay, psychological testing, sophisticated communication mechanisms and so on. It has been noted by Legge (1995), Storey (1992) and Townley (1994) that these practices are significant in their focus on individual employees. Townley (1994), in particular, contends that HRM seeks knowledge of the individual employee for instrumental and humanistic reasons. Implicit in this suggestion is the notion that work effort is maximised under conditions that permit the unleashing of individual potential. HRM posits that these conditions are created through sophisticated practices that motivate, develop, reward and manage employees, producing individual satisfaction and commitment. In this way, maximising effort extraction and individual satisfaction and commitment become complementary objectives.

Unfortunately, the data on process individualism in Australia are limited; what is available arises from a small number of case studies and surveys. With respect to the former, Kitay and Lansbury (1997) report some movement towards individualised HRM systems in their review of six case studies of Australian industries. Their review indicates

growth in direct communication schemes and in individualised pay arrangements. Performance appraisal systems, they argue, have become more popular and are often linked to individual employees' remuneration. However, despite this growth, Kitay and Lansbury (1997, p. 234) argue that individualised payment systems are but one of a variety of payment systems that have emerged in the past decade. Similarly, van Barneveld and Arsvoska (2001), drawing on AWA and certified agreement data, have found that the incidence of contingent pay arrangements linked to individual performance is higher in AWAs than in certified agreements.

Turning to survey research, Deery and Walsh (1998) used Australian Workplace Industrial Relations Survey data from 1995 to examine the characteristics of workplaces that had a majority of their workforce on individual employment contracts (what they call 'individualisers') and compared them with 'collectivised' workplaces, which are those workplaces with no non-managerial employees on individual contracts (Deery & Walsh 1998, p. 6). They discovered that although individualisers were more likely to use performance-related pay and systems for monitoring performance, they were less likely than collectivists to use high-trust HRM techniques such as elaborate participative schemes. They argue, therefore, that:

(Australian) individualists have developed a calculative, instrumental and business orientated approach to managing employees … (which) appears to lack procedural justice and fairness and appropriate voice mechanisms at the workplace.

More recently, two surveys point to increasing use of individualistic management techniques. The first of these, reported by Kramar (1999), was conducted in 1996 and included 331 Australian organisations with 100 or more employees, 40 per cent in the public sector and 60 per cent in the private sector. The survey was designed to discover 'the principal ways in which human resource policies have changed during the 1990s' (Kramar 1999, p. 24). It found evidence of the widespread use of performance appraisal, with 90 per cent of organisations using appraisals for staff employees and 50 per cent using them for manual employees. Unfortunately, the survey does not reveal the characteristics of the appraisal methods used. The survey also found that 'pay for performance' arrangements and direct communication schemes had become more common in the period between 1993 and 1996.

The second survey, conducted by Fisher and Dowling (1999) in conjunction with the Australian Human Resources Institute, included 322 Australian respondents, who were described as senior HR managers with a base salary of at least $70 000. The survey revealed that 'in the last five years, performance appraisal, recruitment and selection and training and development were identified by senior HR managers as the important new HR policies, programs and initiatives' (p. 12). However, like the survey reported by Kramar (1999), this second survey gave no indication of the characteristics of these policies or any information on whether they were in place in the respondent's organisation.

Deery and Walsh (1999) have also found empirical support for Legge's suggestion that the use of individual contracts may be inconsistent with participatory practices and communication mechanisms. They found that while firms with a majority of their non-managerial workforce on individual contracts (individualisers) were sophisticated and strategic in their approach, their policies and practices resembled 'hard' HRM rather than its 'soft' counterpart. In other words, the extensive use of performance-related pay systems and staff appraisals was not accompanied by 'high-trust', 'high-employee-involvement' strategies.

Roan and colleagues' (2000) study of the contents of 539 AWAs registered between March 1997 and June 1998 confirms Deery and Walsh's earlier findings. Roan et al. (2000, p. 40) found that AWAs tended to adopt the 'hard' HRM approach 'of cost minimisation and maximisation of flexibility of hours', and contained very few indicators of 'soft' HRM, such as family leave, consultation, training and other similar provisions. Pickersgill and Arsvoska (2000) have also observed that collective agreements and awards are more likely to contain training provisions than are individual contracts, which would seem to contradict the argument that individualism promotes 'soft HRM'.

The evidence is clearer on the issue of whether AWAs are associated with extensive communication, consultation and involvement mechanisms. Using data from AWIRS 1995, Deery and Walsh (1999) found that Australian employers with a majority of their non-managerial workforce on individual contracts do not invest in elaborate communication and involvement mechanisms. This suggests that these workplaces are akin to Sisson's (1993) 'bleak house' or Guest's (1995) 'black hole' metaphors, according to which firms ignore progressive people management practices and the employee's voice is effectively silenced.

On balance, the available evidence seems to show that the growth of individual contracts (i.e. procedural individualism), especially AWAs, has led to a corresponding increase in process individualism. However, as Kitay and Lansbury (1997) argue, these new practices appear to have been introduced in a fairly ad hoc and piecemeal fashion, reflecting a pragmatism and lack of strong commitment to individualist philosophies by Australian employers. Furthermore, the growth of process individualism has not necessarily

produced the favourable outcomes for employees that the rhetoric suggested. Although advocates of AWAs claim that their use induces a closer, more trusting relationship, the opposite seems to be the case. As well as the limited consultation over the negotiation of the individual contracts themselves, reported in the previous section, Australian workplaces where individual contracts are the primary industrial instrument seem to have managers who are reluctant to provide employees with a means to speak and be heard at work.

Summary and conclusions

This chapter offered a three-fold categorisation of individualism that is useful in assessing the extent to which employment relations in Australia have been transformed over recent years. First, Australian governments undoubtedly embraced *procedural individualism* during the 1990s and introduced widespread legislative changes that greatly expanded the opportunities for employers and employees to use individual contracts to negotiate the terms and conditions of employment. However, few employers and employees have actually taken up these new opportunities. Common law employment contracts cover only a small proportion of the workforce, while the incidence of individual contracts provided by statute law is even more limited. Second, the limited evidence available so far suggests that a lack of *substantive individualisation* is not widespread. Indeed, Australia seems to be following a pattern similar to that in Britain where, with the possible exception of individualised performance-based pay schemes, the growth of individual contracts has actually produced standardisation rather than differentiation of employment conditions. Third, while the incidence of *process individualism* has grown considerably over recent years, this has been across the board rather than confined to those companies that have adopted procedural individualism, and it has rarely followed any systematic and comprehensive strategy within companies. Moreover, where both procedural and process individualism occurs in the same company, there seems to be a strong emphasis on cost minimisation and 'hard' HRM rather than productivity-enhancing 'soft' HRM.

What do these trends say about the various arguments used to promote individualisation? First, they certainly suggest that Australian companies and their representative associations are responding to economic imperatives when they embrace individualisation. Individualisation promises change at the workplace that managers hope will improve the competitiveness of their companies. The extent to which these promised economic improvements are achieved is impossible to judge at present.

Second, although individualisation tends to be justified on the grounds that it produces closer and more 'high-trust' relations between employers and employees, this does not seem to be the reality. There may be isolated examples of companies that are motivated by such ambitions and manage to achieve their goals, but the more typical situation appears to be one in which managers are either motivated by more instrumental aims or unwilling or unable to deliver the complete package of HRM policies required to achieve genuine trust with employees.

Third, the bulk of the literature adds weight to the notion that individual contracts have more to do with individualising power relations and undermining collectivism than with tailoring employment relationships to meet the needs of individual employees. If, as its enthusiasts suggest, individualisation is able to more adequately accommodate the needs and aspirations of individual employees, it is in theory rather than practice.

Implications for HR professionals

In this final section of the chapter, we explore the implications of the strategy of individualism. We argue that there are significant risks for employers in pursuing a strategy of individualisation, and that the perceived benefits may be largely illusory. The potential for individualism to result in protracted disputation and undermine attempts to build 'high-performance' organisations indicates that 'the game may not be worth the candle'. Moreover, it is asserted that the strategy of individualism, especially as it has been implemented in recent times, is morally and ethically questionable.

Implications for workplace relations

The experience of individualisers in Australia suggests that trade unions are very likely to resist attempts to individualise employment relationships. The introduction of individual contracts in workplaces with strong collectivist traditions has often produced protracted industrial action and lengthy litigation. For instance, the introduction of AWAs at the Hunter Valley open-cut mine produced a

dispute that continued for three years, with ongoing litigation before industrial tribunals and courts, and periodic bouts of industrial action (Waring 2000). Ironically, industrial tensions at the mine have eased only somewhat, with the certification of a *collective* agreement in October 2000. Moreover, BHP's introduction of individual contracts in its iron ore facilities in Western Australia has also produced significant industrial action and costly court proceedings (Riley 2000). Similarly, the introduction of AWAs in the Australian banking sector, especially at the Commonwealth and ANZ banks, has resulted in acrimonious industrial relations and litigation in the Federal Court and Australian Industrial Relations Commission.

These experiences suggest that individualisation poses significant risks for employers. Employers willing to pursue individualisation should be prepared to encounter costly resistance from trade unions. Also, individualisation can lead to a divisive contest for the loyalty of employees, often resulting in open conflict and dysfunctional workplace relations.

Implications for building high-performance work systems

There is a growing literature within HRM and industrial relations scholarship on what management practices help to create and sustain a high-performance organisation (see Whitfield 2000). This literature suggests that internally consistent 'bundles' of sophisticated HR practices are conducive to the development of 'high-performance work organisation' (HPWO). Central to HPWO is the creation of a learning and problem-solving culture. This begs the question as to whether individualism is compatible with such a work culture.

Legge (1989) has argued that HRM's individualist orientation is likely to be incompatible with team working and group-based problem solving. Moreover, individualising wages (linking them to individual performance) can lead to perceptions of inequities that are antithetical to the encouragement of 'team' philosophy.

The experience of individualism also suggests that it is more likely to be associated with 'hard' HRM (e.g. de-unionisation, cost minimisation, extension of managerial prerogatives and so on) rather than the 'soft' version of HRM implicit in the high-performance work system ideal. The evidence suggests that individualism has not produced the soft HRM outcomes of a closer, trusting relationship in which employees are more strongly committed to the goals of the firm and more likely to provide discretionary effort freely when required.

This is not to argue that there aren't examples of employers combining procedural individualism with 'soft' HRM. Waring's (2001) case study of a greenfield mine observed such an employer strategy, which combined individual contracts with innovative communication systems, high wages and other sophisticated human resource practices. The mine's greenfield status and its novel HR strategy provided the mine with a dedicated, highly motivated and largely non-union workforce. Yet the case study also suggested that unions were employing their own strategies in an attempt to represent the interests of employees. These strategies included communicating with the mine's employees, particularly those who were less than satisfied with management, and attempting to rope the employer into an industry award. It was this possibility of collective representation that focused management's attention on providing employees with adequate levels of consultation and remuneration and, on the whole, investing substantial resources in employment relations matters. From this a curious paradox can be observed — it appeared that the ongoing presence of collective representation ensured that the more extreme possibilities under individualised employment relations remained largely unfulfilled. The threat of collective representation encouraged management to outbid the union in a contest for the 'hearts and minds' of employees.

Moral and ethical implications

We would argue that there are significant moral and ethical questions to be asked about the strategy of individualisation. The current experience of procedural individualism, in particular, suggests that employees have very little influence in the design and construct of their individual employment contract. Moreover, individual contracts are often accepted in circumstances that leave individual employees with very few other options. For instance, the literature suggests that individual contracts have been offered as a condition of employment; in situations where employment alternatives are limited or, indeed, in circumstances where collective bargaining has been deliberately stalled. This raises questions of whether direct or indirect duress has been applied, and whether this breaches not just legal obligations but the employer's moral obligation to its employees.

Moreover, as the literature suggests, individualism typically places the employer and management in a position of strengthened control over employees, which may have the effect of producing a sense of vulnerability and powerlessness in employees. This, then, begs the question of whether this sense of vulnerability is consistent with the creation of 'high-trust' relationships. The dual desire of individualism

enthusiasts to extend management control and promote more trusting relationships appears to be contradictory and ethically questionable.

Despite the moral and ethical questions that shadow individualism, and its attendant costs and risks, there is little doubt that some employers will continue to individualise. Some will be tempted by the capacity of individualism to cut through collective regulation and extend managerial power. Others may simply see individualism as a means to exclude what they regard as a recalcitrant trade union. Still others may be genuinely attracted by the promise of building closer, more trusting relationships with their employees. We hope that this chapter will at least provoke a more thoughtful assessment of individualism in employment relations and of the strategic choices available when managing human resources.

References

ACIRRT (1998) New information about Queensland workplace agreements sheds light on individual agreement making. Newsletter Information Services, *IR Intelligence Report, Quarterly Analysis of Workplace Trends*, Issue 2.

ACIRRT (1999) *Agreements Database and Monitor*, 20, March.

Adams, J (1965) Injustice in social exchange. In L Berkwitz (Ed.), *Advances in Experimental Psychology*, vol. 2. New York: Academic Press.

Australian Industrial Relations Commission (1996) *Aluminium Industry CRA* [Comalco] *Weipa Case Transcript*, Print No. M8600.

Bray, M (1986) The limits of enterprise autonomy: enterprise bargaining in the Australian domestic airline industry. *Economic and Labour Relations Review*, June, 7 (1) 132–64.

Bray, M, and Waring, P (1998) The rhetoric and reality of bargaining structures under the Howard government. *Labour & Industry*, 9 (2) 61–80.

Brown, W, Deakin, S, Hudson, M, Pratten, C, and Ryan, P (1998) *The Individualisation of Employment Contracts in Britain*. Research Paper for the Department of Trade and Industry.

Business Council of Australia (2000) *Managerial Leadership in the Workplace*. Report by World Competitive Practices Pty Ltd commissioned by the BCA.

CCH Limited (1996) Individual AWAs: constitutional problems. *Australian Industrial Law News*, Newsletter 2/96, 3 April.

Creighton, B, and Stewart, A (2000) *Labour Law: An Introduction* (3rd ed.). Sydney: Federation Press.

Crouch, C (1982) *Trade Unions: The Logic of Collective Action*. London: Fontana.

Dabscheck, B (1995) *The Struggle for Australian Industrial Relations*. Melbourne: Oxford University Press.

Deery, S, and Mitchell, R (1999) *Employment Relations: Individualisation and Union Exclusion — An International Study*. Sydney: Federation Press.

Deery, S, and Walsh, J (1999) The character of individualised employment relations in Australia: a model of 'hard' HRM. In S Deery and R Mitchell (Eds), *Employment Relations: Individualisation and Union Exclusion*. Sydney: Federation Press.

Edwards, PK (1995a) From industrial relations to the employment relationship. *Relations Industrielles*, 50 (1).

Edwards, PK (1995b) The employment relationship. In PK Edwards, *Industrial Relations: Theory and Practice in Britain*. Oxford: Blackwell.

Ellem, B (1998) Trade unionism in 1998. *Journal of Industrial Relations*, March, 41 (1).

Epstein, R (1983) A common law for labor relations: a critique of the new deal legislation. *Yale Law Journal*, 92, 1357–86.

Fisher, C, and Dowling, P (1999) Support for an HR approach in Australia: the perspective of senior HR managers. *Asia Pacific Journal of Human Resources*, 37 (1).

Ford, B (1998) Changing the dynamics of bargaining using and refusing state employment agreements, *Individualisation and Union Exclusion in Employment Relations Conference*, Centre for Employment and Labour Relations Law and Centre for Human Resource Management and Organisation Studies, University of Melbourne, 3–4 September.

Fox, A (1974) *Man Mismanagement*. London: Hutchinson.

Fox, C, and Teicher, J (1994) Victoria's employee relations act: the way of the future? *Australian Bulletin of Labour*, 20, 191.

Frazer, A, McCallum, R, and Ronfeldt, P (Eds) (1997) *Individual Contracts and Workplace Relations*, ACIRRT Working Paper 50, University of Sydney.

Gollan, P (2000) *Trends in Processes in the Making of Australian Workplace Agreements*. Sydney: Office of the Employment Advocate.

Gorman, P (1996) *Weipa: Where Australian Unions Drew Their 'Line in the Sand' with C.R.A.* Published by the Weipa Industrial Site Committee.

Guest, D (1987) Human resource management and industrial relations. *Journal of Management Studies*, 24 (5).

Guest, D (1995) Human resource management, trade unions and industrial relations. In J Storey (Ed.), *Human Resource Management: A Critical Text*. London: Routledge.

Gunnigle, P (1996) Collectivism and the management of industrial relations in greenfield sites. *Human Resource Management Journal*, 5 (3).

Hamberger, J (1995) Individual contracts: beyond enterprise bargaining? ACIRRT Working Paper No. 39, December.

Hamberger, J (2001) *The Future of Individual Contracts*. Presentation to the Human Resources Institute, Melbourne, 8 May.

Houlihan, P (1986) A brief history of Mudginberri and its implications for Australia's trade unions. In HR Nicholls Society, *Arbitration in Contempt*. Proceedings of the HR Nicholls Society, Melbourne.

Jacques, E (1998) On leaving the Tavistock Institute. *Human Relations,* 51 (3).

Kessler, I, and Purcell, J (1995) Individualism and collectivism in theory and practice: management style and the design of pay systems. In P Edwards (Ed.), *Industrial Relations: Theory and Practice in Britain*. London: Blackwell.

Kitay, J, and Lansbury, R. (Eds) (1997) *Changing Employment Relations in Australia*. Melbourne: Oxford University Press.

Kramar, R (1999) Policies for managing people in Australia: what has changed in the 1990s? *Asia Pacific Journal of Human Resources*, 37 (2).

Legge, K (1989) Human resource management: a critical analysis. In J Storey (Ed.), *New Perspectives on Human Resource Management* London: Routledge.

Legge, K (1995) HRM: rhetoric, reality and hidden agendas. In J Storey (Ed.), *Human Resource Management: A Critical Text*. London: Routledge.

Long, S (1999) Unions admit hundreds of members have signed on BHP's dotted line. *Australian Financial Review*, 31 December.

Ludeke, JT (1996) *The Line in The Sand: The Long Road to Staff Employment in Comalco*. Melbourne: Wilkinson Books.

Macdonald, D (1998) Public sector industrial relations under the Howard government. *Labour & Industry*, December, 9 (2) 43–59.

Macdonald, I (1995) *Understanding Organisational Change*, CRA Services.

McAndrew, I, and Ballard, M (1995) Negotiation and dictation in employment contract formation in New Zealand. *New Zealand Journal of Industrial Relations*, 20 (2) 119–41.

McCallum, RC (1997) Australian workplace agreements — an analysis. *Australian Journal of Labour Law*, April, 10 (1).

Moore, D (1998) *The Case for Further Deregulation of the Labour Market*. Canberra: Commonwealth of Australia.

Morehead, A, Steele, M, Alexander, M, Stephen, K, and Duffin, L (1997) *Changes at Work: The 1995 Australian Workplace Industrial Relations Survey.* Melbourne: Longman.

Norington, B (2001) Anti-union email may cost Telstra $420 fine. *Sydney Morning Herald*, 2 July, 3.

Pickersgill, R, and Arsvoska, B (2000) Individualism and training: evidence from enterprise agreements and federal Queensland and Western Australian Workplace Agreements. In J Burgess and G Strachan (Eds), *Proceedings of the 14th AIRAANZ Conference*, Newcastle, February.

Purcell, J (1995) Corporate strategy and human resource management. In J Storey (Ed.), *Human Resource Management: A Critical Text* London: Routledge.

Riley, J (2000) Individual contracting and collective bargaining in the balance. *Australian Journal of Labour Law*, June, 13 (1) 92–8.

Roan, A, Bramble, T, Healy, J, Lafferty, G, and Tomkins, M (2000) AWAs: the story so far. In J Burgess and G Strachan (Eds), *Proceedings of the 14th AIRAANZ Conference,* vol. 3. Newcastle, February.

Ronfeldt, P (1997) The Workplace Relations Act: the implications for representation, rights and reform. Seminar paper presented to the Faculty of Commerce, Charles Sturt University, Bathurst.

Sisson, K (1993) In search of HRM. *British Journal of Industrial Relations*, 31 (2).

Stewart, A (1999) The legal framework for individual employment agreements in Australia. In S Deery and R Mitchell (1999), *Employment Relations: Individualisation and Union Exclusion — An International Study.* Sydney: Federation Press.

Storey, J (1992) *Developments in the Management of Human Resources.* Oxford: Blackwell.

Thornthwaite, L, and Sheldon, P (1996) The Metal Trades Industry Association, bargaining structures and the Accord. *Journal of Industrial Relations*, June, 38 (2).

Timo, N (1997) The management of individualism in an Australian mining company. *Employee Relations*, 19 (4).

Timo, N (1998) Precarious employment and individual contracts in an Australian mining company. *Labour & Industry*, April, 9 (1).

Townley, B. (1994) *Reframing Human Resource Management: Power, Ethics and the Subject at Work.* London: Sage Publications.

van Barneveld, K (1999) Under the covers: negotiating Australian Workplace Agreements: two cases. In C Leggett, R Shanahan, E Stern, G Treuren and P Wright (Eds), *Proceedings of the 13th AIRAANZ Conference*, 4–6 February, Adelaide, vol. 2.

van Barneveld, K (2000) Freedom v. duress?: AWAs and the Federal Court. In J Burgess and G Strachan (Eds), *Proceedings of the 14th AIRAANZ Conference,* February, Newcastle, vol. 1.

van Barneveld, K, and Arsovska, B (2001) AWAs: changing the structure of wages. Paper presented to Special Conference on Ten Years of Enterprise Bargaining, 3–4 May, Newcastle.

Wailes, N (1997) The (re)discovery of the individual employment contract in Australia and New Zealand: the changing demands on industrial relations institutions in a period of economic restructuring. In A Frazer, R McCallum and P Ronfeldt (Eds), *Individual Contracts and Workplace Relations*, Working Paper No. 50. Sydney: Australian Centre for Industrial Relations Research and Training.

Waring, P (1999) The rise of individualism in Australian industrial relations. *New Zealand Journal of Industrial Relations*, October, 24 (3).

Waring, P (2000) Individualism and collectivism in contemporary employment relations: the Australian black coal mining industry experience. Unpublished PhD thesis, University of Newcastle, Australia.

Waring, P (2001) A greenfield in black coal: the case of the Bengalla Mine. *Personnel Review*, 30 (3) 280–96.

Waring, P, and Lewer, J (2001) The no disadvantage test: failing workers? Paper presented to Special Conference on Ten Years of Enterprise Bargaining, 3–4 May, Newcastle.

Waring, P, and Lynch, C (1997) The case of the Hunter Valley open cut mine dispute: 'coalfields collectivism versus corporate individualism'. *Proceedings from the 12th AIRAANZ Conference*, Wellington, New Zealand.

Webb, S, and Webb, B (1897) *Industrial Democracy.* London, reprint 1902). New York: Longman Green and Co.

Weeks, P (1995*) Trade Union Security Law: A Study of Preference and Compulsory Unionism.* Sydney: Federation Press.

Whitfield K (2000) High-performance workplaces, training, and the distribution of skills. *Industrial Relations*, January, 39 (1).

Williams, P (1997) *The Victory.* Sydney: Allen & Unwin.

Workforce (1997) Commission opens door for interveners. *Newsletter Information Services*, Issue 1143, 28 November.

Workplace Relations Act 1996, Parliament of the Commonwealth of Australia. Canberra: Australian Government Publishing Service.

CHAPTER 11

Managing the new workforce: the challenge of mixed employment relationships

by Linley Hartmann
University of South Australia

Introduction

Human resource management in contemporary organisations frequently involves not only dealing with issues that arise in maximising the potential of a diverse workforce, but also in managing a workforce that incorporates a variety of employment relationships including, for example, part time, casual and fixed-term staff. The transformation of the Australian labour market from a highly unionised, centrally regulated, male-dominated, mainly full-time workforce has resulted in a diverse range of direct employment and contractual arrangements that, it has been argued, better meet the needs of employers and employees. In organisations, the use of a variety of employment relationships has been credited with providing greater flexibility in meeting work demands, but for employees the outcomes arising from this flexibility have been more controversial. Blyton and Morris (1992, p. 120) assert that the controversies arising from the introduction of mixed employment options within organisations 'has represented a key issue ... if not *the* key issue in employment relations in several industrial societies' during the 1990s.

This chapter begins by outlining alternative forms of employment and organisational employment structures. It then examines Atkinson's (1984) organisational framework depicting the alternative employment relationships available to organisations, before discussing the differences these alternatives bring to the employment relationship as identified by Pfeffer and Baron (1988) and others. The focus of the chapter then moves to the incidence of

alternative forms of employment in Australia and the issues and challenges of multiple employment relationships for organisations, for managers and for individual workers. The challenges for organisations discussed in this chapter include determining the right employee mix, contracts and commitment, equity and fairness, broader social impacts, and legal implications as illustrated by occupational health and safety issues. These challenges are then explored in terms of their implications for managers and employees.

Alternative forms of employment and organisational employment structures

Since the early 1980s, as downsizing has accelerated in Australia (Kramar 2000), the development of a wide range of employment options has reduced the dominance of the standard employment pattern of a full-time, approximately 40-hour week, worked within a limited range of hours and supplemented by additional pay loadings for work outside these times. This system, which was primarily designed to preserve job opportunities for male breadwinners, and which determined the pattern of many social activities and the provisions of many services in the community, allowed little flexibility either to employers in their use of production technology and the provision of services, or to other workers with diverse, competing interests, such as women with carer responsibilities, and an increasing number of tertiary students (Allan, Brosnan & Walsh 1998). Nevertheless, 'standard' employment, like the so-called 'traditional' career of hierarchical organisational progression and job permanence, has always been characterised by widespread exceptions. For example, in the tourism, retail and construction employment sectors, casual and independent contract employment have been common, and in manufacturing, those who were subject to 'last-on first-off' lay-off rules in times of reduced demand also experienced uncertain employment.

Initially, discussion about flexible work arrangements focused on providing employees with more options for meeting their individual and family needs through the introduction of permanent part-time work and innovations such as flexitime (Allan, Brosnan & Walsh 1998). However, the widespread introduction of casual work, fixed-term contracts, and outsourcing of work to contractors and labour hire organisations has radically extended these initial ideas.

The advantages arising from greater flexibility in employment arrangements for organisations, and the external circumstances that have made these changes seem so necessary, are subject to much debate. The general theme of the debate concerns whether alternative work arrangements provide opportunities for organisations to achieve cost savings and improve productivity, and the extent to which this is a fully considered strategy rather than an ad hoc response to perceptions of global competition, technological change, exposure to low-cost labour markets and changes in labour markets (Blyton & Morris 1992). The primary focus of this chapter is not on the issues of this debate but rather on the consequences of these activities. As summarised by Rousseau and Wade-Benzoni (1995), the consequences are that established bureaucracies are slowly being replaced by 'adhocracies', which involve changes in the nature of work and structure of occupations, and 'a diverse array of employment patterns [within the same organisation, which] necessitates attaching adjectives, descriptors, and modifiers to the term employee…'. Associated with this trend is the need for recognition of work performed beyond organisational boundaries and of the development of a range of commitments between labour and the organisation. In other words, the 'standard' employee is no longer, and mixed employment relationships within organisations are to be expected. We now examine the different types of employment relationships to be found within organisations and use Atkinson's (1984) model as a descriptor of these relationships.

Atkinson's model of the flexible firm

When Atkinson (1984) introduced the concept of the 'flexible' firm as a means to establish competitive advantage, he identified a variety of forms of employment relationships that could enable firms to access the skill mix and people they required from inside and outside their organisation. By considering the organisation of their workforce within a number of distinct categories, Atkinson suggested that firms could pursue four distinct types of flexibility simultaneously. These included *functional* flexibility, which refers to ensuring the availability of required skills; *numerical* flexibility, to ensure the required number of people; *temporal* flexibility, or using alternative work schedules to ensure work completion; and *wage* flexibility, or the capacity to align pay with labour demand while controlling pay costs for the work.

His model of the flexible firm identified three levels of 'work provider' categories. The central level is a core primary labour market that provides functional flexibility to the organisation and generally comprises full-time, permanent employees within the organisation. Peripheral to this level is a secondary labour market providing numerical flexibility through casual, temporary and part-time employees; self-employed and contracted workers; and trainees, who by definition have less job security. Atkinson considered these peripheral workers were most likely to be either lower-skilled and lower-paid or more specialised, skilled workers who were therefore more highly paid and perhaps self-employed. A third ring of contractors and agency staff not directly employed by the organisation provide further externality and flexibility.

The extent to which Atkinson's (1984) model effectively links the different configurations with strategies adopted by organisations is subject to much critical debate, with the categorisation of employment relationships into core or peripheral viewed as too simplistic to be useful (Burgess 1997; Clifford, Morley & Gunnigle 1997). Nevertheless, the model provides a useful way of visualising the changing balance between employment categories. By changing the size of different employment categories it is possible to visualise the range of employment relationships within an organisation. A firm with a small core workforce may be considered to have maximised all aspects of flexibility if the core workforce is sufficient to manage the acquisition and distribution of work; the range of skills required is available outside the organisation; and people with these skills are available for employment at the time required and at a cost that still allows the organisation to be profitable.

It is possible to envisage within this arrangement different configurations that describe the mix of relationships, for example, within a tourist hotel. Twenty years ago, to cope with changing demand, casual labour with variable hours would have been an integral part of the employment mix, just as it is today. Then, as now, it may not have been appropriate to describe the casual workforce as peripheral to the organisation since their use was a long-term strategy. However, it is unlikely that contractors would have been involved to the same extent, and the possibility that restaurants and laundry services, for example, are managed under contract is now greater. Hence, the range and use of alternative employment relationships has increased, and this shift has reduced the relative size of the core workforce in some hotels over recent decades. Another example is that of a car manufacturing organisation: twenty years ago the core workforce was a major part of the organisation, with mostly full-time employees and limited use of external suppliers; with technological changes, the size of this full-time workforce has diminished relative to the increasing size of temporary labour hire and other outsourcing relationships. In this organisation, not only has the periphery become larger but the core has diminished, thereby enhancing the effect.

Although Atkinson's model identifies the key categories of work providers to an organisation, the implications of peripheral or core status are also developed in other frameworks, such as that developed by Pfeffer and Baron (1988). It is useful to remember that both Atkinson in the United Kingdom and Baron and Pfeffer in the United States formulated their ideas in a work environment that is barely recognisable today. Technological changes that now allow on-line communications between distant locations were in the early stages of development; globalisation of business as we know it today was only just emerging; and family-friendly policies in organisations were almost nonexistent.

Rousseau and Wade-Benzoni (1995) argue that the two basic dimensions to employment relationships are time and *embeddedness*. Time refers to whether a short- or long-term time frame drives the relationship, and this largely reflects the extent to which organisations consider they can anticipate the future. Embeddedness refers to the extent of 'internalisation' or 'externalisation' of the role of the work provider, and hence whether the worker is an insider or an outsider. When Pfeffer and Baron (1988) refer to internalisation and externalisation of the workforce they are identifying the degree of attachment between the organisation and those who are considered long-term, core 'internal' employees in contrast to those who are more peripheral and 'external' to the long-term functioning of the organisation.

Pfeffer and Baron consider that work providers would have less attachment to an organisation when:

1. physical proximity was reduced, such as through working at home or another location
2. administrative control was reduced, such as when work is contracted or employees leased
3. when the anticipated length of employment was reduced, such as for casual and temporary workers.

High internalisation, which means a significant core workforce, implies a strategy in which existing and future needs for skills and competencies are met by existing employees with the development of firm-specific skills. For employees, this provides opportunities for training, development and career progression within a reasonably secure employment context; and for organisations it provides opportunities for control. For example, bureaucracies maintain control by encouraging employees to remain insiders through long-term benefits such as superannuation and accumulated sick leave.

High externalisation implies that only a small core workforce has access to these opportunities and therefore a distinctly reduced investment by management in the larger part of the organisational workforce. Before pursuing discussion about the issues and challenges associated with these choices, it is useful to assess the extent to which alternative employment forms located within a core/peripheral framework are evident in Australia.

Alternative employment forms in Australia

The extent to which alternative forms of employment prevail in Australia has become easier to ascertain as data collection through the Australian Bureau of Statistics has begun to more clearly define and differentiate the interactions between the distinct employment categories of part-time and full-time, permanent and casual work, one-person self-employment and business ownership employing others. For example, part-time work may be permanent or casual, full-time work may be short term, and working in an individual business in a defined contractual relationship is quite different from managing a workforce.

Year 2000 data confirm previous trends indicating that since the early 1980s part-time work has steadily increased to 13 per cent for men and 43 per cent for women, and that whereas high part-time rates for young men decline with age, high part-time rates for young women dip only slightly with age and remain higher for married women (ABS 2000a). Knowing that more women than men work part time does not distinguish between casual and permanent part-time work, which may be higher for women.

The lowest part-time rates of men or women are to be found in employment sectors traditionally dominated by men, where high unionisation has always restricted casual or part-time work. In contrast, in traditionally female employment sectors, part-time rates for men and women are higher overall but middle-aged and older men are more likely to be employed full time than are similarly aged women. More part-time work and casualisation is associated with employment sectors in which this has been traditional, and in business services, a major new growth area, this pattern of work has also become evident.

Data from 1998 (ABS 2000b) indicate that 'permanent' full-time and part-time employees (defined as those who receive paid recreation and sick leave benefits) comprise 59 per cent of the Australian workforce. One-third of all part-time employees were employed in 'permanent' positions, and these comprised 12 per cent of the 'permanent' workforce. Casual employees accounted for approximately 18 per cent of the total workforce and 23 per cent of the employee workforce. Seventy-two per cent of the casual workforce worked part time, with almost half of these wishing they could work longer hours. The retail and hospitality industries employed 43 per cent of these workers, nearly two-thirds of whom were women, with the result that two in three employees in the hospitality sector and three in five employees in the retail sector worked on a casual basis.

Other work categories illustrate the extent of externalised employment in Australia. People who identified themselves as 'owner-managers' of their businesses, a group that has not previously been so clearly defined, comprised 12 per cent of the workforce. These ABS (2000b) data indicate that 60 per cent of this group worked in one-person businesses and 15 per cent depended for their work on a limited number of contracting relationships — often just one, with a former employer. Whereas women dominated casual employee numbers, men dominated the 'owner-manager' category at 69 per cent, which included 20 per cent tradesmen, 30 per cent professionals and 15 per cent managers, and reflects the growth of individual consultants and professional practices as an alternative to casual employee relationships for these occupational groups.

Pfeffer and Baron (1988) identify a further mode of externalisation in work distributed to a 'distant' site, such as home-based work. Telecommuting is a recent variant of this option; other teleworking, in call centres for example, has also expanded, although this may also be viewed as an outsourced, contracted service. The numbers of people involved in telecommuting have been difficult to establish but appear to be lower than would be expected even where organisational policies have allowed the practice. Lindorf (2000) points to a lack of research evidence in the human resources literature on the cost benefits and travel savings associated with telecommuting, which is defined as 'undertaking work normally performed in the usual office work site in a home, satellite office, client office, or neighbourhood work center' (p. 3). Lindorf notes that definitions vary according to whether they include, for example, work undertaken outside the office in the employee's own time, occasional home use, and single or multiple employers, and that rates could be distorted by the inclusion of self-employed and independent contractors. Of the 'Top 100' companies in Australia, which employ more than 1 million employees, 55 had no home-based employees and most who did reported that these were women working in a temporary arrangement, usually following maternity leave. Only 11 organisations reported a formal policy supporting home-based workers. Even in a sample of organisations in which teleworking would seem a highly reasonable option, approximately half had no employees working from home unless under a short-term, individually negotiated arrangement (Lindorf 2000).

These data, which further clarify the employment status quo in 1998, need to be considered in the context of other data showing that overall job creation in Australia during the 1990s has been greatest in non-permanent, less than full-time work; that the use of contracting and outsourcing of work has increased; and that this employment growth has been strongest in small and large organisations. ABS data during the 1990s consistently indicated that most employment growth has been in the casual/part-time category, although the figures varied across Australia. The data cited above indicate how this form of employment has expanded in sectors in which it was strongest. Kramer's (2000) study of organisations employing more than 100 people indicates that about one in three of these organisations employed more than 10 per cent of their workforce on a temporary or casual basis. Between 1993 and 1996 just over half reported increasing their use of contracting and outsourcing and of casual, part-time and fixed-term employees.

A majority of Australians are employed in organisations with more than 100 employees, but the small business sector is also considered an important source of employment. Although only one-third of employees worked in organisations with fewer than 20 people, this proportion increases to 50 per cent when one-person owner-manager firms are included; this sector was identified as the fastest-growing employment sector in Australia between 1987 and 1998 (DEWRSB 1998). This is important information because small businesses often provide more precarious employment, since they lack the resources to carry staff through slack times, or to provide training and development, and they may need to close rather than shed staff. This is well demonstrated by what has been described as the 'churnover' effect. In 1996–97, 952 000 jobs were created but 527 000 jobs were lost, 40 per cent of these when businesses closed. Although nearly one-third of new jobs were created by small businesses, for every job generated by the creation of a new business, one job was lost through business closure. Nearly one quarter of newly created small businesses close within three years (DEWRSB 1998).

In recent decades the mix of employment relationships in organisations has involved a new range of configurations that may reflect not only an increase in alternative forms of employment but also the relative decline of traditional full-time employment options for the core workforce. These new relationships indicate a reduced level of 'attachment' between organisation and employee that has been characterised as externalisation and is distinct from the qualities of the internalised relationship that dominated many organisations. The changes appear to be in the early stages of definition, and although further evolution towards small core, highly networked organisations is predicted, changes in circumstances may yet create new surprises. Managing a workforce involving these mixed employment relationships provides new challenges for organisations and managers. For some groups within the labour force these new options have created positive opportunities; for others they have curtailed opportunities for development; but all groups of work providers have been required to think of their careers within a new framework. These topics are now addressed.

Challenges and issues for organisations

During the late 1990s an increasing number of books and articles (e.g. Flood, Gannon & Pauuwe 1996; Barker & Christensen 1998; Herzenberg, Alic & Wial 1998) focused on the issues of managing a workforce that includes non-traditional employment relationships. The organisational issues and challenges discussed in this chapter include:

1. the right mix for the strategic future of the organisation
2. the contractual and commitment relationship
3. equity and ethical issues
4. broader social impacts
5. briefly, the implications for legislated issues such as occupational health and safety.

The right mix of employment relationships

Rousseau and Wade-Benzoni (1995) assert that from a Strategic Human Resource Management perspective the key issue facing the organisation is to determine whether it has sufficient core people proficient in areas representing its current and long-term strategic interests. As these interests change, the appropriate mix may also change. Another way to address this question is to ask whether the organisation can continue to obtain the additional resources it requires from a non-core workforce.

In another paper, Hartmann (in press) identifies evidence suggesting that some organisations may be reconsidering their reliance on high levels of externalised labour sources, and proposes a number of issues that may influence current trends towards small core workforces. The evidence is by no means conclusive, but a recent Morgan and Banks Job Index survey (2000) indicates that fewer employers (one quarter of those polled in 1998) were planning to increase their contract and casual employment, even in the tourism sector where this growth has been highest. Slightly more than one-third of the 3000 organisations in the survey planned to increase their recruitment of long-term staff; this was most evident in the legal services, telecommunications, information technology and tourism employment sectors for jobs in sales and information technology and accounting and clerical/administrative positions. Research by Salzman (1998) of medical imaging and insurance firms in the United States indicates that a reliance on flexibility in staff numbers may be followed by an emphasis on more stable organisational employment; and in Australia Lafferty (1998) found evidence that large international hotel chains were now seeking to enhance staff retention and reduce their casual workforce. Such developments challenge the view that outsourcing and externalising mark the beginning of a new relational form of organisation that includes a variety of alliances, joint ventures and other long-term associations that may involve selling outsourced non-core businesses (Gome 1998).

Hartmann (in press) argues that labour market developments may influence some organisations to reconsider their reliance on peripheral work providers. These developments are associated with changing demographics and the globalisation of employment opportunities. First, the growth in casualisation and outsourcing has been facilitated by growth in the supply of available workers. Since the early 1980s many women who were ill prepared for lifetime careers have returned to the labour market and, with limited options, have joined the casual, low-skilled, low-paid labour force. Similarly, growth in tertiary education has created a large pool of student labour willing to accept casual work during their studies. Redundancies in a wide range of occupational groups have also provided a large pool of qualified tradespeople and administrative/managerial staff, many of whom were in the last 10 years of their working careers and were funded by good redundancy payments. It is possible that each of these sources of labour will not expand and will even contract as women prepare better for long-term careers, the numbers of young people entering the labour market decrease and redundancy levels of older workers decline. Second, as skill shortages associated with demographic changes and economic growth become more evident in North America and Europe, skilled workers will be in greater demand across national and organisational boundaries. Hence, organisations may find the skills they require are not so readily available, and they may be vulnerable to increased costs in training a less employable casual workforce and in buying in skilled labour services.

Organisational costs have not necessarily been the only motivation for reducing the size of core workforces, although for organisations that have traditionally relied on their internal labour markets, the development of organisation-specific skills over long periods of on-the-job training and on-costs of other long-term benefits have been important (Ehrensal 1995). Where technology and skill demands are changing rapidly, outsourcing can provide rapid access to staff with these resources without long-term commitments and on-costs, and these new resources, even though temporary, have been seen as an opportunity for more rapid organisation renewal and change than would otherwise be possible. From case studies of three Australian organisations that introduced outsourcing — a hospital, a local government call centre and a shipyard — Hall (2000) reports that, in addition to numerical flexibility, two key benefits were immediate access to labour with new skills and technologies (without recruitment, training and long-term costs), and changes in the way costs were managed through a more disciplined management of costs through tendering, both of which stimulated change. In these settings the introduction of alternative employment relationships brought rapid change into the organisations.

Pfeffer and Baron (1988) argued that the presence of a flexible workforce 'buffer' could provide organisational benefits by enhancing perceptions of job security for the more secure, stable core workforce and could reduce structural differentiation within the organisation because benefits would be targeted to a more limited range of employees, thereby making the sharing of values, activities and orientations easier, and encouraging perceptions of wage equity by externalising high- or low-paid positions. These conclusions are controversial in view of recent developments. For Rousseau and Wade-Benzoni (1995), this view is too simplistic and ignores the impact of downsizing on the whole workforce in terms of the nature of careers and the psychological contracts of employees, both core and peripheral. For Nisbet and Thomas (2000), it makes too many assumptions about 'core' and 'peripheral' employees and does not recognise that within these categories workers can differ widely in their employment preferences. Both these issues provide challenges for organisations in determining the structure of their workforce.

The contractual and commitment relationship

Rousseau and Wade-Benzoni (1995) argue that differences in employment contracts are further defined by psychological contracts within organisations that reflect the employee's and employer's understanding of the terms of the employment relationship. They identify temporary employment as a *transactional* contract that involves an economic exchange for a limited period of time for well-defined performance. *Relational* contracts, on the other hand, imply an open-ended and longer-term relationship involving investment by both the employer and employee and incomplete or flexible performance requirements. *Balanced* contracts involve a highly interactive relationship based on the individual's capacity to perform and the needs of the organisation to access that performance. *Transitional* contracts reflect the inability of individuals, or more often organisations in unstable circumstances, to identify what performance is expected or what commitments can be made. Rousseau and Wade-Benzoni (1995) find that relational contracts, which were normative for core employees, have been replaced by balanced contracts or in some cases transitional contracts, and organisational loyalty has little long-term payoff even for core employees.

Faced with uncertainty, organisations can expect to find new career orientations in their employees that should influence management strategies. Rousseau and Wade-Benzoni (1995) suggest that these orientations include 'short term insiders' who may be *careerists* expecting to make their career within an industry rather than a specific firm and who look for career growth, or *jugglers* for whom employment is not a central life interest, who want to integrate work with their personal lives, and who offer the organisation some flexibility without requiring promotion or advancement. 'Long term insiders' should align themselves within the *careerist* category in order to ensure they maintain their employability. Stroh & Reilly (1997) found that many managers considered themselves free agents who transferred their loyalty readily from organisation to organisation while proactively managing their careers. The second category comprises temporary employees and independent contractors who are 'short-term outsiders' or 'peripheral workers'. Independent contractors often have occupation-based rather than industry- or firm-based careers, for example in accounting or trades, and are usually used in core activities only when they have specific experience and experience within the firm. Part-timers overlap into many employment relationships, and particular circumstances will vary from temporary employment with limited training to long-standing relationships.

Although there is considerable agreement that the changes occurring in employment relationships have implications for human resources (HR) policies and practices, there is less agreement regarding the nature of the changes, including on the key issues of what employers should expect from employees and what expectations employees bring to the workplace. Roehling, Cavanaugh, Moynihan and Boswell (2000) undertook a content analysis of 51 articles on the new employment relationship published since 1995. They note a lack of recognition of the importance of multiple relationships, with more than half of the scholarly publications and three-quarters of the trade magazine articles referring to a single employment relationship. Their analysis indicates three aspects to strategic management. First, effective employment relations are not driven solely by strategy, but subject to human resource constraints that include the availability of skills and the training required to meet desired skill levels. The cost of these is influenced by what target employees are willing to accept. Second, employers need to distinguish between essential requirements that may meet minimum levels of acceptability and 'wants' or valued outcomes desired by employees.

Effective employment relationships involve a combination of characteristics that a) meet the requirements implied by the employer's strategy, b) meet the essential requirements of the employee target group and c) although not essential to either party, are either valued by the employer or the employee target group. (Roehling et al. 2000, p. 312)

These considerations mean that when required labour is in high demand, the 'wants' of target employees take on increased importance and are reflected in the employment relationship, even though their only value to the employer is their role in attracting and retaining employees. For example, for new graduates development opportunities may be critical and if not provided by an employer may lead to high turnover; and parents who require some flexibility in their time at the work site may need at-home work options. Third, there are likely to be systematic differences across target employees in what they require and what they value,

for example across cultures, career stages and occupational groups, and between peripheral and core employees. Employees and employers need to identify the elements of reciprocity in their employment contract in terms of the psychological contracts identified by Rousseau and Wade-Benzoni (1995), and to explore a variety of approaches appropriate to different types of commitment.

The development of new employment relationships has challenged traditional views about the level of organisational commitment that can be expected when the incentive of job security is no longer available. Many organisations are willing to accept low commitment in exchange for low labour costs or because it enables them to focus on high performance without creating unrealistic expectations among employees. Others regard commitment as important because of its effect on employee identification with the organisation, level of effort and turnover (Stroh & Reilly 1997).

The nature of organisational commitments can be usefully examined through the definitions provided by Meyer and Allen (1997), who identified three types of employee commitment: affective, normative and continuance. *Affective* commitment, which refers to feelings of belonging and a sense of attachment to the organisation, is likely to reflect a psychological appreciation of equity and expectancy. *Continuance* commitment relates to the perceived costs, both financial and non-financial, of leaving and the perceived lack of alternatives. In the past, arrangements such as promotion based on tenure, accrued pensions and sick leave increased the cost of leaving the organisation prematurely; other potential costs included lost investment in firm-specific skills, disruptions to personal life and loss of valued future opportunities. Perceptions of few alternative job opportunities could have a varying effect on commitment depending on the level of satisfaction experienced by the individual, and neither costs nor alternatives alone were thought to determine high or low commitment. *Normative* commitment is concerned with the obligation employees feel to remain with an organisation in response either to cultural expectations about rates of job change or to 'rewards in advance' such as training, payment of study costs and consideration of special needs. The extent to which an organisation conveys its expectations may affect feelings of obligation within employees and the duration of any extra effort. Normative commitment may last only until the 'debt' is considered paid and hence is subject to rationalisation if other circumstances change (Meyer & Allen 1991). In summary, Meyer and Allen (1991) argue that employees with high affective commitment continue because they want to, those with high normative commitment because they think they should and those with high continuance commitment because they need to.

When job security is low among individuals, the need for self-interest and career management seems self-evident and a lower level of organisational commitment is likely among core and peripheral employees. The manifestations of this are demonstrated in a study of white-collar graduate employees in the United States. King (2000) reports that perceptions of job insecurity are significantly related to lower levels of organisational loyalty, higher levels of career loyalty, less effort towards quality work, less organisational citizenship behaviour, and more job search activity. However, time at work, one of the most observable aspects of employee behaviour, does not vary, which suggests that employees are concerned to maintain an appearance of commitment. King (2000) concedes that organisations need to be prepared for increased voluntary turnover, and consequently need to give constant attention to succession planning and the state of the external labour market.

Equity and fairness

Issues of equity and fairness are raised by the previously reported suggestion by Pfeffer and Baron (1988) that mixed employment relationships within an organisation can be used to separate the treatment of groups critical to the organisation's core functioning from other 'externalised' groups. Differences in approaches to pay, conditions of employment and opportunities for development are examples of this discrimination. However, Rousseau and Wade-Benzoni (1995) consider that the creation of two classes of employee — high-paid, long-term staff and lower-paid, short-term workers — particularly when these groups differ demographically in terms of sex, race or religion for example, can potentially lower productivity and increase conflict. These distinctions can also be linked to potentially unwarranted differences in management assumptions about work providers in different categories and their consequent treatment.

Lack of management consideration of casual employees is evident from a study of casual employees in the 'club' industry of New South Wales. Lowry (2001) refers to indications that managers typically view casual staff as less committed and self-motivated than long-term employees, and are less willing to provide them with access to training and development activities. Casual workers indicated most dissatisfaction when:

1. flexibility in scheduling benefited employers only and did not consider employee needs
2. there was inadequate training and too much reliance on 'on-the-job' methods
3. they lacked opportunities for promotion
4. good work received little recognition

5. divisions between permanent and casual staff produced a sense of inequity in their treatment.

Employees on low wages relied heavily on penalty rates. Even so, these issues were more important to those who preferred full-time work and were less of an issue for the minority who were satisfied with their hours.

Sometimes perceptions of inequity can operate in the reverse direction. Contractors and casual staff may receive higher compensation than continuing employees, giving these employees the impression that the organisation is willing to take advantage of them by paying lower rates (Pearce 1993). The importance of employee perceptions of fairness is highlighted by the finding of Rousseau and Wade-Benzoni (1995) that employees value respect from employers very highly and are likely to be increasingly sensitive to this issue when their job is insecure.

Broader social impacts

A range of employment options, and therefore mixed employment relationships within organisations, may provide benefits to a small section of the labour market while seeming mainly to disadvantage more vulnerable sections. Tregaskis (1997) identifies a key positive effect of casual or outsourced employment to be in creating work opportunities for those who are unable to work a standard week, for example those with carer responsibilities. On the other hand, negative outcomes associated with the lower wages and fewer fringe benefits available in peripheral employment include:

- greater uncertainty, which limits financial commitments considered by employees — for example in buying a home and committing to a mortgage
- people juggling more than one job and needing to manage competing employer demands
- people being unable to find permanent employment and accepting non-permanent jobs as a substitute.

As argued by Hendry (1997), the development of a large casual employment sector with reduced development opportunities can create and reinforce low expectations in workers regarding their life chances.

Researchers have also noted that labour inequalities are perpetuated by the lack of negotiating power of peripheral workers, whether they are employed directly by organisations or through contracting organisations. Contracted service providers often tender within very tight budgets that make little allowance for training and development, and pay only minimum rates to their employees (Hall 2000). Strachan and Burgess (1998) note that, as work schedules have become less predictable and shifts longer, increasing pressure has been placed on parents with family commitments, with the consequences of reduced opportunities for occupational advancement and the reinforcement of traditional sex roles for women, who dominate the casual labour market and whose careers are regarded as secondary to meeting family responsibilities (Deery, Plowman & Walsh 1997). When opportunities for further training are not provided to casual staff, who have fewer financial resources to pursue these directly for themselves, their situation is further circumscribed.

Legal implications — occupational health and safety

The distinction between categories of employees also present some as yet unresolved issues concerning the responsibilities of employers that will not be explored in this chapter except by way of example in the area of occupational health and safety. In a recent paper, Quinlan and Mayhew (2000) cite extensive data indicating that a higher incidence of health and safety problems is commonly found among self-employed workers, contractors and casual employees; this finding is directly attributable not only to long hours, low pay and the pressure of tight work schedules but also to a fracturing of responsibilities for OHS issues within organisations. Small organisations, which were identified earlier as contributing strongly to casual employment, often lack resources to develop and monitor OHS procedures; in large organisations multiple employment relationships may serve to weaken the monitoring and control of responsibilities across these different groups, even though the responsibilities of major contractors in these circumstances is becoming increasingly clear.

Challenges for managers

The management of work providers across a mix of employment relationships is a task for which most managers receive no training, yet effective functioning across a range of relationships is a key skill for managers building their careers. Nisbet and Thomas (2000) express the view that it is essential to understand attitudes and perceptions of different classes of employees and how these may vary with circumstances over time. For example, attitudes to job security may change as job opportunities change from poor to good. Similarly, categorising employees with different employment contracts can be misleading, since workers within these categories can differ widely in their preferences

concerning, for example, self-employment and temporary contractual status or casual work.

From a different perspective, Gome (1998) refers to 'confusion among managers [that] is compounded by gurus on the speaking circuit, preaching that only devoted, empowered employees who can provide excellent service can build a successful business'. Other issues concerning the management of contract labour highlighted in this article in *Business Review Weekly* include that managers:

1. use flexible labour to provide a quick fix for problems and to reduce their fixed costs, rather than addressing long-term cost issues
2. hire contract labour for core competency tasks (which they have not defined appropriately), and risk losing valuable company knowledge
3. need to define their performance requirements clearly and to have a system for introducing and assessing new labour quickly to gain high performance
4. need to focus on performance and keep their 'soft' skills for their permanent staff.

In addition to these points, Hall (2000) stresses that managers need skills in preparing tenders and contractual details and in monitoring and managing these outputs when they may often have little control of inputs. They also need negotiating and people skills in resolving situations of inconsistent and divided supervision and loyalties, role ambiguities and problems when equipment, tools or training provided by labour hire firms is inadequate. Among their own continuing staff, they need to deal with concerns about job security and a possible lack of trust between different groups of staff.

The ideas expressed here all relate to good employee management and the implication that managers need to be able to address performance management issues effectively whether work providers are continuing, casual or temporary, in direct employment or indirect employment through labour hire firms, or working in outsourcing contracts. More debatable is the right balance between hard and soft management approaches that may have implications for future access to external work providers, when they are needed. The 'soft' skills that ensure a manager is considered ethical and trustworthy, provides useful feedback on performance and gives some consideration to work providers' needs may be critical in building effective external networks for times of tight labour demand.

King (2000) draws some conclusions regarding the management of core employee expectations that could apply to all employment relationships within the organisation. These stress the importance for organisations to be consistent in their management activities by not indicating to employees that they will provide job security and by not implying this from their interactions, for example in discussions about future career moves within the organisation or in building a sense of reciprocal obligation. Rather, compensation and incentive plans could be used to provide obligation-free indications to employees of their value, and key personnel could be targeted through these processes. As an illustration of how this message can be transmitted, US attorneys surveyed by Klein, Berman and Dixon (2000) considered that organisations were most likely to respond positively to requests for part-time work from valued performers with strong organisational connections who would be difficult to replace and who threatened to leave if requests were denied. This, then, is another form of organisational recognition. Part-time workers appear to be motivated by a mix of features in their reward packages and their work — a mix that varies between workers and is different from that of full-time workers (Fenton-O'Creevy 1992). Recognition may be enhanced by not treating part-time workers the same as full-time workers and by ensuring that working hours allow for other employee time demands.

For some managers, dealing with staff from a distance, and focusing on performance and cost issues rather than the actions that may facilitate the achievement of these aims, is personally less demanding. Flexible working and the associated mixed employment relationships challenge traditional management styles (Sparrow 2000) by demanding more versatility of managers in dealing with the hard and soft issues of employee management.

Challenges for employees

The challenges for employees in organisations with mixed employment relationships can best be identified by examining the circumstances of different categories of employees within an overall framework of varying levels of job insecurity and the objective of maintaining their employability. Kanter (1989) suggests that employability refers to the accumulation of valued skills and reputation, which thereby increase the employment options available to the individual. Inherent in this conclusion is the idea that individuals now need to manage their careers and exercise more influence and direction as they negotiate a series of deals with employers (Herriot & Pemberton 1995).

Continuing employees who provide core organisational services are in the most favourable position to achieve this, since it is these employees that organisations are most likely to view as worth the ongoing investment of training and other development opportunities. However, for these employees a key task may be ensuring that the skills they develop do not become too firm-specific, thereby limiting their attractiveness to other organisations. One of the advantages of involvement in multi-organisational networks is that they keep core employees in touch with other job opportunities and help them build networks of contacts. Ensuring that they become involved in projects that provide opportunities for them to develop high-demand skills increases their value to the organisation and their employability.

For casual employees, two major challenges are, first, to convey to the managers for whom they work a sense of commitment to high performance and, second, to seize 'free' opportunities for skill development whenever these are available. As noted, managers are likely to view casual employees as poorly motivated, with limited development potential, whose time should always be available to fit their employer's scheduling needs. Hence, casual employees who can identify the key issues for managers and meet their expectations in this regard have a better chance of being viewed positively and gaining some scheduling consideration. Taking opportunities to develop their skills is important for their future employability. For casual employees, these opportunities often arise through on-the-job training, and because their pay is often low and schedules unpredictable other training or education may be difficult to access. Equally important is developing an accurate record of their achievements and performance in different jobs as a means to helping them sell their skills to future employers. The problem for many casual employees whose experience may be limited is that they lack the confidence to begin a process of 'impression management'. Bambacas and Hartmann (2000) note that the use of career planning strategies such as 'networking', 'self-nomination' and 'seeking career opportunities' is a function of the sense of optimism and feelings of potential success experienced by casual academic staff. Casual employees may therefore need to seek a mentor within their community who can provide them with the support and advice they need to begin this process.

For temporary employees or employees who work under contract through labour hire agencies, depending on the level of skills they hold and the demand for their labour, maintaining their employability may involve similar processes but at two levels, one within the organisations in which they are placed and one with the labour hire organisation. Particularly for work providers from labour hire firms, employers are likely to have immediate performance requirements in order to fulfil their expectations, and it is important to understand these requirements. Increasingly, labour hire firms have the potential to offer regular employment across a variety of settings, and individuals need to be careful to ensure they have access to work that increases their overall employability and helps them build networks.

Conclusion

This chapter has examined the challenges and issues for organisations, managers and work providers associated with the range of employment relationships that can be found in most contemporary organisations. A framework for identifying the employment contracts associated with these relationships and the main relational effects associated with these different levels of organisational attachment have been discussed. The current trends and some potential direction in the development of these types of employment have been raised.

In Australia, organisations have rapidly adopted alternative forms of employment, and this has created a great deal of uncertainty within the labour force. The extent to which different sections of the workforce, and individuals within them, will find these changes to their advantage or disadvantage may change as their experience and understanding of these new labour market dynamics develop. Human resource management of this new labour force requires new levels of adaptability in managing these changing mixed employment relationships.

References

ABS (2000a) *Labor Force, Australia*. Australian Bureau of Statistics. Cat. no. 6203. Canberra: Australian Government Publishing Service (AGPS).

ABS (2000b) *Forms of Employment, Australia*. Australian Bureau of Statistics. Cat. no. 6359. Canberra: AGPS.

Allan, A, Brosnan, P, and Walsh P (1998) Non-standard working-time arrangements in Australia and New Zealand. *International Journal of Manpower*, 19 (4) 234–49.

Atkinson, J (1984) Manpower strategies for flexible organisations. *Personnel Management*, August, 28–31.

Bambacas, M, and Hartmann, LC (2000) *Casual staff and career strategies*. Proceedings of the Australia and New Zealand Academy of Management Conference. December, North Ryde: ANZAM.

Barker, K, and Christensen, J (Eds) (1998) Contingent work: American employment relations in transition. Ithaca, NY: Cornell University Press.

Blyton, P, and Morris, J (1992) HRM and the limits of flexibility. In P Blyton and P Turnbull, *Reassessing Human Resource Management*. London: Sage, 116–30.

Burgess, J (1996) Workforce casualization in Australia. *International Employment Relations Review*, 2 (1) 33–53.

Clifford, N, Morley, M, and Gunnigle, P (1997) Part-time work in Europe. *Employee Relations*, 19 (6) 555–67.

Deery, S, Plowman, DW, and Walsh, J (1997) *Industrial Relations: A Contemporary Analysis*. Roseville, Australia: McGraw-Hill.

DEWRSB (1998) *Portrait of Australian Business*. Department of Employment, Workplace Relations and Small Business, Canberra.

Ehrensal, KN (1995) Obscuring the changing labour processes of managerial work. *Journal of Organizational Change Management*, 8 (5) 5–16.

Fenton-O'Creevy, M (1992) Moderators of differences in job satisfaction between full-time and part-time female employees: a research note. *Human Resource Management*, 5 (5) 75–81.

Flood, PC, Gannon, MJ, and Paauwe, J (1996) *Managing without traditional methods: international innovations in human resource management*. Wokingham, UK: Addison-Wesley.

Gome, A (1998) Labor hire: the edge is in the contract. *Business Review Weekly*, Sydney, 16 November.

Hall, R. (2000) Outsourcing, contracting-out and labour hire: implications for human resource development in Australian organisations. *Asia Pacific Journal of Human Resources*, 38 (2) 23–41.

Hartmann, LC (in press) Flexible employment: trends and influences in Australia. *Journal of the International Association of Management*.

Hendry, C (1997) *Human Resource Management: A Strategic Approach to Employment*. Oxford, UK: Butterworth-Heinemann.

Herriot, P, and Pemberton, C (1995) *New deals: the revolution in managerial careers*. Chichester, UK: John Wiley & Sons.

Herzenberg, SA, Alic, JA, and Wial, H (1998) New rules for a new economy: employment and opportunity in postindustrial America. Ithaca, NY: Cornell University Press.

Kanter, RM (1989) Careers and the wealth of nations: a macro-perspective on the structure and implications of career forms. In MB Arthur, DT Hall and BS Lawrence, *Handbook of career theory*. Cambridge, UK: Cambridge University Press, 506–522.

King, JE (2000) White-collar reactions to job insecurity and the role of the psychological contract: implications for human resource management. *Human Resource Management*, 39 (1) 79–92.

Klein, KJ, Berman, LM, and Dickson, MW (2000) May I work part time? An exploration of predicted employer responses to employee requests for part time work. *Journal of Vocational Behavior*, 57, 85–101.

Kramar, R (2000) *Cranfield–PricewaterhouseCoopers Survey on International Strategic Human Resource Management*. Sydney: Macquarie Graduate School of Management.

Lafferty, G, and Roan, A (2000) Public sector out-sourcing: implications for training and skills. *Employee Relations*, 22 (1) 76–85.

Lindorf, M (2000) Home-based telework and telecommuting in Australia: more myth than modern work form. *Asia Pacific Journal of Human Resources*, 38 (3) 1–11.

Lowry, D (2001) The casual management of casual work: casual workers' perceptions of HRM practices in the highly casualized firm. *Asia Pacific Journal of Human Resources*, 39 (1) 42–62.

Meyer, J, and Allen, NJ (1991) A three component conceptualisation of organisational commitment. *Human Resource Management Review*, 1 (1) 61–89.

Meyer, JP, and Allen, NJ (1997) *Commitment in the workplace: theory, research and application*. Thousand Oaks, CA: Sage.

Morgan & Banks (2000) *Job Index Survey — Australia*.

Nisbet, P, and Thomas, W (2000) Attitudes, expectations and labour market behaviour: the case of self-employment in the UK construction industry. *Work, Employment and Society*, 14 (2) 353–68.

Pfeffer, J, and Baron, JN (1988) Taking the workers back out: recent trends in the structuring of employment. In BM Staw and LL Cummings, *Research in Organizational Behaviour: an annual series of analytical essays and critical reviews*. London: JAI Press, 10, 257–303.

Quinlan, M, and Mayhew, C (2000) Precarious employment, work re-organisation and the fracturing of OHS management. In K Frick, P Jensen, M Quinlan and T Wilthagen (Eds), *Systematic Occupational Health and Safety Management*. Oxford: Elsevier: 175–98.

Roehling, MV, Cavanaugh, MA, Moynihan, LM, and Boswell, WR (2000) The nature of the new employment relationship: a content analysis of the practitioner and academic literatures. *Human Resource Management*, 39 (4) 305–320.

Rousseau, DM, and Wade-Benzoni, KA (1995) Changing individual-organizational attachments: a two way street. In A Howard, *The changing nature of work*. San Francisco: Jossey-Bass, 290–322.

Salzman, H (1998) Restructuring and skill needs: will firms train? *Annals*, AAPSS, 559, September, 126–40.

Sparrow, PR (2000) New employee behaviours, work designs and forms of work organization: what is in store for future of work? *Journal of Managerial Psychology*, 15 (3) 202–218.

Strachan, G, and Burgess, J (1998) Towards a new deal for women workers in Australia? Growing employment share, enterprise bargaining and the family friendly workplace. *Equal Opportunites International*, 17 (8) 1–13.

Stroh, L, and Reilly, AH (1997) Loyalty in the age of downsizing. *Sloan Management Review*, 38 (4) 83–8.

Tregaskis, O (1997) The 'non-permanent' reality. *Employee Relations*, 19 (6) 535–54.

CHAPTER 12

The management of contractors: challenges for human resource management

by Simon Peel
University College London

Introduction

Traditional models of human resource management (HRM) and traditional styles of managing are increasingly challenged by the variety of employment arrangements used in contemporary organisations. In a climate of ever-increasing competitive pressures, managers seek cost containment, productivity improvement and flexibility, and are forced to question and rethink traditional ways of doing things. For example, the use of contractors challenges managers and others interested in HRM to think differently about their practices and the assumptions that underpin them. Much HRM and management theory and practice is based on assumptions of a traditional employment relationship. These assumptions are increasingly called into question in organisations in which employees under radically different terms and conditions of employment work side by side. This chapter takes a contemporary issue — the widespread use of contractors — and explores some of the issues and implications for managers and organisations.

The chapter examines six ways in which the presence of contractors in organisations challenges HR thinking and practice. This examination starts with the drive for flexibility, in its various forms, which is often at the heart of decisions regarding employment structures. The quest for flexibility, it is argued, is inherently paradoxical, in that seeking flexibility in one form may reduce it in others. Next, it is suggested that changing employment relationships require that we must rethink what is considered a 'normal' employment relationship and where the basis for distinction between groups of

employees lies. This leads to the next challenge to conventional thinking — learning to think about people as resources of the firm, and consequently reassessing what HR is all about. The fourth challenge relates to the implications of contracting for managing intellectual capital in the firm, and the fifth to how we define the 'core', or the part of the business from which distinctive competence and competitive advantage are drawn. The final challenge is for managers to make considered and sound decisions about whether to contract or employ workers for certain work. This section identifies four areas for managers and HR professionals to consider when making these decisions.

The paradox of flexibility

Management interest in 'non-standard' or more flexible forms of employment, such as contracting, has grown in recent years. Economic pressures, such as international competition, the increasing need for competitiveness, unprecedented levels of economic uncertainty and the shift from manufacturing towards service-based industries, are often cited as creating a need for greater flexibility. Deregulation and globalisation expose companies to increased overseas competition, to which firms respond by attempting to reduce costs. In a climate of anxiety over prospects for economic growth, many employers are unwilling to commit themselves to increased investment or additional staff. In an environment characterised by economic uncertainty, the ability to change, innovate and diversify becomes increasingly important. Labour flexibility makes an essential contribution to overall organisational flexibility in responding to these pressures (Blyton 1996).

The concept of flexibility has been the subject of considerable debate. Atkinson (1987) suggests that this is due to the wide range of subjects that it encompasses and the fact that it means different things to different people, and he argues that the term is ideologically loaded. In fact, it may be more a rhetorical slogan than an analytical instrument (Hyman 1991). Hyman comments that flexibility is an elastic concept (1991, p. 280) and points out that it is an ambiguous, generic term that confuses several different dimensions. As generally understood, however, flexibility in the workplace encompasses three main dimensions — functional flexibility (the ability to move a worker from one task to another), numerical flexibility (the ability to quickly vary the number of workers), and financial flexibility, through which labour costs closely reflect the supply and demand of the external labour market (Atkinson 1985).

The paradox is that the pursuit of one kind of flexibility can have unintended negative impacts on other aspects of flexibility. Contractors offer the employer numerical flexibility, since they can be brought into the organisation as and when required, which means that the organisation does not have to pay them when there is little work. However, this reduces functional flexibility, since the contractor will typically be engaged to perform a narrow range of tasks, and renegotiation may be needed before the contractor is able to do other work. In seeking financial flexibility by drawing labour from external labour markets, companies expose themselves to the possibility of paying too much for labour or of not being able to locate the labour they need when they need it, another inflexibility. Should the decision be made to bring a contractor into the internal labour market, the organisation may face the difficulty of fitting that person's externally determined rate of pay into an existing remuneration structure. In seeking numerical and financial flexibility, an organisation may find that both are affected by the practicalities of acquainting a contractor with the particular project and of transferring work between individuals as they enter and exit project teams.

The 1980s 'excellence' literature (e.g. Peters & Waterman 1982) emphasised the importance of building a strong organisational culture embodying high levels of organisational commitment and the pursuit of quality. Seeking flexibility can create problems for the kind of 'excellent' environment that Peters and Waterman had in mind. Part-time, temporary and contractual workers offer numerical flexibility but have less involvement in the day-to-day running of the organisation. They are likely to miss meetings and be left out of formal and informal communication channels. These individuals will probably be less involved than their full-time, permanent counterparts. They will probably not have the same level of understanding of organisational procedures, rules and processes, and they are less likely to be involved in organisational training programs.

Another potential pitfall of flexibility is the possibility of undermining stability and continuity within the organisation. Blyton (1996, p. 278) suggests that many numerical flexibility initiatives are pursued for their cost-cutting and control potential rather than for wider considerations of the overall contribution to the organisation. In fact, the desire for flexibility may clash with other organisational initiatives, such as the use of teams, quality initiatives and many others. In these cases it may be that pursuing numerical flexibility is a short-term strategy that needs to be carefully balanced against other business factors.

The pursuit of financial flexibility creates problems of its own. Increasing the heterogeneity of wages may offer greater equity to high-performing workers, but it can create a different set of problems related to inequality. Workers offered inferior terms and conditions may see this, in turn, as unfair and unjustifiable. In any situation where workers are engaged under different terms and conditions of employment (for the same or similar work), there is the possibility of perceptions of unfairness and injustice. Equity theory (Adams 1965) suggests that individuals are powerfully motivated to act to reduce perceived inequity, and the consequences of this may be negative for the organisation. It may lead to less flexibility through loss of organisational citizenship behaviours.

Beer, Spector, Lawrence, Mills and Walton (1984) use a somewhat broader conception of flexibility when they talk of organisational adaptability. They state:

In the long run, organisational effectiveness means that the firm has been flexible and responsive to its market and social environment. (p. 35)

This goal is achieved through the development of high levels of commitment, competence, cost effectiveness and congruence. It can be argued that creating numerical flexibility, in particular, jeopardises an organisation's ability to develop the four Cs. Beer and colleagues (1984) believe that the kind of flexibility and responsiveness needed for organisational effectiveness comes from developing these qualities within the organisation, and this clearly presents a problem with the use of contractors. Legge (1995) agrees and states that both numerical and functional flexibility often conflict with notions of commitment and quality. Walton (1985) argues that in an increasingly turbulent business environment, flexible, involved and committed workers are a vital part of the organisation.

An important distinction here is that in achieving flexibility, firms can either look within the firm or attempt to gain flexibility from outside. In the former case firms seek flexibility through adaptability; in the latter case, to use the words of Hyman, they seek flexibility through disposability. Geary (1992) found support for this in his study of electronics firms where one firm relied on the recruitment of temporary labour to gain flexibility, and another firm developed flexibility internally through technology, changes to the production process and the organisation of work. As Streeck (1987) points out, these approaches are not mutually exclusive, and employers have the opportunity to capitalise on the best of both worlds.

The fact that flexibility can be facilitated by contradictory and mutually exclusive HR practices hints at its paradoxical nature. A further problem with the pursuit of flexibility is that in some cases flexible employment practices create tensions, which can ultimately detract from organisational effectiveness. A study by Geary (1992) found a number of reasons why managers were concerned about the use of temporary employees as a way of promoting flexibility. Some of the key factors were difficulties training the workers, the jeopardising of management's efforts to maintain a committed workforce, the difficulty of terminating temporary workers once they had become integrated within the workforce, the creation of conflict between staff, conflict between management groups over the use of temporaries, and the feeling that the organisation was adopting ambiguous HR strategies through its dual standards for different groups of workers. According to Geary, the reasons why management does not make greater use of flexible employment practices are under-researched. Clearly, managers feel keenly the challenge of managing 'non-standard' groups of employees.

Perhaps the main paradox of flexibility is that attempts to create a secondary group of employees on inferior terms and conditions runs contrary to much thinking regarding the development of employees as a key resource. It also conflicts with specific initiatives such as the use of teams. Several writers have highlighted this paradox. For example, Cappelli (1995) talks about the paradox of the weakening attachment between workers and firms and the importance of teamwork and other idiosyncratic skills. These skills need strong attachments to make them pay off. Stability is essential to any team-based initiative because of the team-specific skills that are developed and that need to be captured (Benson 1995). Cappelli points out that operating on a flexible, low-commitment model creates long-run challenges for the firm, especially in a climate in which supervision and monitoring are cut back.

How firms deal with these paradoxes will vary, and whether the paradoxes will remain over time is debatable. Benson (1995) suggests that some of the flexibility strategies that firms use are survival strategies that may be retreated from in the longer term, if negative consequences arise. Experimentation is a feature of how managers deal with some of these issues (Streeck 1987). According to Benson (1995), the:

> *inherent contradiction of attempting to maintain a competitive advantage with a contingent workforce will be recognised. While firms may enjoy some short term financial advantages by adopting more market based staffing arrangements, that strategy will do little to meet the competitive challenges of the future.* (p. 607)

Flexibility is a multidimensional and multifaceted concept. Therefore, managers and writers on HR must adopt a critical stance towards the concept. The paradoxical nature of flexibility demands a deeper level of analysis than is often applied, particularly in the context of so-called flexible employment practices.

The changing employment relationship

Another challenge posed by the array of employment relationships that can be seen in organisations is the idea of what we consider to be 'normal', 'standard' or 'typical'. It is important to note that the employment arrangements adopted today have not always been the norm, nor are they assured to remain so in the future. A glance at how employment relationships have changed and evolved over the years reveals that contracting arrangements that might today be regarded as controversial were once very common. Rousseau (1995) describes employment relations as having gone through a number of historical stages including emergent, bureaucratic and adhocratic. Each of these stages has given rise to different forms of employment and contracts. Rousseau (1995) describes the employment relations and contract forms of the late eighteenth century as *emergent*. According to Cappelli (1995, 2000), the employment relations of the same period were primarily market-based. This period, around the time of the industrial revolution, saw the widespread avoidance of direct employer–employee relationships (Littler 1982).

Emergent employment relations and contract forms gave way to a bureaucratic phase, characterised by complex hierarchical organisations with internal labour markets (Rousseau 1995). An array of forces acted to bring about this change. Littler (1982) describes the greater economic pressures resulting from the great depression at the end of the nineteenth century, and the growth of the labour movement and opposition to the harsh and oppressive employment conditions of the time. Rousseau (1995) attributes the change to pressures for greater efficiency and predictability.

The *bureaucratisation* phase corresponds to what Pfeffer and Baron (1988) described as internalised employment. This model is characterised by long-term relationships between the employee and the firm, administrative control over the individual by the firm, and physical proximity between the firm and the individual worker. Employees develop firm-specific skills and climb the rungs of the company ladder. The creation of internal labour markets facilitate long-term retention, assimilation into an organisation's culture and delayed rewards for contributions to the organisation. Competitive advantage is provided through the minds and skills of the employees and managers, in whom investments are made (Rousseau 1995). The nature of the relationship facilitates commitment and identification with the goals of the firm.

Rousseau (1995) labels the present and future of employment relationships and contracts as *adhocratic*, because of what she sees as a fundamental shift in the nature of work. Pressure is placed on the old bureaucratic structures, since organisations need to become more flexible and responsive. Various authors (e.g. Handy 1989) have identified the emerging features of contemporary employment relationships. Rousseau summarises them as the emergence of differentiated employment relations within one firm — for instance, maintaining long-term relational contracts with certain core workers and adopting short-term transactional contracts with peripheral workers; decreased emphasis on upward career mobility within an organisation; increased emphasis on the development of new skills, and a proliferation of contract forms and terms according to the needs of the organisation (1995, p. 96).

There are several similarities and differences between the employment relations and contract forms we see today and those that were common around the end of the nineteenth century. For example, many of the harsh and oppressive conditions and employment practices no longer exist. Also, the workforces of the early twenty-first century differ in many ways from their predecessors, and are supervised by managers who benefit from the existence of a large body of knowledge about individuals and organisations. Among the similarities are that one can no longer assume that workers within a firm are engaged under the same terms and conditions, or even work for that firm at all. Not only will a variety of contractual arrangements apply, but also the subcontracting arrangements entered into by many organisations bear a direct resemblance to their nineteenth-century counterparts. Witness, for instance, a contractor taking over a small part of the operations or maintenance of a large

industrial site, and hiring and managing a gang of employees. It could be said that the consultants of today are modern equivalents of the many skilled craftspeople who operated within and outside the boundaries of firms around the time of the industrial revolution. What seems clear is that the HR managers of today have at their disposal an array of options in the structuring of employment relations in their firm. The assumptions of the bureaucratic phase that a single model of employment will offer the most efficient and effective method of engaging labour no longer hold.

If employment relationships and structures are constantly changing, what then do we mean by 'employment relationship'? Part of the complexity of the relationship between the individual and the firm comes from the terminology involved. Despite the fact that the word 'employment' is casually used in everyday discourse, it has a specific legal meaning. A distinction is made between contracts *of* and contracts *for* service. It is an important distinction for those involved in the relationship, since how it is conducted is in each case governed by a very different legal framework. Each implies different duties, rights and liabilities, and there are tax and pension implications, too. Not surprisingly, then, the distinction between employee and contractor status lies at the heart of many industrial disputes. Unions and employees are often suspicious of companies' use of contractors, which can be seen as a way of avoiding their legal responsibilities by disguising an employment relation with a contractual one.

Despite the apparent clarity of legal definitions of an employment relationship, courts have often been asked to decide whether or not an individual can be deemed to be an employee. In order to determine whether an individual is an employee, a number of tests are applied. The control test, the organisation test, the mixed test, the intention of the parties, the totality test, the business test and the 'ordinary person' test have all been used by courts to determine the existence of an employment relationship.

If legal practitioners sometimes have difficulty in keeping up with contemporary employment contracting, then it can be of little surprise that managers sometimes face difficulties as well. Szakats (1981) has suggested that the evolution of more complex forms of contracting, increasing mobility and borderline contracts will result in the disappearance of the distinction between contractor and employee altogether.

Many labels are attached to different types of employment relationship. A brief survey of the relevant literature reveals terms such as *employee, contractor, contingent, permanent, insider, outsider, entrepreneurial worker, interim worker, consultant, independent contractor, dependent contractor, labour contractor, professional contractor, networked worker, primary* or *secondary worker, flexible worker, atypical worker, standard* or *non-standard worker, precarious worker, interim worker, temporary worker, self-employed contractor, sub-contractor, ad hoc worker, casual worker, part-time worker, full-time worker, complimentary worker, fixed-term worker, peripheral worker, just-in-time worker,* and *core* and *non-core workers.* This abundance of terminology hints at the difficulty that researchers, theorists and practitioners have had in developing a clear conceptualisation of the employment relationship. At workplace level someone described as a 'contractor' might actually be a fixed-term employee, an agency temporary, an employee of an outside organisation or a self-employed consultant. Managers and researchers alike must be careful to specify the types of employment they are interested in.

Each of the above terms conveys something of the connection between the worker and the firm. Several are practically synonymous, while others convey some nuance of the relationship. There is such a variety of potential employment arrangements that to attempt a taxonomy would be a major undertaking. Different writers use some of these terms in different ways; some terms are more significant and more widely used than others.

Given that the very notion of being an 'employee' is increasingly questioned at a practical level, interesting theoretical questions are also raised about the relationship between the individual worker and the firm. How, and on what basis, can we distinguish between groups of workers in a meaningful way?

Complicating our attempts to define contracting and employment is that it is sometimes referred to not as a relationship but as a *process for organising work.* Aside from 'contracting', one often hears the terms 'subcontracting', 'contracting in' and 'contracting out'. Essentially, contracting in and contracting out refer to the same phenomenon. Work needing to be done by an organisation is offered by contract to an individual or individuals. This contract is typically regarded as a contract for services. Depending on how one looks at a given situation, the difference between contracting in and contracting out may relate to the degree of attachment to the firm doing the contracting (consider, for example, Rousseau's (1995) distinction between insiders and outsiders, or Baron and Pfeffer's (1988) internalisation–externalisation continuum). How exactly one conceives of attachment may vary. It may be related to physical location — that is to say, whether the work is being undertaken on the premises of the contracting company or elsewhere. Is the work being contracted to an outside organisation or to an outside individual? Is the work being undertaken using the resources of the contracting company or is it being undertaken completely independently? Is the work subject to the control or supervision of the contracting organisation? Is it

part of the 'core' business of the firm or is it a peripheral activity? Is the contractor working for the contracting company and for no other? Depending on how one answers these questions, one might be inclined to describe a situation as contracting in or out. Furthermore, depending on how one answers the questions, one might argue that it is not a contracting situation at all, but that an employment relationship has been entered into.

According to Davis-Blake and Uzzi (1993), research on employment externalisation has been hampered by the lack of a theoretical framework. This causes difficulties for researchers because:

> *Failure to understand the similarities and differences between diverse aspects of the employment relationship hampers progress towards developing a coherent theory of the employment relationship.* (Davis-Blake & Uzzi 1993, p. 197)

The employment relationship is multidimensional, and it may not be possible to develop a single conceptualisation of it. Several writers have used specific features of the relationship to serve as a basis for a conceptual model. For example, one of the most fundamental dimensions, along which employment relationships can be said to vary, is that of contractual stability. One might even argue that the long-term/short-term employment idea is the fundamental defining dimension of the employment relationship (Ouchi 1980). Pfeffer and Baron (1988) suggest a continuum of contractual arrangements ranging from long-term, 'permanent' attachments to the firm at one end to relatively weak, flexible attachments at the other. They describe the trend towards the latter end of the continuum as employment 'externalisation'.

Pfeffer and Baron's (1988) externalisation–internalisation continuum is a conceptual construct similar to ones used by other writers on employment relationships. Belous (1989), for example, talks about relative affiliation to the firm and suggests, on the one hand, strong affiliation under a model of lifetime employment and, on the other, weak affiliation under the day-labourer model. Whereas Pfeffer and Baron's model tends to combine duration of employment and other concepts such as 'connection' and 'attachment', Rousseau (1995) separates them into a two-dimensional model. One dimension is the short- or long-term duration and the other is 'insiders versus outsiders'. Rousseau uses the term *internalisation* to describe the embeddedness of the individual in the organisation. She defines it in terms of the depth of knowledge some individuals acquire about the organisation, its technology and markets, and the psychological attachment of those individuals to the organisation. The model yields a two-by-two matrix that can classify workers. Under this classification a long-term insider is a core employee, long-term outsiders are casual workers called in on an as-needed basis, short-term insiders are 'careerist' individuals who are employees using the job as a stepping stone to another, and, finally, a short-term outsider is a temporary worker or a contractor.

Rousseau and Wade-Benzoni (1994) attempted to classify employees' contracts according to two key contract terms — first, the time frame of the contract (long or short term); and second, the performance requirements and whether they are well or weakly specified. As with the previously described model, this approach produces the sort of two-by-two matrix often favoured by social science researchers.

Although stability of contract is clearly an important defining characteristic of an employment relationship, there may be others that tell us more about the true nature of that relationship. For example, Deeks, Parker and Ryan (1994) suggest that how management views labour is important. They suggest that, in addition to stability, a second variable is the extent to which labour is seen by the employing organisation as a cost or an investment. According to their model, there are important differences between, for example, workers on stable contracts who may be treated as a cost of business, and those who may be more involved in the business and in whom investments may be made by the company. Gaertner and Nollen (1989) support the idea that such investments send a clear signal about the organisation's commitment to those workers. According to Deeks and colleagues, the 'participative worker' is so named because the organisation is prepared to invest in the worker and offer contractual stability in order to ensure a return on that investment. This status is contrasted with that of an 'entrepreneurial worker' who is offered neither contractual stability nor investment. Investment takes place primarily according to the individual; it is up to the worker to ensure that he or she has the skills and knowledge that can be sold to the organisation.

Investment by the organisation is likely to be restricted to firm-specific training that will allow the worker to function more effectively in that environment. It is obviously in the interests of the worker to develop skills that are in demand and transferable, since that worker's attachment to the employing organisation is short term or for the life of a project. Deeks et al. identify several groups of worker who have traditionally operated in this way, including truck and taxi drivers, couriers, consultants and freelance journalists. Deregulation has increased opportunities for this kind of work, and researchers such as Kanter (1989), Hakim (1987), Arthur and Rousseau (1996), and Bridges (1994) write enthusiastically of the possibilities for this group.

Investment and tenure are, of course, not totally unrelated dimensions. The shorter the tenure, the less likely investment in worker skills becomes. Investment in training provides the functional flexibility demanded of longer term core employees, and allows for one of the potential benefits of a core workforce — development of areas of distinctive competence for the organisation (Pfeffer & Baron 1988). Nevertheless, investment is an important added dimension to contractual stability for what it reveals about how the employer views the employment relationship. Gaertner and Nollen (1989) confirm this point by observing that career-oriented employment practices such as training and job security are more fundamental than other aspects of work life; they reflect the organisation's philosophy *vis-à-vis* the employment relationship.

The philosophical distinction suggested by the Deeks et al. model is well expressed by Miles and Snow (1980), who identify 'make'-oriented firms and 'buy'-oriented firms. 'Buy'-oriented firms follow a strategy of purchasing specific skills for specific needs at specific times, and do not offer long-term employment or developmental opportunities. 'Make'-oriented firms tend to hire at entry level and train and develop employees through the organisation, providing long-term employment. Tornow (1988), similarly, distinguishes between 'building' and 'buying' employees.

In examining how different theorists and writers have conceptualised employment relationships, it is important to note that firms are not monolithic in their choices of employment arrangements. As the work of Osterman (e.g. 1982, 1987) illustrates, firms often adopt different approaches with different groups of workers, and it is useful to examine components of the firm, rather than the firm as a whole. Osterman argues that within a firm several distinct employment sub-systems may coexist, and that the relationship to the firm of the individuals in each of the sub-systems differs in some important respects.

In critiquing previous attempts to provide a framework for understanding employment relationships, Sherer (1996) suggests what he believes is a more robust framework. His Organisation and Labour Relationships (OLR) framework focuses on *agency* as the key dimension of difference among relationships. Labour operating under the direct control of management is an 'employment' relationship; labour operating as a quasi-agent under indirect control is a 'contracting-in' relationship; finally, labour acting as both an agent and an owner is an 'ownership' relationship.

The most useful classification system will be the one that most accurately reflects the fundamental points of difference between the relationships. For example, it would be misleading to suggest that all contractors are necessarily unattached to the organisation, since many have quite strong attachments for various reasons. Some contractors may enter and exit the organisation scarcely noticed; others may have very strong social networks within the organisation. Some may have no explicit promises of long-term work but may have a large degree of de-facto job security, or even implicit or informal promises. Some contractors may perform work that is peripheral to the core business of the organisation, while others may be involved in key strategic decisions. As Sherer (1994) points out, an externalised relationship does not necessarily signify a casual or unstructured one.

While there have been many attempts to map or categorise the relationship between the worker and the organisation, none of the existing models seem satisfactory. However, an examination of these models points to the multidimensional and multifaceted nature of the employment relationship. Each of the models contributes a piece of the puzzle, yet none provides the full picture. Over the past several years our understanding of what is 'normal' in employment relationships has been challenged. A historical perspective suggests that relationships that may now appear novel were once commonplace. Furthermore, employment relationships that are new or controversial in one industry may be less so in another context. The foregoing discussion highlights the danger of inadequate specification of concepts when discussing employment structures, and shows how our understanding of the employment relationship is constantly challenged.

How we define and think about human resource management

The utilisation of contractors challenges traditional notions of what HRM is all about. Perhaps the most widely used definition of HRM belongs to Beer and colleagues (1984):

HRM involves all management decisions and actions that affect the relationship between the organisation and its employees — its human resources. (p. 1)

In the Beer et al. model, commitment is a central feature, and employment, rather than contracting, is assumed. Similarly, Storey (1995) offers the following definition:

a distinctive approach to management which seeks to achieve competitive advantage through the strategic deployment of a highly committed and capable workforce, using an integrated array of cultural, structural and personnel techniques. (p. 5)

Storey's is a highly loaded definition that contains certain beliefs, priorities and assumptions. Perhaps of greater usefulness would be a more global definition of the HRM terrain that encompasses the wide variety of employment arrangements in use today. Boxall (1995) describes HRM as being about the management of labour in its widest sense and suggests that it is concerned with the management of all employment relationships in the firm (p. 2). This definition encompasses managerial as well as non-managerial employees, along with the wide range of HRM practices that may be found in various segments, sub-markets, or sub-systems. In this sense, a firm might use a number of discrete 'HRM models' simultaneously.

A key feature of the first two definitions is commitment. Defining commitment is problematic, and debate surrounds the operationalisation and usefulness of the concept. However, much of the HR literature assumes that commitment should be developed and leads to positive outcomes for the organisation.

The use of contractors presents challenges to other aspects of contemporary HR thinking. The resource-based view of the firm (RBV) suggests that human resources are a potential source of competitive advantage for the firm. According to the RBV, firms develop resources and capabilities that are unique to the firm. These resources and capabilities provide the firm with economic benefits. They cannot be copied, and therefore become powerful sources of sustained competitive advantage (Lado & Wilson 1994). Resources are either strengths or weaknesses of a firm whose assets are tied semi-permanently to the firm (Wright, McMahan & McWilliams 1994). It follows from both of these views that employees can be regarded as human resources in ways that contractors cannot. The Wright et al. (1994) definition of human resources — as a pool of human capital under the control of the firm through an employment relationship — explicitly recognises that the connection between the individual and the firm must be strong for the individual to be considered a resource of the firm.

Contemporary HR thinking (e.g. Pfeffer 1995) holds that human resources are a key resource of the firm and can contribute to competitive advantage. Nowhere is this more apparent than in professional services firms that compete on the basis of the capabilities of their staff. This means that managers must think carefully about the mixture of employment structures that they use. It is in the nature of independent contracting that workers are highly mobile. If they were not mobile and worked exclusively for one firm, it is likely that some of the advantages of contracting would disappear or that the basis of their relationship with the firm would change. However, it is mobility that creates the key problem in terms of competitive advantage. While a contractor can certainly add value to a firm, and it may be that his or her skills are rare, competing firms can easily imitate and substitute by engaging the services of a particular contractor or contractors. Employees, on the other hand, are much less mobile and incur substantial transaction costs in moving from one employer to another (Wright et al. 1994).

It is clear from the resource-based view of the firm that people, and the attributes and competencies they possess, are valuable and a potential source of sustained competitive advantage for the firm. As contractors can, at best, bring only a temporary advantage to the firm, it becomes important to recognise, develop and protect those organisational capabilities that offer sustained advantage. The resource-based view of the firm highlights the problematic nature of the use of contractors, and can be seen as providing strong arguments for using contractors with great caution. Managers are therefore challenged to balance the short-term, pragmatic considerations of what type of worker is needed to do the job with certain important, and possibly strategic, long-term considerations.

Managing intellectual capital

It has been argued (e.g. Snell, Lepak & Youndt 1999) that increasing competitive advantage depends on organisations being able to develop and leverage the knowledge that their workers possess. The increasing use of contractors forces managers to think more carefully about the dynamics of knowledge acquisition and deployment within their organisations. It is of vital importance to have a workforce of known skills and abilities who are trained and developed and able to respond to the needs of clients. In contexts in which the product the company is selling is the professional expertise of its people, building up the intellectual capital of the firm is a vital strategic issue.

The use of contractors can either add to or deplete the intellectual capital of the firm in several different ways. On the negative side, contractors move on, taking with them the skills and knowledge they have acquired. They do not contribute to the building up of knowledge within the firm, unless management can devise ways to ensure that the knowledge and skills are passed on. They may not be well integrated into the company's networks for sharing and storing information, so information that might otherwise be passed on is not. On the other hand, contractors can assist the organisation in developing its intellectual capital. Contractors with a wide experience of different systems and

techniques may be able to offer advice or share the knowledge and experience gained by working in a number of different organisations.

Managers must find ways to use the intellectual capital advantages of contractors while minimising the costs to the organisation of loss of capital or insufficient accumulation of capital. The foregoing discussion, however, hints at the need for a more sophisticated conceptualisation of intellectual capital. Snell and colleagues (1999) identify three specific constructs that underlie intellectual capital. These are human capital (the knowledge, skills and abilities of employees), social capital (the flow of knowledge within a system), and organisational capital (the institutional knowledge embedded in manuals, policies, databases etc.). This more detailed conceptualisation enables a closer examination of how contractors may add to or detract from intellectual capital. However, not all knowledge and skill is of high strategic value to an organisation. Clearly, some forms require more careful nurturing and others offer opportunities for possible contracting out. Managers need to be aware of what forms of intellectual capital are of strategic importance and ensure that the employment structures they utilise support rather than undermine these intellectual sources.

Where is the 'core'?

Following on from the previous discussion of human resources as a source of competitive advantage and the importance of intellectual capital, we need to reconsider what we mean by the 'core'. What constitutes the core or central part of the organisation, from an HR perspective? Interest in defining the core comes from the suggestion that core parts of the organisation may be those that are sources of distinctive competence or that contribute to competitive advantage.

Atkinson's (1984) model of the flexible firm locates full-time permanent employees in the core surrounded by a second layer of workers, the peripheral group. These jobs may also be full-time but tend to be less skilled; little training is needed or given. Turnover will occur at a naturally higher rate, assisting numerical flexibility. A second peripheral group constitutes part-time workers and those on limited-term contracts, also providing a degree of numerical flexibility. The external groups are those sourced outside the organisation, such as contractors. This idea of a dual labour market is well supported in the literature, although it is not without its critics. Pollert (1988), for instance, criticises the core periphery model for oversimplifying the situation. The reality, according to Pollert (1991), is much more complex and uneven, and she would like to see 'a more complex perspective which relates to the untidy dynamics of the real world' (p. 31).

The idea that core equals skilled, and periphery equals unskilled is a gross oversimplification, and the many different modes of atypical or non-standard employment cannot be easily collapsed into a peripheral category (Hyman 1991). Pollert (1991) attacks the model of core versus periphery for being confused, circular and value-laden. It seems to be true that firms define their core idiosyncratically, and some define the core in terms of where they stand in relation to it. Hakim (1990) defends the flexible firm model as being something of a Weberian 'ideal type': it simplifies in order to aid our understanding, without necessarily being true to the 'real world'.

Despite the many criticisms that can be made of the core–periphery model, it evidently has enduring appeal for practitioners and academics alike. The widespread use of contracting across organisations, however, forces managers to reassess what is meant by the core of the business. Managers can find defining the 'core' of a business, and thus the core workforce, problematic (Purcell 1996, 1999). For example, an electricity company might view meter readers as simply 'data harvesters' or as front-line customer service representatives. In the former case, they are deemed to be non-core and are managed as a cost to be reduced as much as possible. The company brings in contractors to do the work. In the latter case, they are deemed to be core and are managed as an asset to be developed so as to contribute to competitive advantage.

For models of 'core' and periphery to have any real meaning, they must be founded on a clear conception of what parts of the organisation are sources of distinctive competence or contribute to competitive advantage. Ideally, this conception is linked to a clear vision and competitive strategy. When this linkage does not occur, managers' assertions of what parts of the business are more important or central than others will be open to question.

Deciding whether to contract or employ

Given the widespread acceptance and availability of contractors in many industries and occupations, managers are challenged to consider what form of employment structure best meets the needs of the firm. But how to do this systematically is problematic, since the context and circumstance

of each organisation and each decision will vary widely. However, it is suggested here that any employment or contracting decision should involve four broad sets of analysis.

A logical starting point might be to consider the operational requirements of the job itself. A work process analysis (WPA) would investigate factors related to the job itself: the interdependencies of the job, the supervisory requirements, and factors related to workflow and process. Questions should be asked regarding the importance of flexibility and the ongoing need for labour or the variability of demand for labour. This would provide a strong argument for certain kinds of job rather than others. Is the job in question a discrete unit of work that can be 'detached' and performed in relative isolation from other tasks? Does the work involve a high level of firm-specific skills for which a stable arrangement is needed that retains those skills within the firm? Does the firm need to be able to control how the work is done in terms of both outputs and processes? For example, in customer contact situations the behaviour of the worker reflects on the organisation. What kind of performance is being sought? Among the behavioural implications of employment contract choice are how different contracts 'incentivise' productivity and performance. While this link is a complex one, some arrangements are likely to promote these kinds of behaviours better than others. Other questions to be asked in the WPA would relate to the need for functional flexibility, and the impact of employment structures on the ability of management to move workers around, redeploying them to a variety of tasks. Finally, questions should be asked regarding whether the firm has the managerial capabilities to manage the employment relationships in question.

A second analysis would relate to the strategic and philosophical implications of employment structure choice. The Strategy Analysis (SA) would examine the set of management philosophies and preferences and business strategies in the organisation. Also relevant to an SA are the extent to which an arrangement develops skills that are highly firm specific, whether these skills are a source of dependency, and whether an employment structure better facilitates organisational learning and innovation. There are several strategic considerations. Importantly, managers should examine closely what the core business of the organisation is and where sources of competitive advantage lie. Understanding sources of competitive advantage offers a clearer sense of which groups of workers should be kept within the boundaries of the firm.

In attempting to understand how a group of workers may contribute to competitive advantage, one needs an understanding of how the knowledge skills and abilities of the group of workers in question contributed to the overall intellectual capital of the firm. Key questions here relate to whether the work involves acquisition of knowledge or skills that would be beneficial to the firm. In addition, how knowledge is acquired and passed on in the organisation may be relevant. While certain kinds of information may be helpful but not critical, all organisations depend to some extent on certain knowledge, skills or abilities. These resources may be readily accessible or in relative short supply. Managers face choices about how best to deal with these dependencies. If the dependency is likely to be significant, then the organisation may wish to internalise it in order to ensure access. Alternatively, they may seek alternative sources or reduce dependence in other ways. The literature reveals that companies respond in different ways to this problem.

Also important in the SA is an acknowledgement of how management philosophies, styles of management and preferences affect choices of employment structures. Management beliefs and ideologies have powerful effects on decision-making, and as such should be made explicit as part of the decision-making process. Less directly, structural issues also need to be considered to the extent that they may allow or facilitate the operation of certain employment structures. If these issues are not assessed, they may, deliberately or accidentally, create pressures or incentives towards one structure or another.

No rational decision on contracting and employment would be complete without a consideration of financial cost. The Financial Cost Analysis (FCA) involves analysis of the direct and indirect factors that comprise the cost of a particular employment structure. A full accounting of the actual financial cost differences between employment structures might examine the labour cost, or cost per unit of work completed. This should include direct and indirect costs, such as holiday and sick pay. Costs related to training and orientation, and to administering the relationship, are also relevant, as are sundry legal and compliance costs. For some types of work, equipment represents a significant business cost, while in some cases it might be desirable to pass these on to others.

Finally, a Relationship Acceptance Analysis (RAA) would entail an assessment of whether the particular employment structure being considered would be acceptable to both parties. This judgement assumes that relationships with mutuality are more likely to produce optimal outcomes for management. Management may be in a position to offer certain work to contractors, but that may prove less than ideal for the person doing the work or unacceptable to other sections of the workforce. Workers might accept particular terms and conditions because they feel pressured to do so or because there is no attractive alternative option. The power dynamics that underlie choices should be recognised as influencing the acceptance of a relationship.

To this end, viewing matters from the perspective of workers and anticipating how management actions might be perceived by the workforce are important. The idea of psychological contracts provides a framework for understanding why we should pay careful attention to contract formation, content and any attempt subsequently to change the contract. The perspective of those groups of workers less directly affected is also important. Certain managerial actions may enhance the development of mutual acceptance. These may include paying particular attention to communication and workers' needs for certain kinds of support.

The analyses outlined here address the basis and criteria for a decision to favour one employment arrangement over another. Although there is clearly no 'one right way' to make such decisions, such a rigorous process is most likely to produce desirable outcomes.

Conclusion

This chapter has suggested that the use of contractors in organisations presents challenges of a theoretical and practical nature. The benefits of using contractors are often readily apparent, and contractors can be found in many organisational contexts and roles. Contracting has costs as well as benefits, and while the costs may not outweigh the real and tangible benefits of using a contractor, they should be acknowledged. Often the costs can be hidden and will be revealed only by close examination. Nowhere is this more apparent than when considering the paradoxical nature of flexibility, with managers challenged to balance the multiple ways in which flexibility can be gained or lost. This chapter has suggested that contemporary employment practices such as the use of contractors challenge some traditional views of what HRM is all about and force a re-examination of fundamental concepts such as what we mean by the business 'core' and what we mean by referring to people as 'resources'. Finally, this chapter has suggested how those responsible for managing the firm's most important resources might accept the challenge of considering alternative employment structures. They should do so by employing a more rigorous style of analysis that accounts for the many ways in which people add value to organisations.

References

Adams JS (1965) Inequity in social exchange. In L Berkowitz (Ed.), *Advances in Experimental Social Psychology*. New York: Academic Press.

Arthur, M, and Rousseau, D (1996) *The Boundaryless Career: A New Employment Principle for a New Organisational Era*. New York: Oxford University Press.

Atkinson, J (1984) Manpower strategies for flexible organisations. *Personnel Management*, August, 28–31.

Atkinson, J (1985) The changing corporation. In D Clutterbuck (Ed.), *New Patterns of Work*. Aldershot, UK: Gower.

Atkinson, J (1987) Flexibility or fragmentation? The UK labour market in the eighties. *Labour and Society*, 12 (1) 87–105.

Beer, M, Spector, P, Lawrence, D, Quinn Mills, D, and Walton, R (1984) *Managing Human Assets*. New York: Free Press.

Belous, RS (1989) Human resource flexibility and equity: difficult questions for business, labour, and government. *Journal of Labour Research*, 10 (1) 67–72.

Benson, J (1995) Future employment and the internal labour market. *British Journal of Industrial Relations*, 33 (4) 603–8.

Blyton, P (1996) Workforce flexibility. In B Towers (Ed.), *The Handbook of Human Resource Management*. Oxford: Blackwell.

Boxall, P (1995) Human resource management: a conceptual framework. In P Boxall (Ed.), *The Challenge of Human Resource Management: Directions and Debate in New Zealand*. Auckland: Longman Paul.

Bridges, W (1994) *Job Shift: How to Prosper in a Workplace without Jobs*. Reading, MA: Addison-Wesley.

Cappelli, P (1995) Rethinking employment. *British Journal of Industrial Relations*, 33 (4) 563–602.

Cappelli, P (2000) Market mediated employment: the historical context. In MM Blair and TA Kochan (Eds), *The New Employment Relationship: Human Capital in the American Corporation* (pp. 66–101). Washington, DC: Brookings Institute Press.

Davis-Blake, A, and Uzzi, B (1993) Determinants of employment externalization: a study of temporary workers and independent contractors. *Administrative Science Quarterly*, 38, 195–223.

Deeks, J, Parker, J, and Ryan, R (1994) *Labour and Employment Relations in New Zealand*. Auckland: Longman Paul.

Gaertner, KN, and Nollen, SD (1989) Career experiences, perceptions of employment practices, and psychological commitment to the organisation. *Human Relations*, 42 (11) 975–91.

Geary, JF (1992) Employment flexibility and human resource management: the case of three American electronics plants. *Work, Employment and Society*, 6 (2) 251–70.

Hakim, C (1987) Trends in the flexible workforce. *Employment Gazette*, November, 546–60.

Hakim, C (1990) Core and periphery in employers' workforce strategies: evidence from the 1987 E.L.U.S. survey. *Work, Employment and Society*, 4 (2) 157–88.

Handy, C (1989) *The Age of Unreason*. Boston, MA: Harvard Business School Press.

Hyman, R (1991) Plus ça change? The theory of production and the production of theory. In A Pollert (Ed.), *Farewell to Flexibility*, 59–83. Oxford: Basil Blackwell.

Kanter, RM (1989) From climbing to hopping: the contingent job and the post-entrepreneurial career. *Management Review*, 78 (4) 22–7.

Lado, A, and Wilson, M (1994) Human resources systems and sustained competitive advantage: a competency-based perspective. *Academy of Management Review*, 19 (4) 699–727.

Legge, K (1995) HRM: rhetoric, reality and hidden agendas. In J Storey (Ed.), *Human Resource Management: A Critical Text*. London: Routledge.

Littler, CR (1982) *Labour Process Development in Capitalist Societies*. London: Heinemann.

Miles, RE, and Snow, CC (1984) Designing strategic human resources systems. *Organisational Dynamics*, 36–52.

Osterman, P (1982) Employment structures within firms. *British Journal of Industrial Relations*, 20, 349–61.

Osterman, P (1987) Choice of employment systems in internal labor markets. *Industrial Relations*, 26 (1) 46–67.

Ouchi, WG (1980) Markets, bureaucracies, and clans. *Administrative Science Quarterly*, 25, 129–41.

Peters, T, and Waterman, R (1982) *In Search of Excellence*. New York: Harper & Row.

Pfeffer, J (1994) *Competitive Advantage through People: Unleashing the Power of the Workforce*. Boston, MA: Harvard Business School Press.

Pfeffer, J, and Baron, JN (1988) Taking the workers back out: recent trends in the structuring of employment. In BM Staw and LL Cummings (Eds), *Research in Organisational Behaviour*, 10. Greenwich, CT: JAI Press.

Pollert, A (1988) The 'flexible firm': fixation or fact? *Work, Employment, and Society*, 2 (3) 281–316.

Pollert, A (1991) The orthodoxy of flexibility. In A Pollert (Ed.), *Farewell to Flexibility*, 3–31. Oxford: Basil Blackwell.

Purcell, J (1996) Contingent workers and human resource strategy: rediscovering the core-periphery dimension. *Journal of Professional HRM*, 5, 16–23.

Purcell, J (1999) High commitment management and the link with contingent workers: implications for strategic human resource management. In P Wright, L Dyer, J Boudreau and G Milkovich (Eds), *Research in Personnel and Human Resources Management (Supplement 4: Strategic Human Resources Management in the Twenty-first Century)*. Stamford, CT: JAI Press.

Rousseau, DM (1995) *Psychological Contracts in Organizations: Understanding Written and Unwritten Agreements*. Thousand Oaks, CA: Sage Publications.

Rousseau, DM, and Wade-Benzoni, K (1994) Linking strategy and human resource practices: how employee and customer contracts are created. *Human Resource Management*, 33 (3) 463–89.

Sherer, PD (1996) Toward an understanding of the variety in work arrangements: the organisation and labour relationships framework. In CL Cooper and DM Rousseau (Eds), *Trends in Organisational Behaviour*, 3, 99–122. Chichester: John Wiley & Sons.

Snell, SA, Lepak, DP, and Youndt, MA (1999) Managing the architecture of intellectual capital: implications for strategic human resource management. *Research in Personnel and Human Resource Management*, 4, 175–93.

Storey, J (1995) HRM: still marching on, or marching out. In J Storey (Ed.), *Human Resource Management: A Critical Text*. London: Routledge.

Streek, W (1987) The uncertainties of management and the management of uncertainty. *Work, Employment and Society*, 1 (3) 281–308.

Szakats, A (1981) *An Introduction to the Law of Employment*. Wellington: Butterworths.

Tornow, WW (1988) Contract redesign. *Personnel Administrator*, 34 (10) 97–101.

Walton, R (1985) From control to commitment in the workplace. *Harvard Business Review*, March/April, 77–84.

Wright, P, McMahan, G, and McWilliams, A (1994) Human resources and sustained competitive advantage: a resource-based perspective. *International Journal of Human Resource Management*, 5 (2) 301–326.

CHAPTER 13

Legal regulation of the workplace

by Suzanne Jamieson
University of Sydney

Introduction

The role of law in the regulation of the employment relationship in Australia has always been a highly political debate. At the time of Federation, significant opinion supported an abstentionist state (Macintyre & Mitchell 1989). In the Constitutional Convention debates, the principle of federal conciliation and arbitration power had been adopted by a close margin, but the eventual adoption of the compulsory conciliation and arbitration system by the new federal Parliament in 1904 was not a foregone conclusion. One hundred years later the debate is just as urgent, although the economic environment has changed completely. The deregulation debate of the past ten years is not, of course, limited to discussions on the employment relationship (Gunningham & Johnstone 1999); also of concern is the way in which collective relations between employers, their employees and those employees' unions are to be regulated (Dabscheck 1995). This debate follows a period of increased regulation in the workplace by means of anti-discrimination legislation, which has occurred in every Australian jurisdiction within the past 25 years. Since most of this anti-discrimination legislation is based on enforcement following the complaint of a single individual, this epochal shift in our labour laws may be seen as entirely consistent with the move towards individualisation evident in wider labour law (see Creighton & Stewart 2000: 22–3).

Individualisation is not an altogether unexpected response when we consider that the employment relationship is essentially based on a contract between employer and individual worker. What this chapter will attempt to do is to map out the way in which the law regulates the employment relationship in Australia, from the creation of the contract through to its conclusion. First, however, a few things need to be said about the Constitution and the powers it provides the various parliaments to address labour and human resource management (HRM) issues, and about the important question of just who is a worker.

The Australian Constitution is a federal document — that is, it contemplates a central government co-existing alongside state governments, with a more or less clear division of authority and legislative power and capacity between the two. This form of government is not unique to Australia; it may be seen in the United States and Canada, too (La Nauze 1972). After considerable debate at the Constitutional Conventions in the 1890s, an industrial relations power was established that gave the proposed Commonwealth Parliament power to legislate with respect to 'Conciliation and arbitration for the prevention and settlement of industrial disputes extending beyond the limits of any one state (s. 51 xxxv)'. This section remains the most relevant of the Constitution to the field of labour regulation; however, sections relating to trade, corporations, external affairs, defence, territories and the federal government's own employees also have a part to play.

These words from section 51 have been interpreted by the High Court of Australia as providing a fundamentally *collective* basis for the regulation of the Australian workplace. Trade unions and *groups* of workers, rather than individual workers, were always in the minds of the framers of the Constitution and the early versions of the legislation.

The settlement of industrial disputes extending beyond the limits of any one state (and therefore beyond the capacity of any state tribunal to make a general settlement) has been recorded in the creation of awards that have also served to lay down legally enforceable minimums on wages and conditions. These awards laid down rights and responsibilities between employers (either singly or, in some cases, across a national industry) and trade unions representing the interests of workers in those organisations and industries. Once established within an industry, these minimums applied also to non-union workers, so long as their employer was a party to the award. These mechanisms were designed to provide a legally enforceable, collective approach to labour regulation in Australia. They afforded security for trade unions; they also meant that employers could not undercut one another in the employment of labour. Similarly, the enterprise agreements (or certified agreements) that have largely replaced awards at the federal level are also seen as collective agreements involving groups of workers. Only Australian Workplace Agreements, available since the introduction of the *Workplace Relations Act 1996*, have been designed to regulate relationships between employers and individual employees.

The federal nature of the Australian Constitution, which reflects the political realities of forging a single nation from a collection of colonies at the time of Federation, has meant that much labour regulation also occurs at the level of the state and territory governments. Not only do all the states (with the exception of Victoria) have extensive conciliation and arbitration systems of their own (some of which are older than that of the Commonwealth), but they also have legislation covering workers' compensation, occupational health and safety, long-service leave and annual holidays, and (more recently) extensive statutory controls over issues of discrimination in the workplace. To add to the complexity of workplace regulation, federal and state legislation may apply concurrently in the area of anti-discrimination. Privacy legislation at both federal and state level, which has enhanced the rights of employees and added to the responsibilities of employers, now also has a role to play. This overlap has led to a very complex web of labour regulation. Some of these issues are discussed in greater detail in the following pages.

Most of these regulations were designed to apply to individuals known in law as *employees*. As already stated, at the heart of this area of the law is the contract of employment between employer and individual worker. When labour and industrial legislation was formulated (much of it in the nineteenth century) the issue of just who was a worker or employee hardly arose, except in sectors such as the building and construction industry. This industry has always included a large number of direct employees and an equally large cohort of subcontractors, who are generally tradespeople working on their own account. Some of these subcontractors may have established themselves as proprietary limited companies for tax reasons. Today the situation is much more complex and has drawn the attention of the High Court of Australia, which historically has clarified those areas in which statute law or the common law is silent or unclear. Much of this complexity is driven by a desire on the part of many businesses to access a more flexible workforce. For example, many large manufacturing organisations that formerly employed a mechanical maintenance staff supported only at annual 'shutdown' by outside skilled labour may now 'contract out' all their mechanical maintenance requirements, with the result that they have no permanent skilled staff in these matters. In the event of an injury occurring at a workplace, workers employed by labour hire firms are clearly 'employees' for the purposes of, say, the relevant workers' compensation legislation (that is, they are employees of the labour hire firm rather than of the organisation for whom the work is being done). However, in the same circumstances the question of who is in control of the workplace for the purposes of possible criminal prosecutions under the occupational health and safety legislation may not be so clear-cut. This is just one example of the greater complexity experienced in typical workplaces in which direct employment is no longer the norm for many workers (Burgess & Campbell 1998).

Regulation of the workplace by law is not limited to employment matters, of course, although that is the focus of this chapter. Other legal regulation relates to environmental protection, taxation, the Corporations Law, the law of partnership, local government issues and a range of other matters peculiar to particular industries. There is also a large body of law concerned with the regulation of collective relationships in the workplace that is beyond the scope of this chapter, which focuses squarely on the individual aspects of HRM. That broader law of collective relationships covers matters such as trade unions and industrial action (including statutory controls within the industrial legislation and other statutes such as the *Trade Practices Act 1974*, and common law economic torts such as interference with contractual relations, intimidation and conspiracy).

The following review provides a very 'broad brush' picture of the current law regulating the workplace. The picture is necessarily complex because of the federal/state dichotomy described above. It is also changing as regulation becomes increasingly individualist in approach. Change, however, is endemic to labour law, which is always subject to changing political attitudes.

Recruitment: creating and maintaining the relationship

Many employers today meet their recruitment needs via employment agencies. Increasingly, workers are engaged by means of labour hire companies, which provide organisations with flexibility. Labour law, which, as we have seen, is largely collective in nature, has not had a great deal to say about recruitment, except where it has had a bearing on other matters, such as whether a closed shop may exist or whether members of certain unions should be preferred over other employment candidates (including members of other unions). This means of guaranteeing union membership, now unenforceable at law in every Australian jurisdiction, has in fact contributed to the falling levels of union membership that have been such a feature of the Australian workplace over the past ten years. Trade unions in certain industries have maintained lists of eligible potential employees. The maritime and waterside industries are sectors where this kind of recruitment has been the norm for much of the past hundred years, although the practice is not encouraged today, particularly by the federal government. Such practices are seen to contravene the right to freedom of association, which is now a prominent feature of federal industrial legislation (see *Workplace Relations Act 1996*, Part XA). Historically, the public sector in Australia has concerned itself with relatively stringent codes of practice in relation to most aspects of its personnel functions (beginning with the recruitment process), recognising the need to be seen to be acting in a way that shows not only fairness to its citizens but also a careful regard to the expenditure of public funds. Anti-discrimination laws, on the other hand, have focused on how organisations recruit their labour.

Australian anti-discrimination legislation is a complex patchwork of federal and state laws that owe their origins not to the traditional collective approach of labour law but to the human rights legislation developed in the 1960s in the United Kingdom and, particularly, in the United States, where significant legislation arose from the struggle of the descendants of black slaves for equal civil rights. This kind of legislation follows an individualised complaint model. In its Australian form it involves conciliation (not unlike that followed in industrial relations); where judicial determinations are needed in the event that conciliation fails, damages are one possible form of reparation.

Discrimination on the basis of particular personal attributes is unlawful in the workplace under both federal and state laws. For example, it is unlawful under the New South Wales *Anti-Discrimination Act 1977* to discriminate against an employee or applicant for a job on the basis of race, sex, transgender status, marital status, disability, carer's responsibility, homosexuality or age; vilification of transgender or homosexual persons and/or those with HIV/AIDS is also unlawful. To take another example, under similar legislation in Western Australia (*Equal Opportunity Act 1984*) it is unlawful to discriminate on the basis of sex, marital status, pregnancy, family responsibilities and status, race, religious or political convictions, impairment or age. Here, too, the protection extends to job applicants as well as existing employees and contract workers.

As with most substantive workplace issues, the responsibility for maintaining discrimination-free hiring practices falls squarely on the shoulders of the employer, reflecting the old common law position that the employer has ultimate control over the workplace. This onus extends to the actions of the employer's other employees: for example, if the HR manager were to act in a discriminatory way during a job interview, the employer would be potentially liable for any damages or other reparations to the aggrieved party (i.e. the applicant). The offending manager would potentially also be personally liable.

Discrimination-free practices are also specifically mandated in the terms and conditions offered to and enjoyed by successful applicants for jobs, as are opportunities for promotion, transfer or training. These are areas in which the wider collective labour law has traditionally been silent (Creighton & Stewart 2000). Opportunities for possible redress are available through individual complaint to the state anti-discrimination board or to the federal Human Rights and Equal Opportunity Commission. All these bodies have a common procedure for initially investigating complaints before attempting to conciliate between the parties. In the event that this conciliation fails, the complaint may be heard in a judicial proceeding with the usual appeal rights. Damages awarded vary between jurisdictions, as does the waiting time for access to conciliation and formal hearings. Aggrieved persons have some choice between jurisdictions and against whom the grievance is brought. For example, in the scenario described above an aggrieved person applying for a job in the private sector in New South Wales might lodge a complaint with the New South Wales Anti-Discrimination Board or the federal commission against the employer or the HR manager or both. Clearly, grievances cannot be pursued in both jurisdictions. Human rights issues at work, in particular harassment and bullying, will be taken up later in this chapter.

Wages and conditions

The setting of wages and conditions for most Australian workers is at the centre of the ongoing debate in Australian labour law over the degree of decentralisation and deregulation that should occur within the workplace. This debate hinges on the level of intervention that either the state or trade unions should enjoy in the way wages and conditions are established, and whether these matters should be left to negotiations between employers and employees.

Historically, Australian wages and conditions have been set collectively as legally enforceable minimums by tribunals established as part of the conciliation and arbitration system. Set in response to industrial disputes between employers and trade unions, these minimums were expressed in industrial awards that have the force of law. The awards were set at federal or state level according to which tribunal had settled the dispute and according to industry. Other wage increases resulted from National Wage Cases. From 1907 wage levels for the poorest workers were always kept just above subsistence levels, which made them relatively high in international terms. Minimum conditions for the vast majority of Australian workers were set in this way until the advent of enterprise bargaining in the 1990s. Very few ordinary workers fell outside the purview of the conciliation and arbitration system at its zenith. Senior executives employed outside the public sector were one major group whose salaries and conditions were set according to the traditional contractual processes of the common law, which by their nature were highly individualised. Interestingly, however, in some state jurisdictions even these individuals continue to have access to a form of contract supervision by the industrial tribunal, although the common law courts are also available, as in the case of ordinary commercial contracts. Some contributors to the ongoing deregulation debate argue that all employment disputes should be settled in the common law courts rather than in specialist employment tribunals.

Beyond the minimums set through conciliation and arbitration, additional benefits continue to be provided for Australian workers through state legislation covering long service leave (i.e. leave accruing after long periods with one employer and designed to encourage employee loyalty in periods of low unemployment) and annual leave (generally set at four weeks for full-time workers) and by means of federal legislation covering superannuation.

The wages of most ordinary workers continue to be set collectively either through industrial awards or through enterprise agreements, whether they fall within federal or state jurisdiction (Buchanan & Callus 1993). The federal *Workplace Relations Act 1996* specifically requires that before moving to certify an agreement the Australian Industrial Relations Commission be satisfied that no overall disadvantage accrues to employees compared with the relevant award conditions (see s. 170 XA). The past decade has seen the development of the legislated capacity for individual contracts to be struck for ordinary workers within the overarching arbitration system, although, in terms of the federal jurisdiction at least, these individual contracts (from which trade unions are specifically excluded) depend on the corporations power found within the Australian Constitution (s. 51 xx). Some state governments have also provided for contracts of this kind to be created, although the existence of these alternative frameworks for setting wages and conditions seems to be subject to political change at parliamentary level.

Women's wages in Australia tend to be closer to men's than in many comparable economies, and this is no doubt the direct product of a long national history of centralised wage fixing (Whitehouse 1992). Men and women have been paid the same rate for the job since an arbitrated federal decision in 1972. Until the advent of enterprise bargaining in the early 1990s the gender pay gap (measured on an hourly basis) was diminishing. This is not to suggest that men and women earn the same total remuneration, because clearly they do not. Women work fewer hours on average than men, are not promoted at the same rates, work in less remunerative occupations and industries, and generally have less access to other employment benefits such as overtime pay and various kinds of bonuses. In 1993 formal equal pay provisions were inserted into the then *Industrial Relations Act 1988* and carried over into the new *Workplace Relations Act 1996*, but as yet they have not been much used (see s. 170 BA). Rather more activity on the equal pay front has occurred in state jurisdictions since the end of the 1990s, with several states launching inquiries into equal pay issues and some states following up the inquiries with equal pay cases designed to address historical undervaluation of typical female jobs and skills. Maternity leave is currently under debate. Few women have access to paid maternity leave. Although 12 months' unpaid leave with a right of return is generally available, this allowance is considered to be significantly less generous than those offered in many comparable economies.

Human rights at work

As outlined above, Australian anti-discrimination laws have their origins in British and American legislation. We have seen that discriminatory behaviour cannot be condoned in the recruitment process or in the provision of training, transfer and promotion opportunities. We have also noted that the employer may be held to be vicariously liable for the discriminatory behaviour of *all* employees within an organisation. Finally, we have noted that when a grievance or complaint arises, the complainant may often seek satisfaction through more than one complaint mechanism. Additionally, all the anti-discrimination legislation also makes unlawful certain discriminatory acts against non-employees, too. For example, in the provision of goods and services, not showing prospective Aboriginal tenants available rental accommodation or refusing to serve women alcohol in licensed premises are both unlawful discriminatory acts. Interestingly, most complaints lodged with the human rights authorities around Australia relate to some form of sex discrimination, including sexual harassment, in respect of employment.

The increased focus on human rights in a global political sense and in the employment context in Australia is intimately connected with the growing influence of international instruments such as human rights conventions and charters. Interestingly, this increased interest in human rights in the workplace, which follows an individual approach to dispute and grievance resolution, is matched by an apparent diminution in traditional collective rights that have for so long been at the centre of the regulation of the Australian workplace. Australia is a signatory to many of these international instruments; many of them stem from the International Labour Organisation, of which Australia is a founding member. These treaties are concerned with issues such as equality between men and women workers, equal pay, termination of employment, freedom of association and family responsibilities for workers. Where rights in these areas exist, they are subject to an individual complaint process, the most commonly accessed being those involving harassment of various kinds (Graycar & Morgan 2002). Before this very significant area of law and practice is discussed, however, a brief mention must be made of the one area of human rights law in the workplace that does not have an individual complaint process at its core.

The federal *Equal Opportunity for Women in the Workplace Act 1999* replaced the *Affirmative Action (Equal Opportunity for Women) Act 1986*. Never designed to reproduce the American use of quotas for so-called minority persons, the Act, in both its incarnations, has been designed to focus the attention of large organisations on the place of women in their structures. The Acts have required organisations with one hundred or more employees to survey and analyse their workforces and to prepare forward estimates of the direction in which they foresee their organisational profile moving. The legislation, which contains no complaint processes, has been designed to use a form of gentle persuasion to encourage organisational reform rather than resorting to coercive regulation.

As we have seen, numerous laws in Australia make it unlawful to discriminate against employees on the basis of certain personal attributes. Harassment on such grounds is equally unlawful. The most well known example of this is sexual harassment, which before it was legislatively defined (initially in the *Sex Discrimination Act 1984*) was seen as a form of sex discrimination. Sexual harassment can take many forms and is not limited to physical harassment; nor does the law apply only to women. All the statutes envisage same-sex harassment or harassment of men by women as well as of women by men. In spite of the publicity given to case decisions, the incidence of sexual harassment does not seem to be decreasing in our society. This might be because, with more publicity, people (women in particular) are no longer willing to put up with his kind of behaviour in the workplace. Also, sexual harassment might be appearing more frequently in human rights complaints because — unlike, say, sex discrimination — it is often easier to establish by means of emails, notes, phone messages, witnessed behaviours or other victims in the same workplace. Sex discrimination, on the other hand, may be covert and difficult to establish in the face of denial. Many incidences of direct discrimination may not even be detected by the victim. Similarly, when compulsory job requirements unrelated to the needs of the job operate disproportionately against one group of people, it may not always be obvious to those individuals most affected by the process. This kind of indirect discrimination is also unlawful.

Where these offences are confirmed by a human rights tribunal, the penalties may consist of pecuniary damages to the victim of the discriminatory behaviour, apologies, written references, payment of the costs of the action and so on. For many organisations, however, the greater cost is the loss of public reputation incurred in a public hearing of these kinds of complaints. Circumstances in which discrimination grievances do not surface as complaints may also see other costs to an organisation, for example in staff turnover or a failure to recruit good staff because of an organisation's reputation.

The physical environment

Organisations may be required to observe general community standards of environmental protection that have been developed in response to the degradation of the physical environment first perceived in the 1960s. Long before that, however, employers were legally required to make certain arrangements for the immediate protection of their workers. The earliest occupational health and safety legislation in the English legal world was the *Health and Morals of Apprentices Act 1802*, which was designed to provide some protection for very young workers by mandating regular whitewashing of factory walls to prevent lung-damaging dust accumulation, directing that apprentices receive clean clothes twice a year, and insisting that not more than two workers share a single bed. While such regulations may now appear quaint, the Act set the pattern for state intervention in the physical workplace by prescribing certain industry-specific standards.

It would be another 75 years, however, before real compensation for injury and disease sustained at work would be available for British workers, and Australian workers would have to wait even longer. The principal approach of the state today remains one of prevention, compensation and rehabilitation. The greater part of this regulation occurs at the state level. Rudimentary arrangements were already in place within the colonial governments at the time of the Constitutional Conventions. The debate about providing any federal industrial relations power proved so divisive that it was considered wiser to leave that area of regulation where it was, although any desire to centralise these laws in a new federal Parliament seems unlikely. Current federal occupational health and safety (OHS) laws are those establishing the National Occupational Health and Safety Commission (Worksafe Australia) and those covering the federal government's own employees and Australian merchant seamen.

All Australian state jurisdictions have adopted British-style Robens legislation — so called for the British executive who, after conducting an extensive inquiry into British OHS in 1970–72, had recommended greater self-regulation in the workplace and the replacement of the older, industry-specific, factory-style legislation that had developed piecemeal since the Act of 1802. From the 1870s the Australian colonies had also adopted this factory-style legislation. In more recent times, again like their British counterpart, these legislative regimes found it increasingly difficult to keep up with rapid technological change and labour market and other economic shifts. At the time of the introduction of the initial New South Wales legislation in 1983, for example, workplaces in many industries simply had no enforceable standards of OHS (Bohle & Quinlan 2000).

The new legislation requires that employers will maintain safe and healthy workplaces (in some states 'to the extent practicable') not only in relation to their employees but also in relation to visitors to the workplace. These visitors might be customers (e.g. if the workplace is a café in a shopping mall), patients' visitors in a hospital, or plumbing subcontractors, if the workplace is a building site. Suppliers,

designers and manufacturers also have obligations under this type of legislation, as do employees. Self-regulation by the workplace parties is taken up by means of joint employer–employee committees in each workplace. In some jurisdictions this includes rights of consultation with trade unions; in some, health and safety representatives must be appointed, or elected by the workforce; these delegates have formally enumerated rights and responsibilities under the relevant legislation.

All these arrangements have been subject to considerable criticism in both Australia and the United Kingdom as representing a retreat by the state from the more specific, detailed enforcement that the older style factory legislation offered. Sceptics suggest that all OHS legislation is only as good as the enforcement by the state that accompanies it, and in some states that is very limited indeed. Trade unions, which in most Australian jurisdictions have the ability to initiate prosecutions, very rarely do so — perhaps because of the resource implications involved in bringing a criminal matter before the courts. The self-regulation debate preceded the wider debate on deregulation of the workplace by at least a decade in Australia. Other critiques have focused on the fact that under the more recent, performance standard legislation, employers are given no real guidance as to what to do in any specific situation. This can be problematic, as the enforcement of these laws can result in criminal prosecutions requiring the criminal standard of proof (beyond reasonable doubt). More recent amendments to the New South Wales legislation have seen some fines reach a potential maximum of well over $750 000 (Jamieson & Westcott 2001); in Victoria a new crime of industrial manslaughter has been introduced. These fines do not accrue to any person injured as a result of an employer's failure to comply with the OHS legislation but are paid into consolidated revenue, as with any other criminal penalties such as speeding fines.

Compensation to workers injured or diseased in the course of their employment is made through statutory workers' compensation schemes introduced into the Australian colonies at the end of the nineteenth century on a British model, which in turn had drawn inspiration from Bismarck's Germany. These schemes generally work on a no-fault basis — that is, the injured worker does not have to show that the injury is the result of the negligence of either an employer or a co-worker, but merely that there is a causal nexus between the employment and the injury or disease and that economic loss has resulted because of the inability to work. The compensation is designed as income replacement, with increasingly parsimonious limits on the weekly amounts paid and the period for which compensation is paid. Additionally, medical expenses arising from the injury or disease are also paid. In circumstances in which there is a dispute over whether the injured person is a worker for the purposes of the relevant legislation, or in which there are questions about causation or other medical issues, there may be recourse to a system of legal appeals.

Today there is less and less access to common law negligence actions for injured workers who think they can establish a nexus between the negligence of someone at the workplace (e.g. an employer or fellow employee) or a manufacturer (e.g. a producer of asbestos) and their disability and economic loss. This is because of rapidly rising costs in workers' compensation and fears on the part of all state governments that workers' compensation liabilities will not be met. Workers' compensation is paid from insurance premiums compulsorily paid by all employers of labour according to the size of their payroll, the nature of their industry and their claims experience.

Ending the relationship: termination and unfair dismissals

The common law traditionally recognised the employer's right to select staff. As we have seen, however, this right is now circumscribed by the anti-discrimination laws, which also impinge on an employer's right to fire. No one can be dismissed on the grounds of their sex, their racial or ethnic background, or their sexuality, to pick just three examples. Industrial relations laws in all Australian jurisdictions now also recognise a right for employees to complain if they believe they have been unfairly dismissed or their position unlawfully terminated, and the parliaments have developed a remedy of reinstatement that was unknown in common law, where damages was the only remedy. These laws are politically controversial, however, and at a federal level at least have been the subject of regular amendment and ongoing debate. Many critics believe an employer's right to hire and fire should be completely unfettered, and that the laws restricting this right constitute an unnecessary intervention by the state in the employment relationship.

Employers have always had the right to summarily dismiss an employee for certain kinds of misconduct. In an era in which access to industrial tribunals for relief from unfair dismissal is widely available, an employer needs a degree of certainty before initiating a summary dismissal. For example, if theft is suspected (and this clearly falls within the rubric of misconduct) a sensible employer would require convincing evidence and would ensure the accused employee had an opportunity to put his or her side of the story. Similarly, care

must be taken in situations in which poor performance is a problem (e.g. habitual lateness, excessive coffee breaks or a marked failure to meet sales targets). Most prudent organisations now provide written and verbal warnings and keep careful records of these events. Employers are increasingly using subcontractors and resorting to other forms of outsourcing by means of which the person who requires the labour is not actually the employer of the labour. The industrial tribunals have been particularly sensitive where a real possibility of reinstatement has existed as a remedy. For this reason, in creating the unfair dismissal laws the federal Parliament made clear that the overriding principal guiding these arrangements would be one of 'a fair go all round', a peculiarly Australian conception indicating that the rights and interests of both employers and employees must be taken into account in these determinations (s. 170 CA, *Workplace Relations Act 1996*).

At other times it may be necessary for an employer to reduce the size of a labour force or to lay off all employees for economic reasons. Both industrial legislation and the particular conditions found in awards and enterprise agreements may dictate that employees are given certain periods of notice when such downsizing occurs.

Other employment relationships may end when professionals, in particular, are no longer able to practise their profession because of a failure to satisfy the requirements of outside regulatory bodies or because professional standards have not been met. This form of state regulation (generally with very significant involvement of the relevant profession) is particularly prevalent in medical settings. Employment relationships may also end when a necessary employment qualification is no longer held by the employee — for example with the withdrawal of certain licences, such as those issued to drivers.

Conclusion

This chapter has mapped out the extensive regulation of the employment relationship in Australia during a time of fundamental change. Many of the old certainties of state regulation no longer appear so certain, and hostility to the collective regulation of the employment relationship is now articulated within government in a way that would have been unthinkable a generation ago. Whether as a reaction to the decline in the dominance of the collective nature of historical regulation, or as a phenomenon that has assisted in the decline of that collective hegemony, the individual regulation of the employment relationship is a corollary of the perceptible retreat by the state from the Australian workplace.

References

Bohle, P, and Quinlan, M (2000) *Managing Occupational Health and Safety in Australia: A Multidisciplinary Approach*. Melbourne: Macmillan.

Buchanan, J, and Callus, R (1993) Efficiency and equity at work: the need for labour market regulation in Australia. *Journal of Industrial Relations,* 35, 515–37.

Burgess, J, and Campbell, I (1998) The nature and dimensions of precarious employment in Australia. *Labour and Industry,* 8, 5–21.

Creighton, B, and Stewart, A (2000) *Labour Law: An Introduction*. Sydney: Federation Press.

Dabscheck, B (1995) *The Struggle for Australian Industrial Relations*. Melbourne: Oxford University Press.

Deery, S, Plowman, D, Walsh, J, and Brown, M (2001) *Industrial Relations: A Contemporary Analysis*. Sydney: McGraw-Hill.

Graycar, R, and Morgan, J (2002) *The Hidden Gender of Law*. Sydney: Federation Press.

Gunningham, N, and Johnstone, R (1999) *Regulating Workplace Safety: Systems and Sanctions*. Oxford: Oxford University Press.

Jamieson, S, and Westcott, M (2001) Occupational Health and Safety Act 2000: a story of reform in New South Wales. *Australian Journal of Labour Law,* 14177–89.

La Nauze, J (1972) *The Making of the Australian Constitution*. Melbourne: Melbourne University Press.

Macintyre, S, and Mitchell, R (Eds) (1989) *Foundations of Arbitration*. Melbourne: Oxford University Press.

Whitehouse, G (1992) Legislation and labour market gender inequality. *Work, Employment and Society,* 6, 65–86.

Contemporary issues in managing performance and development

CHAPTER 14

Contemporary issues in recruitment and selection

by Diana du Plessis
HR Management Consultant

Introduction

Globalisation, advances in technology and labour market conditions have created an external environment dominated by increasing competition (Anthony, Perrewe & Kacmar 1996). Central to managing these organisational challenges is the effective management of the human resources within an organisation (Caudron 1999; Wright, McMahan & Williams 1994). It is the unique combination of individuals employed within an organisation that is the source of its sustainable competitive edge (Pfeffer 1995; Lado & Wilson 1994; Kydd & Oppenheim 1990); and achieving and maintaining a sustainable competitive advantage is fundamental to the long-term survival of an organisation (Flanagan & Desphande 1996). It is easier to replicate technology than to replicate the unique combination of individuals employed within the organisation (Hitt, Ireland & Hoskisson 1995). Effective human resource management (HRM) is therefore of critical importance to all organisations.

Lundy (1994) and Wright and Snell (1991) singled out selection and recruitment, compensation, training and development, and performance appraisal as key HRM practices that organisations need to develop in order to maintain a sustainable competitive advantage. If these practices are managed effectively, an organisation is able to:

attract and retain qualified employees who are motivated to perform and there will be outcomes of greater profitability, low employee turnover, high product

quality, lower production costs and more acceptance of the organisational strategy. (Lundy 1994, p. 697)

Without the right blend of people within an organisation, it will have difficulty achieving its missions and strategic goals, and its very survival could be jeopardised (Anthony, Perrewe & Kacmar 1996, p. 9). This idea is echoed by Kramar, Mcgraw & Schuler (1997, p. 309):

Getting the right people in the right jobs in the organisation is a fundamental basis for getting value added performance from people and a key mechanism for aligning the management of people with organisational vision and mission and hence ensuring that strategic goals are achieved.

If the right people are recruited, selected and developed continuously within an organisation, the employees are likely to be more strongly committed to achieving the organisation's objectives (Anthony, Perrewe & Kacmar 1996).

Recruitment is defined succinctly by Kramar, Mcgraw and Schuler (1997) as a process undertaken by an organisation in order to:

search for, and obtain, in compliance with legal regulations, potential job candidates in sufficient numbers and quality, and at the right cost, for the organisation to select the most appropriate people to fill its jobs. (Kramar, Mcgraw & Schuler 1997, p. 310)

Selection is defined by Gatewood and Field (1998) as:

the process of collecting and evaluating information about an individual in order to extend an offer of employment. Such employment could be either a first position for a new employee or a different position for a current employee. The selection process is performed under legal and environmental constraints and addresses the future interests of the organisation. (Gatewood & Field 1998, p. 4)

However, the recruitment and selection process is not a one-sided activity but a reciprocal process in which, while the employer assesses the applicant for the position, the applicant also interviews and assesses the organisation to see if it meets his or her needs (Laabs 1998). Employment is a two-way decision process (Schwab, Rynes & Aldag 1987), and job applicants are active participants during the recruitment and selection process (Granovetter 1974), because one of the main purposes of recruitment and selection is to ensure that the correct 'person fit' is achieved.

'Fit' in the recruitment and selection of job applicants has long been a cornerstone of HRM. The traditional conception of fit focuses on matching applicants' knowledge, skills and abilities (KSAs) to the job requirements (O'Reilly, Caldwell & Mirable 1992). Matching the values, beliefs and personality traits of applicants with the values, beliefs and norms of an organisation (person–organisation fit) has also become an integral part of 'fit' research and practice (Bowen, Ledford & Nathan 1991; Bretz, Rynes & Gethart 1993; Chatman 1991; Kristof 1996; O'Reilly, Chatman & Caldwell 1991; Rynes & Gerhart 1990). Research in this area has found that perceptions of fit and actual fit relate to job attitudes and behaviour (Kristof 1996). For example, fit has been found to be positively related to job satisfaction, organisational commitment, intentions to remain, job involvement, career success, health and adaptation, and organisational effectiveness, and to lower stress and turnover (Blau 1987; Bretz & Judge 1994; Cable & Judge 1996; Chatman 1991; Edwards & Cooper 1990; Meglino, Ravlin & Adkins 1989; Moos 1987; O'Reilly et al. 1991; Ostroff 1993; Stumpf & Hartman 1984; Vancouver & Schmitt 1991). Poor hiring decisions are associated with low employee morale, absenteeism, employee turnover and reduced output (Naidoo 1997).

The challenge for all organisations, therefore, is to ensure person–job fit and person–organisation fit for each individual candidate for employment. A poor selection decision can be an expensive mistake for the organisation. Recent research by DDI Asia Pacific found that hiring the wrong person cost the organisation between $2000 and $20 000.

The first major challenge facing any organisation undertaking recruitment and selection is how to attract and select the right people. Once recruitment and selection have taken place, the focus shifts to motivating and retaining the new employee, and other HRM activities such as training and development, compensation and performance appraisal become the focus.

Impact of the external and internal environment on recruitment and selection

The recruitment and selection process is not a single, one-off activity but rather a series of activities and processes undertaken by an organisation to attract sufficient numbers of high-quality candidates. These activities do not occur in isolation; all organisations operate in a dynamic environment and are influenced by factors and challenges. Understanding these factors and the opportunities and constraints they present is a major challenge for organisations contemplating recruitment and selection.

The external environment includes economic, social, political, technological and industry variables; competition; labour market conditions; and legislation governing recruitment activity in Australia. *Economic* factors such as inflation, interest rates and industry competition may provide constraints or opportunities for employment across different sectors of the Australian economy at different times (Stone 1998). Higher inflation and interest rates mean the costs associated with running a business increase. Higher labour costs can restrict the organisation's ability to recruit new employees and its opportunities to invest in new technology. Equally, lower inflation and interest rates can increase opportunities for organisational growth, recruitment and investment in new technology. The availability of capital to finance investment is vital for continued organisational growth (ABS 1990).

Social factors such as industrial initiatives, quality of work life, and occupational health and safety issues could affect the number of applicants responding to advertised positions (Compton & Nankervis 1998). For example, it can be difficult to attract experienced, high-quality applicants with their families for a long-term position in a remote location where there is no infrastructure, and facilities to provide for their health needs and schooling for their children.

Political and social issues such as government policies influence labour supply, because the structure and levels of funding provided to educational and training institutions affect the numbers, training, and availability of apprentices and graduates for employment (Compton & Nankervis 1998).

Industry competition is a challenge for organisations needing to recruit new employees in terms of both the goods and services offered by the organisation and the potential impact on labour costs. For example, if there is a skill shortage in a particular area, the organisation might have to pay high wages to attract new employees or to keep their highly skilled employees.

Labour market conditions and employment levels vary across Australia according to locality, industry (ABS industry sector) and occupation (Compton & Nankervis 1998). For example, although Australia currently enjoys high levels of employment, there are still shortages of technical specialists in the IT industry, and doctors and allied health professionals willing to work in the rural areas.

All recruitment activity in Australia is governed by *legislation*. Relevant state and federal legislation pertains to industrial relations, equal employment opportunity (EEO), affirmative action (AA), occupational health and safety (OH&S) (Anthony, Perrewe & Kacmar 1996), and privacy (the new *Privacy Amendment (Private Sector) Act 2000*).

EEO, AA, OH&S and privacy legislation have implications for recruitment and selection. Employers need to be aware of their recruitment and selection policies and of procedures to ensure that they are not discriminatory. State and federal guidelines covering these aspects of the recruitment and selection process are very clear and specific. For example, the *Equal Opportunity for Women in the Workplace Amendment Act 1999* amends the former *Affirmative Action (Equal Employment Opportunity for Women) Act 1986*. It still requires all private sector employers of 100 or more employees to establish workplace programs for women and to submit annual reports on the progress of their programs to the Equal Opportunity for Women in the Workplace Agency (CCH Newsletter 2000). Another example is the federal *Privacy Amendment (Private Sector) Act 2000*, which came into force on 21 December 2001 and enforces the National Privacy Principles (Fenton-Jones November 2001). The National Privacy Principles apply to personal and/or sensitive information collected and held on record during and after the recruitment and selection process. The NPP allow unsuccessful candidates access to all documentation relating to the processing of their application for employment. Companies that do not conform to the stringent standards of non-discriminatory recruitment and selection could face expensive litigation from employees along

with other consequences such as bad publicity, lowered productivity and a negative impact on employee morale (Naidoo 1997). Furthermore, to remedy an incorrect selection decision, an organisation might have to decide either to maintain the employment of the individual concerned or to initiate the difficult dismissal process (Kramar, Mcgraw & Schuler 1997; Brumback 1996). Other legislation, such as that relating to migration, also affects recruitment from overseas if suitable candidates cannot be found in Australia. The ease or difficulty of bringing an employee into Australia will determine whether an organisation, or the individual applicant, pursues such a strategy.

The internal environment describes the characteristics of the organisation, including such factors such as the number of staff in the organisation, whether there is an HR manager, whether or not the business engages in strategic or business planning, and the number of locations in which it operates. Evidence of a strategic plan and the conduct of strategic business planning can have an important bearing on the nature and extent of recruitment activities and processes required by the organisation in order to meet all its business needs, particularly with regard to maintaining or extending its skill base. If new employees are needed, the strategic business plan should help identify how many employees the organisation needs to meet its business objectives, what skills these employees need to bring to the business and how the organisation will go about seeking employees with these skills (Dessler et al. 1999).

Both external and internal environment contextualise the organisation's recruitment activities and processes, and influence the organisation's recruitment decisions — for example, decisions on how many employees need to be recruited, the skills required of these employees and how to set about the recruitment process. Once these decisions have been made the organisation then must decide which internal and external sources and methods of recruitment are best suited to meet their recruitment needs. The choice it makes will depend on the resources available and the person(s) responsible for the recruitment process (Compton & Nankervis 1998).

Internal and external sources of recruitment

The two main sources for recruitment are internal and external applicants. Internal recruitment refers to recruiting those employees who have past or present links with the organisation. External recruitment refers to hiring employees who do not currently have links with the organisation.

The main sources of internal recruitment are present employees, friends of employees, former employees and former applicants (Kramar, Mcgraw & Schuler 1997). The most important source is current employees because they can refer their friends to the organisation, and they themselves may be applicants for promotion or transfer.

Potential benefits of promoting existing employees within an organisation include strengthening employee morale and loyalty; saving on the costs associated with external recruitment; minimal orientation for the employee, who is already familiar with the way the organisation operates; and a prior knowledge of the employee's strengths and weaknesses (Stone 1998). Attracting applicants from outside the organisation can be an expensive process (Flynn 1995). The costs may include advertising, time spent processing the applications and interviewing and selecting the right applicant, and relocation costs for the new employee. A new employee will also be unfamiliar with the organisation's policies, work methods and performance standards, and will therefore require time to adjust and become familiar with the way the organisation operates. They may even require training in this area. Whether the organisation undertakes internal or external recruitment, finding the best candidate to fill the position can be a lengthy process, as the results of the 1999 Annual InfoHRM Benchmarking Report showed. This study found that the median for time taken to fill positions was 50 days per recruit (Ellerby & Barrett 1999).

Bringing a new employee into the work environment also has an impact on the existing workforce. For example, existing employees might be resentful if they felt they were passed over in favour of the new employee, particularly if the new employee is paid a higher salary for doing a similar job. However, there are also disadvantages to promoting from within. Existing employees may not possess the required skills or relevant experience and may have become entrenched in the way in which they perform their job (Flynn 1995).

Considering these advantages and disadvantages, it is not surprising to find that organisations tend to promote positions internally while collecting applicants from external sources. In addition, they tend to obtain particular types of employees from particular sources. For example, many organisations are more likely to hire highly trained professionals and high-level managers from outside than to promote from within (Kramar, Mcgraw & Schuler 1997). In a study comparing the recruitment practices of large and small organisations in Canada, Golhar and Desphande (1997) found that internal vacancy advertising was the preferred approach for both groups, although larger organisations were more likely to rely on transfers and recruitment from educational institutions and employment agencies.

Another way for organisations to recruit internally is to transfer current employees without promotion. This may provide existing employees with alternative career options, but again it depends on the size of the organisation and the number of locations in which it operates. It is easier for large organisations to explore this option, but this option is not available for a small or medium-sized organisation with only one operation. For large organisations it is a way of developing their employees, because a transfer offers opportunities for learning new skills, enriching their jobs and avoiding the staleness that can come from remaining in the same job for too long.

Internal methods of recruitment

The two most frequently used methods of internal recruitment are job posting and reviewing internal human resource records (Gatewood & Field 1998; Kramar, Mcgraw & Schuler 1997). Job posting is a formal method of notifying members of the organisation about job openings and the method of applying for these openings. Most often the vacancy is announced on an internal organisation bulletin board, in the organisational newsletter, via email or, more recently, on the company website. All organisations, whether large, medium or small, are likely to make use of some if not all of these methods of recruitment.

The main difficulty in using this technique is to ensure that this information is conveyed to everyone in the organisation. In small firms it is easier to circulate this information among all employees because the workforce is smaller and contact between management and all employees tends to be more frequent. In medium-sized organisations, as the number of employees increases, communication, and ensuring the 'right' people receive the information, becomes more difficult. The primary advantages of this method of recruitment are that it provides employees with an opportunity for job variety and the position can be filled at a low cost (Kleinman & Clark 1984).

Human resource (HR) records are an important source of employee information. They include information about employee qualifications, skills and interests as well as various assessment activities such as performance appraisal. Small and medium-sized employers (SMEs) usually rely on more informal storage methods, such as manual systems, for recording employee data. Neiger (2000) has suggested that SMEs will face increasing pressure to formalise their HR information systems in the face of events such as unfair dismissal actions or industrial accidents. This pressure on SMEs is unlikely to be reduced as the Australian Government continues to regulate industrial relations.

Most large organisations have a computer-based information system, or Human Resource Information System (HRIS) (Dessler et al. 1999), such as Peoplesoft, Oracle,

SAP or Aurion (Neiger 2000). However, these information sources are only as good as the data they contain. It is highly unlikely that HR records will be the only source of recruitment information. In practice, a variety of sources usually informs and guides the recruitment process (Dessler et al. 1999). The HRIS is nevertheless a powerful tool. If used effectively, it can assist in individual career development, since it identifies and tracks an individual's continuing professional development (Kirk 1999). It can also be used as a tool for organisational planning, since employee performance can be rated against the organisation's key performance indicators (Kirk 1999).

External methods of recruitment

Recruiting internally may not always produce a large enough pool of applicants, in which case it becomes necessary to recruit externally. This is particularly true when organisations are new, or growing rapidly, and have a large demand for specific skilled employees. A recent example of a large demand was the opening of the Colonial Stadium in Melbourne in March 2000. Redding Consulting Group was commissioned to find 1300 customer services employees within six months. Only online applications were accepted, and Redding received 15 000 of these in three weeks. These applications were processed and the positions filled in less than two months at a saving of $35 000 (*HR Monthly* December 2000).

The main advantages of external recruitment include bringing in people with new ideas and insights, increasing the talent pool within the organisation, and hiring a skilled employee or trained professional (Stone 1998). Outside employees are also not members of existing cliques. This can be of great benefit, for example when trying to introduce a change in work procedures within an organisation, because it may help counter employee resistance to the change (Stone 1998).

Disadvantages to external recruitment include the associated time, advertising and processing costs, and the time needed by the new employee to adjust to the way the organisation operates (Flynn 1995). Morale among existing employees may suffer if they feel they have been passed over in favour of an outside employee. It is also possible that the new employee does not perform as expected or that there is a mismatch between the employee's personality and the organisational culture (Stone 1998).

The major *external sources* for recruitment include walk-in applicants; referrals by existing employees; the use of private and government employment agencies; search firms; trade unions; professional associations; TAFEs and universities; and high schools.

Advertising in the newspapers, magazines and/or trade journals; on radio or television, or through direct mail are the principal *methods* used for external recruitment. Mergers and acquisitions have also become a means by which organisations have increased their employee numbers.

Walk-ins were defined by Gatewood and Field (1998, p. 12) as 'unsolicited individuals initiating contact with the organisation'. The incidence of walk-ins depends on factors such as the image of the company, its physical proximity to the labour market and the perception in the marketplace of the availability of positions. While walk-ins may be a valuable source for an individual employer, they leave much to chance, and cannot be relied upon as a regular, dependable means of attracting new employees.

The most common method of external recruitment used in all organisations is word-of-mouth (Gatewood & Field 1998; Kramar, Mcgraw & Schuler 1997). Here current employees are provided with information about job openings and are asked to refer suitable individuals to the organisation. The importance of this external recruitment method was supported by an article in the *Australian Financial Review* in which a Sydney-based executive recruitment consultant endorsed the commonly held view that 'only one in three jobs is ever advertised (Main 2001, p. 31).

There is evidence to suggest an increase in the use of consultants and external recruitment agencies for all recruitment activity (Compton & Nankervis 1998). Recruitment agencies may be either public or private, and the job seekers may be either employed or unemployed. Private employment consultants or agencies charge fees to the employer. In Australia these fees vary from 10 to 30 per cent of the annual starting salary of the employee depending on the level of the position (Compton & Nankervis 1998; Jasper 2000).

Government employment agencies operate in every state in Australia and are coordinated by the Department of Employment, Education, Training and Youth Affairs. Unemployed people register with Centrelink, which then refers them to Job Network providers located around Australia as well as the government-owned Employment National, the largest provider in the network (Mitchell 1998; Stock 1998). Using the computer-listed job information, agency staff counsel applicants about suitable jobs available in their geographic area. Job seekers can also access this information directly and contact the relevant agency or employer (Bennett 1998). Although public agencies are a major source of blue- and white-collar workers, the experience of employers with the service from these agencies has been mixed (Dessler et al. 1999).

There has also been an increase in private employment agencies offering temporary secretarial, clerical or semi-skilled labour on a short-term basis (Dessler et al. 1999). These agencies can be useful for organisations trying to cope with peak loads or seeking staff to fill in for employees who are on leave. The recent trend towards outsourcing a wide range of jobs, from cleaning to computer programming and HRM, has led to an increase in the number of agencies and specialist organisations offering such services. Many employers also supplement their permanent employee base by hiring temporary or short-term non-executive and executive contract workers (Dessler et al. 1999; Leighton 2001).

Private employment agencies are an important source of clerical, white-collar and managerial employees. Figures on use by Australian firms vary, but Drake Consulting recently estimated that somewhere between 20 and 30 per cent of Australian companies use recruitment firms to hire permanent staff and up to 50 per cent use recruitment firms to hire temporary staff (Kramar, Mcgraw & Schuler 1997). Bainbridge (1998) has suggested that if organisations are not able to find the right candidate for a job vacancy through networking, recruitment consultants or agencies should be their next option.

Many professional associations and unions have regional, state and national bodies that run regular meetings, provide training for their members, and publish newsletters and journals. Often these bodies run job placement advertisements in their newsletters or journals. For example, the agency Skilled Engineering has grown rapidly in recent years and, with some 10 000 employees, is now a major employer. The company's 1998–99 report to shareholders reported sales revenue of $536.3 million, up 39.7 per cent on the previous year (Skilled Engineering Limited: Annual Report 1999).

McEnvoy (1984) found that media advertising, particularly in newspapers, is used extensively by all organisations. Radio advertising was used to a lesser extent and television as a means of recruiting was hardly ever used. The lack of interest in television recruitment is hardly surprising given the cost involved. The main advantages of using the media as a means of advertising job vacancies are that the message can include information about both the job and the organisation, and, more important, it can be used to target either the general public or a specific segment of the population, whether locally, regionally or nationally.

In Australia the local newspaper is seen as the best source of blue-collar, clerical and lower-level administrative positions (Dessler et al. 1999). For more specialised employees, national newspapers such as the *Australian* and professional journals are used. Daily capital city newspapers such as the *Sydney Morning Herald*, the *Age* or the *Courier-Mail* are used successfully to advertise middle or senior management positions (Dessler et al. 1999). Of all the media options for recruitment, the newspaper remains the preferred option among employers and employees (Jones 1996; Morehead et al. 1995). Newspapers account for more than 90 per cent of all employment advertising (Levy 1999). In a review of the

ANZ job advertising series, Rose (1999) noted that job advertisements in major newspapers were at their highest levels since March 1990. For example, the *Sydney Morning Herald* alone carried 7000 job advertisements on a single day, 16 January 1999 (Rose 1999). These advertisements are placed either by the organisation seeking a new employee or by external recruiters.

Easy access to the Internet has seen a dramatic increase in its use as a method for recruitment overseas in countries such as the United States and the United Kingdom, as well as in Australia (Callander 1999; Greengard 1998; *Management Today,* September 1996, March 1998; Rance 1997). It has become standard practice for newspapers such as the *Age* and the *Sydney Morning Herald* to place their classified advertisements on the Internet. Recruitment agencies, universities and some professional associations also advertise positions on the Internet (Compton & Nankervis 1998). Recruitment consultants advertise information about job vacancies on the Internet and use their web pages as data-gathering sites where potential job seekers are able to add their curriculum vitae for consideration by the consultants for future job positions (Greengard 1998; *Management Today,* April 1997). Typical sites are Seek.com.au, Careerone.com.au, Mycareer.com.au, Employment.com.au and Monster.com.au. When the site was launched in June 1999, Monster.com contained one million jobs around the world (Abernethy 1999). Even the Australian Government has extended its Jobs Network by using online vacancy information (Bennett 1998).

Online job advertising is being used increasingly by large organisations for recruitment purposes. Examples include Sony, Siemens, Kellogg's, Ericsson, AT & T, Procter, Goodman Fielder, AMP and ORICA (Kramar, Mcgraw & Schuler 1997). At least one large organisation uses two websites, one for internal recruitment and one for external recruitment purposes (Flynn 1996). The most obvious advantage of using web sites is that organisations can provide detailed information about the company and specific jobs, and details about the knowledge, skills and abilities needed while also presenting video displays of the work environment and employees (Gatewood & Field 1998). The relatively low cost of providing a great deal of current information about the organisation and job vacancies will be an attractive reason for organisations to continue to develop this source of recruitment (Greengard 1998). While there is evidence in the literature about the use of this recruitment medium by large organisations, it is unclear about the extent of its use by SMEs. However, the value of this strategy for large organisations is questioned. Levy (1999) questions how effectively large organisations screen the unsolicited résumés streaming into the organisation through their websites, and suggests that organisations that fail to reply to online job applications may be tarnishing their own reputation. Despite the increase in Internet usage, Callander (1999) feels that Australian recruitment agencies in particular have been slow to explore the use of the Net as a tool for locating and tracking potential applicants, especially those candidates who are not actively searching for new positions. Recruiters have limited their use of this new technology to the online placement of job advertisements and acceptance of applications via e-mail. They are not using specialised search tools to seek out résumés of suitable candidates either within the company or on personal websites (Callander 1999).

The challenge of managing the selection process effectively

While recruitment focuses on attracting a pool of suitable applicants for employment, selection is the means by which this pool is reviewed, assessed and reduced to an individual or group of individuals most suitable for employment for a specific position (Dessler et al. 1999; Anthony, Perrewe & Kacmar 1996; Kramar, Mcgraw & Schuler 1997; Stone 1998). Selection is not a one-off activity but rather a series of steps aimed at processing placement decision information. Steps typical of a full-scale selection process are described in figure 14.1 (Stone 1998; Nankervis, Compton & McCarthy 1996; Compton & Nankervis 1998; Anthony, Perrewe & Kacmar 1996).

The steps illustrated in figure 14.1 are typical of a full-scale selection process. Organisations may not undertake each step each time they select employees. For example, step 5 (psychological or other testing), and step 6 (reference checking) may not be required if the applicant is already employed within the organisation, although larger organisations might still deem them necessary according to their policies and procedures. In SMEs, on the other hand, step 5 (testing) may never be used, and an internal applicant's knowledge, skills and abilities might be known to the person(s) undertaking the selection process, so that step 6 (reference checking) might also not be required.

The challenge of choosing the right selection device

A number of methods can be used as selection devices. These include:
- job analysis
- job descriptions
- person specifications and competency profiling
- application form
- reference checking
- selection interviews
- psychological, aptitude or ability testing
- medical examinations
- assessment centres.

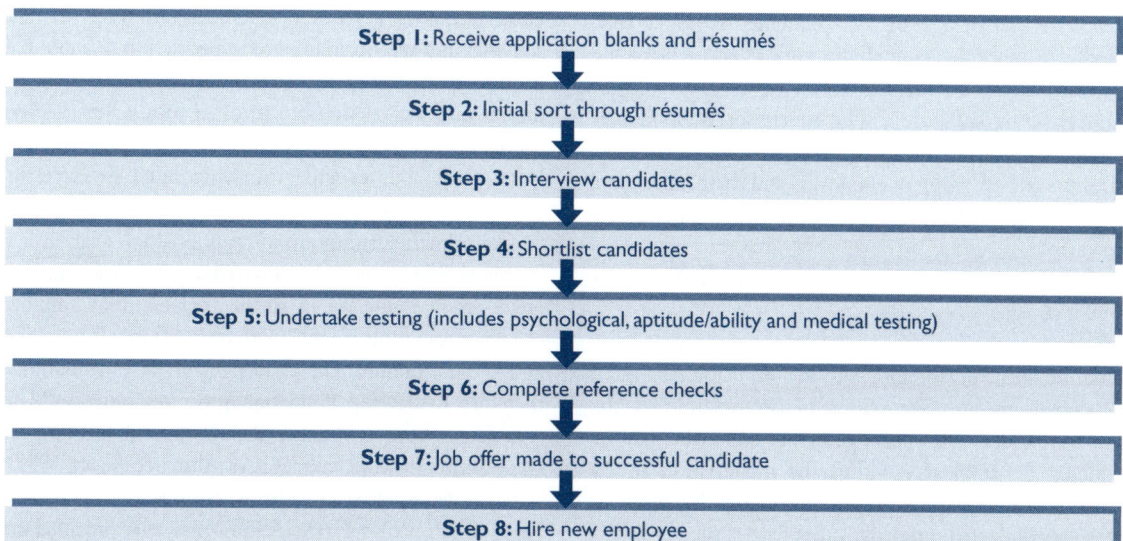

Step 1: Receive application blanks and résumés

Step 2: Initial sort through résumés

Step 3: Interview candidates

Step 4: Shortlist candidates

Step 5: Undertake testing (includes psychological, aptitude/ability and medical testing)

Step 6: Complete reference checks

Step 7: Job offer made to successful candidate

Step 8: Hire new employee

Figure 14.1: Steps in the selection process ***Sources:*** Adapted from Stone (1998); Nankervis, Compton and McCarthy (1996); Compton and Nankervis (1998); and Anthony, Perrewe and Kacmar (1996).

Each of these methods will now be examined individually. Selection design and selection decision making will also be discussed.

Job analysis

Job analysis is a crucial determinant of employee performance and influences other HRM activities including employee training and development, compensation, performance management, occupational health and safety, and recruitment and selection (Dessler et al. 1999). It is the main means by which information is gathered about a job position within an organisation and the type of person needed to fill the position. If, for example, an organisation was downsizing, upsizing or restructuring, the roles of people within the organisation, and their job descriptions, could change. Ideally, job analysis is used to identify and develop revised or new job descriptions. It can also be used as a means to identify a need to recruit an individual. Compton & Nankervis (1998, p. 28), addressing all of these facets, define job analysis as follows:

> *A systematic process of identifying the component tasks, responsibilities and outcomes of jobs, and the knowledge, competencies, skills and abilities required to adequately perform these duties.*

Organisations use a number of methods to gather the information required for job analysis. Typically, information-gathering techniques include:
- *Observation:* The job analyst observes the person doing the job being analysed.
- *Employee diaries or logs:* The jobholder keeps a daily, weekly or monthly log of all the work activities he or she performs.
- *Written or verbal surveys:* The supervisor or jobholder completes surveys.
- *Expert panels:* A group of employees and their supervisors meet, discuss and develop a list of the key elements of a job.
- *Individual or group interviews.* (Compton & Nankervis 1998, p. 30).

The best method is determined by the size, complexity and nature of the organisation and the job being assessed.

Organisations may use one or a combination of the above techniques. These data-gathering strategies may be conducted by employees within the organisation or by external consultants specifically employed for this purpose. If they are conducted internally, other parties such as supervisors, line managers, HR practitioners and other employees could be involved. However, there is evidence to suggest that line managers, in conjunction with relevant employees, are most frequently involved in selection (Anthony, Perrewe & Kacmar 1996; Dessler et al. 1999). Other evidence points to the interview technique as the preferred method of job analysis for all organisations, regardless of size (Gatewood & Field 1998; Caudron 1994; Dessler et al. 1999). The main drawback of gathering information using interviews is the possibility of distortion through falsification or misunderstanding (Gatewood & Field 1998). Obtaining valid information can therefore be a slow process.

If external consultants are called in to undertake a formal job analysis, it is likely they would use either Functional Job Analysis (FJA) or the (PAQ) Position Analysis Questionnaire (Compton & Nankervis 1998). However, both of these techniques are highly structured and require specific training to administer them. This can be a costly exercise for an organisation. There is considerable research evidence of validation and use of the FJA and the PAQ within larger organisations (Dessler et al. 1999). However, there is little evidence of its use in SMEs in Australia. This is probably linked to the costs associated with bringing in an external consultant, and possibly a perception among SMEs that other techniques such as observation, employee diaries or logs, surveys, expert panels, and individual or group interviews produce the results they require.

Job descriptions, person specifications and competency profiling

A job description is the practical outcome of job analysis. Usually, this is a written statement outlining the tasks, activities and responsibilities of a specific job. It should also include details about expected work outcomes, work conditions and the relationship to other jobs. Often a person specification is also included, describing the personal knowledge, skills abilities and attitude required to successfully perform a job (Dessler et al. 1999).

The primary assumption in traditional job analysis is the existence of ongoing stable, analysable jobs consisting of discrete sets of tasks. Yet in smaller organisations employees often perform multiple roles with unclear job role boundaries and responsibilities. The challenge for all organisations is therefore to develop evaluation processes using valid and reliable methods to predict the short- and medium-term composition of work roles (Visser, Altink & Algera 1997).

If job descriptions and person specifications are based on accurate job analysis, crucial information is provided with which to develop selection criteria. This facilitates the choice of suitable candidates as well as ensuring compliance to equal employment law (Dessler et al. 1999). Job descriptions and person specifications need to be written clearly and to be specific.

The Australian Bureau of Statistics, in conjunction with the Department of Employment, Education, Training and Youth Affairs, produces the Australian Standard Classification of Occupations (ASCO 1997). This resource can be used by any organisation as a national standard for analysing, comparing and classifying jobs (Pithers, Athanasou & Cornford 1995).

Recently in Australia, the UK, the US and New Zealand, there has been a trend towards the use of competency profiling for recruitment and selection (Hearn, Close, Smith & Southey 1996; Stickels 1994). The focus in competency profiling is on determining the unique behavioural dimensions affecting job performance. Typically, this is done by developing a 'list' of approximately 9 to 12 characteristics or competencies, and detailed behavioural descriptions relating to the effort required by each employee within an organisation. The objective is to facilitate the effective contribution of individuals to organisational success. Recruitment and selection processes seek to identify potential employees who have these desired characteristics or competencies and best meet the criteria for the person–environment fit (Borman, Hanson & Hedge 1997).

Some researchers regard competency profiling as just another term for job analysis (Nankervis, Compton & McCarthy 1996). Others regard it as more than traditionally described job skills (Sparrow 1997); rather, as the performance of a range of activities, including transferring skills and knowledge to new situations and managing a variety of tasks within the job (Rutherford 1996).

Problems with the use of job analysis

Despite the widespread use in all organisations of job descriptions and person specifications, some still believe that they are a waste of time and irrelevant, given that the written information quickly becomes outdated and inaccurate (Compton & Nankervis 1998). While most of these criticisms are valid, they can also be readily countered. Information contained in these documents should be regularly updated and reviewed if it is not to become irrelevant, outdated or inaccurate. For example, if an organisation conducts an annual performance appraisal of each of its employees, this would be the ideal time to review these documents. Before the event each employee, as well as the person conducting the performance review, should examine these documents, discuss any changes that need to be made and then incorporate these afterwards.

There is still considerable debate in Australia about the use of professional competencies and the relevance of competency standards for Australian managers (Hearn, Close, Smith & Southey 1996; Stickels 1994). Indeed, there is some disagreement about what constitutes a competency. This debate centres on two main issues — namely, the lack of studies evaluating the effectiveness of this technique, and a lack of international standardisation of what constitutes competencies (Compton & Nankervis 1998). Given the newness of the concept, it is not surprising that there is as yet insufficient empirical evidence evaluating the technique.

It could be said that the competency movement is still in its infancy in Australia, despite the recommendations in the Karpin Report for their development and use (Hunt & Wallace 1997; *The Enterprising Nation* 1995). Attempts have been made to define generic professional competencies, and the British competencies model developed by the Management Charter Initiative has been adapted to meet the needs of more than 100 Australian government departments and companies (Hearn et al. 1996; Stickels 1994). Perhaps, as Burgoyne (1993) says, we should develop management competencies for individual companies rather than industry-wide descriptors of competencies. The main benefits of this approach are that it is less prescriptive, and it provides more flexibility for organisations and employees across jobs and job families in times of change and increased competition (Peake 1994).

The criticism levelled against job descriptions and person specifications, namely that they quickly become outdated, inaccurate and irrelevant, could also apply to competencies. This is because organisations are dynamic, and competencies will not remain the same for extended periods. For example, different managerial competencies are required depending on the strategic situation faced by each enterprise as it moves through its life cycle.

The main benefit of competency profiling for recruitment and selection is the provision of clear guidelines. It assists internal and external recruiters with information about the type of people required and the behavioural characteristics they need to display for maximum benefit to the organisation. It also forms a basis for the development of criteria used by selectors during the selection process. Before selection this information can be used for advertising purposes to promote the organisation to prospective applicants.

Application form

In general, the application form refers to a form designed by an organisation specifically for the purpose of recruitment and selection. The forms might vary from position to position within the organisation, or there might be a standardised form to be completed by each individual seeking employment in the organisation (Anthony, Perrewe & Kacmar 1996). The main purpose of such a form is to document biographical information, which can then be used in the selection process as a standardised means of comparing job applicants with the job criteria. Following the initial screening process, the information can also be used as the basis for a selection interview. Once the selection process is complete, the details contained in the application form can be used as a record of the successful applicant's particulars.

There is considerable variation among organisations as to the length of the form and the amount of detail required for its completion. Large organisations, having a greater staff turnover and need for mass recruiting, find the forms a time-saving device for screening applicants (Compton & Nankervis 1998). By contrast, SMEs, with a low staff turnover rate, are able to deal directly either by telephone or in person with job applicants and successful candidates, without necessitating the completion of an application form.

When designing an application form, careful attention should be paid to the nature and level of detail of the information requested of applicants. Only those facts essential to deciding whether an individual should be interviewed or not should be included. Personal details, such as religion, nationality and marital status, should be excluded, because the inclusion of such variables could lead to charges of unlawful discrimination. More in-depth information about an individual candidate may be sought during the selection interview and a résumé may be requested.

Reference checks

The main purpose of reference checking is to establish the accuracy of data provided by job applicants about themselves. Usually, this check is undertaken after a selection interview and with the applicant's permission. The process includes verifying applicant information from people with whom the applicant has previously been closely associated. Typically, the information sought includes education and employment histories, skills, achievements, job responsibilities, and character and interpersonal abilities. The check can be carried out either through a telephone interview with a previous employer or by asking another person at the applicant's previous employment to comment in writing on the extent to which the applicant meets the selection criteria.

Usually, a representative of the potential employer conducts a telephone reference check with at least one referee nominated by the applicant. The representative conducting the check may be either an external consultant employed by the organisation to undertake recruitment and selection on

their behalf, or an internal representative of the organisation, such as the HR manager or a line manager.

In the past, job applicants included personal written references prepared by friends or relatives as statements of their character. For the most part this information was not considered an important aspect of the selection process. However, more recently reference checking has become a crucial element in the selection process. Compton and Nankervis (1998) cite three major reasons for this development: first, the increasing costs of selection and its consequences; second, an awareness of 'credential distortion'; and finally, research evidence supporting the premise that past work experience and behaviour are a predictor of future work performance.

A reference check that is not handled appropriately and thoroughly could result in costly financial and public relations consequences for the organisation (Brown 1993; Dunn 1995). The media frequently report cases in which individuals have 'faked' their qualifications, skills and experience. Care must be exercised by the referee as well as the person seeking the information. A referee should provide factual information that can be substantiated in order to minimise defamation or negligent referral claims (Barada 1996; Perry 1995; Leonard 1995). This is not as straightforward as it might appear. For example, a referee must be very careful about how he or she handles a request for a report on a previous employee who has been dismissed for poor performance or misconduct. Inaccurate reporting might lead to the referee's being sued for defamation (Muchus 1992). A job applicant might also sue the prospective employer if he or she perceived the selection process as inequitable. The *Commonwealth Privacy Act 1988*, the *Freedom of Information Act* and equal opportunity legislation applies to the recruitment and selection process in Australia, protecting the rights of applicants and their referees. It ensures that information gathered during the recruitment and selection process remains confidential and that the process of gathering the information is handled with due care by everyone involved.

Given that applicants usually suggest their own referees (Compton & Nankervis 1998), whether clients, customers or previous supervisors, 'credential distortion' is also an issue in the recruitment and selection process. Naturally, they are likely to submit names only of referees who will provide favourable reports of their work performance. In order to ensure that the credentials of the applicant do not become distorted, it is important to select more than one referee nominated by the applicant, and to make sure that all the relevant questions are asked (Barada 1996; Perry 1995; Leonard 1995).

Information gathered through reference checking affords the prospective employer an opportunity to review the candidate's past performance and to verify the information provided by the candidate. This provides a broader picture of the applicant's experience, skills and behavioural competencies, and should facilitate the hiring decision.

Survey research evidence in Australia suggests that 90 per cent of organisations use systematic reference checking as part of their selection process (Compton & Nankervis 1998). In a recent study of 432 manufacturers in Queensland, Wiesner and McDonald (1998) found that only 3 per cent of respondents to their survey did not check prospective employees' references. The results of a national recruitment and induction practice survey undertaken by the Australian Graduate School of Management and CCH in 1994 found that the telephone interview was the most frequently used method of reference checking in Australia (CCH 1994).

Interviews

This selection technique is discussed in detail in this section owing to the popularity of selection interviews and the wide use of interviews by all organisations. Research shows that the interview is the most frequently used aid in the selection process (Graves & Karren 1996; Kramar, Mcgraw & Schuler 1997; Campion, Pusell & Brown 1988; Maurer & Fay 1988; Raza & Carpenter 1987). Most organisations use this method for selection.

An interview is a two-way communication process between a job applicant and a potential employer. From the employer's viewpoint it is an opportunity to meet with applicants and assess their personality, competencies and appearance and the manner in which they conduct themselves. It is also an opportunity to discuss, confirm and expand on the information already provided by the applicant via an application form or letter. At the same time the interview allows the applicant an opportunity to assess the job and the organisation to see whether they suit his or her needs.

An interview usually involves a face-to-face meeting between the candidate and the employer. However, a recent innovation in interviewing uses computers to conduct preliminary screening. Typically, a computer-aided interview has about 100 questions and can be completed in less than 20 minutes. More sophisticated versions generate information about the candidate's intelligence, leadership qualities, verbal assertiveness, drive, emotional control and other personal attributes (Abernethy 1997). A well-designed computer interview avoids the weaknesses of a face-to-face interview such as the interaction between interviewer and interviewee. However, Martin and Nagao (1989) found that applicants for higher level positions felt that more

personal attention was warranted. This method is therefore best suited for use as an initial screening device for lower level positions (Stone 1998).

Another innovation in employment interviewing is the use of videoconferencing (Galen & Kroenck 1995; Johnson 1991). This procedure is particularly useful for organisations wishing to interview interstate or overseas candidates. It can save management time as well as accommodation and transport costs. Some candidates may be reluctant to be video interviewed; the main complaint seems to be the lack of feedback and of the human element (Rimmer-Hurst 1996).

Despite increased access to computers and other technology, the face-to-face interview remains the most widely used technique for employment selection. Milia and Smith (1997) found that 99.6 per cent of Australian organisations participating in their survey used face-to-face interviews as part of their selection process.

Types of interviews

Compton and Nankervis (1998, p. 178) identified five different types of face-to-face interview. These were:
- structured or directive interviews
- unstructured or non-directive interviews
- panel interviews
- stress interviews
- group interviews.

In the *structured or directive interview*, which Sawyers (1992) claimed is the most widely used type of interview, the interviewer(s) asks each candidate a series of specific questions from a list that includes an assessment rating to help summarise the information obtained during the interview. Research indicates that the structured interview provides more accurate results than those gained from an unstructured approach, particularly because it ensures consistency, which facilitates the evaluation and comparison of applicants (Campion, Pursell & Brown 1988; Starke 1996). It is also the easiest type of interview for an inexperienced interviewer to conduct and is considered the most time-efficient method for interviewing. The main disadvantage of using a structured interview is that its rigidity can limit the information-gathering process. Instead of exploring an applicant's responses by further questioning during the interview, the process is often rushed in order to get through all the questions on the schedule, and the assessment of the applicant can be inaccurate as a result. Also, since the interviewer takes the lead during the interview process, he or she may sometimes dominate the process, denying the applicant sufficient time to provide a considered and accurate response (Compton & Nankervis 1998).

In an *unstructured or non-directive interview* the questions tend to be unplanned, following the lead of the applicant rather than the interviewer. The main advantage of a less structured interview is that the applicant may be more relaxed and may therefore provide more considered responses. The main disadvantage is the difficulty of controlling the interview. With the discussion drifting towards irrelevant or less important topics, important questions may not be asked. Also, since the questions asked of each applicant will differ, it is very difficult to make meaningful comparisons between applicants (Campion, Pursell & Brown 1988).

In a *panel interview* the applicant is usually questioned by a group of two or more interviewers. This group may include the HR manager, a department head and other departmental staff. This is an expensive method of interviewing, particularly because of the time lost to the organisation while panel members are interviewing. Aside from cost, the other main disadvantage of the panel interview is that the applicant may feel intimidated and outnumbered, and may therefore not perform well in the interview. This method is generally used in large organisations and for high-level and managerial positions. Its main advantage is a greater likelihood of impartiality and reliability, since the panel needs to reach a consensus of opinion about the outcome of the interview. Also, one panel member might notice something missed by the others (Cascio 1991).

The *stress interview* is often used at the second or third interview stage for jobs in the diplomatic or military services. The main purpose of such an interview is to assess how the individual will behave in an emotionally stressful situation. In a stress interview the interviewer may initially appear casual and relaxed, then become openly hostile and critical of the applicant's character and performance, before once more adopting a relaxed and informal manner. In this way the interviewer can examine the applicant's behaviour under stress, and the time taken to recover his or her composure. This technique requires a very skilled interviewer, and it has limited applicability to SMEs. Indeed, there is a risk that a suitable applicant would find this approach offensive and objectionable, and might even consider withdrawing his or her application.

The *group interview* is often used in an assessment centre situation. In this instance, a number of applicants are brought together for a set time period and are assigned to participate in various activities, such as solving a business problem. The applicants are then observed for their qualities of leadership and adaptability and their problem-solving and interpersonal skills. The main advantage of this method is being able to observe and compare applicants' behaviour, responses and interactions over an extended period. Its main disadvantage is the considerable time and effort required to set up and run such an event.

Despite its wide acceptance and popularity, recent research suggests that the interview is not a particularly effective predictor of future performance success (Martin & Lehnen 1992). Its low reliability and validity relates to the subjective nature and complexity of the variables affecting the interview process. The interaction between interviewer and interviewee will differ from interview to interview. Interviewer skills will vary, and the personality of each party will affect the candidate's responses (Spector 1996). Multiple interviewers may also have difficulty agreeing on their evaluation of the candidate's potential (Fisher, Schonfeldt & Shaw 1996). Compton and Nankervis (1998) succinctly summarised the complexity of the variables affecting an interview. Their findings are outlined in table 14.1.

Table 14.1: Variables affecting an interview

Features of the applicant	Features of the interviewer	Features of the environment
Physical appearance	Physical appearance	Interview structure and type
Personal characteristics (age, sex, race etc.)	Personal characteristics (age, sex, race etc.)	Role of interview (whether supplemented by tests, reference checks etc.)
Interview experience/training	Interview experience/training	Outside forces (e.g. political, social, cultural, economic)
Verbal/nonverbal behaviour	Verbal/nonverbal behaviour	Number of applicants
Education/work experience	Education/work experience	Physical aspects of interview (e.g. location, timing, length, privacy, number of interviewers, forms used etc.)
Psychological aspects (attitude, motivation etc.)	Psychological aspects (attitude, motivation etc.)	
Ambitions, career plans, interests	Knowledge/ perception of job requirements	
Perception of job, organisation, interviewer	Interviewing experience and training	
	Knowledge of applicant	

Source: Compton and Nankervis (1998), 134–5.

Despite its difficulties, the selection interview has many advantages for employers. These include the following:

- It can be an effective screening technique when there are many applicants.
- It can provide a means for further probing the results of psychometric testing (e.g. work motivation).
- It is an opportunity to inform the applicant about the organisation.
- It is an opportunity to meet with the applicant face-to-face to consider the person–environment fit (although this does not guarantee a successful placement).
- It is a relatively 'easy' means of considering and reviewing applicants for employment.
- It is a chance to elicit information that can be checked by other means such as reference checks and medical examinations.

Psychological, aptitude and ability testing

A number of different psychological, aptitude and ability tests are available for use in Australia for screening purposes during a selection process. They may either form part of a battery of tests or stand as a single test for use by recruitment consultants, organisational psychologists or HR managers. The results of psychological, aptitude and ability tests should not be the only criteria used for selection (Anonymous 1997; Murphy & Shiarella 1997). Rather, they should be viewed as additional sources of information on a job applicant's specific skills, competencies and aptitudes. Aptitude and ability tests attempt to match applicant and job requirements. Examples of such tests include tests of mechanical and clerical ability and manual dexterity. When these tests relate to the job they tend to be more accurate predictors of particular skills needed (Murphy & Davidshofer 1991). Psychological, aptitude and ability testing can be undertaken either before or after the selection interview. The tests chosen as part of the selection process need to accurately reflect job content outlined in the job description, advertisements and the selection criteria (Murphy & Shiarella 1997; Murphy & Davidshofer 1991).

Psychological, aptitude and ability tests used as part of a selection process are defined as:

an objective and standardised measure of a sample of applicant behaviour in order to determine job suitability and predict future job performance. (Anastasi 1988, p. 23)

The three main types of tests used in selection are:
- *general ability tests*, which measure the job applicant's verbal, numerical, spatial, coordination and perceptual skills

- *specific aptitude or work sample tests*, which measure specific skills such as keyboard or machine operation required to perform the job
- *'personality' or psychological profile tests*, which assess individual personality characteristics.

Examples of general ability and aptitude tests include computer and office skill tests and the mechanical concept test. Examples of personality tests include the Minnesota Multiphasic Personality Inventory, the California Psychological Inventory, the Cattell 16PF Questionnaire and the Myers-Briggs Type Indicator (Hogan & Roberts 1996; Gardner & Martinko 1996). Well-designed and job-relevant tests, used properly, can inject a measure of objectivity into the selection process. They can also be extremely useful as a screening device, saving time and effort when there are many applicants for a specific job (Lawson 1996).

Only reliable and valid tests should be used in selection. Test reliability refers to the ability of the test to yield consistent results each time the test is used. Test validity refers to the degree to which the test measures what it purports to measure. Ignorance about these aspects could expose the organisation or individuals conducting the selection process to the possibility of litigation if an applicant feels he or she has been discriminated against.

As already stated, although psychological tests can be very useful, they should not be used as the sole criteria for assessing an applicant's suitability for a job; rather, they should be viewed as predictors of future job performance (Martin & Lehnen 1992). It is unwise to reject an applicant on the basis of test results who appears to be acceptable on all other criteria, because there are numerous problems associated with using psychological tests for selection. For example, psychologists themselves disagree about the concept of 'personality' since no adequate definition has been agreed on. Other criticisms of personality testing include the potential for dishonesty, test 'anxiety' or 'faking' of applicant responses (Martin & Lehnen 1992). More recently, selection tests have been scrutinised under equal opportunity legislation for their job relevance (Dessler et al. 1999). The types of tests used depend on the type of job applied for, the cost of the test and the qualifications of the candidate (Hicks 1991; Lawson 1996).

Medical examinations

A medical examination is usually conducted by a medical doctor approved and paid for by the organisation. Its main purpose, of course, is to obtain medical information about the candidate. Stone (1998, p. 235) summarises possible uses for this information as:

- ensuring that people are not assigned to jobs for which they are physically unsuited

- safeguarding the health of present employees through the detection of contagious diseases
- ensuring that applicants are not placed in positions that will aggravate an existing medical condition
- protecting the organisation from workers' compensation claims by identifying injuries and illnesses present at the time the employee was hired
- determining the applicants' eligibility for group life, health and disability insurance.

Pre-employment medical examinations are not a prerequisite for employment in all organisations. They are used only when the employer is able to demonstrate that a legitimate job requirement is involved. Only then will EEO authorities sanction their use (National Committee on Discrimination in Employment and Occupation 1984). AIDS and drug testing remain controversial issues (Walsh & Maltby 1996). In a national policy statement the Confederation of Australian Industry, the National Occupational Health and Safety Commission and the ACTU recommend employers against testing their staff for AIDS (Stone 1998).

Assessment centres

In contrast to their low usage in Australian organisations (Vaughan & McClean 1989; Patrickson & Haydon 1988), assessment centres have been widely used in the United States for recruitment and selection purposes (Shippman, Hughes & Prien 1988). Some evidence suggests use of these centres in large Australian organisations grew rapidly in the 1990s (Kramar, Mcgraw & Schuler 1997), although they are considered time-consuming and expensive to run (Gatewood & Field 1998).

An *assessment centre* usually consists of a number of different selection activities run back to back over a period of one to three days. For example, job applicants may be interviewed by a panel, undergo a battery of psychological tests including intelligence, aptitude and personality testing, and be presented with an 'in basket' exercise or a role-play activity. The main purpose of such an exercise is to collect more in-depth and detailed information about the applicant.

Assessment centres can be very useful when undertaking large-scale recruitment and selection — for example with the opening of a new large manufacturing operation or mine. They can also help organisations identify and assess individual and organisational strengths and limitations after a merger or downsizing. Here the main purpose is to discover where 'the talent pool lies' (McGibbon & Ball 1997).

Issues in selection design and decision

An individual or group of individuals within or outside the organisation can undertake the design of the selection procedure and decision. This procedure generally takes place before recruitment and selection begin (Gatewood & Field 1998). The issues to be considered in selection design include: what information will be provided to possible candidates; how this information will be presented; who will be involved in the applicant reviewing process; and how the review will be undertaken.

The selection design approach to be adopted depends to a large extent on the resources available to the organisation. In a small organisation the owner or manager will probably take responsibility for the recruitment and selection of new employees as well as the promotion of existing employees. Other members of the organisation may be consulted or included in this process, but research within SMEs has shown that the owner or manager usually assumes all HR responsibilities (Marlow & Patten 1993). As the size of the organisation increases, so does the likelihood that an HR manager and/or department will take on this role (Wiesner & McDonald 1998). Not only is this likely to increase the use of a more formalised recruitment and selection design, but it is more likely that a team approach will be adopted to undertake this process.

Team members may include an HR manager or a representative from the HR department in the case of a larger organisation; in a smaller organisation, the section or departmental head seeking the new employee, or a line manager or supervisor, is typically included in the process. Other significant members of the organisation may also be involved. If an external agent, such as a recruitment consultant, has assisted in recruitment and selection, he or she would certainly be engaged in the design and execution of the process. However, the final selection decision rests with the organisation.

Conclusion

Globalisation, advances in technology, labour market conditions and the legislative framework in which organisations operate have created an external environment dominated by increasing competition. Not only are organisations facing greater challenges from their external environment, but their internal environment now presents them with as many challenges. Central to the management of these challenges is the effective management of human resources. It is easier for organisations to duplicate competitors' technology or manufacturing processes than to replicate their unique combination of human resources. It is critical for organisations to hire the right mix of employees in terms of their knowledge, skills and abilities, for without the right blend of people the organisation would find it difficult to achieve its missions and strategic objectives. Indeed, its very survival could be jeopardised.

The organisation's first major challenge in effectively managing their human resources is the attraction and selection of the right employees. Other HRM activities, including compensation, training and development, and performance appraisal, will follow on once the right employee has been recruited.

The internal and external environments in which organisations operate present them with many challenges, among them decisions on how to handle the recruitment and selection process, which method is best suited to achieving success and who should be involved in this process. Furthermore, recruitment and selection is not simply a one-sided activity, for while the organisation assesses prospective employees, the candidates are also seeking to determine whether the organisation will meet their needs.

The variety of recruitment and selection methods available, the advantages and disadvantages of each and the bilateral nature of the process add to the complexity of the decision-making process. Making the appropriate choices is the greatest contemporary challenge facing organisations.

References

Abernethy, M (1997) The selector weeds out corporate pretenders. *Australian Financial Review*, 14 March, 54.

Abernethy, M (1999) Jobs down the line. *Bulletin*, 20 April, 72–5.

Anastasi, A (1988) *Psychological Testing* (6th ed.). Englewood Cliffs, NJ: Prentice Hall.

Anonymous (1996) Email us your CV please? *Management Today*, September, 21–4.

Anonymous (1997) Send in number 95 … *Management Today*, April, 9–11.

Anonymous (1997) IPD advises employers not to base recruitment decisions solely on the results of personality tests. *Journal of Managerial Psychology*, 12 (3/4) 220–22.

Anonymous (1998) Recruiters take up the net and improve their catch. *Management Today*, March, 13–14.

Anthony, WP, Perrewe, PL, and Kacmar, KM (1996) *Strategic Human Resource Management* (2nd ed.). Florida: The Dryden Press, Harcourt Brace College Publishers.

ASCO (1997) *Australian Standard Classification of Occupations, Second Edition Manual Coding System: Occupational Level*. Cat. no. 1220.0. Canberra: Australian Government Publishing Service.

Bainbridge, J (1998) How do I fill the job? *Management Today*, February, 82–4.

Barada, P (1996) Reference checking is more important than ever. *HR Magazine*, November, 41 (11) 49–51.

Bennett, B (1998) Download a job. *Bulletin*, 24 November, 58.

Blau, GL (1987) Using a person–environment fit model to predict job involvement and organizational commitment. *Journal of Vocational Behavior*, 30, 240–57.

Borman, WC, Hanson, MA, and Hedge, JW (1997) Personnel selection. *Annual Review of Psychology*, 48, 299–338.

Bowen, DE, Ledford, GE Jr, and Nathan, BR (1991) Hiring for the organisation, not the job. *Academy of Management Executive*, 5 (4) 35–51.

Bretz, RD Jr, and Judge, TA (1994) Person–organisation fit and the theory of work adjustment: implications for satisfaction, tenure, and career success. *Journal of Vocational Behavior*, 44, 32–54.

Bretz, RD Jr, Rynes, SL, and Gerhart, B (1993) Recruiter perceptions of applicant fit: implications for individual career preparation and job search behavior. *Journal of Vocational Behavior*, 43, 310–27.

Brown, M (1993) Checking the facts on a résumé. *Personnel Journal*, January, 72 (1) 6–8.

Brumback, GB (1996) Getting the right people ethically. *Public Personnel Management*, Fall, 25 (3) 267–77.

Burgoyne, JG (1993) The competence movement: issues, stakeholders and prospects. *Personnel Review*, 22 (6) 6–13.

Cable, DM, and Judge, TA (1996) Person–organisation fit, job choice decisions, and organisational entry. *Organisational Behavior and Human Decision Processes*, 67, 294–311.

Callander, P (1999) Technology outpaces recruiters. *HR Monthly*, May, 54.

Campion, MA, Pusell, ED, and Brown, BK (1988) Structured interviewing: raising the psychometric properties of the employment interview. *Personnel Psychology*, Spring, 25–42.

Cascio, WF (1991) *Applied Psychology in Personnel Management* (4th ed.). Englewood Cliffs, NJ: Prentice Hall, 276.

Caudron, S (1994) Team staffing requires new HR role. *Personnel Journal*, May, 73 (5) 88–94.

Caudron, S (1999) Nothing's trivial about people issues. *Workforce*, January, 78 (1) 23–6.

CCH Australia (1994) National Survey of Human Resource Practices. *Human Resource Management,* 78 (1) 1461–94.

CCH (2000) Newsletter no. 109, Australian & New Zealand Equal Opportunity Law and Practice, 27 January.

Chatman, JA (1991) Matching people and organisations: selection and socialization in public accounting firms. *Administrative Science Quarterly,* 36, 459–84.

Compton, RL, Morrissey, WJ, and Nankervis, AR (2002) *Effective Recruitment and Selection Practices* (3rd ed.). Sydney: CCH.

Dessler, G, Griffiths, J, Lloyd Walker, B, and Williams, A (1999) *Human Resource Management.* Sydney: Prentice Hall.

Dunn, PA (1995) Pre-employment referencing aids your bottom line. *Personnel Journal*, February, 74 (2) 68.

Edwards, JR, and Cooper, CD (1990) The person–environment fit approach to stress: recurring problems and some suggested solutions. *Journal of Organisational Behavior*, 11, 293–307.

Ellerby, A, and Barrett, K (1999) Increased costs eat into profits: findings from the 1999 Annual Info HRM Benchmarking Report. *HR Monthly*, June, 22–6.

Fischer, CD, Schoenfeldt, FF, and Shaw, JB (1996) *Human Resource Management* (3rd ed.). Boston, MA: Houghton Mifflin, 326.

Flanagan, DJ, and Desphande, SP (1996) Top Management's perceptions of changes in HRM practices after union elections in small firms. *Journal of Small Business Management*, October, 23–34.

Flynn, G (1995) Overall cost per hire is still on the rise. *Personnel Journal,* December, 74 (12) 26–7.

Flynn, G (1996) CISCO turns the internet inside (and) out. *Personnel Journal*, October, 75 (10) 28–34.

Galen, A, and Kroenck, K (1995) Video conferencing maximises recruiting. *HR Magazine*, August, 40 (8) 70–72.

Gardner, WL, and Martinko, MJ (1996) Using the Myers-Briggs type indicator to study managers: a literature review and a research agenda. *Journal of Management*, 22 (1) 45–83.

Gatewood, RD, and Field, HS (1998) Human Resource Selection (4th ed.). Florida: The Dryden Press, Harcourt Brace College Publishers.

Golhar, DY, and Desphande, SP (1997) HRM practices of large and small Canadian manufacturing firms. *Journal of Small Business Management*, 35 (3) 30–39.

Granovetter, MS (1974) Getting a job: a study of contacts and careers. Cambridge, MA: Harvard University Press.

Graves, LM, and Karren, RJ (1996) The employee selection interview: a fresh look at an old problem. *Human Resource Management*, 35 (2) 163–80.

Greengard, S (1998) Putting online recruiting to work, *Workforce*, August, 77 (8) 73–7.

Hearn, G, Close, A, Smith, B, and Southey, G (1996) Defining generic professional competencies in Australia: towards a framework for professional development. *Asia Pacific Journal of Human Resources*, 34 (1) 44–62.

Hicks, RE (1991) Psychological testing in Australia in the 1990s. *Asia Pacific Journal of Human Resource Management*, 29 (1) 94–101.

Hitt, M, Ireland, RD, and Hoskisson, RE (1995) A mid-range theory of the interactive effects of international and product diversification on innovation and performance. *Journal of Management,* Summer, 2, 297–326.

Hogan, J, and Roberts, BW (1996) Personality measurement and employment decisions. *American Psychologist*, 51 (5) 469–77.

Hunt, JB, and Wallace, J (1997) A competency-based approach to assessing managerial performance in the Australian context. *Asia Pacific Journal of Human Resources,* 35 (2) 52–6.

Jasper, M (2000) Recruitment from the other side. *HR Monthly*, September, 44–5.

Johnson, M (1991) Lights, camera, interview. *HR Magazine*, April, 36 (4) 68.

Jones, N (1996) People still look where the jobs are — in the newspapers (still). *HR Monthly,* May, 18–19.

Kirk, D (1999) A systems approach. *HR Monthly*, June, 43.

Kleinman, LS, and Clark, KL (1984) An effective job posting system. *Personnel Journal*, February, 20–25.

Kramar, R, Mcgraw, P, and Schuler, RS (1997) *Human Resource Management in Australia*. Melbourne: Addison-Wesley Longman.

Kristof, AL (1996) Person–organisation fit: an integrative review of its conceptualizations, measurement, and implications. *Personnel Psychology*, 49, 1–49.

Kydd, C, and Oppenheim, L (1990) Using human resource management to enhance competitiveness: lessons from four excellent companies. *Human Resource Management,* Summer, 29 (2) 145–66.

Laabs, J (1998) Pick the right people. *Workforce*, November, 77 (11) 50–53.

Lado, AA, and Wilson, MC (1994) Human resource systems and sustained competitive advantage: a competency-based perspective. *Academy of Management Review,* October, 19 (4) 699–727.

Lawson, M (1996) Why psych tests are just the job, *Australian Financial Review*, 24 June, 1.

Leighton, J (2001) Executive Contracting. *HR Monthly*, December, 32–3.

Leonard, B (1995) Reference checking laws: now what? *HR Magazine*, December, 40 (12) 57–62.

Levy, H (1999) Making the most of online recruitment. *HR Monthly*, May, 50.

Lundy, O (1994) From personnel management to strategic human resource management. *The International Journal of Human Resource Management*, 5 (3) 687–720.

Main, A (2001) How to turn goodbye into a victory song, *Australian Financial Review*, 27 October, 31.

Marlow, S, and Patton, D (1993) Managing the employment relationship in the smaller firm: possibilities for human resource management. *International Small Business Journal*, July–September, 11 (4) 57–64.

Martin, SM, and Lehnen, LP (1992) Select the right employees through testing. *Personnel Journal*, June, 71 (6) 46–50.

Maurer, SD, and Fay, C (1988) The effect of situational interviews and training on interview rating agreement: an experimental analysis. *Personnel Psychology*, Summer, 329–44.

McEnvoy, GM (1984) Small business personnel practices. *Journal of Small Business Management*, October, 1–8.

McGibbon, A, and Ball, A (1997) Assessment centers or assassination centers? *HR Monthly*, June, 32.

Meglino, BM, Ravlin, EC, and Adkins, CL (1989) A work values approach to corporate culture: a field test of the value congruence process and its relationship to individual outcomes. *Journal of Applied Psychology*, 74, 424–32.

Milia, D, and Smith, P (1997) Australian management selection practices: why does the interview remain popular? *Asia Pacific Journal of Human Resources*, 35 (3) 90–103.

Mitchell, B (1998) Private problems, *Age*, Employment Section 6, 25 July, 1–2.

Moos RH (1987) Person–environment congruence in work, school, and health care settings. *Journal of Vocational Behavior*, 31, 231–47.

Morehead, A, Steele, M, Alexander, M, Stephen, K, and Duffin, L (1997) *Changes at Work: the 1995 Australian Workplace Industrial Relations Survey*. Melbourne: Addison-Wesley Longman.

Muchus, G (1992) Check references for safer selection, *HR Magazine*, June, 37 (6) 75–7.

Murphy, KR, and Davidshofer, CO (1991) *Psychological Testing* (2nd ed.). Engelwood Cliffs, NJ: Prentice Hall, 329–30.

Naidoo, M (1997) Poor hiring policy can prove costly. In G Dessler, J Griffiths, B Lloyd Walker and A Williams (1999), *Human Resource Management*. Sydney: Prentice Hall.

Nankervis, AR, Compton, RL, and McCarthy, TE (1996) *Strategic Human Resource Management* (2nd ed.). Melbourne: Thomas Nelson.

Neiger, D (2000) Vendors weave web into new releases. *HR Monthly*, September, 20–21.

Neiger, D (2000) Putting the HRIS into SMEs. *HR Monthly*, November, 38–9.

O'Reilly, CA, Caldwell, DF, and Mirable, R (1992) A profile comparison approach to person–job fit: more than a mirage. Academy of Management Best Papers Proceedings, 237–41.

O'Reilly, CA, Chatman, JA, and Caldwell, DM (1991) People and organisational culture: a Q-sort approach to assessing person–organisation fit. *Academy of Management Journal*, 34, 487–516.

Ostroff, C (1993) Relationships between person–environment congruence and organisational effectiveness. *Group & Organisation Management*, 18, 103–122.

Patrickson, M, and Haydon, D (1988) Management selection practices in South Australia. *Human Resource Management in Australia*, 26 (4) 96–104.

Peake, D (1994) Competency analysis provides a bridge for HR. *HR Monthly*, 24 April.

Perry, C, Riege, A, and Brown, L (1998) Realism rules OK: paradigms in marketing research about networks. *Proceedings of the Australian and New Zealand Marketing Academy Conference*, University of Otago, Dunedin.

Pfeffer, J (1995) Producing sustainable competitive advantage through the effective management of people. *Academy of Management Executive*, 9 (1) 55–72.

Pithers, RT, Athanasou, JA, and Cornford, IR (1995) Development of a set of Australian occupational descriptors. *Asia Pacific Journal of Human Resources*, Spring/Summer, 33 (3) 140.

Rance, C (1997) Cost savings for councils using Internet for tenders and staff recruitment. *Age*, Employment Section, 8 March, H16.

Raza, SM, and Carpenter, BN (1987) A model of hiring decisions in real employment interviews. *Journal of Applied Psychology*, November, 596–603.

Reddin Consulting (2000) Standing room only. *HR Monthly*, December, 46.

Rimmer-Hurst, R (1996) Video interviewing — take one. *HR Magazine*, November, 41 (11) 100–104.

Rose, S (1999) Placing job ads that work. *HR Monthly*, May, 46–9.

Rutherford, PD (1996) *Competency Based Assessment: A Guide to Implementation*, Melbourne: Pitman, p. 158.

Rynes, SL, and Gerhart, B (1990) Interviewer assessments of applicant 'fit': an exploratory investigation. *Personnel Psychology*, 43, 13–35.

Sawyers, PC (1992) Structured interviewing: your key to the best hires. *Personnel Journal,* December, 71 (12) 1–4.

Schwab, DP, Rynes, SL, and Aldag, RJ (1987) Theories and research on job search and choice. In KM Rowland and GR Ferris (Eds), *Research in Personnel and Human Resources Management,* 5, 129–66. Greenwich, CT: JAI Press.

Shippman, JS, Hughes, GL, and Prien, EP (1988) Raise assessment centre standards. *Personnel Journal,* July, 69–79.

Skilled Engineering Limited (1999) Annual Report to Shareholders.

Sparrow, PR (1997) Organisational competencies: creating a strategic behavioural framework for selection and assessment. In N Anderson and P Herriot (Eds), *International Handbook of Selection and Assessment.* Chichester, UK: John Wiley & Sons.

Spector, PE (1996) *Industrial and Organisational Psychology.* Chichester, UK: John Wiley & Sons, 120.

Starke, AM (1996) Tailor interviews to predict performance. *HR Magazine,* July, 41 (7) 49–54.

Stickels, G (1994) The right stuff: standards for model managers. *Business Review Weekly,* 6 June, 90–91.

Stock, S (1998) *Weekend Australian,* Recruitment Section, 25–26 July, 33.

Stone, RJ (1998) *Human Resource Management* (3rd ed.). Brisbane: John Wiley & Sons.

Stumpf, SA, and Hartman, K (1984) Individual exploration to organisational commitment or withdrawal. *Academy of Management Journal,* 27, 308–329.

The Enterprising Nation (The Karpin Report) (1995) Industry Task Force on Leadership and Management Skills. Canberra: Australian Government Publishing Service.

Vancouver, JB, and Schmitt, NW (1991) An exploratory examination of person–organisation fit: organizational goal congruence. *Personnel Psychology,* 44, 333–52.

Vaughan, E and McClean, J (1989) A Survey and Critique of Management Selection Practices in Australian Business Firms. *Asia Pacific HRM,* 27 (24) 20–34.

Visser, CF, Atlink, MM and Algera, J (1997) From job analysis to work profiling — do traditional procedures still apply? In N. Anderson and P Herriot (Eds), *International Handbook of Selection and Assessment.* Chichester, UK: John Wiley & Sons.

Walsh, JM, and Maltby, LL (1996) Is workplace drug testing effective? *HR News,* April, 15 (4) 5.

Wiesner, R, & McDonald, J (1998) Managing organisational change through teams: implications for SMEs. Proceedings of ANZAM 1998.

Wiesner, R, and McDonald, J (1997) Organisational change and enterprise bargaining in regional SMEs. In T Bramble, B Harley, R Hall and G Whitehouse (Eds), Current Research in Industrial Relations, *Proceedings of the 11th AIRAANZ Conference,* 30 January–1 February, Brisbane, 485–92.

Wright, PM, and Snell, S (1991) Toward an integrative view of strategic human resource management. *Human Resource Management Review,* 1, 203–225.

Wright, PM, McMahan, C, and Williams, A (1994) Human resources and sustained competitive advantage: a resource based perspective. *International Journal of Human Resource Management,* 5 (2) 301–326.

The rhetoric and reality of e-cruitment: has the Internet really revolutionised the recruitment process?

by Susan Hinton
Monash University

Introduction

The spectacular growth in the Internet employment industry, if we are to believe claims made in the business press, has created a revolution in the way employers recruit staff at a time when recruiters are faced with labour market conditions that necessitate increasingly aggressive, targeted and expensive recruitment activities (Sunderland 2000; Piturro 2000; Thomas & Ray 2000). Internet-based recruitment methods are faster, cheaper and more effective than traditional, paper-based recruitment methods.

Whether you are a graduate applying for an entry-level position on line, a recruitment consultant embarking on a specialised recruitment campaign or a currently employed job seeker ready to post her résumé on line, it is hard to ignore the impact of the Internet on the recruitment process. Today, as organisations face massive changes in their environments brought about by the growth of technology and increased competition, the recruitment process is seen as a strategic component of the human resource (HR) function (Stone 1998).

In an environment characterised by uncertainty and change, an organisation's survival and ongoing success will depend on managers' ability to attract, select and retain workers who have the skills, qualifications, experience and values necessary to achieve the organisation's strategy (Stone 1998, pp. 174–6). Within this context, Internet-based recruitment methods are changing the way people come together and communicate in the job market (see, for example, Bigelow 1999; Jones 2000; Rudich 2000).

E-cruitment is the application of technologically sophisticated tools and techniques to facilitate staff recruitment. Internet-based computer technologies are used to advertise job vacancies; search, sort and categorise résumés; and match job applications to vacant job positions, thereby eliminating the need for newspaper advertisements and manual search activities (Rothstein 1999; Stone 1998).

While the pundits enthuse about the cost and time savings of e-cruitment and calculate the competitive advantage derived by recruiters who use Internet recruitment methods, Thomas and Ray (2000) caution that the Internet should not be viewed as a staffing panacea. Sandilands (2000) argues that many of the claims made by proponents of e-cruitment are naive in that they fail to take account of the challenges that e-cruitment presents to recruiters along with the advantages.

More important, Internet recruitment methods raise a number of crucial issues yet to be explored in detail in the literature. Although the explosive growth of the Internet has facilitated communication across the globe, not everyone has access to the Internet. This is an issue for employers who seek a diverse pool of job applicants and for job seekers wanting the best chance of finding suitable employment. Privacy is also an issue. Once job seekers or employers place confidential personal or business information in the public realm via the Internet, they forfeit control over who has access to it (Thomas & Ray 2000; Fisher 2000; Radcliff 2000).

To develop a better understanding of the challenges and advantages e-cruitment offers managers and HR professionals, we first need to survey the claims made by proponents of e-cruitment. What are the costs and benefits of e-cruitment? To what extent do recruiters rely on the Internet as a recruitment tool, and for what purpose? What kind of recruitment outcomes does e-cruitment provide?

This chapter addresses these questions by first providing an overview of 'e-cruitment' as it is popularly[1] understood, and then examining claims that it is an effective, low-cost alternative to traditional (face-to-face and paper-based) recruitment methods. After this discussion we take a short break to surf the Net and learn what Internet job sites have to offer employers and job seekers. The chapter then goes on to argue that despite the hype surrounding the popularity and effectiveness of e-cruitment methods, the take-up of Internet technology in the recruitment industry is relatively slow. The evidence suggests that many businesses still rely on a mix of cyber-free technologies and traditional recruitment methods to assist them in their staffing activities. The point to be made here is that e-cruitment is better understood as a new method of recruitment (one of many available to employers) that brings new challenges to an already complex and increasingly strategic process (Thomas & Ray 2000; Rothstein 1999).

The chapter concludes by examining a number of important issues for job seekers, employers and HR professionals that arise out of recruitment, an already extremely complex and important HR function. These are privacy, access and diversity.

The growth of the Internet and the rise of e-cruitment

The Internet has experienced phenomenal growth across Western industrialised nations[2] over the past 10 years (Slevin 2000, p. 40). According to Slevin (p. 40), the total number of Internet users worldwide numbered between 150 and 180 million at the end of 1999. This figure is expected to rise to 1 billion by 2005. Research conducted in Australia indicates that in February 2001 52 per cent of Australian adults used the Internet and 89 per cent of 16- to 20-year-olds regularly log on to their favourite websites (Lowe 2000).

E-commerce, the development of Internet-based businesses, has been part of the Internet revolution; the growth of Internet-based job sites and employment advertising over the Internet is also part of this revolution. In the United States the predicted turnover of the electronic recruitment market (a market that did not exist in 1995) in 2001 was US$7.5 billion (Interbiznet 2001). Internet job advertisement statistics continue to show strong growth as employers struggle to recruit suitably qualified workers to fill available job positions in the face of a severe skills shortage (Thomas & Ray 2000; Rothstein 1999).

In Australia the Internet employment industry is growing steadily. During the year 2000, 200 000 job seekers lodged their résumés on the Internet, and the number of Internet job advertisements placed by recruitment agencies and employers doubled (Sunderland 2000). A simple search of Australian corporate web sites and commercial job sites can take the interested job seeker to information about career and employment opportunities in a multitude of industries.

The changing context of recruitment

The growth and acceptance of Internet-based recruitment methods must be understood in terms of the environments in which they were developed. Employers in the US information technology industry first used the Internet as a recruitment tool to attract IT professionals during the 1990s. At a time when there was a severe shortage of skilled labour, the Internet offered employers eager to recruit qualified staff in an extremely competitive labour market a fast, cost-effective and efficient alternative to traditional methods (Thomas & Ray 2000).

The reasons for the successful take-up of Internet-based recruitment methods in the IT industry are easy to identify. IT employers had the tools and technology to communicate with people in the industry, and were already linked into and familiar with the Internet. At the click of a mouse button, employers had almost instant access to a large pool of suitably qualified potential applicants. In this context, the Internet was an appropriate and efficient recruitment method when compared with more costly and time-consuming word-of-mouth or print-based search methods.

The rise of Internet recruitment across other industries has been similarly influenced by significant environmental changes. Technological innovation, rapid change, expanding markets and globalised competition have changed the ways in which work is performed. The 'new workplace' (Rothstein 1999) brought about by these changes is characterised by changes in attitudes to work, life-long careers and permanent

---

1. In the absence of academic research in the area, much of the evidence for these claims comes from articles found in business and professional magazines and journals.
2. The growth in countries outside Western Europe, the United States and Japan is less spectacular, accounting for about 1 per cent of total Internet traffic (Slevin 2000, p. 40).

employment. Firms are increasingly operating with a two-tier workforce made up of a small, highly flexible and broadly skilled 'core' of permanent workers who work side by side with a contingent workforce made up of contractors and temporary employees who contribute to the organisation on an as-needed or just-in-time basis (Piturro 2000). Consequently, job markets now consist of a growing number of workers who compete for outsourced non-core work previously performed by permanent, career-oriented employees (Rothstein 1999, p. 69–73).

Demographic changes and skills shortages have contributed to an increasingly volatile and uncertain labour market. The baby boomers are getting older and leaving the workforce, while the next generation of workers is much smaller, creating a shortage of skilled labour (Hale 1999; Leonard 2000; Way 2000). Demographic factors have been particularly important in shaping labour market conditions in the United States, where the mismatch between workers' skills and the skills demanded by employers has created a structural imbalance in the labour market (Rothstein 1999; Hale 1999; Toppy 1999; Thomas & Ray 2000).

The implications of these changes for staffing are significant. The job of attracting, recruiting, selecting and retaining workers is difficult and potentially expensive. Employers seeking qualified workers must widen their searches — a potentially expensive exercise — and must be able to respond quickly to secure staff when they find them. Also, many employers face increasing costs in terms of handling and sorting through greater volumes of job applications and résumés (Rothstein 1999, p. 69).

In response to these conditions, employers are constantly searching for a competitive edge in their recruitment efforts; the Internet, if we are to believe the pundits, offers employers the advantages they are looking for. It promises lower costs, speed and instant access to a huge pool of computer-literate job seekers (Thomas & Ray 2000; Rothstein 1999; Toppy 1999).

Before we move on to examine the claims that Internet recruitment methods are cheaper, faster and more effective than traditional methods, it might be useful to conduct a brief survey of the Internet to see what it has to offer employers, HR professionals and job seekers.

Online job sites: what does the Internet offer?

On-line recruitment sites offer a vast array of services, ranging from a relatively simple noticeboard listing of available positions (the equivalent to print-based employment pages) to web sites managed by professional recruitment consultants. A well-resourced professional recruitment site typically offers a sophisticated range of tools including a résumé builder, career advice, on-line psychological and aptitude tests, and advice on taking tests and interview techniques.

Alternatively, you can log on to the Internet and search for some niche sites managed by professional associations and interest groups. For example, if you are a graduate engineer you can access the Institution of Engineers Australia site (www.ieaust.org.au/members/career.html) and find information on career development, career counselling, résumé preparation, outplacement advice and job search strategies. This site also has links to other niche (as well as more general) job sites including New Generation Australia (www.nga.net.au), an online system specifically set up to link engineering students and graduates with employers from their preferred industry in the engineering sector.

You can also access a host of dedicated commercial employment sites, such as hotjobs.com and monster.com, if you are looking for new job prospects. These sites vary enormously in the kinds of information and services they offer, as well as ease of use. Some sites simply offer a job bank service where employers post jobs and potential candidates can search the site according to location and/or type of work. The sites listed here offer a sophisticated range of products and services including a résumé builder, career information and career or job expo sites, where employers and potential candidates can meet and greet in cyberspace.

Many large corporations offer employment links on their corporate web sites. BHP-Billiton (www.bhp.com), for example, has a link on its corporate home page to a 'People and Recruitment' page. The page contains information about the company's graduate recruitment program and provides prospective recruits with an online application form. The links to employment opportunities in Coles Myer (www.colesmyer.com) are rather more difficult to find. First you have to access the Coles Myer corporate web page, which then takes you to one of the company's business sites. For example, by clicking on the Bi-Lo site you can find information about Bi-Lo's retail trainee programs and career pathways at Bi-Lo.

The Internet affords you instant access to overseas corporate employment sites, too, if you are looking for a career further afield. If you visit the Texas Instruments site in the US (www.ti.com), for instance, following the prompts will help you match your skills and experience to available positions by taking you to a page that provides job descriptions for each vacant job position (Rothstein 1999).

Some sites offer job seekers chat rooms and/or newsgroup services. The New Generation site (described above) offers a chat room service for engineering students and graduates. HRNet in the US offers a newsgroup site for job seekers and HR professionals.

Interbiznet (www.interbiznet.com) offers an extensive range of information, newsletters and reports for those interested in Internet recruitment. You can subscribe (free) to the *Interbiznet Bugler*, an Internet recruiting newsletter delivered by email several times a week. The service offers news about employment statistics, recently published articles and data about Internet recruitment, and information about unusual recruitment sites (see, for example, www.6figurejobs.com for those who are aiming high in the job market, or http://NeuroHub.com for online career and staffing services for neurologists and pain medicine specialists). The site also provides HR professionals with information about software innovations and improvements to help them develop their Internet recruitment programs.

Finally, government-provided or -sponsored sites offer services for job seekers, employers and professional recruitment organisations. The Recruitment Consulting Services Association (http://rcsa.com.au/) is the peak body that represents the recruitment consulting industry in Australia. This site, which provides a gateway to Australian Job Search (http://jobsearch.gov.au/), a job network set up by the Commonwealth Government, offers job seekers a range of employment services including information on apprenticeships, volunteer work, Indigenous employment, skills training and retraining, and help for unemployed job seekers.

E-cruitment: advantages, disadvantages and challenges

The Internet offers employers and job seekers a comprehensive and diverse range of tools, techniques and services. However, it is still unclear whether the Internet, with all its bells and whistles, provides effective and efficient recruitment outcomes. The review of the literature (such as it is) offers at best a 'two steps forward, three steps back' account of the advantages and disadvantages derived from e-cruitment. For nearly every benefit or advantage gained from Internet-based recruitment methods identified in the literature there are corresponding costs, disadvantages and/or challenges (see, for example, Thomas & Ray 2000; Rothstein 1999).

The most popular and oft-cited claim is that Internet-based recruitment technologies and tools offer employers and professional recruitment agencies a competitive advantage in the employment market. This claim is based on the belief that Internet recruitment methods increase the quality and size of the applicant pool, lower recruitment costs and increase the speed of the recruitment process, thereby improving recruitment outcomes (Thomas & Ray

2000; Menagh 1999; Bigelow 1999; Rothstein 1999; Zall 2000). The following discussion will examine each of these sources of advantage and identify the disadvantages or challenges that simultaneously arise from them.

Increase in the size and quality of the applicant pool

Proponents of e-cruitment argue Internet recruitment methods increase the size of the applicant pool because the Internet offers a communication medium that transcends regional, state, international and even temporal boundaries that limit more traditional print-based recruitment methods (Thomas & Ray 2000; O'Connell 1996; Toppy 1999).

Writers argue that e-cruitment methods are far superior to traditional 'manual' recruitment methods because they facilitate access to a diverse, computer-literate and highly skilled pool of potential job candidates who regularly visit Internet sites to look for jobs (LaVine 2000; Rudich 2000). Thompson and Ray (2000) claim that while there is no doubt that the Internet increases the *quantity* of applicants, there is little evidence to suggest that their *quality* is any higher. The best applicants do not automatically log on to the Internet in search of a job vacancy.

The experience of the IT industry has demonstrated that the Internet is a very good means of recruiting highly skilled technical workers; however, it has proved to be of limited success in the recruitment of certain types of job applicants. Those who visit job sites are not necessarily active job seekers, whereas passive job seekers — those already employed and not actively looking for a job — may be bypassed. Internet-based recruitment methods are also not very successful for recruiting senior or executive positions; in this sector, traditional search methods are often more useful for attracting suitable candidates. Similarly, when employers are looking for job seekers located within a specific geographic area, local advertising may be more effective than a message broadcast on a job site (Thomas & Ray 2000; Piturro 2000).

More important, increasing the size of the applicant pool does not automatically ensure that the applicant pool is more diverse. This claim has implications for the quality of recruitment outcomes for recruiters wishing to access a pool of applicants with a wide range of skills and experience. Any bias built into the recruitment process will not only reduce employers' choice but also risk potential legal problems as a result of possible breaches of equal employment and anti-discrimination legislation.

This issue requires further research and discussion, because there is strong evidence to support the view that Internet-generated applicant pools are relatively homogeneous. Recent research in the area of 'e-business' and 'e-entrepreneur' activity reveals that Internet-based activities remain very much a 'guy thing' — more men than women use the Internet for a range of activities including finding a job (Cave 2000). The stereotypical Internet user is male, highly educated, affluent, young (average age 35 years) and white and resides in a metropolitan area of a Western industrialised nation (Slevin 2000, p. 42; Rothstein 2000, p. 76). In the United States more males than females access the Internet and the largest proportion of Internet users are aged between 18 and 34. Seventy-five per cent of Internet users are college educated, and they usually work in computer-related, professional and management positions (Slevin 2000, pp. 40–1).

In Australia the characteristics of Internet users mirror those in the US: 89 per cent of 16- to 20-year-olds use the Internet, and usage is highest in households with middle to high levels of income (Red Sheriff 2000); only 21 per cent of households with incomes below $35 000 have Internet access; men are the heaviest users, and women in the 50+ age bracket are least likely to use the Internet, even if they have access to a computer (Red Sheriff 2000).

Another source of homogeneity in the applicant pool reflects the gap between 'information haves' and 'information have nots', particularly in countries such as Australia and the United States (Slevin 2000; Red Sheriff 2000). From a global perspective, countries outside the Western industrialised nations account for approximately 1 per cent of Internet usage (Slevin 2000, p. 40). This gap has an ethnic as well as an economic dimension. In the United States there is a large gap between Internet access and usage of African Americans and white Americans (Slevin 2000, p. 42). In Australia these patterns are repeated across categories such as gender, economic class and geographic location (Red Sheriff 2000, p. 2).

These statistics bring into question the view that Internet recruitment offers organisations competitive advantage in terms of access to a large group of diverse applicants, although they do support the view that those who access the Internet tend to be well-educated, career-oriented professionals. Nonetheless, an argument can be made that Internet recruitment is very restricted in that it is accessing a relatively homogeneous group of job seekers and ignoring older applicants, women, and applicants from lower socioeconomic groups and minority groups (Rothstein 2000, p. 76).

Increased speed and reduced costs

E-cruitment is believed to lower recruitment costs and increase the speed at which employers can post and fill a job vacancy (Jones 2000; Piturro 2000; Toppy 1999). But does it? There is very little hard evidence to support claims that e-cruitment lowers recruitment costs or that it produces better recruitment outcomes than traditional methods (Thomas & Ray 2000; Jones 2000; Piturro 2000).

Evidence from the United States indicates that Internet recruiting has cut the cost of hiring senior staff by about US$5000 and has sped up the process by one-third (Way 2000). Menagh (1999) and Daniels (1997) confirm this trend. Moreover, the trend towards posting basic HR services on line is lowering costs by letting computers do some of the menial, mundane work previously undertaken by recruitment staff. The shift away from print media to the Internet has produced major cost savings because not only is it much cheaper to lodge a job advertisement, but the medium has a much wider, more comprehensive reach than daily newspapers. Time savings are also made because employers are not constrained by newspaper deadlines and publication schedules.

Much of the discussion about cost savings, however, does not account for areas of potential cost increases. Online job advertisements are cheap and can be posted or deleted at the click of a mouse button, and job seekers can respond almost instantaneously by filling out online applications and emailing their résumés. But with technology-enabled speed comes the potential for additional costs — for example the cost of handling large numbers of job applications and inquiries efficiently and effectively. Internet-generated increases in the quantity of responses to job advertisements need to be supported by sufficient staff to process inquiries and applications; otherwise any gains will soon be lost as staff become overloaded and systems begin to collapse. Moreover, job seekers expect a prompt response and employers — particularly those facing a tight job market — must be able to provide prospective candidates with a timely response to their inquiries. To derive competitive advantage from speeding up the recruitment process, Internet recruitment programs must be supported by increased investment in resources, including staff, technology and structures to handle the influx of responses to job postings (Thomas & Ray 2000).

Employers also derive savings from being more efficient in their HR management practices. Some organisations have saved on hiring agency fees by using the Internet to manage their own recruitment programs. Others use Internet-based technologies to achieve a better match between current staff and existing job vacancies, thereby retaining staff and saving money on unnecessary recruitment programs (Toppy 1999). For businesses that rely on contract labour or consultants, the Internet provides fast and efficient access to employees on demand, enabling employers to better manage 'just in time' recruitment practices (Piturro 2000; Toppy 1999).

Taking up the technology, including software development and hiring the staff to support and service the website, can add significant costs. The savings offered by Internet recruitment methods rely on the installation of fast and modern computer hardware as well as sophisticated and appropriate screening and sorting software to ensure the system works with accuracy, convenience and speed (Jones 2000; Piturro 2000; O'Connell 1996).

Competitive advantage

While there can be no doubt that the Internet offers employers advantages, Thomas and Ray (2000) argue that any competitive advantage derived by firms is quickly whittled away by competitors who copy sites and use the same or similarly powerful software. Nonetheless, there is some evidence that small to medium-sized enterprises gain a competitive advantage over larger organisations by using Internet recruitment methods. This is because they are able to advertise their job vacancies more widely and at a lower cost than the more traditional print-based methods. Also, by utilising Internet technology, small to medium-sized organisations may make themselves appear more attractive to job seekers through the use of well-designed websites.

In the absence of hard data, the jury remains out on whether organisations enjoy a sustained competitive advantage through the use of Internet recruitment methods (Thomas & Ray 2000). Currently, we have only anecdotal evidence and some limited statistical information to support the view that e-cruitment offers employers effective recruitment outcomes. Similarly, there is scant empirical evidence to support the view that Internet-based screening; sorting and evaluating technologies generate better outcomes than traditional manual methods. Therefore, although we might speculate that employers derive cost and time savings from the technological sophistication of the recruitment process, we cannot predict this outcome with any certainty.

Other contemporary issues

A number of other issues arise from the growing use of Internet recruitment methods. These issues are not well covered in the literature, but they need to be highlighted to encourage further discussion and research.

Over-reliance on technology

Technological innovation in the recruitment process is both expensive and risky, and although database software and search engines are improving all the time, there are limits to the technology that must be acknowledged. Writers are beginning to ask whether technology-rich e-cruitment tools are losing sight of the human aspects of the recruitment process, ignoring the importance of social networks and face-to-face contact as essential elements in the search for suitable job candidates (Rothstein 1999; Miller & Cardy 2000).

Rothstein (1999) emphasises the importance of a two-way exchange of information between the job candidate and employing organisation and argues that over-reliance on the technological aspects of Internet recruitment may compromise this important stage in the recruitment process. Prospective employees require information about the job and the organisation in order to decide whether their skills match the job position and whether they want to leave their present job and join a new organisation. On the other hand, employers need to meet job candidates not only to evaluate whether they are the 'right' candidate for the job but also to ascertain whether the job seeker's values and attitudes match those of the hiring organisation — to ensure a good fit between the person, the job and the organisation (see also Way 2000).

Privacy

There are privacy implications for both employers and job seekers to placing information in the public realm. The Internet offers limited privacy protection; according to Piturro (2000), job sites are routinely 'mined' by consultants and recruiting organisations looking for interesting résumés.

Job seekers on commercial job board sites have no control over who accesses their résumés once they are posted in cyberspace. This means that job seekers may face unwanted approaches from recruitment consultants or risk being discovered looking for new positions by their current, Internet-literate bosses. Corporate sites, on the other hand, are more reliable because employers have more control over their own sites, and the likelihood of résumés moving beyond the individual site is low (Thomas & Ray 2000; Anonymous, 2000).

Employers also face privacy risks by placing important staffing and commercial information on the Internet. The ability to access important information about business operations or staffing plans may provide opportunities for competitors to gain competitive advantage.

Summary and implications for HR management, organisations and employees

In the absence of empirical research on the operation and efficacy of e-cruitment it is difficult to judge the degree to which employers and recruitment consultants are making extensive use of the Internet for their recruitment needs. Moreover, it is almost impossible to judge the quality of Internet recruitment outcomes in order to compare Internet recruitment with more traditional recruitment methods. The current literature, drawn mostly from the business press and HR industry journals, offers at best mixed messages about the success and effectiveness of Internet recruitment compared with traditional print-based and face-to-face recruitment methods.

Despite the rhetoric about the enthusiastic take-up of Internet-based recruitment methods, there is no real agreement or statistical evidence on the degree to which people rely on e-cruitment as their prime method of recruiting staff (Thomas & Ray 2000). Stewart (1998, cited in Thomas & Ray 2000) states that HR professionals are slow to take up Internet technology because of a lack of expertise and understanding of what the Internet has to offer. Piturro (2000) cites statistics that indicate that only 2 per cent of employment advertisements in the United States are placed on the Internet. Similarly, Menagh (1990) argues that many recruitment consultants have taken up 'cyber-free' technologies — for example videoconferencing and teleconferencing — to facilitate their recruitment efforts.

The message for HR professionals is clear. Internet recruitment presents HR practitioners with the challenge to develop ways of working with technology to achieve quality recruitment outcomes. HR practitioners need to consider the cost of removing the human element from the recruitment process and finding ways to address this issue of how to automate the process and still bring job seeker and employer face to face in the early stages of the recruitment process (Rothstein 1999).

For organisations, managers must consider the cost of using sophisticated technology to achieve recruitment outcomes. The cost of hardware, software, human technical expertise and technical support must be assessed when planning an online recruitment campaign.

There are also serious access issues. Organisations must ensure that their Internet recruitment methods yield a diverse and representative pool of applicants. Current research indicates that those who log on to the Internet are a relatively homogenous group defined by age, sex, income and ethnic demographics.

Those employees who use the Internet as a job search tool must be aware of the limits of Internet-based search and match software as well as the lack of human contact that characterises the early stages of Internet job searches (see, for example, Fisher 2001). By posting a résumé on the Internet the job seeker sacrifices control over who can access vital information about themselves. Employees also face the problem of how to differentiate themselves from other job seekers in cyberspace. There is a risk that a job seeker's posted résumé may fail to be picked up in searches by appropriate recruiting organisations.

Future directions

More research needs to be conducted into the operations and outcomes of Internet-based recruitment methods; only then can we move beyond the hype surrounding 'e-cruitment' to a better understanding of the advantages and limitations of Internet-based recruitment. The literature suggests that firms tend to use a range of recruitment methods depending on the recruitment task and the environment in which they are operating.

E-cruitment may be considered by hiring organisations as a legitimate recruitment method alongside a number of more traditional 'cyber-free' processes depending on the needs of the organisation. For example, Internet-based recruitment methods may be used when a manager is looking for highly qualified technical workers or when an organisation is faced with a mass recruitment task such as the Sydney Olympics. Similarly, there is evidence that the Internet is extremely effective for managing graduate recruitment programs. On the other hand, when organisations are seeking to recruit senior or executive staff, traditional, personal network and search methods may be more appropriate.

References

Anonymous (2000) 'More pros and cons to Internet recruiting', *HR Focus*, May, 77(5), 5.

Bigelow, M (1999) Recruitment online: reinventing the process. *Ohio CPA Journal*, July–September, 58 (3) 30–32.

Click, J (1997) Blend established practices with new technologies. *HR Magazine*, November, 59–64.

Conhaim, WW (1998) The Internet as an employment resource. *Link-Up*, 1 November, 5–14.

Fisher, A (2001) Enjoy being unemployed? Keep job hunting online. *Fortune*, January, 143 (2) 164.

Goldsborough, R (2000) Job hunting on the Internet. *Link-Up*, November/December, 17 (6) 23.

Hale, B (1999) The staff squeeze. *Business Review Weekly*, May, 76.

Holley, R (1999) Despite the Web, recruiting is still a contact sport. *Computer Reseller News,* December, 125.

IBN (Internet Business Network) (1999) Electronic recruiting index: the industry matures, Executive Summary, www.interbiznet.com (Road Mill Valley, CA).

Jones, S (2000) Logged on … or hands on. *HR Monthly*, December, 42–5.

LaVine, J (1999) How to land a job using the Web. *R & D Magazine*, April, 42 (4) E25–6.

Leonard, B (2001) Quality of online recruiting sites vary widely. *HR Magazine*, February, 46 (2) 32.

Lowe, I (2000) Australia's e-generation takes shape. Red Sheriff: www.redsheriff.com.

Menagh, M (1999) IT cost per hire: finding Net (and other) savings. *Computerworld* 18 January, 44.

Millers, J, and Cardy, R (2000) Technology and managing people: keeping the 'human' in human resources. *Journal of Labour Research*, 21 (3) 447–61.

O'Connell, S (1996) Technology in the employment office. *HR Magazine,* August, 41 (8) 31.

Piturro, M (2000) The power of e-cruiting. *Management Review*, January, 33–6.

Radcliff, D (2000) Diary of an online job seeker. *Computerworld,* July, 34 (31) 36–7.

Rothstein, H (1999) Recruitment and selection: benchmarking at the millennium. In A Kraut and A Korman (Eds), *Evolving Practices in HRM: Responses to a Changing World of Work*. San Francisco: Jossey-Bass.

Rudich, J (2000) Job hunting on the Web. *Link-Up*, March–April, 17 (2) 21.

Sandilands, B (2000) Net hunters spinning a tangled web. *Australian Financial Review*, 6 December, 2.

Slevin, J (2000) *The Internet and Society*. Cambridge: Polity Press.

Stone, R (1998) *Human Resources Management* (3rd ed.). Brisbane: John Wiley & Sons.

Sunderland, K (2000) The rise and rise of e-cruitment. *HR Monthly*, December, 34–41.

Thomas, SL, and Ray, K (2000) Recruiting and the Web: high tech hiring (Industry Overview). *Business Horizons*, May, 43 (3) 43.

Toppy, S (1999) Cyber-savvy recruitment. *Nursing Management,* February, 30 (2) 37.

Way, N (2000) A new world of people power. *Business Review Weekly,* June, 62.

Zall, M (2000) Internet recruiting. *Strategic Finance*, June, 81 (12) 66–72.

CHAPTER 16

Reward philosophy, workplace climate and performance management: three key issues in implementing a 'total reward' framework

by Graham O'Neill
Hay Group

Introduction

Typically, when we think of employee rewards, we focus on direct remuneration such as wages and salaries, bonuses or incentive payments, and perhaps other financial benefits such as superannuation and employee share plans. This traditional perspective is founded on a rational economic view of the employment contract based on payment for time and services, underpinned by relative work value and the notion that further monetary opportunity (in the form of performance incentives) will encourage greater productivity.

There are three major problems with this approach. First, the orthodox rational economic view of behaviour is widely seen as out of touch with modern economic thinking (for example, see Heilbroner & Milberg 1995; Ormerod 1994). Second, the empirical evidence for linking pay to performance is at best inconclusive, and where it is positive, it is typically associated with factors that are intrinsic to the work and work environment (see O'Neill 1995 for a comprehensive review). Third, and more generally, the world of work has moved on. In the challenge to attract, develop and retain talented and capable employees at all levels, organisations will need to acknowledge these traditional remuneration components as only one part of the answer in the context of a need for more innovative solutions to employee reward (Wright 2001).

Paradoxically, this is potentially good news for employers. Few organisations can absorb the continuous upward push of fixed costs indefinitely and remain profitable. Further, pay and pay-based incentives are often the least effective

retention mechanism because they can be — and are — matched by competitors. This means that the investment required needs to be directed at a better understanding of the needs and wants of those employees required to ensure the sustained success of the enterprise.

The problem is that many private and public sector organisations are relatively uninformed of the needs of their workforces. Many have spent the past two decades downsizing, outsourcing and restructuring. The notion of loyalty between employer and employee has largely disappeared, leaving the workforce distrustful and suspicious of employer actions and motives. Advances in technology, the decline of job security and greater demands on remaining employees heighten their concerns and anxiety. Add to this the huge increase in dual income families, single parents, and generation and cultural differences, and we have a social framework in the work environment that is radically different from that of 20 years ago. For employers, this workforce diversity further invalidates the 'one size fits all' reward programs of the past.

Remuneration is clearly an important element in the employment contract. We don't need to test the proposition that if you stop paying people, they won't come to work! But when pay is set at levels perceived by employees to be internally and externally fair and equitable, other non-financial criteria assume a greater influence in attraction and recruitment. Issues generally reported by employees to be important in their employment decisions include *interesting and challenging work, opportunities for training and further development, reputation of the employer, workplace climate* and issues related to *work–life balance* (see, for example, Onsman 1999; Prewitt 1999; Tabakoff 2000).

What is reward 'best practice'?

Before proceeding further, it is relevant to address the meaning of 'best practice' in the broader reward area. The notion of 'best practice' grew out of the Total Quality Management movement (TQM) in the mid to late 1970s. A major tenet of the approach to quality, particularly in manufacturing and like environments, is the necessity for process and outcome measurement and comparison against selected external benchmarks. This measurement and comparison is a critical basis for system improvement. The external benchmarks are typically selected to represent best practice within an industry or comparator group where similar systems and processes are used. This provides a common and consistent process by which the individual firm can set targets and track progress.

Application of the term 'best practice' to remuneration gained currency in the mid to late 1980s and early 1990s. As new and innovative remuneration practices arrived, or in some cases were resurrected, they were often labelled 'reward best practice'. This was true of pay solutions ranging from *performance-based pay* (in its various forms), *skill- and competency-based pay*, *broadbanding* and *team-based pay* to *employee share/option plans* and a variety of *recognition schemes*.

No one or combination of these approaches to employee remuneration is inherently 'best practice'. They are pay solutions that may be adopted or modified depending on the organisation's business objectives, its commercial operating environment, culture, values and employees' needs. A reward solution that works for company A will not necessarily work for company B, even if it is in the same industry. The diversity and uniqueness of organisations means that reward programs need to reflect the environments in which they are to operate.

For these reasons, 'reward best practice' is best regarded as: *the deliberate and systematic integration of reward plans and programs with the company's culture and values, its business plans and objectives, and other people management processes, to maximise the motivational impact on employees and return on investment to the employer.*

The notion of 'total rewards'

Employers have always had the challenge of attracting, retaining, developing and motivating their employees. And while the charge has traditionally been led by remuneration, particularly through more competitive pay rates and performance bonuses, we know from a significant body of research since the 1950s that intrinsic rewards are also critically important. These rewards include the positive impact of job design, learning and development opportunities, management style, organisation climate and the general quality of work life in attracting and retaining staff, and winning their commitment to the organisation's broader goals and objectives (Campbell & Pritchard 1976; Pfeffer 1998).

If there is one major global trend in the broad arena of employee rewards, it is the growth of the idea of *Total Rewards*. In effect, this approach is aimed at providing a tailored and integrated approach encompassing direct remuneration, financial security and benefits, individual development, work environment and corporate image. Other labels used to capture the essence of this approach include *Employee Value Proposition*, *Employee Brand Proposition*, *Rewarding Work Environment*, *Employee Engagement* or the more traditional *Employer of Choice*.

Figure 16.1 illustrates a framework for thinking about the Total Rewards approach to designing a reward program.

Work environment
- Work culture and climate
- Management style
- Work design and flexibility
- Work relationships
- Work–life balance

Corporate image
- Company reputation
- Brand image
- Community standing

Direct remuneration
- Fixed pay
- Incentives
- Employer benefits
- Recognition plan

Personal development
- Performance management
- Professional development opportunities
- Career growth

Financial security
- Superannuation
- Employee share plan

Figure 16.1: Framework for planning a Total Reward program

Establishing a reward philosophy

Few companies have a clear statement of the philosophy and rationale underlying what they want their reward program to deliver to employees. Remuneration programs tend to evolve over time, usually through designing and managing individual components (e.g. wages, salaries, incentive or bonus payments, superannuation, share plans, car policy and other benefits available). Typically, these changes occur without consideration of how each individual element fits within the total package. As a result, the overall program is often independent of the business plans and objectives, and the company's work culture and values.

One of the surest ways to maximise the return on this investment is to develop a deliberate framework that includes all reward mechanisms available to the organisation. This strategy should define the role of each element in the reward process to achieve three specific objectives. These are to:

- directly promote and support the company's philosophy and values
- reinforce the short-, medium- and long-term business goals and objectives
- provide a basis for evaluating the effectiveness and return on investment of the reward program.

The starting point for developing a planned and systematic approach to establishing or reviewing the reward program is to provide clear answers to the following three questions:

- What does the company want its reward program to communicate to employees?
- What are the policy implications?
- What will be visible and meaningful to employees?

Consider the statement shown in figure 16.2 as an illustration of how one company attempted to address these three questions in developing a reward and recognition philosophy.

Figure 16.2: A reward and recognition philosophy

ACME MANUFACTURING LTD
REWARD AND RECOGNITION PHILOSOPHY

We acknowledge that the success of Acme Manufacturing is based on maintaining the committed engagement of all employees. And we know that it is important that the Company rewards and recognises people for their commitment. Our reward structure and processes are designed to meet four key values related to how we engage people in our enterprise; in this respect, we will:

1. Ensure that reward determination is fair and equitable with reference to internal and external comparisons.
2. Provide opportunities for employees to meet career development goals where these are consistent with the needs of the business.
3. Build direct links between Acme's financial performance and employee rewards.
4. Provide a constructive and supportive approach to planning, managing and assessing each employee's contribution to Acme's business objectives.

Acme Manufacturing Will Provide a Total Rewards Structure that:

- Is competitive with leading industry practice in the Australian manufacturing market;
- Has direct links between performance and individual and work group rewards;
- Encourages greater personal responsibility by reinforcing individual empowerment;
- Builds future capability at all levels;
- Supports multi-discipline teamwork;

- Provides an equal emphasis on recognition through non-financial rewards; and,
- Is based on transparency and open communication to maximise employee ownership and commitment.

Reward Principles
The following principles apply to the design of management reward structures to support this philosophy.

Internal Comparability — Fixed pay levels are based on established work relativities within job families/work streams underpinned by a consistent process for assessing work relativities at all levels.

Fixed Pay — The fixed component of pay is based on median pay for job size within the Australian manufacturing sector. Individual fixed pay is based on an employee's demonstrated level of acquisition — and consistent application — of competencies required for his/her role.

Performance-based Pay — Each employee's total remuneration consists of fixed and variable pay. The variable component is performance-based, and payable for achievement of agreed individual, work team, business unit and/or company objectives. Target performance-based pay levels will vary across employee levels and operating areas of the company.

Individual Choice — Employees will have the opportunity to 'salary sacrifice' their fixed pay to meet individual need within company guidelines.

(*continued*)

Performance Management — The performance management process defines and assesses employees against two work-related criteria:

- **Acquisition and application of specific knowledge, skill and behavioural requirements for the role**. Assessment in this aspect determines the individual development plan, and is used as part of the annual fixed pay review process.
- **Contribution to individual, team, business unit and/or corporate achievements**. Assessment of this aspect determines the variable, performance-based component of pay.

Performance assessment may involve ratings by supervisor, peers and subordinates depending on the nature of the role, employee level and work area within the company.

Career and Job Opportunity — Our commitment to building capability, through ongoing development of skill and competency levels, supports the aim of providing continual growth and development opportunities for employees at all levels. We will seek to provide career growth and challenge consistent with employees' capability and Acme's business requirements.

Open Communication — We believe that all employees have a right to know how their pay and other rewards are determined. Free and open communication also ensures that the company reinforces the principle of equity and fairness in reward determination and distribution.

Figure 16.3 is a useful tool for developing the final section of the blueprint. The matrix shown below can be used to audit an existing reward program, or as a basis for designing a new plan. Assuming a new plan is being designed, the matrix prompts the design team to consider the following issues:

- What is our overriding reward objective?
- What are the key focus areas required to meet this overriding objective?
- What reward components will be used to meet these objectives?
- How will each component contribute to meeting one or more of these objectives?

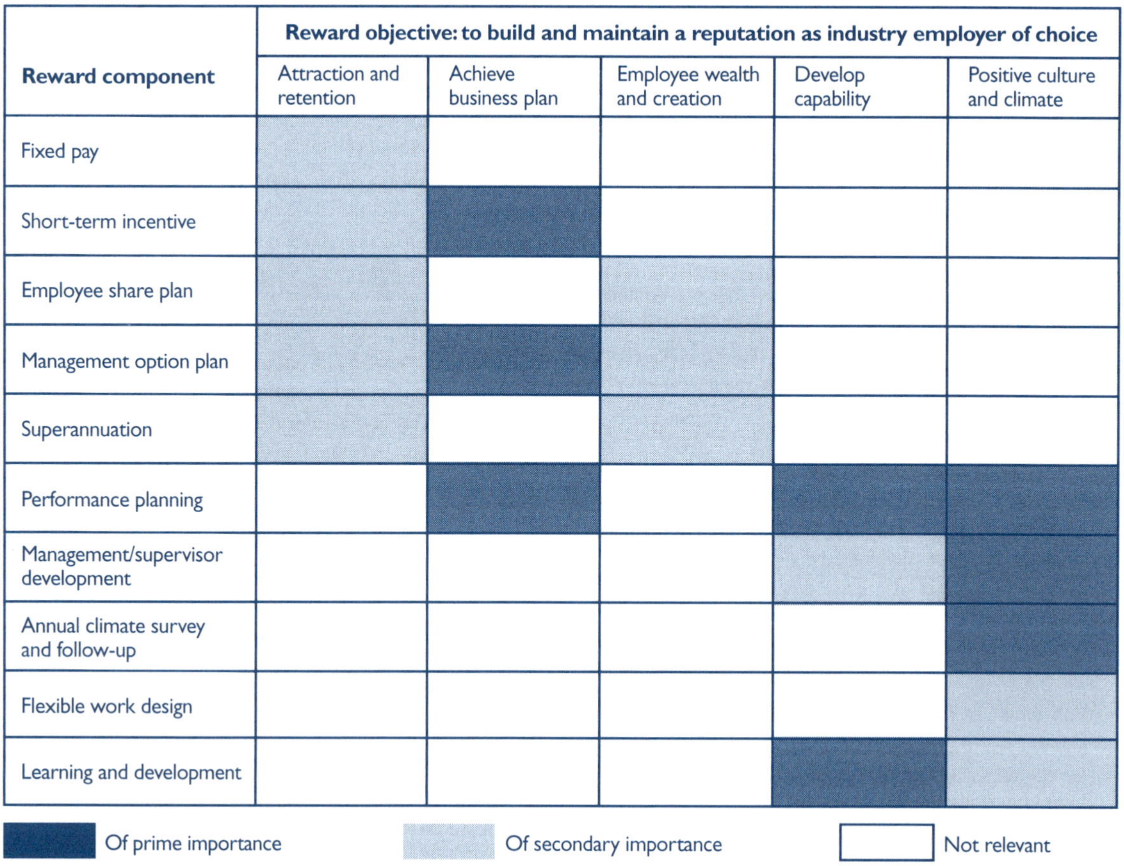

Reward component	Reward objective: to build and maintain a reputation as industry employer of choice				
	Attraction and retention	Achieve business plan	Employee wealth and creation	Develop capability	Positive culture and climate
Fixed pay	Secondary				
Short-term incentive	Secondary	Prime			
Employee share plan	Secondary		Secondary		
Management option plan	Secondary	Prime	Secondary		
Superannuation	Secondary		Secondary		
Performance planning		Prime		Prime	Prime
Management/supervisor development				Secondary	Prime
Annual climate survey and follow-up					Prime
Flexible work design					Secondary
Learning and development				Prime	Secondary

Legend: ■ Of prime importance   ▨ Of secondary importance   ☐ Not relevant

Figure 16.3: A reward strategy matrix

Culture, climate and management style

Intuitively, we all recognise that an organisation's culture and its workplace climate shape and determine much of the environment experienced by employees. But the terms themselves are not always distinguished clearly. Culture refers to the behaviours expected of people within the organisation; it is the established expectations that people have of each other, often expressed in terms such as 'This is what you can expect of your manager (or colleague), and this is what your manager (colleague) can expect of you'. Climate is an individual (or group) expression of what it feels like to be part of the organisation or work group, and is typically measured in employee attitude surveys. Culture is about expectations. Climate focuses on the individual's personal experience of the organisation.

Experience shows us that all organisations have a dominant culture. That culture may be the result of a systematic and planned process that articulates, communicates and reinforces expectations. Or, in the absence of a deliberate attempt to design a work culture, it may simply be acceptance and practice of the things you can get away with in the company.

Since 1997 the Hay Group has partnered with the US *Fortune* magazine to compile an annual listing of the world's most admired companies. In the 1998 survey (Kahn 1998), the firm asked teams of executives from the ten companies that ranked at the top of their industry sectors to complete their proprietary *Targeted Culture Modeling*[SM] instrument. The responses were compared with the Hay Group database of more than 300 international companies. The profiles of these top companies were dramatically different from the average corporations, as shown in figure 16.4 below.

Key priorities of top companies	Key priorities of average companies
• Teamwork	• Minimising risk
• Customer focus	• Respecting the chain of command
• Fair treatment of employees	• Supporting the boss
• Initiative	• Making budget
• Innovation	

Figure 16.4: Work culture priorities of top global companies compared with average companies

Not only did the top companies differ in their priorities, but they showed far more consistency within their senior teams than did executives in average firms. And it is the very issue of consistency and unanimity that defines a successful culture: *'We all understand it, we all believe it, and we all practise it!'*

Management style, organisation climate and the 'bottom line'

During the mid 1990s the Hay Group undertook separate global leadership and management development engagements with two major US multinational firms. In each instance, the firm was requested to evaluate the programs with particular reference to their impact on organisational outcomes. The firm's longitudinal study of each organisation included an assessment of the work climate created by managers within their work groups, and the contribution that this work climate made to the organisations' results. The results indicated that management style accounted for 68 per cent of the variance found within the work climate; in turn, work climate accounted for 28 per cent of the variance in organisation effectiveness. Put simply, managers create the climate that employees experience at work, and their experience of that climate accounts for almost one-third of the reasons why a company does or does not achieve its objectives.

These findings are reinforced by an article in the *Harvard Business Review* reporting on the link between employee attitudes and company performance at Sears Roebuck and Company (Rucci, Kirn & Quinn 1998). Over a five-year period, Sears had sought to radically transform its business as a means of dramatically improving its financial results. One key component of this process was to develop a model that tracked success from management behaviours through employee attitudes to customer satisfaction and financial performance. Sears acknowledge that management style is a primary driver of employee attitudes. The model developed includes an algorithm that follows the impact of employee attitudes on customer satisfaction, and the link between the customer satisfaction index and next quarter revenue. The illustration provided by the authors shows that a 5-point improvement in employee attitudes at a given store location will drive a 1.3-point improvement in customer satisfaction; which leads to a 0.5 per cent improvement in revenue for the next quarter.

The Hay Group's experience in working with clients on issues of management style and work climate over the past decade or so suggests some specific characteristics that differentiate a high-performing organisation:

- Expectations are clear.
- Employees understand how their jobs link to the broader picture.
- Performance standards are known and understood.
- Lines of accountability are clear.
- Goals are achievable but challenging.
- Performance is recognised.
- People demonstrate pride.

If we accept the proposition that people are the key to achieving success for any organisation (see, for example, Pfeffer 1998), then these work climate characteristics of successful enterprises represent 'enabling' processes for all employees. It is these workplace characteristics that make for a rewarding work environment.

Recognising and rewarding employee performance

An effective reward structure needs to recognise individual capability and performance contribution. Many firms have introduced performance-based pay programs as a means of recognising individual or work group contribution to organisation outcomes. However, attracting and retaining capable employees is becoming a critical issue for all organisations. As part of the reward framework, there needs to be recognition of the sustained performance and capability of executives, managers, senior professionals and high-value operational employees who have demonstrated their long-term value and future potential.

There are good reasons for designing a reward process to recognise the two issues separately. Too often the remuneration system unintentionally provides a 'double jackpot or double jeopardy' outcome. Employees who achieve their performance targets for the year maximise their incentive payments, and are consequently at the top of the list for pay increases. Conversely, employees who, for whatever reason, miss this year's targets also miss the incentive amount, and are likely to be given a low priority for pay increases.

Figure 16.5 illustrates a performance management and reward process that separates the two issues in terms of *inputs* and *outputs*. The input side aims to build and develop technical, professional and managerial capability across the organisation. It does this by allowing for an assessment of the person–job capability fit against predetermined requirements

for the role. Three criteria must be met to make this an effective and credible developmental process for individuals, and to deliver long-term gains to the firm. The input side must involve:

- a capability model that specifies the required level of skills, behaviours and competencies for each role
- a process that assesses individual capability against job requirements
- an outcome that can be translated into a level of fixed reward that appropriately recognises the individual human capital value of the person to the firm.

The output side is designed to reward people for their role in delivering outcomes to the company. Similarly, this side of the process also requires:

- a process that establishes performance outcome requirements at the beginning of the planning period
- a credible and defensible means of assessing achievements against target
- a transparent method for translating outcomes into financial recognition.

Reward structures are essentially a means of sending messages to employees. These messages are about what the organisation values, and how it recognises and delivers on those things. The approach outlined above is simply one way of using the direct remuneration program to differentiate between two things that are important: building future capability and recognising current contribution.

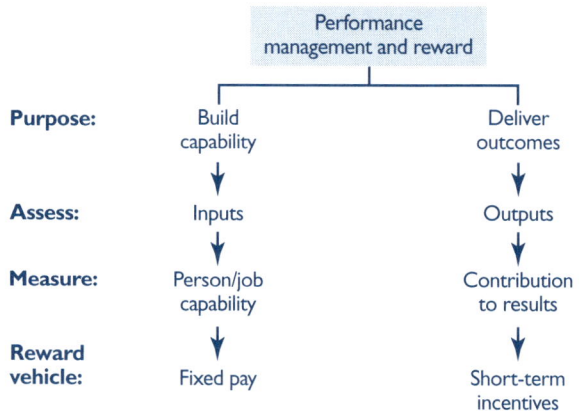

	Performance management and reward	
Purpose:	Build capability	Deliver outcomes
Assess:	Inputs	Outputs
Measure:	Person/job capability	Contribution to results
Reward vehicle:	Fixed pay	Short-term incentives

Figure 16.5: Using performance management to reward capability and achievement

Good practice for performance-based pay

There are two critical design factors related to performance-based pay at all levels within the organisation. In particular, where performance pay is applied under negotiated

Enterprise Agreements, the transparency of these factors provides comfort to the Australian Industrial Relations Commission. The two factors are *procedural justice* and *fairness of reward distribution* (see Greenberg 1986 for a detailed explanation). Both factors relate to the degree of credibility, defensibility and transparency of the system.

'Procedural justice', or due process, refers to the perceived fairness and equity in making decisions about performance. In essence, what are the rules and procedures by which decisions are made? Ultimately, the aim of any performance-based pay system is to discriminate in favour of higher performers. This requires a system by which performance is assessed. In turn, assessment itself requires a process that clearly establishes performance requirements. The most defensible design criteria to meet the requirements of *due process* include the following.

Accuracy of performance data

At a basic level this means that the performance requirements are established against measurable criteria relevant to the position. This does not mean that qualitative requirements (e.g. behaviours and capabilities) can't be set. It does mean that there must be a credible means of measuring and assessing performance against those requirements. It also means that issues need to be documented throughout the performance period. This documentation should not be limited to an annual — or even half-yearly — assessment process. Ongoing documentation, especially where there are performance shortfalls, provides reinforcement and support for any final assessment.

Rater bias

Rater bias (or, just as important, *perceived* bias) can occur in several ways. Most commonly, it is viewed as unfair bias against an individual and inconsistency across raters (i.e. one supervisor is seen as a 'harder marker' than another).

Employee input

Award-level performance management systems typically require formal processes for employee input. This is usually done in two ways: first, the employee has the opportunity to contribute directly to his or her own assessment (self-rating); and second, an aggrieved employee may seek resolution through formal channels.

'Fairness of reward distribution' refers to the way in which rewards contingent on performance are distributed to employees. In effect, how fair, consistent and equitable are the means that determine the distribution of outcomes to participants?

Perceptions of fairness can be looked at with respect to consistency among employees within any one work group, across the whole of the organisation, and over time (this year versus last year). Furthermore, fairness, equity and consistency also include notions of transparency and credibility regarding what the employee views as within or outside his or her control. This does not mean that profit sharing (for example) is not appropriate because no individual employee is likely to see his or her efforts as directly related to profit. It does mean that the full plan and rationale need to be communicated to all participants.

Issues in team-based performance management and reward

Managing team performance is a major issue with the growing trend towards team-based work structures. However, traditional approaches to performance management are individual, rather than group oriented. This distinction is particularly noticeable in organisations that have adopted quality and continuous improvement as strong cultural values and key performance indicators. Among significant criticisms of traditional performance appraisal methodologies applied to team structures are the following:

- Individual performance appraisal systems confuse people with systems and processes by assuming that the person being evaluated is primarily responsible for the results. This ignores the influence of work systems and processes in determining final outputs.
- Traditional appraisal systems focus on the individual's personal performance as evaluated by the supervisor. This is often inconsistent with the need to build and maintain teamwork, especially when employee performance appraisal is combined with individual rewards.

Performance appraisal overlooks continuous improvement when it focuses on individual goals and objectives as performance standards. This has three disadvantages:

(a) There is little incentive to exceed the set standard.
(b) The importance of continuous improvement is reduced when the focus is on setting absolute standards; the incentive is to keep the goal as low as possible.
(c) It encourages employees to focus on short-term achievements at the expense of longer term success.

- Appraisal systems can often 'blame' the individual when performance depends on factors outside his or her control. Most people depend on co-workers, equipment, operating policies and procedures, and a range of other factors that can adversely affect performance.

Tables 16.1 and 16.2 contrast traditional performance management processes and reward systems with those adopted by 'high involvement' organisations.

Table 16.1: Traditional versus high involvement performance management processes

	Traditional	High Involvement
Who appraises and sets performance standards?	Supervisor/Manager	Individual, supervisor, co-worker, internal and external customers
Whose performance is planned and appraised?	Individual employee	Individual employee, supervisor, work team, work process and systems
What is the basis for setting performance standards?	Individual job goals and standards set for employee	Performance levels are set for the work team and defined on the basis of business mission/ objectives, customers and nature of work processes and systems
What is the process for planning and managing employee performance?	Focus on review of individual's past performance. Directed by the supervisor and generally one-way communication. Minimum training is provided, usually limited to the appraiser. Process is administratively driven and annual.	Focus is on reviewing past, planning ahead and ensuring required resources are available. Mutual review encourages two-way feedback. Training provided to all participants. Reviews are periodic as needed and on natural performance cycles.
Why is the performance management process undertaken?	Personal development, identify training needs, succession planning and pay	Personal development, identify training needs, succession planning and pay. Feedback provided to team to identify and correct structural problems in work processes and systems leading to variance in output and quality. Individual receives feedback on personal team contribution.

Table 16.2: Linking performance and reward in high involvement organisations

Criticisms of traditional approaches	Performance management responses	Performance reward responses
Confuses people with the system and processes	Plan and manage performance of the system, processes and team.	Determine system and process baselines and reward for improvements to baseline standards.
Undermines team work	Focus on individual's contribution to the team and its goals.	Ensure work rewards are based on team performance.
Overlooks continuous improvement	Manage through goal setting, not goal achievement.	Ensure reward structures emphasise and pay for continuous improvement.
Short-term focus	Define goals in terms of corporate mission, business strategy and customer service criteria.	Design reward systems that pay on corporate mission, business strategy and customer service criteria.
Blames the individual	Assess team performance and allow team and individual self-ratings.	Reward the individual for contribution to team performance.

Implications for HR managers

For some years the Hay Group has used the phrase *People before Strategy* to draw attention to the primary importance of people in achieving organisational objectives. This is not simply a matter of making sure that the managing director's message in the company's Annual Report somewhere contains the (now somewhat tired) phrase 'people are our most important asset'. The true expression of the notion of *People before Strategy* can be seen in enterprises where people-oriented values predominate, and leaders manage these values to build and maintain high-performance work environments.

The concept of people as the key to success came out of the 1997 *Fortune* magazine survey of the world's most admired companies (Fisher 1997). Several basic themes emerged from a series of interviews with executives from companies that ranked at the top of their respective industry sectors:

- Top managers at the most admired companies take their mission statements seriously and expect everyone else to do likewise. Their mission statements form the basis of their culture and values, which in turn provides a basis for managing people.
- These companies see career development as an investment in their future success.
- They measure — and act on — employee opinion surveys. All these companies seem genuinely interested in what their employees think, and they use a variety of internal surveys and 360° evaluations to determine workforce satisfaction.
- The most admired global firms have clear programs that reward performance, and they value long-term more than short-term performance. This accounts for the fact that these companies show eligibility for options and share ownership schemes, as well as annual performance-based bonus plans.

This view of people in organisations runs counter to the traditional rational economic perspective with its emphasis on the need for control and financial incentives as the basis for managing employees. In the clearest sense, it is about providing a genuinely rewarding work environment that encourages employees to become committed to the objectives of the enterprise. This organisational approach contrasts significantly with that of firms that maintain a simplistic reliance on individual financial rewards as the basis for managing people and their work experience. As Pfeffer (1998, pp. 299–300) comments: 'Putting people first means having articulated values and goals, organizational language and terminology, measurements, role models in senior leadership positions, and specific practices that make real the noble sentiments so often honoured in the breach.' The implication for HR managers is to develop strategies that promote and reinforce such values in relation to the normal routines and behaviours of their organisations.

References

Campbell, J, and Pritchard, R (1976) Motivation theory in industrial and organizational psychology. In M Dunnette (Ed.), *Handbook of Industrial and Organizational Psychology*. Chicago: Rand McNally.

Fisher, A (1997) The world's most admired companies. *Fortune*, 27 October, 220–6.

Greenberg, J (1986) Organizational performance appraisal procedures: what makes them fair? In R Lewicki, B Sheppard and H Bazerman (Eds), *Research on Negotiation in Organizations*, vol. 1. Greenwich: JAL, 219–34.

Heilbroner, R, and Milberg, W (1995) *The Crisis in Modern Economic Thought*. Cambridge: Cambridge University Press

Kahn, J (1998) The world's most admired companies. *Fortune*, 26 October, 173–88.

O'Neill, G (1995) Linking pay to performance: conflicting views and conflicting evidence. *Asia Pacific Journal of Human Resources*, 33 (2) 20–35.

Onsman, H (1999) The secret of a happy office. *Business Review Weekly*, 11 June, 46–7.

Ormerod, P (1994) *The Death of Economics*. London: Faber & Faber.

Pfeffer, J (1998) *The Human Equation: Building Profits by Putting People First*. Boston, MA: Harvard Business School Press.

Prewitt, E (1999) To keep your star employees, try a little tenderness. *Business Review Weekly*, 3 September, 48–50.

Rucci, A, Kirn, S, and Quinn, R (1998) The employee–customer profit chain at Sears. *Harvard Business Review*, January–February, 83–97.

Tabakoff, J (2000) Happy workers: it's not just about money. *Age*, 16 August, 1–3.

Wright, V (2001) Reward for a new workforce. In C Fay, M Thompson and D Knight (Eds), *The Executive Handbook on Compensation: Linking Strategic Rewards to Business Performance*. New York: The Free Press, 75–85.

CHAPTER 17

Human resource development and the management of knowledge capital

by Brian L. Delahaye
Queensland University of Technology

Introduction

Twentieth-century management theories were predicated on the assumption that there were two basic resources — time and money. Furthermore, it was held that these two basic resources could be exchanged. For example, if a project was falling behind schedule, more equipment could be purchased or more staff hired to catch up. This old dictum is no longer true (Delahaye 2000).

Knowledge has now become an equally important resource. Unfortunately, there is no simple relationship between time and money, on the one hand, and knowledge on the other. Although gaining knowledge may take time and money, the relationship may be variable. Sometimes new knowledge costs nothing. A staff member may simply come up with a brilliant idea. On other occasions the new knowledge may have to be purchased. For example, someone with the new idea may have to be hired or a patent bought.

Complicating this relationship between the three basic resources is the fact that implementing the new idea will cost time and money. Further, this new idea will have to be maintained as staff leave the organisation or move to other parts of the organisation. In addition, current valuable knowledge must also be maintained. This means that an organisation will have to make continuing investments in this maintenance process.

Managing the knowledge capital (sometimes referred to as the knowledge asset or knowledge resource) of an organisation has become one of the key activities for organisations in the twenty-first century (Delahaye 2000; Sveiby 1997), and it is this key activity of managing knowledge that is addressed in this chapter. It is a basic contention of this chapter that the Human Resource Development (HRD) function has the central role in managing the critical asset of knowledge.

The chapter will first examine the change in organisational emphasis from the early 1900s concept of 'training and development' to 'human resource development' to 'managing knowledge'. The unique nature of knowledge as an asset will then be discussed. A basic model will then be presented as a means of examining the processes involved in managing an organisation's knowledge capital. This model comes from complexity theory (Stacey 1996), which suggests that all organisations have two fundamental systems — a legitimate system and a shadow system. While the legitimate system pulls the organisation towards stagnation, the shadow system pulls the organisation towards chaos. It should be noted that neither system is 'better' than the other. Both systems are needed and should be kept in balance, in what is referred to as a state of *bounded instability*. This model of two interacting systems — the legitimate and the shadow — will be used to examine the critical role each has to play in managing the organisation's knowledge capital. In addition, the interrelationship between the two systems needs to be carefully and subtly managed to ensure that one system does not become too powerful.

Historical developments

We can thank Frederick Taylor for being one of the first writers on management to recognise the need for training staff in organisations. His third principle for managing organisations emphasised the 'scientific education and development of the worker' (Stoner, Collins & Yetton 1985). The first and second world wars, with their demand for the rapid transformation of ordinary working men into soldiers with the complex skills needed to use the increasingly sophisticated weapons and machines, highlighted the need for the efficient training of people. Behind the front lines, women were making an equally rapid transformation as they replaced the skilled artisans in the workforce.

By the 1950s most managers recognised the importance of training and development, and training courses became an accepted part of good management practice. These training courses, however, concentrated on what could be called 'procedural matters' — for example, how to use a certain machine or how to complete a form correctly. For the type of business environment facing most organisations at that time — featuring constant growth and a predictable long-term future — such procedural training was quite suitable. Tasks could be broken down into sub-parts (adhering to Taylor's first principle, the development of a true science of management), staff could be trained in these sub-parts, and such skills would remain relevant for a number of years.

The 1970s saw the start of a change in the external environments businesses faced. The constant growth that had been fed by the post war expansion of nations was declining; Middle East oil-supplying countries flexed their economic muscles, increasing the price of petrol; machinery and equipment were becoming more complex; and computers were starting to change the way people viewed information. In general, society had become more educated and social expectations were changing. Managers began to recognise that people were an important resource for an organisation. In this increasingly complex world, people were needed to make critical judgements, and the lead time to institute change was decreasing. Staff, and their motivations for working, became a pivotal factor in ensuring the smooth and viable operation of industry and business.

In short, the staff of an organisation became an important strategic resource for the prosperous future of any organisation. Accordingly, in the 1980s staff planning became a strategic factor: 'personnel management' was upgraded to 'human resource management', and 'training and development' was replaced by 'human resource development'. The functions of human resource management (HRM) and HRD were finally given the recognition they deserved, and many people in the HR professions felt that their time had finally arrived. They were now included in the strategic decision making of their organisations.

The changes in the external environments that business faced did not slow down or even level out; change increased exponentially. By the early 1990s, with information doubling every three years or so, new inventions pouring onto the market, computer power growing at an unbelievable rate and globalisation becoming a significant force, organisations faced enormous pressures. Managers reacted by focusing on the most obvious resource — the finance of the organisation. Rational economics became the catch-cry, and cost savings were sought in every corner of the business. This search for cost efficiencies was not a totally misguided objective. The 1980s had been a somewhat profligate decade, with many organisations acquiring serious inefficiencies. However, some of the new strategies were pursued too vigorously, especially those relating to outsourcing and flatter structures. Staff were retrenched or encouraged to take early retirement, and with them went their knowledge.

By the mid-1990s academic writers and business leaders were acknowledging this loss of knowledge and were beginning to float the idea that knowledge itself might be an important organisational resource. By the start of the new millennium, successful organisations were actively examining ways to strategically manage their most unique and important asset — their knowledge capital.

Knowledge resides in a variety of areas in an organisation. Some is located in the business systems — for example in computer programs and databases — but the predominant reservoir of knowledge is located in the minds of the organisation's staff. This means that the most significant HRD task is the appropriate governance of the organisation's knowledge resource.

When knowledge is viewed as an asset, it soon becomes clear what an unusual asset it is. Writers such as Delahaye (2000) and Sveiby (1997) suggest that knowledge is a unique resource for the following reasons:

- There is *no law of diminishing returns*. The law of diminishing returns states that, as long as output increases, there will come a time when the cost per unit will begin to rise, and this principle is valid in a world of limited physical resources. However, unlike petrol or minerals, knowledge is not intrinsically scarce. Knowledge can be conjured up by the human mind without the use of costly external resources.
- There is a *difference between information and knowledge*. Information is what is printed on this page and is also contained in the data banks of computers. In itself,

information is inert. When it is accessed and acted on appropriately by an individual, this information becomes knowledge.

- *Knowledge cannot be hoarded.* The competitive edge provided by knowledge is only temporary, since competitors learn from each other, and if knowledge is created once, it can be created again.
- *Knowledge grows from sharing.* Unlike physical resources, knowledge does not disappear from the 'giver' when shared or sold. The 'giver' retains exactly the same level of knowledge. So, when knowledge is shared with someone else, it is doubled. In addition, the very act of dredging up knowledge from the unconscious mind brings new insights to the 'giver' through a process called *externalisation*.
- *Knowledge can be created by anyone.* This means that one organisation's competitive edge can be eradicated overnight.
- Unlike information, *knowledge is not subject to copyright or patents.* No person or organisation can copyright or patent an idea; only physical expressions of the idea can be protected in this way.

Two basic systems related to managing knowledge

The idea that knowledge is a unique and important asset presents two vital challenges to modern organisations:

1. How can the organisation's current valuable knowledge be maintained?
2. How can new knowledge be imported and created by the organisation?

Of course, organisations are very complex systems. As a first step towards understanding these complexities, we need a basic but robust model that will allow us to explore the various processes used by organisations to maintain, import and create knowledge.

Stacey (1996), using complexity theory as an analytical base, suggests that any organism, including organisations, can be viewed as having two basic systems — the legitimate system and the shadow system. This chapter will now describe the assumptions that underlie the activities carried out in each system and will then discuss the role of the two systems in managing the knowledge assets of the organisation. At the end of the chapter we will examine the complexities of the relationship between the two systems.

The legitimate system

The legitimate system uses negative feedback loops and single-loop learning to maintain the status quo. Negative feedback loops dampen any behaviour that is seen as aberrant by the legitimate system (Stacey 1996). If a staff member continually turns up to work late, for example, the manager will hold a discipline interview with the errant employee. Single-loop learning passes on current knowledge without challenging the veracity or the underlying values of the knowledge (Argyris 1992). Staff members, new to the organisation, receive orientation training during which the employment policies of the organisation are explained. The new staff member is not expected to challenge the employment policies (for example commencing work at a certain time) but to conform to the expected behaviour prescribed by those policies.

The responsibility of the legitimate system is to:

- ensure that the organisation survives the immediate future by the efficient use of its resources
- examine the short-term future of the organisation
- organise its structure so that resources are distributed efficiently
- pull the organisation towards a state of equilibrium or stability. It is in that state of equilibrium that the organisation is at its most efficient.

The underlying goals of the legitimate system, then, are efficiency and short-term effectiveness.

The shadow system

The shadow system, on the other hand, provides the organisation with the energy, usually in the form of knowledge, that will ensure the organisation's long-term future. The shadow system is predicated on positive feedback loops and double-loop learning. Positive feedback loops enhance behaviour and increase energy (Stacey 1996). For example, a staff member may come to a manager with a new idea for improving one of the processes in the department. The manager may ask the staff member to form a group and allow the group to meet for four hours each week to develop the new idea. By giving his or her imprimatur and investing time to investigate the idea, the manager is providing positive feedback loops. Double-loop learning occurs where an individual or group challenges the underlying values of an idea, assumption or concept (Argyris 1992). If the new idea of the staff member challenges one of the employment policies, then the group will examine the values and assumptions that underpin the employment policy, thereby using double-loop learning.

The responsibility of the shadow system is to:

- import or create new knowledge for the organisation so that, when unpredictable challenges occur, the organisation has a sufficient reservoir of energy, skill and knowledge to survive any future challenges
- continually examine the organisational culture of the legitimate system and change this culture where it has become inappropriate
- pull the organisation towards a state of non-equilibrium or instability. It is in a state of non-equilibrium that the organisation is at its most creative.

The underlying goal of the shadow system is to be creative. Double-loop learning encourages the shadow system to challenge the existing culture of the legitimate system, and positive feedback loops reward this creativity.

Managing knowledge capital in the legitimate system

Delahaye (2000) points out that robust and practical theories about HRD have evolved over the years. Writers such as Dewey (1938), Tyler (1949), Knowles (1950), London (1960), Goldstein (1974) and Brookfield (1984) have all contributed to the notion that there are four stages to HRD — needs investigation, design, implementation and evaluation. Most important, the four stages are the legitimate system's main contribution to managing the knowledge capital of the organisation. The four stages conform to the basic assumptions of negative feedback and single-loop learning. They provide negative feedback, in that the learning objectives are formulated in the investigation stage and the progress is checked and brought back into line if necessary by the evaluation stage. Single-loop learning is the main learning process; the underlying values of the knowledge to be imparted are rarely challenged since efficiency must be maintained. To be fair, in most legitimate systems there is some challenging of the knowledge values in the investigation stage, but such challenges are usually constrained by the short-term focus of the needs investigations, the power within the hierarchy of the organisation and the organisational culture.

The four stages of HRD, then, allow the legitimate system to make its major contribution to the management of the organisation's knowledge capital. That the legitimate system uses negative feedback loops and single-loop learning is quite reasonable. The organisation survives in its present external environment because it has valuable knowledge capital (for example on how to effectively and efficiently service its present client base). This current valuable knowledge is sometimes referred to as its *core competencies* (Prahalad & Hamel 1990). By using the four stages correctly, the legitimate system ensures that the organisation's core competencies are continually circulated around the organisation. We will now examine some issues that need to be emphasised during the four stages to ensure that the legitimate system undertakes its role appropriately.

Needs investigation

Fundamentally, a needs investigation is a process that identifies the gap between what is currently happening and what should be occurring. Delahaye and Smith (1998) believe that the organisation should act on two levels as far as needs investigations are concerned. At the surveillance level, the organisation constantly monitors its control systems to identify any aberrations to predetermined objectives or behaviours (this is a classical negative feedback loop in action). These controls include quality assurance systems, financial systems, safety reports, and staff monitoring systems such as staff turnover and discipline. So, for example, a quality assurance system may identify a sudden increase in customer complaints. A needs investigation may show that, with the resignation of two staff members, other untrained staff have taken their place. Since the solution to the service problem is the development of these staff members, they will need to attend a training course in customer service.

Once an aberration is identified in the surveillance stage, the next phase comes into action — the investigation stage. During this stage, data specific to the aberration are gathered and analysed. Data gathering processes include interviews, focus groups, questionnaires, observations and scrutiny of organisational records. Qualitative and quantitative data analysis processes appropriate to the raw data gathered are then used. A number of texts (e.g. Delahaye 2000; DeSimone & Harris 1998; Goldstein 1993) describe these data gathering and analysis processes in detail, and these processes should be familiar to anyone involved in HRD.

However, for the HR developer several issues need specific attention:

- While the needs analysis stage is linked closely to the various control systems in the organisation, the HR developer must also monitor the strategic plan of the organisation, since it is a crucial indicator of possible new knowledge. For example, if new equipment is to be purchased, the HR developer will need to design a training course to develop staff in the skills needed to operate the new equipment. Note that it is via this link between the strategic plan and the needs analysis that the legitimate system imports new knowledge into the organisation.

- The HRD or training needs investigation is really a research process, so any such project should be based on acceptable research methods (see, for example, Cavana, Delahaye & Sekaran 2001; Ticehurst & Veal 1999; Zikmund 1997). Every research project has weaknesses, and any limitations need to be fully acknowledged by the HR developer so that appropriate risk management procedures can be planned.

Finally, the results of any needs investigation have to be compared with the organisational strategic plan to ensure that the learning objectives identified will contribute to the strategic direction established by the plan.

Design

Few texts in HRD provide full practical advice on designing learning experiences. Perhaps this is because designing learning experiences is, in many ways, part art and part science. We often need to turn to educational writers for guidance (e.g. Caffarella 1994; Gagne, Briggs & Wagner 1992; Print 1993). Two other major challenges facing HR developers when considering the design of learning experiences for the legitimate system of the organisation are balancing the needs of the stakeholders and designing appropriate learning strategies.

In the legitimate system, the needs of the two major stakeholders in a learning experience have the potential to come into strong conflict. One major stakeholder is the upper management of the organisation; their needs are represented by the organisational strategic plan and by the results of the approved HRD investigation report. Note the power of negative feedback loops and single-loop learning here. Both these documents — the strategic plan and the approved needs analysis report — have become the predetermined standard for the legitimate system. The underlying values of the knowledge presented in these documents are not to be challenged, and any behaviour that is different from that approved in the documents will be considered aberrant and therefore will need to be dampened (i.e. brought back to the required standard). However, the other major stakeholder in the learning experience is the body of learners. In most organisations these people are adult learners, who, as Knowles (1990) points out, are often a 'neglected species'. Even today the needs of adult learners — their learning styles, personal conceptual maps and currently perceived knowledge deficiencies — often come a poor second to the needs of the legitimate system. One can empathise with the

HR developer who feels that championing the needs of the adult learner is fighting a losing battle. This is a significant personal and moral challenge for the HR developer, because if the developer, as the steward of the organisation's knowledge capital, does not champion the adult learner, who will? Not all organisations have such a strong and uncaring legitimate system but, in an era that still reflects the problems of an overly enthusiastic application of rational economics, short-term, easily measured activities (for example sending the learners an instructional manual) are often favoured to the disadvantage of long-term benefits (for example giving the learners sufficient instruction and practice that they can be assessed as competent).

To understand the second challenge for the HR developer when developing learning experiences, the differences between learning types must be recognised. Mezirow (1990) has suggested that there are three types of learning for adults — instrumental, communicative and emancipatory. *Instrumental learning* allows the learner to manipulate her or his own environment. A typical example of instrumental learning occurs when the organisation upgrades to a new computer system. The staff have to be developed in the knowledge and skills they will need to use the new system. Most research into human learning has focused on instrumental learning, which has led to the acknowledgement of such principles of learning as *spaced learning*, *active learning*, *multiple-sense learning* and *meaningful material* (see, for example, Delahaye & Smith 1998; DeSimone & Harris 1998). *Communicative learning* occurs where two parties interact with an open communication style. Each party has two responsibilities — to understand the inner world of the other party, and to help the other party to understand his or her own inner world. Communicative learning is about understanding the beliefs and values of others. Mezirow (1990) believes such communicative learning can occur only with rational discourse, which is the opposite of debate. In a debate, one party tries to convince the other party that only one point of view is correct. In rational discourse the emphasis is on understanding the other party's point of view. *Emancipatory learning* occurs when a learner is freed from a hegemonic frame of reference. (A frame of reference is a deeply held belief or value system. We all have frames of reference that help us make hundreds of decisions automatically during our daily lives.)

A frame of reference is classed as hegemonic when it causes an individual, or the people the individual interacts with, long-term hurt or pain. For example, I may have a frame of reference that values hard work and a 'never-say-die spirit'. When I come across a learner who will not try hard or who gives in easily, I may lose my temper — an automatic response governed by my frame of reference. But if I am to be a successful adult educator, I will need to change that hegemonic part of my frame of reference (of placing an absolute value on hard work). This change is called emancipatory (being freed) learning. For a fuller discussion on instrumental, communicative and emancipatory learning, see Delahaye (2000).

The heart of this second challenge is designing *appropriate* learning strategies — instrumental learning for skills and knowledge to manipulate the environment; communicative learning for understanding the belief systems of others; and emancipatory learning for changing hegemonic frames of reference. One of the problems faced by HR developers is that instrumental learning is usually cheaper (in immediate time and money) than communicative or emancipatory learning. For the legitimate system, with its focus on efficiency, the short-term cost savings of instrumental learning appear much more attractive than the long-term effectiveness (and, incidentally, long-term cost savings) of communicative and emancipatory learning. Time and again we see organisations attempting to change organisational culture by using instrumental learning (a three-hour 'workshop', based on a series of lectures and some short but highly structured learning experiences, is typical). Such an approach is worse than useless, since it invariably engenders negative feelings among the participants. At the other end of the continuum, of course, there is the example of the overly enthusiastic HR developer using emancipatory learning to develop skills. This can also engender negative feelings in the learner and is invariably a waste of money.

It is interesting to note that the second challenge in designing appropriate learning experiences is often caused by the first challenge, when upper management focuses on short-term cost at the expense of long-term effectiveness.

Implementation

At the implementation stage, the learning experience and the learner come together. In the legitimate system, this conjunction of learning experience and learner is usually envisaged as occurring in the formal setting of a classroom. Indeed, often such an environment is the most conducive to effective learning, since the learner is isolated from distracting intrusions. This option is also attractive to the legitimate system because it enhances the power and control of negative feedback loops. Again, a number of basic texts provide advice on how such a learning experience should be managed (see, for example, Delahaye & Smith 1998; DeSimone & Harris 1998; Wexley & Latham 1991).

At the implementation stage, however, there are at least two issues for the HR developer to consider, namely developing *tacit* as well as explicit knowledge, and enhancing the value of 'informal' learning.

Explicit knowledge is held in the conscious mind and can be expressed in words and shared, for example in the form of data, written ideas, specifications and manuals. Tacit knowledge — for example subjective insights, intuition and hunches — is held in the subconscious mind and is highly personal and hard to formalise. Tacit knowledge is encompassed in the saying 'We can know more than we can tell' (Polanyi 1997). While explicit knowledge can be transmitted easily between individuals, tacit knowledge is not easily expressible and is difficult to share with others. Tacit knowledge has two dimensions (Nonaka & Konno 1998). One component is personal skills and abilities, for example those exhibited by a craftsperson. The second dimension is cognitive and consists of the individual's various schemata — mental models that the individual has built up over a lifetime of experience, particularly in a trade or profession. This tacit knowledge also links with, and overlaps, the individual's frames of reference. Importantly, tacit knowledge is seen as the foundation and catalyst of most decisions the individual makes.

Using this differentiation between tacit and explicit knowledge, Nonaka and Takeuchi (1995) have identified four processes for the creation of knowledge — combination, externalisation, internalisation and socialisation. Unfortunately, most legitimate systems value only combination. *Combination* involves the conversion of explicit knowledge into more complex sets of explicit knowledge. Your reading this book is an example of combination. Since they are expressed in words, the ideas in this book represent explicit knowledge. As you read the book, the explicit knowledge it contains is combined with your own explicit knowledge. Through a process of sorting, combining and categorising your current knowledge and the explicit knowledge of the book, you reconfigure your existing knowledge.

This process of combination is valuable, especially in instrumental learning. For the legitimate system, the big advantage of combination is that the results can be measured — that is, single-loop learning can be proven and the power of negative feedback loops is maintained. However, by undervaluing the other three knowledge generation processes, the typical legitimate system loses critically important opportunities to harness the dynamic learning possibilities that these processes offer. The first challenge for the HR developer, then, is to encourage the use of these three knowledge-generating processes during the learning experience.

- *Externalisation* (tacit to explicit). The externalisation process occurs when tacit knowledge is translated and expressed in forms that are comprehensible to the conscious mind of the individual and to others. Externalisation always occurs when an individual commits thoughts and ideas to paper. Although certain aspects of the conscious mind are easily transposed into the written word, the writer usually finds that some ideas, embedded in the subconscious mind, also surface and give the original, conscious thoughts a richer meaning and context. Reflection, through writing, discussions with others or contemplative thinking, is one of the main forms of externalisation.

- *Internalisation* (explicit to tacit). The process of internalisation is most easily confirmed when an individual is 'learning by doing'. For example, there is a big difference between your reading about the techniques in this book and your putting them into practice. Consider the skills of interviewing. Reading about interviewing skills, they seem logical and straightforward. However, when we actually try to interview someone — and attempt to combine questioning, paraphrasing, summarising and probing, to say nothing of taking notes — we realise we still have much to learn. It is this *whole body experience* of 'learning by doing' that converts explicit knowledge into tacit knowledge. Internalisation may also occur through re-experiencing another's experiences, for example through oral stories or diagrams and models.
- *Socialisation* (tacit to tacit). Socialisation is an osmotic process through which complex information is exchanged. It is seen, for instance, when a learner watches and interacts with an expert. While often accompanied by the combination process, socialisation is also a whole body experience during which various nuances and non-verbal messages are received and synthesised into a complex appreciation of an intricate archetype.

The legitimate system values classroom training because of the control such a learning situation affords. Again, it must be emphasised that such training courses do have an important place in the legitimate system's role in managing organisational knowledge. The first challenge for the HR developer, then, is to ensure that all four knowledge-generating processes — combination, internalisation, externalisation and socialisation — are used as much as possible in learning experiences.

However, the less controllable aspect of learning — what could be referred to as *informal learning* — is also critical for the transfer of learning from the classroom to the workplace. In ensuring that the legitimate system is fulfilling its role in managing the organisation's knowledge capital, the transfer of learning is the second challenge for the HR developer, who must ensure that a 'positive transfer climate' (Tennant 1999) prevails in the workplace by developing a supportive, workplace culture that:

- provides the learner with opportunities to practise 'routinised problem-solving' knowledge and skills (i.e. internalisation)

- gives the learner feedback that is both informational and motivational
- allows the learner opportunities to observe models of expert performance (i.e. socialisation)
- provides the learner with opportunities that are progressively more complex and accountable
- continually encourages the learner to develop expertise using the process of progressive approximations.

For a more detailed discussion on developing a supportive workplace culture, see Billett (1999).

Evaluation

The overall purpose of the evaluation stage is to ensure that the knowledge considered important by the legitimate system is successfully and efficiently circulated within the organisation. One of the most frequently cited models of evaluation is that proposed by Kirkpatrick (1994). This model identifies the following four levels of evaluation:

1. The Reaction level, where the learner's liking of the learning experience is assessed
2. The Learning level, where the learner's knowledge is assessed by using tests
3. The Behaviour level, where the extent that the learner has transferred the knowledge back to the job is assessed (usually through the performance appraisal process)
4. The Results level, where the impact of the learning episode on the organisation as a whole is assessed.

Brinkerhoff (1987) adds to these four levels by suggesting that the other three stages of HRD (needs analysis, design and implementation) should also be evaluated.

Evaluation is an important stage in managing the knowledge capital of the organisation. In the legitimate system, evaluation is used to:

1. measure what change has occurred
2. see if the change is attributable to the learning episode
3. see if the amount of change is worthwhile.

This fourth stage of HRD, evaluation, shows the operation of negative feedback loops in action. The predetermined standards used to make these judgements are drawn from the strategic plan and the needs analysis. The emphasis is on what is observable, what is measurable and bringing any perceived aberration back to the predetermined standard. For the legitimate system, the evaluation process needs to be efficient, so single-loop learning is emphasised — that is, the underlying values of the strategic plan and the needs analysis should not be challenged. Of course, the values may be challenged but the challenger is operating in the shadow system rather than in the legitimate system (this will be discussed later in the chapter).

The HR developer confronts at least three challenging issues at the evaluation stage:

- One common difficulty faced by HR developers in the evaluation stage occurs when the predetermined standard is based on the organisational culture or frame of reference of senior management. The frustration is caused by the covert nature of the formulated predetermined standard. To add to this frustration, this predetermined standard (based on organisational culture or senior management's frame of reference) is usually not articulated until after the event. It is simply assumed that the HR developer would have 'sensed' such requirements.

- The second difficulty in the evaluation stage is the assumption by the legitimate system that all learning can be observed and measured. As evidence of this, consider the value placed on 'competencies' in the past decade. The idea that all learning should be observable and measurable assumes that worthwhile learning can only be instrumental learning and must focus solely on explicit knowledge. The measurement of instrumental learning and explicit knowledge should certainly be carried out. The problem occurs when the sensate option (that is, that the outcome must be observable and measurable) is assumed to be the only option. As we have seen, tacit knowledge cannot be measured, yet it is probably the most powerful determinant in the individual's decision-making process. If this is so, then the sensate prerequisite of the legitimate system bypasses a significant reservoir of knowledge — the individual learner's tacit knowledge.

- The third difficulty faced by the HR developer is caused by the legitimate system's predilection for efficiency. A lot of money and energy could be saved, in the short term, by not conducting an evaluation. This would certainly be 'efficient', but it would not be wise.

The basis for these three challenging issues confronting the HR developer at the evaluation stage can be found in the organisational culture and the frames of reference of the key stakeholders, and these are difficult to change. As discussed earlier, we know that instrumental learning using the combination process of knowledge generation will in all likelihood fail. To change a frame of reference (that is, a basic value and belief system), emancipatory learning is needed, and this presents a catch 22 situation. How can one use emancipatory learning on someone who only values instrumental learning? Furthermore, during periods of slowly changing external environments, the goal of equilibrium — where everything is highly predictable and tasks and behaviours are constant — is a reasonable ambition for organisations. In today's rapidly changing environment, such a goal is inappropriate. A state of equilibrium in such a business environment would mean that the organisation's

processes become antiquated and ineffective, with the organisation very soon stagnating and ceasing to be competitive. The answer to these quandaries lies, not in the legitimate system, but in the successful management of the shadow system.

Managing knowledge capital in the shadow system

Any organism that uses all its energy merely to ensure the efficient use of its resources will be doomed to failure. Complexity theory suggests that an organism needs to use some of its energy to avoid redundancy. In other words, the organism needs to continually explore and test new options. This is the role of the shadow system. To survive, an organisation needs to import and create new knowledge. This knowledge is then either transferred to the legitimate system for immediate use or stored in what are sometimes referred to as 'knowledge silos'. Knowledge silos may be created by the organisation as storage systems (for example an interactive database in a computer) or, more likely, will occur in the minds and memory of the organisational staff members. This new knowledge is stored in this way until unforeseen problems and challenges arise.

Ordinary management — with its use of negative feedback loops and single-loop learning — is appropriate for the legitimate system. However, ordinary management would suffocate the shadow system. Stacey (1996) believes that the proper governance of the shadow system needs a process he calls extraordinary management. *Extraordinary management* is based on positive feedback loops and double-loop learning. Positive feedback loops enhance creative behaviour and increase energy, encouraging growth and wellbeing. Double-loop learning occurs when an individual or group challenges the underlying values of an idea, assumption or concept. Therefore, the assumptions underlying extraordinary management are the opposite to those of ordinary management used to administer the legitimate system.

These opposing assumptions create a significant tension between the legitimate system and the shadow system for a number of reasons. First, the legitimate system has the credibility of being an 'observable' entity, usually represented by the organisational hierarchy chart. Second, the illusion of control that is promised by negative feedback loops and single-loop learning is very attractive to managers who are under severe pressure to produce. Third, by its very action of double-loop learning, the shadow system constantly threatens the values and beliefs of the legitimate system. The legitimate system, then, invariably uses its considerable power to nullify the actions of the shadow system. However, the innate creativity of human nature — and this is the force that the shadow system nurtures — can never be eradicated. So the legitimate system finds itself under what it perceives as a constant threat from the shadow system — and so the tension continues.

The shadow system is a hotbed of learning and, as such, it must be managed and nurtured appropriately by upper management. To carry out this responsibility, managers must:

1. recognise the basic nature of the shadow system,
2. be able to manage the shadow system, and
3. be able to manage the tension between the shadow system and the legitimate system.

As the steward of the organisational knowledge capital, the HR developer provides the professional assistance needed to develop the managers and systems required, and this is a major challenge for the HR developer in the new millennium.

The nature of the shadow system

It is tempting to view the shadow system as an entity that is separate from, and as easily identifiable as, the legitimate system. It is better to view the shadow system as overlapping the legitimate system. As we will see, it is sometimes difficult to identify where one system ceases and the other begins. Only in certain specific cases is the shadow system a separate area of the organisation where some people work and others do not. In fact, most probably the only examples of this are research and development departments and special project groups charged with investigating specific phenomena.

More usually, the shadow system occurs as members of the organisation (either physically or mentally) leave their usual work tasks in the legitimate system and think up or come across new ideas. As Andrews (1999) comments, knowledge generation in an organisation is more about the everyday actions of many than the plans of a few. For example, the manager of the Registry and Records branch of an organisation may be driving to work one morning listening to the radio when a comment by the DJ triggers an idea in the manager's mind. This idea inspires an improved way of managing the records of the organisation. Once at work, but over a period of several months, the manager works steadily towards introducing the change. The manager does not spend this period of months working solely on the new idea. Rather, a few minutes one day, an hour

the next and ten minutes the next may be invested in the idea. Most of the manager's time is still spent in the legitimate system. However, the time spent thinking about the new idea, and working to introduce it, represents time the manager has spent in the shadow system.

This view of staff moving in and out of the shadow system several times a day probably accounts for most of the activity in the shadow system. If we use the metaphor of large and small business, it is reported that more than 60 per cent of business in Australia is conducted within the small business stream. Similarly, it is likely that more than 60 per cent of the activity in the shadow system is conducted by the staff's frequent daily visits. The more conspicuous examples of the research and development department and the special project team probably represent only 30 to 40 per cent of the activities in the shadow system. For the CEO, managing the special projects in the shadow system is relatively straightforward. However, supporting the frequent visits of staff to the shadow system requires discrimination and subtlety — discrimination in that the intention of some staff (albeit a minority) may be detrimental to the welfare of the organisation, and subtlety in that heavy-handed support of the well-intentioned can sometimes kill off the creative endeavour.

Self-organising groups

Often, the creative processes do not confine themselves to one person. As adult educators such as Knowles (1990) and Revans (1982) have emphasised, adult learning is invariably a social process. So the shadow system tends to comprise self-organising groups who come together for a mutual purpose. This mutual purpose may or may not be sanctioned by management. One of the most well known of these self-organising groups are the 'whinge-and-bitch' cliques. For the legitimate system, such cliques are anathema; for the shadow system, they are a potentially rich source of energy. Whether this potentially rich source of energy leads to chaos or becomes the basis of valuable knowledge for the organisation depends on how the self-organising groups are managed. Of course, not all cliques are of the 'whinge-and-bitch' variety. A large number of self-organising groups come together through a desire to solve a problem or to meet a common challenge. It is this natural curiosity, this inclination to question, to solve puzzles, to implement solutions, that has to be harnessed in the shadow system.

Harnessing this energy requires systems that encourage positive feedback and double-loop learning so that the shadow system is managed appropriately.

Managing the shadow system

Earl (1997) suggests that knowledge building is a multi-faceted endeavour and, at its simplest, requires a combination of technological and social actions. He believes that at least four components are required — knowledge systems, networks, knowledge workers and a learning culture.

Knowledge systems

The organisation needs to develop and maintain systems that will capture, store and make available information on any new experience. Developing such a corporate database does not mean simple information storage. First, the people involved in the new experience need time to arrange the storage of the data. Second, the knowledge systems need decision-support tools and computer screen-based analyses to interrogate the data at an appropriate time.

The decision on what data to store and what to ignore requires critical judgement. The data may come from a regular surveillance of the Internet, access to particular journals, a special one-time survey of non-customers or reports from self-organising groups. Of course, the more data gathered and stored, the higher the immediate cost. On the other hand, the less data gathered, the higher the potential long-term costs — usually measured in terms of the risk of not having appropriate knowledge available when an unexpected problem arises.

An overly powerful legitimate system will tend to discount any knowledge capture system, usually based on a rational economic decision. A well-balanced organisation with appropriately powerful legitimate and shadow systems will make a rational decision not on whether a knowledge capture system is needed — that will be assumed to be a given — but on the likely importance of data in the future, the ease of gathering data and the level of investment that can be afforded. The problem is, of course, that what appears to be inconsequential data now may become critical knowledge in the future. The consolation, though, is that an established and robust knowledge capture system has the capacity and processes to quickly make up any leeway at the time the omission is recognised.

Networks

Networks appear to be significant in knowledge capture, knowledge building and knowledge dissemination (Earl 1997). Having access to other parties outside the organisation enhances the ability of the organisation to gather data. A number of commercial and government organisations are aligning with universities for just this purpose.

Having a network of associates so that ideas, written work and questions can be exchanged and explored is vital to the knowledge generation process. Finally, a network of contacts within the organisational system facilitates the sharing of knowledge.

The importance of networks cannot be emphasised enough. Knowledge grows by sharing, and this introduces the element of risk. Few of us enjoy having our basic frames of reference and favourite models of understanding challenged. Yet knowledge will not grow unless this challenging process becomes a constant theme. It is this constant challenging, this constant questioning of the status quo, that is the heart of action learning (Revans 1983).

Closely linked to networking are the ideas of loose links (sometimes called loose couplings) and the six degrees of separation. The assumption of loose links recognises that the impetus for new knowledge comes, not from familiar networks, but from unusual sources. So, for example, significant new insights into customer needs come, not from current customers, but from that part of the population that has nothing to do with the organisation. The 'six degrees of separation' idea suggests that no more than six steps separate any person in the world from any other (Paulos 1990). In searching for new knowledge, the learner must move beyond the first contact to discover new sources.

Knowledge workers

In the processes of learning, knowledge acquisition and knowledge generation, people become the core resource, since only the human mind has the capacity to be creative within such a complex web of activities. Most importantly, the actors in the shadow system must be allocated that valuable resource — time. Other resources in the organisation are given time to be developed, maintained and upgraded. Knowledge has to be given the same consideration.

Knowledge workers need time because they operate in an environment of discovery learning. Cavaliere (1992) has proposed a five-stage model of discovery learning. Within each of these stages, there are four repetitive cognitive processes — goal setting, focusing, persevering and reformulation. The five stages are:
- *inquiring*, in which the individual sees a need to solve a particular problem
- *modelling*, in which the learner casts around and observes similar phenomena (for example watching birds fly before designing an aeroplane). Similarities and differences are noted and, gradually, a prototype model or solution is developed. Undoubtedly, the observations of similar phenomena are absorbed into the individual's

tacit knowledge, and then metaphors, analogies and models slowly surface. Some of these will be discarded until a viable model is identified.

- *experimenting and practising*, in which the learner builds a model or representation of the solution and tests it against various standards of reality. This may mean trying out the prototype (for example testing a model of the aeroplane) or having the solution assessed by experts. For the actors in the shadow system, the proposed solution may be previewed by certain trusted members of the legitimate system.
- *theorising and perfecting*, in which the model or solution is constantly refined from a stage where it solves the problem in a barely acceptable manner to a stage where the model or solution gains high acceptance from the potential clients. The actor in the shadow system will continually ask the question 'What possible objections could be made to this solution?'; or the actor could use a decision-making model such as force-field analysis.
- *actualising*, in which the individual (who has been both a learner and an actor in the shadow system) receives recognition for the product of their learning efforts.

To progress through these five stages, and to use the four repetitive cognitive processes of goal setting, focusing, persevering and reformulation within each of the five stages, however, needs more than an investment of time. The actors will also need to be *self-directed learners*. Being a self-directed learner means:

1. having a high level of the *skills of learning*. We have already discussed several aspects of learning — the three levels of learning (instrumental, communicative and emancipatory) and the four knowledge generation processes (combination, externalisation, internalisation and socialisation). The learners also need high levels of competency in the four stages of needs analysis, design, implementation and evaluation. These four stages still provide the overarching theme of learning in the shadow system — they simply occur with such bewildering speed that each learner must manage the four stages rather than having someone else do it for them.
2. having the self-confidence and motivation to be a self-directed learner. Much has been written on becoming a self-directed learner, so the discussions will not be repeated here (see, for example, Brookfield 1987 and Knowles 1990).

What can be noted is that becoming a self-directed learner takes time, energy, commitment to life-long learning and an endless curiosity. These qualities are needed, not only by the individual, but also by the organisation. Such qualities in an organisation are reflected by its organisational culture.

A learning culture

The fourth component of the shadow system is the need for a robust and dynamic organisational culture that values learning. One very good test of such a culture is evidence of how the organisation views failure: a robust learning culture sees failure as merely one step in the learning process. Another feature of a robust learning culture is the presence of what Argyris (1992) termed 'theory-in-use model II', which essentially describes double-loop learning, through which an individual or organisation examines and/or changes the underlying governing variables or its master programs. In theory-in-use model II:

- the interaction is based on valid information
- the participants have free and informed choice
- the participants keep testing the validity of the choices, especially as the choices are being implemented.

A culture that recognises the value of failure and adheres to the assumptions of theory-in-use model II is well on its way to becoming a learning organisation.

However, more is needed. According to Billett (1999) and Tennant (1999), a learning culture in the workplace encourages learning by:

- starting with 'routinised problem-solving' knowledge and skills (i.e. combination and instrumental learning)
- being given time to practise and learn these basics (i.e. internalisation and externalisation)
- encouraging the development of expertise using the process of successive approximations (i.e. communicative learning)
- providing opportunities to become engaged in tasks that are progressively more complex and require greater accountability (i.e. communicative and emancipatory learning)
- giving feedback that is both informational and motivational (i.e. the steps of implementation and evaluation)
- giving opportunities to observe models of expert performance (i.e. socialisation)
- operating in a supportive atmosphere (i.e. an organisational culture that values learning).

Managing the shadow system is not a controlling process. Rather, it is based on trust and respect for the organisational staff. Any hint of negative feedback loops will kill the creativity on which complex learning is based. The four components discussed in this section — knowledge systems, networks, knowledge workers and a learning culture — provide a basis for understanding the complexities involved. The HR developer needs to fully understand the dynamics of learning in the shadow system, since this role will become more important as organisations realise that the only way to survive is to maintain a rich and extensive reservoir of knowledge capital.

Managing the tension

To this point we have discussed the legitimate and shadow systems as separate entities. This is useful in order to gain an understanding of the role of each system in the management of knowledge. However, they are *not* two separate systems; indeed, they are enduringly intertwined and interconnected. I often view them as overlapping circles. At times, it is difficult to see whether one is in the shadow system or the legitimate system — that is, where the two circles overlap.

However, keep in mind the basic assumptions of each system:

- The legitimate system is based on negative feedback loops and single-loop learning. Its role is to ensure the current viability of the organisation by emphasising the efficient use of resources. Recognise, though, that the legitimate system drags the organisation towards stable equilibrium — a dangerous state in a changing external environment. If the legitimate system becomes too strong, it will stagnate and the organisational culture will become toxic, poisoning everyone involved.
- The shadow system is based on positive feedback loops and double-loop learning. Its role is to ensure the future viability of the organisation by generating sufficient knowledge to permit the organisation to meet unknown and unpredictable challenges. Recognise, though, that the shadow system drags the organisation towards instability. If the shadow system becomes too strong, the organisation will enter chaos.

The aim, of course, is to achieve a state of bounded instability. In this state, the organisation is constantly hovering between toxic stagnation and chaos. This state is achieved by ensuring that each system is given an appropriate level of power and resources so that neither will dominate. Given this appropriate distribution of power and resources, each system has specific duties in ensuring that new, pertinent knowledge is introduced into the organisation.

The transfer duties of the shadow system

Making new discoveries in the shadow system can be an exciting and emotional experience. This is the actualising stage of Cavaliere's learning model. However, these ecstatic reactions are a form of positive feedback loop and are guaranteed to encourage the learners to move further into chaos. Sensing a strong move towards chaos, the legitimate system will immediately begin to organise a strong defence. Rather than allow a 'declaration of war', the shadow system needs to:

- recognise that the actualisation stage needs to be celebrated but that this stage marks the end of learning and the beginning of the transfer of knowledge to the legitimate system.
- review and package the new knowledge as a product that will be more acceptable to the legitimate system. This means that the learners involved in the discovery of new knowledge need to think realistically about how the new knowledge will benefit the organisation. In other words they need to move from creative thought to rational thought.
- prepare the way for the new knowledge. This is a political process (Stacey 1996). Key stakeholders need to be identified and approached. This is communicative learning and the 'approachee' needs to be a skilled adult educator. Any other possible barriers also need to be identified and overcome.

The transfer duties of the legitimate system

For the legitimate system, anything new is a threat to efficiency. Its immediate reaction is to revert to defence, and an impressive array of defensive tools have been developed by the legitimate system over the years. Argyris (1992) calls these 'defence mechanisms'. Three of the more common are:

1. *The undiscussables.* Certain issues in organisations cannot be discussed. The reasons for this are often clouded by history, but most people in the organisation know that the issue should not be discussed. New members are soon enculturated into recognising the undiscussability through the use of 'non-verbals' or public 'put-downs'. If the new member does not take the hint, then someone with higher power will take on the responsibility of 'straightening him out'. Eerily, this enculturation into the world of undiscussables is overt, with the 'teacher' requiring no instruction to carry out the task. The process becomes even more bizarre when the undiscussability of the issue itself becomes undiscussable.

   A classic example is the role of the 'Assistant to' the CEO. We are not talking about a secretary or personal assistant here. The 'Assistant to' is usually a professional (an engineer in an engineering company; an academic in a university). Most research has found that the 'Assistant to' tends to be involved in secondary or even tertiary tasks that the CEO does not wish to be bothered with. Often, these tasks only exist because the CEO has not had the courage to say 'we will not be involved in this'. Any questioning of the role of the 'Assistant to' is often met with a brusque comment from the CEO: 'Don't talk to me about that' (indicating that the issue is undiscussable) or 'She does a very valuable job. I'm very disappointed that you would even raise it' (not only is the issue undiscussable but the undiscussable nature of the issue is also undiscussable).

2. *Defensive routines.* Organisational defensive routines are highly protective. They are designed to protect key members of the organisation from embarrassment, threat and surprises, or to ensure that the organisation does not move in a direction that would cause discomfort to key members. Note that key members do not necessarily occupy the higher levels of the organisation but are 'power centres' — people with a resource that gives them potency. This potency may derive from a variety of sources — for example being the reservoir of critical knowledge or from occupying an indispensable position in the information flow of the organisation. The defensive routines used by organisations are many and varied and are often unique to a particular organisation.

Defensive routines are often disguised as 'normal' operating activities. One common defensive routine is the meeting that identifies a series of issues but never decides on what must be done about those issues. Some defensive routines that use meetings are expert at proliferating other meetings and committees. Another common defensive routine (and one of which the HR developer must be particularly aware) is the training course based on instrumental learning when communicative or emancipatory learning is needed. For a toxic legitimate system, the attraction of both these defensive routines is that the managers *appear* to be taking constructive action (note theory-in-use model I here), but the new idea is doomed to failure because negative feedback loops automatically strangle creativity.

Defensive routines are very powerful. Several attributes can be recognised:
- The organisation is avoiding double-loop learning.
- Defensive mechanisms are invariably partnered with undiscussables.
- Defensive routines proliferate and grow in an underground manner.
- There is a heavy reliance on instrumental learning by the organisation, since this does not challenge underlying frames of reference but still gives the illusion of progress.

For the legitimate system to contribute positively to the management of knowledge capital, it must avoid such defensive mechanisms. Rather, the legitimate system must carry out an *auditing role*. This auditing role ensures that:
- new ideas that are totally alien to the good governance of the organisation are filtered out. Alien ideas cause confusion to both the organisational staff and its customers.
- new idea overload does not occur. Staff can be 'burnt out' quite easily if expected to continually import and consolidate new ideas.
- the organisation has sufficient resources to fully introduce the new idea
- standing plans (policies, procedures and rules) and single-use plans are promulgated to ensure the successful integration of the new idea (see Davidson & Griffin 2000).

The promulgation of standing plans and single-use plans bring us back to the legitimate system's primary method of managing knowledge — the four stages of HRD (needs analysis, design, implementation and evaluation). The new idea from the shadow system needs to be supported by standing plans. In other words, policies, procedures and rules have to be created. So, for example, if new equipment is to be used, policies on its maintenance should be formed. To carry out these policies, procedures for conducting the maintenance of the equipment need to be listed and any rules that are essential for the safe operation of the equipment have to be identified. Once the standing plans have been established, a needs analysis can identify the skills and knowledge that need to be learned by the operators. The results of this needs analysis then form the foundation for the design of a training program. The program of the designed training course is, in fact, a single-use plan. This single-use plan is then implemented and, after all appropriate staff have been trained, the evaluation stage is conducted.

And so the process of managing the organisation's knowledge capital continues. The shadow system identifies more areas of new knowledge, and the legitimate system audits the new ideas and implements them through standing and single-use plans and the four stages of HRD. In due course the new idea becomes part of the organisation's accepted knowledge and this accepted knowledge is eventually challenged by the shadow system.

Managing the interaction between the shadow system and the legitimate system is an important but delicate process. Each system needs to have sufficient power and resources, and appropriate procedures need to be recognised as part of their roles in transferring new ideas that will revitalise the organisation.

Conclusion

Managing the organisation's knowledge capital is the responsibility of Human Resource Development (HRD). It is the central theme of this chapter that HRD is pivotal to the effectual management of the organisation and, to effectively fulfil this central role, the HR developer must become the steward of the organisational knowledge capital.

Managing the knowledge assets of an organisation is now the most critical challenge facing organisations around the world. Because of its close association with adult learning, this challenge must be supervised by the HR developer. In other words, the HR developer must become the steward of the organisational knowledge capital.

To accept and mobilise this stewardship role, the effective HR developer:

- recognises that knowledge is a unique asset
- recognises the different roles of the legitimate system and shadow system in the management of the knowledge capital
- ensures the effective and efficient operation of the four stages of HRD — needs investigation, design, implementation and evaluation
- overcomes the specific challenges within each of these four steps:
  - that needs investigation is a research process and should conform to the acceptable research methods, and that the needs investigation is the start of the learning process
  - to balance the needs of the two major stakeholders — upper management and the adult learners — and design appropriate learning strategies
  - to ensure that all four knowledge-generating processes of combination, internalisation, externalisation and socialisation are used when implementing learning, and that a positive transfer climate prevails in the workplace
  - that evaluation of learning accounts for tacit knowledge as well as explicit knowledge
- recognises the processes — knowledge systems, networks, knowledge workers and a learning culture — needed to support learning in the shadow system, encourages the development of the processes required, and develops managers who can effectively manage these processes
- assists with managing the tension between the legitimate system and the shadow system by ensuring that the shadow system prepares the new knowledge for the acceptance of the legitimate system, that the legitimate system has an authentic and reasonable auditing process for evaluating new knowledge, and that the legitimate system then promulgates the new knowledge by using standing plans and single-use plans so that the new knowledge becomes accepted knowledge.

References

Andrews, K (1999) Knowing, learning and unlearning in a knowledge creating company: an inductive, theory-building case study. Unpublished doctoral thesis, Centre for Professional Practice in Education and Training, Queensland University of Technology, Brisbane.

Argyris, C (1992) *On Organizational Learning*. Cambridge, MA: Blackwell.

Billett, S (1999) Guided learning at work. In D Boud and J Garrick (Eds), *Understanding Learning at Work*. London: Routledge.

Brinkerhoff , RO (1987) *Achieving Results from Training*. San Francisco: Jossey-Bass.

Brookfield, S (1987) *Developing Critical Thinkers: Challenging Adults to Explore Alternative Ways of Thinking and Acting*. San Francisco: Jossey-Bass.

Caffarella, RS (1994) *Planning Programs for Adult Learners*. San Francisco: Jossey-Bass.

Cavana, RY, Delahaye, BL, and Sekaran, U (2001) *Applied Business Research: Qualitative and Quantitative Methods*. Brisbane: John Wiley & Sons.

Davidson, P, and Griffin, RW (2000) *Management: Australia in a Global Context*. Brisbane: John Wiley & Sons.

Delahaye, BL (2000) *Human Resource Development: Principles and Practice*. Brisbane: John Wiley & Sons.

Delahaye, BL, and Smith, BJ (1998) *How to Be an Effective Trainer*. New York: John Wiley & Sons.

DeSimone, RL, and Harris, DM (1998) *Human Resource Development* (2nd ed.). Fort Worth, TX: Dryden.

Dewey, J (1938) *Experience and Education*. New York: Kappa Delta Pi.

Earl, MJ (1997) Knowledge as strategy: reflections on Skandia International and Shorko Films. In L Prusak (Ed.), *Knowledge in Organisations*. Boston, MA: Butterworth-Heinemann, 1–15.

Gagne, RM, Briggs, LJ, and Wagner, WW (1992) *Principles of Instructional Design* (4th ed.). New York: Holt, Rinehart and Winston.

Goldstein, IL (1974) *Training: Program Development and Evaluation*. Belmont, CA: Brooks/Cole.

Goldstein, IL (1993) *Training in Organizations* Belmont, CA: Brooks/Cole.

Kirkpatrick, DL (1994) *Evaluating Training Programs: The Four Levels*. San Francisco: Berrett-Koehler.

Knowles, MS (1950) *Informal Adult Education: A Guide for Administrators, Leaders and Teachers*. New York: AAAE.

Knowles, MS (1990) *The Adult Learner: A Neglected Species* (4th ed.). Houston, TX: Gulf.

London, J (1960) Program development in adult education. In MS Knowles (Ed.), *Handbook of Adult Education in the United States*. Chicago: AAAE.

Mezirow, J (1990) *Fostering Critical Reflection in Adulthood: A Guide to Transformative and Emancipatory Learning*. San Francisco: Jossey-Bass.

Nonaka, I, and Konno, N (1998) The concept of Ba: building a foundation for knowledge creation. *California Management Review*, Spring, 40 (3) 1–15.

Nonaka, I, and Takeuchi, H (1995) *The Knowledge Creating Company: How Japanese Companies Create the Dynamics of Innovation*. New York: Oxford University Press.

Paulos, JA (1990) *Innumeracy: Mathematical Illiteracy and Its Consequence*. Vancouver: Vintage.

Polanyi, M (1997) The tacit dimension. In L Prusak (Ed.), *Knowledge in Organizations*. Boston, MA: Butterworth-Heinemann.

Prahalad, CK, and Hamel, G (1990) The core competencies of an organisation. *Harvard Business Review*, May–June, 79–81.

Print, M (1993) *Curriculum Development and Design* (2nd ed.). St. Leonards, NSW: Allen & Unwin.

Revans, RW (1983) *ABC of Action Learning*. Kent: Chartwell-Bratt.

Stacey, RD (1996) *Strategic Management and Organisational Dynamics*. London: Pitman.

Tennant, M (1999) Is learning transferable? In D Boud and J Garrick (Eds), *Understanding Learning at Work*. London: Routledge.

Ticehurst, GW, and Teal, AJ (1999) *Business Research Methods: A Managerial Approach*. Sydney: Longman.

Wexley, KN, and Latham, GP (1991) *Developing and Training Human Resources in Organizations*. New York: HarperCollins.

Zikmund, WG (1997) *Business Research Methods* (5th ed.). Fort Worth, TX: Dryden.

CHAPTER 18

Does mentoring deserve another look?

by Brian Hansford, Lisa Ehrich and Lee Tennent
Queensland University of Technology

Introduction

In recent decades, mentoring has been identified as a worthwhile workplace learning activity in a variety of organisational settings, including large and small corporations, government departments, hospitals, universities and schools. Mentoring has received enormous coverage in both the popular and academic literature. Some of these sources have hailed the mentoring process as a panacea for a variety of personal ills (Torrance 1984), while a smaller body of work has cautioned about the 'dark side' of mentoring (Long 1997). The purpose of this chapter is to report on findings from empirical research conducted in the area of mentoring in order to draw more than tentative conclusions about its benefits and limitations, as well as its implications, challenges and future directions for human resource (HR) managers and other organisational stakeholders affected by it.

We begin this chapter by defining mentoring and identifying the two types of mentoring arrangements that operate in organisations — formal and informal mentoring. Of the two, formal mentoring arrangements are most likely to be of interest to HR managers, since they tend to influence the development and implementation of mentoring programs within organisations. The chapter then provides a brief discussion on some of the theories and conceptual models that have been proposed to explain the mentoring phenomenon. An analysis of the research literature identifies the benefits and drawbacks of mentoring for key stakeholders such as mentors, 'mentees' (traditionally known as 'protégés') and

the organisation. To assist us in identifying these benefits and difficulties, we draw upon findings from our structured analysis of 151 pieces of mentoring research (Hansford, Tennent & Ehrich 2001). Finally, the chapter discusses some important issues, implications, challenges and future directions associated with mentoring for human resource management (HRM).

A definition

Although mentoring has received wide coverage in recent decades, researchers have yet to reach a consensus on a functional definition. It is evident, however, that researchers and notable writers in the area have been influenced by the Greek poet Homer, who first introduced the term 'mentor' in about 700 BC. In Homer's epic *The Odyssey*, Mentor was the wise and dear friend of Odysseus, who entrusted his son, Telemachus, into Mentor's care while he fought in the Trojan War. Mentor acted as a father figure to the young Telemachus and guided him as any prudent parent would — thus, the generic meaning of mentor as a 'father' figure who guides and instructs a younger individual. In the traditional sense, mentors are experienced individuals (both men and women) who use their knowledge, power and status to assist, promote and develop others (protégés or mentees) in their chosen field.

Two seminal studies that brought a great deal of attention to the phenomenon of mentoring during the 1970s were conducted by Kanter (1977) and Levinson, Darrow, Klein, Levinson and McKee (1978). The authors of both studies proposed that mentoring was a process that was beneficial for mentor and protégé alike. The mentor benefited from career rejuvenation and the satisfaction gained from helping another develop his or her abilities, while the protégé benefited from learning new skills and competencies and improved prospects for career development and promotion. Kanter's (1977) ethnographic study of men and women in corporations revealed that individuals who were mentored secured the most desirable jobs and accessed the power structures within the organisation. The longitudinal study conducted by Levinson et al. (1978) found that mentoring was not only concerned with 'sponsorship' (Kanter 1977) but, more importantly, construed as a developmental phase in an adult's life. Mentors were those important people who acted as 'peer and parent' and took on roles such as teacher, sponsor and friend. Since these analyses were first published, studies on the topic of mentoring have proliferated. Some of this work has been concerned with informal mentoring, while some has focused on formal mentoring. It is to these types of mentoring arrangements that we now direct our attention.

Types of mentoring relationships

In the studies by Kanter (1977) and Levinson et al. (1978), the mentoring relationship that developed between mentors and protégés could be distinguished as 'informal' or 'traditional' mentoring. This type of arrangement is typified by an experienced, older mentor initiating a relationship with a younger protégé who is recognised as having potential or talent. Informal or traditional mentorship can be a highly selective and elitist process since selection depends on the mentor's discretion and interest in the novice. As can be expected, mentors exhibit biases towards some potential protégés and not others (Odiorne 1985). For example, Odiorne (1985) suggests that some mentors have strong biases towards individuals of their own cultural background and religion. Kanter (1977) noted that in corporate settings it was not culture and religion that influenced mentor choice of protégés, but rather gender. She used the term 'homosocial reproduction' to refer to the practice of male mentors selecting male protégés. Her study prompted research into the area of women and mentorship in the 1980s and early 1990s. Much of this research was concerned with the

particular barriers women faced when they sought mentoring relationships (see Bogat & Redner 1985; Byrne 1989; Marshall 1985, Noe 1988; Ragins & Cotton 1991), as well as some of the potential risks, such as sexual attraction, marital disruption and damaging gossip, in male–female mentoring dyads (see, for example, Clawson & Kram 1984; Bowen 1985; Henderson 1985). Thus, this literature revealed that informal mentorship can be problematic, particularly for women.

A fundamental distinction between informal and formal mentoring arrangements is the extent of the involvement of the organisation concerned. While informal mentoring arrangements are spontaneous, occur at the discretion of the mentor and are rarely recognised by organisations, formal mentoring arrangements are programs that are developed and subsequently managed and monitored by organisational managers (Chao, Walz & Gardner 1992; Douglas 1997). Formal mentoring programs are of interest to HR managers because they are usually responsible for establishing, designing and implementing mentoring as a tool for learning in organisations.

Formal mentoring programs began to emerge in the 1970s in both private and public organisations in countries such as the United States, Australia and the United Kingdom. The movement by organisations towards institutionalising mentoring occurred, not only because organisations could see the benefits of mentoring for the mentor, mentee and organisations, but also because mentoring was perceived as an affirmative action strategy that ensured women and members of minority groups had access to the mentoring process (Sheridan 1995). Formal mentoring arrangements have the advantage of giving a wider range of employees access to mentors, an opportunity often denied to them under informal mentoring arrangements. However, the success of a formalised mentoring program is not automatic; rather, its success depends on a range of factors that will be discussed later in the chapter.

Theoretical underpinnings of mentoring research

The business literature abounds with exhortations for researchers, program developers and curriculum designers to underpin their work with a sound theoretical or conceptual framework. Yet a number of authors in the mentoring field (e.g. Gibb 1999; Jacobi 1991) have noted that very few studies locate mentoring within a wider theoretical framework. For example, Gibb (1999) commented that 'a substantive theoretical analysis of mentoring has been absent, implicit or underdeveloped' (p. 1), while Jacobi (1991), in a comprehensive review of the research literature on mentoring, noted a general 'lack of theoretical analysis' (p. 522). As Healy and Welchert (1990) caution, this absence of theoretical grounding has led to definitional problems for mentoring.

In light of this, a focus for our structured analysis of the mentoring literature was the use of theory in the 151 reviewed studies. Our review revealed no shortage of theoretical insight, with 34.4 per cent of studies espousing at least one theoretical perspective. These theories were derived from fields such as economics (human capital theory; exchange theory), philosophy (Foucault's 1983 analysis of discipline and control; post-Confucian theory), organisational behaviour (contingency theory; the competing values framework), sociology (structuration theory) and psychology (social learning theory; developmental theory). Interestingly, 42.4 per cent of studies also referred to the seminal work of Kram (1985). An important contribution of Kram's (1985) work is her conceptualisation of the mentor role into two discrete functions. First, mentors provide career functions to mentees through sponsorship, protection, visibility and exposure. Second, mentors provide psycho-social functions to mentees in the form of role modelling, counselling and friendship.

While a substantial number of studies were underpinned by theory or a conceptual framework, it is noteworthy that a majority of the reviewed studies were not. We would argue that if mentoring research is to be taken seriously by researchers and practitioners alike, it is incumbent upon researchers to articulate the theoretical underpinnings of their empirical research. This will help eliminate the definitional confusion that surrounds mentoring and strengthen its place in the academic research community. The chapter now examines some of the key outcomes of mentoring that emerged from our structured analysis of the business literature.

Outcomes of mentoring

A further focus of our investigation was to examine the outcomes of mentoring from a variety of perspectives. MacCallum and Baltiman (1999, p. 1) have argued that 'little of the research literature considers mentoring from the perspective of the different stakeholders'. Likewise, Lauland (1998, www.ed.gov/pubs/YesYouCan/) suggested that stakeholders' expectations should be taken into consideration in mentoring programs. In our study (Hansford et al. 2001), we examined positive and negative outcomes as experienced by three of the major stakeholders, namely the mentors, the mentees, and the business or organisation in which the mentoring program was offered. To achieve this, the 151 studies were coded and analysed according to descriptive and factual data. Descriptive data comprised the positive and negative outcomes of mentoring for all of the stakeholders; factual data included year of publication, source, sample size, data collection techniques employed, theoretical perspectives evident, country of study, and from whom the data were collected (i.e. mentor or mentee or others). We felt it was important to code factual data so that we could obtain a profile of the mentoring research in terms of the type and nature of research carried out in this area. Some of the key findings from our structured analysis of the mentoring literature are now discussed.

Factual data

Almost all (98 per cent) of the research studies in our structured analysis of the mentoring literature were published in journals between 1986 and 2000. The remainder were derived from monographs, research reports and book chapters published during the same period. The majority of studies (70 per cent) came from the United States, which was not surprising given that the US is the birthplace of formal mentoring programs in organisations. A further 13.6 per cent of studies came from the UK, 3.3 per cent from Canada and only 2.6 per cent from Australia and Asia, respectively. In terms of the study respondents, 53 per cent of the studies sought responses exclusively from mentees, while only 7.9 per cent of the studies sought responses exclusively from mentors. A further 23.8 per cent of studies sought information from both mentees and mentors. In the remaining studies, data were obtained from such sources as HR personnel, training consultants and executives in the business as well as mentors and mentees. In all, approximately 90 per cent of the database contained data from mentees while approximately 32 per cent contained data from mentors. This seems to indicate that business researchers or the personnel supporting the studies are more interested in the outcomes for mentees than for mentors. We did not code the studies according to the type of mentoring arrangement used (i.e. formal or informal), because very few of them acknowledged this distinction.

Initial general findings

Of the 151 studies reviewed, 67.5 per cent reported only positive outcomes as a consequence of mentoring programs. A further 24.5 per cent of the studies reported a mix of positive and negative outcomes. By way of contrast, only 6.6 per cent of the articles reported exclusively negative outcomes. In order to elaborate these general findings we will present data that relate to both positive and negative outcomes. The following sections discuss such outcomes specifically for mentors, mentees and the organisations involved.

Positive and negative outcomes for mentors

It should be kept in mind from the outset that approximately two-thirds of the studies did not elicit responses from mentors. Numerous positive and negative outcomes were reported; however, we have limited our discussion to the eight most frequently cited outcomes. As can be observed in table 18.1, the most frequently cited positive outcome, reported in almost 8 per cent of the studies, related to the mentors' belief that networking, collegiality and reciprocity were constructive outcomes from a mentoring experience. In 7.3 per cent of the studies, mentors indicated that their involvement in a program was associated with career satisfaction and even promotion. Mentors also perceived that their participation could be linked to improved skills and job performance (6.6 per cent of studies) and pride or personal satisfaction (6.6 per cent). Table 18.1 also reports that the mentors considered that taking on the role potentially offered them the benefits of assistance and ideas (6.0 per cent), respect and empowerment (6.0 per cent), insight into other roles (6.0 per cent), and interpersonal development and confidence (6.0 per cent).

Negative outcomes were reported less frequently. As can be seen in table 18.1, 6 per cent of the mentors reported lack of time to perform their mentoring role. Mentors also reported negative attitudes by the mentee in more than 5 per cent of the studies, a lack of training, knowledge and understanding (4.6 per cent), jealousy and negativity from others (4.0 per cent), pressure from other components of their workplace responsibilities (3.3 per cent), unrealistic expectations of the mentee (2.6 per cent), negative outcomes if the mentee is unsuccessful (2.6 per cent) and difficulties in ending the mentor–mentee relationship (2.6 per cent).

Table 18.1: Nature of outcomes for mentors

Positive outcomes	(N)	%
Networking/collegiality/reciprocity	12	7.9
Career satisfaction/motivation/promotion	11	7.3
Improved skills/job performance	10	6.6
Pride/personal satisfaction	10	6.6
Assistance/ideas/support/feedback	9	6.0
Respect/empowerment	9	6.0
Insight into other's roles/divisions	9	6.0
Personal/interpersonal development/confidence	9	6.0
Negative outcomes	**(N)**	**%**
Lack of time	9	6.0
Negative mentee attitude/lack of trust/cooperation	8	5.3
Lack of training/knowledge/understanding	7	4.6
Jealousy/negative attitudes of others	6	4.0
Pressure/conflicting demands/roles	5	3.3
Mentee expectations unrealistic	4	2.6
Negative exposure/failure if mentee unsuccessful	4	2.6
Difficulty ending relationship	4	2.6

Positive and negative outcomes for mentees

Mentees were largely positive about their mentoring experiences. The eight most frequently identified positive and negative outcomes for mentees in business studies are presented in table 18.2. The most frequently occurring positive outcomes related to career satisfaction, motivation, developing plans and possible promotion. This was reported by mentees in 50.3 per cent of the 151 studies examined. Mentees indicated in 30.5 per cent of the studies that their mentors had coached them and given them ideas, feedback and strategies. A further 23.3 per cent of mentees' responses noted that they had been given challenging assignments that had led to improved workplace skills and overall performance. The fourth most positively cited mentee outcome (21.9 per cent of studies) focused on the benefits that accrued as a consequence of counselling, listening, supporting, understanding and encouraging. In 16.6 per cent of the studies, the mentees reported that being mentored gave them access to resources, information and personnel. In 15.5 per cent of the studies, the mentees indicated heightened self-confidence, respect and interpersonal growth as a result of their involvement in the mentoring program. Other mentees suggested that mentoring had helped with their socialisation in the company (14.6 per cent of studies) and their sponsorship, protection and advocacy within the specific businesses (13.9 per cent).

Table 18.2: Nature of outcomes for mentees

Positive outcomes	(N)	%
Career satisfaction/motivation/plans/promotion	76	50.3
Coaching/ideas/feedback/strategies	46	30.5
Challenging assignments/improved skills/performance	35	23.2
Counselling/listening/support/understanding/encouragement	33	21.9
Access to resources/information/people	25	16.6
Self-confidence/respect/personal/interpersonal growth	23	15.2
Company socialisation/involvement in policies/issues	22	14.6
Sponsorship/protection/advocacy	21	13.9
Negative outcomes	**(N)**	**%**
Gender-/race-related problems	12	7.9
Cloning/conformity/limited autonomy/overprotection	11	7.3
Mentor untrained/ineffective	10	6.6
Negative attitude of others	9	6.0
Mentor competes/takes credit/exploits	8	5.3
Career blocked by mentor	6	4.0
Lack of mentor interest/support/communication	6	4.0
Mentor lacks time/availability	6	4.0

In terms of negative mentoring outcomes, almost 8 per cent of the studies reported problems associated with gender and race differences. This is in keeping with Fulop and Linstead (1999), who argued that diversified mentoring, which involved personnel of differing power and status, can produce difficulties. They suggest that these power and status problems are frequently based on gender, sexuality, race and ethnicity. In our study, other negative mentoring outcomes included cloning, conformity, limited autonomy and overprotection (7.3 per cent of the studies),

mentors being untrained and ineffective (6.6 per cent), negative attitudes from others in the business (6.0 per cent), mentors taking the credit (5.3 per cent), careers being blocked by mentors (4.0 per cent), lack of interest and support from the mentor (4.0 per cent) and lack of mentor time or availability (4.0 per cent).

Positive and negative outcomes for organisations

Involvement in a mentoring program may have an impact on the personnel involved, but it is suggested that there are also potential positive and negative outcomes for the business organisation itself. Among the 151 research studies, 30.5 per cent cited one or more positive outcomes for organisations, and only 8.8 per cent commented negatively concerning the impact on the business. The outcomes affecting the organisation were more frequently described by the researcher or a participant other than the mentor or mentee. It seems appropriate to point out that the focus of the research in many of the studies was on mentors and mentees. It seems highly likely that studies with a more specific focus on the organisation would yield greater evidence of both negative and positive outcomes.

Table 18.3 indicates the positive outcomes that may accrue to a business as a consequence of a mentoring program. Negative outcomes are not included in this table as the percentages are so small.

Table 18.3: Nature of positive outcomes for organisations

Positive outcomes	(N)	%
Improves productivity/contribution/profit by employees	21	13.9
Retention/attraction of talented employees	18	11.9
Promotes loyalty/empathy/team spirit	10	6.6
Improved workplace/communications/relations	6	4.0
Facilitates change/learning	3	2.0
More control over employees	2	1.3
Bridges gap between training and workplace	2	1.3

It is no surprise that in a business setting the most significant positive outcome was identified as improved productivity, contribution or profit by employees. In total, 13.9 per cent of the studies from the business database identified this as a positive outcome. The other positive organisational outcomes were grouped as retaining or attracting talented employees (11.9 per cent); promoting loyalty, empathy or team spirit (6.6 per cent); improving workplace communications and relations (4.0 per cent); facilitating change and learning (2.0 per cent); obtaining more control over employees (1.3 per cent); and bridging the gap between training and the workplace (1.3 per cent).

In terms of negative organisational outcomes, there was mention of the potential to increase staff turnover, the creation of gender or race bias, a decline in sales if mentors were overburdened, a difficulty in controlling mentoring programs, the financial outlay and the constant need to evaluate such programs.

Summary of mentoring outcomes from the business database

Based on the 151 studies examined in this analysis, mentoring in business settings is generally associated with positive outcomes. In fact, more than 90 per cent of the studies involved reported some evidence of positive and beneficial outcomes. However, enough studies mention negative outcomes to suggest that mentoring can have a 'dark side'.

From the mentors' point of view, involvement in a program can facilitate and foster networking and collegiality, career satisfaction, respect, empowerment and new ideas. Performing the role of mentor can also facilitate greater confidence and personal growth. However, mentors also indicated that time restraints can minimise potential benefits, that they are not always fully trained, that others in the organisation may exhibit negative attitudes towards them, and that mentees can develop unrealistic expectations about what the mentor can provide.

Mentees perceived that career satisfaction, increased motivation and possible promotion could flow from participation in a mentoring program. Mentees also contended that the feedback they received could result in the development of new ideas and strategies. Further, some mentees benefited from interpersonal growth and socialisation in the organisation. The negative perceptions of mentees included those associated with gender and race differences, the need to conform to the mentor's expectations, the lack of mentor training and mentor time, and negative attitudes expressed by others in the organisation.

For the organisation, the positive mentoring outcomes included improving productivity, attracting and retaining talented staff, and developing team spirit. Negative outcomes, on the other hand, included problems relating to gender and race, implementation costs and the danger of decreasing profits if mentors are overburdened.

Implications of findings from the analysis of the mentoring literature

An examination of the positive outcomes for mentors, mentees and organisations suggests that implementing a mentoring program can be a productive strategic decision for the business. The main positive mentoring outcomes include networking, greater collegiality and understanding, improved career satisfaction and workplace skills, more motivated and confident staff, enhanced interpersonal skills, and increased productivity and profit. Although such outcomes conjure up an image of a utopian workplace, they tend to be counterbalanced by the problems associated with mentoring, such as the overburdening of staff; lack of time and training of staff; conflict stemming from race and gender difficulties; unrealistic expectations of staff, who may also believe that their careers have been blocked; pressure to conform; and the difficulties associated with developing and funding a worthwhile program.

Clearly, organisations considering implementing a mentoring program should attempt to maximise the potentially positive outcomes and minimise the potentially negative outcomes of mentoring. A spontaneous, 'spur of the moment' mentoring program risks at least some of the negative outcomes that we have identified in our study, since the design and implementation of programs requires considerable planning and preparation. Successful mentoring programs are more likely to be realised when management, and HR management in particular, include such programs in long-range strategic planning. Many texts and articles set out a range of developmental and implementation tasks required for implementing successful mentoring programs. Before we outline what we consider to be the vital aspects of such a program, it seems appropriate to highlight an issue raised by Goodlad (1999). Goodlad (1999, p. 20) points out that peer tutoring and mentoring have 'exciting possibilities' but that 'we need to be careful not to claim too much … In short, we need to be aware of overselling, and thereby discrediting, exciting and eminently useful ideas' (p. 20). We have also made this point elsewhere. In a paper entitled 'Mentoring: A panacea for all times' (Hansford & Ehrich 1999, p. 1), it was suggested that 'much of the writing on mentoring provides an unproblematic view of its potential gains for mentors, mentees and organisations'. Managers need to fully appreciate the positive and negative outcomes reported here.

Challenges and future directions facing HR managers

The following points highlight important challenges and future directions for HR managers and others in organisations who may be endeavouring to maximise the outcomes from mentoring. These challenges and considerations include obtaining organisational support for mentoring; clarifying aims, roles, expectations and rules; training mentors; selecting personnel and possible matching procedures; keeping logistics simple; and ongoing monitoring and evaluation.

Obtaining organisational support

It is difficult to imagine a mentoring program in a business functioning well without organisational support. Indeed, Douglas (1997, p. 91) indicates that 'the support of top managers is probably the most frequently mentioned success characteristic in the literature'. Furthermore, Douglas (1997) states:

> *Organizational support is defined as encouragement and support of a program by the organization as a whole. More specifically, program-development efforts should be integrated into strategic needs, organizational systems (for example, performance-appraisal process, reward systems, and communication systems), and other management-development systems. (p. 91)*

Burke and McKeen (1989) note that if senior managers are to become involved in a program, it is important for them to see there is visible support from top management. If it is known that there is little or no support from senior management for a mentoring program, it would be extremely difficult to create an organisational culture in which the program could flourish. But there is a difference between general support from management and support associated with the day-to-day running of a scheme. Goodlad (1999) has pointed out that in a mentoring scheme, 'there is one person with whom the buck stops', and this in turn suggests keeping a scheme 'to a scale where one organiser can be in touch with what is going on' (p. 11). Sustaining a mentoring program is very much about sustaining the necessary organisational support.

Clarification of aims, roles, rules and expectations

At a very early stage of mentoring planning, there is a need to articulate the aims of the program, the roles that personnel are to perform and the rules operating during the program. The program's aims should be outlined and discussed with mentees. Douglas (1997) recommends that program aims should not only be defined, but they should be 'communicated to relevant individuals, potential mentors, top management, non-participants, and programme coordinators' (p. 95). Such communication would reduce the likelihood of misunderstandings surrounding the roles and expectations of participants. Tovey (1998) argues that in order to minimise misunderstandings, a minimal set of rules should be developed. It is likely that such rules would differ from program to program, but Tovey suggests as a starting point the following:

- The mentee's personal life and experiences will be discussed only by invitation of the mentee.
- Mentors will not make excessive demands on the time of mentees.
- Mentees will not make excessive demands on the time of mentors.
- Mentors will assist mentees to achieve their goals but will let them run their own show.
- Knowledge of the mentee will be passed on only with the permission of the mentee.

Program rules would most likely be developed following discussion between participants, but individual mentors and mentees might need to agree on specific rules covering their own association in the program.

There should be frank and open discussion about expectations for the program. Mentors and mentees need to spend time discussing their respective expectations. Jorgenson (1992) contends that there should be a no-fault exit clause in mentoring arrangements in order to minimise criticism of retaliation following a decision to exit a program.

Training of mentors

The mentor role needs to be outlined by an appropriate internal staff member, possibly the program coordinator or a suitably trained member of human resources. Alternatively, the training of mentors may be carried out by suitably qualified external consultants. Mentors need to know what is expected of them, the sort of questions they will be asked, the nature of tasks they can set mentees and the time restraints on themselves and mentees. The type and length of training of mentors would vary according to the work site involved and the nature of the aims or goals established for the program. Regardless of the context, however, Tovey (1998) believes that 'in-depth training must be provided for mentors' (p. 5) and that a 'willingness to undertake training for the role' (p. 16) be a prerequisite. One component that should be included in mentor preparation relates to what Tovey (1998, p. 33) describes as a knowledge of *scaffolding* and *fading*. It must be made clear to mentors that they have a responsibility to provide support in the form of scaffolding for mentees. This scaffolding is constructed in accordance with the skill and knowledge levels of individual mentees. At the same time, mentors must be aware of the need to fade, or gradually remove the scaffolding, as mentees become more accomplished.

Another issue that may need to be addressed in mentoring programs is whether or not mentees also require training. Certainly, they need to be included in discussions of rules and expectations. However, they should also be consulted or briefed during the development and implementation of the program, thereby facilitating an open and effective communication system.

Selection of participants and possible matching

In our preliminary reading relating to mentoring we were inclined to agree with MacCallum and Baltiman (1999), who suggested that there is an assumption 'that if anyone were to follow the guidelines then the mentoring programme would be successful' (p. 1). MacCallum and Baltiman (1999) also stress that mentoring 'is not always successful and unsuccessful matches can be worse than no mentoring at all' (p. 1). Dondero (1997) agrees and points out the dangers of 'drive-by mentoring' (p. 22). The work of Long (1997) and Ehrich and Hansford (1999) reinforces the possibility of a 'dark side' in mentoring. These views strengthened our resolve to explore the positive and negative outcomes of business mentoring.

It is unlikely that all experienced staff in an organisation would want to be mentors. Indeed, it is likely that some would not have the appropriate personal qualities to perform the role. Consequently, the selection of mentors can be a difficult task. Tovey (1998) has indicated that having relevant expertise in a field is not in itself sufficient qualification for the role of mentor. He recommends a number of essential characteristics for successful mentors. These characteristics include the ability to build and manage relationships, a willingness to share knowledge, organisational knowledge, expertise in the field, a commitment to the facilitation of learning, and a willingness to commit the time and effort required.

Douglas (1997) suggests that participation by mentors and mentees should be voluntary and comments that if 'participation is not perceived as voluntary, the effectiveness of the initiative will be diminished by participant resistance' (p. 97). Douglas (1997, pp. 96–7) goes further, arguing that the effectiveness of a program might well be linked to the extent that mentors, mentees and senior managers perceive that they have a sense of choice and a role in decision making.

Antal (1993) has suggested that there are several possible methods for identifying and selecting participants. These include self-nomination, nomination by other potential mentors, nomination by senior managers and supervisors, and nomination of potential mentors by other participants.

Goodlad (1999) believes that the jury is still out on the question of matching mentors and mentees, but this view is not shared by Tovey (1998) or Douglas (1997). Tovey (1998) suggests that, where possible, mentors and mentees choose each other, but that gender and cultural differences should be taken into consideration. Douglas (1997) favours a matching process based on program objectives and a predetermined set of criteria. In addition, she raises issues such as position in the firm, similar interests, personalities, accessibility, geographical location and functional area.

Keeping logistics simple

As the organisation and program increase in size and complexity, the potential for difficulties also increases. Goodlad (1999) suggests that mentoring and peer tutoring programs should start small and simple. Freedman (1995) identifies time as one of the major logistical problems. This view is in keeping with the findings of our structured analysis, which found that lack of time was perceived by mentors and mentees to be a significant impediment to the success of mentoring programs.

Freedman (1995) suggests that 'mentors are often better at signing up than showing up' (p. 221). An important issue, then, is whether the mentor has the time to perform the role in a professional manner. How long should meetings be scheduled for, and has the mentee's line manager been informed about them? For both mentor and mentee there is a potential for work overload. There are also considerations regarding a suitable meeting place, which Goodlad (1999, p. 16) suggests 'must ... be geographically accessible [and] must make both mentors and mentees comfortable — culturally as well as physically'.

Monitoring and evaluating

Monitoring and evaluation procedures must be clearly defined and articulated during the developmental stages of the program. Kram and Bragar (1991) encourage ongoing monitoring and assessment through the use of such procedures as interviews, focus groups and surveys. These authors also argue that the monitoring process should be linked to the strategic challenges and requirements of the workplace.

Conclusion

An important implication of the findings from our analysis of the research literature discussed in this chapter is that mentoring has many spin-offs for mentors, mentees and the organisations concerned. Thus, we would argue that HR managers view mentoring as an important learning tool and professional development strategy in the workplace. This said, careful long-term planning and skilful and sensitive HR leadership will be needed to minimise the potentially negative aspects of mentoring.

The successful implementation and management of any mentoring program requires a careful mix of many important ingredients, and this chapter has identified some of these. A further essential ingredient that cannot be over-emphasised is the provision of adequate levels of resourcing. It is evident that the overall planning, the training of mentors, the appointment of a coordinator, and the evaluative process require both financial and human resources. We believe that positive outcomes are unlikely in the absence of sufficient funding. Thus, it is essential that ongoing and visible organisational support (demonstrated in dollars and in kind) for mentoring programs not be overlooked.

References

Antal, AB (1993) Odysseus' legacy to management development: mentoring. *European Management Journal*, 11 (4) 448–54.

Bogat, GA, and Redner, RL (1985) How mentoring affects the development of women in psychology, *Professional Psychology: Research and Practice*, 16 (6) 851–9.

Bowen, DD (1985) Were men meant to mentor women? *Training and Development Journal*, February, 30–34.

Burke, RJ, and McKeen, CA (1989) Developing formal mentoring programs in organisations. *Business Quarterly*, 53 (3) 76–9.

Byrne, EM (1989) Role modelling and mentorship as policy mechanisms: the need for new directions. Brisbane: Department of Education, University of Queensland.

Chao, GT, Walz, PM, and Gardner, PD (1992) Formal and informal mentorships: a comparison on mentoring functions and contrasts with nonmentored counterparts. *Personnel Psychology*, 45, Autumn, 619–36.

Clawson, JG, and Kram, KE (1984) Managing cross-gender mentoring. *Business Horizons*, 27 (3) 22–32.

Dondero, GM (1997) Mentors: beacons of hope. *Adolescence*, 32 (128) 881–6.

Douglas, CA (1997) *Formal Mentoring Programs in Organizations: An Annotated Bibliography*. Greensboro, NC: Centre for Creative Leadership.

Ehrich, LC, and Hansford, BC (1999) Mentoring: pros and cons for HRM. *Asia Pacific Journal of Human Resources*. 37 (3) 92–107.

Foucault, M (1983) Afterword: the subject and power. In HL Dreyfus and P Rabinow (Eds), *Michel Foucault: Beyond Structuralism and Hermeneutics*. Chicago: University of Chicago Press.

Freedman, M (1995) From friendly visiting to mentoring: a tale of two movements. In S Goodlad (Ed.), *Students as Tutors and Mentors*. London: Kogan Page.

Fulop, L, and Linstead, S (1999) *Management: a critical text*. Melbourne: Macmillan.

Gibb, S (1999) The usefulness of theory: a case study in evaluating formal mentoring schemes. *Human Relations*, 52 (8) 1055–75.

Goodlad, S (1999) Never knowingly oversold: a watchword for tutoring and mentoring schemes? Second Regional Conference on Tutoring and Mentoring. Perth, 30 September–2 October.

Hansford, BC, and Ehrich, LC (1999) Mentoring: a panacea for all times? Queensland HR Practices Day, Australian Human Resources Institute, Brisbane, 18 February.

Hansford, BC, Tennent, L, and Ehrich, LC (2001) Business mentoring: help or hindrance? Unpublished paper.

Healy, CC, and Welchert, AJ (1990) Mentoring relations: a definition to advance research and practice. *Educational Researcher*, 19 (9) 17–21.

Henderson, DW (1985) Enlightened mentoring: a characteristic of public management professionalism. *Public Administration Review*, November–December, 857–63.

Jacobi, M (1991) Mentoring and undergraduate academic success: a literature review. *Review of Educational Research*, 61 (4) 505–532.

Jorgenson, J (1992) *Mentoring Programs: An Overview.* Washington, DC: National Academy of Public Administration.

Kanter R (1977) *Men and Women of the Corporation.* New York: Basic Books.

Kram, KE (1985) Improving the mentor process. *Training and Development Journal*, 39 (4) 40–43.

Kram, KE, and Bragar, MC (1991) Development through mentoring: a strategic approach. In D Montross and C Shinkman (Eds), *Career Development: Theory and Practice.* Springfield, IL: Charles C. Thomas.

Lauland, A (1998) Yes you can: a guide for establishing programs to prepare youth for college. USA Department of Education, www.ed.gov/pubs/YesYouCan/ (viewed April 2001).

Levinson, DJ, Darrow, CN, Klein, EB, Levinson, MH, and McKee, B (1978) *The Seasons of a Man's Life.* New York: Ballantine.

Long, J (1997) The dark side of mentoring. *Australian Educational Research*, 24 (2) 115–83.

MacCallum, J, and Baltiman, S (1999) Mentoring: an old idea that works — or does it? Second Regional Conference on Tutoring and Mentoring, Perth, 30 September–2 October.

Marshall, C (1985) The stigmatised woman: the professional woman in a male sex–typed career. *Journal of Educational Administration*, 23 (2) 131–51.

Noe, RA (1988) Women and mentoring: a review and research agenda. *Academy of Management Review*, 13 (1) 65–78.

Odiorne, GS (1985) Mentoring — an American management innovation. *Personnel Administrator*, 30 (5) 63–70.

Ragins, BR, and Cotton, JL (1991) Easier said than done: gender differences in perceived barriers to gaining a mentor. *Academy of Management Journal*, 34, 939–51.

Sheridan, AJ (1995) Affirmative action in Australia — employment statistics can't tell the whole story. *Women in Management Review*, 10 (2) 26–34.

Torrance, EP (1984) *Mentor Relationships: How They Aid Creative Achievement, Endure, Change and Die.* New York: Bearly.

Tovey, MD (1998) *Mentoring in the Workplace: A Guide for Mentors and Managers.* Erskineville, NSW: Prentice Hall.

CHAPTER 19

CHAPTER 19

The internal team: the socio-emotional dynamics of team(work)

by Susan Long
Swinburne University of Technology

Introduction

In the past 30 years or more much has been written about the development of teams in work organisations. The team was first recognised as a focused and effective way of working that encourages members to cooperate in performing a task; it is now increasingly regarded as a structural solution for organisations that can replace several layers of hierarchy and achieve a flatter organisational structure. The team may also improve communication and accountability. Semi-autonomous teams, together with project management, are nowadays regarded by many as a superior organisational form to older, cumbersome layers of bureaucracy. They achieve a kind of 'mini business unit' structure, with the attendant advantages of mobility, flexibility and independence. As well as achieving task focus, this allows teams more readily to be 'consumer' as well as producer units within a broader organisation, a distinct advantage in the new, consumer-dominated culture of organisational life (Long 1999a).

With this focus, a process-consultancy industry has grown up around teamwork through educating and training people at all levels to be 'team players', yet even today little is understood about the *psycho-dynamic* and *unconscious* processes in teams. Most of the literature is centred on the ideas and basic assumptions of organisational culture (e.g. Schien 1990; Schneider & Shrivastava 1988) or on types of team players (Belbin Year). Bion (1961) wrote largely about less structured groups, as have most of the psycho-dynamic writers that followed him. Among those who consider teams from

a psycho-dynamic perspective, Hirschhorn (1991) writes of the 'new team environment' and the need for collaboration. In exploring the unconscious dynamics, however, he draws mainly on the work on group culture and group defence mechanisms. Stokes (1994) also considers multidisciplinary teams in a health care setting, again emphasising collaboration and the particular dynamics of the sophisticated work group. While these approaches have much to offer, understanding the specific dynamics of teams in organisations requires further exploration.

What, then, is the specific nature of a team, and how are the team members related to one another? This chapter argues that effective and satisfying teamwork relies on a complex and specific psychological capacity among team members — that is, the ability to work creatively with other team members and the team-as-a-whole as *internalised objects*. When this capacity is not exercised or cannot be achieved, teamwork is impaired. To build my argument:

- an examination of the nature of work is required. I will argue here that, in essence, psychic work involves transformative and representative processes that engage the psyche (or mind) with reality. Lawrence (1999) describes work organisations as 'ideas in the mind' for working with products and services. Organisational work can be similarly characterised — that is, as a process involving transformation and representation that engages the psyche with reality.
- an exploration of the nature of teams as a special form of group is necessary
- the complex dynamic of work with internal objects must be articulated and illustrated through research examples.

I will endeavour to address each of these areas in this chapter, and will also consider the nature of identificatory dynamics and the accompanying emotional experiences for members within a team. I will argue that, compared with other, 'looser' forms of psychological group, the team relies heavily on identifications between members to achieve a task. Specifically, this is a partial identification in which members retain their own specific role identities while understanding and relating to the roles and tasks of other team members. This is achieved through a capacity to:

1. be in the presence of the other team members (Long, Newton & Dalgleish, forthcoming)
2. internalise other team members
3. refer to and negotiate with the internalised team members when forming judgements.

I will suggest that, in successful teamwork, there are many occasions when direct reference to others is not possible. Communication takes on subtle forms, and members rely heavily on their 'internalised team'. At other times, members are able to verify, challenge, reshape and renew their internalised team. Successful teamwork requires attention to team dynamics so that members' internal teams reflect reality.

Teamwork is less successful when members are unable to engage partial identifications based on realistic internalisation. Sometimes a full and immediate identification with others may occur, so that one's own role identity is lost, and the team cannot operate with complex and sophisticated role divisions. This happens in basic assumption experience (Bion 1961) and is driven by anger, fear and anxiety. Also, often linked to this, members may internalise phantasy based on projected identifications that are poorly mediated by reality. Such dynamics may be due to intense emotional experiences, or the inability of members to realistically internalise the team or to renew their 'internal teams' in light of changed circumstances.

The chapter will develop an argument around these ideas, drawing on case material from working teams.

Contemporary issues in team dynamics

Work and the group

Before examining teams specifically, I will review some thinking about groups and the nature of work within groups. Lawrence (1999) suggests that organisations are no longer necessarily the 'containers' of work and that work extends beyond the boundaries of particular organisations into the non-specific environment, which includes new contexts such as cyberspace. The group, then, more than ever has to be seen in terms of its psychic space (Schlachet 1986) rather than in terms of a concretely defined organisation. People who never meet face to face may nonetheless form a group. This is the domain of virtual groups.

Identification

Following traditional psychoanalytic thinking, this section will argue that the basic 'glue' for groups is identification and the primary identification for work group members is achieved through a common task.

The psychoanalytic literature, from Freud through Bion to current socio-analytic formulations (Bain 1999), often centres on the problem of how group members work collectively to achieve a task. Freud's seminal definition of a primary group (i.e. a group with a leader) is centred on identification. For him:

a primary group of this kind is a number of individuals who have put one and the same object in the place of their ego ideal and have consequently identified themselves with one another in their ego. (Freud 1921, p. 147)

I have described some implications of this definition elsewhere (Long 1992, 1999b). In brief, we can say that identification is the primary 'glue' of a group; it is what holds members together. A person (the symbolic leader) or idea is collectively valued and held in esteem and, through identification, becomes an internalised ideal. Different group members identify with one another because of this collective internalised ideal. They recognise an affinity that binds them and brings with it feelings of loyalty and solidarity. Such feelings are not developed in isolation. One doesn't simply manufacture trust or loyalty. They are the outcome of a perceived similarity that can be tested. Once established, however, trust and loyalty can be shaken. Although they may be built initially on a perceived point of similarity, they are sustained and developed only through ongoing mutual testing during interactions in reality, for example through day-to-day work relations.

Some social psychologists have demonstrated that people don't even have to meet others whom they believe to have similar ideals to identify with them (Turner et al. 1987). Finding their names on the same list as others is enough to begin the process. Further, they are likely to identify with them even with respect to characteristics completely unknown or seemingly irrelevant to the initial point of identification. This has implications for those who find themselves communicating across the Internet, for instance. Bion's notion of valency is relevant: it is a kind of immediate, spontaneous 'falling into identification' with another.

Of course, the strength of ties within a group varies, and people may have identificatory ties with many groups, which may present contradictions. Nonetheless, it is the identifications among members, or what is more properly described as partial identifications, that provide the foundation for collective work together. Bion (1961) described a group as a number of individuals with a common task. His exploration of basic assumptions points to an unconscious and implicit task shared by members — of defending the group from an enemy, for instance, or giving obeisance to a god-like leader. He compared the dynamics of such assumption groups with those of the work group whose task is explicit and tied to reality rather than to phantasy, linked to science rather than to magic. In this, Bion links work to reality testing and the scientific method of gaining knowledge — that is, not simply a 'working *with*' thoughts and emotions but a 'working through' of thoughts and emotions. For Bion, the 'task' replaces Freud's 'leader' as the object supplanting the ego-ideal, or, at least, the task provides legitimacy for the leader.

The nature of work

If the work group is held together by members' identification with a task, the nature of work itself must be questioned. I argue here that work is a transformative and representative process that also involves sublimation of affect and engagement with reality. Without these features, what appears to be work is rather a process of conforming to actions or processes that maintain a status quo or make translations in phantasy alone. This is not work but repetition or distortion (Freud 1915). It may involve physical or mental effort, but I am distinguishing this from work.

Take, as an example, the task of writing a report on an inmate undertaken by a prison officer, working as a case manager in a prison unit. Writing an incident report in a case file requires the case manager to transform various pieces of information into a meaningful account. This may require making judgements about what is good or poor information, reconciling differing pieces of evidence, checking information, talking with different people (including the prison inmate and others involved), and deciding what really occurred. If, instead of this process, the case manager decides simply to reproduce the account of just one of many sources of information, then his labour is not real work. Or, if he

decides to 'fill in the gaps' with what he assumes happened or with what he wishes happened, rather than investigating the incident thoroughly, then the result will be a laborious distortion.

Thus, the first way of approaching the task requires the transformation of information, hunches and observations. It involves the representation of a multitude of thoughts and feelings surrounding the issue, and several reality checks. The case manager must become engaged in a process first of *suspending judgements* while checking facts, and then, after having gathered as much information as possible, of *applying judgements*. This process of suspension followed by application of judgement is transformative. Personal feelings about the situation are held in check or classed as hunches — sublimated, if you will, into a form of curiosity. This is the condition for 'evenly suspended attention'.

The second way of approaching the task with unchecked assumptions involves avoidance. Perhaps questioning the account of a fellow officer or superior feels dangerous or provokes anxiety, so the inquiry goes no further. The prisoner's own account may be too easily dismissed ('he's a troublemaker') or too readily accepted, according to how he or she is generally viewed. Such a failure, even when detected, is not easily overcome.

Nonetheless, avoidance of this kind may be overcome by what psychoanalysis describes as *working through*. Here transformation can occur, and reality (including emotional reality) is engaged rather than avoided. The process of working through is, I believe, akin to the process of suspending and applying judgement at critical points in the engagement of reality. It involves self-understanding and the development of symbolisation in contrast to acting out of primitive impulses (O'Shaughnessy 1988).

Psychoanalysis has always regarded 'work' as an important life motive. But what do we *mean* by work, and how is it linked to the group task as described by Bion? In the Freudian literature, work is discussed primarily in terms of 'work of the intellect'. Although we can distinguish between physical and intellectual work, the collective work of a group or organisation should be seen primarily in terms of the ideas and the emotions of the members. An idea, for example, may involve creating a product or performing a service, carrying out a manoeuvre or fulfilling a ministry. Team members also have feelings about what is created. Here I distinguish work from 'labour'. Psychic work is that of transformation and representation. The instincts and emotions are given meaning and a place in personal or organisational history. Thought emerges both from action and from its suspension.

A transformation takes place. For instance, Freud traced how work is done unconsciously in the formation of dreams and symptoms, as well as consciously in the processes of 'working through', in which situations and issues are faced realistically and their implications examined, and in which emotional experiences are relived and new responses found. Lacan (1977) linked this work to linguistics, demonstrating how the unconscious processes of condensation and displacement are psychically equivalent to the linguistic processes of metaphor and metonomy. Bion traced the transformations (through container/contained) of emotional experience in his theory of thinking from primitive alpha and beta elements to scientific hypotheses and mathematical formulations.

In psychoanalytic formulations, psychic work is inextricably linked to the subject and its attempts to transform emotional experience. Organisational work, too, is transformative. Open systems theory emphasises this when work is understood as a process through which inputs are transformed into outputs (Miller 1993). Organisational work occurs when ideas and experiences are represented and transformed largely into services and products.

Work as sublimation and engagement with reality

There is a difficulty in seeing work simply as transformation, however. Psychic work also involves an attempt to reconcile this transformation to an often-painful reality. Reiff (1979), for example, understands Freud's view of the world as reconciliatory and believes that this is the basis of Freudian morality.

> It is exhilarating yet terrifying to read Freud as a moralist, to see how compelling can be the judgement of a man who never preaches, leads us nowhere, assures us of nothing except perhaps that, having learned from him, the burden of misery we must find the strength to carry will be somewhat lighter. (p. xi)

In his comments 'Thoughts for the times about war and death', Freud (1915) considers civilisation as a true transformation of the instincts. He contrasts this to forms of society that, while appearing to be civilised, on closer analysis are only superficially so. Although psychic work may be rational, it may also be a rationalisation. There may be a kind of transformation 'work' for the pleasure principle as much as for the reality principle. Hence, what is seemingly civilised may yet be based on quite uncivilised motives. Freud saw the disillusionment brought on by the Great War as the result of an inability to distinguish between the truly civilised (a society built

on sublimation) and the superficially civilised (a society built on compliance). This failure to distinguish was due to a failure to question motives. Many Europeans had hoped that the so-called civilised world would not experience such an atrocious war. Freud tries to understand why what had seemed to be civilised was just a veneer; a compliance in order to serve a selfish phantasy. Much like the veneer of work illustrated earlier, when a case manager might report an incident without clearly checking the circumstances, so the veneer of civilisation might be based on a dynamic of avoidance. In the case of the Great War, Freud identifies this with avoiding the emotional reality of unconscious destructive impulses. Much the same analysis might be made of many twentieth-century wars.

Such a distinction is necessary for understanding work. Two forms of work are implicit, just as Freud saw two forms of civilisation — that is, a true sublimation or *transformation* in the service of the reality principle, and work that is but a shadow of this, in which transformation is in the service of phantasy alone. I am calling this *distortion* rather than work. This distinction is one that Bion draws in comparing his 'work' and 'basic assumption' groups. Basic assumption groups distort reality. It is a distinction often not made when considering the nature of work predominantly in terms of 'added value'. Is 'added value' a real development or a transformation in phantasy only? Certainly the 'added value' of the speculative processes that marked the 1980s proved to be no real work (Sykes 1994).

The other aspect of work is as *representation*. Much as *mind* is a social process (Harre 1984), work is also a social process even when seemingly performed by a single individual. Individual minds represent something in the wider psyche. Individual thinkers transform the thoughts that are present in the culture. Individual work, therefore, represents a broader task. The conscious division of labour in work organisations is represented in organisational charts and job descriptions; each unit of this division represents something of the whole. The unconscious division of work into a system of roles, constantly negotiated across slightly shifting boundaries, represents the tasks of the organisation in a different way, and includes the emotional tasks of the organisation (Hirschhorn 1988). Work both represents and is represented in organisational structures and dynamics. This is the nature of the process of representation — it flows across boundaries.

In short, the essence of psychic work involves transformative and representative processes that engage the psyche with reality. Just as work organisations are 'ideas in the mind' for working with products and services, organisational work can be described in a similar way.

Teams and work

A team is a special form of primary group. First, it is an organised group in that roles within a team are usually highly differentiated. Whereas undifferentiated group members identify generally with one another in that they share a view of the leader or task as ideal, and may take on specialised roles during the development of the group, team members identify with particular specialised aspects of the task from the onset of the team's operations. Specific team roles are defined. For example, a surgical team will have an anaesthetist, a surgeon, an orderly, surgical nurses and other relevant technicians; members of a football team will fill specified roles according to their abilities and the game's rules; and a management team may have managers accountable for particular organisational functions or projects. Such specialised roles are normally part of the team's definition, although this may change over time.

Second, because of the team's specialised organisation, team members have a heightened sense of their own role in relation to the roles of other team members. To play a role within a team requires a strong sense of the operation as a whole. You have to know how your special tasks fit with those of other team members, so that the team works as an integrated whole on a common enterprise. This means that team members have to have a good sense of what one another do. The work of team members should be clearly engaged with a collective goal.

This leads to a third point about work teams. Because members need a good sense of what their fellow team members do and how they each work to effect transformations, they must move from a position of *role narcissism* to a position of *role centredness*. These terms, first defined in Long, Newton and Chapman (1999), identified some aspects of work roles observed in a project involving work role analysis. What we found was that many people saw themselves as fulfilling the single most important role in the organisation, without which the organisation would cease to function effectively. This attitude, which we termed *role narcissism*, gave role holders a kind of single-mindedness in daily negotiating the conditions and boundaries of their tasks. Yet in order to interact collaboratively with others, this narcissistic attitude had to be tempered. Role dialogue — that is, dialogue between people in roles rather than interpersonal dialogue between individuals — could take place when role holders became centred in their roles, seeing the need for interaction between roles rather than seeing their own roles as paramount. The importance of this for teams is that the energy invested in one's role becomes sublimated from a more directly narcissistic energy into a commonly shared team energy. It describes a kind of 'dynamic altruism' that is built on narcissism but that involves sublimation.

Implications for the internal dynamics of teams

Teams that function well achieve this ability through a particular identificatory process. Each member seems able to internalise a version of his or her fellow team members and then to draw on this internal object during teamwork. This is done through three linked capacities.

The first is the capacity to be in the presence of the other team members (Long, Newton & Dalgleish 2000). This might seem to be easily achieved, but it is often a difficult process because there are many anxieties that prevent us from really being in the presence of others. More often we live and act in the presence of 'phantastic' others who are vehicles for our projections and are distorted by our desires. We see in the other what we want to see, or what we fear to see. The more we can work with the reality of other team members and what their role requires of them, the more the team as a whole will engage reality and, hence, work effectively.

The second capacity is the ability to internalise the other team members. As with a group, identifying with others through the task is an important aspect of this. The required internalisation of other team members is more specific, however. General identification is not enough. 'The other' must be understood in more depth. Differences between members become as important as similarities. A differentiated and individuated other must first be recognised. Team members may be internalised not simply as generalised group members through partial identification, but also as distinctive individuals — an individual member of the team rather than a 'membership individual', to use Turquet's (1975) term.

The third capacity is to be able to refer to and negotiate with the internalised team members when forming judgements.

These ideas came to me when I was working on an action research project in a team with two others. The project involved examining case management within a correctional services organisation. Most field aspects of the research would involve at least two members of this team working together at a particular organisational location. There would be ongoing opportunities to confer about issues that required interpretation or decision making about interventions. Also, the three of us would have regular meetings during which we discussed the ongoing data, the dynamics of the project and our own experiences.

The work we did together involved attempts to transform the ideas in the organisation through analysis, interpretation and working through the emotional experiences present *in* us, yet *of* the organisation (Armstrong

1996). It also involved working directly with the real experiences of people in the organisation. This joint work led to a close understanding of each other in role, as well as a more general understanding of each other as individuals. We came to see one another's valencies for particular types of experiences. For example, throughout the project one of us tended to feel fearful, another sickened and the third somewhat voyeuristic. Whereas this led both to a deeper understanding of the emotional dynamics present in prisons, because we were introjecting these feelings from the system, and to a deeper understanding of how people react when experiencing in each of these ways, it also led to a deeper understanding of one another in our researcher roles. Thus we learned about (a) the emotions and reactions aroused by the environment of the system we were studying, and (b) each other in the role of researcher. I came to know my fellow researchers' particular ways of thinking about the issues.

This became most evident when one of the team was away from Australia and the other was unavailable because of other work commitments. I had to make some decisions but had no one from my team with whom to confer. As project leader I had the authority to make the required decisions, but I felt isolated. I found myself automatically thinking through the issues the way John would, and then the way Jane might. It wasn't that I consciously thought, 'What would John be saying here?' and 'How would Jane be approaching this?' Rather, it was as if I was having an internal conversation with John and Jane. What's more, I felt myself making internal adjustments — adopting postures, both mental and physical, that were similar to those of my colleagues. I literally 'caught myself in the act' of doing this and realised the extent to which I was drawing on my internal John and Jane. I was then able to do this deliberately, and after the 'conversation' I was able to make my decisions.

Later it struck me that this was a good description of how teams work. The literature on teams often refers to the need for good communication between clearly distinguished and authorised roles, but what I am describing goes beyond that. There are a few distinct points to be made.

First, what is an internal object? Simply, it is the representation or image of an 'other' felt, in phantasy, to live within oneself. When members are able to internalise the other, they are able to draw on a living representation of the other, not simply a memory or a cognitive representation. By this I mean that it is not a static image or idea that is internalised; the internal object is dynamic and alive. My internal team-mates were able to engage in a discussion and even to change their position throughout the discussion as it developed. During this process I could either stand back (metaphorically) as they had this discussion, or engage with

them in it. Although this sounds strange, it is the 'aliveness' of internal objects that forms the basis of the creative imagination. This quality of being alive is due, I believe, to the identification I was able to have with my internal team-mates. It is a phenomenological quality akin to that described by Winnicott (1971) as belonging to the transitional object — for instance a child's teddy bear.

Second, the internal object must also be subject to change, renewal or transformation in the face of reality. For instance, I later discussed my experience with my colleagues, recounting how I had drawn on my internal John and Jane. As we compared our current thoughts we were able again to modify our internal team. John and Jane saw how the views of my internal objects might well have been theirs had they been there to consult at the time. This is not to say that they would have said exactly the same to me, or that they would not have had other views to add. But by now the whole situation had moved on, and anyway no one could be sure of what they *might have said*. But this 'comparing notes' allowed for further modification.

One can say, then, that the internal team members, while subject to change in response to their own inherent dynamics, are also regularly modified through contact with the living team members. It is through such reality checking and modification that the internal team remains creative and effective in the real world of work.

Third, the internal team members provide the real external team members with ongoing support and interaction when direct contact is not possible. The crucial importance of the internal team members was that at the time of making my decisions I had been able to work with more confidence and with a greater range of ideas than if I had acted independently rather than as part of a team. I didn't feel I was on my own. This was particularly important because my fellow team members were unavailable at a critical time for the project.

Fourth, there are situations in which team members are together, yet direct contact or discussion is broken or impossible. At these times, it is as if the members internalise the *team-as-a-whole* as well as the individual team members. This is evident in the following observations by psychiatric nurses who work as part of a team in an adolescent in-patient facility. They were discussing 'restraints' — that is, the process by which a patient is restrained because he or she is acting dangerously. The need for a restraint may emerge quite suddenly under tense and unpredictable circumstances. There is no time for discussion; action must be taken quickly.

Teamwork is especially important during restraints. You feel safer when you are with a team-mate you know. One of you goes in first to do the main restraint. There's no real decision about this. It's kind of automatic. Whoever goes in first will be backed up. The other person just stands back a bit and then helps. But a restraint should be a last resort. You should be trying to de-escalate the situation; calm them down. There may be two of you and you have to sense the need to work together, either to talk them down or restrain them.

The situation was tense and I didn't want to disturb him even more — there was no back-up; no one within call. It's harder to work with agency staff that you don't really know. You never know how they will react. They'd support you but you can't actually sense how, and there's no time to exchange views.

All the time you're making serious decisions like whether to let a kid go on extended leave when they might self-harm or even suicide. Life and death decisions. No wonder it's stressful. If you've got a good mini-team then you can argue out the decision and they're there to back you when it's made.

In such circumstances nursing staff must act confidently and calmly in a highly emotional setting. They rely on each other and on their judgement that the other will work in role. Working with these nurses as a consultant to a staff support group, I get a strong sense of their each having internalised the team-as-a-whole as well as the individual members. There certainly is *labour* involved in the nursing task. However, I am here referring to their *work*. In this example, if the restraint is appropriate, the work *transforms* an anxiety-ridden and dangerous situation into one that is safer and more emotionally contained. Team members work on the basis of their capacity to internalise the team and work automatically from that internal object.

Finally, I have stressed the dynamics of identification throughout this chapter, but here I want to pause in this emphasis. An internal object — whether a person, a team or even an institution — may be related to the self or other internal objects in a variety of ways. I may identify with the internalised person — that is, I may want to 'be like' them. Or I may want to distinguish myself from them — to be quite unlike them. Also, I may love them, hate them, want to possess them, to dominate or be dominated by them, and so on. The internal object may inspire as strong an emotional response as any person in my external world. The issue for teams is whether the team becomes internalised through identification or through some other kind of relationship — say, libidinal (e.g. love or hate). When the internalisation is through identification with the task, then the team members work more effectively than if members internalise each other via libidinal ties alone.

Implications for human resource management

There are two major sets of implications to be taken from what has been said. The first set involves the maximisation of real transformative work. The second set concerns the optimisation of teamwork using the development of internal teams for members. These implications are interrelated.

Organisations are best served when human resources are operating creatively and efficiently. This involves people in doing real transformative work as well as engaging in labour. Opportunities for reflection, discussion and reality checking need to be built into organisational life rather than being a luxury 'add-on'. Work is not simply done but must also be thought about, difficult as this may be. This involves a need for mentoring. It also requires that senior managers and others check out their hunches, perceptions and data with staff at all levels of the organisation. Reality does not reside in one organisational level alone.

Nowadays, the idea of 'team' is broadly conceived. I have argued here that when teamwork is most successful, members are able to internalise 'other' members, particularly, although not exclusively, in their work roles. In addition, members internalise the team itself. These internalised others and team-as-a-whole act as continuous reference points for teamwork judgements and actions. The accompanying emotions will be complex, because the internalisation of the other requires more than simply taking in an 'idea' of the other. It involves an internalisation of many of the emotional experiences of the other. Work with the internal team requires reference not only to how one might think 'as if' in other team members' roles, but also to how one feels and may be impelled to act. Implications must then be discussed in the overt or real external team. Working through these complexities is essential if one is to use teams as a major organisational structure.

If these arguments are valid, then we must also think about the limitations on the successful and creative use of the internal team.

First, there is the problem of team size and stability. Let me speak by way of analogy. Part of my role as an academic involves supervising the research of doctoral students. I find that I can successfully keep in mind the work of up to 12 or 14 students for any sustained period of time — enough, that is, to help them towards successful completion of their degree. Beyond this number, something less than satisfactory occurs. Too many projects means that I start to forget things. I simply cannot keep all of them in mind in a way that allows me to be actively helpful. The concentration required to assess the research — its conceptualisation, analysis and implications — is greater than I can access, despite an occasional, sometimes random creative thought here and there. My mind cannot remain preoccupied with all of the projects at an unconscious level. There is a limit to my capacity to internalise 'living research projects'.

The size of the team is relevant to the capacity to internalise it. Beyond a certain size, perhaps a small group of 10 to 14 members, the capacity to internalise each of its members in a distinct way may be reduced. The nursing staff on the in-patient unit noted that communication between team members was disturbed when the team size doubled. Also, when there is a large turnover of staff, trust, clear communication and teamwork are diminished. It takes time for people to get to know one another.

This is also linked to ideas of 'span of control'. There is a limit to the number of project teams that a senior manager can internalise.

Another impediment to good teamwork is more subtle. Sometimes a kind of 'full and immediate' identification with others may occur, so that one's own role identity is lost and the team cannot operate with complex and sophisticated role divisions. This happens in basic assumption experience (Bion 1961) and is driven by anger, fear and anxiety. Examples of basic assumption behaviour are fully described in the literature. Extreme examples of such full identification might include the Jonestown massacre and similar cult phenomena. The common symptom of the dynamic is a lack of differentiation among most members.

Team members may internalise others based on projective identifications that are poorly mediated by reality. This impediment to teamwork may involve the incapacity of members to realistically internalise the team due to intense emotional experiences, or the inability of team members to renew their 'internal teams' in light of changed circumstances. This may relate to the influence of powerful archaic internal objects formed during infancy or during traumatic periods of personal history. Such internal objects may be transferred to new internalised team-mates in inappropriate ways. At the national level this was seen during the recent Timor crisis. It was as if Australians had internalised a United States that would always be there for them when they called for help. This internal US must have influenced many an Australian government's policies and decisions. Washington's hesitation in responding to the intervention in Timor was a shock. The internal US in the Australian psyche (if you can talk of such a thing) seemed not to fit with reality. The internalised Australian–US team playing on a world stage seemed suddenly to have evaporated. An adjustment was necessary to this internal object in the national psyche.

In organisational life, such a dynamic is seen when team members do not understand one another's role and hence cannot draw on an internal image of that role when performing their own tasks. For instance, a senior university administrator had no real understanding how one of her colleagues had taken up her role. Consequently, she continued to make judgements and decisions in her own work that cut across the findings of her report. This influenced decisions about university courses and subjects and strongly affected relations between her colleague and students. This, in turn, led to feelings of resentment and anger that further reduced opportunities for mutual understanding. In the long run, this hostility interfered with collaborative work. Each side became a hostile and negative internal object for the other.

The key to successful teamwork is to establish conditions under which each member can understand and internalise the roles of other team members vis-a-vis the common task. As well as communicating with others, team members should have an understanding of the other roles in the system. A helpful human resource consultant can provide supportive conditions to aid this process. These conditions allow team members to develop and change their internal objects in the light of current realities. Team training and mentoring should advance such processes.

References

Armstrong, D (1996) The recovery of meaning. Paper given at the Symposium of the International Society for the Psychoanalytic Study of Organisations, New York.

Bion, WR (1961) *Experiences in Groups*. London: Tavistock Publications.

Freud, S (1915) Thoughts for the times on war and death. In *The Pelican Freud, Volume 12, Civilization, Society and Religion* (1985). Harmondsworth, UK: Pelican Books.

Hirschhorn, L (1988) *The Workplace Within: Psychodynamics of Organizational Life*. New York: MIT Press.

Hirschhorn, L (1991) *Managing in the New Team Environment: Skills, Tools and Methods*. Boston, MA: Addison-Wesley.

Lacan, J (1977) *Ecrits*. London: Tavistock Publications.

Lawrence, GW (1999) Centring of the sphinx for the psychoanalytic study of organizations. *Socio-Analysis* 1 (2) 99–126.

Long, SD (1999a) The tyranny of the customer and the cost of consumerism. *Human Relations* 52 (6) 723–43.

Long, SD (1999b) Who am I at work: an exploration of work identifications and identity. *Socio-Analysis* 1 (1).

Long, SD, Newton, J, and Dalgleish, J (2000). In the presence of the other: developing working relations for organisational learning. In E. Klein, F. Gablenick and P. Herr (Eds), *Dynamic Consultation in a Changing Workplace.* Madison, CT: Psychosocial Press.

Long, SD, Newton, J, and Chapman, J (1999). Bridging the tensions: organisational role analysis with members of the same organisation. Paper given at the Symposium of the International Society for the Psychoanalytic Study of Organisations held in Toronto, June 1999.

Miller, EJ (1993) *From Dependency to Autonomy: Studies in Organization and Change.* London: Free Association Books.

O'Shaughnessy, E (1988) Words and working through. In E Bott Spillius (Ed.), *Melanie Klein Today: Developments in Theory and Practice, Volume 2: Mainly Practice.* London: The Institute of Psychoanalysis and Routledge.

Schlachet, PJ (1986) The concept of group space. *International Journal of Group Psychotherapy* 36 (1) 33–53.

Stokes, J (1994). The unconscious at work in groups and teams: contributions from the work of Wilfred Bion. In A Obholtzer and V Zagier Roberts (Eds), *The Unconscious at Work: Individual and Organizational Stress in the Human Services.* London: Routledge.

Sykes, T (1994) *The Bold Riders.* St. Leonards, NSW: Allen & Unwin.

Reiff, P (1979) *Freud: The Mind of a Moralist.* Chicago: University of Chicago Press.

Turner, JC, Hogg, MA, Oakes, PJ, Reicher, SD, and Wetherall, MS (1987) *Rediscovering the Social Group.* Oxford: Blackwell.

Turquet, P (1975) Threats to identity in the large group. In L Kreeger (Ed.), *The Large Group: Dynamics and Therapy.* London: Constable.

Winnicott, DW (1971) *Playing and Reality.* London: Tavistock.

Managing for the millennium

CHAPTER 20

Power and politics in organisations

by Dianne Lewis
Queensland University of Technology

Introduction

Power is a word that evokes vivid images and associations for most people. Some see it positively (Henry Kissinger once said that power was as good as sex). For others, it has associations of unreasonable authority, coercion or inequality. Many people equate power with authority, but authority implies managerial power, whereas the manager and his or her subordinates both have access to power in a variety of other forms. Understanding power is not simple, especially as it has been, until recently, a topic very rarely discussed in the management and human resources (HR) academic literature; but neither is it impossibly complex and mysterious. Social scientists today have a good understanding of some of the basic components and determinants of power in organisations.

While a knowledge of power has traditionally been considered essential for general managers, it is also important for HR managers and individuals in organisations to understand its workings. Many individuals may never aspire to managerial positions, but this does not mean they will never want to use power. And even if they have no desire to use it, they need to know about it and how it affects outcomes in organisations. Gaining a knowledge of power is an important survival tactic.

This chapter will address the nature of power and politics, the different forms of power and where power comes from. It will also examine such challenging issues as how to recognise and assess power, the relationship between power and conflict, and how to understand when to use power. Controversies such as the unsettling nature of power and politics and the place of politics in organisational life are also discussed. An assessment is made of the directions the study of power seems to be taking in the literature for general managers, HR managers and practitioners, women and individuals who work in the public sector. The chapter concludes with a discussion of the implications of power and politics for organisations, managers (both general and HR) and individuals. The message is that power exists in organisations for good and for ill, and both managers and other individuals need to understand this and recognise the threats power poses and the opportunities it presents.

The nature of power and politics

Probably the best description of the two-edged nature of power is offered by Pfeffer (1992, p. 337), who suggests:

> Power is a process that can be used to advance individuals' and groups' goals, or to frustrate them. That is, power can be a force for good and for ill. Irrespective of whether it is used to achieve good or bad ends, power is central to the process of getting things done in organisations.

But just what is this thing called power? Consider the following definitions:

- the probability that one actor within a social relationship will be in a position to carry out his own will despite resistance (Weber 1947)
- the power of person A over person B is the ability of A to have B do something he would not have done otherwise (Dahl 1957)
- the ability of an actor to produce outcomes consonant with his perceived interests (Emerson 1969)
- the ability to limit the scope of decision making in organisations (Swingle 1976)
- the capability of one social actor to overcome resistance in achieving a desired objective or result (Pfeffer 1981).

All these definitions identify power as a resource, not an act. It is an ability, a capacity, a potential; and it does not have to be used. An interesting question, then, is whether power can be stored like most other resources.

Politics, on the other hand, relates to the things people do to get (or keep) power when it does not come naturally. If power is the resource, politics is the act used to develop that resource.

Forms of power

In examining the different types (or sources) of power, we need to remember that all power is relative. People are not powerful or powerless in general, but only relative to others around them. A person may be powerful in one situation but powerless in another. Power can be classified either by the position held or by the resources commanded. Researchers French and Raven (1960) have identified five sources of power, each of which may occur at all levels in an organisation.

Legitimate power

Legitimate power comes from the position held, where the distribution of power becomes legitimated over time. In bureaucracies this power is called authority — and it is expected; in fact, the more it is used, the more the person in authority is likely to have. Authority can be defined, then, as the ability of an individual to exercise influence because of his or her legitimate position within the organisation.

Authority works because people have been socialised to expect it, although some organisations, for example bureaucracies such as the armed forces and hospitals, use it more than others. However, authority works only if it is used in context; once they are outside their area of jurisdiction authority figures lose that power. The power comes from the ability to ensure that people accept a certain interpretation of the rules, and someone is powerful only if they are able to ensure that such acceptance will occur. Remember that all power is relative.

The sociologist Max Weber was interested in the concepts of power and authority, but Weber saw power and leadership as one and the same, and we know now that there are other forms of power apart from that which comes from leadership and position.

Reward power

Reward power exists when one person is able to exert influence by providing rewards and preventing punishments. It often, but not necessarily, goes hand in hand with legitimate power (authority). Anyone can praise others, and praise is a form of reward power.

Coercive power

If a person is able to influence others through the use of punishment or threat, that person has coercive power. It is often used as a support for legitimate power, but it can have undesirable side effects such as increasing conflict in the organisation.

Referent power

Referent power exists when a person is well liked by others. We tend to be more influenced by people we like, to consider their points of view, ignore their failures and seek their approval. A person who praises others for a job well done is using reward power and gaining referent power.

Expert power

Expert power exists when a person has special expertise that is valued by the organisation. Individuals who are difficult to replace have expert power, although they may not have legitimate power; for example, many technical people possess expert power.

Information/resource power

Information/resource power often goes hand in hand with expert power and is the ability of a person to influence others because those people want the information or resources that the power holder controls. Again, legitimate power is not a necessary prerequisite; information/resource power is often held by such organisation members as secretaries and storeroom attendants.

Figure 20.1 illustrates the sources of power and influence, but it is important to remember that they are only *potential* sources of power. Whether or not influence is actually exerted depends on the actions of at least one of the participants, the type of power each participant possesses and the setting in which the situation occurs. For example, as a part-time worker in a take-away food store, a person may accept the boss's reasonable work requests based on his or her legitimate power. However, if that same boss tries to influence the person's vote in an upcoming election, the chances of that influence being successful would depend heavily on the personal power characteristics of the boss — that is, referent power. Individuals with potential power may also not recognise they have the power, so the potential is lost; or they may choose not to use their power, ignoring the potential or storing it up for later use.

Where power comes from

Broadly, there are two sources of power — membership of a powerful group and individual power.

Group power

Group power comes from organisations being structured in such a way that some groups or sub-units automatically possess power and other groups are made dependent on them. People often consider an organisation's structure to be an impersonal thing — something that simply has to be worked with — but structure is not impersonal; it is actually a very powerful mechanism by which people and processes can be controlled. The choice of structure will automatically favour some groups and disadvantage others. Authority can be highly centralised, as in a functional structure, or decentralised, as in a divisional or network structure. As Burnes (2000) argues:

> *A person or group's position in the structure will determine such things as their influence in planning, their choice of technology, the criteria by which they will be*

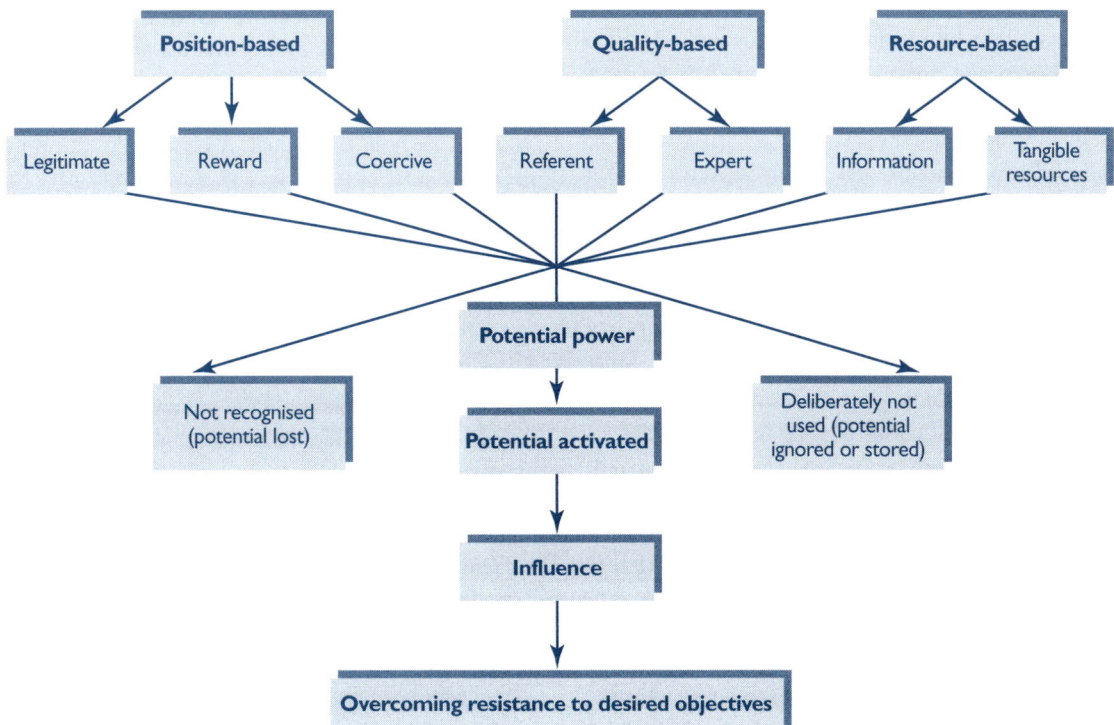

Figure 20.1: Forms of power

evaluated, allocation of rewards, control of information, proximity to senior managers, and their ability to exercise influence on a whole range of decisions. (p. 182)

People in managerial positions are invariably in dominant coalitions — that is, small groups of people who hold power of one sort or another in the organisation. The most common dominant coalition in any organisation is the top management team, but other groups may become dominant if they possess skills or resources that are valued by the organisation. Where the top management team is the dominant coalition, they will have the power to determine the organisation's structure.

Almost certainly, power will be delegated to some extent by the setting up of formal groups consciously created by management to meet organisational objectives, for example task forces, work teams, quality circles and self-managing work groups. When one sub-unit's tasks are essential to the success of the organisation and cannot be performed by anyone else, that sub-unit holds substantial power. This is much the same as 'expert' power: subgroups like audiovisual services hold a lot of power because all requests for technical equipment often have to go through them.

But in any organisation there is also a complex network of relationships among different members who are attracted to one another for non-formal reasons — groups that have nothing to do with the formal hierarchical line in the organisation. They have no formal authority but still seek to exert influence and exercise power. These *informal work groups* were the groups that Elton Mayo (1933) was interested in.

Informal work groups aim to make relatively less powerful people more powerful through their association with other like-minded people. That, of course, was not what Mayo had in mind; his idea was that managers had to replace this informal work group with something that would work in management's interests. But informal work groups do aim to influence decision outcomes both within and outside organisations.

A particular type of informal group is the *interest group*, which is a collection of people who share common aims or viewpoints about work. These people may be concerned about the division of limited resources, or may be struggling to survive in a competitive workplace; they may share similar technology or have similar goals. Professional bodies and trade unions are two examples of interest groups that are not part of any particular formal organisational structure but that exert great influence (wield great power) on the outcome of decisions within organisations.

Individual power

While certain groups can wield a lot of power in organisations, there are a number of ways in which individuals can also acquire power (apart from legitimate power).

By making people dependent on them

According to Pfeffer (1981):

Power derives from having something that someone else wants or needs, and being in control of the performance or resource so that there are few alternative sources, or no alternative sources, for obtaining what is desired. (p. 99)

In other words, individuals wishing to use this form of power must make people dependent on them for what they really want. But power holders have to ensure that they can provide the most critical and difficult to obtain resources in the organisation, and that *only* they can provide them. The more those resources are valued as important by the person who wants them, the greater the power of the person who can provide them.

People who control money in an organisation have a great deal of power, because money is the most negotiable of all resources. Monetary control is usually the prerogative of top management, but there are many other, less tangible or obvious resources too, such as prestige, rewards, sanctions, comforts and services. Neither does a person have to provide the bulk of the resources to wield the power; he or she may just have some control over the *slack*.

Most resources in organisations are committed to a particular area of the enterprise; 'slack' refers to resources that have not yet been committed. A person who can provide slack gains a lot of power because, once people have had a taste of the extra resources, they come to depend on them and no longer see them as slack. Individuals who have supplied those extra resources have created a resource dependency and therefore a power base for themselves.

By being irreplaceable

A second thing people can do to acquire power is to make themselves irreplaceable. People use a number of strategies to achieve this, including:
- not writing down information that could make the power holder's expertise available to others. According to French and Raven (1960), expert power is quickly eroded if others can access the information easily.
- using jargon to make the power holder's expertise even less understandable to outsiders. Jargon can be a good facilitator of communication between people in the same field, but it is also often used to exclude outsiders. Those of us trained in non-technical fields struggle with

computer language that we often suspect technical staff use to keep other academic staff 'in their place'.

- making sure that if the power holder does have to call for outside help to solve a problem, as few people as possible know about it. The power holder (or would-be power holder) cannot be seen to need outside help.
- ensuring that people either inside or outside the organisation who could do the same work as the power holder do not get the opportunity to display their knowledge or skills. This tactic may involve the use of *politics*, which will be discussed later.

By being able to affect the decision-making process

The third way in which people obtain power is by affecting the decision-making process, either when the boundaries and premises are being laid down or when the alternatives are being considered, or alternatively by making themselves gatekeepers of information.

Decisions are usually made according to some premise laid down by an organisation member. For example, once the premise 'We need to cut our electricity bill next financial year' has been accepted, very few people will challenge it, and all discussion will be confined to how electricity costs may be cut. This makes it very difficult for those sections of the organisation that have to use a lot of electricity. The power resides in resource holders' ability to withhold electricity from an area for which they may want to create a difficulty.

Not every alternative to a problem is considered in the decision-making process. We all tend to see things from our own perspective, and what may be seen as a financial problem by the accountancy department may be seen as a communication problem by the communication department. Each group would want to put forward different alternatives for solving the problem. The power over the final decision resides in the people who can determine which alternatives will be brought forward as possible solutions.

People who are able to make themselves gatekeepers of information — that is, channels through whom information flows — have an opportunity to affect the decision-making process by making sure that the 'right' information is supplied and the 'wrong' information is suppressed. People such as private secretaries and finance professionals can wield a lot of power this way.

Kipnis (1990) identifies a number of strategies that both managers and other organisation members use to exert influence or wield power. These are:

reason	using facts and data to support development of a logical argument
friendliness	using impression management and flattery, and the creation of goodwill
coalition	mobilising support from other people in the organisation
bargaining	using negotiation through the exchange of benefits or favours
assertiveness	using a direct and forceful approach
higher authority	gaining support at higher levels in the organisation to back up requests
sanctions	using organisationally derived rewards and punishments.

According to Kipnis (1990), people fall into one of three categories in the strategies they use to influence people; they are *shotgun*, *tactician* or *bystander*. 'Shotgun' people attempt to get their way by using the full range of influence strategies. People who take the shotgun approach use all seven strategies, from reason to sanctions, with above-average frequency to influence others. They seem to want a great deal from others, and as a result they must keep trying out different strategies.

'Tacticians' rely heavily on reason to influence others, but they have at least average scores on the other strategies. Tacticians get their way by using facts and data in logical arguments. Using a rational approach, they try to exert an influence in a deliberate manner. 'Bystanders' have below-average scores on all seven influence strategies. They exercise little influence in their organisations. Kipnis suggests two possible reasons for this:

- They are so powerful that others continually anticipate their needs. They do not have to exercise influence, because they get their way without effort.
- They have so little power that they feel it is futile even to try to influence others.

Where do you think you fit in the power strategy categories?

Challenging issues

Many managers will not admit the existence of a power influence in the decision making of their organisations, but prefer to stress a reliance on the rational model of objective analysis of all data. In addition, many HR managers are not privy to the power goals of senior organisation members or to the strategies being used to realise them. But if, as is argued here, power interests do exist, then a recognition of a power influence in decisions poses many challenges for general and HR managers and for individuals. It is important, therefore, that all organisation members recognise and assess the distribution of power in the organisation, and that they understand when to use power and when power is being used by others. They also need to recognise that most HR theories neglect the role of power and politics in the workplace and the effect these have on conflict. The greatest challenge is to bring a discussion of power and politics into the open.

How to recognise and assess power

Recognising and assessing power is an important skill for people to learn if they want to survive and progress in an organisation; it is an essential one if they themselves want to play the power game. Recognising and assessing power is not always easy because, by its very nature, power is not always used openly; but there are a few methods that can be used to identify the power holders in an organisation.

It is usually possible to work out what is valued by the organisation and see who has expertise in this area. This does not mean that the people who have the potential power will necessarily use it. They may not even recognise they have it (see figure 20.1). It may also be possible to see which people win most of the contested issues in the organisation. Symbols such as the size of offices, the quality of the furniture and the privacy of workspace are also possible indicators of power when differences occur among members on the same organisational level. It is also possible to ask people directly or to examine such things as membership on influential boards and committees.

But this information is not always readily available, again because power is not always used openly and because most organisations like to believe they make decisions according to the impersonal rational model. Probably the most reliable approach to recognising and assessing power, therefore, is to look at a number of these indicators and try to see links between them. This combination of methods will often reveal where the real power lies in any organisation.

Power and conflict

A major challenge for HR students and professionals is understanding the role of power in the causes and resolution of conflict in organisations. Morgan (1997) suggests we can use the metaphor of a political system in which all people pursue their own interests to view power and conflict in organisations. Researchers have identified three major perspectives on conflict — unitarist, pluralist and radical — which differ primarily in their views on the role power plays in organisations.

Unitarist approaches to conflict

Unitarists see the need to control conflict either by minimising it or by getting rid of it altogether. Conflict is seen as wrong or bad, as something that must be eliminated. Most schools of management thought — Scientific Management and Human Relations theories for example — are unitarist.

Certainly they differ in their ideas of 'economic versus social man' but the assumption is nonetheless that management can satisfy employees' needs, whether economic or social.

Unitarists believe in the 'managerial prerogative', and make no distinctions between conflict and power. Management has the power; and conflict, if it does occur, is pathological, because it upsets harmony in the organisation. There is no consideration of differing goals of management and workers; it is presumed that all have the same overall goals.

Most leadership theories, too, are unitarist; for example, according to Trait Theory certain people have specific qualities (or traits) that make them natural leaders. Transformational leadership theories are also unitarist, because again they take a managerial perspective in believing that management knows best and can decide what 'meanings' everyone will eventually adhere to (Lewis 1996).

In fact, most management and leadership models are based on a unitarist perspective and the idea that conflict is abnormal. This means that most of our theories are biased in favour of management. Since management theories, in contrast to scientific theories, tend to be value-laden — that is, they are *prescriptive* as well as *descriptive* — a conflict of ideological positions is likely. Any theory that prescribes actions by one group while being biased in favour of another is going to result in conflict.

However, it is very difficult to recognise the unitarist bias in the various management and leadership theories because people often do not consider power and the effect it has on conflict in the workplace. The unitarist view of conflict does not take power into consideration because it operates from a viewpoint of the managerial prerogative and the universal needs of all workers, which it is believed management can satisfy. Thus, until recently power has tended to be neglected in the literature.

HR theorists and practitioners have until recently accepted the traditional Organisation Development (OD) model of change, which stresses slow, planned change that concentrates on organisational effectiveness and employee wellbeing without disruption to the organisation's life cycles and with the use of participation, teamwork and collaboration. As Davis says, it is:

> *an intervention strategy that uses group processes to focus on the whole culture of an organisation in order to bring about planned change.* (1981, p. 221)

This view indicates that OD is attempting to create an overall culture (system of shared meanings) that all organisation members will adhere to; that is, OD — and HR in general — sees the organisation from a unitarist point of view.

Pluralist approaches to conflict

According to the pluralist approach to conflict, there are actually many different groups in organisations — employers, workers, shareholders, unions, government — and all these groups have different goals. Pluralists see conflict as coming from many different sources, so they have tried to devise different techniques for resolving that conflict, depending on the specific situation. They hold, therefore, that there is no 'one best way' of resolving conflict.

Pluralists also argue that conflict can be beneficial for an organisation if it can be properly integrated into the processes and if differing viewpoints can be brought out into the open. Unitarists believe conflict is never beneficial and should be checked. The school of management thought that comes closest to a pluralist approach is Contingency Theory (Woodward 1965; Burns & Stalker 1966; Lawrence & Lorsch 1967); the school of leadership that comes closest is Situational Leadership (Fiedler 1967; Dunphy & Stace 1988). As yet, there appears to be no coherent HR theory that adopts a pluralist approach to conflict. Participative decision making comes closest, but even then there is no guarantee that all participants' interests will be considered.

A challenging question that all students, managers and HR professionals should ask themselves is whether it will ever be possible to have a prescriptive theory that is pluralist.

Radical approaches to conflict

The radical approach to conflict is also a pluralist one, in that it views conflict as inevitable; but, whereas some pluralist approaches see conflict as healthy and manageable, the radical approach views it as a never-ending struggle between management and labour. Goals pursued by the two groups are seen as irreconcilably different, so that conflict is bound to be dangerous and disruptive. Any conflict is seen from a win–lose point of view, because it is assumed that any gains one side makes are necessarily at the expense of the other. This point of view has not been popular with management because it suggests that management does not have complete power and control in the workplace.

Using power to resolve conflict

Sometimes, in spite of what many of the elementary textbooks say about the choices in conflict resolution, power is the *only* way to resolve conflict. The Thomas and Kilmann Conflict Grid, for example (adapted in figure 20.2), ranks people as either high or low on concern for self and for others (Thomas 1976, p. 900). It classifies the *competing* approach (the power approach) as low on concern for

others and high on concern for self; its creators claim that people who adopt this approach create win–lose situations and use rivalry and power plays to get their own ends and to force submission. The Grid is, therefore, very *unitarist* and does not take into consideration the particular situation in which the conflict occurs. Sometimes a power approach, with the possibility of accompanying political action, is the *only* way to resolve a conflict. Use of the power approach may not indicate that a person has low concern for others and high concern for self at all.

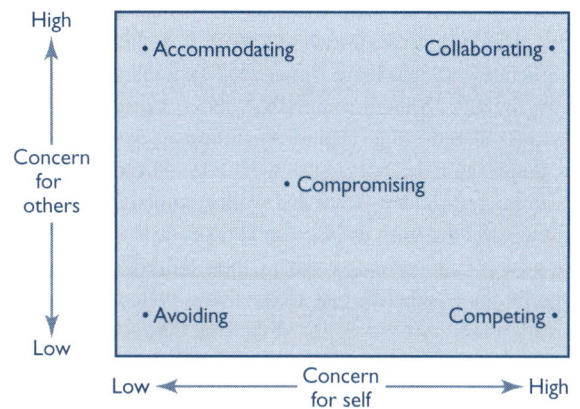

Figure 20.2: The Thomas and Kilmann Conflict Grid

However, when a combination of certain conditions occurs, power is the only way to resolve a conflict. The first condition is *interdependence*, a situation in which what happens to one person affects what happens to others. If there is no interdependence, there is no conflict, so there is no need for power to be used. The second condition is *heterogeneous goals*, or goals that are inconsistent with one another. If interdependence exists, so may heterogeneous goals — but not necessarily. The third condition is *scarcity*. If there is enough of a resource for everybody, in spite of the interdependence and the heterogeneous goals, there would still be no decision problem. And the greater the scarcity, the greater the power and effort that will be expended in resolving the decision.

The presence of these three conditions will produce conflict, but whether this conflict will result in the use of power, or even politics, depends on two other conditions. The first of these conditions is the importance of the decision issue or the resource; the second is the distribution of power in the organisation. Political activity, bargaining and coalition forming occur mainly where power is dispersed. If one person has all the power, that person can usually make rules and decisions according to his or her own values, without regard to outside conditions. But when all these conditions are present in a situation, power of some sort is the only way to reach a decision.

Controversies

There are a number of controversial issues relating to the discussion of power and politics in organisations.

The unsettling notion of power and politics

Probably the most controversial issue in the discussion of power politics is the unsettling feelings it evokes in people, particularly people in countries like Australia. Australians have always felt uncomfortable about power, perhaps because it seems to go against our culture of egalitarianism, mateship and the 'tall poppy syndrome'. Hofstede (1980) examines attitudes to work and work relations in 40 countries, including Australia. He found that one key dimension in which cultures varied was in their attitudes to power, specifically whether people accepted and preferred large or small power differences (or distances) between superiors and subordinates. Australia was found to belong to a group of mainly English-speaking countries (e.g. the UK, US and Canada) in which the dominant value was for relatively small power distances between 'leaders' and 'led'. That is, the dominant value was for consultative, democratic styles of leadership. Power and politics are just not things with which the average Australian feels particularly comfortable.

According to Hofstede, another cultural attribute of Australians — and many other Western cultures — that causes us to feel uncomfortable with the concept of power is individualism. Individualism refers to the loosely knit social framework in which members are supposed to take care of themselves and their immediate families only. Power is about dependence by one person or group upon another and, in general, dependence is not something that the average Western adult values. Australians tend to see growing up as the process of acquiring independence, so the idea of dependence in our adult life has connotations of a failure 'to be one's own person' — that is, a loss of individuality. This creates a mix of (sometimes unconscious) feelings, which often involve a degree of fear and dislike of the person with power over us.

The place of politics in organisations

As stated earlier, power is the resource and politics the act of developing that resource. The two are intricately bound up with each other; but power, being more abstract, is the more acceptable and respectable term. Why do we find politics distasteful, and why are we reluctant to talk about it?

First, while power is about dependence by one person or group on another, politics implies that one person or group has been *manipulated* by another. This idea goes against our ethic of independence. Second, people who consistently win contested decisions often do not want other people to know how much power they have or some of the tactics they may have used to get it. By the same token, losers do not want to show how *little* power they have or how they have been outmanoeuvred.

Yet politics plays an important role in organisational life. Since it is the art of getting and keeping power, managers and other individuals in organisations use it more often than they are willing to admit. Politics may be considered as just another 'tool' in a manager's or worker's 'toolkit' of strategies; it does not have to be used all the time; people will not always choose to use political action to get things done, but at least it gives them options. In this sense, politics is a form of control.

Some students find the whole topic of politics distressing, especially those who adhere strongly to unitarist theories of management; but politics is a fact of organisational life, and HR professionals are confronted with its consequences all the time in the conflict that occurs when they try to involve organisation members in general management decisions or inform them of management policies and actions.

Political action is not all bad. Organisations are *not* structures or strategies; organisations are *people*, collections of individuals who, if one adheres to a pluralist view, have widely differing interests. Politics helps them fit into the organisation and get things done when they feel the formal structure hinders them.

There are at least five very useful functions of politics, and probably many more that individuals will uncover for themselves.

Overcoming personal inadequacies

Some people in important positions are just not suited to, or capable of doing, their assigned duties. Politics may be necessary to allow other people to get things done, circumventing the person with the legitimate power when necessary. In lay language, this is called 'working around the boss'.

Coping with change

Sometimes changes occur very quickly and without notice, and the organisational structure may be too cumbersome to allow an equally quick response. Politics may be necessary to allow people and resources to be moved around to cope with the changes and prevent a small problem from becoming a much larger one.

Coping with crises

As stated earlier, the traditional OD model of change stresses slow, planned change using participation, teamwork and collaboration. However, sometimes crises occur that require immediate organisational changes to be made; according to Dunphy and Stace (1988, p. 321), 'radical times may demand radical remedies'. An example of such a crisis might be 'when the organisation is markedly out of fit, or the environment changes dramatically, and for the organisation to survive, fit must be achieved by more discontinuous change processes' (Dunphy & Stace 1988, p. 321). Politics may be necessary to make fast changes.

Channelling personal contacts

In large organisations people cannot liaise with everyone. Politics may be necessary to allow people to access the people they need (or want) to influence, even if the formal structure does not make provision for it.

Helping in conflict management

Politics may be used to resolve conflict when the existence of power is widely dispersed in an organisation. Even if all the other conditions for the use of power — interdependence, heterogeneous goals, scarcity and importance — are present, if legitimate power exists and the power holder is prepared to use it, political action can be avoided. But when power is widely dispersed in an organisation, or the power holder is not prepared to use it, then someone will resort to political action.

Future directions

Power has always been of interest in the sociology and ethics literature, but it is now making inroads into the literature of general management, human resources, women's issues and the public sector.

Power in the general management literature

In the general management literature, with publications such as those by Kramer and Neale (Eds) (1998), Oliga (1996), Jernier, Knights and Nord (1994), Hardy (1994) and Hardy and Clegg (1996), the topics of power and politics are being openly discussed as researchers and practitioners in the field begin to admit the reality of power in organisational life.

Bjoe and Winsor (1993) argue that Total Quality Management (TQM) programs are no more than another resurrection of Taylorism, using corporate culture to facilitate 'the use of psychological and social control and coercion' (Bjoe & Winsor 1993, p. 68). This argument is supported by Knights and McCabe (1999) and investigated further by Lewis (2001).

Power in the HR literature

The HR literature has been slower to recognise the importance of power, as is evidenced by the relative rarity of chapters such as this one in HR textbooks. The OD model of organisational change, for example, has traditionally been a unitarist model, and only recently have researchers such as Hardy and Redivo (1994) suggested a new model of OD that takes power into consideration as a primary, legitimate strategy for change. Most other HR theories of recruitment, selection, training and development have also traditionally been unitarist. Yet power is coming into this literature too. Ferris, Galang, Thorton and Wayne (1995) confront the topic of power and politics in human resource management (HRM); and Russ, Galang and Ferris (1998) explore how HR departments in organisations gain influence. They argue that HR departments have particular problems with power because they need to influence people yet they lack legitimate authority and have no objective measures of success. They are faced with having to manage impressions through symbolic actions. HR's boundary-spanning role may be the basis for an evolutionary model of information management.

Other works dealing with power in the human resource area include those by Elangovan and Xie (2000), who explore the relationships between perceptions of supervisor power and subordinate work attitudes, and by Lewis, French and Phetmany (2000), who look at the relationship between perceived leadership behaviour and subordinate job satisfaction in different cultural groups.

Power and gender

The place of women in the power stakes is another area being pursued in the literature. Mann (1995) highlights the ways in which sources of power are balanced in favour of male employees, and argues that it is the politicking and power-mongering in organisations that tends to put women off applying for managerial positions.

Foster (1999, p. 316) argues that 'women as senior managers present a challenge both to the occupational status of management and to the structures of power in a patriarchal society', and that men try to minimise these challenges by excluding women from management roles and denying them the legitimate authority that comes with such roles. According to Ledet and Henley (2000), women who do achieve high positions are perceived as more masculine than men and women in low positions and as masculine as men in high positions.

The literature on power and gender will most likely continue to grow rapidly as women attempt to make further inroads into the male domain of senior management.

Power in the public sector

The use of power in the public sector is also gaining attention with the idea that the re-emergence of bureaucracies is a sign that organisations are becoming more politically centralised and governed (Courpasson 2000).

Against the general trend of power in the HR literature, Oswick and Grant (1996) argue that HR in the public sector is losing power. They claim that the very change of name from personnel management to human resource management indicates a change in role for the personnel practitioner in terms of power and influence in the organisation. They argue that HR departments are 'likely to continue to be reshaped to play an increasingly subservient support role — a role which more suitably reflects personnel's inferiority in terms of organisational power' (Oswick & Grant 1996, p. 16).

There is still not enough literature on power in either the HR or the public sector fields to be able to predict a trend at this stage. What is encouraging in the literature in all areas, though, is the new interest in power as an important facet of organisational life. Only when we are prepared to openly and honestly explore power relationships and political actions will we be able to truly understand the workplace and our own place in it.

Implications for organisations, managers and individuals

Implications for organisations

From this short discussion, we can conclude that power is not confined to managers or to others with legitimate power but may reside in formal groups set up as part of the organisational structure to work in the organisation's interests; in

informal groups, which may or may not work in the organisation's interests; and in individuals working mainly in their own interests. In fact, power is ubiquitous, even in what may seem to be the most rational of systems.

Power can help or hinder people and the organisation in the achievement of their goals; as Pfeffer (1992) says, it may be a 'two-edged sword', used to reward or punish. For both the organisation and the individuals in it to survive, people need to be able to view power in both positive and negative ways.

Implications for human resource managers

Much of the responsibility for handling power in organisations falls on the general managers and how they manage the political process. But it will be the task of the human resource managers to implement many of the strategies of the general managers and to deal with any resulting conflict. This means HR managers need to have an intimate knowledge of the goals of general managers and the effects the implementation of strategies to achieve them will have on organisation members.

First, both general managers and HR managers will need to work out the different interests in the organisation. This will require them to adopt a pluralist view of power and to recognise that not all people in the organisation are working towards the same goals or have the same motives as the managers themselves. As Robbins et al. (2000, p. 212) say, 'Organisations are made up of divergent interests that make it difficult, even impossible, to create a common effort towards a single goal. Decisions are therefore rarely directed towards achieving an overall organisational goal.'

Recognition of this pluralism may not come easily to some managers, and particularly HR managers, brought up on unitarist theory and the belief that conflict is abnormal and must be eradicated. Most HR policies and practices start from a base assumption of unitarism. Some general managers may feel uncomfortable having to acknowledge that subordinates do not always think the same way they do, but that subordinates' views have to be considered and not necessarily changed or quashed.

Second, general and HR managers need to understand how to manage the political process. Not only must they be able to analyse interests; they must also understand conflicts and explore power relations, so that situations can be brought under a measure of control.

Third, general managers need to understand the strategies and tactics through which they may develop and use their power. Should they adopt the 'shotgun' or the 'tactician' approach? It is assumed that few managers will choose the 'bystander' approach, although some very powerful managers may be able to afford that luxury. The approach they eventually choose will most likely be the one that sits most comfortably with their own personality. The HR manager, charged with the task of implementing the chosen strategy of the general manager, needs to have a very good knowledge of how to handle the conflict that will invariably result.

Thomas and Kilmann (see figure 20.2) suggest that managers have five different choices in how they manage conflict. These are:

- *avoidance*, in which the manager tries to ignore conflicts and hopes they will go away, is uncooperative and unassertive, and attempts to withdraw from conflict
- *compromise,* in which the manager looks for deals and trade-offs, and tries to find satisfactory or acceptable solutions; this approach will lead to a lose–lose situation, because both parties have to give up something they value
- *competition,* an aggressive and combative strategy in which one party tries to disempower the other
- *accommodation*, in which one party submits to the other, satisfying the interests of the other party at their own expense
- *collaboration*, in which the conflicting parties adopt a problem-solving stance, confronting their differences and sharing ideas and information; this approach involves trying to satisfy all parties' interests in order to achieve a win–win outcome.

It is obvious that collaboration is the style Thomas and Kilmann prefer, but they promote this as a 'one best way' style rather than being open to the value of other styles. Sometimes it might be best to collaborate, sometimes to accommodate and sometimes to compete; it all depends on the situation. Just as there is no 'one best way' to manage, so there is no 'one best way' to handle conflict. As stated earlier, sometimes a power approach is the *only* way.

A strong case can therefore be made that general and HR managers have much more choice in the strategies they use than they would have organisation members believe.

Implications for organisational members

Managers are not the only organisation members who may have difficulty accepting a pluralist view; the first 'rule' for employees entering an organisation is to recognise that the rational model of decision making is not always used. Many young employees enter organisations believing in rational

decision making and are rudely awakened to the realities of organisational life. They can then become very disillusioned when their best schemes and ideas seem to fall on deaf ears. But the fault may not lie with the ideas themselves; it may simply be that they have not yet deciphered the power and politics of the organisation.

Organisation members usually have a choice in whether they play the power game. However, even if they decide to opt out of direct involvement in power, they still need to be able to recognise and assess power in their organisations, and they still need to know how to survive the political process. Advice in this chapter may go a small way towards assisting them in survival. On the other hand, individuals who decide to play the power game themselves may wish to explore some of the strategies suggested by Kipnis (1990) or even Machiavelli (1513 [1958]).

Conclusion

While we may espouse democratic and rational decision making, participation and collaboration, power still exists as a force for both good and ill in organisations. We need to see it, therefore, as a source of both positive and negative outcomes, and not try to eliminate it altogether. Future HR professionals will need to recognise its influence and learn to use it to implement general managers' policies and handle conflicts, and organisational members will need to understand its workings and how they may use it either in pursuit of their own ambitions or simply to survive in a power environment. Power is indeed a 'two-edged sword'.

References

Bjoe, DM, and Winsor, RD (1993) The resurrection of Taylorism: total quality management's hidden agenda. *Journal of Organizational Change Management*, 6 (4), 57–70.

Burnes, B (2000) *Managing Change: A Strategic Approach to Organisational Dynamics* (3rd ed.). London: Pearson Education.

Burns, T, and Stalker, GM (1966) *The Management of Innovation*. London: Tavistock.

Courpasson, D (2000) Managerial strategies of domination. Power in soft bureaucracies. *Organization Studies*, 21 (1) 141–61.

Dahl, RA (1957) The concept of power. *Behavioral Science,* 2, 201–215.

Davis, K (1981) *Human Behavior at Work: Organizational Behavior* (6th ed.). New York: McGraw-Hill.

Dunphy, D, and Stace, D (1988) Transformational and coercive strategies for planned organizational change. *Organization Studies*, 9 (3) 317–34.

Elangovan, AR, and Xie, JL (2000) Effects of perceived power of supervisor on subordinate work attitudes. *Leadership and Organization Development Journal*, 21 (6) 319–28.

Emerson, RM (1969) Power-dependence relations. *American Sociological Review*, 27, 31–40.

Ferris, GR, Galang, MC, Thornton, ML, and Wayne, SJ (1995) A power and politics perspective on human resource management. In GR Ferris, SD Rosen and DT Barnum (Eds), *Handbook of Human Resource Management*. Oxford, UK: Blackwell.

Fiedler, F (1967) *A Theory of Leadership Effectiveness*. New York: McGraw-Hill.

Foster, J (1999) Women senior managers and conditional power: the case in social services departments. *Leadership and Organization Development Journal*, 14 (8), 316–24.

French, JRP Jr, and Raven, B (1960) The bases of social power. In D Cartwright and AF Zander (Eds), *Group Dynamics: Research and Theory*. New York: Harper & Row, 607–623.

Hardy, C (1994) Power and politics in organizations. In C Hardy (Ed.), *Managing Strategic Action: Mobilizing Change*. London: Sage.

Hardy, C, and Clegg, S (1996) Some dare call it power. In S Clegg, C Hardy and W Nord (Eds), *Handbook of Organizational Studies*. London: Sage.

Hardy, C, and Redivo, F (1994) Power and organizational development: a framework for organizational change. *Journal of General Management*, 20 (2) 1–13.

Hofstede, G (1980) *Culture's Consequences: International Differences in Work-Related Values*. London: Sage.

Jermier, J, Knights, D, and Nord, W (1994) *Resistance and Power in Organizations*. London: Routledge.

Kipnis, D (1990) *Technology and Power*. New York: Springer-Verlag.

Knights, D, and McCabe, D (1999) Are there no limits to authority?: TQM and organizational power. *Organization Studies*, 20 (2) 197–224.

Kramer, RM, and Neale, MA (Eds) (1998) *Power and Influence in Organizations*. Thousand Oaks, CA: Sage.

Lawrence, PR, and Lorsch, JW (1967) *Organization and Environment: Managing Differentiation and Integration*. Graduate School of Business Administration. Boston, MA: Harvard University.

Ledet, LM, and Henley, TB (2000) Perceptions of women's power as a function of position within an organization. *Journal of Psychology*, 134 (5) 515–26.

Lewis, D (1996) New perspectives on transformational leadership. In K Parry (Ed.), *Leadership Research and Practice: Emerging Themes and New Challenges*. Sydney: Pitman, 17–28.

Lewis, D (2001) Organisational culture: theory, fad, or managerial control. In R Wiesner and B Millett (Eds), *Management and Organisational Behaviour*. Brisbane: John Wiley & Sons.

Lewis, D, French, E, and Phetmany, T (2000) Cross-cultural diversity and its challenges for leadership and workplace relations. *Asia Pacific Business Review*, Autumn, 7 (1) 105–124.

Machiavelli, N (1513) *The Prince*. Transl. WK Marriott (1958). London: JM Dent & Sons.

Mann, S (1995) Politics and power in organizations: why women lose out. *Leadership and Organization Development Journal*, 50 (11) 1403–1422.

Mayo, E (1933) *The Social Problems of an Industrial Civilization*. Reprinted 1952. London: Routledge and Kegan Paul, 31–50.

Morgan, G (1997) *Images of Organization*. California: Sage.

Oliga, JC (1996) *Power, Ideology and Control*. New York: Plenum Press.

Oswick, C, and Grant, D (1996) Personnel management in the public sector: power, roles and relationships. *Personnel Review*, 25 (2) 4–18.

Pfeffer, J (1981) *Power in Organizations*. Cambridge, MA: Pitman.

Pfeffer, J (1992) *Managing with Power: Politics and Influence in Organisations*. Boston, MA: Harvard Business School Press.

Robbins, SP, Bergman, R, Stagg, I, and Coulter, M (2000) *Management*. Sydney: Prentice Hall.

Russ, GS, Galang, MC, and Ferris, GR (1998) Power and influence of the human resources function through boundary spanning and information management. *Human Resource Management Review*, Summer, 8 (2) 125–43.

Swingle, P (1976) *The Management of Power*. London: John Wiley & Sons.

Thomas, KW (1976) Conflict and conflict management. In MD Dunette (Ed.), *Handbook of Industrial and Organizational Psychology*. Chicago: Rand McNally.

Weber, M (1947) *The Theory of Social and Economic Organization*. London: Oxford University Press.

Woodward, J (1965) *Industrial Organization: Theory and Practice*. London: Oxford University Press.

CHAPTER 21

Quality culture as a critical factor for quality performance

by Dianne Waddell

Monash University

Introduction

Quality is unquestionably one of the hottest topics in the media today, frequently addressed in books, journals and training seminars (Neergaard 1999). Reeves and Bednar (1994, p. 419), for example, claim that quality 'is perhaps the most frequently repeated mantra among managers and executives in contemporary organisations'.

However, the quality movement has had a troubled past. Seeking a magic elixir or 'quick fix', many organisations in the early part of this decade appear to have hastily implemented pre-packaged quality programs without fully appreciating what they were doing (Sitkin, Sutcliffe & Schroeder 1994). In their zeal, early proponents of quality management failed to recognise the importance of tailoring the quality program to the specific needs of the organisation. Not surprisingly, such action led to lacklustre economic results, a proliferation of articles focusing on the 'failure of TQM' (Holoviak 1995; Conner 1997; Feinberg 1998) and the view that 'TQM died a quiet death, never fulfilling its initial promise' (DeCock & Hipkin 1997, p. 663).

Consequently, a range of alternative business models, such as supply chain management, business process re-engineering and time-based competition, have recently emerged (Hendricks & Singhal 1999). However, many of these paradigms also appear to have produced mixed results. For example, the failure rate of re-engineering programs has been estimated at as high as 70 per cent (Ashkenas, Hsaffer and associates 1994; Higginson & Waxler 1994).

The inability of such models to provide managers with better economic results, and the growing realisation that survival depends almost entirely on the ability to provide quality products and services, has once again shifted the interest of academics and practitioners back to quality management.

Large-scale neglect of the 'soft stuff' (Redman & Grieves 1999, p. 47), or the social, psychological and emotional needs of employees, is now seen as the predominant reason for the failure of many early quality programs. As a result, it has been suggested that organisations attempting to implement or manage quality programs need to pay more attention to the development of the appropriate 'quality culture' (Saraph & Sebastian 1993; Van Donk & Sanders 1993; Dellana & Hauser 1999).

This argument is based on the premise that if the culture of the organisation does not support and reinforce a quality philosophy, the entire quality effort will be significantly undermined. Indeed, research indicates that without the supporting value system, most quality programs 'run out of steam' 18 to 24 months after being launched (Smith, Transfield, Foster & Whittle 1993). The purpose of this chapter is to:

- Identify which quality culture factors (top management leadership, teamwork, employee empowerment and commitment to customers) have the greatest impact on quality performance outcomes (financial performance, service performance, employee satisfaction and customer satisfaction); and
- emphasise the extent to which HR managers recognise the importance of establishing and maintaining such a quality culture.

The concept of quality culture

Culture may be defined as 'the combination of beliefs, values and underlying assumptions supporting behaviour patterns and artefacts' (Zeitz, Johannesson & Ritchie 1997, p. 418). Such a definition is adopted by what is probably a majority of writers on the issue (Deal & Kennedy 1982; Peters & Waterman 1982; Lewis 1996a, 1996b), and recognises that culture embodies both implicit and unmeasurable elements such as values and beliefs and observable, tangible elements such as behaviour.

Given the above interpretation, a 'quality culture' can be viewed as incorporating those quality-related beliefs, values and subsequent behaviours that typically exist in an organisation that has adopted a quality philosophy. For the purpose of this chapter, it is accepted that an organisational culture creates an environment that supports behaviour consistent with that culture. Such behaviour, in turn, leads to outcomes that are consistent with that culture (Schlesinger & Balzer 1985).

In the past, a number of authors have investigated the relationship between quality and organisational culture (Linklow 1989; Hames 1991; Rubin & Inguagiato 1991; Westbrook 1993). Most of these studies point to the importance of establishing and maintaining a culture that reflects the organisation's underlying quality philosophy. Van Donk & Sanders (1993, p. 5), for example, claim that culture is the 'missing link' in quality management. They argue that it is necessary to study, measure and make use of the existing culture in order to increase the success of a quality program. Similarly, Saraph & Sebastian (1993, p. 73) suggest that quality efforts 'might not achieve their true potential if an organisation fails to develop its corporate quality culture'.

These views appear to be supported by more recent research. Bardoel & Sohal (1999), for example, used the case study technique to investigate issues relating to the adoption of quality management in seven Australian organisations. They found that the most common reason for quality programs 'not being entirely successful' was that 'employees did not perceive the program to be part of a corporate vision for quality and consequently had no enthusiasm' (Bardoel & Sohal 1999, p. 268). This led the authors to believe that 'sustained commitment is more likely if employees share the same mental models of quality in the organisation' (Bardoel & Sohal 1999, p. 272).

Tata and Prasad (1998), who studied the relationship between quality practices, culture and organisational structure, reached a similar conclusion. They suggested that successful quality implementation requires 'a fundamental change in the way individuals and groups approach their work … from working as individuals to working as teams; from an autocratic management style of direction to a softer style of team leader and coach; and from power concentrated at the top to power shared with employees' (p. 710).

Each of these research studies suggests that establishing a quality culture can significantly increase the success of an organisational quality improvement program. As Lewis (1996a, p. 12) points out, 'while TQM had separate origins from the culture movement, the two fields have recently converged with the idea that to achieve "excellence" and "quality", it is necessary to change or work with the culture of the organisation'.

Relationship between quality culture and quality performance outcomes

In the past, commentators have focused on how a range of quality tools or techniques affect product or service quality. This single-minded interest in certification and documentation has resulted in a serious neglect of the 'softer' quality factors that are essential for organisations if they are to meet or exceed their performance targets.

Critical quality culture factors

The challenge is to implement, or 'operationalise', the concept of quality culture. Extensive examination of past research has confirmed the findings of a recent study completed by Adebanjo and Kehoe (1998, p. 275), which listed those factors considered to be 'indicative of attributes which practitioners generally agree should be present in quality organisations'. These included:
- top management leadership
- teamwork
- employee empowerment
- commitment to customers.

Since these factors have also been singled out by a variety of other authors who have attempted to identify the key dimensions of quality management (Stoner-Zemel 1989; Brocka & Brocka 1992; Goetsch & Davis 1994; Dale et al. 1994; Prescott 1995; Kaye & Anderson 1999), it is generally accepted that these factors could reasonably be used to characterise or describe a quality culture. The following sections illustrate the practical importance of each factor and highlight the relevant research findings for each respective area of interest.

Top management leadership

Leadership is consistently reinforced in the literature as a fundamental requirement for any organisation implementing a quality program (Saraph et al. 1989; Drensek & Grubb 1995; Flynn et al. 1995; Hoff 1995; Roosevelt 1995; Hemphill 1996). A lack of top management leadership is frequently cited as the primary reason for the failure of quality programs (Masters 1996; Krumwiede et al. 1998). The role of top management therefore appears to be critical for the articulation of a new vision and the establishment of a quality culture (Abraham et al. 1999).

The importance of top management leadership has been recognised by quality gurus (Crosby 1979; Juran 1981), through formal acknowledgements such as the Baldridge Award (Garvin 1991) and by a variety of authors who have examined the role of top leadership in quality organisations. Garvin (1991, p. 20), who found that 'high product quality does not exist without strong top management commitment', completed one of the earliest of these studies. In another study, Powell (1995, p. 23) tested the hypothesis that 'TQM performance (measured by financial indicators such as profit) is positively associated with committed leadership'. By evaluating the strength of the correlation between variables, Powell (1995, p. 30) concluded that the hypothesis could be 'supported conclusively'. This finding was later reinforced in a larger, international study in which senior management involvement was described as 'one of the primary factors predicting financial performance' (Adam et al. 1997, p. 865).

Not surprisingly, other research has also found that top management leadership is 'critically important' to the success of the quality effort (Ahire & O'Shaughnessy 1998, p. 15). Similar results were obtained in a large international study involving 411 organisations in seven countries (Dahlgaard et al. 1998). After an analysis of the survey responses, the primary recommendation was that 'top management should sustain their commitment to quality improvement efforts and take an active role in all quality management activities. The high level of visibility of top management will provide the much needed motivation to lower level employees' (Dahlgaard et al. 1998, p. 825).

Teamwork

Teamwork occurs when a group of individuals work together to solve problems or carry out tasks (Hackman 1987). Many authors emphasise the role of teams in quality organisations (Manz & Sims 1980, 1987; Alpander & Lee 1995; Harrington 1996; Vass 1998; Barnard 1999; Connors & Smith 1999; Spreitzer et al. 1999). Korukonda and colleagues (1999, p. 31) observe that 'there seems to be no question that teams occupy a central role in the quality movement'.

This central role is no doubt due to the wide range of benefits believed to result from teams and teamwork. Waterman (1994, p. 33), for example, claims that teams 'can make enormous gains in productivity and morale'. Deming (1982, p. 36) suggests teams 'can accomplish important improvements in the design of products and services'. Teams have also been associated with job satisfaction and commitment (Cordery et al. 1991), problem-solving skills (Harris & Harris 1996) and high productivity (Wellins et al. 1990; Cohen & Ledford 1994). These favourable consequences are essentially a direct result of the synergistic nature of teams in which individual contributions are enhanced through cooperation with others (Connor 1997; Laszlo 1998).

International studies (Lackritz 1997; Epstein & Epstein 1998; Liu 1998; Sohal 1998) also regularly emphasise teamwork. For example, in a recent study Batt (1999, p. 73) found that 'participation in self managed work teams was associated with a statistically significant improvement in service quality and a 9.2% increase in sales per employee'. Similar findings have caused other authors to conclude that it is absolutely imperative for organisations to develop a 'culture of teamwork and co-operation ... and an atmosphere of trust and sharing' (Dahlgaard et al. 1998, p. 825).

Employee empowerment

Although 'empowerment' has been given a range of meanings in recent times, this research views it as the 'process of giving employees greater responsibility, authority and accountability' (Hamzah & Zairi 1996, p. 40). Since empowered employees have greater opportunity to exercise discretion in their work roles, empowerment may be understood as the antithesis of authoritarian management (Kelly 1993; Ledford & Lawler 1996). Although management has to relinquish some decision-making power, employee empowerment is advocated as essential for any organisation attempting to provide high levels of service quality. This is because employees dealing with situations on a daily basis are the best qualified to make decisions regarding those situations (Hamzah & Zairi 1996; Perry et al. 1999).

The importance of employee empowerment has led to a proliferation in descriptive and empirical research on the topic. Past studies have addressed, among other things, which personal and external factors influence empowerment levels. Koberg et al. (1999), for example, found that tenure with the organisation, leader approachability, group effectiveness and position in the formal organisational hierarchy all influence feelings of empowerment. Other studies have found that elements of the work context itself may influence employee perceptions of empowerment. According to Conger & Kanungo (1988), empowerment levels are influenced by supervisory style and reward and recognition systems.

Much of the literature consistently reaffirms the need for empowerment in quality organisations. Empowerment has been associated with the provision of quality services (Terziovski & Dean 1998), employee satisfaction and motivation (Kappelman & Prybutok 1995; Purser & Cabana 1997; Wilkinson et al. 1997), high levels of employee morale (Sohal 1998), problem solving (Barnard 1999; Silos 1999) and business performance (Ripley & Ripley 1992; Ledford & Lawler 1996, Lin 1998; Oakland & Oakland 1998).

Perhaps the key factor driving these outcomes is that people want to 'experience meaningfulness' (Connor 1997, p. 503) from their work and will accept a decision more readily when they have been involved in making it (Rodrigues 1994). One respondent in the Koberg study stated that 'administration gives departments control over decisions, and input is allowed during the process; we are more committed as a result' (1999, p. 81). Empowerment thus creates an environment of trust and is a source of motivation for employees to commit themselves to improving the quality of the organisation (Lam 1995).

Commitment to customers

Dean & Bowen (1994, p. 394) state that the 'goal of satisfying customers is fundamental to quality management and is expressed by the organisation's attempt to design and deliver products and services that fulfil customer needs'. The 1991 national Baldridge Award reinforces this view with the statement that 'quality is judged by customers ... therefore all product and service characteristics that contribute value to customers must be a key focus of a company's management team' (cited in Massnick 1996, p. 95).

Meeting the needs and requirements of customers is therefore the main thrust of quality management (Dale et al. 1997). However, for employees to satisfy customer needs, management must consistently communicate customer requirements. Not only does this help maintain enthusiasm for the quality initiative, but clear communication also ensures that employee efforts are directed towards the appropriate goals (Hamzah & Zairi 1996). In addition, the organisation should allow for upward and lateral communication so that employees can 'present their ideas and vent their feelings' (Thiagarajan & Zairi 1997, p. 345).

Another essential aspect of maintaining a consistent commitment to customers is to allow the customers themselves to express their views about the level of service provided by the organisation. The need to obtain feedback from customers has been identified by a range of empirical studies (Saraph et al. 1989; Flynn et al. 1995). More recently, a survey of 1300 organisations in Australia and New Zealand found that leading organisations know what their customers' 'current and future requirements' are by systematically and regularly measuring customer satisfaction (Samson 1997, p. 223). Similarly, Liu (1998, p. 598) found that regular measurement of customer perceptions of quality allows the 'voice of the customer' to be translated into measures of performance.

Any attempt to satisfy the customer must begin with a genuine desire to fulfil customer expectations. There seems little doubt that the best companies have a passionate and shared commitment to serve customers to the best of their abilities (Peters & Waterman 1982).

Quality performance outcomes

The previous sections have discussed the past research that has been completed on each of the four major factors of quality culture. However, quality outcomes and their relationship with quality culture need to be clarified before their impact on HR managers can be considered. An examination of the literature suggests that quality organisations typically assess performance through both 'hard' (financial and service performance) and 'soft' (employee and customer satisfaction) measures. These four performance outcomes will therefore now be discussed in more detail.

Financial performance

Various empirical studies appear to support the general proposition that quality practices are related to financial performance (Adam 1994; Roth & Jackson 1995; Forker et al. 1996; Adam et al. 1997; Chapman et al. 1997; Terziovski & Samson 1999).

Some of the earliest empirical investigations into quality and business performance were conducted under the Profit Impact of Marketing Strategy (PIMS) database study (Buzzell & Wiersema 1981; Craig & Douglas 1982; Phillips et al. 1983). Using a database of 3000 US and European organisations, the researchers found a 'strong positive correlation between quality and market share and between quality and financial measures of profitability such as return on investment' (Schoeffler et al. 1974; Craig & Douglas 1982). These results led the authors to conclude that for every 2 per cent improvement in the rating of an organisation's quality by its customers, there is a 1 per cent increase in the company's return on investment (Phillips et al. 1983). Although it could be argued that the results are limited to the manufacturing industry, the PIMS studies demonstrated that quality improvement practices have a significant and direct effect on financial performance.

Shortly after the PIMS studies, the US Government Accounting Office Study (GAO 1991) examined the impact of formal quality improvement strategies on the performance of 20 US companies presented with the Malcolm

Baldridge National Quality Award. Not surprisingly, the study found a significant 'cause and effect relationship between quality practices … and corporate performance'. These findings have since been replicated by Ernst & Young in the International Quality Study (1992), and expanded on by Powell (1995, p. 15), who found that certain 'tacit features such as employee empowerment and executive commitment can produce financial advantage'.

Dow, Samson and Ford (1999) have produced a similar result. After surveying approximately 4000 organisations across Australia and New Zealand, the authors concluded that, 'when combined together, several of the softer quality management practices do have a positive relationship with financial performance' (Dow et al. 1999, p. 18). Taken overall, these studies provide conclusive evidence that quality management has a positive effect on financial performance.

Service performance

In the past, the evaluation of 'service performance' has been influenced largely by the service quality literature, which has focused on identifying those factors that affect customer expectations and perceptions of quality (Sasser et al. 1978; Lewis & Booms 1983; Gronroos 1984; Parasuraman et al. 1991). This clearly reflects the generally accepted view that 'quality is whatever the customer says it is, and the quality of a particular product or service is whatever the customer perceives it to be' (Buzzell & Gale 1987, p. 111).

This line of research has in turn led to the development of a number of models that, according to the authors, reliably measure service quality (Parasuraman et al. 1988; Freeman & Dart 1993; Cronin & Taylor 1994). An alternative measure of service performance, and one that is easily interpreted by quality managers, is reliability, or the ability of the organisation to perform a service 'dependably and accurately' (Parasuraman et al. 1991, p. 41).

Reliability has been identified as 'the single most important feature in judging service quality' on the basis that 'little else matters to customers when a company is not dependable' (Berry & Parasuraman 1994, p. 34). The critical importance of reliability is also recognised by other authors, who suggest that 'management must place a premium on company service reliability' (Caruana & Pitt 1997, p. 605). The fact that 'negative word of mouth can have a devastating impact on the credibility of an organisation' (Ghobadian et al. 1994, p. 44) reaffirms the significance of reliability as a key measure of service performance.

However, a full appreciation of service performance, especially from a managerial viewpoint, must incorporate some measure of quality costs, or 'the costs that are attributable to achieving quality' (Evans & Lindsay 1989, p. 29). Cost reduction has traditionally stood at the core of quality

management (Crosby 1979). This is because quality costing is one tool that has been used to 'justify the adoption of quality improvement efforts to top management' (Thiagarajan & Zairi 1997, p. 351). Thus, a focus on quality costs creates an incentive for ensuring that future investments in quality endeavours are targeted towards 'key areas of business improvement and success' (ASQ Quality Costs Committee 1999, p. 84).

Employee satisfaction

Decades of job design research show that employees are more satisfied when they have a 'sense of control and of doing meaningful work' (Bowen & Lawler 1992, p. 305). In recent years a number of empirical studies have investigated the relationship between employee satisfaction and a range of other constructs.

In an extensive survey of 1277 employees and 4269 customers of a personal insurance organisation in the United States, Schlesinger & Zornitsky (1991, p. 146) tested the hypothesis 'Efforts successfully directed at enhancing service capability will improve job satisfaction'. They found that the variable 'service capability' explained 18 per cent of the variation in overall job satisfaction levels. From this result, the authors concluded that 'focussing on activities that enable employees to better serve customers is generally the most significant service related initiative an organisation can make' (Schlesinger & Zornitsky 1991, p. 149).

External factors, such as customer satisfaction, have also been related to employee satisfaction levels. Schneider and Bowen (1985), for example, found a direct relationship between well-designed service encounters, enhanced bank customer satisfaction and the satisfaction of tellers. The presence of a two-way relationship between customer and employee satisfaction has more recently been identified in the 'cycle of success' (Schlesinger & Heskett 1991, p. 99) and by the term 'satisfaction mirror' (Heskett et al. 1997, p. 101). Taken overall, these studies suggest that if customers are satisfied, then employees should also be satisfied (and vice versa).

Another empirical study, completed by Lam (1995), examined the effect of quality improvement programs on employee satisfaction levels. While agreeing with the general argument that 'working conditions which minimise role conflict and provide employees with interesting work' lead to increased levels of job satisfaction, the findings also suggested that 'quality programs made work more demanding' (Lam 1995, p. 77). The explanation given for this was that 'while the ability of employees to achieve customer satisfaction goals was enhanced', the nature of the quality program 'did not necessarily allow for the enhancement of employee satisfaction levels' (Lam 1995, p. 78). This suggests that although the benefits of employee satisfaction are generally recognised (Simmerman 1993; Oakland & Oakland 1998), organisations may need to pay more attention to mechanisms that facilitate employee satisfaction.

Customer satisfaction

Customer satisfaction is closely linked to the concept of service quality. As Gabbot & Hogg (1997, p. 171) point out, 'the close conceptual links between satisfaction and service quality have led to considerable disagreements about how these two dimensions are related'. Much of this debate has centred on the direction of causality. Some writers argue that customer satisfaction is a prerequisite for service quality, in that a consumer's overall assessment of the service is based on an accumulation of satisfying or dissatisfying experiences (Bolton & Drew 1991; Boulding et al. 1993; Cronin & Taylor 1994). Others prefer to focus on transaction-specific assessments, with the result that high service quality is seen as the determinant of customer satisfaction (Woodside et al. 1989).

Nevertheless, the most widely adopted view of customer satisfaction is that of 'expectancy disconfirmation', whereby satisfaction is viewed as based largely on meeting or exceeding expectations (Churchill & Surprenant 1982; Bolton & Drew 1991; Oliver 1993).

Despite the operational difficulties associated with customer satisfaction, most authors agree that customer satisfaction is a critical organisational objective (Barnes & Cumby 1995; Rust et al. 1996). According to Reichheld & Sasser (1990, p. 105), 'customer defections can have more to do with a service company's profits than scale, market share and many other factors usually associated with competitive advantage'. An investigation into the defection rates of a variety of companies operating in the United States suggested that 'companies can boost profits by almost 100 per cent by retaining just 5 per cent more of their customers' (Reichheld & Sasser 1990, p. 106).

In a large-scale examination of Swedish firms, Anderson et al. (1994) confirmed that firms that achieve high customer satisfaction levels also enjoy superior economic performance. They found that an annual one point increase in customer satisfaction results in a net present value that represents an increase of 11.5 per cent over five years for the typical firm in Sweden (Anderson et al. 1994).

Satisfying customers is therefore a critical objective for any organisation. As Muffatto & Panizzolo (1995, p. 154) point out, past research suggests that customer satisfaction may be one of 'the most important competitive factors for the future and one of the best indicators of a firm's future profits'. Quality organisations are thus advised by the literature to use a range of tools, such as customer surveys, focus groups and advisory panels, to ensure that employees

develop an appreciation of customer desires (Flanagan & Fredericks 1993; Thiagarajan & Zairi 1997; Oakland & Oakland 1998).

Summary

With quality viewed increasingly as a means of creating and maintaining competitive advantage, articles have proliferated on all aspects of the quality process. However, despite the diverse range of research, few studies have viewed quality as a complex cultural process that requires the integration of more than one core quality dimension.

For example, authors such as Ahire & O'Shaughnessy (1998) and Dahlgaard et al. (1998) have examined the specific role and contribution of top management leadership; Sohal (1998) and Batt (1999) have investigated the importance of teamwork; Koberg et al. (1999) have highlighted the implications of employee empowerment; and Samson (1997) and Liu (1998) have reaffirmed the importance of establishing a customer focus. Although these studies are significant in their own right, little research has attempted to combine these elements in one empirical study.

Similarly, there has been much interest in determining how quality management practices influence particular performance outcomes. By far the most commonly investigated outcome is that of financial performance (Ernst & Young 1992; Powell 1995; Dow et al. 1999). A range of other studies have helped define service quality (Caruana & Pitt 1997), and more recently the concepts of employee satisfaction (Schlesinger & Zornitsky 1991) and customer satisfaction (Muffatto & Panizzolo 1995; Reichheld & Sasser 1990) have gained popularity. Once again, however, few empirical studies have examined in a single study how quality management influences all of these outcomes. This chapter highlights this deficiency, suggests approaching the quality concept from a cultural perspective and examines how a range of quality culture factors can influence multiple performance outcomes.

Recent empirical research

As previously stated, an overview of the literature identified four critical quality culture factors and four common performance outcomes. This construct suggests a total of sixteen testable relationships between the four independent and four dependent constructs (see figure 21.1).

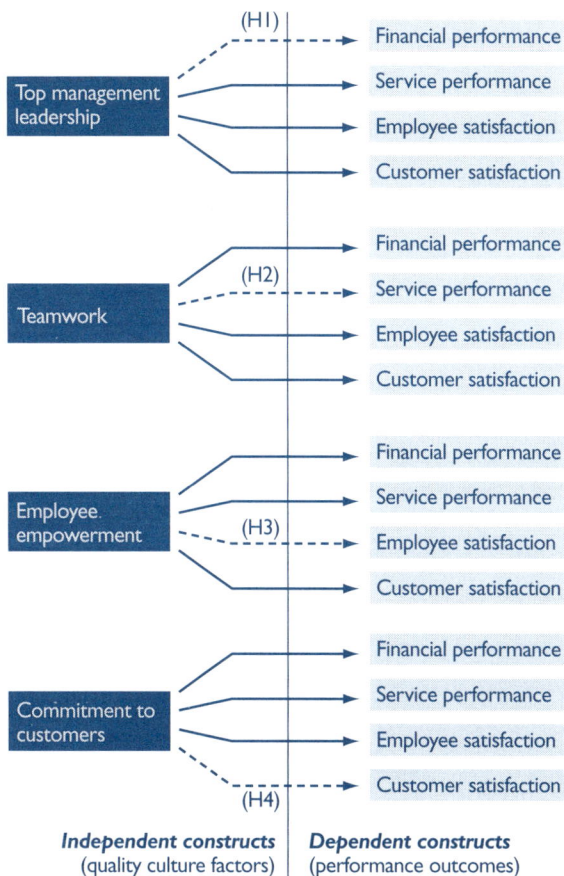

Independent constructs
(quality culture factors)

Dependent constructs
(performance outcomes)

Figure 21.1: Testable relationships between the research constructs

Using this model, Barrett and Waddell (2001) examined a random sample of five hypotheses:

- There is a significant positive relationship between quality culture factors and quality performance outcomes (general hypothesis).
- There is a significant positive relationship between top management leadership and financial performance (H1).
- There is a significant positive relationship between teamwork and overall service performance (H2).
- The empowerment of employees has a significant positive relationship with employee satisfaction levels (H3).
- A genuine commitment to customers has a significant positive relationship with overall customer satisfaction levels (H4).

They surveyed 365 organisations including both private and government-owned organisations listed under the title 'Business Management Services' in the JAS–ANZ Register of Accredited and Certified Organisations for Australia and New Zealand (November 1998). Single organisations formed the unit of analysis, while individuals responsible for implementing and monitoring organisational quality programs, typically the Quality Manager, were considered to be the

ideal respondents. The survey included open and closed questions (with a Likert scale of 1 to 5), and five follow-up interviews were completed. The responses were analysed using the Version 9.0 SPSS for Windows program. Although what follows is a summary of simple mean score results, they were confirmed by techniques that included univariate, bivariate, factor, multivariate and reliability analyses.

Quality culture practices

A brief examination of table 21.1 suggests that most responses to the statements pertaining to quality culture practices were positive. Top management and teamwork were both measured by attitudes towards four separate statements. The overall scores were 3.77 and 3.96 respectively, with few respondents indicating that either of these constructs was extremely important.

The construct of employee empowerment was also measured by the responses to four statements; however, in this case two items were negatively worded ('Our organisation has low levels of morale' and 'Employees can be confused about what is expected of them in their job'). Negatively wording some statements was a deliberate attempt to reduce acquiescence or positive response bias (Edwards & Thomas 1993, p. 425). In order to calculate the overall score for employee empowerment, the scores attached to each of these negatively worded statements were reversed. This process resulted in an overall score of 3.67, suggesting once again that although respondents believed in employee empowerment, the overall level of interest was by no means significant.

The final independent construct, named 'Commitment to customers', was measured by responses to three separate statements. Interestingly, the overall score for this construct was 4.20, indicating that of all the quality culture factors, a commitment to customers was considered to be the most critical.

Quality performance outcomes

Consideration was also given to the mean and overall scores for each dependent variable. Table 21.2 indicates that financial performance and employee satisfaction were given the lowest scores (3.29 and 3.12 respectively). This suggests that most organisations in the sample have reached positive, but only moderate, gains in both financial return and employee satisfaction levels. Such a conclusion can also be extended to the 'service performance' outcome. Although an overall score of 3.63 is higher than the scores attached to financial performance and employee satisfaction, respondents were generally reluctant to associate large gains in service performance with quality practices.

Table 21.1: Mean and overall scores for independent variables

Construct	Variable	Mean score	Overall score
Top management leadership	• A common mission / purpose is frequently communicated to employees by top management.	3.75	
	• Employees are committed to a common mission or purpose.	3.76	
	• Goals and priorities are related to top management to the business mission.	3.74	
	• The work environment supports continual learning.	3.82	**3.77**
Teamwork	• There is a feeling of cohesiveness or community in our organisation.	3.93	
	• Employees are excited about the work they do.	3.61	
	• Employees take pride and satisfaction in their work.	4.25	
	• Employees coordinate their efforts when necessary.	4.06	**3.96**
Employee empowerment	• Our organisation has low levels of morale.	3.76	
	• Individual employees have the freedom to use their own judgement.	3.95	
	• There is a feeling that employees can overcome almost any obstacle.	3.56	
	• Employees can be confused about what is expected of them in their job.	3.42	**3.67**
Commitment to customers	• Employees are committed to satisfying customers and helping the organisation meet its goals.	4.34	
	• Employees are determined to meet whatever challenges may arise.	3.96	
	• Employees put in a great deal of extra effort to meet customer demands.	4.29	**4.20**

Table 21.2: Mean and overall scores for dependent variables

Construct	Variable	Mean score	Overall score
Financial performance	• Return on investment (ROI)	3.42	
	• Profit	3.07	
	• Market share	3.38	**3.29**
Service performance	• The reliability of our product / service	4.16	
	• Cost reduction	3.03	
	• Timeliness (delivery in full on time to customers)	3.76	**3.63**
Employee satisfaction	• Employee education and training levels	3.55	
	• Employee recognition and performance measurement	3.30	
	• Employee turnover	2.50	**3.12**
Customer satisfaction	• Customer feedback on service / product performance	3.83	
	• Overall level of commitment to the customer	4.20	
	• Ability to meet customer requirements and expectations	4.02	**4.02**

Perhaps the most surprising result was the extremely high level of (perceived) customer satisfaction. With an overall score of 4.02, there seemed little doubt that respondents view customer satisfaction as one of their most important quality performance outcomes. Such a result partly explains the heavy emphasis placed on creating a work environment that supports a strong customer orientation.

The general hypothesis that quality culture factors are significantly and positively related to both 'soft' and 'hard' objectives was confirmed by the analysis of the multiple regression results. These indicated that not only was the model highly significant (F = 48.85, p = .000) but 52.1 per cent of the variability in quality performance could be accounted for by quality culture factors.

This finding raises two significant implications for quality organisations. The first, and most obvious, is that overall performance can be increased by establishing a quality culture that focuses on most, if not all, of the cultural elements considered in this study. However, organisations cannot expect to achieve 'bottom line' results overnight. A common theme running through all survey responses was that there is a two- or three-year 'time lag' before substantial increases in performance are achieved. This was clearly demonstrated by one survey respondent who, in response to an open-ended question, replied that 'this company has spent an absolute fortune on team building, empowerment and cultural change programs; yet the results some 12 to 18 months later are not that dazzling'.

Thus, while the study results indicate that organisations can benefit substantially from the establishment of an appropriate quality culture, managers should recognise that quality management is not a short-term investment (Laszlo 1998), and that even after effective implementation, it usually takes a couple of years before performance starts to improve (Henricks & Singhal 1999).

The second implication derived from these results is that successful quality initiatives are rarely the outcome of quality programs that focus on only one or two aspects of the quality process. Although not immediately apparent from the statistical output reported here, this proposition was clarified during the interview process. One interviewee, for example, specifically referred to the synergistic nature of quality: '*All the quality culture factors work together; if there is a weakness in any particular part then the others will suffer*'. This suggests that organisations should establish a work environment in which quality initiatives work in concert and are integrated with the broader strategic direction of the organisation.

Summary

The following conclusions were drawn from the findings of this study.

Organisations that establish and maintain a 'quality culture' are more likely to enjoy higher levels of overall performance in the long term. This statistically significant relationship was confirmed by subsequent interviews.

The commitment of the top management leadership team is positively and significantly related to financial performance. Although only a small proportion of overall financial performance (10.7 per cent) could be directly accounted for by the efforts of top management, the qualitative data indicate that top management plays a critical 'facilitative' role in the articulation of a new vision and the establishment of a quality culture.

Team-based organisations provide significantly better levels of service than organisations that have adopted a different structural form. This assertion was confirmed by the qualitative data to apply to small, large, public and private organisations.

Empowered employees are more satisfied than employees who are not empowered. That is the general conclusion to be drawn from the data. Although analysis of the qualitative data indicated that in a small minority of cases employees do not wish to be empowered, the study found that overall there is a statistically significant relationship between empowerment and the personal job-related satisfaction of employees.

Organisations that encourage and communicate their commitment to customers will record higher levels of customer satisfaction than those that do not. Of all the findings, this was without doubt the most conclusive. It suggests that organisations wishing to remain competitive should foster a work environment that is highly customer focused.

Implications for human resource managers

This chapter identifies two specific implications for human resource managers and employees currently operating in both service and manufacturing industries in Australia and New Zealand.

First, supporting the general proposition that quality culture factors are positively related to quality performance outcomes produces results indicating that it is absolutely imperative for managers in general and human resource managers in particular to establish and maintain a quality culture in their organisation.

Setting up a quality system is no easy feat. The transition to a quality organisation requires significant structural changes in the way work is organised. Typically, the traditional autocratic hierarchy is replaced with a flatter, team-based structure in which employees are given greater decision-making freedom. In many cases, the structural realignment required for change of this magnitude represents what Nadler and Tushman (1989, p. 194) describe as 'frame bending', by which the organisation 'breaks out of its current pattern of congruence and develops a completely new configuration'.

This type of alteration is by no means insignificant and can generate a range of additional complications. However, the success of these structural changes is highly contingent on the ability of management to re-calibrate the existing corporate culture by identifying, communicating and engendering a key set of quality-related values. Over time, these values will become part of the work culture and will be reflected in the subsequent behaviour of employees (see figure 21.2).

Since organisations with an established quality culture perform better overall, all managers should either work to establish a quality culture or attempt to strengthen the existing quality culture in their organisation (see figure 21.3). Responding to such a challenge involves a long, slow process but one that is necessary to ensure that the organisation remains competitive.

Management values
- Managers must believe in continuous quality improvement.
- Managers must consider quality to be a strategic business variable.
- Quality must be the central organisational value for managers.

Employee values
- Every employee is responsible for the quality of his or her work.
- Every employee must strive to do things right the first time.
- Employee participation is very important to the quality improvement process.
- Continuous problem solving should be the norm.

Customer-related values
- Customer satisfaction is of primary importance to the organisation.
- Understanding internal and external customers' requirements is crucial.

(Adapted from Saraph & Sebastian 1993.)

Figure 21.2: Examples of universally desired quality values

1. Identify quality competitors and their attributes.
2. Identify necessary organisational quality values to suit competitive environment.
3. Identify target groups that must have the desired values listed in Step 2.
4. Identify the current quality values of the target groups and compare them to the desired quality values.
5. Decide on formal and informal mechanisms to introduce the desired quality values in the targeted groups.
6. Review each target group's quality performance and repeat the appropriate steps where necessary.

(Adapted from Saraph & Sebastian 1993.)

Figure 21.3: Process of quality culture development

The second implication is that the need to create a quality culture reaffirms the critical role played by top management in the quality program. Successful large-scale change requires visible and active leadership (Abraham et al. 1997; Bardoel & Sohal 1999). During the move towards quality, employees are likely to feel disrupted, uncertain, insecure and possibly even threatened. In order to manage resistance to change and to facilitate the transition towards quality, senior managers should act as role models and emphasise critical values and practices. Once the desired cultural mindset has been established, management needs to continuously demonstrate leadership in quality matters, both as an example to others and to communicate the seriousness with which the quality approach is viewed (Bricknell 1996).

The quality of leadership within an organisation is a crucial factor when developing a true quality culture. The key responsibilities of the leadership team should be:
- to establish a clear vision of the quality plan
- to develop communication strategies and programs to ensure that everyone in the organisation understands their role in helping to establish the quality program
- to provide leadership based on ethical values and moral principles
- to establish training and development programs to fully support both the quality initiatives and a continuous improvement philosophy
- to foster the development of a highly participative, supportive and flexible work environment
- to develop a win–win performance management system based on the organisation's quality objectives and closely linked to the remuneration system
- to lead by example
- to develop this leadership potential throughout the entire organisation.

For leadership to be effective, it must be consciously responsible for the influence it has on the people within the organisation.

Conclusion

Although an underlying principle of quality is to improve output by working constantly to improve the process, in most cases it is the people who drive the process. Thus, it could be said that quality is predominantly about people, not processes. It is about behaviour, attitude, involvement, empowerment, commitment and, above all, change. As Stephen Covey (1991, p. 253) stated, 'Approaching quality from the human side harmonises systems with processes, unleashes latent creativity and energy, and creates other benefits that go right to the bottom line'.

Few writers give as much emphasis to the people management side as the technical side of W. Edwards Deming's proposals. According to Deming, we must understand people, their relationships, and the systems in which they work and learn — their motivations, intrinsic and extrinsic. Although Deming says that 90 per cent of all problems in variation or defects are the result of the system rather than the individual, it is still the people who design, develop and control all other elements of the systems driving these processes. In fact, attention to the remaining 10 per cent is well warranted, since it is the people who are the most variable, unstable and unpredictable component of any business system or process.

In *Beyond TQM*, Robert Flood states: 'Treating and managing organisations as if they are cultures is a potentially powerful way of getting things done … Establishing a different organisational culture means influencing people to think or act in a particular way' (1993, p. 157). From his analysis of the most recognised quality principles and methodologies, he developed the following 'Ten Principles of TQM':

1. There must be agreed requirements for both internal and external customers.
2. Customers' requirements must be met first time, every time.
3. Quality improvement will reduce waste and total costs.
4. There must be a focus on the prevention of problems, rather than an acceptance of the need to cope in a fire-fighting manner.
5. Quality improvement can only result from planned management action.
6. Every job must add value.
7. Everybody must be involved, from all levels and across all functions.
8. There must be an emphasis on measurement to help assess and meet requirements and objectives.
9. A culture of continuous improvement must be established.
10. An emphasis should be placed on promoting creativity.

Each of these principles contains a cultural component, confirming that there needs to be a change in people's values, behaviours and beliefs for each of these principles to be accepted as an integral part of an organisation's work environment. To this end the human resource manager must be a proactive champion for the quality movement and a catalyst for continuous improvement in the organisation.

References

Abraham, M, Crawford, J, and Fisher, T (1999) Key factors predicting effectiveness of cultural change and improved productivity in implementing Total Quality Management. *International Journal of Quality and Reliability Management*, 16 (2) 112–32.

Abraham, M, Fisher, T, and Crawford, J (1997) Quality culture and the management of organisational change. *International Journal of Quality and Reliability Management*, 14 (6) 616–36.

Adam, EE (1994) Alternative quality improvement practices and organisation performance. *Journal of Operations Management*, 12, 27–44.

Adam, EE, Corbett, LM, Flores, BE, Harrison, NJ, Lee, TS, Rho, B, Ribera, J, Samson, D, and Westbrook, R (1997) An international study of quality improvement approach and firm performance. *International Journal of Operations and Production Management*, 17 (9) 842–73.

Adebanjo, D, and Kehoe, D (1998) An evaluation of quality culture problems in UK companies. *International Journal of Quality Science*, 3 (3) 275–86.

Ahire, SL, and O'Shaughnessy, KC (1998) The role of top management in quality management: an empirical analysis of the auto parts industry. *International Journal of Quality Science*, 3 (1) 5–37.

Alpander, GG, and Lee, CR (1995) Culture, strategy and teamwork: the keys to organisational change. *Journal of Management Development*, 14 (8) 4–18.

Anderson, EW, Fornell, C, and Lehmann, DR (1994) Customer satisfaction, market share, and profitability. *Journal of Marketing*, 58, 53–66.

Ashkenas, RN, Hsaffer, RH, and associates (1994) Beyond the fads: how leaders drive change with results. *Human Resource Planning*, 17 (2) 25–44.

ASQ Quality Costs Committee (1999) Profiting from quality in the service arena: using cost-of-quality applications in non-manufacturing organisations. *Quality Progress*, May, 81–4.

Bardoel, AE, and Sohal, A (1999) The role of the cultural audit in implementing quality improvement programs. *International Journal of Quality and Reliability Management*, 16 (3) 263–76.

Barnard, J (1999) The empowerment of problem solving teams: is it an effective management tool? *Journal of Applied Management Studies*, 8 (1) 73–87.

Barnes, JG, and Cumby, JA (1995). The cost of service quality: extending the boundaries of accounting systems to enhance customer value. In WJ Glynn and JG Barnes, *Understanding Service Management*. Chichester, UK: John Wiley & Sons.

Barrett, B, and Waddell, D (2001) Quality culture and its impact on quality performance. *Quality Australia*, 15 (2) 30–1.

Batt, R (1999) Work organisation, technology and performance in customer service and sales. *Industrial and Labour Relations Review*, 52 (4) 539–69.

Berry, LL, and Parasuraman, A (1994) Prescriptions for a service quality revolution in America. *Organizational Dynamics*, 20 (4) 5–15.

Bolton, RN, and Drew, JH (1991) A multistage model of customers' assessment of service quality and value. *Journal of Consumer Research*, 17, 375–84.

Boulding, W, Kalra, A, Staelin, R, and Zeithamal, VA (1993) A dynamic process model of service quality: from expectations to behavioural intentions. *Journal of Marketing Research*, 30, 7–27.

Bowen, DE, and Lawler, EE (1992) The empowerment of service workers: what, why, how and when. *Sloan Management Review*, 33 (3) 31–9.

Bricknell, G (1996) Total quality revisited. *Management Services*, 40 (1) 18–20.

Brocka, B, and Brocka, MS (1992) *Quality Management: Implementing the Best Ideas of the Masters*. Homewood, IL: Richard Irwin.

Buzzell, RD, and Gale, BT (1987) *The PIMS Principles: Linking Strategy to Performance*. New York: The Free Press.

Buzzell, RD, and Wiersema, FD (1981) Modelling changes in market share: a cross sectional analysis. *Strategic Management Journal*, January/March, 27–42.

Caruana, A, and Pitt, L (1997) INTQUAL — an internal measure of service quality and the link between service quality and business performance. *European Journal of Marketing*, 31 (8) 604–616.

Chapman, RL, Murray, PC, and Mellor, R (1997) Strategic quality management and financial performance indicators. *International Journal of Quality and Reliability Management*, 14 (4) 432–48.

Churchill, GA, and Surprenant, C (1982) An investigation into the determinants of customer satisfaction. *Journal of Marketing Research*, 19, 491–504.

Cohen, SG, and Ledford, GE (1994) The effectiveness of self managing teams: a quasi experiment. *Human Relations*, 47, 13–43.

Conger, J, and Kanungo, R (1988) The empowerment process: integrating theory and practice. *Academy of Management Review*, 13, 471–82.

Connor, PE (1997) Total quality management: a selective commentary on its human dimensions, with special reference to its downside. *Public Administration Review*, 57 (6) 501–9.

Connors, R, and Smith, T (1999) Align your team. *Executive Excellence*, 16 (5) 12–15.

Cordery, JL, Mueller, WS, and Smith, LM (1991) Attitudinal and behavioural effects of autonomous group working: a longitudinal field study. *Academy of Management Journal*, 34, 464–76.

Covey, S (1991) *Principle-Centred Leadership*. New York: Simon and Schuster.

Craig, CS, and Douglas, SP (1982) Strategic factors associated with market and financial performance. *Quarterly Review of Economics and Business*, 22 (2) 101–112.

Cronin, JJ, and Taylor, SA (1994) SERVPERF versus SERVQUAL: reconciling performance based and perceptions-minus-expectations measurement of service quality. *Journal of Marketing*, 58, 125–31.

Crosby, P (1979) *Quality Is Free: The Art of Making Quality Certain*. New York: McGraw-Hill.

Dahlgaard, JJ, Kristensen, K, Kanji, GK, Juhl, HJ, and Sohal, A (1998) Quality management practices: a comparative study between East and West. *International Journal of Quality and Reliability Management*, 15 (8/9) 812–26.

Dale, BG, Boaden, RJ, and Lascelles, DM (1994) Total quality management: an overview. In BG Dale (Ed.), *Managing Quality*. Hertfordshire: Prentice Hall Europe.

Dale, BG, Boaden, RJ, Wilcox, M, and McQuater, RE (1997) Sustaining total quality management: what are the key issues? *The TQM Magazine*, 9 (5) 372–80.

Deal, TE, and Kennedy, AA (1982) *Corporate Cultures. The Rites and Rituals of Corporate Life*. Reading, MA: Addison-Wesley.

Dean, JW, and Bowen, DE (1994) Management theory and total quality: improving research and practice through theory development. *Academy of Management Review*, 19 (3) 392–418.

DeCock, C, and Hipkin, I (1997) TQM and BPR: beyond the beyond myth. *Journal of Management Studies*, 34 (5) 659–74.

Dellana, SA, and Hauser, RD (1999) Toward defining the quality culture. *Engineering Management Journal*, 11 (2) 2–8.

Deming, WE (1982) *Quality, Productivity, and Competitive Position*. Cambridge, MA: Centre for Advanced Engineering Study, MIT.

Dow, D, Samson, D, and Ford, S (1999) Exploding the myth: do all quality management practices contribute to superior quality performance? *Production and Operations Management*, 8, 1.

Drensek, RA, and Grubb, FB (1995) Quality quest: one company's successful attempt at implementing TQM. *Quality Progress,* 28 (9) 91–5.

Edwards, JE, and Thomas, MD (1993) The organisational survey process. *American Behavioural Scientist*, 36 (4) 419–42.

Epstein, DG, and Epstein, MZ (1998) Hand in hand. *HR Magazine*, 43 (8) 102–8.

Ernst & Young and the American Quality Foundation (1992) The international quality study best practices report: an analysis of management practices that impact performance, 49.

Evans, JR, and Lindsay, WM (1989) *The Management and Control of Quality*. New York: West Publishing Company.

Feinberg, S (1998) Why managers oppose TQM. *The TQM Magazine*, 10 (1) 16–19.

Flanagan, TA, and Fredericks, JO (1993) Improving company performance through customer-satisfaction measurement and management. *National Productivity Review*, 12 (2) 239–58.

Flood, R (1993) *Beyond TQM*. Chichester: John Wiley & Sons.

Flynn, BB, Schroeder, RG, and Sakakibara, S (1995) The impact of quality management practices on performance and competitive advantage. *Decision Sciences*, 26 (5) 659–91.

Forker, LB, Vickery, SK, and Droge, CLM (1996) The contribution of quality to business performance. *International Journal of Operations and Production Management*, 16 (8) 44–62.

Freeman, KD, and Dart, J (1993) Measuring the perceived quality of professional business services. *Journal of Professional Services Marketing*, 9 (1) 27–47.

Gabbot, M, and Hogg, G (1997) *Contemporary Services Marketing Management: A Reader*. Sydney: The Dryden Press.

GAO Study (1991) *Report to the House of Representatives on Management Practices: US Companies Improve Performance Through Quality Efforts*, United States General Accounting Office, Washington, DC.

Garvin, D (1991) How the Baldridge Award really works. *Harvard Business Review*, November–December 80–92.

Ghobadian, A, Speller, S, and Jones, M (1994) Service quality: concepts and models. *International Journal of Quality and Reliability Management*, 11 (9) 43–66.

Goetsch, DL, and Davis, S (1994) *Introduction to Total Quality: Quality Productivity, Competitiveness*, New York: Macmillan College Publishing Co.

Gronroos, C (1984) A service quality model and its marketing implications. *European Journal of Marketing*, 18 (4) 36–44.

Hackman, JR (1987) *The Design of Work Teams*. In J Lorsch (Ed.), *Handbook of Organizational Behaviour*. Englewood Cliffs, NJ: Prentice Hall, 315–42.

Hames, RD (1991) Managing the process of culture change. *International Journal of Quality and Reliability Management*, 8 (5) 14–23.

Hamzah, A, and Zairi, M (1996) People management: where is the evidence of best practice? Part 3, *Training for Quality*, 4 (4) 37–44.

Harrington, JH (1996) National traits in TQM principles and practices. *The TQM Magazine*, 8 (4) 1–6.

Harris, PR, and Harris, KG (1996) Managing effectively through teams. *Team Performance Management: An International Journal*, 2 (3) 23–36.

Hemphill, D (1996) Leave your soft drinks (and sanity) at the door. *Quality Progress*, 29 (4) 69–73.

Hendricks, KB, and Singhal, VR (1999) Don't count TQM out. *Quality Progress*, 32 (4) 35–41.

Heskett, JL, Sasser, WE, and Schlesinger, LA (1997) *The Profit Service Chain: How Leading Companies Link Profit and Growth to Loyalty, Satisfaction and Value*. Sydney: The Free Press.

Higginson, T, and Waxler, R (1994) Communication, commitment and corporate culture: the foundation for TQM and reengineering. *Industrial Management*, 36 (6) 4–7.

Hoff, JS (1995) TQM: old wine in a new bottle? *CPCU Journal*, 48 (4) 202–6.

Holoviak, S (1995) Why TQM fails to change behaviours or attitudes. *Journal for Quality or Participation*, 18 (4) 86–9.

Juran, JM (1981) Product quality: a prescription for the West. *Proceedings, 25th Conference EOQC*, Paris, June, 3, 221–42.

Kaye, M, and Anderson, R (1999) Continuous improvement: ten essential criteria. *International Journal of Quality and Reliability Management*, 16 (5) 1–12.

Kappelman, L, and Prybutok, V (1995) Empowerment, motivation, training and TQM program implementation success. *Industrial Management*, 37 (3) 12–15.

Kelly, SW (1993) Discretion and the service employee. *Journal of Retailing*, 69 (1) 104–126.

Koberg, CS, Boss, RW, Senjem, JC, and Goodman, EA (1999) Antecedents and outcomes of empowerment. *Group and Organisation Management*, 24 (1) 71–91.

Korukonda, AR, Watson, JG, and Rajkumar, TM (1999) Beyond teams and empowerment: a counterpoint to two common precepts in TQM. *S.A.M. Advanced Management Journal*, 64 (1) 29–36.

Krumwide, DW, Sheu, C, and Lavelle, J (1998) Understanding the relationship of top management personality to TQM implementation. *Production and Inventory Management Journal*, 39 (2) 6–10.

Lackritz, R (1997) TQM within Fortune 500 companies. *Quality Progress*, 30 (2) 69–72.

Lam, SK (1995) Quality management and job satisfaction: an empirical study. *International Journal of Quality and Reliability Management*, 12 (4) 72–8.

Laszlo, GP (1998) Implementing a quality management program: three C's of success: commitment, culture, cost. *The TQM Magazine*, 10 (4) 281–7.

Ledford, GE, and Lawler, EE (1996) Research on employee participation. *Academy of Management Review*, 19 (4) 633–6.

Lewis, D (1996a) The organisational culture saga: from OD to TQM: a critical review of the literature: Part 1 — concepts and early trends. *Leadership and Organization Development Journal*, 17 (1) 12–19.

Lewis, D (1996b) The organisational culture saga: from OD to TQM: a critical review of the literature: Part 2 — applications. *Leadership and Organization Development Journal*, 17 (2) 9–16.

Lewis, RC, and Booms, BH (1983) The marketing aspects of service quality. In L Berry, G Shostack and G Upah (Eds), *Emerging Perspectives on Services Marketing*, Chicago: American Marketing.

Lin, CY (1998) The essence of empowerment: a conceptual model and a case illustration. *Journal of Applied Management Studies*, 7 (2) 223–38.

Linklow, P (1989) Is your culture ready for total quality? *Quality Progress*, 22 (11) 69–71.

Liu, CK (1998) Pitfalls of total quality management in Hong Kong. *Total Quality Management*, 9 (7) 585–98.

Manz, CC, and Sims, HP (1980) Self management as a substitute for leadership: a social learning theory perspective. *Academy of Management Review*, 5, 361–7.

Manz, CC, and Sims, HP (1987) Allowing workers to lead themselves: the external leadership of self managing work teams. *Administrative Science Quarterly*, 32, 106–9.

Massnick, F (1996) Consult your customers before making plans. *Quality Progress*, 29 (11) 95–7.

Masters, R (1996) Overcoming the barriers to TQM's success. *Quality Progress*, 29 (5) 53–5.

Muffatto, M, and Panizzolo, R (1995) A process based view for customer satisfaction. *International Journal of Quality and Reliability Management*, 12 (9) 154–69.

Nadler, DA, and Tushman, ML (1989) Organisational frame bending: principles for managing reorientation. *Academy of Management Executive*, 3 (3) 194–204.

Neergaard, P (1999) Quality management: a survey on accomplished results. *International Journal of Quality and Reliability Management*, 16 (3) 1–7.

Oakland, JS, and Oakland, S (1998) The links between people management, customer satisfaction and business results. *Total Quality Management*, 9 (4/5) 185–90.

Oliver, RL (1993) A conceptual model of service, quality and service satisfaction: compatible goals, different concepts. In TA Swartz, DE Bowen and SW Brown (1993), *Advances in Services Marketing and Management*, 2. Greenwich, CT: JAI Press.

Parasuraman, A, Berry, LL, and Zeithaml, VA (1988) Understanding customer expectations of service. *Sloan Management Review*, Spring, 39–48.

Perry, ML, Pearce, CL, and Sims, HP (1999) Empowered selling teams: how shared leadership can contribute to selling team outcomes. *Journal of Personal Selling and Sales Management*, 19 (3) 35–51.

Peters, TJ, and Waterman, RH (1982) *In Search of Excellence*. Sydney: Harper & Row.

Phillips, LW, Chang, DR, and Buzzell, RD (1983) Product quality, cost position and business performance: a test of some key hypotheses. *Journal of Marketing*, 47, Spring, 26–43.

Powell, TC (1995) Total quality management as competitive advantage: a review and empirical study. *Strategic Management Journal*, 16, 15–37.

Prescott, BD (1995) *Creating a World Class Organisation: 10 Essentials for Business Success*. London: Kogan Page.

Purser, RE, and Cabana, S (1997) Involve employees at every level of strategic planning. *Quality Progress*, 30 (5) 66–71.

Redman, T, and Grieves, J (1999) Managing strategic change through TQM: learning from failure. *New Technology, Work and Employment*, 14 (1) 45–61.

Reeves, CA, and Bednar, D (1994) Defining quality: alternatives and implications. *Academy of Management Review*, 19 (3) 419–45.

Reichheld, FF, and Sasser, WE (1990) Zero defections: quality comes to services. *Harvard Business Review*, September–October.

Ripley, RE, and Ripley, MJ (1992) Empowerment: the cornerstone of quality: empowering management in innovative organisations in the 1990s. *Management Decisions*, 30 (4) 20–43.

Rodrigues, CA (1994) Employee participation and empowerment programs: problem definition and implementation. *Team Performance Management: An International Journal*, 2 (2) 29–40.

Roosevelt, B (1995) Quality and business practices: essential ingredients for success. *Quality Progress*, 28 (7) 35–40.

Roth, AV, and Jackson, WE (1995) Strategic determinants of service quality and performance: evidence from the banking industry. *Management Science*, 41 (11) 1720–33.

Rubin, I, and Inguagiato, R (1991) Changing the work culture. *Training and Development Journal*, 45 (7) 57–60.

Rust, RT, Zahorik, AJ, and Keiningham, TL (1996) *Service Marketing*. New York: HarperCollins.

Samson, D (1997) Progress in total quality management: evidence from Australasia. *International Journal of Quality Science*, 2 (4) 214–35.

Saraph, JV, and Sebastian, RJ (1993) Developing a quality culture. *Quality Progress*, 26 (9) 73–8.

Saraph, JV, Benson, PG, and Schroeder, RG (1989) An instrument for measuring the critical factors of quality management. *Decision Sciences*, 20 (1) 810–29.

Sasser, WE, Olsen, RP, and Wyckoff, DD (1978) *Management of Service Operations: Text and Cases*. Boston, MA: Allyn & Bacon.

Schlesinger, LA, and Balzer, RJ (1985) An alternative to buzzword management: the culture performance link. *Personnel*, September 45–51.

Schlesinger, LA, and Heskett, JL (1991) Breaking the cycle of failure in services. *Sloan Management Review*, Spring, 17–28.

Schlesinger, LA, and Zornitsky, J (1991) Job satisfaction, service capability, and customer satisfaction: an examination of linkages and management implications. *Human Resource Planning*, 14 (2) 141–9.

Schneider, B, and Bowen, DE (1985) Employee and customer perception of service in banks: replication and extension. *Journal of Applied Psychology*, 70, 423–33.

Schoeffler, S, Buzzell, R, and Heany, D (1974) Impact of strategic planning on profit performance. *Harvard Business Review*, March–April, 137–45.

Silos, IM (1999) Employee involvement: a component of total quality management. *Production and Inventory Management Journal*, 40 (1) 56–65.

Simmerman, SJ (1993) Achieving service quality improvements. *Quality Progress*, November, 47–50.

Sitkin, SB, Sutcliffe, KM, and Schroeder, RG (1994) Distinguishing control from learning in total quality management: a contingency perspective. *Academy of Management Review*, 19 (3) 537–64.

Smith, S, Transfield, D, Foster, M, and Whittle, S (1993) Strategies for managing the TQ agenda. *International Journal of Operations and Productions Management*, 14 (1) 75–88.

Sohal, AS (1998) Assessing manufacturing / quality culture and practices in Asian companies. *International Journal of Quality and Reliability Management*, 15 (8/9) 920–30.

Spreitzer, GM, Cohen, SG, and Ledford, GE (1999) Developing effective self managing work teams in service organisations. *Group and Organisation Management*, 24 (3) 340–66.

Stoner-Zemel, J (1989) *PAVE: indicators of excellent organisations*. Organisation Design and Development.

Tata, J, and Prasad, S (1998) Cultural and structural constraints on total quality management implementation. *Total Quality Management*, 9 (8) 703–710.

Terziovski, M, and Dean, A (1998) Best predictors of quality performance in Australian service organisations. *Managing Service Quality*, 8 (5) 359–66.

Terziovski, M, and Samson, D (1999) The link between total quality management practice and organisational performance. *International Journal of Quality and Reliability Management*, 16 (3) 226–37.

Thiagarajan, T, and Zairi, M (1997) A review of total quality management in practice: understanding the fundamentals through examples of best practice applications — Part 2. *The TQM Magazine*, 9 (5) 344–56.

Van Donk, DP, and Sanders, G (1993) Organisational culture as a missing link in quality management. *International Journal of Quality and Reliability Management*, 10 (5) 5–15.

Vass, V (1998) Quality: making a lasting impression. *Metal Centre News*, 38 (9) 60–65.

Waterman, RH (1994) *Frontiers of Excellence: The Journey Toward Success in the 21st Century*. USA: Allen & Unwin.

Wellins, RS, Wilson, R, Katz, AJ, Laughlin, P, Day, CR, and Price, D (1990), *Self Directed Teams: A Study of Current Practice*. Pittsburgh, PA: DDI.

Westbrook, JD (1993) Organisational culture and its relationship with TQM. *Industrial Management*, 35 (1) 1–3.

Wilkinson, A, Godfrey, G, and Marchington, M (1997) Bouquets, brickbats and blinkers: total quality management and employee involvement in practice. *Organisation Studies*, 18 (5) 799–819.

Woodside, AG, Frey, LL, and Daly, RT (1989) Linking service quality, customer satisfaction, and behavioural intention. *Journal of Health Care Marketing*, 9 December, 5–17.

Zeitz, G, Johannesson, R, and Ritchie, EJ (1997) An employee survey measuring total quality management practices and culture. *Group and Organization Management*, 22 (4) 414–44.

CHAPTER 22

Ethical challenges for human resource management

by Michelle R. Greenwood

Monash University

Introduction

The development of the human relations school in the 1950s was perhaps the most significant occurrence in the history of management since the Industrial Revolution. Indeed, the idea that the owner–worker relationship could be built on communication and cooperation was revolutionary. By the 1980s the belief that the effective management of people could affect organisational outcomes was gaining acceptance. With it evolved the concept of human resource management (HRM), commonly defined as the 'productive use of people in achieving the organisation's strategic business objectives and the satisfaction of individual employee needs' (Stone 1998, p. 4). It took another twenty years, however, for this idea to be examined from an ethical perspective. This chapter explores the existence of a pervasive positivist perspective of HRM, the response of an alternative critical paradigm and the development of an ethical perspective of HRM. Gaps and challenges in the existing ethical discourse of HRM are debated, and the implications for organisations, managers and employees are discussed. Finally, future directions for the ethical perspective of HRM are identified.

Ethical issues in HRM have been addressed increasingly in the literature since the mid 1990s. To appreciate the development of the ethical perspective of HRM, existing perspectives of HRM must be understood. To this end, this section will identify and describe a positivist and 'critical' perspective of HRM.

The positivist tradition in HRM

The existence of a 'positivist' perspective of HRM, although rarely acknowledged, has been alluded to recently by several authors (Kamoche & Mueller 1998; Warren 2000). It is argued in this chapter that a common paradigm pervades research and practice in HRM. The features of this positivist viewpoint are that:

- it tends to be US based and practitioner focused
- its content is prescriptive
- it often relies on naive generalisations that assume the value of HRM.

Much of the writing is concerned either to offer practical advice or to present empirical data (Wright & McMahan 1992). It takes a systems maintenance or functionalist approach and reflects concerns with improvements in efficiency that derive from classical management theory (Townley 1993). It also tends to assume an individualistic and unitarist perspective of the employment relationship (see table 22.1).

The values and practices of this positivist view of HRM developed within the individualistic enterprise ideology of the 1980s and continue to reflect this ideological climate. This perspective continues to be dominant and pervasive. A number of reasons for this managerialist orientation of HRM can be suggested.

First, there is the strategic focus of HRM. The link between strategy and HRM developed from a need to establish importance and distinctiveness for what in the 1980s was a new discipline. One implication of this focus is that HRM is primarily concerned with those who determine and implement strategy, namely senior managers (Clark, Mabey & Skinner 1998).

Second, in countries like the United Kingdom, Australia and New Zealand, a shift from centralised, union-negotiated, award-based industrial relations to enterprise-based individual employment agreements has resulted in a significant change in the employment relationship (Moorhead, Steele, Alexander, Stephen & Duffin 1997). Managers now have greater control over employment relations, employees are more likely to be employed on staff (or on contract), and there is less likelihood of a union being involved as a third party. The result is a more individualistic and unitarist environment.

Third, popular management writers and theories exercise a significant influence. Books written by Peters and Waterman (1982) and Covey (1989) have sold in the millions and reached the best-seller lists. These writers present simple, prescriptive, 'new' ways of organising and communicating that will (supposedly) bring about more effective and successful individuals and organisations. Influential and prolific HRM academics present a quasi-empirical literature that parallels the work of the popular writers (see, for example, Ulrich 1998; Pfeffer & Veiga 1999).

Finally, the dominant epistemological approach in HRM is positivism (Legge 1995). Positivism seeks to explain and predict what happens in the social world by searching for regularities and causal relationships between its constituent elements. The sorts of questions asked in HRM research tend to reinforce the status quo rather than question it.

Table 22.1: Characteristics of HRM paradigms

Positivist HRM	*Critical HRM*
US based	UK based
individualist	collectivist
unitarist	pluralist
prescriptive	analytic
practitioner oriented	academic oriented
empirical investigation	conceptual investigation
positivist methodology (quantitative large-scale data analysis)	social constructivist methodology (in-depth case analysis)
HRM as a valuable tool	HRM as a control device
reinforces power inequities	questions power inequities

Some writers have expressed concern about the lack of a theoretical framework in HRM (Wright & McMahan 1992). Kamoche and Mueller (1998) find the 'apparent reluctance of many HR scholars, practitioners, and consultants to acknowledge the rationale underpinning the practice of HRM' to be 'remarkable'. Alvesson and Willmott (1996) speak of a silence about issues such as inequality, conflict, domination and subordination, and manipulation within both orthodox and more progressive accounts of management and organisational theory. At the very least, the problem with 'how-to' models of HRM is that, without theoretical underpinning, guidelines alone can be ambiguous. Rules without reasons can be interpreted and applied in a variety of ways. Wright and McMahan (1992) argue that a strong theoretical model is of great value to both researchers and practitioners. For practitioners, a cogent theoretical model will provide better predictions for better decision making. For researchers, strong theoretical models provide greater depth and understanding, and thus potential for further development in the discipline.

The work of Wright and McMahan (1992) and Jackson and Schuler (1995) advances 'positivist' quality HRM beyond the 'how-to' atheoretical stance. They present theoretical models of strategic HRM drawn from macro-level organisational theory, finance and economics. Several of these models (the resource-based and behavioural approaches, human capital theory, general systems theory and the agency/transaction costs model) explain HRM in strategic and rational terms. The focus of these theories is efficiency. The models both assume and explain organisational control of employees in order to achieve strategic goals. Other theories, in contrast, focus on the relationship between an organisation and its constituencies and, thus, on instrumental and political determinants of HRM practices. Institutional theory sees organisations as social entities that conform in order to attain legitimacy, while the resource dependence/power mode suggests that organisations and groups gain power over each other by controlling valued resources. Both these theories emphasise the irrational and dysfunctional characteristics of HRM and, thereby, challenge the centrality of efficiency. The political perspective of HRM assumes that unwritten, informal activities influence the design and implementation of HRM (Ferris, Hochwarter, Buckley, Harrell-Cook & Frink 1999). It is these positivist theories that come closest to questioning or challenging the philosophy and practice of HRM. Jackson and Schuler (1995, p. 252), however, note that 'available theories are inadequate … each deals with pieces of the larger phenomenon; none addresses the whole domain of HRM in context'. Nevertheless, in their opinion, research driven by incomplete theory is better than research driven by no theory at all.

The critical view of HRM — an alternative perspective

A more significant critique of HRM has been offered by British authors writing from a 'critical perspective' (Legge 1996; Guest 1997). The development of an alternative and critical perspective of HRM was inevitable and necessary. Writers in the fields of sociology, political economy and labour relations have distinct and important perspectives on the workplace. In general, the critical perspective sees HRM as rhetorical and manipulative and, thus, a tool of management control over workers (see table 22.1). Rather than being a way for employees to fully develop and contribute within the organisation, HRM practices are a way of intervening in employees' lives in order to ensure they make a greater sacrifice to the needs of the organisation. HRM is accused of redefining the meaning of work and the organisation–employee relationship in order to gain the acceptance of such intolerable actions. As early as 1990 HRM was cleverly depicted by Keenoy as 'a sheep in wolf's clothing' (cited in Legge 1995). The suggestion that the 'soft' HRM[1] promoted by the popular theorists is just a 'hard' HRM in disguise has been pursued by many sceptical commentators.

Several theorists identify positivist HRM's employment of a unitarist framework (Guest 1987; Kamoche 1994; Legge 1995). Kamoche (1994) identifies the revival of a unitarist ethos of the organisation in order to achieve congruence of purpose within the organisation. He claims that the ideology of unitarism is being used to control any divergence of interest between managers and subordinates in order to achieve economic goals. In contrast to positivist writers, 'critical' theorists tend to assume a pluralist and collectivist nature in the workplace (see table 22.1). They conclude that the various parties involved in the workplace have differing views and thus, potentially, differing goals. This view of the workplace resonates with the stakeholder perspective of the organisation, which will be discussed later.

In a significant example of this type of analysis, Townley (1993) presents an interpretation of HRM based on the work of French theorist Michel Foucault. She argues that HRM techniques are a means of evaluating individuals in order to render them 'calculable' and therefore manageable. Individuals can be 'known' through the two processes of examination and confession. Examination is a method of observing in order to measure, rank and classify. External features such as skill, performance and behaviour are commonly measured in the workplace. Increasingly, the internal dimensions (such as attitudes and sentiments) of the individual are also being objectified. An individual's confession, or the exposure of their self-knowledge, allows for them to be 'known' in two ways: first, the confession requires that the individual break the bounds of discretion; and, second, it produces information that becomes part of the individual's self-understanding. The technique of confession is evident in survey and application forms and, particularly, in performance appraisals. Thus, HRM practices function to constitute the individual in a particular manner (Townley 1993). According to Townley (1993, p. 538), HRM practices are:

> examples of procedures that constitute the subject with varying degrees in individual engagement and participation. There is the inculcation of required habits, rules, and behaviour and socially constructed definitions of the norm. However, the status of the individual, that is, the individual's right to be different and everything that makes the individual truly individual, tends to get lost in the process.

Particular aspects of the modern corporation are targets of critical analysis. Sennett (1999) describes a 'chameleon' organisation. Its form is a network of semi-autonomous teams in constant flux. Workers are added or shed in response to market demand. Power is centralised in an elite technical-managerial class. The inner management core gives orders to isolated cells or teams, who are told what to achieve but not how to achieve it. The people in power do not witness what they command. Labour is seen as purely contractual. There is no commitment, no dependence; and there is no social cohesion. Such an organisation no longer carries on the pretence of 'soft' HRM.

---

1. The distinction between 'hard' and 'soft' models of HRM policies and practices was first made by Storey (Guest 1987; Guest 1999). The 'hard' version of HRM explicitly presents workers as a key resource for managers to exploit, thus reflecting the capitalist view of the worker as a commodity. According to this view, the employment relationship is an economic exchange to be terminated when no longer profitable for the employer. In contrast, the 'soft' version of HRM views objects as means rather than objects. This view sees HRM as a way of gaining the commitment of employees in order to achieve organisational goals. The focus is therefore on winning the 'hearts and minds' of the workers. These models should be understood as 'ideal' types that are unlikely to be seen in their pure form.

An ethical view of HRM — a developing perspective

The introduction of ethical theory and stakeholder theory into the discussion of HRM is still an unusual occurrence. While the abovementioned writers ruthlessly expose HRM practices as objectifying individuals (Townley 1993), as suppressing resistance and confrontation (Sennett 1999) — in short, as manipulating employees — they resist passing judgement. Questions such as 'Is this right or wrong?' or 'How should organisations behave?' do not seem to be addressed by HRM researchers. The fact that the way employees are managed may invite ethical scrutiny is not addressed (Winstanley & Woodall 2000). In their lengthy review of 80 years of HRM science and practice, Ferris et al. (1999) identify the issue of justice and HRM as an interesting and potentially important direction for future work in HRM. The focus of the research cited in this review is on the micro level of procedural fairness of selection, performance evaluation and compensation systems. Broader ethical issues are ignored, or mentioned in passing, even though they are arguably central to the discussion. In the discussion of accountability and HRM, the authors note 'the presence of multiple audiences', 'accountability perceptions' and the 'moderating effects of context and personality differences' (Ferris et al. 1999, pp. 402–3), yet they overlook theories of ethical development, corporate social responsibility or stakeholder management. Such theories can offer insights into HRM that are different from, yet equally important to, other theories of the organisation. It is this area that will be the focus of the remainder of this discussion.

To date only a few theorists have attempted to apply ethical theory directly to HRM. Legge (1996), for example, uses both deontological (principle-based) and teleological (outcome-based) ethical theories to evaluate 'hard' and 'soft' HRM. She arrives at the predictable conclusion that the outcome of any evaluation of a particular form of HRM will depend upon which ethical principles are applied. In contrast, Miller (1996) provides a micro-level analysis of HRM systems, procedures and outcomes based on a framework of procedural justice. He argues that ethical HRM can be achieved by applying principles of fairness and equality. He concludes that ethical or 'good' HRM depends on good employment conditions, which in turn depend on good organisational strategy. This conclusion would come as no surprise to many HRM researchers or practitioners. If ethical arguments are too philosophical and unattainable, and positivist 'how-to's too scripted and atheoretical, then what form of critique do we need?

A perceived need to be more practitioner focused has led Winstanley, Woodall and Heery (1996a) to reconceive these ethical theories in more user-friendly ethical frameworks for HRM. Rowan (2000) also offers managers a set of more user-friendly guidelines for the moral foundation of employees' rights. Although these frameworks are less abstract and more accessible than the doctrines of philosophical ethics employed by Legge (1996), they still represent a set of ideals to which individuals and organisations may aspire.

Challenges to the ethical perspective of HRM

Debate on the ethics of HRM has tended towards the extremes of either the macro level (Is the totality of HR 'ethical'?) or the micro level (Is the individual HR practice 'ethical'?) (Winstanley & Woodall 2000). The value of ethical assessment of micro-level practices is limited. HRM research has moved well beyond the exploration of individual practices (see, for example, Guest 1997). Mere lists of employees' rights can be ambiguous, permitting a variety of interpretations and applications (Rowan 2000). At the macro end of the scale, an attempt has been made to draw ethical theory into HRM theory. This analysis is at an early stage, faces many challenges and requires significant development.

First, the implications inherent in assuming that employers have affirmative obligations to their employees need to be addressed. Second, the ethical considerations of the outcomes of HRM need much greater attention. Related to these two points is the third problem — the fact that the role of employees as stakeholders has been overlooked in this debate. Stakeholder theory has a significant role in the debate on business ethics and has many obvious connections to HRM.

Assumptions of affirmative obligation

The assumptions underlying the acceptance of these ethical theories must be explicit. To even begin to apply these ethical stances to HRM is to make significant assumptions about the purpose of the organisation, the roles and responsibilities of managers, and the rights and obligations of employees (and other stakeholders). Most ethical analysis assumes, at the very least, that employers have positive moral obligations towards their employees. The significance of the acceptance of affirmative moral obligation on the part of business cannot be underestimated.

It should be understood that classic economic constructs of the firm assume the opposite stance — that business has no moral obligations beyond that of making a profit for its shareholders (Friedman 1970). The middle ground is occupied by concepts of the 'moral minimum'. This stance is distinguished by the rejection of an obligation for businesses to undertake affirmative duties. Simon, Powers and Gunneman (1993), for example, maintain that all individuals and social institutions ought to adhere to certain moral standards, but that these are negative injunctions. There is a difference between requiring the organisation not to cause harm and requiring it to do everything it can to promote the good. The precept that there is a minimum standard of behaviour expected of business by society was acknowledged even by Milton Friedman (1970) in his manifesto of the narrow view of corporate social responsibility. He wrote that business, in its pursuit of profit, must 'stay within the rules of the game, which is to say, engage in open and free competition without deception or fraud'.

At the other end of the spectrum are ethical frameworks and models that assume positive obligation. These include stakeholder theory and utilitarianism. To argue that business organisations have affirmative obligations to society has far-reaching implications (Beauchamp & Bowie 1993). These include:

• the concern that the obligations of the corporation to do 'good' can be expanded without limit
• the concern that the injunction to take social responsibilities into account and to assist in solving social problems may make impossible demands on a corporation
• the view that any such injunction ignores the impact that such activities might have on profit
• the question of who defines the social problems and determines which has priority.

Friedman (1970) went as far as to call the principle of social responsibility a 'fundamentally subversive doctrine' in a free society.

Attending to stakeholders

The identification of employees as stakeholders in a firm is conspicuously absent from many discussions regarding the theoretical underpinning of HRM (Wright & McMahan 1992; Jackson & Schuler 1995; Ferris et al. 1999), even though the belief that employees are legitimate stakeholders in the organisation is often taken for granted either explicitly or implicitly (see, for example, Handy 1991; Legge 1998). The stakeholder approach has become increasingly prominent in recent years owing to greater coverage in the media,

public interest and concern about corporate governance, and its adoption in 'third-way' politics (Metcalfe 1998). The examination of practices at the level of social transactions and interactions between organisation members (managers, employees and other stakeholders) could help bridge the gap between academic theory and practice (Cornelius & Gagnon 1999). The stakeholder perspective is in keeping with a pluralist view of employment relations that assumes there are distinct groups with their own valid needs and interests with respect to the organisation. Credit is due to Winstanley and Woodall (2000) for recently beginning a dialogue on the employee as a stakeholder.

The stakeholder theory of the corporation, as developed by Freeman (1984), is characterised by the notion that managers have a duty to attend to all those who have a stake in or claim on the organisation. This contrasts with the classic view (sometimes called shareholder value theory) that managers bear a special relationship with the owners of the organisation (see, for example, Friedman 1970; Rappaport 1986). The obvious questions raised by the stakeholder view are, who is a legitimate stakeholder, and what is the nature of the stakeholder relationship? These issues have been addressed periodically in the literature, with some pattern developing in the responses (for a more detailed discussion, see Mitchell, Agle & Wood 1997; Greenwood 2001).

Stakeholders may be seen in one of two manners: instrumental or functional; or normative. Goodpaster (1991) noted that stakeholders may be considered in a manner that has nothing to do with ethics. A company might analyse its action in order to take into account any positive and negative effects on stakeholders for no other reason than that offended stakeholders might resist and retaliate. Just as a company has the potential to affect its stakeholders, so the stakeholders have the capacity to affect the company. It is the stakeholders' capacity to affect the company positively and (especially) negatively through political or market mechanisms that concerns the company. Hard HRM, in which employees are viewed instrumentally as a means to achieve organisational goals, aligns with this strategic consideration of stakeholders. However, soft HRM practices are not always without strategic intent. According to Ojeifo and Winstanley (cited in Winstanley & Woodall 2000, pp. 13–14):

> it is too easy for approaches to involvement based on stakeholding to be used manipulatively and duplicitously by employers anxious to bind employees into a rhetoric of excellence and enterprise, for example where employee empowerment is introduced for cost-cutting reasons but promoted on the basis of its involvement of staff in decision making.

This, of course, has significant implications for soft HRM.

On the other hand, stakeholders may be considered from an ethical perspective apart from their instrumental, economic or legal potential to affect the organisation. Adopting this moral view of the stakeholder, the interest of various stakeholders may involve a trade-off, balancing the economic advantage of the shareholders against the interest of others. The primacy of the manager's relationship with the shareholder is no longer assumed, and is replaced with the notion that managers must act in the interests of all stakeholders in the organisation (Evan & Freeman 1988). Stakeholder theory is cast as a form of Kantian[2] capitalism (i.e. based on the principle that no individual should be used as a means to an end). Soft HRM, which suggests that the employee be seen as more than instrumental, is more in line with the moral account of stakeholders. In organisational terms, each of the stakeholder groups has a right not to be treated as a means to an end, and therefore must participate in determining the future direction of the firm in which it has a stake. It is, therefore, the company's potential to affect the stakeholder that is of concern. Such a view of the organisation, its purpose and responsibilities is quite revolutionary, or, as Friedman (1970) would say, subversive. It implies a reconceptualisation of capitalism.

Assessing HRM by its outcomes

A great deal of utilitarian thinking is present in the way in which business justifies itself … Business and any other practical activity must pay attention to results to remain viable and to remain ethical. (Grace & Cohen 1998, p. 12)

Ethical justification of actions based on their outcomes is fundamental to consequentialist theories. Utilitarianism[3] advocates producing the greatest good for the greatest number of people. HRM policies and practices, therefore, can be viewed as ethical so long as it can be proved that their outcomes do indeed maximise the benefits for those involved. By this measure, both soft and hard types of HRM can be judged as ethical. This analysis, however, requires greater attention. There are three significant problems: that of 'proving' outcomes, the question of who do we mean by 'everyone', and the issue of determining what is considered 'best'.

First, how can the outcome of a particular HRM practice, or 'bundle' of practices, be 'proved'? The link between HRM and organisational outcome is the focus of much HRM research. As previously noted, many positivist writers (e.g. Wood 1995; Huselid 1995, as cited in Purcell 1999) suggest that there is HRM 'best practice' that can be universally applied for organisational success. Other writers question both the methods and the findings of much of this research (Becker & Gerhart 1996; Purcell 1999). Guest (1999) suggests that any analysis of influences on company profits or factory outputs or even absence levels quickly leads to the conclusion that factors other than HRM are involved. Purcell (1999) identifies a number of significant problems with large-scale quantitative analysis that could potentially result in unreliable data. Becker and Gerhart (1996) also suggest that the use of large numbers of firms in order to test the relationship between HR and firm performance provides little insight into the process involved. They describe a 'black box'[4] of intervening variables between a firm's HR system and its bottom line that must be investigated and tested with more complete models. Without such knowledge, it is difficult to explain how HR influences firm performance and to rule out alternative explanations such as reverse causation. For example, Becker and Gerhart note that the fact that profit sharing is often correlated with higher profits can be interpreted in at least two ways: profit sharing causes higher profits; or firms with higher profits are more likely to implement profit sharing. They suggest that studies within a single industry or company, case studies of single firms or plants, provide a clearer, if narrower, picture of the process of HRM. They call for deeper qualitative research to complement the large-scale multiple firm studies.

Second, we must consider the issue of whom we mean by 'everyone'? According to stakeholder theory, corporations

---

2. From the ethical theory of Immanuel Kant (1724–1804) based on the respect-for-persons principle that people should be treated as ends and never only as means. This respect is founded on the belief that human beings possess a moral dignity and therefore cannot be treated as if they have merely conditional value. 'Respect for persons' has sometimes been expressed in corporate contexts as 'respect for the individual'. (Beauchamp and Bowie 1993)

3. Utilitarianism is based on the writings of Jeremy Bentham (1748–1832) and John Stuart Mill (1806–1873). Utilitarian theories hold that the moral worth of actions or practices is determined solely by their consequences. Utilitarianism is committed to the maximisation of the good and the minimisation of harm and evil (Beauchamp and Bowie, 1993, pp. 21–2).

4. The question of the nature of the 'black box' of internal HRM processes and outcomes has been debated at length for many years. For Shuler and Jackson (1987) the 'black box' referred to employee outcomes such as employee commitment, job satisfaction, motivation and employee role behaviours. The debate is still continuing (see for example Academy of Management (2000).

have stakeholders who are individuals or groups who benefit from or are harmed by corporate actions (Evan & Freeman 1988). However, according to Mitchell et al. (1997), stakeholder theory 'offers a maddening variety of signals on how questions of stakeholder identity might be answered'. In considering the outcomes of HRM, we naturally consider outcomes for the organisation (commonly interpreted as value for shareholders) as well as outcomes for the employees themselves. But what about the managers? We are strongly encouraged by Willmott (1997) to see the manager as more than an agent of capitalist priorities, but rather as a human subject who also sells labour and is a target of control. In terms of stakeholder theory, managers have the potential to be stakeholders in the organisation, as do customers, suppliers and the community. But what about competitors, government, the environment, future generations? Are they not legitimate stakeholders? They also potentially have an interest in the organisation. To what extent is the organisation obliged to take into account the outcomes of its actions?

Third, how do we know what is in people's best interests? We can make certain assumptions, but what if we are wrong? Is not the act of assuming we know what is best for someone else an ethical problem in itself? Clark, Mabey and Skinner (1998) suggest that 'the voice of those at the receiving end has tended to be under-represented in the HRM literature'. The predominance of a mangerialist orientation in positivist HRM research was identified earlier in this chapter, yet it is the employees who are the recipients and consumers of HRM. Normative stakeholder theory suggests that employees have a legitimate claim that should be addressed. Furthermore, employees have a right to be involved in decisions regarding their wellbeing. According to Evan and Freeman (1988, p. 82):

The corporation should be managed for the benefits of its stakeholders: its customers, suppliers, owners, employees, and local communities. The rights of these groups must be ensured, and further, the groups must participate, in some sense, in decisions that substantially affect their welfare.

Yet the interests of employees are overridden by the organisation's imperative to achieve economic goals (Kamoche 1994). The difficulties involved in recognising employees as stakeholders in the corporation are clearly significant. It has been argued that to accept such an ethical relationship with stakeholders is almost as problematic as ignoring stakeholders (ethically) altogether (Goodpaster 1991). This is even recognised by the authors when they state 'the task of management is akin to that of King Solomon' (Evan & Freeman 1988, p. 81).

Implications for organisations, managers and employees

Legge (1998) suggests that only HRM that treats employees as more than a means to an end is ethical. Corporations would be expected, for example, to offer training and development that focused on the enhancement of the employee's career path, not just on the skills required by the workplace. In contrast, Vallance (1995) suggests that any practice not 'productive of the business aim' is unjustifiable on the grounds that it may interfere with an individual's liberty. Stakeholder theory claims a moral relationship with employees (and all other stakeholders). Shareholder value theory, on the other hand, denies such a relationship. Sennett (1999) argues that organisations should be paternalistic; Handy (1989) argues that they should not. Such a range of ethical approaches offers little guidance on how to proceed. What are the implications for the employment relationship? In order to further this debate, two issues will be explored: the nature of HRM practice and the nature of the employment 'contract'.

The dual nature of HRM in modern organisations

The soft–hard dichotomy has been well established in normative models of HRM, and this distinction needs to be taken into account in conceptualisations of HRM (Truss, Gratton, Hope-Hailey, McGovern & Stiles 1997). However, a study by Truss et al. (1997) showed that no pure example of either form of HRM existed. Legge (1995) notes that most normative statements of HRM contain elements of both soft and hard models.

It is the soft model of HRM, the version that purports to care for the employee, that is of greatest concern from an ethical standpoint because it is viewed as more subtle and potentially insidious (Guest 1997; Warren 2000). Popular theorists describe the modern organisation as characterised by a number of practices including flexibility, teamwork, cultural management and a focus on core competencies. The rhetoric of the positivist paradigm suggests that these practices provide employees with the opportunity to participate, gain greater skills, perform a wider range of tasks and have more control over their work. The suggestion is that the organisation feels an obligation to care for its employees. Measured against the Kantian dicta of seeing employees as an end in themselves and respecting the rights of the individual, soft HRM appears to score well. Critical theorists, however, have identified the other side of a double-edged sword. An absence of clear lines of authority, for example, encourages greater contribution and cross-skilling, but also frees management to shift and adapt and rationalise without the need to justify its actions (Sennett 1998; Warren 2000). Team working encourages employee involvement and sharing but also allows the avoidance of managerial responsibility and suppresses resistance and confrontation (Sennett 1998). Even if the rhetoric is soft, the reality is almost always hard. If the potential duality of these practices is accepted and we are no longer assured that individuals' rights are being respected, then their approval under the conditions of Kantian ethics must come under scrutiny.

Soft HRM practices are evaluated against Kantian criteria as ethical if the individual is seen as not entirely a means to an end — that is, the intrinsic value of the employee is recognised. Hard HRM practices are seen as unethical from the same perspective since they treat employees only as a means to an end. There is, however, an alternative way of looking at this argument. If we cannot be assured of the soft nature of HRM practices (of whether, that is, we are dealing with a wolf in sheep's clothing), then it is more dangerous for employees to be exposed to such practices than for them to face blatant hard HRM practices. We *know* to approach a wolf with caution. In fact, could the removal of soft HRM rhetoric have an empowering and liberating effect on employees? Vallance (1995) suggests that any practice not 'productive of the business aim' is unjustifiable on the grounds that it may interfere with an individual's liberty. This blurring of the line between soft and hard HRM raises a question of significant ethical concern: Under what, if any, circumstances is it permissible for employees to be 'used' as a means to an end.

The employment 'contract': loyalty or autonomy?

The changing nature of the employment contract has been acknowledged (Robinson, Kraatz & Rousseau 1994), particularly in relation to issues of obligation and commitment (Dunford 1999; Sennett 1999). According to Rousseau and Parks (1992), mutual obligations are the essence of a 'psychological contract' between employers and employees. Legal and contractual models of the employment relationship need to be 'stretched to encompass a psychological dimension' (Winstanley, Woodall & Heery 1996b, p. 191). Various deep changes in working relationships between

employers and employees over recent years have been identified (Anderson & Schalk 1998). Organisational restructuring has significantly changed the nature of this contract (Dunford 1999). Where a contact is not fulfilled or is changed without agreement, it can be seen as having been 'violated'. Such violation can 'run the gamut from subtle misinterpretation to stark breaches of good faith' (Rousseau 1995, p. 111). Managers have described the decline of loyalty among employees who have been counselled not to rely on job security or employer commitment but rather to take charge of their own employability (Robinson et al. 1994). It has been claimed that contract violation is the norm rather than the exception (Robinson & Rousseau 1994). The trend in modern management is to command and then to depart; to sacrifice authority and leadership for self-protection. Any kind of dependency such as existed in bureaucratic hierarchies of command is shunned (Sennett 1999). The new 'chameleon' organisation, therefore, has enormous problems generating commitment and loyalty among its employees. Dunford (1999) suggests two contrasting positions that can be taken with respect to this experience.

An employment relationship free from obligation and commitment may be characterised as challenging, mature, free and creative (Dunford 1999). Loyalty and commitment can have negative connotations, suggesting a less-than-mature stage of individual development, narrow-mindedness and oppression. Noer (cited in Dunford 1999, p. 73) describes the traditional employment relationship as one of 'co-dependency' in which individuals 'enable the system to control their sense of worth and self-esteem' and in doing so 'make themselves into permanent victims'. That labour is seen as freed of any paternalistic taint is widely proclaimed as a virtue (Sennett 1999). Loyalty is seen as a concept whose time has passed, yet there is a striking resonance with much earlier conceptualisations of the employment relationship. Hayek (cited in Sennett 1999) and Friedman (1970) argued long ago that the workplace was not a source of social fulfilment. This version of the employment relationship is thus in keeping with a narrow or classic view of the organisation and also with a hard model of HRM.

Alternatively, an employment relationship free from obligation and commitment may be characterised as cynical, evasive, meaningless and exploitative. The claim that 'our employees are our most valued asset' is common in many organisations. The importance of commitment and involvement in the organisation has been identified both conceptually and empirically (Walton 1985; Lawler 1992). Any benefit the organisation may derive is likely to be threatened by practices that are inconsistent with such rhetoric. Senior management may find their own rhetoric thrown back at them and a degree of cynicism may develop among employees (Dunford 1999). Sennett (1999) argues that the problem with the modern organisation is a lack of commitment and dependence in the name of autonomy. The result is a loss of social cohesion at work. He suggests that the failures, betrayals and inadequacies people experience in their dealings with one another serve as reasons for withdrawal rather than for coming together: 'There is a kind of negative magnetic charge' (Sennett 1999, p. 27). He argues that mutual obligation, indeed paternalism, is necessary to restore social cohesion in the workplace, thereby re-establishing the dignity of men and women as workers. Such an argument can be seen as promoting the soft model of HRM. This debate introduces the ethical question, to what extent, if at all, should the 'organisation' care for or protect employees?

Challenges and future directions

Many corporate mission statements contain claims that the organisation values and cares for its employees. What do these claims imply about the ethical responsibility of the organisation to its employees? The answers to this and other questions are the subject of the developing ethical perspective of HRM. This perspective has been differentiated in the HRM literature only recently. Seminal works by Legge (1995, 1996, 1998) and Winstanley et al. (1996a, 2000) have furthered thinking in this area. This chapter has sought to both analyse and further develop the conceptualisation of these issues. Particular emphasis has been given to the use of stakeholder theory, which has hitherto been neglected in the literature.

Managers have traditionally been expected to act as agents for owners in the pursuit of earnings. Are they now expected to act as agents for other parties in the pursuit of social responsibility? What does this mean, and is it possible? In order to discuss this, stakeholder theory and ethical theory have been considered. Evan and Freeman (1988) label stakeholder theory as 'Kantian capitalism'. The implications of treating all stakeholders in accordance with the first principle of stakeholder theory (Evan & Freeman, 1988, p. 79) — that 'the corporation and its managers may not violate the legitimate rights of others to determine their own future' — are immense. Does this mean, for example, that employees may never be used as a means to an end? Such an imperative would render the employment relationship, as we understand it, untenable. It may be more realistic to suggest that employees cannot be used *exclusively* as a means to an end. But this begs the question raised earlier in the chapter: Under what circumstances, if any, is it allowable for employees to be so 'used'?

The nature of the employment relationship should also be considered. It is overly simplistic to argue that soft, paternalistic HRM practices are ethical because they show consideration for the employees as individuals. First, soft and hard HRM probably do not exist in their pure form (Truss et al. 1997) but more likely occur in combination (Legge 1995). Second, the paternalistic behaviour of an employer may have sinister motivations (Winstanley & Woodall 2000). As noted earlier, the debate between high-commitment and low-commitment employment relationships introduces the ethical question: to what extent, if at all, should the organisation care for or protect employees?

The introduction of ethical issues into the research and practice of HRM is essential to advance the field. The debate so far is only a beginning. In order to understand more fully the ethical dimension of HRM, the employer–employee relationship must be further explored from the perspective of business ethics. It is time not only to 'make room for labour in business ethics' (Leahy 2001) but to bring ethics into HRM.

References

Academy of Management (2000) *Academy of Management 2000 Proceedings*. Academy of Management, Toronto, Canada.

Alvesson, M, and Willmott, HC (1996) *Making sense of management: a critical introduction*. London: Sage.

Anderson, N, and Schalk, R (1998) The psychological contract in retrospect and prospect. *Journal of Organizational Behaviour*, 19 637–47.

Beauchamp, TL, and Bowie, NE (1993) *Ethical Theory and Business Practice*. Englewood Cliffs, NJ: Prentice Hall.

Becker, B, and Gerhart, B (1996) The impact of human resource management on organizational performance: progress and prospects. *Academy of Management Journal*, 39 (4) 779–95.

Clark, T, Mabey, C, and Skinner, D (1998). Experiencing HRM: the importance of the inside story. In C Mabey, D Skinner and T Clark (Eds), *Experiencing Human Resource Management*. London: Sage.

Cornelius, N, and Gagnon, S (1999) From ethics 'by proxy' to ethics in action: new approaches to understanding HRM and ethics. *Business Ethics: A European Review*, 8 (4) 225–35.

Covey, SR (1989) *The Seven Habits of Highly Effective People: Powerful Lessons in Personal Change*. New York: Simon and Schuster.

Dunford, R (1999) If you want loyalty get a dog!: loyalty, trust and the employment contract. In SR Clegg, E Ibarra-Colado and L Bueno-Rodriquez (Eds), *Global Management: Universal Theories and Local Realities*. London: Sage.

Evan, WM, and Freeman, RE (1988) A stakeholder theory of the modern corporation: Kantian capitalism. In TL Beauchamp and N Bowie (Eds), *Ethical Theory and Business*. Englewood Cliffs, NJ: Prentice Hall.

Ferris, GR, Hochwarter, WA, Buckley, MR, Harrell-Cook, G, and Frink, DD (1999) Human resource management: some new directions. *Journal of Management*, 25 (3) 385–423.

Freeman, RE (1984) *Strategic Management: A Stakeholder Approach*. Boston, MA: Pitman.

Friedman, M (1970) The social responsibility of business is to increase profit. *The New York Times Magazine*.

Goodpaster, KE (1991) Business ethics and stakeholder analysis. *Business Ethics Quarterly*, 1 (1) 53–73.

Grace, D, and Cohen, S (1998) *Business Ethics: Australian Problems and Cases*. Melbourne: Oxford University Press.

Greenwood, MR (2001) The importance of stakeholders according to business leaders. *Business and Society Review*, 106 (1) 29–49.

Guest, D (1987) Human resource management and industrial relations. *Journal of Management Studies*, 24 (5) 503–521.

Guest, D (1997) Human resource management and performance: a review and research agenda. *International Journal of Human Resource Management*, 8 (3) 263–76.

Guest, D (1999) Human resource management — the workers' verdict. *Human Resource Management Journal*, 9 (3) 5–25.

Handy, C (1989) *The Age of Unreason*. IL: Century-Hutchinson.

Handy, C (1991) What is a company for? *RSA Journal*.

Jackson, SE, and Schuler, RS (1995) Understanding human resource management in the context of organizations and their environments. *Annual Review of Psychology*, 46 (1) 237–65.

Kamoche, K (1994) A critique and a proposed reformulation of strategic human resource management. *Human Resource Management*, 4 (4) 29–47.

Kamoche, K, and Mueller, F (1998) Human resource management and the Appropriation-Learning perspective. *Human Relations*, 51 (8) 1033–60.

Lawler, EE (1992) *The Ultimate Advantage: Creating the High-involvement Organization*. San Francisco: Jossey-Bass.

Leahy, JT (2001) Making room for labor in business ethics. *Journal of Business Ethics*, 29 (1/2) 33–43.

Legge, K (1995) *Human Resource Management: Rhetorics and Reality*. London: Macmillan.

Legge, K (1996) Morality bound. *People Management*, 25 (2) 34–6.

Legge, K (1998) The morality of HRM. In C Mabey, D Skinner and T Clark (Eds), *Experiencing Human Resource Management*. London: Sage.

Metcalfe, C (1998) The stakeholder corporation. *Business Ethics: A European Review*, 7 (1) 30–36.

Miller, P (1996) Strategy and ethical management of human resources. *Human Resource Management Journal*, 6 (1) 5–18.

Mitchell, RK, Agle, BR, and Wood, DJ (1997) Towards a theory of stakeholder identification and salience: defining the principle of who and what really counts. *Academy of Management Review*, 22 (4) 853–86.

Moorhead, A, Steele, M, Alexander, M, Stephen, K, and Duffin, L (1997) *Changes at Work: The 1995 Australian Workplace Industrial Relations Survey*. Melbourne: Longman.

Peters, T, and Waterman, R (1982) *In Search of Excellence*. New York: Harper & Row.

Pfeffer, J, and Veiga, JF (1999) Putting people first for organizational success. *The Academy of Management Executive*, 13 (2) 37–48.

Purcell, J (1999) Best practice and best fit: chimera or cul-de-sac? *Human Resource Management Journal*, 9 (3) 26–41.

Rappaport, A (1986) *Creating Shareholder Value: The New Standard for Business Performance*. New York: The Free Press.

Robinson, SL, Kraatz, MS, and Rousseau, DM (1994) Changing obligations and the psychological contract: a longitudinal study. *Academy of Management Journal*, 37 (1) 137–52.

Robinson, SL, and Rousseau, DM (1994) Violating the psychological contract: not the exception but the norm. *Journal of Organizational Behavior*, 15, 245–59.

Rousseau, DM (1995) *Psychological Contracts in Organizations*. Thousand Oaks, CA: Sage.

Rousseau, DM, and Parks, JM (1992) The contracts of individuals and organisations. *Research in Organizational Behavior*, 15 1–47.

Rowan, JR (2000) The moral foundation of employee rights. *Journal of Business Ethics*, 24 (2) 355–61.

Sennett, R (1998) *The Corrosion of Character*. New York: W.W. Norton.

Sennett, R (1999) How work destroys social inclusion. *New Statesman*, June, 25–7.

Shuler, RS, and Jackson, RE (1987) Linking competitive strategy and human resource management practices. *Academy of Management Executive*, 1 (3) 207–219.

Simon, JG, Powers, CW, and Gunneman, JP (1993) The responsibilities of corporations and their owners. In TL Beauchamp and NE Bowie (Eds), *Ethical Theory and Business*. Englewood Cliffs, NJ: Prentice Hall.

Stone, RJ (1998) *Human Resource Management*. Brisbane: John Wiley & Sons.

Townley, B (1993) Foucault, power/knowledge, and its relevance for human resource management. *Academy of Management Review*, 18 (3) 518–46.

Truss, C, Gratton, L, Hope-Hailey, V, McGovern, P, and Stiles, P (1997) Soft and hard models of human resource management: a reappraisal. *Journal of Management Studies*, 34 (1) 53–73.

Ulrich, D (1998) A new mandate for human resources. *Harvard Business Review*, 76 (1) 125–34.

Vallance, E (1995) *Business Ethics at Work*. Cambridge, UK: Cambridge University Press.

Walton, RE (1985) From control to commitment in the workplace. *Harvard Business Review*, 63, 77–84.

Warren, RC (2000) *Putting the person back into human resource management*. Third Conference on Ethics and Human Resource Management. Imperial College Management School, London.

Willmott, H (1997) Rethinking managerial work: capitalism, control, and subjectivity. *Human Relations*, 50 (11) 1329–59.

Winstanley, D, and Woodall, J (2000) The ethical dimensions of human resource management. *Human Resource Management Journal*, 10 (2) 5–20.

Winstanley, D, Woodall, J, and Heery, E (1996a) Business ethics and human resource management themes and issues. *Personnel Review*, 25 (6) 5–12.

Winstanley, D, Woodall, J, and Heery, E (1996b) The agenda for ethics in human resource management. *Business Ethics: A European Review*, 5 (4) 187–94.

Wright, PM, and McMahan, GC (1992) Theoretical perspectives for strategic human resource management. *Journal of Management*, 18 (2) 295–321.

CHAPTER 23

Virtual assignments: a new possibility for IHRM?

by Denice Ellen Welch and Marilyn Fenwick

Mt Eliza Business School | Monash University

Introduction

International human resource management (IHRM) has become well established as a field of scientific inquiry, with a growing body of literature pertaining to issues surrounding the management of people in an international context. Over the past two decades, research has focused on key differences between domestic and international HRM activities and functions: expatriate management, including repatriation of staff; the impact of cultural adjustment — of both the employee and the accompanying partner/family members — on performance during the foreign assignment; and the HR consequences of strategic staffing decisions. This interest reflects the need to understand the impact of international operations on the staff concerned as well as the HR activities involved. There are also implications for the HR department as its role expands to handle more cases of international relocation, even if some of the activities (such as cross-cultural awareness training) are outsourced.

In IHRM, the terms Parent Country National (PCN), Third-Country National (TCN) and Host Country National (HCN) are used to denote staff categories based on home location. For example, an Australian-based international firm may transfer Australians (PCNs) and Indians (TNCs) to its English subsidiary, and transfer English subsidiary staff (HCNs) to its Australian headquarters. A criticism of IHRM has been its apparent research preoccupation with expatriate management issues relating to PCN expatriates (Dowling, Welch & Schuler 1999; Welch & Welch 1994). In its defence, one could argue that HCN management issues have

been taken up by scholars and researchers in the comparative and cross-cultural HRM fields. However, this work is yet to be integrated into a holistic approach to IHRM. Further, little work has been conducted into TCN expatriate issues (Chadwick 1995), the dynamics of PCN and HCN relations at the subsidiary level (Hailey 1996, 1999; Vance & Ring 1994), and the HR issues of transferring TCNs and HCNs into headquarters operations (Novicevic & Harvey 2001).

If one accepts the above criticism, one can argue that concentration on expatriate management has meant that other types of international assignments have been overlooked. Many of a firm's international management activities involve travelling — to attend meetings and training programs, conduct sales visits, oversee new ventures, negotiate with clients and key host government officials, undertake performance monitoring and the like. These trips may last for days or weeks, and may often involve visits to several countries. Such travel may comprise the majority of a person's job description. For example, an export sales manager may spend, in total, the equivalent of three months a year travelling to foreign markets. However, the HR implications of frequent international business travel on staff health and performance have received little attention from researchers in the IHRM and international management fields. Further, international assignments vary in duration, from a week to several months (even up to a year), before they are treated as expatriate postings. Some of these trips may not even come under the aegis of the HR department.

In this chapter we draw on results of a recent survey suggesting that the use of what is being termed 'non-standard' international assignments is growing, partly as a substitute for the more traditional form of longer term expatriate assignments. Non-standard forms include short-term, contractual, rotational, commuter and virtual assignments. We attempt to draw out the HR management implications of what is emerging as a new form of international assignment — the 'virtual assignment'. Given its newcomer status, the central question we investigate is: is the virtual assignment a new form of international assignment initiated to complement existing forms as the organisational context of multinational enterprise changes? Or is it merely repackaging elements of existing practice to capitalise on advances in communication media to overcome barriers to staff mobility and to contain the rising cost of expatriate management? If the former, what are the implications for IHRM?

'Expatriate' is used in this chapter as an umbrella term to describe staff working temporarily in a foreign location. Lately, some US researchers have begun to refer to foreign staff brought into parent operations as 'inpatriates' (see, for example, Novicevic & Harvey 2001). However, we shall be using the term 'expatriate' to refer to all transfers of staff — PCN, TCN and HCN — that require temporary relocation to a foreign country, regardless of purpose, nature and duration of that relocation. Various terms are used in the relevant literature to denote international relocation — for example, international assignments, overseas assignments, foreign assignments or expatriate postings. As these terms are used interchangeably, we shall follow suit.

International assignments

For managers of internationalising firms, their key distinction from domestic operations is the perceived increased risk, since, by its very nature, international business involves moving into foreign markets that are geographically and culturally distant. Research evidence indicates that the more distant the operation, the higher the perception of risk and uncertainty in the minds of management (see, for example, Buckley & Ghauri 1999; Benito & Welch 1994). Using staff from the home office or headquarters in key positions in the foreign market operation is one way of reducing the level of perceived risk and enhancing control. Although the reasons for moving staff in and out of foreign locations will vary according to the nature of the receiving operation and the role to be performed, three main reasons for staff transfers are generally recognised in the IHRM literature: to fill a specific corporate position; for management development;

and for organisational purposes, such as control and coordination, knowledge transfer and inter-unit communication, and corporate identity and relationship-building (Fenwick, De Cieri & Welch 1999; Edström & Galbraith 1977). These purposes have remained fairly consistent over time. The latest Global Relocation Trends Survey (conducted by GMAC GRS/Windham International, in conjunction with the US National Foreign Trade Council and the SHRM Global Forum, 2000) asked respondents to indicate their primary objectives for international assignments. The most common reason was to fill a skills gap, followed by organisational purposes such as the launch of a new endeavour, and technology transfer.

Naturally, the duration of the assignment varies depending on the nature and purpose of the staff transfer. Short duration assignments (from three to six months) are usually related to troubleshooting or project supervision, or are a stopgap measure until a more permanent arrangement can be found. Longer term assignments (for two to five years) tend to involve a clearly defined role in the receiving operation, perhaps as managing director of a subsidiary (Welch & Welch 1994; Dowling & Welch 1988), or as a senior technical expert (Fenwick 2000).

Although Kobrin (1988) noted a reduction in the use of expatriates by US multinationals in the early 1980s, there is no clear evidence that 'the expatriate' is a threatened species. Rather, the use of expatriate assignments, in various guises and for various purposes, has been a consistent staffing strategy over a considerable period of time, and recent surveys indicate an increasing requirement for internationally mobile staff. The results of a 1997–98 survey of 184 companies operating in 15 European countries indicated that participating companies anticipated the number of expatriates to grow in all regions over the following five years (Price Waterhouse 1997). The Global Relocation Trends survey mentioned above found that 58 per cent of the 154 (predominantly US-based) participating companies expected the number of expatriates to increase in 2001. A similar finding emerged from recent research conducted across 650 countries, including Australasia, by Organization Resources Counsellors (Stanley 2001).

When trying to determine trends in expatriate management, the variation in terms used by international firms to describe the different types of assignments employed makes comparisons between surveys somewhat problematical. For example, some firms in the 1997–98 Price Waterhouse survey defined a business trip as involving a stay of up to one month (37 per cent) or up to three months (32 per cent); 49 per cent defined a short-term assignment as up to one year, 8 per cent as up to three months, and 26 per cent as up to six months; and 50 per cent of the companies considered transfers of over one year to be long-term assignments. There is also confusion over the use of the term 'expatriate'; responding companies may use it to refer to employees on both short-term and longer term assignments, and even those on business trips, whereas others may regard an expatriate as someone on a traditional longer term assignment while those on shorter assignments are deemed to be 'business travellers'.

The dilemma for multinationals in the twenty-first century is that they still depend on mobile international staff to maintain and develop global operations, but expatriates are expensive (figures vary, but the 'rule-of-thumb' is two to three times their home cost). Relocation expenses and support packages (cost-of-living adjustments, education allowances, subsidised housing, for example) comprise typical compensation costs in addition to the person's normal salary entitlement. While shortening the duration of the assignment does not necessarily remove these additional remuneration expenses, the shorter the assignment, the less likely it is that the partner and/or family members will also relocate, thus lowering some of the compensation costs.

Taking the above concerns into account, it is possible to identify an increase in the use of other forms of international staffing such as shorter assignments. The central IHRM issue related to the longer term expatriate assignments has been that of on-assignment performance, with most empirical investigation concerned with expatriate adjustment to the foreign location, along with accompanying partner and family adjustment. Underperformance and 'failure' (defined as early recall from the foreign location) have been critical aspects of this line of research (see Dowling, Welch & Schuler 1999 for an overview of this literature).

The inability of the expatriate to adjust has been suggested as a primary factor in expatriate population reduction as firms seek to minimise the personal and monetary cost of failure, but it is not the only barrier to the use of expatriates (Welch 1994). Recent surveys of expatriate relocation suggest that cost containment and staff immobility are more likely to affect the size of the expatriate population, and appear to explain the trend towards non-standard assignments. For example, in the 1997–98 Price Waterhouse study mentioned above companies indicated unwillingness of employee and/or family to relocate and cost containment as the major reasons for their move towards non-standard assignments. Fifty-eight per cent of companies highlighted dual careers as a factor in assignment refusals. The GMAC survey likewise reports that companies see the most critical relocation challenge as finding candidates. Reluctance to move may also relate to the assignment location. For example, in the GMAC 2000 survey, responding firms listed China (33 per cent), Brazil (22 per

cent), Russia (18 per cent), India (16 per cent) and Japan (14 per cent) as countries presenting the greatest assignment difficulties.

Alternative forms of multinational enterprise such as collaborative, intra- and inter-organisational networks, and 'born globals' have proliferated in recent years (Bartlett & Ghoshal 1992; Oliver & Liebeskind 1997; Oviatt & McDougall 1995). These new forms significantly challenge prevailing views of multinational enterprise and, therefore, of international management and IHRM. They are implemented only through high levels of interdependence between their parts, and may require different approaches to international staffing. Therefore, the likelihood of alternatives to traditional expatriation being adopted in such organisations will continue to increase.

Non-standard assignments

As previously mentioned, the 1997–98 Price Waterhouse survey identified a trend away from the longer term, traditional international assignment to 'non-standard' arrangements. These are depicted in figure 23.1.

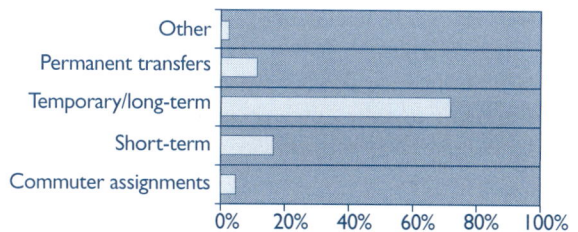

Figure 23.1: Assignment categories **Source:** Compiled from data reported in Price Waterhouse (1997).

For the purposes of the survey, short-term assignments were defined as those longer than a business trip but shorter than the typical long-term assignment. Generally, responding firms classified short-term assignments as between one and twelve months' duration. The main reason given for an increase in the use of short-term assignments was cost pressures, and most seemed to be targeted at operations in developing markets.

Commuter assignments are special arrangements under which the employee commutes from his or her home country on a weekly or biweekly basis to the place of work in another country. The family remains in the home country. The employee is not a daily commuter. While these arrangements are partly cost reduction strategies, they tend to be responses to overcome barriers to staff mobility, particularly in the case of dual-career couples and other family-related circumstances (Dowling et al. 1999). The use of these assignments perhaps is more feasible where geographic distances are minimal, such as in the European Union.

An interesting development noted in this study was the emergence of the 'virtual assignment' — a situation in which the employee, rather than relocating to a host location, manages the international job requirements from the home country. Forty-three per cent of companies indicated that they had utilised a virtual assignment. The dictionary defines *virtual* as 'equivalent in so far as effect is concerned'. In other words, the means may differ but the end is the same. Of course, the notion of the 'virtual organisation' (Boudreau, Loch, Robey & Straud 1998, p. 121) has been the focus of considerable attention in the past decade. Within strategic HRM, the notion of virtuality has also previously been applied to '*virtual HR:* a network-based structure built on partnerships and typically mediated by information technologies to help the organization acquire, develop and deploy intellectual capital' and as a means of gaining strategic flexibility (Lepak & Snell 1998, p. 216).

In 2000 PricewaterhouseCoopers (PwC) conducted a follow-up study into the virtual assignment, along with other permutations of the 'non-standard' assignment. To quote the study's authors:

> With no sign of any decline in the demand for internationally mobile employees, organisations are increasingly seeking alternatives to the standard two to five year assignment in order to source the demand and address the growing barriers to mobility. (PwC 2000, p. ii)

The survey involved 82 multinationals across 13 countries but predominantly based in Europe. Commuter, short-term and virtual assignments were explored, along with two other types of employee not addressed in the 1997–98 study: rotators — those who commute from the home country to a place of work in another country for a short, set period followed by a holiday in the home country (used on oil rigs, for example); and contractors — those with specific skills vital to an international project assigned for a limited duration of six to twelve months.

The usages of all five types of non-standard assignments among the respondents are shown in figure 23.2.

Of all survey respondents, 28 per cent anticipated an increasing use of virtual assignments, compared with 17 per cent in the 1997–98 Price Waterhouse survey. Sixty-five per cent of respondents who use virtual assignments reported having seen an increase in the number of virtual assignments used by their company, and the same proportion indicated an expected increase in the next two years.

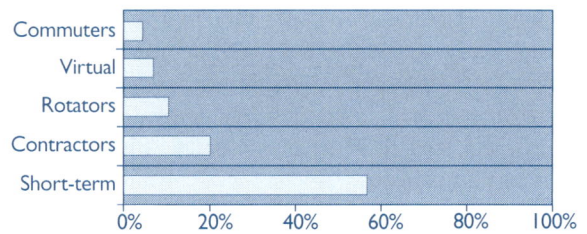

Figure 23.2: Use of non-standard assignments *Source:* Compiled from data provided in PricewaterhouseCoopers (2000).

Given the expected increase in the use of the virtual assignment, in the following section we attempt to establish whether the end is the same, and to draw out the IHRM implications for both the international firm and the virtual assignee.

The virtual assignment

The 'virtual assignment' is defined as an assignment in which 'an employee does not relocate to a host location, but has international responsibilities for a part of the organisation in another country which they manage from the home country' (PricewaterhouseCoopers 2000, p. 31). It replaces a traditional international assignment rather than one in which business travel is a normal part of the employee's role. However, it does involve frequent business trips to the host country, and between such trips it relies on the use of telecommunication and information technology such as telephone, email and videoconferencing as a substitute for physical presence in the foreign location.

The appeal of the virtual assignment is that it removes or reduces some of the barriers to the traditional assignment, notably staff immobility and rising costs. At least superficially, the virtual assignment is a cost containment strategy, since the virtual assignee is not required to relocate in the foreign country and the family is not compelled to move, which saves on relocation expenses and other aspects of the support required for a traditional assignment. It also provides a more flexible way of approaching the international assignment to accommodate dual-career concerns and other family-related barriers to staff mobility. Within 'born globals' and collaborative networks, there may be no necessity to relocate staff. Rather, network relations, for example, can be managed through virtual assignment.

However, possible hidden or indirect costs related to the virtual assignment may need to be taken into account, since they may counter its advantages. Figure 23.3

provides a useful conceptual framework for analysing aspects relating to the virtual assignment and factors that may influence its success.

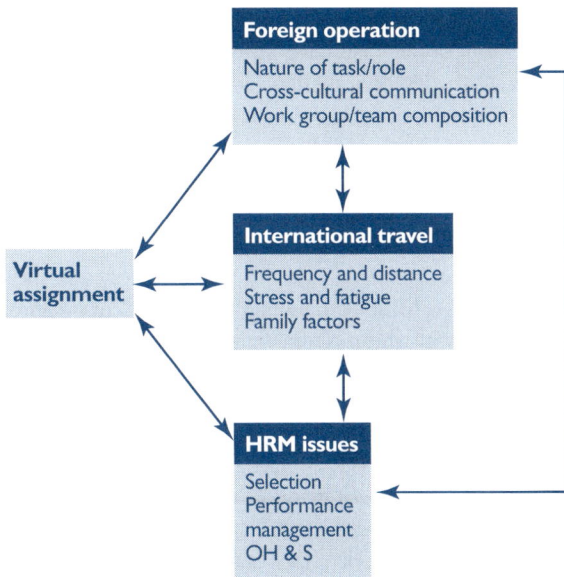

Figure 23.3: Influences on the virtual assignment

Foreign operation

The location of the foreign operation, the nature of the task, and the person's role can be expected to determine the appropriateness of a virtual assignment.

Nature of task/role

Analysis of the PwC survey data indicates an industry bias: 69 per cent of respondents who indicated that they used such an arrangement were in the oil and gas industry. The oil and gas industry has tended to drive assignment practice (it is often used as a benchmark in areas such as expatriate compensation packages). The industry has tended to use more flexible work arrangements such as the rotational concept (a certain number of days on an oil rig, followed by the same number of days on shore leave). It is not surprising, therefore, to find that this industry was the highest user of virtual assignments in the PwC 2000 survey (69 per cent). The findings of the Global Relocation Trends study mentioned above support an industry relationship for non-standard assignments: short-term assignments were found to be concentrated in the high-tech, pharmaceutical and healthcare sectors (virtual assignments were not covered in this survey). However, the suggestion of an industry bias should also encourage caution in the extrapolation of survey findings across all industries.

The specific nature of work also appears to influence the use of virtual assignments. Respondents in the PwC survey indicated they were using virtual assignments to manage local operations (55 per cent); for troubleshooting, establishing a global company culture and project operations; and to open new operations (35 per cent respectively). The survey data available, however, do not indicate the precise nature of the local operations being managed virtually. The international project literature highlights supplier–client relationships and maintaining a local presence as critical success factors (Luostarinen & Welch 1990). A comment from a respondent in the PwC survey provides some insight into how a virtual assignment may be viewed in an international project: 'When you're not sure how the project will go, virtual assignments can work'.

It may be that virtual assignments turn into short-term assignments, or even longer assignments, as the project evolves. For example, in one instance revealed during interview research with expatriates, the corporate lawyer in a petroleum company responsible for negotiating and finalising a contract for an international joint venture to extract oil in Vietnam was expatriated with the project team for three years during the implementation phase. However, before this he had been on virtual assignment, with regular short-term assignments to Vietnam over the previous four years, in order to experience first-hand the local legal environment and to initiate negotiations (Fenwick 2000). Following repatriation to his headquarters base, this executive then resumed the virtual assignment of responsibility for contract renegotiation and eventual withdrawal from the project by the company. It is hard to solve complex managerial and technical problems without being physically 'on site'. The literature on internationalisation has long stressed the role of tacit, experiential knowledge and learning in assisting the development of foreign operations. As Johannesen, Olaisen and Olsen (2001, p. 4) point out, 'tacit knowledge is difficult to communicate to others as information, and can at best be difficult to digitalize'. Such knowledge is highly 'person-bound'. The transfer of knowledge and learning into local operations, and between units of the global organisation, and its dissemination is a perennial international management challenge (Roberts, Kossek & Ozeki 1998). Given the role played by the traditional expatriate in transferring skills, and the tacit nature of 'know-how' and 'show-how' that is a major component of skills and knowledge transfer, one can question how effective the virtual assignee would be in performing this role. Perhaps this difficulty is the reason that only 20 per cent of respondents in the PwC survey indicated they would use a virtual assignment to fill a skills gap, and only 15 per cent would use it to train staff.

Cross-cultural communication

Certain cross-cultural barriers may be lessened in the virtual assignment situation. Given that most time is spent in the home country, social interaction takes place predominantly within the confines of the person's social and family networks. Daily interaction with foreign staff is largely work related and directed from the executive's usual office. This does not mean that he or she is removed from 'all things foreign'. Cross-cultural interaction remains a critical component of the virtual assignment, and the virtual nature of the assignment may introduce or irritate areas for conflict. High-context cultures rely more heavily on ability to read the non-verbal cues than do low-context cultures (Hall 1976). Virtual expatriates who come from a culture where direct, plain speaking is the norm may send brusque email messages that cause offence, but without non-verbal feedback the sender may not realise that offence has been taken. Lack of non-verbal cues and feedback is recognised as a barrier to effective communication; this is exacerbated in the virtual assignment setting, given its heavy reliance on electronic media. Of course, non-verbal messages are also open to misinterpretation, particularly in cross-cultural settings. For example, as face-to-face communication is reduced with the use of faxes, emails and telephone calls, the potential for misunderstanding and unintended offence increases. Emerging research on the use of email illustrates how culture-bound this medium of communication may be. Clarke and Lipp (1998, p. 22) examined interaction between local and Japanese workers in US-based Japanese subsidiaries, and found many instances of differing expectations around the use of communication. One Japanese executive explained:

> The Americans also rely too much on written communication. They send us too many memos and too much email. They seem content to sit in their offices creating a lot of paperwork without knowing how people will react.

In a study of language as a facet of multinational inter-unit communication, the importance of face-to-face communication and personal contact was stressed. One expatriate interviewed explained:

> I think that to know the people helps in communication. Having met the person one knows how he may express himself, how he can formulate a problem. Communication between strangers is more distant and more difficult. To be able to communicate directly eliminates the possible misunderstandings. Otherwise by fax ... or phone ... it's more complex, harder. (Lahtinen 2000, p. 72)

It appears that, to be effective, a virtual assignment requires investment initially in face-to-face settings in order to establish at least a degree of personal interaction and perhaps trust that will provide the underpinnings of a long-distance working relationship. Videoconferencing was encouraged by 35 per cent of the responding firms in the PwC 2000 study as a way of addressing the lack of face-to-face contact and daily informal contact. However, it is not a perfect substitute. As Kezsbom (2000, p. 34) points out, 'Even in the best of videoconferencing, facial expressions can be difficult to pick up if the transmission is poor, if someone is off camera, or when the mute button is pressed'. Some people find video-conferences constraining, and this may be reflected in their body language. Misunderstandings may arise if, for instance, discomfort with the medium is interpreted as discomfort with the person receiving the message.

Work group/team composition

Another factor is the nature of the role and the work group. Increasingly, work *teams* are being considered as the more effective form of work group and an important part of multinational enterprise. They are distinguished from work groups in that teams assign jobs to members, manage themselves, plan and schedule work, make production or service-related decisions, and take action to remedy problems (Kirkman & Shapiro 1997). Therefore, another factor is the nature and role of the work team.

For example, if the assignment involves managing the local operations, as indicated by 55 per cent of the PwC respondents, then one can assume a hierarchical separation between the virtual assignee and the local work group involved. The resulting status distance may affect the degree to which the parties can build the required level of interaction and trust that will foster adequate performance and productivity so that the virtual assignment can achieve the same ends as would be achieved in the traditional, standard assignment. Jones and George (1998) regard the organisation's ability to create the appropriate setting as important in the development of trust within work groups. The PwC survey did reveal that the local set-up was important, with the size of the local team and the degree to which the role required direct managerial responsibilities mentioned as two aspects. What is not certain, from the limited data available, is the effect that the lack of the consistent presence of the virtual assignee has on the work group dynamics, performance and motivation. Even assuming that personal interactions occur, the very nature of the virtual assignment might exacerbate problems with the use of expatriate assignments reported in the past. At the subsidiary level, a demoralised HCN workforce has long been suggested as a disadvantage of staffing with PCNs (see the review in Dowling et al. 1999).

Other, more recent research has indicated that HCNs have expressed resentment towards expatriates with whom they worked (Hailey 1996). In the PwC survey, 55 per cent of responding firms mentioned the lack of assignee integration into the local workplace or community as a main problem encountered; 35 per cent identified resentment from host company employees as a further problem with virtual assignments. Short visits to the subsidiary by headquarters staff, or to the headquarters by subsidiary staff, may be negatively perceived by HCNs as signifying paternalism, mistrust or lack of interest in local concerns. HCNs may interpret the non-assignment of a person full-time to the subsidiary as evidence of a downgrading of either the job or the subsidiary, thus reinforcing resentment and the perception of increased centralisation. Perhaps indicative of host location concerns, 40 per cent of companies in the PwC survey reported sending frequent updates to the host country operations so employees were kept informed about what was happening in the company.

While the virtual assignment cannot be equated with the virtual team, since it tends to take the place of a more traditional assignment, there may be some parallels between issues faced by leaders of virtual teams and those of virtual assignees. Both evidently rely on trust. Mazneviski and Chudoba (2000) found that successful global virtual teams focused more on building relationships to increase trust. More important, these authors found that as task complexity increased, so did message complexity, and that complex messaging required a rich medium such as face-to-face meetings and lengthy conference calls.

Of course, if the virtual assignment involves an international project, then the emerging literature on virtual teams may be informative when considering the IHRM implications of virtual assignments. Further, those with the responsibility for managing intra- or inter-organisational networks could also be considered members of virtual teams, if the network management remains embedded within the participating entities rather than assuming an independent structure.

International travel

As the PwC report recognises, the virtual expatriate is required to make frequent trips to the foreign location, and will tend to work in a multicultural team. As discussed above, frequent travel may assist in establishing face-to-face contact and relationship building with the foreign employees involved, but it may also generate friction. While alleviating some of the problems associated with electronic forms of communication, it will place the virtual expatriate in the foreign location, and the resulting 'reality check' may provoke cross-cultural issues similar to those experienced in other forms of international assignment. Recognising this potential source of conflict, 30 per cent of firms in the PwC survey provided virtual assignees with cultural awareness training in at least some circumstances, with half of these providing such training in all circumstances.

Apart from the cross-cultural issues, there are other factors related to international travel that may influence the effectiveness of the virtual assignment.

Frequency and distance

Sixty per cent of the firms in the PwC indicated the use of frequent visits as part of the virtual assignment. The frequency of these visits may have an impact on the virtual assignee's ability to function.

The time taken in travel was also a recognised problem (25 per cent), although this factor was, of course, greater for commuters (77 per cent) and might be a reason for some firms switching from commuting to virtual assignments.

There is a link between use of virtual assignments and geographical distance. Since respondents in the PwC 2000 survey were predominantly based in Europe, it is perhaps not surprising to find that 85 per cent of virtual assignments were used in Western Europe, with none in Australasia, whereas 18 per cent used short-term assignments in Australasia.

Stress and fatigue

International travel may create health and productivity problems. Stress and fatigue were listed as problems encountered by 35 per cent of the PwC respondents who utilised the virtual assignment. Travel stress is defined by DeFrank, Konopaske and Ivancevich (2000, p. 59) as 'the perceptual, emotional, behavioral, and physical responses made by an individual to the various problems faced during one or more of the phases of travel'. However, even if the virtual assignee does not travel extensively, psychological and physical stress may result from the nature of home-based work. Consider, for example, one marketing executive of a computer corporation responsible for worldwide marketing of a particular product. She is required to teleconference across time zones, often for one to two hours between two and four o'clock in the morning, then to continue to perform at a high level throughout the 'normal' local business day. Depending on the frequency and intensity of such activity, and the extent to which HR policy and practice acknowledges and accommodates such work practices, her wellbeing, and therefore ultimately her performance in this virtual assignment, might be negatively affected. A related implication concerns the blurring of the work–life boundaries of those involved in virtual assignments.

Family factors

This factor was more pronounced in the commuter group in the PwC survey (54 per cent compared with 15 per cent of the virtual assignment group). However, frequent absences from the family situation can have an impact on the virtual assignee. The emotional costs of frequent international travel have been identified with what is termed the Intermittent Spouse Syndrome (ISS): the rapid and unrelenting cycle of partings and reunions caused by frequent international visits can lead to psychological problems for the virtual assignee and family members. Anxiety, depression, sexual difficulties and sleep problems have been associated with frequent flyers (Kahn 1997). Family relationships can suffer as the frequent absence of the spouse can result in disengagement from family events, placing additional stress on the spouse. The combination of all these aspects is likely to affect performance both in the home and host locations.

HRM issues

The virtual assignment is used by international firms as a substitute for the traditional longer term expatriate posting. As indicated in figure 23.3, the nature of the foreign operation and the task will influence the HR activities involved in managing the virtual assignee during the period of the assignment. Although empirical evidence is limited, it is possible to speculate on the implications of a virtual assignment for selection criteria, performance management including training and development and compensation, and occupational health and safety (OH&S).

Selection

The expatriate literature has identified aspects that may serve as predictors for success in international assignments. Dowling et al. (1999) list technical ability, cross-cultural suitability and family requirements as factors in individual expatriate selection; they add three situational factors: country-cultural requirements, language and multinational enterprise (MNE) requirements. These general factors can be adapted to suit the virtual assignment. Since there is no physical transfer to the host location, the assignee's family situation need not be considered to the same extent. Technical ability assessment should perhaps be extended to include electronic media literacy — particularly the use of intranet, email and related software such as groupware and videoconferencing — given the heavy reliance on such tele-communication to support the virtual assignment.

The virtual assignee must be comfortable with the lack of direct control of day-to-day work situations and be prepared to delegate (Picot 1999). In addition, the capacity to function in an environment characterised by ambiguity of job role, job context and job content may be a feature of virtual assignments. Such ambiguity is typified in the role of the virtual assignee as boundary spanner — someone who must simultaneously manage the interests of the home office and those of the international job requirements. Studies into telecommuting arrangements may provide some insight, given that the virtual assignee has 'remote' staff to control (see, for example, Cascio 2000). Common to all these factors is the importance of interpersonal communication, and those with the skills to build and sustain effective communication irrespective of the media and channels employed will be advantaged in the competition for employment on virtual assignments.

As discussed earlier, cross-cultural issues are important, and these are contingent on the situation in the foreign operation (see figure 23.3). We would argue, however, that selection of the HCN work group needs to be 'factored' into the equation. The virtual nature of the work situation means that most, if not all, HCNs involved need access to electronic media and a level of competence in their use. Most multinational companies use English as the common corporate language for internal, inter-unit communication and information dissemination (Marschan-Piekkari, Welch & Welch 1999). The need for competence in English (or whatever language is used between the home and host location) is increased, given the reliance on telephone and email in the virtual assignment situation, and may influence the composition of the work group.

Performance management

Broadly, performance management relates to any intervention designed to improve employee performance. According to Lewis (1998, p. 67), the term is 'used to describe an integrated set of techniques which have had an independent existence under their own names, e.g. performance appraisal'. Although it has been variously defined in the literature, performance management is typically a bundling of performance appraisal, compensation, and training and development. While no one definition of performance management prevails, it has become common practice to extend the concept beyond its core HR activity of performance appraisal to a holistic or integrated, strategic approach — for example, as:

a process for establishing shared understanding about what is to be achieved, and an approach to managing and developing people in a way which increases the probability that it will be achieved in the short and longer term. (Armstrong 1994, p. 23, author's emphasis)

Integrated performance management has therefore been characterised by links to organisational strategy; setting individual performance goals; providing regular feedback on progress towards those goals; providing opportunities for improving performance through appraisal feedback and training and development; and links between results and rewards (Armstrong 1994). In an MNE, performance management occurs across national and cultural boundaries. Therefore, each of the characteristics of an integrated performance management system already mentioned must be considered for all MNE employees (Fenwick 2000). These characteristics provide a useful framework for considering the performance management implications of virtual assignments.

Links to organisational strategy

This aspect involves a requirement for the relationship between each individual's performance and the achievement of strategic goals and objectives to be clearly established and understood. To achieve links with MNE organisational strategy, the identification of relevant, practical and reliable performance criteria, upon which performance goals are based, must recognise the context in which the virtual assignment takes place. Thus, for those involved in virtual assignments — as for expatriates — despite their home-based nature, there is a need for a broader perspective, perhaps encompassing several sub-strategies across multiple operating environments, in addition to the superordinate enterprise-wide strategy. As a result, the already difficult challenge of effectively communicating the strategic links between the assignee's performance and organisational strategy is likely to be magnified.

Setting individual performance goals

This characteristic of performance management has both content and process implications for HRM in virtual assignments. With regard to content, effective individual performance goals are defined as specific, measurable, achievable, realistic and timely (Flamholtz, Das & Tsui 1985). They should also reflect critical success factors or key performance indicators of the job role. What are the critical success factors of virtual assignments? Perhaps the most obvious implication for HRM of this aspect of performance management is to determine performance criteria and goals related to the effective conduct of the virtual assignment. This involves making explicit tacit knowledge held by effective performers. With regard to process, in order to be effective, the goal-setting element of the performance management process is generally advocated as a highly participative process between

supervisor and employee. However, virtual assignments cross cultural and national boundaries, and cultural differences in the nature of performance goals and acceptability of individual participation in goal setting have been noted (Rubienska & Bovaird 1999). For example, in her case study research of a large Finnish MNE, Tahvanainen (1998) found that employees in Germany and Sweden commonly participated in goal setting for their jobs, but those in the US tended to have their job goals assigned.

Providing regular feedback on progress towards those goals

This aspect is usually managed through performance appraisal. For the MNE and those on virtual assignment within it, issues central to the process of performance management may become more complex managerial challenges. For example, the enduring concerns of who conducts performance appraisals, how and based on what performance data may be compounded when those outside head office with whom the virtual assignee is working are involved. Recent emphasis on participative methods of performance appraisal, such as 360-degree feedback, may resolve some of these challenges, while creating others (London & Smither 1995). For example, providing relevant and timely performance-related feedback across spatial, temporal and cultural boundaries might not necessarily be facilitated or improved through increased access to electronic communication. Individual interpersonal skills and abilities have always moderated the performance appraisal process, and effective performance feedback continues to depend on personal and cultural factors. Further, the extent to which performance appraisal and feedback are received with distrust or interpreted as insulting differs across cultures (Rubienska & Bovaird 1999). Like those for expatriate assignments, performance criteria and standards for virtual assignees will need to generate feedback for assignees relevant to the international context in which they are performing (Harvey 1997). In this context, the cultural distance and the extent to which they share the language of those with whom they are working, or their fluency in the company language, are critical (Marschan-Piekkari et al. 1999). Additionally, depending on the goals set, determining individual performance levels, outstanding performance, underperformance or failure in virtual assignments will be a challenge for the performance appraisal process, since separating the international dimensions of job performance may not be as clear-cut as in traditional expatriate assignments.

Opportunities to improve performance through feedback and training and development

One key function of performance appraisal feedback is that it contributes to training needs analysis by identifying performance gaps that may be eliminated with training and development. Much of the literature and research related to training and development for performance improvement in MNEs has focused on expatriate employees. For example, expatriate training and development appears to have been focused on developing their ability to adjust to a new culture before departing their home countries (Dowling et al. 1999). As already indicated, cross-cultural awareness and competence training will still be relevant for those on virtual assignment, although preferred modes of communication will perhaps be emphasised. For MNEs and virtual assignees, the effectiveness of training and development may be a function of the extent to which tacit knowledge held by effective performers may be made explicit for the training and development of potential virtual assignees. A process such as Critical Incident Technique could be useful in identifying effective and ineffective performance (Fenwick & De Cieri 1995). Given that effective performance of virtual assignments is most likely to rely substantially on competence with communication technology and interpersonal communication, training in, and maintenance and updating of, those competencies may well emerge as a development priority. Also, in the PwC survey the need for language training was recognised by 10 per cent of companies using virtual assignments, and a further 40 per cent of these companies provided language training in some circumstances. Of course, these same implications apply to HCNs.

Links between performance and rewards

The more direct and immediate these links, the more rewards reinforce effective behaviour. In MNEs, management of links between performance and rewards is complex owing to the specialised local knowledge required across multiple employment and legal environments. Further, the objectives of international compensation present significant challenges (Bonache & Fernández 1997). These objectives are to achieve and maintain internal consistency, to attract and retain staff in the requisite areas in the MNE, to facilitate efficient international staff transfers, and to appropriately consider equity and ease of administration (Dowling et al. 1999).

Particularly from the perspective of employees, compensation is one of the most visible aspects of SIHRM (Reynolds 1997) and a major element of collaborative interaction with the organisation. Equity is a central concern in compensation strategy. Individuals compare their compensation to referent standards of people most like themselves (Graham & Trevor 2000). Equity has long been a theme in the expatriate compensation literature, with some compensation approaches resulting in differential compensation provided to PCNs, TCNs and HCNs for comparable roles and responsibilities (Bloom & Milkovich 1996; Dowling et al. 1999; Harvey 1993). These distinctions may reflect 'national cultural norms of fair treatment' (Graham & Trevor 2000, p. 141), and result in conflict and dissatisfaction. The virtual nature of the international assignment does not dispose of the equity issue, since informal and formal interactions between virtual assignees necessary for effective performance bring together individuals from all participating organisations to form ongoing relationships. In both intra- and inter-organisational networks, for example, referent standards for virtual assignees are most likely to be individuals with similar qualifications in similar work roles. Questions such as 'What are the compensable factors in virtual assignments?' and 'How might compensation for virtual assignees fit with global compensation strategy?' will need to be resolved.

Occupational health and safety (OH&S)

The above discussion of the HRM implications of virtual assignments has centred on content and process implications for the selection and performance management functions. However, there are also implications for OH&S. Although the area of OH&S has been extensively covered in the domestic context, it has tended to be overlooked in the IHRM literature — a curious omission given the range of OH&S issues related to international business travel and short-term assignments. As discussed earlier, frequent flying and short international assignments can raise stress and fatigue levels. Recent attention to the incidence of deep vein thrombosis among longer distance frequent flyers is another health concern. Sleep deprivation, lack of regular exercise and poor diet are some of the physical stresses encountered by frequent travellers. For virtual assignees in the PwC survey, host country accommodation was typically a hotel. International business often involves social dinners and banquets, and may require the consumption of food and drink that later causes stomach ailments. Metabolic disorders and disturbed sleep patterns are health concerns that have been studied extensively in relation to the impact of shift work but practically ignored in relation to international assignments, including their cross-cultural adjustment demands. When virtual assignments do extend the work day, the increased stress may place demands on employee relations and workplace agreements.

Conclusion

In this chapter we have explored the emergence of the virtual assignment as part of the trend towards non-standard assignments. We began with the question of whether the virtual assignment is a new form — a logical extension of improved communication systems and new forms of multinational enterprise that are conducive to the achievement of strategic objectives without the need for a longer term physical presence in the host country. From the limited data available, however, it seems that the virtual assignment is a variation of the traditional, standard assignment — the spatial dimension being its main distinction, in that a geographical distance separates the assignee from the organisation's day-to-day operations located in a distant foreign country. Perhaps a more relevant question is, what makes a virtual assignment different from situations in which international activities are supervised from a central location?

Traditionally, a considerable amount of international activity is managed from the 'home office', using a combination of mechanisms such as expatriates and frequent supervisory visits for control and coordination purposes. In her account of medieval trade, Origo (1992) reconstructs the way a medieval merchant in the Italian city of Prato in the 1390s was able to supervise his agents in southern France and Spain via the communication technology of the period: letters delivered by couriers on horseback, supplemented by visits by trusted partners to the remote locations, and the use of expatriate assignments in key foreign branches. One expatriate was given overall responsibility for the three Spanish branches — he was what we would term today a 'country manager'.

In the twenty-first century, export managers perform similar roles: they control foreign market activity from the home location, with frequent personal visits to monitor and control foreign agent/distributor activities (which may be extended into periods of short assignments). Even when a sales subsidiary is established to replace a foreign agent, the export manager is often the reporting line to head office management. The fine distinction here is when the sales subsidiary is staffed, not by a local, but by someone within, say, the export/marketing department who did not relocate but managed the sales subsidiary from the home country as a virtual assignment. It appears, however, that there is scope for further research into the interaction between the nature of the assignment and the type of international operation, as indicated in figure 23.3.

Exploring the HRM implications of virtual assignments has been valuable in highlighting specific issues that may apply to other forms of non-standard international assignments (see figures 23.1 and 23.2). Further empirical work on these issues is indicated. Such research would also be useful in determining whether distinct differences exist between the various types of assignments; and to settle the question we raised at the beginning of this chapter: is the virtual assignment a new form or a variant of old forms? Another consideration is the predominance of European-based firms in the PwC survey. Australian firms adopting various non-standard forms, including the virtual assignment, may encounter different issues.

We have identified and discussed a recognised trend in IHRM, and in the process tried to draw out implications for HR management and for employees. It appears that the virtual assignment is a new opportunity for IHRM, but whether it is a proactive development or a reactive response has yet to be determined.

References

Armstrong, M (1994) *Performance Management.* London: Kogan Page.

Bartlett, CA, and Ghoshal, S (1992) *Transnational Management: Text, Cases, and Readings in Cross Border Management.* Boston, MA: Irwin.

Benito, GRG, and Welch, LS (1994) Foreign market servicing: beyond choice of entry mode. *Journal of International Marketing*, 2 (2) 7–27.

Bloom, MC, and Milkovich, GT (1996) Issues in managerial compensation research. In CL Cooper and DM Rousseau (Eds), *Trends in Organizational Behavior*, 3, 23–47.

Bonache, J, and Fernández, Z (1997) Expatriate compensation and its link to the subsidiary strategic role: a theoretical analysis. *International Journal of Human Resource Management*, 8, 457–75.

Boudreau, M-C, Loch, KD, Robey, D, and Straud, D (1998) Going global: using information technology to advance the competitiveness of the virtual transnational organization. *Academy of Management Executive*, 12 (4) 120–28.

Buckley, PJ, and Ghauri, PN (1999) *The Internationalization of the Firm: A Reader* (2nd ed.). London: International Thomson Business Press.

Cascio, WF (2000) Managing a virtual workplace. *Academy of Management Executive*, 14 (3) 81–90.

Chadwick, WF (1995) TCM manager policy. In J Selmar (Ed.), *Expatriate Management: New Ideas for International Business*. Westport, CT: Quorum Books.

Clarke, CC, and Lip, GD (1998) Conflict resolution for contrasting cultures. *Training and Development Journal*, 52 (2) 20–33.

DeFrank, RS, Konopaske, R, and Ivancevich, JM (2000) Executive travel stress: perils of the road warrior. *Academy of Management Executive*, 14 (2) 55–71.

Dowling, PJ, and Welch, DE (1988) International human resource management: an Australian perspective. *Asia Pacific Journal of Management*, 6 (1) 39–65.

Dowling, PJ, Welch, DE, and Schuler, RS (1999) *International Human Resource Management: Managing People in a Multinational Context* (3rd ed.). Cincinnati, OH: South-Western.

Edström, A, and Galbraith, JR (1977) Transfer of managers as a coordination and control strategy in multinational organizations. *Administrative Science Quarterly*, 22 (2) 248–63.

Fenwick, M (2000) *Control and Expatriate Performance Management in Australian Multinational Enterprises.* Doctoral thesis, University of Melbourne.

Fenwick, M, and De Cieri, H (1995) Building an integrated approach to performance management using Critical Incident Technique. *Asia Pacific Journal of Human Resources*, 33 (3) 76–91.

Fenwick, MS, De Cieri, HL, and Welch, DE (1999) Cultural and bureaucratic control in MNEs: the role of expatriate performance management. *Management International Review*, 39 (3) 107–124.

Flamholtz, EG, Das, TK, and Tsui, AS (1985) Toward an integrative framework of organizational control. *Accounting, Organizations and Society*, 10 (1) 35–50.

GMAC GRS/Windham International /US National Foreign Trade Council and the SHRM Global Forum (2000) *Global Relocation Trends 2000 Survey Report.*

Graham, ME, and Trevor, CO (2000) Managing new pay program introductions to enhance the competitiveness of multinational corporations. *Competitiveness Review*, 10 (1) 136–55.

Hailey, J (1996) The expatriate myth: cross-cultural perceptions of expatriate managers. *The International Executive*, 38 (2) 255–71.

Hailey, J (1999) Localization as an ethical response for internationalization. In C Brewster and H Harris (Eds), *International Human Resource Management: Contemporary Issues in Europe*. New York: Routledge, 89–101.

Hall, E (1976) *Beyond Culture*. New York: Doubleday.

Harvey, M (1993) Developing a global compensation system: the logic and a model. *Columbia Journal of World Business,* 28, 56–72.

Harvey, M (1997) Focusing the international personnel performance appraisal process. *Human Resource Development Quarterly*, 8 (1) 41–61.

Johannessen, J-A, Olaisen, J, and Olsen, B (2001) Mismanagement of tacit knowledge: the importance of tacit knowledge, the danger of information technology, and what to do about it. *International Journal of Information Management*, 21, 3–20.

Jones, GR, and George, JM (1998) The experience and evolution of trust: implications for cooperation and teamwork. *Academy of Management Review*, 23 (3) 531–46.

Kahn, F (1997) Living in fear of frequent flying. *Financial Times*, 3 November, 14.

Kezsbom, DS (2000) Creating teamwork in virtual teams. *Cost Engineering*, 42 (10) 33–6.

Kirkman, B, and Shapiro, D (1997) The impact of cultural values on employee resistance to teams: toward a model of globalized self-managing work team effectiveness. *Academy of Management Review*, 22 (3) 730–57.

Kobrin, SJ (1988) Expatriate reduction and strategic control in American multinational corporations. *Human Resource Management*, 27 (1) 63–75.

Lahtinen, M (2000) *Language Skilled Employees in Multinationals — Implications to Communication and International Human Resource Management*. MS thesis, Helsinki School of Economics, Finland.

Lepak, DP, and Snell, SA (1998) Virtual HR: strategic human resource management in the 21st century. *Human Resource Management Review*, 8 (3) 215–34.

Lewis, P (1998) Managing performance-related pay based on evidence from the financial services sector. *Human Resource Management Journal*, 8, 66–77.

London, M, and Smither, JW (1995) Can multi-source feedback change perceptions of goal accomplishment, self-evaluations and performance related outcomes? *Personnel Psychology*, 48, 803–839.

Luostarinen, R, and Welch, L (1990) *International Business Operations*. Helsinki: Kyriiri Oy.

Marschan-Piekkari, R, Welch, D, and Welch, L (1999) Adopting a common corporate language: IHRM implications. *International Journal of Human Resource Management*, 19 (3) 377–90.

Maznevski, ML, and Chudoba, KM (2000) Bridging space over time: global virtual-team dynamics and effectiveness. *Organization Science*, 11, 473–92.

Novicevic, MM, and Harvey, MG (2001) The emergence of the pluralism construct and the inpatriation process. *International Journal of Human Resource Management*, 12 (3) 333–56.

Oliver, AL, and Liebeskind, JP (1997) Three levels of networking for sourcing intellectual capital in biotechnology: implications for studying interorganizational networks. *International Studies of Management & Organization*, 27 (4) 76–103.

Origo, I (1992) *The Merchant of Prato*, London: Penguin Books.

Oviatt, BM, and McDougall, PP (1995) Global start-ups: entrepreneurs on a worldwide stage. *Academy of Management Executive*, 9 (2) 30–43.

Picot, A (1999) Management in networked environments: new challenges. *Management International Review*, 39 (3) 19–26.

Price Waterhouse (1997) *International Assignments: European Policy and Practice*. Price Waterhouse Europe.

PricewaterhouseCoopers (2000) *Managing a Virtual World: International Non-standard Assignments, Policy and Practice, 2000*. PricewaterhouseCoopers Europe.

Reynolds, C (1997) Expatriate compensation in historical perspective. *Journal of World Business*, 32 (20) 118–32.

Roberts, K, Kossek, EE, and Ozeki, C (1998) Managing the global workforce: challenges and strategies. *Academy of Management Executive*, 12 (4) 93–106.

Rubienska, A, and Bovaird, T (1999) Performance management and organizational learning: matching process to cultures in the UK and Chinese services. *International Review of Administrative Sciences*, 65, 251–68.

Stanley, P (2001) *Trends in International Assignments*. Australian Human Resource Institute Special Interest Group in International Human Resource Management (Victoria) Seminar, Melbourne, 6 March.

Tahvanainen, M (1998) *Expatriate Performance Management*. Helsinki: Helsinki School of Economics Press.

Vance, CM, and Ring, PS (1994) Preparing the host country workforce for expatriate managers: the neglected other side of the coin. *Human Resource Development Quarterly*, 5 (4) 337–352.

Welch, DE (1994) HRM implications of globalization. *Journal of General Management*, 19 (4) 52–67.

Welch, D, and Welch, L (1994) Linking operation mode diversity and IHRM. *International Journal of Human Resource Management*, 5 (4) 911–26.

CHAPTER 24

Human resource management: the challenges of globalisation

by Beverley McNally
Open Polytechnic of New Zealand

Introduction

As firms pursue their short- and long-term goals, they are finding that success depends on a successful global presence (Ghoshal & Bartlett 1989). Winston Churchill once said: 'we are shaping the world faster than we can change ourselves and we are applying to the present the habits of the past' (Brake 2000, p. 59).

We live and work in a turbulent global economy and this new world poses radically different challenges for us. (Brake 2000, p. 59)

At the centre of these challenges is the globalisation of business. Globalisation has been defined as:

a new international system that is shaping domestic and international politics and changing the rules of trade. A dynamic and ongoing process, globalisation involves the integration of markets and nation-states enabling individuals, corporations and countries to reach the world farther, faster, deeper and cheaper. (Rosen, Digh, Singer & Phillips 2000: p. 16)

Even purely domestic businesses cannot avoid the globalisation process. The globalisation tsunami is such that the ability to work with a global focus and an understanding of the dynamics of the current business environment is becoming critical for all businesspeople. They must understand who their current *and* potential competitors (often large multinationals) are and, more important, how they can maximise the

opportunities and minimise the threats confronting them. Domestic companies must still confront the effects of the global movement of people and the challenges that result. Increasingly, domestic companies, faced with the difficulty of recruiting the required skilled, talented people from the local market, are being forced to search globally in order to fill vacancies. This trend has resulted in an increasingly diverse workforce. Even in domestic companies this is just one of the challenges arising from globalisation. The growing cognitive diversity within many organisations will lead to increased expertise, particularly global expertise, and a reduction in the tendency to strategise narrowly; it will also allow some organisations to develop a set of core competencies that are difficult for competitors to copy (Miller, Burke & Glick 1998).

Globalisation is a strategic issue whose impact is felt not only by larger companies. Small to medium businesses are not exempt from having to address the people issues resulting from globalisation. Such organisations generally employ fewer people with the knowledge, skills and abilities to enable them to make sense of the changes occurring, and this can cause stress. If the globalisation process is not handled with care, this stress may affect not only the organisation's physical and financial resources, but also its human resources. So the human resource management (HRM) role in any company, whatever its size or strategic focus, is critical (Joynt & Morton 1999).

Because of the need for a successful global presence, it is increasingly important that organisations operating in the global environment continue to improve their competitiveness. In doing so, they look to the people within these organisations, and in particular the proactive human resource (HR) development of those individuals, to give them this competitive edge. A competitive strategy is truly effective only if it is unique to a particular organisation. As brands, technology and capital became common commodities in the domestic market, firms could distinguish themselves, and thereby gain a competitive advantage, only through the uniqueness of how they managed their human resources (Reich 1991). In short, for many organisations, it is its people who have become the critical success factor that will lead to competitive advantage in the global marketplace.

In order to survive, therefore, organisations will have to ensure that their people are ready, willing and able to manage in the global environment. There is an oft-used quotation from Duerr & Roach (1973) found in many articles that deal with international human resource management (IHRM):

Virtually any type of global problem, in the final analysis, either is created by people or must be solved by people. Hence, having the right people in the right place at the right time emerges as the key to a company's successful international growth. If the firm is successful in solving that problem then it can cope with all others. (p. 43)

That this observation is so often reiterated does not make it an empty cliché. If anything, it has become more relevant today than it was when first uttered. While creating opportunities for organisations, especially in the areas of strategy, markets and operations, globalisation is also creating challenges for HR professionals — notably, how they can ensure their discipline contributes to the organisation's overall strategic objectives. What must organisations do to be competitive in this global environment? What role should HR play in building and sustaining global competitiveness? What habits do we need to break and what new approaches do we need to develop (Brake, in Joynt & Morton 1999)?

This chapter outlines several HRM challenges relating to globalisation, including the development of an IHRM discipline along with an HR system with global strategies, a strategic partnership, and the global HR specialist and global employee.

Contemporary HRM challenges of globalisation

The progressive development of the IHRM discipline

Rhinesmith (1991) believed that a company might consider itself a global organisation in terms of strategy but not of its skills, attitudes and culture. Often no one within the company will have a clear understanding of how to make globalisation work — that is, how to meet the challenges of managing people in the global environment.

In order to turn the challenges posed by globalisation into opportunities, the discipline of HRM is progressively evolving into the broader, more complex discipline of IHRM, a response to the diversity of national contexts and operations (Tung 1993).

IHRM has been defined as:

the progression of the skills and knowledge of formulating and implementing policies and practices that effectively integrate and cohere globally dispersed employees, while at the same time recognising and appreciating local differences that impact the effective utilisation of human resources. (Sparrow, Schuler & Jackson 2000, p. 44)

There is a general consensus that IHRM is far more complex than domestic HRM, and that failure to address these complexities will compromise an organisation's strategic competitiveness. However, for this to happen, it is necessary for the IHRM discipline to play a more active part in the field of human resources, especially with regard to research and the development of theory and practice within the discipline. Briscoe (1995) noted evidence (McEvoy & Buller 1992) indicating that despite the increasing pace of globalisation, the number of published articles on HRM has not increased significantly in recent years. Bird and Beechler (2000, p. 70) support this view commenting that while research output may have grown in recent years, much of this research has been limited to the area of staffing. Only a few writers have examined the role of IHRM in formulating and implementing business strategy at an international level. Even fewer have focused on its role as an enhancer and/or implementer of strategy.

Buckley (1996, p. 8) suggested that:

international business theory and research has been dominated by neoclassical (economic) theory of the firm with institutional elements.

The result is that the overall body of knowledge and practice of IHRM is more private than public. Therefore, perhaps the first challenge for the discipline of IHRM is to move out of the shadows of other management disciplines, such as economics, marketing operations and even domestic HRM, and firmly establish its own place in the sun.

Many organisations are breaking new ground with the development of IHRM functions. Wells and Rioux (2000, p. 79) assert:

Although operations, sales and marketing functions have generally made great strides in adapting to the global reality, most human resource functions are still breaking new ground in developing policies, structures and services that support globalisation.

It is critical that all aspects of IHRM meet a world standard, but, as Rhinesmith (1995, p. 36) observed, 'to become world class requires a clear understanding of what world class means for the profession'. Therein lies a problem. Given the limited research and writing available as a source of learning, determining what 'world class' really means is a challenge in itself. Pucik (1997) believed that for an organisation to enhance its global competitiveness via its human resources, the HR function itself needs to focus on developing its international competence. A key challenge is to develop HR specialists capable of operating successfully in the global environment.

Developing the global HR specialist

To understand what it means to be a world-class organisation, Rhinesmith (1995) believes the HR profession must develop a much broader view of the world within which it operates. Internationally experienced HR executives on a global development track are still relatively rare, and the development of a cadre of HR professionals with an international perspective and capabilities requires a thorough understanding of global strategy and cultural differences (Briscoe 1995). In other words, those working within the HR discipline must develop a *global mindset* if they are to become truly world-class practitioners of IHRM.

Developing the mindset

What could prevent the IHRM discipline meeting and overcoming the challenges confronting the discipline in the twenty-first century is the ability of the HR professional to develop a global mindset. Laurent (1986) stressed that the internationalisation of HR functions owes more to a *way of thinking* or mindset than to behaviour. To become global managers with *geocentric* mindsets, HR professionals must develop a blend of knowledge, skills and abilities.

Thinking globally means extending the imagination from one-to-one models and relationships to multiple, simultaneous realities and relationships, and then acting skilfully in this more complex reality (Lane, DiStefano & Maznevski 1997). This broader view of the world is crucial

if the HR professional is to be proactive in encouraging the development of a global mindset in others. Furthermore, a global mentality may also be required further down the organisation. The manager initiating change must understand the reasons for change and appreciate that global competition is changing the rules of the game to such an extent that no one remains unaffected (Hedlund 1995).

Each manager needs a global mindset to understand the organisation's interdependence in the global economy. However, this mindset cannot exist in isolation. The condition that sustains a global mindset is the interrelation between this mindset and the manager's knowledge and skills (see figure 24.1) (Kedia & Mukherji 1999).

Figure 24.1: The global mindset as the root of all activities.
Source: Adapted from Kedia and Mukherji (1999), 235.

Even when the firm's activities are ostensibly confined to the domestic environment, a manager needs knowledge of different aspects of the interdependent global world. This is still more critical for HR professionals, since they are often first in an organisation to encounter the ramifications of globalisation (Rhinesmith 1993, p. 24).

This kind of knowledge is difficult to achieve in the short term. The HR discipline needs to adopt a longer-term perspective with a view to developing a geocentric mindset early within all HR professionals.

Developing a strategic partnership

HR policies must be integrated into the business strategy, growing from it and contributing to it (Storey 1995). In order to meet its strategic business needs, the company must achieve its people-related global needs. This correlation indicates that HR professionals and HR systems need to be strategically focused (Carrell, Elbert & Hatfield 2000).

If we are to see people as the organisation's most important asset rather than, as so often happens, a significant cost, then HR's role becomes one of proactively developing policies and practices that add value to the organisation's activities at all levels.

Many HR professionals today do not address the impact of globalisation proactively because they are not as involved in all aspects of the business strategy as they should be (Rothwell 1999). There is a perception that the HR role is marginalised, making it difficult for HR managers to take their place at the executive table (Brake 2000). Even when executives value the firm's people, they may not value the HR department. In some instances, the HR department is seen as redundant to the organisation's needs (Carrell et al. 2000) — that is, HR is perceived as an obstructer to rather than an enabler of the achievement of the organisation's strategic goals.

The HR professional should not merely be brought in to fix problems when they occur (Anfuso 1995). HR must be involved from the first hint of global activities or influences. This will be more difficult for some organisations than for others, depending on their level of centralisation. When a company goes global, it is an opportunity for HR to become involved at a strategic level. HR can influence how successfully the company will operate in the global environment. For example, the HR professional might investigate the cultural climate of the countries with which the firm will be working. Appropriate IHRM policies and practices could then be developed to ensure that the manner in which the company operates is culturally sensitive.

The management of human resources must develop beyond its traditional operational, employee relations and cost-cutting modes. Carrell et al. (2000, p. 8) argued:

How to avoid extinction and earn a place at the table as a strategic partner is one of the more important issues facing HR professionals today.

HR practitioners must position themselves as part of the executive team and become highly valued strategic partners, especially if they are operating in a global environment. The HR manager will take his or her place at the executive table by becoming a strategic partner, connecting in radically new ways and undertaking activities that truly add value to the business. More important, the factor most likely to propel businesses and the HR professional into the future is the ability to unleash the minds and creativity of the workforce (Losey 1998; Brake 2000). Such a factor should not be seen as simply an exercise in empowerment but taken in a broader context of innovation.

Developing the global employee

Deploying skills, disseminating information and identifying talent have long been basic HR challenges. In the global environment, as Roberts et al. (1998) observed, these issues are overlaid by the complexities of distance, language and cultural difference. The HR challenges in a global organisation, then, become recruitment, selection, training and succession planning on a global scale (Rhinesmith 1991).

International organisations need people who can think, lead and act (Kim 1999). Equally, a global mindset is required by all staff within the organisation.

A number of international writers (Friedman 1998; Laabs 1991, 1996; Pasher 1996; Ioannou 1994; Scullion 1992) have highlighted the growing shortage of experienced executives able to lead in the new corporate environment. Global success or failure in the future could hinge on the ability to attract and retain competent managers. This talent shortage applies not only to executives able to manage in a domestic environment but also, more importantly, to those qualified to operate in a global environment. Whatever form organisations take in the future they will always need skilled, competent people.

The growing complexity of the business environment suggests that, rather than branding, economies of scale or even capital, talented people at all levels could ultimately become the key strength of an organisation. Talented people will be the factor most likely to distinguish the top-performing companies from the mediocre.

In some industry sectors HR practitioners believe that organisations do not need to develop their own global staff — that they will be able to recruit leaders from outside their organisations (McNally & Parry 2000a). This is a naïve view. Organisations are increasingly competing with the rest of the world for staff; no longer can they be confident of sourcing suitable talent locally, let alone globally. There is no evidence to suggest that there will be sufficient talent available to staff the organisations of the twenty-first century; if anything, the opposite appears to be true.

An ongoing challenge for HR professionals is the development of a global corporate culture that aligns with and supports the global strategy and structure (Carrell et al. 2000). This objective may seem like something of a tall order; however, some organisations are discovering that if they focus on global HR strategies and begin the process early, they can build the competence in their core people that is required for competitive success. The first stage in developing the competencies in working across cultures is awareness. Organisations need to develop people who are adept at exchanging ideas, knowledge and processes across borders (Carrell et al. 2000). Without an awareness of the differences between cultures, we tend to measure others against our own cultural standards (Hall 1995).

There is no point in pretending that operating in this new environment is going to be easy. For organisations to operate effectively in the global environment, HR practitioners must be proactive, leading the changes that will enable this to happen.

What should corporations do to develop people with the skills to implement global strategies? How can they take an integrated approach to globalisation that allows a global strategy and structure to be supported by a global corporate culture and a globally skilled workforce (Rhinesmith 1995)? Strategic human resources are the primary means by which corporate culture is built, strategies are formulated and implemented, integrated with and adapted to corporate objectives. HRM must be:

• fully integrated with the strategy and strategic needs of the firm
• coherent across areas and across hierarchies
• adjusted, accepted and used by line managers and employees in their everyday work (Schuler 1992).

Developing the global HR system

If the HR role in any organisation is critical, then having a system that supports the HR professional is a fundamental necessity, particularly in an organisation that is actively involved in the global environment. Having the right people in the right place at the right time is the key to an organisation's success. Even if the external environment supports a global strategy, without the internal competence needed, the organisation is destined to fail. The structure and approach of the HR function is a critical factor in developing this internal competence. The HR manager must establish the core principles and values by which the business operates. By establishing the core and non-core principles, they will begin to understand what can be adapted, where compromises may be made, and how to utilise flexibility and creativity to meet people's needs in any situation (Joynt & Martin 2000).

Adler and Bartholomew (1992) propose three key components for a successful transnational HR system: scope, representation and process.

Transnational scope

Transnational scope refers to the geographic context within which all major decisions are made. To achieve global scope, executives and managers must frame major decisions and

evaluate options in the context of worldwide business dynamics. Moreover, they must benchmark their own and their firm's performance against world-class standards.

Transnational representation

To achieve *transnational representation*, the firm's portfolio of key executives and managers should be as multinational as its worldwide distribution of production, finance, sales and profits.

Transnational process

Transnational process reflects the firm's ability to include representatives and ideas from many cultures in its planning and decision making. Firms create transnational process when they consistently recognise, value and effectively use cultural diversity within the organisation. This is achieved by a genuine belief in cross-cultural learning (Adler & Bartholomew 1992).

Roberts, Kossek and Ozeki (1998) found that executives' vision of the ideal labour market had three broad features:

• deployment
• disseminating knowledge and innovation
• identifying talent on a global scale.

To be successful, any HR system must incorporate and deal with these three processes.

Deployment

The HR challenge is to develop alternative ways to get the right people to the right place when they are needed. New technologies, new markets and new talent require that the best human resources be available anywhere in the world at any time. Often talent will be found in the most unlikely places.

For example, one New Zealand organisation has utilised the skills of people nearing the end of their career to enable it to grow as a multinational. The company recognised that a number of its talented staff, who were a driving force behind the reorganisation resulting from deregulation of the New Zealand business environment in the early 1980s, did not necessarily have the knowledge, skills and abilities required in the twenty-first century. However, their experience and their passion for the industry sector within which they operated made them uniquely suited to undertake the reorganisation of similar business systems in countries such as South Africa, Uzbekistan, Jamaica and Zimbabwe. Furthermore, they had reached a stage in their lives at which their children had left home and the responsibilities (e.g. the children's education) that might have constrained their undertaking a global assignment in the past were no longer a factor.

Disseminating knowledge

Global organisations require structures in which all units concurrently receive and provide information, spreading state-of-the-art knowledge and practices throughout the organisation, regardless of where they originate (Roberts et al. 1998, p. 95). New technology has made it possible for all companies to disseminate knowledge proactively, and even to maintain contact with staff on leave or in remote parts of the world. One General Manager, Human Resources, reported:

> I pay for their Internet link and I talk to them — we have created chat rooms for people to talk to each other despite being separated geographically. I send them our job net — we've got a job news bulletin that goes right across the company, and jobs are arrayed in there, so I send them updates. I send them information. We have people in different countries that are contact points, so these people are on retainers as contacts.

Whether staff are in Bolivia or England, she pointed out, the use of technology plays a vital role in ensuring knowledge and ideas are transferred freely and quickly.

Identifying and developing talent

Not everyone will thrive in a global environment, so identifying who has the ability to function effectively in a global organisation is a critical function of the HR system. Managing a global labour force is about identifying who will best grasp the complexities of the transnational operations and then function well in that sort of environment (Roberts et al. 1998, p. 95). The global movement is such that New Zealand and Australian companies may not be able to source international workers from traditional sources. Rather, every employee will require some form of global awareness, so the organisation must start sourcing this competency at the recruitment and selection stage. For example, Tetra Pak International, a Swedish multinational, looks for international potential every time it recruits. Expatriates are selected from within the company, which is interested in people who could eventually relocate internationally and cope with that adjustment well (Talbott 1996).

When Nordson made the strategic decision to enter the Japanese market, its HR policies were already in place. For two years the company scoured the world for young people with Japanese language ability and cultural awareness — and a good game of customer golf. These recruits were then trained and managed by the corporation to ensure that their performance and goals matched the firm's business needs (Solomon 1994).

Global HR strategies

Having staff with a high level of global awareness is one of the key strategic goals of any organisation's HR development strategies. Much has been made of organisations' need for competent mobile managers with an open disposition, high adaptability to different conditions in their various assignments and a constant readiness to be transferred from one country to another (Phatak 1987). Such staff may not be easy to find in the short term, but every organisation must start somewhere, and HR practitioners must take a longer view if all staff are to develop the desired global mindset.

Strategies for achieving this global awareness in organisations include:
- classifying managers according to their mobility
- keeping an inventory of global skills and talent
- regularly assessing the skills gap
- identifying leadership capital
- retaining talent
- adopting repatriation programs
- capitalising on OE
- adopting career development measures.

Each of these strategies is now dealt with in turn.

Classifying managers according to their mobility

If companies classify managers according to a mobility pyramid such as that shown in figure 24.2, an HR department can look beyond the traditional 'movable' or 'non-movable' categories to develop a broader view of international placement (Quelch & Bloom 1999). This sort of classification allows the evaluation of managers in terms of their willingness to move as well as their knowledge, skills and abilities.

Using the mobility pyramid in conjunction with a global skills inventory database may encourage a more open attitude to international placement. In particular, it should encourage HR managers to be more proactive in encouraging international placements, allowing a wider group of employees to obtain experience in the global business environment.

Figure 24.2: Mobility pyramid for global managers *Source:* Adapted from Quelch and Bloom (1999).

Keeping an inventory of global skills and talent

An important tool of transnational HR policy in countries such as New Zealand and Australia is the development of a *skills inventory database*. New Zealand is a small, geographically isolated country that is often far removed from a company's head office. Although Australia is much larger, with a larger population, it can often still be far removed from head office. The skills inventory database identifies those employees with the skills, or skill potential, necessary to succeed in the global environment.

Frequently, this type of database focuses on the top levels of management within an organisation. However, a database is needed that also identifies middle managers and potential stars further down the organisation hierarchy. Such an inventory would include individuals previously neglected because they were far removed from head office, or those whose skills, overseas experience or foreign language ability was recognised within their own area but unknown to a wider audience. Sophisticated technological systems, which have replaced the cumbersome paper-based systems of the past, make such a strategy viable.

Regularly assessing the skills gap

Organisations using a skills inventory database should conduct ongoing analysis of the skills of the company in order to identify skill gaps. Once identified, current competencies should be used as a baseline; the company should then be able to identify skills that it requires over and above the baseline. Ongoing assessment and planning will help identify knowledge, skills and abilities that should be addressed in personal development programs in order to close the identified gaps.

Identifying leadership capital

Gregersen et al. (1998, p. 26) noted that, to succeed, global business leaders need superior talent, abundant opportunity, and excellent education and training. Companies need to assess whether they are hiring enough young managers with the required base level of leadership talent to ensure that, given normal turnover, they will have the future global leaders they need. Peter Drucker

(1993, 1996) has developed a view of leadership in the twenty-first century that encourages the conversion of knowledge within the organisation into productive acts. It is important that organisations identify early the leadership capital they possess if they are to use this capital productively.

Once companies have successfully identified their leadership capital, they can formulate strategies to develop the knowledge, skills and abilities required. It takes many years to develop individuals with potential into successful leaders. Corporations that do an above-average job of developing leadership potential put an emphasis on creating challenging opportunities for relatively young employees (Kotter 1990). Graduate recruitment programs can be used to ensure that the knowledge, skills and abilities required in the future will be available. Graduates with foreign language ability should be encouraged, and the use of international secondments would help to broaden the outlook of these young people.

It is important for IHRM specialists to adopt strategies that expose potential leaders to unfamiliar situations, risk and challenge, particularly in the international arena. Failure could cost the firm significantly more than the cost of any development programs. Black and Gregersen (1991) estimated that expatriate failure rates among US companies sometimes reached 80 per cent. The direct costs of such failures range between US$50 000 and US$250 000 per case (Adler 1997; Guzzo & Noonan 1992).

Retaining talent

Retaining competent managers and leaders in the context of intensifying international competition will present the next major challenge for transnational firms. Competent managers able to operate in the global environment will be highly sought after. Executive retention reduces turnover, recruitment and opportunity costs. If long-term strategies are not put in place to minimise them, companies in countries such as New Zealand and Australia could face significant increases in these costs in the future. World-class performance incentives, rewards and career opportunities are crucial if companies are to retain top performers within the industry. Overseas assignments, cross-border project teams and horizontal promotions are excellent ways to meet the challenges identified as critical by Kotter (1990) and could assist in the retention of superior talent. As well, companies should seek to promote features of the resident country and region such as lifestyle and schooling as an added incentive for retention.

Adapting repatriation programs

Repatriation is one of the most neglected areas of international HRM. Black and Gregersen (1999) reported that between 10 and 20 per cent of all US managers sent overseas returned early because of job dissatisfaction or difficulties in adjusting to a foreign country. More problematically, the study found that a quarter of those who completed an assignment left their company, often to join a competitor, within one year of returning. The principal goals of international assignments — the generation of knowledge and the development of international managers — will not be achieved if managers leave the company when they return home.

Proactive induction programs are critical if managers sent to New Zealand and Australia on secondment are to maximise their development potential. These programs should focus on the New Zealand and Australian *way of life* and, in particular, the idiosyncrasies of the two countries' management styles and how these differ from those in Europe or the US. It would be useful to address the differences between New Zealand and Australian management styles to dispose of some of the myths that the two countries are one and the same.

New Zealand and Australia could lead the world in the development of innovative induction and orientation programs for those arriving 'down under'. These programs will target not only people arriving from head offices around the world (*inpatriates*) but also expatriate employees coming home and young people returning from their overseas experience. Failure to manage induction and repatriation effectively risks reinforcing the perception within the organisation that an international assignment is a high-risk strategy rather than a career advantage (Welch 1994). Furthermore, if not dealt with fully and effectively, this area could be the weak link in an otherwise strong HR strategy.

Overseas experience (OE) versus expatriate assignment (EA)

One uniquely Australasian method of encouraging global awareness is the tradition of OE — that is, young people travelling abroad to gain some overseas experience — an area not covered in the literature emanating from Europe or the United States. Here the initiative for the international experience comes from the individual. Typically she or he will save money to bankroll the trip, will resign from work, or take time out from university, and set off overseas for a few months or longer. The expatriate assignment (or EA), on the other hand, is most often the initiative of an international company that decides the destination and funds the trip (Inkson, Pringle, Arthur & Barry 1997).

Inkson et al. (1997) examined differences between expatriate assignment and overseas experience as sources of international experience (see table 24.1). The relative importance of EA and OE varies across countries. This study took place in New Zealand, where OE has a long tradition and where multinational head offices, and therefore opportunities for EA, are more limited. Inkson et al. argued that OE offers greater flexibility to leverage the career development of the individuals involved, the competencies of specific companies and the human resources of the countries through which they move.

Table 24.1: Contrasting qualities of expatriate assignment (EA) and overseas experience (OE)

	Expatriate assignment (EA)	*Overseas experience (OE)*
Initiation	Company	Individual
Goals	Company projects (specific)	Individual development (diffuse)
Funding	Company salary and expenses	Personal saving and casual earnings
Career type	Organisational career	Boundaryless career
Research literature	Large	Nil

Source: Inkson, Pringle, Arthur and Barry (1997), 352.

Characteristics of OE

Cultural experience as important as work

Geographical mobility

Curiosity-driven

Personal learning agendas

Individual is self-supporting

Weak company attachments

Figure 24.3: Characteristics of overseas experience (OE)
Source: Inkson, Pringle, Arthur and Barry (1997), 358.

A sample of tertiary-educated New Zealand women in mid life who had undertaken OE earlier in their lives were interviewed regarding the impact of OE on their lives. Most reflected on the importance of their broadened perspectives and knowledge, their increased awareness and appreciation of cultural differences, and the confidence and independence built (Park 1995, p. 127).

Figure 24.4 outlines some of the common themes in OE stories. These themes consistently fit with the espoused knowledge, skills and abilities required of managers operating in the global environment. For example, increased interest in self-employment could be an indicator of a willingness to try new things, experiment and take risks. As careers change and as the economy becomes increasingly global, the benefits of OE may be widely recognised in cultivating global managers. It is important that the basic success factor of OE as outlined by the Inkson study is not ignored.

In OE it is the freedom from fixed purpose or formula, the implicit invitation to 'broaden oneself', the release of the human spirit to determine its own learning, which give it its potential as a major source of learning for both those who undertake it, and the companies which subsequently employ them. (Inkson 1997, p. 366)

Common themes in OE stories

Self-directed experimentation

Self-designed apprenticeships

Cast off negative past legacies

Find occupational/industry identity

Develop confidence and self-reliance

Return with clearer career focus

Increased interest in self-employment

Figure 24.4: Common themes in OE stories *Source:* Inkson, Pringle, Arthur and Barry (1997), 364.

Rather than seeing the departure of graduates after two years as a negative, as happens so often in New Zealand (McNally 1999), organisations should be encouraging this independence and broadening of perspective. Organisations should be asking: What will attract these young people back to the company when they have finished seeing the world? The key to success will be the ability of the company to look

outside the conventional HRM frameworks and package itself as an attractive option to return to. This may involve:
- paying the return airfare of the traveller
- arranging an international career placement following the OE
- revamping the notion of 'career'.

Career development

Organisations need to re-examine their attitudes towards career development and take a proactive approach to using the notion of career as a strategic HR tool. The prevailing view that it is for the individual to manage his or her own career is not a reason for organisations to opt out totally from career development programs. This is not to advocate a return to the paternalistic attitudes of the past (with the individual dependent on the company for career and career progression), but neither should career management be designed only to manage people out of the business. Career development takes place across a spectrum — from self-assessment to organisational succession planning (see figure 24.5). It is important to recognise that career planning and career management can be complementary activities, providing a win–win situation for all parties.

Succession planning does not have to be the identification of a need to identify, not the individual, but rather the core knowledge, skills and abilities required in the future, so that when a person leaves the firm, a plan exists to ensure the appropriate skills are available in the future. The individual also gains transferable knowledge, skills and abilities.

Organisations cannot assume that, in taking responsibility for their own careers, individuals are always aware of the options available to them. Environmental changes are occurring with such rapidity, and people are working under such pressure, that individuals frequently find it difficult to envision the key knowledge, skills and abilities that will be required in the future.

Training and development

In speaking of *transnational scope*, Adler and Bartholomew (1992) recognise that all experiences throughout people's working lives may help prepare them to work anywhere in the world. These experiences include formal, on-the-job and informal training and even off-the-job experiences. Truly global developmental programs may be difficult to plan, given budgetary and other constraints. It is critical that companies begin to develop this global outlook early in an individual's career, since this will help overcome some of the barriers imposed, for example, by family commitments and dual careers that often occur later in the individual's career. International training and development take much longer than the few days allotted to most training programs; becoming proficient in a second language, for example, can take a number of years. However, if a broad international understanding is to be achieved at all levels within the organisation, then more intensive development activities are critical.

Language can also be used as a competitive weapon. While English may be the language of international business, the ability to communicate in the language of the country of operation gives the multinational a competitive advantage over firms without this ability. Because language serves as a window to the culture of a society, many international business experts believe that even a modest level of language training gives clues about cultural norms and attitudes that may prove helpful in doing business.

Development programs specifically designed to maintain a strong talent pool for the industry in the future are essential if New Zealand and Australian organisations are to take their place on the world stage. Examples of development activities that could be used to ensure a depth of experience include:
- Job assignments, lateral promotion, special projects and the use of international assignment as a mandatory part of early experience. International experience must be

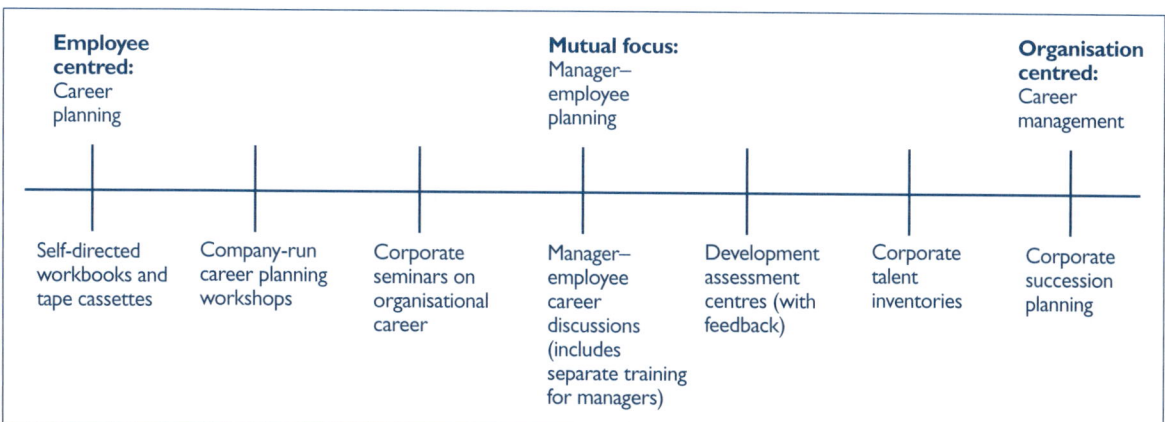

Employee centred: Career planning			Mutual focus: Manager–employee planning			Organisation centred: Career management
Self-directed workbooks and tape cassettes	Company-run career planning workshops	Corporate seminars on organisational career	Manager–employee career discussions (includes separate training for managers)	Development assessment centres (with feedback)	Corporate talent inventories	Corporate succession planning

Figure 24.5: Spectrum of career development activities *Source:* Adapted from Hall (1986).

obtained as early as possible. Family considerations, such as children's education or a partner's career, strongly influence people's willingness to move freely internationally (Adler & Bartholomew 1992; McNally & Parry 2000b; Rhinesmith 1995), which reinforces the importance of instilling the required knowledge, skills and abilities early in a person's career. Early exposure to international experience and opportunities can also break down some of the misconceptions that produce resistance towards facilities and international opportunities.

- Active support of the spouse in dual-career families. Truly transnational companies are finding opportunities for the spouse that will ensure his or her career progression and development, too.
- Language skills and cross-cultural awareness training should be included in all development programs.
- Task force or committee assignments with a global focus.
- Mentoring or coaching from senior executives.
- Attendance at meetings outside the firm and outside the person's core responsibility.
- Special projects. United Parcel Service (UPS), for example, conducts a Community Internship Program in which managers are sent on month-long sabbatical to work on community aid programs. UPS believe this not only helps the communities but also helps the managers to broaden their perspectives and become better supervisors.
- Assigning special development roles — for example, as executive assistants working with senior managers, especially those working and travelling internationally.

Realignment of recruitment and selection strategies

The level of sophistication in international recruitment is still relatively low (Sparrow 2000). Realigning an organisation's recruitment and selection strategies is one area that can make a crucial difference to global competency. Most companies will realign recruitment strategies after reassessment of job evaluations and job descriptions. Recruitment methods also need to change — for example, the increasing use of Internet recruitment has broadened the pool of potential recruits.

The knowledge, skills and abilities and competencies required for various roles also need to be re-evaluated. Candidates for recruitment will be assessed on their potential for working globally. They should possess qualities such as:
- flexibility
- high levels of proven interpersonal skills
- multiple language ability, especially in international languages

- completed overseas experience (OE) or similar international experience
- a demonstrated willingness to take risks.

Companies can ill afford selection systems that provide skills and experience that were appropriate 10 years ago, or even today. Sparrow (2000) argued that selection criteria are shifting, albeit slowly from being based on technical and intelligence criteria to favouring a wider range of skills and personality traits that are essential for the flexible manager. They must secure people with the potential and skills needed for the future. Ensuring that global awareness is built into the process will help to create a base from which the *geocentric mindset* can develop. Setting up selection systems that are free from bias and that take into account the new sets of knowledge, skills, abilities and competencies needed, is essential for the development of a pool of talented individuals capable of operating in the new global world.

Conclusion

The development of global capabilities will depend greatly on an organisation's approach to international human resource management.

The numerous challenges include:
- rapid growth
- issues of culture and diversity
- new technology
- globalisation
- competitive pressures.

Given these rapid changes, managers may have to struggle to keep up with the new skills required of them.

As the globalisation process continues unabated, the challenge for business is to fundamentally change the way in which people understand doing business in this environment. It is no longer about taking frequent short business trips, attending conferences or meeting people from other cultures at company headquarters. It is about developing a *geocentric mindset* which requires a global perspective. It is about being comfortable doing business in a country with a different culture, and on that country's terms. There is no reason why a manager from New Zealand or Australia should not have the knowledge, skills and ability to lead their organisation at a transnational level, should they choose that career option.

The traditional business mould has been broken, and it is unlikely to be repaired in a form that is easily recognisable today. The challenge facing all companies in the current business environment will be to recruit, select, train, develop and retain managers who know how to manage in the global environment.

Creating an organisation that adds value for customers will form the basis of the competitive battleground for many organisations in the next decade. You will need to match your competitor's products, prices and services. You will also have to match their ability to create organisations with the capabilities necessary to win (Kerr & Ulrich 1995).

People create revenue. Only by looking past the rhetoric of cost reduction will organisations be able to position their talent pool strategically in order to maximise their potential. By creating revenue, people will help to ensure the continuing profitability of their organisation.

To summarise:

Globalisation is a reality.

- For continuing success, managers and leaders will have to be more transnational in their focus.
- Human resources must be proactive in making this happen.

References

Adler, NJ (1997) *International Dimensions of Organisational Behaviour*. Cincinnati, OH: South Western Publishing.

Adler, NJ, and Bartholomew, S (1992) Managing globally competent people. *Academy of Management Executive*, August, 6 (3) 52–65.

Bartlett, CA, and Ghoshal, S (1992) What is a global manager? *Harvard Business Review*, 70 (5) 124–32.

Brake, T (1999) The HR manager as a global business partner. In P Joynt and B Morton (Eds) (1999), *The Global HR Manager: Creating the Seamless Organisation*. London: The Institute of Personnel and Development.

Briscoe, DR (1995) *International Human Resource Management*. Englewood Cliffs, NJ: Prentice Hall.

Buckley, PJ (1996) The role of management in international business theory: a meta-analysis and integration of the literature on international business and international management. *Management International Review*, 36 (1) 7–54.

Drucker, P (1993) Tomorrow's manager. *Success*, October, 40 (8) 80.

Drucker, P (1996) Leaders are doers, *Executive Excellence*, April, 13 (4) 8.

Duerr, M, and Roach, JM (1973) *Organisation and Control of International Operations*. New York: The Conference Board.

Carrell, MR, Elbert, NF, and Hatfield, RD (2000) *Human Resource Management: Strategies for Managing a Diverse Global Workforce*. Orlando, GA: The Dryden Press.

Friedman, S (1998) Management talent battle heating up. *National Underwriter*, August, 102 (31) 42–3.

Guzzo, RA, and Noonan, KA (1992) International assignments require more personal and family support than what is being provided now. *SHRM/CCH Survey*. Chicago, IL: The Commerce Clearing House.

Hall, DT (1986) *An Overview of Current Career Development Theory, Research and Practice*. San Francisco: Jossey-Bass.

Hedlund, G (1995) The hypermodern MNC — a heterarchy? In PN Ghauri and SB Prasad (1995) *International Management: A Reader*. London: The Dryden Press.

Inkson, K, Pringle, J, Arthur, M, and Barry, S (1997) Expatriate assignment versus overseas experience: contrasting models of international human resource development. *Journal of World Business*, Winter, 32 (4) 351–68.

Ioannou, L (1994) Catching global managers. *International Business*, March, 7 (3) 60–6.

Joynt, P, and Morton, B (Eds) (1999) *The Global HR Manager: Creating the Seamless Organisation*. London: Institute of Personnel and Development.

Kedia, B, and Mukherji, A (1999) Global managers: developing a mindset for global competitiveness. *Journal of World Business*, 34 (3) 230–51.

Kerr, S, and Ulrich, D (1995) Creating the boundaryless organisation: the radical reconstruction of organisation capabilities. *Planning Review*, 23 (5) 41.

Kim, PS (1999) Globalisation of human resource management: a cross-cultural perspective for the public sector. *Public Personnel Management*, Summer, 28 (2) 197–215.

Laabs, J (1991) The global talent search. *Personnel Journal*, August, 70 (8) 38–44.

Laabs, J (1993) Building a global management team. *Personnel Journal*, August, 72 (8) 75.

Lane, HW, DiStefano, JJ, and Maznevski, ML (1997) *International Management Behaviour* (3rd ed.). Cambridge: Blackwell.

Laurent, A (1986) The cross-cultural puzzle of international human resource management. *Human Resource Management*, Spring, 25 (1) 91–103.

Losey, M (1998) HR comes of age. *HR Magazine* (SHRM 50th Anniversary), 40–53.

McEvoy, GM, and Buller, PF (1992) International human resource management publications: even in the eighties and needs for the nineties. Paper presented at the Western Academy of Management International Conference, Lueven, Belgium, June, 21–4.

McNally, BA (1999) Tomorrow's managers: preparing managers in the New Zealand finance sector for the global environment. Unpublished Master's in Business Administration Dissertation, Henley Business College, Henley, UK.

McNally, BA, and Parry, KW (2000a) The phenomenon of systemic future talent shortage: a challenge for the competitive advantage of the finance industry in New Zealand. Australia and New Zealand Academy of Management (ANZAM) Annual Conference, Sydney, 3–6 December.

McNally, BA, and Parry, K (2000b) Global managers? Meeting the transnational challenge: an investigation into the development of transnational competencies in the New Zealand finance sector. *Asia Pacific Journal of Human Resources*, 38 (1) 84–101.

Miller, C, Burke, L, and Glick, W (1998) Cognitive diversity among upper-echelon executives: implications for strategic decision processes. *Strategic Management Journal*, 19, 39–58.

Pasher, VS (1996) Global skills lacking expert warns. *National Underwriter*, 25 November, 13 (33) 13–15.

Phatak, AV (1989). *International dimensions of management*, 2nd ed. Boston: PWS-Kent Publishing.

—— (1992) *International dimensions of management*, 3rd ed. Boston: PWS-Kent Publishing.

Park, J, Pringle, JK, and Tangri, S (1995) *New Zealand Women's Life Paths Study*. Working Paper, Departments of Anthropology and Management and Employment Relations, University of Auckland.

Pucik, V (1997) Human resources in the future: an obstacle or champion of globalisation. *Human Resource Management*, Spring, 38 (1) 163–8.

Quelch, JA, and Bloom, H (1999) Ten steps to a global human resource strategy. *Strategy & Business*, 14 (1) 18–29.

Reich, R (1991) *The work of nations: preparing ourselves for 21st century capitalism.* New York: Knopf.

Rhinesmith, SH (1991) An agenda for globalisation. *Training and Development Journal*, 45 (2) 22–30.

Rhinesmith, SH (1995) Open the door to a global mindset. *Training and Development Journal*, March, 49 (5) 35–43.

Roberts, K, Kossek, E, and Ozeki, C (1998) Managing the global workforce: challenges and strategies. *Academy of Management Executive*, 12 (4) 93–107.

Rosen, R, Digh, P, Singer, M, and Phillips, C (2000) *Global literacies: lessons on business leadership and national cultures.* New York: Simon & Schuster.

Rothwell, WJ (1999) Transforming HR into a global powerhouse. *HR Focus*, March, 7–9.

Schuler, RS (1992) Strategic human resources management: linking the people with the strategic needs of the business. *Organisational Dynamics*, Summer, 21 (1). As contained in *Human Resource Issues Course Readings*, University of Southern Queensland.

Scullion, H (1992) Attracting management globetrotters. *Personnel Management*, January, 24 (1) 28–35.

Sparrow, P (2000) International recruitment selection and assessment. In P Joynt and B Morton (Eds) (1999), *The Global HR Manager: Creating the Seamless Organisation.* London: The Institute of Personnel and Development.

Sparrow, P, Schuler, RS, and Jackson, SE (2000) Convergence or divergence: human resource practices and policies for competitive advantage worldwide. In M Mendenhall and G Oddou (Eds) (2000), *Readings and cases in international human resource management.* Cincinnati, OH: South Western College Publishing.

Stone, RJ (1998) *Human resource management*, 3rd ed. Brisbane: John Wiley & Sons.

Storey, J (Ed.) (1995) What is human resource management? *Human resource management*. London: Routledge.

Talbott, SP (1996) Building a global workforce begins with recruitment. *Personnel Journal* (recruitment staffing sourcebook supplement), March, 9–12.

Tung, RL (1993) Managing cross-national and intranational diversity. *Human Resource Management*, 32 (4) 461–77.

Welch, D (1994) HRM implications of globalisation. In *Journal of General Management*, Summer, 19 (4), as reprinted in R Stone (1998), *Readings in Human Resource Management*. Brisbane: John Wiley & Sons.

Wellins, R, and Rioux, S (2001) Solving the global HR puzzle. *Workspan*, February, 44 (2) 26–9.

CHAPTER 25

Company change and human resources: in pursuit of flexibility?

by Patrick Dawson
University of Aberdeen

Introduction

Flexibility is a key business concept in the twenty-first century. For example, companies need to rapidly adjust to changes in the business environment, staff must learn new skills or shift into new areas of operation, and households must juggle the competing demands of work and family life. In practice, the work–family balance demanded by flexible working arrangements may be far from the ideal suggested by the 'how to' recipes for managing change that promise employee harmony and collaboration.

In this chapter we examine change management and, in particular, the growing pressure for employees to accommodate flexible work practices and job arrangements. As we shall see, although it is not uncommon for change models to recognise the importance of gaining the support of employees, the view from the shop floor or in the branch office reflects a growing weariness and cynicism in the face of what appears to be an endless barrage of change initiatives to extract ever more from a dwindling pool of employees.

In critically evaluating some of these issues, the chapter begins by examining the main reasons why companies embark on change initiatives. First, a number of definitional concerns are discussed and some key dimensions are identified. Next, attention is directed towards change strategies — such as employee participation, communication and building collaborative relations at work — that seek labour flexibility and yet stress the importance of the human dimension. The push towards flexible working arrangements is then critically appraised and the benefits to employees of such changes are evaluated. The notion of employee resistance to change is addressed and a range of reasons why people are often unwilling to accept change are specified. Change theories that emphasise the importance of communication and employee involvement are outlined and the planned organisational development approach to change is critically assessed.

The chapter concludes by charting the benefits of a processual approach that is able to draw attention to the lived experience of change and unmask the rhetoric behind many of the change initiatives associated with the 'culture-excellence' school (see Burnes 2000). Taken as a whole, this chapter questions traditional change models and modern change initiatives that advocate a human-centred approach, for while they support strategies that supposedly promote flexibility and empowerment, these initiatives actually result in increased workloads and greater pressure on employees to conform to new, imposed behaviours.

Reasons for embarking on company change initiatives

There are many reasons why companies embark on change initiatives. Within the business media, it is not uncommon to hear of the need to introduce change in order to remain competitive, or indeed to survive. The perceived need to rapidly adapt to changing market conditions has led to the development of human resource (HR) strategies that promote labour flexibility. In practice, however, these new work arrangements may not benefit all parties, as was illustrated when Vauxhall laid off 2200 flexible workers in response to market-driven change (Spence 2001). Similarly, although employees at Corus's steel plants in Wales had achieved productivity improvements under new flexible arrangements, the company still announced 6000 redundancies in January 2001 (Gow, Bannister, Wintour & Black 2001). Even after change has been accepted and new working arrangements agreed to by employees, senior management may still decide to switch production to plants elsewhere. Corus, for example, argued that an overvalued pound meant that more profitable output could be achieved from their Dutch operations.

Such experiences at the very least tend to dampen employee enthusiasm for change, and yet employees increasingly find themselves in these uncertain circumstances. As we shall see, it is naïve to expect employees to be willing enthusiasts of change strategies that weaken their labour market position. But first, what are the major drivers for change?

In the examples above, management strategy, the development of more flexible work arrangements, and the external pressure on costs and profitability as a result of fluctuating exchange rates may all be identified as triggers to change. Within the literature the main external drivers for change are seen to include:

- government laws and regulations (for example, legislation on age discrimination, world agreements and national policies on pollution and the environment, and international agreements on tariffs and trade)
- globalisation of markets and the internationalisation of business (the need to accommodate new competitive pressures both on the home market and overseas)
- major political and social events (for example, some of the changing relationships and tensions between the United States and countries in the Middle East, and Australia and its Asian neighbours)
- advances in technology (for example, companies who specialise in high-technology products are often prone to the problem of technological obsolescence and the need to introduce new technology)
- organisational growth (resulting in increased complexity of the organisation, which requires the development of appropriate coordinating mechanisms)
- fluctuations in business cycles (for example, changes in the level of economic activity both within national economies and within major trading blocks can significantly influence change strategies).

In examining internal reasons for company change, the management literature has identified four broad areas:

- technology
- primary task
- people
- administrative structures (Leavitt 1964).

Technology here refers broadly to the plant, machinery and tools (the apparatus) and the associated philosophy and system of work organisation that are integrated in the production of goods or services. Thus, a change in an organisation's technology may involve the installation of a single piece of equipment or the complete redesign of a production process. The *primary task* of an organisation refers to the core business, whether this is providing a health service, refining oil or developing computer software. *People*, or human resources, refers to the individual members and groups who constitute an organisation. *Administrative structures* refer to elements in the administrative control of work, such as formalised lines of communication, established work procedures, managerial hierarchies, reward systems and disciplinary procedures.

With the growing recognition of the need for change, the managerial careers and political aspirations of business leaders can also promote visions and strategies for change. External influences and internal factors may interlink and overlap in determining the speed, direction and outcomes of change within an organisation. As already indicated, a central driver of company change is the pursuit of flexibility. Attempts to increase company flexibility have raised a number of important HR issues, particularly in the reshaping of employment relations and workplace practice. As David Jaffe argues:

> *Flexibility is now the single most popular trait of the new organizational form. New organizations are praised for being more flexible than old organizations. Almost all of the positive changes attributed to new organizations are couched in the language of flexibility. The assumption that flexible is good and rigidity is bad is based on the belief that organizations must be malleable in an environment characterized by rapid change, innovation and emerging markets. Flexible implies the ability to restructure, reengineer, learn more quickly, and adapt to changing circumstances.* (Jaffee 2001, pp. 150–1)

In addressing this issue in more detail, the next section sets out to explain what we understand by the term 'flexibility'. The section is also concerned with a consideration of the consequences of change for employees' experience of work.

Flexible human resources and employee experience of work

Company strategies for change, developments in communication and information technologies, and the changing nature of business markets are all having a significant influence on the nature of work and employment (Purcell, Hogarth & Simm 1999). Awareness of these changes has stimulated a debate about the nature, process and consequence of new management techniques for flexibility and employees' experience of work. This debate is supported by new empirical evidence that demonstrates an increase in both job insecurity and the intensity of work (Burchell 2000), and the limits to flexible work and employment practices (Dawson & Webb 1989). Much of the work restructuring currently under way is seen to represent a movement towards the development of multiskilled self-regulatory workgroups who liaise with teamwork supervisors/facilitators on the shopfloor (Clark 1995). However, as the following report on the experience of an aircraft dispatcher captured in a newspaper article highlights, the demands of flexible work arrangements can severely disrupt the work–life balance:

> The biggest problem is the shifts, which change at a moment's notice. There are early shifts (from 6 am to 2 pm) and late (2 pm to 10 pm) but those times alter according to flight patterns ... Basically this is a job where you're given no flexibility but expected to give plenty yourself. It's impossible to plan any private life because of the shifts. We're constantly reminded we're expendable. (Spence 2001, p. 28)

With neo-Taylorite or Fordist work structures replaced by a more flexible model of management practice (e.g. Storey 1994; Thompson & Warhurst 1998), the rhetoric behind this new method of work organisation emphasises the importance of worker involvement, multiskilling, and a team approach to production and process work tasks (Oliver & Wilkinson 1988; Procter & Mueller 2000). The latter involves shopfloor employees in elements of industrial engineering, which, in turn, influences worker involvement through placing greater emphasis on the quality rather than the quantity of output (Dawson & Palmer 1995). In conjunction with other innovations, such as the push for quality management, cellular work arrangements, business process re-engineering, best practice management and just-in-time manufacturing, these changes raise serious questions about teamwork, supervision and management control (Garraham & Stewart 1992). In the United States (Womack, Jones & Roos 1990) and the United Kingdom (Oliver & Wilkinson 1988), the adoption of these management concepts has been ongoing, but whether they result in 'greater empowerment for workers' (Hammer & Champy 1993) or a deterioration in the quality of work life remains contentious (e.g. Thompson & Warhurst 1998). As Knights and Willmott have suggested:

> the kind of empowerment envisioned by BPR is seen to involve a form of false charity: 'Charity' because it seeks to bestow the gift of greater discretion and involvement upon employees; and 'false' because it is motivated less by any concern to reduce the hierarchical relations of authority than it is by a calculation that such a change will engender enhanced performance and profitability. The employee is expected, in a self-disciplined manner, to respond enthusiastically to new responsibilities. (Knights & Willmott 2000, p. 11)

In the management literature, flexibility has been a central concept and has generally been used in four main ways (Atkinson & Meager 1986; Clutterbuck 1985):

- *functional flexibility* with regard to resources, which is taken to refer to a 'firm's ability to adjust and deploy the skills of its employees to match the tasks required by its changing workload, production methods and/or technology' (NEDO 1986).
- *manufacturing flexibility*, which is generally taken to refer to the ability to rearrange and adjust existing plant and equipment to meet the changing requirements of a transformation in operations control, the process of production and/or product design
- *numerical flexibility*, which refers to the ability to rapidly increase or decrease the numbers employed within a firm
- *financial flexibility*, which refers to the ability to adjust labour costs, such as pay, to short-term changes in the level of business and economic activity (Atkinson 1984).

These concepts have been used to explain the emergence of a more general managerial strategy favouring a model of the flexible firm with a core multiskilled and functionally flexible workforce, combined with peripheral groups of temporary or part-time employees (Bradley, Erickson, Stephenson & Williams 2000). Likewise, Handy (1984, 1994) has used the term 'shamrock organisation' to refer to three broad groups of workers (corresponding to the three leaves of a shamrock). Again, he uses the term *core workers* to refer to those who carry out key activities of the firm and are readily able to adapt to change. *Peripheral workers* refers to those who generally carry out less central tasks and are employed on contract, which permits the rapid adjustment of employee numbers. Finally, *external workers* refers to those who are employed on a part-time basis as required. A key feature of shamrock organisations is their small size in relation to productive output. This is achieved by investment in labour-saving technologies and through the use of outsourcing strategies. Under such conditions the management of human resources is far simpler, since the contractual fringe is no longer directly employed on standard contracts. It is argued that the well-paid core workers with good benefits and operating conditions support rapid adjustment, whereas:

> the rest are all scattered in different organisations or their own homes, often linked through sophisticated communication systems. Such organisations, with their flexibility and skills, are well suited to the provision of high-performance products and services to demanding and rapidly changing markets. The beauty of it all, as Handy argues, is that they do not have to employ all of the people all of the time or even in the same place to get the work done. (Burnes 2000, p. 112)

In examining an agenda of issues for flexible labour and non-standard employment, Felstead and Jewson (1999) note that opinions are divided about whether flexible labour practices are simply supporting poorly paid, unsocial forms of work, or whether these HR strategies offer desirable forms of employment for those who seek to fit work around other family commitments. As the author has discussed elsewhere (Dawson, forthcoming), the push for change initiatives in the name of competitive survival may sometimes do little to improve the position of the company while undermining the employee experience of work. Consequently, care should be taken with change initiatives that may worsen employee relations at work.

Some studies have also shown that, in situations where flexibility is valued more highly than commitment and loyalty (Brannen, Lew & Moss 2000), employees are likely to resist any further attempts to introduce change. In the case of teamworking, Procter and Mueller (2000) suggest that employees may feel an 'abuse of flexibility' if change is accompanied by some form of downsizing that intensifies work. In this sense, employees are aware that flexibility that suits the company may render staff more interchangeable and leave them in a weaker position in terms of job security while extending work expectations. Under such circumstances, employee resistance to change is understandable.

Employee resistance to organisational change

Organisational change may break the continuity of a working environment and create a climate of uncertainty and ambiguity. Old, established relationships may be redefined, familiar structures redesigned and modified, and traditional methods of work called into question. Understandably, some employees may seek to maintain the status quo and resist change. Typically, resistance has been identified as resulting from one or a combination of the following factors:
- substantive change in job (skill requirements)
- reduction in economic security or job displacement
- psychological threats (whether perceived or actual)
- disruption of social arrangements (new work arrangements)
- lowering of status (redefining authority relationships).

According to Gray and Starke (1988), a substantive change in the nature of work and the skills required to perform certain functions is likely to engender distrust and resistance, particularly in situations where employees are not informed of the change before its implementation. Even if these threats reflect an individual's perception of change rather than an actual threat, employee resistance is likely to result. Parochial self-interest, misunderstanding and lack of trust are common causes of resistance to organisational change. In practice, individuals will differ in the way they perceive and evaluate change, and some employees are likely to show a lower tolerance for change than others.

In examining reasons why employees may resist change, Eccles (1994) identifies the following possible causes:
- The problem is not understood.
- An alternative solution is preferred.
- There is a feeling that the proposed solution will not work.
- The change has unacceptable personal costs.
- The rewards from change are not sufficient.
- There is a fear of being unable to cope with the new situation.
- The change threatens to destroy existing social arrangements.
- Sources of influence and control will be eroded.
- New values and practices are repellent.
- Willingness to change is low.
- Management motives for change are suspected.
- Other interests are more highly valued than new proposals.
- The change will reduce employee power and career opportunities.

According to Collins (1998), writers on change management tend to view employee resistance as a negative individual problem rather than as a positive response to changing conditions that might require further consideration. As he states:

> Workers who 'resist' change tend to be cast as lacking the psychological make-up to deal with change, and so are said to be weak and fearful of change, whereas those who support or manage change are regarded as 'go-ahead' chaps who have the 'right-stuff' for career success. (Collins 1998, p. 92)

A number of strategies to overcome resistance to change have been identified. These strategies largely range from methods of participation, communication and support at one end of a continuum through to negotiation, manipulation and coercion at the other. As argued in the section that follows, those who adopt an organisational development approach have tended to opt for more participative methods in seeking to secure the support and collaboration of company employees.

Planning the human dimension: the organisational development approach

Although there are many different organisational development (OD) models, the general approach has been described by Huse as 'the application of behavioural science knowledge in a long-range effort to improve an organization's ability to cope with changes in its external environment and increase its internal problem-solving capabilities' (1982, p. 555). This approach is based on an HR perspective that stresses the importance of collaborative management and, according to French and Bell (1995, p. 15), can be defined as 'a long-range effort to improve an organization's problem-solving and renewal processes ... with the assistance of a change agent or catalyst and the use of the theory and technology of applied behavioural science, including action research'.

Typically, the OD approach is planned; it attempts to consider and include all members of an organisation; the proposed change is supported by top management; the objectives of change are to improve working conditions and organisational effectiveness; and an emphasis is placed on behavioural science techniques, which facilitates communication and problem solving among members (Beckhard

1969). A number of steps are associated with such an approach, often beginning with the appointment of a change agent (usually an individual outside the organisation), who intervenes to start the change process. Once a need for change has been identified, it is then necessary to select an appropriate intervention technique. In managing change, OD consultants stress the need to plan the process and to ensure top management support. During implementation, the views of employees should be listened to and accommodated in order to overcome potential resistance to the change initiative. Once completed, the change program should be evaluated (Aldag & Stearns 1991).

In charting the steps of a planned approach, some OD consultants utilise Kurt Lewin's three-phase model of change, an early theory that set the scene for much of what we know as OD today (Weisbord 1988). The main thrust of Lewin's model (also referred to as the Lewin–Schein model) is that an understanding of the critical steps in the change process will increase the likelihood of the successful management of change. The three steps identified by Lewin (1951) are *unfreezing*, *changing* and *refreezing*.

During the unfreezing stage a need for change is recognised and action is taken to unfreeze existing attitudes and behaviour. This preparatory stage is deemed essential to secure employee support and minimise employee resistance. According to Lewin's technique of force-field analysis (1947), two sets of forces operate within any social system — namely, driving forces that operate for change and restraining forces that attempt to maintain the status quo. Using the example of smoking, although there are strong driving forces to stop smoking (such as social pressure, cost, fear of cancer, legal restrictions, disapproval of children and the concern of others), the restraining forces (for example, habit, social pressure, relief of tension, a spouse who smokes and a dislike of coercive constraints) may act to maintain the status quo (Weisbord 1988). If these two opposing forces are equal in strength, then they are in a state of equilibrium. Thus, to bring about change you need either to increase the strength of the driving forces or to decrease the strength of the resisting forces. Furthermore, since these two sets of forces are qualitatively different, it is possible to modify elements of both sets in the management of change. In practice, however, the emphasis of OD specialists has been on providing data that would unfreeze the system through reducing the resisting forces rather than increasing the driving forces (Gray & Starke 1988; Weisbord 1988).

Once these negative forces have been reduced through disconfirming information, the consultant begins to move the organisation towards the desired state. This is the second general step of changing or moving an organisation, and involves the implementation of new systems of operation. Once this has been achieved, the final stage of refreezing is initiated; this process involves the positive reinforcement of desired outcomes to promote the internalisation of new attitudes and behaviours. An appraisal of the effectiveness of the change program is the final element of the last step to ensure that the new way of doing things is assimilated.

This, then, is the basis of Lewin's three-phase model of change, which is still widely used to inform company change practice. The strength of the model lies in its simple representation (which makes it easier to use and understand), yet this is also its major weakness, since it presents a linear and static model of change. As Kanter, Stein and Jick have noted, 'the organisation as an ice cube ... is so wildly inappropriate that it is difficult to see why it has not only survived but prospered' (1992). In an article in the *Harvard Business Review* Beer and colleagues also criticise this traditional approach to change that is based on the underlying assumption that attitude change will drive behavioural change.

> *Most change programs don't work because they are guided by a theory of change that is fundamentally flawed. The common belief is that the place to begin is with the knowledge and attitudes of individuals. Changes in attitudes, the theory goes, lead to changes in individual behaviour. And changes in individual behaviour, repeated by many people, will result in organizational change. According to this model, change is like a conversion experience. Once people 'get religion', changes in their behaviour will surely follow.* (Beer, Eisenstat & Spector 1990, p. 159)

They argue for frameworks that view change as an ongoing process rather than a 'one-off' event. In recognising the dynamic and continuous nature of change processes, the processual perspective provides such an approach.

Understanding human resources and change: a processual perspective

The push to identify and define strategies to aid change management under prevailing contextual conditions in the past led to a tendency to downplay the processual and ongoing nature of organisational change. However, the past decade has witnessed a shift in emphasis, with greater attention given to the importance of *process* for understanding the dynamics of organisational change (Van de Ven &

Huber 1990). For example, the early work of Pettigrew (1985) charted the unfolding and non-linear aspects of change at Imperial Chemical Industries. He has criticised the 'aprocessual' character of much of the material on change management and has argued elsewhere that human conduct is perpetually in a process of becoming. The overriding aim of the process analyst therefore is to 'catch this reality in flight' (Pettigrew 1997).

The processual framework developed below by the author builds on some of this earlier work but, unlike Pettigrew, it incorporates the concept of competing histories and narratives of change and does not attempt to examine change through one particular lens. Consequently, there is no attempt to reconcile the different experiences of change, or to take an employee or mangerialist stance; rather, the aim is to provide a framework for making sense of change processes and the different human experience of these processes (Dawson, forthcoming). This orientation is based on the assumption that companies continuously, and often concurrently, move in and out of many different states during the history of one or a number of organisational change initiatives (Dawson 1994). Although, for analytical purposes, it may prove useful to identify and group a number of tasks and decision-making activities, such as the search for and assessment of implementation options, these should not be treated as representing a series of sequential stages in the process of change (as in conventional stage models). The approach taken here, as already outlined, is that organisations undergoing change embody a number of dynamic states that interlock and overlap, and that processes associated with change should be analysed 'as they happen' so that their emergent character can be understood in the context within which they take place.

A central element of the proposed approach is the need to incorporate an analysis of the politics of managing change (Dawson 1996). On this count, management writers such as Stace and Dunphy (1994) can be criticised for ignoring the political processes associated with trade union and employee actions in response to management's decision to introduce change, whereas political writers such as Braverman (1974) can be criticised for treating management as a homogeneous political group. The position taken here is that an understanding of organisational politics should be central to any approach that seeks to explain change management. For example, the commitment of middle management to strategy implementation cannot be taken for granted (see Porter, Crampon & Smith 1976). As research has shown, variations in commitment can significantly influence the successful management of change (Guth & MacMillan 1989), particularly in cases where differing vested interests between management levels and functions do not align with strategic objectives (Wilkinson 1983). As Buchanan and Badham conclude:

> In the domain of practical action ... management is a contact sport. If you don't want to get bruised, don't play. There is little to be gained by complaining about the turf game, its players, its tricks, its strategies, its tactics and its potential damage. Criticism of the existence of organizational politics is likely to have as much impact as criticism of British weather ... The main argument of this book is that the change agent who is not politically skilled will fail. (Buchanan & Badham 1999, p. 231)

The second major concern of a processual approach is the context in which change takes place. A historical perspective on both the internal and the external organisational context is central to understanding the opportunities, constraints and organisationally defined routes to change (Kelly & Amburgey 1991). As already noted, the coexistence of a number of competing histories of change can significantly shape ongoing change programs. The contextual and historical dimension can both promote certain options and devalue others during the process of organisational change. Here the contextual dimension refers to the past and present external and internal operating environments as well as the influence of future projections and expectations on current operating practice.

This framework also takes account of external contextual factors and the substance of change (for a more detailed discussion, see Dawson 1994, pp. 104–122). All these elements overlap and interplay during the process of organisational change, in which there is an ongoing mutual shaping that renders it difficult to differentiate these elements in practice. For example, it is not uncommon for definitional confusion to surround the introduction of new management techniques and for the content of change to be redefined during the process of organisational adaptation. Moreover, knowledge of the substance of change and clarification of what the change means for a particular organisation can in themselves become political processes, influenced by external contextual views and internal agendas around the management of change.

In short, change is a complex, muddied process that does not follow any simple, linear route, as many 'n-step' models suggest; neither can the various components be treated as discrete, independent entities. But this complexity also draws attention to the human dimension of change and the importance of people's experience in shaping attitudes and expectations. As indicated elsewhere (Dawson 2000), different individuals may recount and construct stories that reflect their own interests; in the case of company change programs, the maintenance of common organisational stories often reflects the influence and political action of certain powerful actors and groups.

These dominant narrators are often actively involved in the political process through which a rational narrative is constructed, revised and modified over time and sustained within the context of other competing voices and views.

In addition to competing narratives, there are some organisational members who may remain silent or whose voices remain unheard, and others who may be 'victims' of change (for example, through redundancy or a shift in status and position). What the processual approach helps us to understand is that there will always be 'casualties' in a major change program; that accepting that a dominant narrative may exist at any given time, and there is always more than one 'story' of change; and that, ultimately, it is this human experience of change that provides us with real insights into the dynamic process of company change.

Conclusion: the human experience of change

It is widely accepted that people are critical to the perceived success or failure of company change initiatives, but what is perhaps more controversial is that it is the narrative or stories of change that count. From this perspective, it is the interpretation of events and outcomes (the social construction and revision of organisational histories) that provides the material for understanding our experiences of change. The political process of change helps to explain how certain accounts come to dominate in the orchestration of change initiatives. However, if there is a mismatch between, for example, the rhetoric of participation and empowerment and the lived experience of employees, then there will be a set of competing narratives that will serve to shape employee attitudes and behaviours. In much of the critical literature on modern change initiatives, it is this mismatch between the casting of a management tale on how to improve competitive advantage while simultaneously improving working conditions (the culture-excellence school) and the lived experience of job intensification, a decline in job security and a labour context of declining trade union membership (e.g. Bradley et al. 2000) that raises doubts about the benefits of these changes for employees.

Participation in strategies that ultimately increase the workload and responsibilities of staff while undermining job security does not create enthusiastic employees (Knights & Willmott 2000). Fear of redundancy in the face of global competition is a common experience among employees today. It is within this context that change, employment and HR needs to be understood. As Coyle-Shapiro and Kessler (2000) have noted in their study of the implications of changes in the employment relationship for the psychological contract:

> The decline in collective responses such as strikes to injustices in the employment relationship diverts attention to individualized responses to unbalanced exchanges with the employer. In this case, employees are redressing the balance in the relationship through reducing their commitment and their willingness to engage in organizational citizenship behaviours, which have been highlighted, as important factors in an organization's survival and well being. (Coyle-Shapiro & Kessler 2000, p. 924)

If ideas behind modern change initiatives, such as the development of high-trust, collaborative relationships, are seen by employees largely as management rhetoric rather than as reflecting their own lived experience, then serious questions need to be asked about the strategic purpose of continuing to engage in an ever growing raft of such change programs. To maintain the present course is to blindly accept the narratives of 'success' offered by a growing army of change consultants and guru-professors, ignoring the real stories of those experiencing change.

We need to move beyond the search for simple, generalisable solutions or recipes for success, accepting that change is a complex dynamic within which employee attitudes and future expectations will be shaped. As such, the pursuit of flexibility should not simply serve a drive for competitive advantage (often resulting in a deterioration of employment conditions), but, rather, it should accommodate the needs of employees, who should also directly benefit from more flexible work arrangements. The agenda needs to be shifted away from company-driven change (with a rhetoric of employee involvement) to greater employee choice in work arrangements that may benefit employee decision-making in the work–home balance.

HR managers need to reflect critically on the nature of any changes proposed and not to assume that because these changes are couched in empowerment rhetoric, they will necessarily lead to greater involvement and empowerment of employees. The HR manager is in a central position in being able not only to identify when to change and when not to change but also to assess attitudes and behaviour of employees and to steer change in particular directions. Fads and fashions should not dictate the nature and pace of change. The HR manager has a critical role in developing programs that harness human resources and do not simply distance staff from their work. Attention should focus on broadening choice, giving employees a say in the development of new work arrangements so that they do not see themselves as merely 'victims' in a never-ending barrage of reactive and externally driven change initiatives.

References

Aldag, R, and Stearns T (1991) *Management*. Cincinnati, OH: South Western.

Atkinson, J (1984) Manpower strategies for flexible organisations. *Personnel Management*, 16, 28–31.

Atkinson, J, and Meager, N (1986) *Changing Working Patterns: How Companies Achieve Flexibility to Meet New Needs*. London: National Economic Development Office.

Beckhard, R (1969) *Organizational Development: Strategies and Models*. Reading, MA: Addison-Wesley.

Beer, M, Eisenstat, R, and Spector, B (1990) Why change programs don't produce change. *Harvard Business Review*, November/December, 68, 158–66.

Bradley, H, Erickson, M, Stephenson, C, and Williams, S (2000) *Myths at Work*. Cambridge: Polity Press.

Brannen, J, Lewis, S, and Moss, P (2000) *The impact of organisational change on family lives: theoretical and methodological developments in an ongoing exploratory study*. Paper presented to an ESRC seminar on the Changing Nature of Work and Family Life, University of Aberdeen, 23 November.

Braverman, H (1974) *Labor and Monopoly Capital: The Degradation of Work in the Twentieth Century*. New York: Monthly Review Press.

Buchanan, D, and Badham, R (1999) *Power, Politics, and Organizational Change: Winning the Turf Game*. London: Sage.

Burchell, B (2000) *Job insecurity and work intensification*. Paper presented to an ESRC seminar on the Changing Nature of Work and Family Life, University of Aberdeen, 23 November.

Burnes, B (2000) *Managing Change: A Strategic Approach to Organizational Dynamics* (3rd ed.). London: Pitman.

Clark, J (1995) *Managing Innovation and Change: People, Technology and Strategy*. London: Sage.

Collins, D (1998) *Organizational Change: Sociological Perspectives*. London: Routledge.

Coyle-Shyapiro, J, and Kessler, I (2000) Consequences of the psychological contract for the employment relationship: a large scale survey. *Journal of Management Studies*, 37 (7) 903–930.

Dawson, P (1994) *Organizational Change: A Processual Approach*. London: Paul Chapman Publishing.

Dawson, P (1996) *Technology and Quality: Change in the Workplace*. London: International Thomson Business Press.

Dawson, P (2000) Multiple voices and the orchestration of a rational narrative in the pursuit of 'management objectives': the political process of plant-level change. *Technology Analysis & Strategic Management*, 12 (1) 39–58.

Dawson, P (forthcoming) *Living with Change*. London: Sage.

Dawson, P, and Palmer, G (1995) *Quality Management: The Theory and Practice of Implementing Change*. Melbourne: Longman Cheshire.

Dawson, P, and Webb, J (1989) New production arrangements: the totally flexible cage? *Work, Employment and Society*, 3 (2) 221–38.

Eccles, T (1994) *Succeeding with Change: Implementing Action-Driven Strategies*. London: McGraw-Hill.

Felstead, A, and Jewson, N (1999) Flexible labour and non-standard employment: an agenda of issues. In A Felstead and N Jewson (Eds), *Global Trends in Flexible Labour*. London: Macmillan Business.

French, W and Bell, C (1995) *Organizational Development and Change* (5th ed.). Minneapolis: West Publishing Company.

Garraham, P, and Stewart, P (1992) *The Nissan Enigma*. London: Mansell.

Gow, D, Bannister, N, Wintour, P, and Black, I (2001) Counterparts of threatened British workers refuse to accept transfer of work to Corus plant in Holland: steel boycott by Dutch unions. *Guardian*, 3 February, 2.

Gray, LG, and Starke, FA (1988) *Organizational Behavior: Concepts and Applications* (4th ed.). Columbus, OH: Merrill Publishing.

Guth, WD, and MacMillan C (1989) Strategy implementation versus middle management self-interest. In D Asch, and C Bowman (Eds), *Readings in Strategic Management*. London: Macmillan.

Hammer, M, and Champy, J (1993) *Reengineering the Corporation: A Manifesto for Business Revolution*. New York: HarperBusiness.

Handy, C (1984) *The Future of Work*. Oxford, UK: Blackwell.

Handy, C (1994) *The Empty Raincoat*. London: Hutchinson.

Huse, E (1982) *Management*. New York: West.

Jaffee, D (2001) *Organization Theory: Tension and Change*. New York: McGraw-Hill.

Kanter, RM, Stein, BA, and Jick, TD (1992) *The Challenge of Organizational Change: How Companies Experience It and Leaders Guide It*. New York: The Free Press.

Kelly, D, and Amburgey, TL (1991) Organizational inertia and momentum: a dynamic model of strategic change. *Academy of Management Journal*, 34 (3) 591–612.

Knights, D, and Willmott, H (Eds) (2000) *The Re-engineering Revolution: Critical Studies of Corporate Change*. London: Sage.

Leavitt, HJ (1964) Applied organizational change in industry: structural, technical and human approaches. In WW Cooper, HJ Leavitt and MW Shelly (Eds), *New Perspectives in Organizations Research*. New York: John Wiley & Sons.

Lewin, K (1947) Frontiers in Group Dynamics. *Human Relations*, 1, 5–42.

Lewin, K (1951) *Field Theory in Social Science*. New York: Harper & Row.

National Economic Development Office (1986) *Changing Working Patterns: How Companies Achieve Flexibility to Meet New Needs*. London: National Economic Development Office.

Oliver, N, and Wilkinson, B (1988) *The Japanization of British Industry*. Oxford: Blackwell.

Pettigrew, A (1985) *Awakening Giant: Continuity and Change in ICI*. Oxford: Basil Blackwell.

Pettigrew, A (1997) What is a processual analysis? *Scandinavian Journal of Management*, 13 (4) 337–48.

Porter, LW, Crampon, WJ, and Smith, FJ (1976) Organizational commitment and managerial turnover: a longitudinal study. *Organizational Behavior and Human Performance*, February, 87–98.

Procter, S, and Mueller, F (2000) *Teamworking*. London: Macmillan Business.

Purcell, K, Hogarth, T, and Simm, C (1999) *Whose Flexibility? The Costs and Benefits of Non-Standard Work Arrangements and Contractual Relations*. York: Joseph Rowntree Foundation.

Spence, R (2001) When flexible. *Guardian*, 13 January, 28.

Stace, D, and Dunphy, D (1994) *Beyond the Boundaries: Leading and Re-Creating the Successful Enterprise*. Sydney: McGraw-Hill.

Storey, J (Ed.) (1994) *New Wave Manufacturing Strategies. Organizational and Human Resource Management Dimensions*. London: Paul Chapman Publishing.

Thompson, P, and Warhurst, C (Eds) (1998) *Workplace of the Future*. Basingstoke, UK: Macmillan.

Van de Ven, A, and Huber, GP (1990) Longitudinal field research methods for studying processes of organizational change. *Organization Science*, 1 (3) 213–19.

Weisbord, MR (1988) *Productive Workplaces: Organizing and Managing for Dignity, Meaning and Community*. San Francisco: Jossey-Bass.

Wilkinson, B (1983) *The Shop Floor Politics of New Technology*. London: Heinemann.

Womack, JP, Jones, DT, and Roos, D (1990) *The Machine That Changed the World*. New York: Rawson Associates.